Morgan, Lewis
& Bockius

MORGAN, LEWIS & BOCKIUS

A Law Firm and Its Times

1873-1993

Park B. Dilks, Jr.

To Jonathan and Robin

■ ■ ■ ■ ■

Editor: Jane Brahms
Project Manager: Denise Elliott
Designer: Alfred Casciato
Typeface: Bookman
Printer and binder: R. R. Donnelley & Sons Company

Library of Congress Catalog Card Number: 94-76567
ISBN 0-9641753-0-4
Printed in the United States of America
1 2 3 4 5 6 7 8 9 0 __

CONTENTS

bar association activities and versatility · Seashells and islands · A lion in winter · All the business the Firm needs · A guardian angel in the prompter's box

ILLUSTRATIONS

(Following page 238)

ACKNOWLEDGMENTS

The author owes a debt to many Morgan, Lewis & Bockius partners past and present. To name a few: W. James MacIntosh (especially regarding the 1920s), Orvel Sebring (especially regarding the 1930s), William Lingelbach, John Bracken, Brady Bryson, J. David Mann, Thomas Lefevre, Benjamin Quigg, John Brittain, Richard Brown, Robert Young, A. A. Sommer, Sheldon Cohen, Donald Scott, William Curtin, Samuel Fortenbaugh, Alan Reed, Richard Hotvedt, Michael Thoyer, William Zeiter, John Lewis, John Quarles, Charles O'Connor, John Linsenmeyer, John Lombard, John Shenefield, Caswell Hobbs, Clive Anderson, William Emanuel, Charles Lubar, Harry Rissetto, Michael Klowden, Joseph Hennessy, Bradford Coupe, Mark Dichter, George Stohner, Lawrence Berger, Joseph Fay, John Hartigan, Frank Mirabello, and Jami McKeon. They provided good stories and useful information.

Donald Scott critiqued the final typescript to good effect. From beginning to end, Denise Elliott typed and retyped the work-in-progress. In addition, she also researched the bulk of the book. Her patience and ingenuity defy praise. Trudy Kuehner also contributed research for the early chapters. Finally, the book benefited immensely from the editorial skills of Jane Brahms. She mixed discipline with compassion.

PREFACE

This book has no illusions. At best, it may interest several thousand readers, comprising those who have spent, are spending or will spend their working lives with Morgan, Lewis & Bockius. In a sense it deals with their roots. It also deals with some clients whose fortunes have been entwined with those of the Firm. They may be curious. Otherwise, *caveat lector!*

Many of the events recounted have been part of the author's life over the past forty years. So objectivity, while laudable, is sometimes elusive. But the record should be kept straight. Consequently, when the narrative concerns the author, he will be called by name like everyone else. When reminiscing, he will be referred to as the author.

Company histories are typically dismissed as dull. Perhaps they are—for *readers*. Their writers feel differently: They fall victim to their material, judging significant what others regard as dross. Familiarity breeds exhilaration.

Still, in the present case, there is a comforting precedent. Twenty years ago, J. Tyson Stokes published a history of the Firm. Entitled *Morgan, Lewis and Bockius, Memoir of a Law Firm, One Hundred Years, 1873-1973*, it was addressed to those who share the faith, as is the present volume. Nevertheless, it has gone through several printings, and about ten thousand copies have been distributed. Stokes called it "a slender tome." Slender tomes are more apt to be read than thicker ones like this, which are more apt to be sampled or skimmed.

Since this work owes its inspiration to Stokes's pioneering effort, he deserves attention at once. Born in 1906, he graduated from the University of Pennsylvania Law School and came to the Firm in 1932. He was made a partner in 1939, retired in 1974, and died in 1983. During World War II, he served as vice-president and general counsel of the Baldwin Locomotive Works, once the Firm's largest client as well as the largest manufacturer of steam locomotives in the world.

Although Stokes returned to the Firm after World War II, he did not fully participate in its active practice. Instead, he maintained important client relationships at a personal level and functioned for some years as the Firm's managing partner. Independently wealthy, he asked that his allocation of partnership profits be modest. Indeed, he received "the breakage," meaning that after all other partners got their allocations in thousands of dollars, he got his in thousands, hundreds, tens, dollars, and even pennies, thus absorbing the balance of the Firm's net income.

During the 1960s, Stokes was known to be working on a centennial history. Since its appearance in 1973, it has charmed a generation of the Firm's family with its stories about the achievements as well as the eccentricities of their predecessors. Stokes's book matched its author's personality as an entertainer. He could pass another lawyer in the hall without any sign of recognition or perhaps just a grunt. But his after-dinner speeches revealed a different side of him. For beneath his starched exterior beat the heart of a stand-up comic whose stentorian presentations (he eschewed microphones) at the Firm's annual dinners left his audiences weak with laughter.

Originally, the idea was simply to update Stokes's book. But such an approach proved unrealistic for several reasons. First, many facets of the Firm's recent history—national practice, for example— were not anticipated in Stokes's time. Thus, there is no backdrop in his book for what happened subsequently. Second, his treatment of the post-World War II period was fragmentary: He was most at home with the Bockius years (1908-1939). Third and foremost, his was a personal view. His father and Morris Bockius were best friends. From childhood forward, Stokes participated intimately in the Firm's history. It was simply not possible to update so unique a piece.

Consequently, a different kind of book has emerged. One aim has been to amass as much firsthand information about the Firm as possible while eyewitnesses and other sources still exist to shed light. (Hence the book's length.) Another aim has been to highlight the Firm's place in history—locally, nationally, and internationally—by considering what was happening around the Firm as its story unfolded. (Hence the subtitle, *A Law Firm and Its Times*.) Applying this approach, the roles played by clients assume greater importance. Clients are after all the raison d'être for a law firm, and their history is often its history.

Looking back, one thing is certain: The practice of law in 1993 contrasts sharply with its practice in the Bockius period so dear to Stokes. That period embraced qualities of stability, warmth, deference, and collegiality at which a cynic might scoff today. Still, it has been precisely in the preservation of those qualities, while coping with revolutionary changes, that the Firm has achieved rare distinction. If this book has a single theme, it is an exploration of how this came to pass.

P. B. D., Jr.
Chestnut Hill
December 1993

CHAPTER 1

IN THE BEGINNING

The Civil War ■ *Battery A of the First Regiment Artillery* ■ *Action at Carlisle* ■ *Philadelphia as the Workshop of the World* ■ *Charles Eldridge Morgan, Jr., and Francis Draper Lewis become partners in 1873* ■ *Getting started at 623 Walnut Street* ■ *Reading law versus law school* ■ *Langdell and the case method* ■ *The advent of telephones and typewriters* ■ *The letterpress archives* ■ *Randal Morgan and Morris Rex Bockius* ■ *The Drexel Building* ■ *State House Row* ■ *A new City Hall* ■ *The Panic of 1873* ■ *The Centennial of 1876* ■ *Caring for the sick* ■ *Early clients and coming attractions*

Morgan, Lewis & Bockius (ML&B) numbers about sixth among the largest law firms in the world today. With eleven offices on three continents, it comprises approximately 650 lawyers and 1,000 supporting personnel. They are the successors to Charles Eldridge Morgan, Jr., and Francis Draper Lewis who founded the Firm on March 10, 1873, under the name Morgan & Lewis.[1]

There was a time when college history courses divided the American experience comfortably into two semesters. The first semester was called *The United States to 1865;* the second semester, *The United States from 1865 to the Present.* Applying this division, the Firm's history fits neatly into the second semester. But since the past is prologue, it is important to recall how the first semester ended.

The country had just suffered the agony of a civil war, testing its will for unity. Almost 4 million Union and Confederate soldiers were in uniform at one time or another. And of these, about 1 million were killed, wounded or stricken by disease—more casualties than in all other wars fought by the United States from the American Revolution to the Persian Gulf. In terms of technology, tactics, and slaughter, the Civil War was the first "modern war."

Although no battles were fought in or near Philadelphia, the city felt the brunt of the war in many ways. Between 1861 and 1865, almost 90,000 Philadelphians saw military service. Thousands more churned out the warships, uniforms, blankets, weapons, and other goods and supplies that advanced the Union cause. Also, the city was the northern terminus of the Philadelphia, Wilmington & Baltimore Railroad and hence the assembly point for hundreds of thousands of troops from New York, New Jersey, and New England. When those troops returned from battle, Philadelphia cared for the sick and wounded. Two dozen military hospitals in the city tended more than 150,000 casualties.

Founding partner Charles Eldridge Morgan, Jr., usually called CEM in the Firm's archives, was a Civil War veteran. He was born in Philadelphia on September 23, 1844. The Morgan family had come to America in 1684 from Llantarnam Abbey, Ponty Pool, Wales. They settled first near Gwynedd, Montgomery County, in the province of Pennsylvania, before relocating to New Jersey and subsequently to Philadelphia in the early 1840s. In about 1860, they moved to Germantown, a northwestern suburb within Philadelphia. CEM's father, a wholesale dry goods merchant, was prominent in the community, and CEM remained a Germantown resident until his death in 1917.[2]

During CEM's brief period of military service, he experienced one of the Civil War's highlights, at least from the Northern viewpoint, by taking part in action near Gettysburg. He was a member of Battery A, First Regiment Artillery, Philadelphia Home Guard, which included many of Philadelphia's young lawyers. Battery A had been organized in 1844 by the Philadelphia bar to help quell local riots among clashing ethnic and religious groups. It was revived after the Battle of Antietam in 1862 when Philadelphia seemed threatened.

That threat became real toward mid-1863 with the crossing of the Confederate army into Pennsylvania. Philadelphia prepared "for the emergency."[3] Every available unit was mobilized and sent westward. Battery A, which became part of the Militia of 1863, comprised 108 men. In addition to CEM, it included John G. Johnson, of whom much more later. The battery was activated on June 19, 1863, and dispatched on July 24 by train to Harrisburg, the Confederates' original target in Pennsylvania. The militia's orders were to help defend the city. Trenches were dug, a telegraph line was strung from Harrisburg to the emplacement, and hogsheads were filled with water from the Susquehanna River to prepare for a siege.

The action lay elsewhere, however, and on July 1 new orders came for a thirteen-mile march to Carlisle, where "[t]he people . . . [had been] despoiled by the Rebels"[4] led by General James Ewell Brown (Jeb) Stuart. Operating independently and out of touch with General Robert E. Lee, Stuart had been marauding behind federal lines in York County for several weeks. CEM's unit reached Carlisle late in the afternoon and was greeted by grateful townspeople.

But any celebration was short, as Stuart returned to shell the town. CEM's battery fired back. A lone rebel "bearing a rag at the end of a switch"[5] rode into town and demanded that the Union troops surrender. The demand was indignantly refused, and the messenger rode off. The shelling resumed, continuing into the night. Then silence fell. Finally, at 3 a.m. on July 2, "a souvenir shell described an arc across the heavens—our 'brothers' had bidden us farewell."[6] Stuart had reestablished contact with Lee, who had summoned all available forces to Gettysburg (twenty-five miles south of Carlisle) where 163,000 men were engaged in the most critical battle of the war. Stuart's cavalry arrived for the final day of that three-day struggle. But it was too late for the South.[7]

CEM's battery remained at Carlisle on July 2 and 3. Then, as day broke on July 4, the first news came of the bloodbath at Gettysburg: The two armies had suffered 51,000 killed and wounded. Lee withdrew his forces below the Potomac. CEM's battery followed the Southern retreat as far as Hagerstown, Maryland, before returning to Philadelphia. There, the battery was mustered out of service on July 30, 1863. CEM had chosen his engagement well. He had been in the war for only six weeks, but at a decisive time; and he was unscathed. Incidentally, the Firm's archives contain a letter dated April 1, 1915, from CEM expressing doubt that any photograph of Battery A was ever taken. Famed Civil War photographer Matthew Brady was probably busy elsewhere.

■ ■ ■ ■ ■

The war left a terrible legacy of hatred, a way of life wiped out, one part of the country under occupation by the other, and millions of former slaves with uncertain roles. It also begat a national debt of $2.8 billion. This approximated half of the then gross national product—shocking in those times, but less than today's share without the excuse of a major war.

By 1873, when the Firm was founded, much of the devastated South had been rebuilt, and the North was experiencing a building boom of its own. In Philadelphia, it was the age of the row house— a hallmark of the city, like pepper pot and scrapple, and in later times the soft pretzel and hoagie. The homes were two stories high, thirty feet deep, and sixteen feet wide. Usually selling for about $1,500, they were constructed of brick with mass-produced trim and were stamped out like cookies by the tens of thousands. With the postwar housing boom and the spread of street-railway systems, wage earners began commuting to work. Factory mass-production methods put out of business small artisan shops that once made shoes, clothing, furniture, and other handcrafted articles.

Philadelphia was blessed. With a population in 1870 of almost 675,000, it was the third-largest English-speaking city in the world, exceeded only by London and New York. It had an ample labor force, access to raw materials, and good transportation systems by rail, river, and road. In the last quarter of the nineteenth century, it was home to an enormous variety of industries, including food processing, textiles, publishing, chemicals, iron and steel, machine tools and hardware, and boots and shoes. The city's diversified economy earned it the sobriquet "Workshop of the World."[8]

Some of Philadelphia's plants were fully integrated, producing their wares from start to finish. But most specialized, thus following Adam Smith's dictum. In the textile field, for example, separate plants spun, wove, dyed, knit, and finished, making Philadelphia "the world's largest and most diversified textile center."[9] All this enormous activity was supported by endless supplies of immigrant labor and of energy from coal mined upstate and transported to Philadelphia by the Reading Railroad, a future client of the Firm.

■ ■ ■ ■ ■

Such was the city's economic climate in 1873 when the Firm was founded. The catalyst, according to J. Tyson Stokes, was Henry Lewis, a successful cotton merchant, who brought together his twenty-three-year-old nephew, Francis Draper Lewis, and CEM, then twenty-eight.[10] They formed a partnership of which CEM was the senior member not only in age but also in partnership income: His share was 75 percent, while Lewis received 25 percent. Again according to Stokes, Uncle Henry gave the two young lawyers $500, which they used to purchase a law library.[11] Not much was needed to get started in those days: some law books, a few chairs and rolltop desks, maybe a high desk and stool for the inevitable Dickensian clerk, and some stationery.

The Firm's first office was at 623 Walnut Street. City directories reveal that CEM was already there as early as 1869, four years before the partnership with Lewis. Horsecars ran on Walnut Street in those days. They would be superseded in the mid-1890s by electric trolley service. The gas lights that illuminated Walnut Street in the 1870s would be replaced by electricity two decades later.

The first office of Morgan & Lewis comprised several rooms in one of a row of converted Georgian residences that lined the north side of Walnut Street facing Washington Square. That square had served in the 1750s as a potter's field, later as a burial ground for Revolutionary War soldiers, and still later as the site of mass burials from the yellow fever epidemic of 1793. The building that housed the Firm's first office no longer stands: Much of the block was demolished in 1908 to make way for the Curtis Publishing Company Building, which remains today as the Curtis Center.

Long before television, indeed long before radio, the *Saturday Evening Post* and the *Ladies' Home Journal* were required reading. These and other publications made Curtis the premier magazine publishing house in America. Although Curtis was not an ML&B client during its heyday, descendants of its founder retained the Firm in the late 1960s to wrest control from an outside investor who had brought the company perilously close to bankruptcy. After high-profile litigation, bankruptcy was averted, and the Firm handled the disposition of Curtis's remaining operations, along with rights to use the names of its famous publications. In 1970, a year after these dispositions, Mary Louise Curtis Bok Zimbalist died at age ninety-three. She was the daughter of Cyrus H. K. Curtis, the company's founder. In ensuing estate matters, the Firm represented her heirs, including her grandson, Derek Bok, later dean of Harvard Law School and president of Harvard University.[12]

Diagonally across from the Firm's first office, on the east side of Washington Square, was a group of four-story buildings called Lawyers' Row. One of those buildings, at 231 South Sixth Street, housed the office of Philadelphia's city solicitor. So it housed CEM part time between 1878 and 1884 when he was first assistant to city solicitor William Nelson West. For his services CEM was paid $2,350 per year while continuing in private practice.

Since the city's work involved substantial litigation, it is likely that CEM was active in the courts, which supports the view passed down over the years that he was an outstanding trial lawyer. As such, he seems occasionally to have bested his Battery A buddy, the redoubtable John G. Johnson. For example, in *Haddock v. Grinnel Manufacturing Corporation*, 109 Pa. 372 (1885), CEM took the high road, arguing for strict compliance with the law. Johnson had to be more imaginative. The high road won.

CEM graduated in 1864 from the College of the University of Pennsylvania. It was then located at Ninth and Chestnut streets, the later site of successive federal courthouses. After college, CEM "read law" in the office of William A. Porter and was admitted to the bar in 1868. Until late in the nineteenth century, most lawyers qualified for the bar by reading law instead of attending law school. Actually, it was not until 1854 that the authorities for bar admission in Philadelphia even took notice of law schools. Then the Philadelphia courts ruled that two years of law school might be substituted for two of the required three years of clerkship with a practicing lawyer. Lawyers pay their clerks today. But it was the other way around in those early times. Lawyers with several clerks in residence could supplement their incomes nicely. They were not apt to favor law schools.

Back then, a law school education was of dubious benefit compared with on-the-job training. Teaching was by lectures, featuring massive doses of Blackstone and Kent. Socrates was definitely not on the rostrum, and participation by students was discouraged, as it interrupted the majestic flow of one legal principle after another. Facts got in the way of theory.

It was not until the school year 1870-71 that Dean Christopher Columbus Langdell pioneered the case method at Harvard Law School. Langdell's approach was initially unpopular. The Boston bar deplored it, and student attendance dwindled. Langdell, never one to take a vote, plowed on and prevailed. Today, lawyers regard the case method as a given.

Unlike CEM, the Firm's other founding partner, Francis Draper Lewis, did attend law school. Born in Boston on August 28, 1849, he graduated from Episcopal Academy in Philadelphia and received degrees from Amherst College in 1869 and Harvard Law School in 1871. Considering his year of graduation, he was probably among the earliest students subjected to Langdell's case method. (Langdell signed Lewis's diploma.) Before his association with CEM in 1873, Lewis practiced in Philadelphia with John C. Bullitt, whose firm is an antecedent of today's Drinker Biddle & Reath. ML&B's archives include some pages from Lewis's 1873 diary. His entry of January 1 states: "at Bullitt office till March 11." Then on March 11, he wrote: "moved table into Morgan's office." A graphic description of the Firm's birth.

■ ■ ■ ■ ■

When Morgan & Lewis was founded, communications with clients were either in person or by letters delivered through the mail or by messengers. Some messengers were employed by their firms. Others simply hung around office buildings as independent contractors hoping for an assignment. If the need arose for a speedy contact at a distance, a telegram could be sent.

In the Firm's early years, documents were handwritten. By that time, steel-tipped pens had replaced quill pens, facilitating the work of scriveners. (Quill pens needed frequent sharpening.) Prototypical typewriters existed in 1873, the year of the Firm's founding. But the early machines were cumbersome: Among other disadvantages, the typist could not see what had been typed. Only in the 1890s did satisfactory typewriters become standard business equipment. The earliest typewritten documents in the Firm's archives date from that decade.

Before the advent of carbon paper, documents were copied by letterpress. This involved writing (or later typing) with special ink. The documents were then inserted in a book under a sheet of very fine paper moistened to absorb some of the special ink. The Firm's archives include a bound collection of typewritten letterpress documents dating from 1902.

Telephones were unknown when the Firm was founded. But three years later, in 1876, that revolutionary technology attracted international acclaim when Alexander Graham Bell demonstrated it to a mystified Brazilian emperor, Dom Pedro II, at Philadelphia's Centennial Exposition. Still, there was no point in having a telephone until others had them—someone had to be at the other end. Consequently, more than a decade passed before telephones were in common use. The first Firm letterhead showing the word "telephone" (no number given) dates from 1890. By then, the number of telephones in America had passed the 200,000 mark. Not to be outdone, the 1896 letterhead shows "long distance telephone" (still no number given).

As the Firm grew, its quarters at 623 Walnut Street probably became cramped, especially with the addition in 1875 of CEM's brother Randal Morgan, who would play an important role in developing the Firm's public utility practice, as traced in Chapter 2. So the two Morgans, Lewis, and their support staff moved to 302 Walnut Street in 1881. After the addition of Morris Rex Bockius in 1883, they moved again the next year to 411-13 Walnut Street. And they moved once again in 1896 to 501-09 Drexel Building, where they remained until 1904.

The Drexel Building was at that time *the* address in Philadelphia. In 1891, *Philadelphia and Popular Philadelphians* noted that the "white marble structure . . . [was] said to be the handsomest private bank in the world." It contained "398 rooms . . . and 22 toilet rooms." To form a "general idea of the magnitude of the building . . . it is necessary to take a ramble through the corridors—nearly three-quarters of a mile long . . . and climb the great staircase through the eleven stories . . . connected by six swift running elevators."[13]

The Drexel Building was built in 1887 by Drexel & Co., of which more in Chapter 11. At various times during the Firm's eight-year tenancy, the Drexel Building housed the Firm's premier public utility client, the United Gas Improvement Company; also the founding partners of Duane, Morris & Heckscher; and Henry & Pepper (the firm of young George Wharton Pepper), which after many name changes would become today's Pepper, Hamilton & Scheetz.

■ ■ ■ ■ ■

All four of the Firm's locations from 1873 to 1904 were within five blocks of one another and within two blocks of State House Row, a complex of buildings on the south side of Chestnut Street between Fifth and Sixth streets. The centerpiece of the complex was the State House, now called Independence Hall. Polymath lawyer Andrew Hamilton "planned and designed"[14] that historic building commencing in 1732. It was Hamilton who journeyed to New York in 1735 to defend John Peter Zenger when he was charged with libel against the Crown. The phrase "Philadelphia lawyer" may have been coined to honor Hamilton's victory in that landmark case.

As Independence Hall, the State House stands today on hallowed ground. It is America's most precious national shrine. But back in 1873, it was simply part of State House Row, the lively seat of Philadelphia's government since 1789. Hemmed in at that time by commercial buildings on three sides, State House Row housed the city council, the state and city courts, the sheriff, the recorder of deeds, the register of wills, and the police and fire commissioners. It was definitely the hub of old Philadelphia.

But that hub had become inadequate by the late 1860s. Complaining of overcrowded and inadequate office and court space, the city government urged a massive relocation. So in 1868, the year CEM was admitted to the bar, an ordinance was passed calling for the replacement of State House Row by a new municipal building to be constructed on the south side of Independence Square, facing Walnut Street. The ordinance provided that the old State House buildings would be torn down once the new City Hall was built. Some Philadelphians were so appalled by the prospect of losing the old State House that they appealed to the Pennsylvania General Assembly.

The Assembly ruled out the demolition of the old buildings and decreed a referendum so the public could choose either Washington Square (across from the Firm's original office) or Penn Square for the new City Hall. Penn Square, previously called Center Square, was at the junction of Broad and Market streets. It had once been the location of the city's pumping station, before the waterworks were moved in the 1820s to the classical buildings that still line the Schuylkill in Fairmount Park behind the Philadelphia Museum of Art.

Hoping to keep City Hall in the old city, some prominent Philadelphians claimed Penn Square was too far from the city's business center. One of the louder protests came from the *Public Ledger*, which had constructed its new building on the southwest corner of Sixth and Chestnut streets in 1867. Nevertheless, when a referendum was held in 1869, Penn Square won. From its beginnings along the Delaware River, the city's center of gravity would now definitely shift to the west.

On July 4, 1874, sixteen months after the Firm was founded, the cornerstone was laid for the new City Hall. It took twenty-six years to build. *Fortune* magazine would later comment that during construction "the entire technology of architecture changed so that City Hall is the last great structure to have been erected on the general principles of the pyramid builders."[15]

The building of City Hall not only continued seemingly forever but also cost an astronomical $25 million. Generations of politicians and contractors were nourished at the trough of this never-ending project. Most of them were active with the Republican party, which enjoyed an unbroken stretch of political dominion in Philadelphia between 1884 and 1951. The machine functioned so efficiently that there were even times when the Republican party paid the rent for the Democratic party's city headquarters. As Lincoln Steffens put it back in 1903, Philadelphia was of all American cities "simply the most corrupt and the most contented."[16]

The new City Hall was finally completed just after the turn of the century. With its tower supporting a statue of William Penn, this enormous Second Empire building was (and still is) the tallest structure with load-bearing walls in North America. Law practitioners inevitably followed lawmakers to Center City. Morgan & Lewis did so in 1904, when the Firm relocated to 934 Land Title Building.[17] That building, at Broad and Chestnut streets, was just a block south of the new City Hall.

With the westward move, the legal community in the old city withered. Lawyers' Row on east Washington Square, where CEM had served as first assistant city solicitor, disappeared in 1913 along with other eighteenth- and nineteenth-century buildings, thus making way for the headquarters of the Penn Mutual Life Insurance Company, which became a Firm client in 1989. Another monument, the Academy of Music, was already standing when City Hall was built. Located in Center City at Broad and Locust streets, it had been completed in 1857. Ulysses S. Grant was renominated there for the presidency at the 1872 Republican National Convention. Since 1900, the Academy has been the home of the Philadelphia Orchestra, which became a Firm client in 1959, as recounted in Chapter 33.

■ ■ ■ ■ ■

In retrospect, the last three decades of the nineteenth century may be viewed as a period of unparalleled economic development for the United States, and consequently a good time for Messrs. Morgan and Lewis to set up shop. But those decades also included several business panics in a nation wholly committed to laissez-faire principles. Two months after the Firm was founded, there were dramatic business failures in Vienna, traceable to the Franco-Prussian war less than three years earlier. One default triggered another, as the Panic of 1873 spread to other European money centers. A worldwide depression ensued, signaled in the United States by the collapse of the New York branch of Jay Cooke & Company on September 18, 1873.

Jay Cooke & Company was a Philadelphia investment banking house with its headquarters on South Fourth Street next to the Girard National Bank, an original client of the Firm. Cooke had marketed an amazing $400 million in government securities to fund the Civil War. And in the postwar period, he had helped finance 50,000 miles of railroad construction in the United States. Much of the capital he raised came from foreign sources: The United States was a debtor nation then, as it remained until World War I and became again in 1985. So when foreign lenders sought to liquidate their holdings, credit disappeared in the United States.

The Panic of 1873 was followed by a five-year depression marked by business failures, unemployment, social unrest, and deflation.

Conditions were so bad that some Irish and German immigrants even fled back to their native countries. It was the longest business contraction in United States history, even longer than the first leg of the Great Depression from 1929 through 1933.

Despite these difficulties, Philadelphia weathered the storm. One reason was its diversified economy. Another was the stimulus of preparing for the Centennial Exposition—where Bell would display his telephone. On May 10, 1876, President Grant declared the Exposition formally open. It was one of Philadelphia's finest achievements. For six months, national and international attention focused on the city. About 10 million people visited the Exposition before it closed in November. The attractions were housed in 180 buildings constructed in Fairmount Park along the Schuylkill northwest of Center City. Just a few of those buildings remain. One of them, Memorial Hall, is visible in the distance from the Firm's present offices at One Logan Square.

■ ■ ■ ■ ■

Since the Firm's surviving records from its earliest years are skimpy, it is difficult to assess the prosperity of the founding partners. By the 1880s, there were roughly 1,500 lawyers in Philadelphia. According to John G. Johnson's biographer, only about one-third were self-supporting, of whom less than a hundred made more than $5,000 per year, and only two or three (Johnson included) had incomes of over $100,000.[18]

Still, Messrs. Morgan and Lewis apparently did well enough. From the time of the Firm's founding, it served the Girard National Bank, as well as the Germantown Dispensary and Hospital (now called the Germantown Hospital and Medical Center). When the Germantown Trust Company was chartered in 1889, it also engaged the Firm. Representations of the hospital and the trust company underscore the prominence of the Morgan family in the Germantown community.

Germantown Hospital is a sometime client even today. *A History of Caring for the Sick Since 1863*, published by the hospital, tells how CEM's legal opinion was requested in 1894 regarding the propriety of admitting *paying* patients. At that time, most hospitals functioned purely as charities, and the admission of patients where money changed hands "required special arrangements which seemed to conflict with the basic purpose of the institution."[19]

CEM's opinion letter to William H. Haines, president of the

hospital's board of managers, was attached to the minutes of the November 1894 board meeting. In it he counseled the hospital: "I do not think that your right to accept persons able and willing to reimburse the hospital for services could be seriously questioned, unless by doing so you should impair your ability to accommodate and care for the class specifically intended to be benefited (as set forth in the Hospital's charter)."[20] Despite Morgan's advice, a majority of the hospital's board resisted the idea of "paying patients," and it was five years before they were regularly admitted. If hospital care were free today, there would be no need for Independence Blue Cross, a major client of the Firm.

When CEM died in 1917, his obituary described him as "one of the leaders of the Philadelphia bar, with a clientele comprised of many of the city's largest banking and public service corporations."[21] He served on Philadelphia's Board of Education, as well as on the Board of City Trusts that administers the Stephen Girard estate. It is Firm lore that he was "an angel of a man." Apparently, he had a propensity for getting involved in pro bono matters and for taking cases "on spec." Morris Bockius had no such propensity. After about 1908, with CEM in decline, Bockius assumed control of the Firm. As he did so, CEM's angelic wings were clipped, again according to Firm lore.

Messrs. Morgan and Lewis arrived on the scene at a generally auspicious time. Philadelphia's industries made fortunes for many Philadelphians whose descendants still enjoy, in decreasing number and amount, the city's "old money." And where there is prosperity for business, there is prosperity for lawyers. By the end of the nineteenth century and into the twentieth century, the Firm would attract as clients the country's leading public utility holding company, the city's largest newspaper, the state's second-largest railroad, a major paper manufacturer, an international glass producer, at least four banks, and the largest manufacturer of steam locomotives in the world.

But all that would take five decades. Like every fledgling law firm, what the founding partners needed during their early years was one really good client. Such a client arrived in 1882. It was the United Gas Improvement Company, still a client of the Firm more than a century later.

CHAPTER 2

A CLIENT FOR ALL SEASONS

UGI becomes a client in 1882 ■ *The country's largest public utility holding company* ■ *Randal Morgan goes in-house* ■ *William Warden as a protégé of John D. Rockefeller* ■ *The heavy hitters organize* ■ *Electricity and gas fight it out* ■ *Philadelphia's longest-running political football game* ■ *The great gas grab of 1905* ■ *The mayor is enjoined in 1937* ■ *Living by the sword* ■ *Lawyers go back and forth* ■ *Fingers in all the pies*

Ⅰf a history of the Firm had to be written by reference to a single client, that client would surely be the United Gas Improvement Company, which changed its name to UGI in 1968. The Firm's work for UGI started in 1882, when UGI was founded and the Firm was nine years old. Although at least two other present clients reach back farther than UGI—indeed they reach back to the Firm's beginning in 1873—neither shaped the Firm's destiny as did UGI.

By the end of the nineteenth century, UGI had become the country's largest gas and electric utility holding company. And, through the representation of UGI, the Firm had become a significant force in the field of public utility law.[1] Work for UGI involved complex financings, mergers and acquisitions, real estate transactions, and tort law.

Tort law was much simpler in those early days, as evidenced by this terse Firm opinion dated March 3, 1903, to UGI:

> Dear Sir:
>
> We have examined and herewith return the statements in [the] above matter, together with letter of Mr. Ambrose to your company, dated February 23, 1903. The injuries to this person were, as shown by these papers, the result of his own negligence in holding a lighted candle over a box from which there was a strong smell of gas. He is a gas fitter by trade and is therefore presumed to know the risk he took in so doing. We are of [the] opinion that

these papers do not disclose a case in which your company is liable.

Yours truly,

/s/ Morgan & Lewis

It is not known whether this was enough to silence Mr. Ambrose. In those days, plaintiffs' lawyers may have been less ingenious. Also the law was more favorable to defendants.[2]

The Firm owes its representation of UGI to Randal Morgan, a younger brother of founding partner CEM. Randal received both his bachelor's degree in 1873 and his master's degree in 1876 from the University of Pennsylvania. After graduating, he maintained a lifelong relationship with Penn, serving as a trustee from 1893 and as chairman from 1922 until his death in 1926. In 1902, he donated to the university the Randal Morgan Physics Laboratory on Thirty-fourth Street. The building remains part of the campus today.

Like CEM, Randal Morgan did not go to law school. Instead he "read law" at Morgan & Lewis. While still at Penn, he was listed in the Philadelphia city directory as having an office at the Firm's address, although no occupation was given for him. Then during his last year at Penn, he was listed at that address as a "notary." Following his admission to the bar in 1877, he was listed as a lawyer, and between 1885 and 1895 he was a partner. It took Randal Morgan only eight years to become a partner, whereas it took Morris Bockius, who arrived in 1883 and became a partner in 1898, fifteen years. Was it nepotism? Was Bockius a slow starter? Or was it because Randal produced UGI as a client?

Upon the organization of UGI in 1882, Randal immediately became its inside general counsel, while maintaining for thirteen more years his relationship with Morgan & Lewis. In 1890, he was elected a director of UGI and served in that capacity until he died. His highest office was first vice-president and chairman of the executive and finance committee. Descriptions of Randal often characterize him as a philanthropist, raising the question whether material rewards are more bounteous for a lawyer inside a company or outside as a partner in a law firm. No reference has been found to older brother CEM as a philanthropist. Nor has any reference been found to CEM as a yachtsman, unlike Randal who crossed the Atlantic and toured the Mediterranean in 1906 aboard his steam yacht *Waturus*, built originally for an Austrian grand duke.

As inside counsel to UGI, Randal was apparently in a position to retain his own firm. The resulting relationship between the two entities has endured for more than a century. In fact, the three most signal events in the Firm's entire history may well have been the employment of Randal Morgan by UGI in 1882, the hiring of Morris Bockius by the Firm a year later, and the acquisition of Souser & Kleeb in 1959. The first event generated clients UGI, Philadelphia Gas Works, Philadelphia Electric Company, and the Bulletin Company, not to mention the Firm's utility practice generally. The second event yielded the Firm's financial practice and strongly shaped its development as an institution. The third event laid the groundwork for ML&B's national preeminence in the field of labor and employment law.

The Firm's early UGI file listings include thousands of collection cases against people who did not pay their gas bills, as well as the defense of tort claims brought by people like the unfortunate Mr. Ambrose. Over the years, generations of the Firm's young litigators would be nourished by these minicontroversies, and later by Federal Employers' Liability Act (FELA) cases for the Reading Railroad. (MLB's representation of the Reading Company is detailed in Chapter 10.)

Beyond routine cases for UGI, there were major corporate matters, as the company made dozens of acquisitions, expanded into the transit business, even owned for a time the largest construction company in the United States, entered into agreements with other utilities for power sharing, and then fought for years to survive the "death sentence" of the Public Utility Holding Company Act of 1935 (PUHCA). Despite the Firm's efforts, directed by William Clarke Mason, UGI was dismembered under that law during the 1940s. Today, although a significant company, it is a pale reflection of what it must have been at its zenith.

At that zenith in 1930, UGI had controlling interests (51 percent or more) in twenty-seven major companies, most of them utilities. Those companies, in turn, controlled another forty-four companies. In addition, UGI had less than controlling interests in another twelve utilities which, in turn, controlled twelve operating companies. It was this pyramiding of public utility companies that made them targets for New Deal legislation.

On the 1930 list of UGI's subsidiaries was Philadelphia Electric Company (PE), also a client of the Firm. PE was formed in 1881 by several of UGI's founders. UGI and PE had talked merger for years. In 1928, UGI finally acquired PE. After an uneasy fifteen-year relationship with its parent, PE was divested by UGI in 1943 pursuant to PUHCA. The Firm represented UGI and PE side by side before the merger, after the merger, and following the divestment. In recent years, the Firm's work for PE has been extensive, as related in Chapter 37.

So omnivorous was UGI that from 1928 to 1938 it owned United Engineers & Constructors, Inc., at that time the country's largest engineering and construction firm. United's operations extended to massive building projects in Europe, Argentina, Brazil, and Hawaii. And it erected two Philadelphia landmarks well-known to present-day Firm personnel—the Franklin Institute and Thirtieth Street Station.

■ ■ ■ ■ ■

When UGI was organized in 1882, the force behind it was William G. Warden, who had been instrumental in founding PE a year earlier. He and his descendants would enjoy many relationships with the Firm. In his early years, Warden had built a Pittsburgh-based business that manufactured oil refining equipment. Warden's equipment was used by operating companies of the Standard Oil trust, controlled by John D. Rockefeller. Rockefeller believed that businesses (or at least his businesses) should be totally integrated both vertically and horizontally. In short, he believed in monopoly and at one time controlled 90 percent of the country's petroleum industry. So he acquired Warden's company with Standard Oil stock, thus making Warden a millionaire.

Rockefeller also acquired Warden and sent him to Philadelphia to manage the Atlantic Refining Company, which Standard Oil had absorbed in 1874.[3] While president of the Atlantic Refining Company, Warden solicited the heavy hitters of his day to join him in creating UGI. They included department store pioneer John Wanamaker, textile manufacturer Thomas Dolan, and traction magnates Peter A. B. Widener and William L. Elkins. (More about Widener in Chapters 13 and 30.)

In those days, it was not clear whether gas or electricity would ultimately prevail as the preferred means of illumination. In 1881, the year before UGI was formed, Chestnut Street became Philadelphia's first electrically illuminated thoroughfare, with forty-nine arc lights extending from the Delaware River to the Schuylkill. At the same time, gas was generally used to light public buildings, homes, hotels, and clubs. For example, it was not until 1893 that electricity superseded gas lighting at Philadelphia's Union League.

Although UGI would work both sides of the street, its initial interest was gas. The words "gas improvement" in its name reflected its objective: to get more light out of gas. It did this by improving both the gas and the illuminating mantles. The gas was improved by being enriched with hydrocarbons from oil. The mantles were improved through the acquisition of the patent rights to the Welsbach process. UGI then created a subsidiary named Welsbach Incandescent Light Company, which manufactured the new mantles at a factory in Gloucester, New Jersey. (That company became a Firm client in 1887.) Between the improved gas and the improved mantles, illumination by gas enjoyed a short renaissance before finally yielding to electricity. Subsequently, gas was used primarily for cooking and heating.

To hedge its bets, UGI acquired its first electricity producer in 1886. It then created additional subsidiaries to manufacture generating equipment, incandescent lamps, and motors. The early UGI management must have moved at lightning speed. By 1891, the *North American* (a Philadelphia newspaper) could write:

> [T]oday The United Gas Improvement Company is the largest concern of . . . [its] kind in the United States, and gas and electric light companies from Maine to Florida and from the Atlantic seaboard to the Rockies are operated under its management.[4]

Toward the turn of the century, UGI even developed street railway systems in Pennsylvania, Delaware, Virginia, Connecticut, Rhode Island, North Carolina, and Iowa. The company's prosperity was also reflected in the twelve-story office building it constructed for itself at Broad and Arch streets in 1899. Now called One City Plaza, the building still stands, although UGI left Philadelphia in 1974 to settle in Valley Forge.

As UGI's acquisitions multiplied, it seemed to have the Midas touch. Its profits increased fivefold from 1922 to 1929. It expanded into the Midwest, where the Firm took part in working out consolidation agreements with that personification of utility holding companies, Samuel Insull. But Insull's house of cards collapsed in the 1930s, and he became a whipping boy for the legislation that led to UGI's dismemberment. (More about Insull and UGI's dismemberment in Chapter 14.)

■ ■ ■ ■ ■

As counsel to UGI, the Firm also played a major role in Philadelphia's longest-running political football game. The game commenced in 1897 and "made headlines regularly"[5] until 1972. It involved the operation and expansion by UGI of the Philadelphia Gas Works (PGW). In 1836, the city had constructed its first gas plant along the Schuylkill near Market Street, where PE's headquarters stands today. But as operated by the city, the system performed poorly, and "[p]olitical affiliation rather than competence determined employment in the gas service."[6]

The solution was an alliance with private enterprise. So in 1897, the city turned over to UGI three gas plants, seven independent gas-holder stations, 1,300 miles of pipes, and 216,000 customers. The turnover took the form of a thirty-year lease by which UGI would operate the system, pay rentals to the city, charge agreed-upon rates, and construct "betterments" that would become the property of the city free of charge when the lease terminated. The Firm drew the lease, which was witnessed by CEM and executed by a UGI founder and then president, Thomas Dolan. Dolan was one of Philadelphia's most prominent businessmen. From modest beginnings, he made a fortune in textiles before turning to utilities. A sometime president of the National Association of Manufacturers, he was also a frequent adviser to the Republican National Committee. Like Warden, he became a Firm client, as did generations of his descendants after his death in 1914.

Although the city's gas service improved dramatically under UGI's aegis, the honeymoon was brief. It ended with the great gas grab of 1905, "one of the most notable political upheavals in the history of the city."[7] Instigating the grab was Israel Durham, a powerful figure in the city's Republican organization at the turn of the century. Toward the end of his career, he wished to "make provision for his own future needs and also reward faithful supporters of the organization."[8] The gasworks was the intended vehicle—not for the first or last time.

As Durham worked out the deal with Dolan, the city would extend UGI's lease from thirty to seventy-five years, for which UGI would pay the city $25 million over three years instead of annual rentals then running $655,000. Thus, the city and presumably Durham would get their money up front, while UGI would effectively buy the gasworks and its valuable monopoly at a bargain price. The press went wild: One newspaper projected UGI's potential profit on the transaction at $884,572,000.[9] Unmoved, City Council passed the requisite ordinance on May 18, 1905, even though "2,000 men and women, jammed like sardines in the chamber and the adjoining corridors, screamed 'Thieves' and other epithets at the Councilmen."[10] Members of the clergy thundered from their pulpits, while ordinary citizens demonstrated in the streets, forcing some city councilmen to escape from their homes through their back doors. When the clamor did not subside, Dolan withdrew UGI's offer on May 18, leaving Durham to provide otherwise for "his future needs."

What about the Firm's role in the great gas grab of 1905? Since the Firm and UGI then functioned virtually as one, involvement is likely. But speculation is pointless: The files have long since been destroyed, unfortunately or perhaps mercifully. So let a veil be drawn over this squalid affair, which happened—or almost happened—at a time of especially venal politics and lusty capitalism.

Memories of the great gas grab long plagued UGI's relationship with the city, despite the unparalleled efficiency UGI brought to running the gasworks. As the thirty-year lease neared expiration in 1927, a study by the Bureau of Municipal Research of Philadelphia noted that Philadelphia's gas rates were approximately at market, that UGI's aggregate net income from the operation had totaled about $21 million, that UGI had paid the city $62 million in rentals while also providing $20 million in free gas and maintenance for street lamps, and that UGI had made betterments to the system of $33.8 million, more than twice the required amount.[11] So in 1927, a friendly City Council—there was not a dissenting vote—authorized a new lease for an indefinite period, terminable by either party at the end of any ten-year interval.

There followed another honeymoon and then a further upheaval in which the Firm was intensely involved. This time it was the city's turn to play great gas grab, with the mayor as grabber and UGI as grabbee. The year was 1937, and the nation was deep in the Depression. Essentially bankrupt and running an illegal deficit, the city desperately needed an asset to hock. A new mayor had taken office the year before. He was S. Davis Wilson, "controversial, overly fond of intoxicating liquors, but colorful."[12] Something of an iconoclast, he opposed both the New Deal and, though a Republican, the city machine. He also sported populist tendencies, playing to the gallery and promising the moon, including lower gas rates. If he could get his hands on the gasworks, which was debt-free, he would have a mortgageable asset, and he could also make good his campaign promise to reduce rates.

Although the gasworks lease was terminable in 1937, termination required that the city pay UGI for any unamortized betterments. Having no money to pay for the betterments, the mayor simply accused UGI of so mismanaging the gasworks that UGI was indebted to the city instead of the other way around. When the mayor gave notice terminating the lease, W. James MacIntosh, later an ML&B senior partner, recalled how all hands at the Firm were turned loose to rebut the mayor's contentions and work for renewal.

The city government was divided on the question. While the mayor fought renewal, City Council was again friendly. It passed an ordinance directing the mayor to execute a new lease with UGI. The mayor vetoed the ordinance. Council overrode the mayor's veto on December 29, 1937. The mayor then announced that he would simply seize the gasworks when the lease expired at midnight on December 31.

On the morning of December 31, the Firm filed a bill in equity to enjoin the mayor from seizing the gasworks, asserted that the Pennsylvania Supreme Court had original jurisdiction, managed to convene a majority of that court, gathered up the city solicitor, and presented its petition, which was argued by William Clarke Mason. During the argument, word reached the courtroom that the mayor had issued a "proclamation." It declared that the lease between the city and UGI would expire at midnight, that the city would take over the gasworks at that time, that a state of emergency existed requiring the mayor to assume command of the city's 4,000-man police force, that gas rates would henceforth be halved, and that employees of the gasworks would receive a 5-percent wage increase. Something for everyone.

But within hours, the Pennsylvania Supreme Court rendered the mayor's proclamation a *brutum fulmen*, as lawyers say. The court granted the relief urged by the Firm, noting that "this is such an extreme case as to make it the duty of the court to take original jurisdiction" and that "defendant Mayor's threats . . . exhibited such disregard for law that it was necessary immediately" to grant the injunction.[13] After further hearings, the court rejected the mayor's allegations that UGI had mismanaged the gasworks and was therefore indebted to the city. (Press headlines quoted Mason as saying "the mayor has been living recently like 'Alice in Wonderland.'"[14]) The injunction was made permanent on June 30, 1938, and a new twenty-year lease between the city and UGI was executed on October 5, 1938.

Although the mayor failed in his effort to seize and mortgage the gasworks, the fiscal cat still had to be skinned. The solution was a "sale" in 1939 by the city to the Reconstruction Finance Corporation of the annual rentals payable by UGI to the city under the lease. The sale covered the period from 1940 to 1957 and raised the $41 million necessary to eliminate the city's deficit. It was during such period, in 1947, that the Firm opened its Washington office, as related in Chapter 20. That office would play an important role in federal regulatory proceedings involving UGI and particularly Philadelphia's gasworks.

Tensions between UGI and the city mounted again when the lease neared its termination date in 1958. As before, ML&B worked closely with UGI to secure renewal. In a memo to City Council dated August 18, 1958, UGI reviewed the sixty-year history of its relationship with the city: The city had received cash payments of almost $200 million from UGI, as well as free services worth at least $20 million. Moreover, through internal financing, UGI had built up a gasworks valued at $335 million.

Although the lease was again renewed in 1958, the relationship was clearly winding down. City Council was no longer friendly: The gasworks was an irresistible political plum crying out to be plucked. Still, the citizenry was wary of a patronage play, approved of UGI's service, and required reeducation. This the city did by sniping endlessly at UGI and encouraging the press to join the fray. No item was too minuscule for criticism: UGI executives should not be permitted to treat any part of their Union League dues as a gasworks expense. Nor was any item too speculative: UGI should not be permitted to keep profits earned from selling gas elsewhere, to the extent that such profits arguably derived from bulk buying made possible by UGI's operation of the city's gasworks. Ultimately, the relationship between the city and UGI was not worth saving, and UGI ceased operating the gasworks in 1972. When turned back to the city, it was valued at $400 million and was the largest municipally owned gas operation in the United States. UGI had done its job well.

ML&B was an early casualty of this political infighting. On November 6, 1962, former Philadelphia Mayor Richardson Dilworth was defeated as he ran for governor of Pennsylvania. Three days later, Dilworth's law firm was appointed counsel for the gasworks, thus succeeding the Firm, which had served in that capacity since 1897. The timing was said to be "a coincidence."[15] MacIntosh called the appointment a "consolation prize for Dilworth."

As political fortunes changed, Dilworth's firm later lost the gasworks to yet another firm. On January 6, 1972, the day Dilworth's replacement was announced in the media, MacIntosh and the author passed Dilworth on the ground floor of the Fidelity Building. MacIntosh greeted Dilworth cheerily, saying, "Live by the sword, die by the sword." Dilworth simply smiled.

The story has a coda. Between 1978 and 1989, the Firm again received assignments from the gasworks, years after its separation from UGI. The work involved rate-making proceedings handled by Philadelphia partners Kenneth Myers and David MacGregor, as well as federal gas regulatory matters handled by Washington partners Frank Saponaro, Mary Baluss, and Roberta Halladay. As it turned out, only ML&B had the required expertise in gas rate-making and federal gas regulation. Law firms are not fungible.

■ ■ ■ ■ ■

For more than a century, UGI has stood alone in terms of the number of lawyers trained by the Firm before going in-house to work for a client. Randal Morgan moved from the Firm to the company in 1882, while maintaining his relationship as a partner in the Firm until 1895. Clarence A. Warden—son of William G. Warden, Rockefeller's partner and a founder of both UGI and PE— became an associate in the Firm in 1903. He left the Firm in 1906 to succeed Randal Morgan as general counsel of UGI, as Morgan moved higher into management. Then Warden was succeeded in 1921 as general counsel of UGI by Garfield Scott, whose son Donald Scott became an ML&B partner in 1964.

In addition, William Findlay Brown was a partner in the Firm from 1898 to 1902 before leaving to become president of Welsbach, the subsidiary that made the improved gas mantles. Also, William Warden Bodine was associated with the Firm between 1914 and 1919, when he left to join UGI's legal department. He advanced through the ranks and served as UGI's president from 1940 to 1943.

Later, Thomas Lefevre, who was made a partner in 1956, left the Firm to become president of UGI in 1979. Then Lon Greenberg severed his ML&B ties in 1980 to join UGI's legal department, subsequently becoming senior vice-president—legal and corporate development, thus taking Randal Morgan's original job and bringing the list full circle.

Some UGI directors also had special relationships with the Firm. In addition to former ML&B lawyers Randal Morgan, William Warden Bodine, and Thomas Lefevre, there were at least three UGI directors supplied over the years by sometime Firm client Drexel & Co. and its New York counterpart, J.P. Morgan & Co. One was Edward Stotesbury, who served on the UGI board from 1915 to 1932. Stotesbury was a close friend of Bockius and an important Firm client. (More about Stotesbury in Chapter 11.)

Another Drexel partner on UGI's board was Thomas Sovereign Gates. He served as president of the University of Pennsylvania from 1930 to 1944 and was a UGI director from 1927 to 1943. A Chestnut Hill neighbor of William Clarke Mason, Gates was a long-time ML&B client whose estate the Firm handled after his death in 1948. Finally, Drexel was represented by Charles D. Dickey, who served on the UGI board from 1930 to 1938. Between 1969 and 1980, his son, Charles D. Dickey, Jr., was president of Scott Paper Company, another client of the Firm, as detailed in Chapter 7.

In the early days, the same people seemed to have their fingers in all the pies, and relationships stood for more than they do now. Society was more cohesive and elitist. But it was an open society. Birth into it was not required. It could be entered by merit, as in the case of Morris Rex Bockius.

CHAPTER 3

THE GREAT PRECIPITATOR

History as biography ■ A change of name ■ Bockius dominates ML&B from 1908 to 1939 ■ The largest law firm in Philadelphia by 1920 ■ Rainmaking ■ Penn Law School in the 1880s ■ A Christmas Carol at Wyndmoor ■ Directorships ■ Disapproval of bar activities and marriage ■ The morning meeting and tales of derring-do ■ Sunday at the Bockius home ■ Construing the Bockius will ■ Clients of the Bockius halcyon years

A year after UGI became a client in 1882, Morris Rex Bockius arrived at the Firm fresh from law school. His middle name may have set his destiny. For with his regal qualities, Bockius completely dominated the Firm from after the turn of the century until a few years before his death in 1939.

Carlyle equated history with the biographies of great men, while Tolstoy denigrated the hero's role, asserting that human events were predetermined by complex and conflicting forces. In the case of the Firm, Tolstoy must yield to Carlyle: The Firm was not a fortuity but largely the creation of one man. And of the three lawyers who gave Morgan, Lewis & Bockius its name, that man was Bockius. He built the Firm so that by 1920 it numbered fifteen lawyers and was the largest in Philadelphia.[1]

In prehistoric times, great hunters who killed more than they ate furnished surpluses for their tribes. In the context of today's law firms, those great hunters have evolved into rainmakers or, in Romance-language terms, precipitators. All law firms require precipitators, of whom ML&B has had its share. But no Firm partner ever made rain of such quality and quantity as Bockius. In fact, it is likely that up to the time of his death only one Philadelphia lawyer surpassed Bockius as a precipitator. That lawyer was the legendary John G. Johnson, whose *New York Times* obituary in 1917 characterized him as arguably "the greatest lawyer in the English-speaking world."[2] Some of the Firm's many contacts with Johnson over the years will be covered in subsequent chapters.[3]

With CEM ailing in his later years (he died in 1917) and Francis Draper Lewis never the Firm's dominant force (he was largely retired by the 1920s and died in 1930), it was Bockius who shaped the Firm and developed its practice. His halcyon years of client attraction and Firm governance started in the first decade of the 1900s and lasted into the 1930s. More than a half century after his death, the Firm still feels his influence.

Bockius was born on October 3, 1859,[4] in Germantown, where his father was a "bespoke tailor."[5] Early Philadelphia city directories show the haberdashery firm of Bockius & Rex on Germantown Avenue, and the elder Bockius's obituary in 1892 recited that the "[d]eceased for many years was the leading merchant tailor of the town, and the most fashionable and aristocratic of citizens led his custom."[6] Bockius's father was in partnership with a Rex and also had Rex ancestors. Hence Morris *Rex* Bockius. Both the Bockius and the Rex names in Germantown date back before 1700, when Bockius's forebears emigrated from the Palatinate.

Bockius studied at Germantown Academy, then located near the family home, followed by the College of the University of Pennsylvania and thereafter its law school, from which he graduated in 1883. He was the Firm's first Penn Law School product, since CEM and Randal Morgan read law, and Lewis graduated from Harvard Law School.

By the time Bockius matriculated at Penn, the university had moved (in 1872) from Ninth and Chestnut streets to its new campus in West Philadelphia. Law school classes were held on the third floor of College Hall, and the course was two years in duration. (It would be extended to three years in 1888.) Until 1889, Penn Law School was essentially a commercial enterprise. The faculty, consisting of practicing attorneys, rented space from the university, sold tickets for admission, and pocketed the proceeds.

After graduating from law school, young Bockius approached Randal Morgan for a job at UGI. Randal had been at UGI only a year and did not need an assistant. But he was impressed by Bockius, whom he referred to brother CEM. CEM hired him. According to Firm lore, Bockius not only worked indefatigably but also was exceedingly deferential to the Morgan family, whom he held in awe. In return, the Morgans virtually adopted Bockius. Later he would be the only non-Morgan invited to the Morgan family gala held each Christmas at Wyndmoor, the baronial Randal Morgan estate, where the many Morgans gathered to perform Dickens's *A Christmas Carol.* Also, when Bockius built his home in 1906 at 528 Church Lane in Germantown, the land he chose was just across the street from CEM's home. The lore also suggests that Bockius remained in awe of the Morgans long after his achievements far surpassed those of CEM.

Bockius did not become a partner until 1898, fifteen years after he arrived at the Firm. He was then thirty-nine years old. But after a slow start, his rise was meteoric. In 1908, his name was added to the Firm name, which once and for all became Morgan, Lewis & Bockius. Every year, the Firm's incoming associates are given the bad news: They will never see their names on the marquee. The name issue—which has torn some law firms asunder—was decided early in the century and is nonnegotiable.

Bockius's obituaries in 1939 were carried by the *New York Times* and *New York Herald Tribune,* as well as by the four leading Philadelphia newspapers: the *Evening Bulletin, Philadelphia Inquirer, Record,* and *Evening Public Ledger.* While each of the four Philadelphia newspapers used a different picture of Bockius, the text was essentially the same, suggesting that it was taken from a press release and not from information accumulated by the newspapers earlier about so celebrated a man. In fact, he was not celebrated in the popular sense. Only the *Record* left the beaten path: "Mr. Bockius, a member of the bar for 56 years, seldom went into court himself. Yet as an expert in corporation finance he played an important part in legal and business affairs in Philadelphia."[7]

While maintaining a low public profile, Bockius was highly visible where he thought it counted—with clients and the business community. He was at various time on the boards of Girard National Bank, Philadelphia National Bank, Fidelity Trust Company, Fidelity-Philadelphia Trust Company, Provident Life and Trust Company of Philadelphia, Provident Trust Company, Provident Mutual Life Insurance Company, Germantown Trust Company, Germantown Mutual Fire Insurance Company, and Philadelphia Electric Company. No lawyer of his time in Philadelphia served on so many boards of such prominence.[8]

Bockius's advice was sought by the first tier of Philadelphia's business leaders. He was a business executive's lawyer with a clear appreciation of the bottom line. Had he been a litigator, he would surely have been more conspicuous. But he took the client's viewpoint that litigation was not cost-effective and should be avoided where possible. When a court battle was inevitable—when conquer we must—he made certain the Firm could field a top gladiator. CEM had been a fine trial lawyer. He was followed by R. Stuart Smith, the Firm's preeminent litigator from 1908 to 1922. After Smith's death, Bockius attracted William Clarke Mason to the Firm. Mason was one of Philadelphia's all-time great trial lawyers.

Bockius was disinterested in the organized bar, even hostile to it. He regarded bar association pursuits as wastes of time and vehicles by which lawyers came together to congratulate one another on their achievements, most of them imaginary. But he did not impose this view upon other partners whose judgments he respected. Mason, for example, would rise to the highest ranks within the Philadelphia, Pennsylvania, and American bar associations.

Those who knew Bockius attest to his quietly dominating personality. Everyone has attended meetings where groups of people, perhaps clients and their lawyers, gather to argue and decide upon a course of action. In such meetings, many opinions and proposals will be advanced, some compelling, some unpersuasive. Gradually one person, without noticeably trying, will take charge of the meeting. That person, not necessarily the most brilliant, knows instinctively how to advance from point A to point B and so on through the alphabet. When the meeting is over, that person's approach will have been adopted. Bockius was such a person. He had presence, and he spoke from preparation and conviction. Clients naturally wanted him on their side.

The business acumen of many lawyers stops with advising their clients. Few lawyers, including some of the most effective practitioners, have the organizational and operational skills required to run a major law firm. John G. Johnson, for example, did not have them and did not care. His firm was a sole proprietorship that died with him.[9]

By contrast, Bockius was the archetypal organization man. For him the institution was paramount, not the individual. A long-range planner, he was totally committed to the Firm and the idea that he should leave it bigger and better for future generations. He started by developing a fine stable of clients. Along the way he added a fine stable of lawyers, including Clement Wood in 1901, A. Allen Woodruff in 1915, Francis Bracken in 1918 (as a partner), Arthur Littleton in 1920, William Clarke Mason in 1922 (as a partner), and W. James MacIntosh in 1926.

Then there was the way Bockius conducted the Firm's practice on a day-to-day basis. Control was total with nothing left to chance.

Currently, the expression is "hands-on management." Office hours were from 8:30 a.m. to 6 p.m. Monday through Friday and from 8:30 a.m. to 1 p.m. on Saturdays. It was not until 1947 that Pennsylvania banks began closing on Saturdays, which meant the financial community, including lawyers, could treat Saturday as a day off. The Firm maintained official skeleton crews for half-day Saturday duty through the 1970s. But obviously all such niceties yield to the overarching principle that busy lawyers have always worked without regard to what day it is—Saturdays, Sundays, and holidays as required.

During the Bockius years, the opening of the mail was like the ritual levee practiced by some royal houses in the seventeenth and eighteenth centuries. At 8:30 a.m. every day (including Saturdays), all partners gathered in Bockius's office. Each piece of mail was opened, read, and the appropriate course of action determined. Assignments were specific, and there was never any doubt about who was charged with doing what and by when.

The levee, actually called the "morning meeting," continued into the 1970s in diluted form before petering out altogether. Post-Bockius, the time was 9:15 a.m., manifesting some weakening of the moral fiber, and the content obviously did not include opening and reading the mail. Instead, the senior partner (or, starting in 1971, the chair for that year of the Executive Committee) would call upon each partner by name, and such partner would respond with the word "nothing" or would report a new client, a new matter, or a major victory.

It was not uncommon for reports of major victories to embody elements of cliffhanging or portray the triumph as against preposterous odds. The recitals were gripping: "The deal almost cratered three times during the closing that lasted sixteen hours before we all broke up at 2 o'clock this morning"; or "The jury returned a verdict for our client, even though the judge was really antagonistic to us in the charge, having recommended earlier that we settle for the other side's demand."

Defeats were rarely reported at the morning meeting, except those in the press or otherwise so well known around the Firm that they could not be ignored. The meeting concluded with "the reading of the checks"—a kind of financial benediction. At one time, a list of the prior day's fee receipts of $1,000 or more was read by reference to the client, the amount, and the lawyer who was responsible for the client. When inflation and the Firm's size rendered this too tedious, the number was raised to $10,000, before the benediction was scrapped altogether.

In addition to long daytime hours, the work schedule during the Bockius years included two or three evenings each week. To a lesser degree, these work habits survived Bockius, and it was common well into the 1960s for lawyers to stay and work one or more evenings each week after "going out for a bite." (If a sizable group of lawyers went out together, bite time expanded exponentially due to camaraderie.) Nevertheless, starting in 1939 with the Mason years, evening service became more sporadic, and it does not appear that the Firm's lawyers were driven as hard as during the Bockius era.

Bockius set a good example by working at least as diligently as his colleagues. He also starched their resolve by patrolling the floor and, in the new Fidelity Building after 1928, by positioning his office at the end of the hall so he could observe the whereabouts of all lawyers as they moved about the premises.

This is not to say that Bockius was a drudge. On the contrary, he was charming and greatly in demand on the social circuit. His large house on Church Lane was the scene of much entertaining of colleagues and clients. According to J. Tyson Stokes, his household staff included a full-time chauffeur, since Bockius never learned to drive. In those days, driving was something done by coachmen, and people of Bockius's standing were not coachmen. Also, the luxury cars of pre-World War I days required skilled attention on a daily basis. In the case of the Bockius car, that attention included the semiannual rotation of its two bodies on the same chassis: One was the touring-car body used between April and October; the other, the limousine body, used during the other months.

Stokes's father and Bockius were best friends. Their houses were within walking distance. Consequently, Bockius was a regular guest at the Stokes's home for Sunday dinner in an age when that meal followed church services and was an important culinary and social ritual. But before Sunday dinner came Sunday breakfast. Let Stokes tell the story:

> Uncle Morris and I breakfasted together every Sunday morning from a menu which never varied and which still stimulates my saliva. Breakfast started with fresh orange juice, followed by smooth Irish oatmeal smothered in heavy cream, then a concoction served from an antique English Sheffield oval hot water dish called, for some reason, "stewed meat," apparently ground steak cooked in a cream sauce, and, finally, English, French or German pancakes, depending on the humor of Annie, the cook. When I was very young, Uncle Morris extended the breakfast hour by reading to me the

"comics" from the *Philadelphia Press*—Hairbreadth Harry, The Katzenjammer Kids, Buster Brown and Happy Hooligan.[10]

Those who knew Bockius find it difficult to think of him as a reader of comics. Stokes paints the picture: "Stern of visage, tall, clean shaven with gray hair, [Bockius] dressed in dark three-piece tailor-made suits and carried (or wore) a walking stick until they went out of fashion."[11] But inside every grown man lurks a little boy, and Bockius was apparently no exception. Perhaps he was lavishing his fathering instinct on young Stokes, since, despite an active social life, Bockius never married and had children.

In an amusing letter to Mason in 1925 as Mason vacationed in New Hampshire, Bockius reminisced that he had been successful for many years in escaping "American widows [who] are more dangerous than English dowagers or Rumanian [sic] queens." (While on a mission for the Baldwin Locomotive Works in Romania, he had become acquainted with that country's Queen Marie.) As a prosperous and distinguished lawyer, it is likely that Bockius had many narrow escapes.

Bockius's aversion to marriage was a cross also borne by his colleagues. Arthur Littleton, who was the Firm's senior partner from 1957 through 1966, remembered when, as an associate in 1922, he approached Bockius with trepidation to announce his forthcoming marriage. Stokes noted that other young lawyers had the same problem when the time came for them to make similar disclosures to the senior partner. Such announcements were not greeted with enthusiasm. According to Stokes, Bockius thought marriage "diluted and interfered with the professional efforts of the lawyers in the firm."[12] In this he agreed with Francis Bacon, the renowned Lord Chancellor of England, who wrote: "He that hath wife and children hath given hostages to fortune; for they are impediments to great enterprises."[13]

Bockius died on April 13, 1939, at The Cabin, his country house near Media, Pennsylvania. He left a sizable estate but no close relatives. Treating the Firm as his family, he made provision in his will for each member of that family according to his or her rank. Benjamin Quigg, who was a partner from 1956 to 1983, has vivid recollections of the Bockius will. Quigg came to the Firm in 1934 at age seventeen as an office boy. He then learned shorthand and became a secretary before going to college and law school. He was a secretary when Bockius died, but he had held that position for less than a year. Now the problem: Bockius left $100 to anyone who had been an office boy at the Firm for more than one year. He left $250 to anyone who had been a secretary at the Firm for more than three years. Quigg had been at the Firm for five years, although for less than one year as a secretary. Should he receive $100 or $250? He benefited from loose construction and received $250—a tidy sum in those days.

Among the elite of Philadelphia during the Bockius era, it was useful to have a name like Biddle or Cadwalader, or an ancestor who signed the Declaration of Independence. It was also useful to be the son of a successful lawyer or wealthy industrialist. Bockius was none of these, but he nevertheless entered the inner sanctum of Philadelphia's business community and apparently also its social circle.

Major clients for which the Firm was active during the Bockius halcyon years (with the dates when the Firm commenced representing them) include: Girard National Bank (1873); UGI (1882); Philadelphia Electric Company (1887); Germantown Trust Company (1889); Provident Life and Trust Company (1908); Bulletin Company (1909); Fidelity Trust Company (1912), later Fidelity-Philadelphia Trust Company and still later Fidelity Bank; Pilkington Brothers Limited (1912), later Pilkington plc; Scott Paper Company (1915); Baldwin Locomotive Works (1917); Victor Talking Machine Company (1920); Drexel & Co. (1921); Provident Trust Company (1922); Provident Mutual Life Insurance Company (1922); Reading Company (1922); and Philadelphia-Girard National Bank (1926), renamed Philadelphia National Bank in 1928 and CoreStates Bank, N.A. in 1990.

A number of these clients will be considered in the following chapters. Some have ceased to exist altogether. Others have evolved beyond recognition. Still others are clients of the Firm even today.

CHAPTER 4

BANKS AND
TRUST COMPANIES

Essential clients ■ *Early history of the Philadelphia National Bank and the Girard National Bank* ■ *Stephen Girard buys the First Bank of the United States* ■ *Bockius and Joseph Wayne* ■ *The merger of 1926* ■ *Trust companies* ■ *Bockius on all the boards* ■ *He sires the Fidelity Building in 1927* ■ *The move to Logan Square in 1983* ■ *Law firms migrate to Philadelphia's northwest quadrant* ■ *CoreStates acquires First Pennsylvania Bank in 1989* ■ *Spreading the business*

In 1950, while the author was serving his clerkship at another law firm, he heard a senior partner of that firm say: "To be a really great law firm, you have to represent a department store, a railroad, and a bank. Two firms in Philadelphia have two of the three, but only one firm has all three."

The firm with all three was Morgan, Lewis & Bockius. Its clients included a department store (Strawbridge & Clothier), a railroad (the Reading), and a bank (the Philadelphia National). Putting aside the representation of a department store, the railroad part was easy: In those days, railroads were still the backbone of the economy. Incidentally, the same senior partner considered no enterprise quite so close to God as the Pennsylvania Railroad, often called the Standard Railroad of the World. That was twenty years before the wreck of the Penn Central in 1970, as discussed in Chapter 35.

About representing a bank, the senior partner was absolutely right then and now. Banks crave legal protection, preferring to wear both belt and suspenders. Also, they tend to be as punctilious in paying *their* bills as they expect their customers to be in paying *them*. Finally, they judge themselves overregulated and underloved. No better client.

Entire law firms have grown up around banks. Before the Depression, there was a plethora of banks, and any law firm worth its salt represented at least one. The relationship of a bank and its law firm was virtually that of joint venturers. The CEO of the bank and the senior partner of its law firm finished each other's sentences as they lunched together to plot strategy.

Now all that has changed. Such lunches are not exactly viewed with fervor by the bank's inside counsel. Anyway, everyone is too busy these days for such niceties. Sadly, something has definitely been lost over the years by both the bank and the law firm. But in those times when relationships with a bank's senior management were the lifeblood of a law firm, Morris Bockius was surely a master at cultivating them. He was on the boards of half a dozen banks, all of which the Firm represented. The most prominent of them was the Philadelphia National Bank (PNB). To understand how the Firm came to represent PNB, the histories of PNB and another bank, the Girard National Bank, must be traced side by side.

■ ■ ■ ■ ■

When PNB (originally called the Philadelphia Bank) was formed in 1803, there were roughly forty banks in the United States. All were state banks but one. Only the First Bank of the United States was a national bank.[1] It had been created by Congress in 1791 at the urging of Alexander Hamilton to act as a depository for government funds. Hamilton was farsighted, but the idea of a central bank remained politically unpopular, and the charter of the First Bank was not renewed when it expired in 1811.[2] Nevertheless, the First Bank was the progenitor of the Girard Bank (later called the Girard National Bank), which was among the first clients of the Firm in 1873 and which merged with PNB in 1926.

How did the First Bank metamorphose into the Girard National Bank? The answer is that the First Bank was not a central bank wholly owned by the government. Only one-fifth of its stock was so owned. The rest had been subscribed by private citizens, including Stephen Girard. When the First Bank's charter expired in 1811, Girard bought up the rest of its stock, as well as its bank building and related assets. With these he created his own private bank, known as the Girard Bank, which played a major role in financing the War of 1812.

Born in France in 1750, Girard came to Philadelphia in 1776. Successively a sea captain, a ship owner, and a merchant, he became a one-man conglomerate. When he died in 1831, he left an estate of $6 million and was said to be the richest man in America. His principal benefaction was Girard College, and his last will and testament spawned litigation that occupied Daniel Webster in the 1840s, as well as ML&B in the 1950s and 1960s. Representing

Girard's heirs, Webster attacked Girard's will and lost. A century and a quarter later, the Firm defended Girard's will on behalf of the trustees and also lost. (More about this in Chapter 16.)

After Girard's death in 1831, a group of private citizens obtained a state charter for the Girard Bank. With its new charter, it resumed operations in 1832. It was located in the First Bank's neoclassical building, constructed between 1795 and 1797 at 120 South Third Street and reputed to be the first edifice with a marble facade in the United States. Today, as part of the Independence National Historical Park, it is America's oldest extant bank building. It remained the headquarters of the Girard Bank (which rechartered in 1864 as the Girard National Bank) until 1926 and was undoubtedly the scene of many meetings involving the Firm's early lawyers as the bank's counsel.

So the Girard National Bank could arguably trace its lineage to 1791 and the First Bank of the United States. Even retreating from that claim, its lineage went back to 1811 when it became Stephen Girard's private bank, or to 1832 when it was chartered as a Pennsylvania state bank. Impressive credentials.

Somewhat less impressive were the credentials of the Philadelphia Bank, which arrived on the scene in 1803. True, its first president was George Clymer, a signer of the Declaration of Independence. But on Clymer's death he was found to be "almost hopelessly in debt to the Bank [so that] his debts were carried on the books for more than a generation."[3]

The Philadelphia Bank had another threshold problem: Its organizers were Jeffersonian Republicans. They were at odds with the Federalists who controlled the city's finances. Consequently, the other three Philadelphia banks conspired (in those pre-antitrust days) to destroy their new competitor by refusing to accept its notes. The Philadelphia Bank retaliated by refusing to accept their notes. In due course, the parties made peace, and by 1842 the Philadelphia Bank was the largest bank in the city, a distinction it would lose and regain several times over the ensuing century and a half. It was number one again just before World War I, by which time it had rechartered (in 1864) as the Philadelphia National Bank. There were then more than thirty national banks, about ten state banks, and roughly sixty trust companies in Philadelphia.

The Girard National Bank, descendant of the First Bank, was at that time Philadelphia's next largest commercial bank after PNB. The Firm was so identified with the Girard National Bank that, starting in 1889 and for some years thereafter, the Firm's entry in the *Hubbell* directory advertised it as "Attorneys to Girard National Bank."[4] The Firm's surviving records include lists of matters handled for the Girard National Bank going back to the Firm's earliest days. Among such matters is an 1888 Pennsylvania Supreme Court case in which the Firm prevailed on behalf of the bank.[5]

Joseph Wayne became president of the Girard National Bank in 1914. He had joined the bank in 1890, and over the years he and Bockius enjoyed close business and personal relationships. Bockius went on the board of the Girard National Bank in 1915, and Wayne was an ML&B client until his death in 1942, after which his estate was handled by the Firm. (More about Wayne in Chapter 13.)

By all accounts, Wayne was a superb banker—so superb that in 1926, with PNB's CEO nearing retirement, PNB's board sought to lure Wayne away from the Girard National Bank. (The PNB board then included Randal Morgan, CEM's brother and a former Firm partner.) As sometimes happens in such situations, they got more than just Wayne. They got the Girard, too. So Wayne became CEO of the newly merged Philadelphia-Girard National Bank. Bockius went on the board of the resulting bank, and the Firm became its counsel.

Wayne and Bockius did not stop to take a breath. In 1928, Philadelphia-Girard National Bank acquired Franklin Fourth Street National Bank, which had become the second-largest bank in the city. (At that point, Girard was dropped from the bank's name, which again became the Philadelphia National Bank.) The Firm handled the transaction for the acquiring bank, which was now four times the size of its nearest commercial bank rival in Philadelphia and nearly three times the size of its nearest trust-company rival. (That trust company was another Firm client, the Fidelity-Philadelphia Trust Company, on whose board Bockius also served.) In 1928, with PNB's "directors forming an assemblage of business leaders unmatched in Pennsylvania . . . [and with its] enlarged capital, lines of five million dollars were granted to the Campbell Soup Company, DuPont, Ford Motor Company, General Electric, General Motors and Philadelphia Electric."[6]

Bockius remained a member of the PNB board until his death in 1939. He was followed on the board by other ML&B partners: William Clarke Mason from 1939 until his death in 1957, Arthur Littleton from 1943 until 1969, and John Bracken from 1969 until 1982. When both Mason and Littleton were on the PNB board during the late 1940s and early 1950s, the Firm's involvement with the bank was so intensive that "ML&B practically ran the bank," according to G. Morris Dorrance, Jr., who was the bank's CEO from 1959 to 1987.[7]

■ ■ ■ ■ ■

Side by side with commercial banks such as the Girard National and PNB, there were trust companies. The oldest in Philadelphia was the Pennsylvania Company, chartered in 1812. Then came the Girard Trust Company (unrelated to the Girard National Bank) chartered in 1836, the Provident Life & Trust Company in 1865, the Fidelity Insurance Trust & Safe Deposit Company in 1866, the Philadelphia Trust Company in 1869, and the Germantown Trust Company in 1889.

Bockius became a director of the Germantown Trust Company in 1899, the Provident Life & Trust Company in 1908, and the Fidelity Trust Company in 1911. As he went on their boards, the Firm's files show that he gathered up their legal business. In 1926, the Fidelity Trust Company swallowed the Philadelphia Trust Company to form the Fidelity-Philadelphia Trust Company, the largest trust company in the city. The Firm represented Fidelity in that important transaction.

Trust companies had originally been formed to serve executors and trustees. The Firm's Germantown, Provident, and Fidelity file listings illustrate the fiduciary nature of such services. Representing those institutions, the Firm handled hundreds of estates and trusts, unlike the lending and collection work handled by the Firm for the Girard National Bank and (after 1926) for PNB.

Trust companies also provided safekeeping services. Such services were particularly in demand after the Civil War, due to the widespread ownership of negotiable bonds issued during that war. The Fidelity Trust Company promoted its safekeeping services by guaranteeing against losses due to bank robberies, which seem to have been numerous in those days. In an advertising brochure, Fidelity declared that its vault was protected by watchmen "provided liberally with Rifles, Pistols and Ammunition and they wear their Arms while on duty."[8]

Fidelity's founder and first president, Nathaniel B. Browne, had been a real estate lawyer. But he did the profession no favor. He pioneered title insurance, which replaced the searches and warranties of conveyancers. In that way, trust and title companies ultimately put out of business those members of the bar who had previously held a monopoly on conveyancing.[9] The Firm's stationery in the 1880s listed Bockius as a conveyancer. He made the adjustment.

■ ■ ■ ■ ■

In addition to serving on the board of the Fidelity-Philadelphia Trust Company, Bockius was a director of its subsidiary, the Fidelity Building Corporation, also a Firm client. The subsidiary's purpose in the 1920s was to construct and operate a thirty-story office building at 123 South Broad Street, to which the Firm moved in 1928. When completed, the structure was the ninth-largest office building in the world. Bockius led the project, and the bank's archives contain pictures of him surrounded by other dignitaries in straw hats as he laid the building's cornerstone with a silver trowel in 1927 and dedicated the finished building in 1928. The bank's archives also contain a silent movie, now on videotape, showing these festivities and the building's progress through various stages of construction. The giant steam shovels were magnificent.

In a sense, the Fidelity Building was not finished until the mid-1950s, when air conditioning was added. That mammoth improvement project cost more than the original building. But the system functioned better than many in newer buildings. Moreover, the Fidelity Building's windows could still be opened. That was a blessing on hot Sunday afternoons in the summer when the system was not working but lawyers were.

Prior to air conditioning, seersucker suits for the Firm's lawyers were *de rigueur* in the summer. Only the most pompous lawyers failed to remove their jackets when in their own offices. And even those who took them off could feel beads of perspiration trickling down their backs. The maintenance people closed the windows when they finished cleaning at night. So the first order of business in the morning was to fling the windows wide open. This sometimes caused papers to blow around the room and out the windows. Paperweights were much in use.

The Fidelity Building as sired by Bockius was superb, especially its multistoried banking floor with balconies, classical motifs, and coffered ceiling. The Italian renaissance-style structure featured imported marble and great bronze doors reminiscent of Ghiberti's masterpieces in Florence. For almost four decades, the Fidelity Building was the premier office structure in Philadelphia.

The building's services were no less elegant than the building itself. Tenants were looked after by Henry Lear, president of the Fidelity Building Corporation. A courtly man who wore a bowler, he presided over a small empire in his building. The empire included construction personnel and a resident architect. They were not workers who came and went. They were his permanent crew.

The Fidelity Building originally housed several hundred tenants. Lear kept a watchful eye on their growth and anticipated how the larger ones would expand and ultimately push out the smaller ones. He arranged the leases of the smaller ones accordingly. As expansion took place, the building architect drew the plans, and the in-house construction workers made the changes.

Occupying the southern wing of the Fidelity Building's twenty-first floor starting in 1928, the Firm adopted the address 2107 Fidelity Building, which remained its Philadelphia address for fifty-five years. The building was H-shaped. Consequently, as the Firm expanded, the next step was to advance northward and take the center of the H. Then an internal stairway was built that permitted expansion upstairs to the twenty-second floor where, at first, the Firm occupied only part of the southern wing. Next, the Firm picked up the remainder of the twenty-first floor, then up again to add the remainder of the twenty-second floor, then the twenty-third floor, and finally the twenty-fourth floor and miscellaneous space elsewhere in the building. By the time the Firm moved out of the building in 1983, it occupied more than 100,000 square feet of space—a far cry from Morgan & Lewis's original rooms at 623 Walnut Street.

The Fidelity Building was sold in 1982 for $63.5 million to a corporation owned by Mahdi Al-Tajir, one-time United Arab Emirates ambassador to Great Britain. The building, which had cost a stunning $10 million in 1927 (without air conditioning), was largely depreciated by the time of the sale. As a result, an extraordinary gain was realized by the bank. The Firm represented the bank in that transaction.

After fifty-five years in the Fidelity Building, the Firm moved in 1983 to more than 150,000 square feet of space in a newly constructed building at One Logan Square. Immediately prior to the move, the Fidelity Building's tenants comprised the Fidelity Bank, one major corporation, and four major law firms. Each tenant desperately needed space for expansion, but there was none in the building. The Firm hated to move. It had been in the building from the beginning and, second to the bank, was its largest tenant. Also, it was Bockius's building.

But the move to Logan Square was farsighted. As it turned out, the once-glorious Fidelity Building was not well maintained by its absentee owner, was resold to another absentee owner, and was ultimately abandoned by its major nonbank tenants before ending up in bankruptcy proceedings in 1992. Moreover, the Firm's site at Logan Square was unique, with its unobstructed views of the Benjamin Franklin Parkway and Logan Square. For many Philadelphians, the Parkway and Logan Square are on a par with the Champs Elysées and the Place de la Concorde in Paris.[10]

ML&B was the first lessee to sign on at One Logan Square, thus becoming the building's anchor tenant and "making the project go," in construction parlance. Of the thirty stories, the Firm occupied floors eighteen through twenty-four at the outset, with options to expand onto floors twenty-five through thirty over the period of the lease, which could extend as long as fifty years.

Buildings along the Parkway are subject to special setback requirements. Consequently, One Logan Square is triangulated at its eastern end. Another unique aspect of the Logan Square complex is the Four Seasons Hotel to the north. Whenever the Firm requires additional space for seminars and Firm meetings, it can expand into the hotel. Together, the office building and hotel surround a terraced garden with lighted pools and waterfalls.

Before the move, no law firm seriously thought of Logan Square as a proper address. The Philadelphia legal community had clustered within two blocks of Broad and Chestnut streets since its relocation from the old city at the turn of the century. Logan Square was at least five blocks away, and even that calculation demanded a diagonally flying crow. In fact, Logan Square was so far off the beaten path that the Firm's relocation committee was concerned about feeding the Firm's flock, since there were few eateries in the neighborhood. The solution was a cafeteria. In addition to feeding the flock, it promoted camaraderie and reduced downtime.

The Firm was not long off the beaten path. Within a few years, the city's second- and third-largest law firms also relocated to the area, as Logan Square became the most prestigious professional address in the city. The Firm had exorcised the spell of Broad and Chestnut streets and led the bar to a new life in the city's northwest quadrant.

■ ■ ■ ■ ■

Now back to banking and what happened to the plethora of banks and trust companies that graced the Philadelphia scene early in the twentieth century. Many fell prey to the Depression and were liquidated. Almost all the rest have disappeared through mergers. Today, only one is still headquartered in Philadelphia—CoreStates Bank, N.A., formerly PNB.

But it might have been otherwise. In 1960, PNB and Girard Trust Bank (again no relation to the Girard National Bank) tried to merge. It was an all-out effort in which senior partner Arthur Littleton led a powerful Firm team representing PNB. The shareholders of both banks approved the merger, as did the Comptroller of the Currency. But before the closing, the Justice Department brought an action in federal court to enjoin the merger on grounds that it violated the Sherman and Clayton acts. After the district judge rejected these contentions,[11] the Justice Department appealed directly to the United States Supreme Court. That Court reversed, holding the Clayton Act applicable.[12] The transaction did not close. Richardson Dilworth, formerly a mayor of Philadelphia, once remarked to the author that the decision kept the city's banks "in short pants."

But the Supreme Court may have done Philadelphia (and the Firm) a favor. After its merger with PNB aborted, Girard Trust Bank was acquired in 1983 by Pittsburgh's Mellon Bank Corporation and lost its identity in Philadelphia. If PNB and Girard had been successful in their merger effort, would Mellon have acquired the resulting bank? If so, PNB and Girard might both have disappeared from the local scene.

As to the other banks, the Provident National Bank was acquired in 1983 by PNC Financial Corporation, also based in Pittsburgh. (Earlier, when the bank was called the Provident Trust Company, the Firm was on retainer to it, with Bockius and later J. Tyson Stokes serving on its board.) The Fidelity Bank was acquired in 1988 by First Fidelity Bancorporation, based in Newark, New Jersey. (When the Fidelity Bank was a major Firm client, three ML&B partners served successively on its board: Bockius, W. James MacIntosh, and Richard Brown.)

One of the Firm's earliest banking clients, the Germantown Trust Company, was acquired by the Pennsylvania Company (subsequently First Pennsylvania Bank) in 1947. First Pennsylvania went through a rough patch in the 1970s, necessitating a rescue effort by the Federal Deposit Insurance Corporation. Subsequently, Marine Midland Bank staked out a position in First Pennsylvania with the apparent intention of acquiring the bank in the 1990s, when evolving interstate banking laws would permit. Marine Midland was controlled by the Hong Kong & Shanghai Banking Group—a long way from Philadelphia.

But in 1989, there was a surprising development. Just as Philadelphians had become reconciled that Marine Midland would ingest so venerable an institution as First Pennsylvania Bank, it became the subject of a bear hug by Meridian Bancorp, Inc., based in Reading, Pennsylvania. Wishing to repulse Meridian's embrace, First Pennsylvania turned to CoreStates Financial Corp., PNB's parent, as a white knight. CoreStates responded and acquired First Pennsylvania. The Firm handled the $745 million transaction, which closed in March 1990. The Firm's team was led by Donald Scott. Twenty-seven years earlier, Scott had assisted Arthur Littleton in the aborted PNB/Girard Trust merger. This time no one kept the Philadelphia banks in short pants.

Before the merger, CoreStates was a $16-billion bank, and First Pennsylvania a $7-billion bank. With its combined $23 billion in assets, CoreStates became the third-largest banking institution in Pennsylvania, exceeded only by the two Pittsburgh giants: PNC with $42 billion in assets and Mellon with $32 billion. Following the merger, CoreStates Financial Corp. changed the name of its major banking subsidiary from Philadelphia National Bank to CoreStates Bank, N.A., which thereafter also did business under the names Philadelphia National Bank and CoreStates First Pennsylvania Bank. In addition, CoreStates Bank, N.A. adopted the charter of First Pennsylvania Bank (which had itself adopted the charter of the Bank of North America), thus pushing its official origin back to 1781 and making CoreStates the oldest bank in the United States.

Today, no major bank does business exclusively with any single law firm. Loyalties are divided. Nevertheless, the Firm continues to receive what CoreStates calls the lion's share of its legal work. At the same time, the erosion of exclusivity has enabled the Firm to enter into exciting relationships with Citibank, Bank of America, Chase Manhattan Bank, Industrial Bank of Japan, Security Pacific National Bank, and Deutsche Bank, to name a few. Collectively, these relationships have been far more rewarding for the Firm than an exclusive relationship with any single bank could have been.

Yes, the senior partner was right who said that a major law firm had to represent a bank. Chapter 10 will deal with the railroad; and Chapter 14, with the department store.

CHAPTER 5

IN PHILADELPHIA NEARLY EVERYBODY READ THE *BULLETIN*

The files are reorganized ■ *Sarah Warden marries William McLean* ■ *The* Bulletin *becomes a client in 1909* ■ *The largest evening newspaper in the Western Hemisphere* ■ *Libel suits and contempt proceedings* ■ *Labor law problems* ■ *Richard Slocum and Kenneth Souser* ■ *A comfortable way of life* ■ *Television kills evening newspapers* ■ *A candlelight vigil* ■ *No buyer is found* ■ *Closing File Number 1*

For years, it was an article of faith that the Bulletin Company was the Firm's first client, because its file was Number 1. But recent research has revealed the fallacy of this claim. The confusion must be laid at the door of Miss Mulligan.

Kitty Mulligan applied for a job with the Firm in 1923. She was hired by Morris Bockius "on a temporary basis," as she would remark years later. By 1928, files were her bailiwick. At some point before she retired in 1970, she became Mrs. Munshower. Depending upon their vintage with the Firm, lawyers called her either Miss Mulligan or Mrs. Munshower. She was a woman of few words, patient, and ponderous. She was also well respected, and she knew where everything was. In the early 1960s, she had two assistants. Together they filed every piece of paper generated by the Philadelphia office. Based on her forty-seven "temporary" years with the Firm, Mulligan/Munshower could somehow put her hands on whatever needed retrieving. She was a computer in a precomputer age.

In 1928, Bockius directed that Mulligan/Munshower overhaul the filing system. Files maintained by lawyers (dangerous) or by secretaries (standards varied) were then in filing cabinets anywhere and everywhere—in lawyers' offices, in hallways, and in nooks and crannies. Some files going back to the Drexel Building days before 1904 had been removed en masse to the Land Title Building, and files that had accumulated after that time lacked centralized organization. The whole agglomeration was transported with the Firm to the new Fidelity Building in 1928.

Following the move, when Mulligan/Munshower reorganized the files, she gave some of them new numbers. By that time, the Firm's first client had ceased to exist, at least for the purpose of having a number. Its identity died with her, and the Bulletin Company simply took its place as Number 1.

Clients beget clients, and it seems likely that UGI begat the Bulletin Company as a client, courtesy of the William Warden family. As noted in Chapter 2, Warden was a trustee of the Standard Oil trust. He came to Philadelphia to preside over one of the trust's holdings, the Atlantic Refining Company. While doing so, he helped found UGI in 1882 and was its first president. At the same time, Randal Morgan became UGI's in-house lawyer, and UGI became the Firm's first major client. Randal arranged to have Morgan & Lewis plan Warden's estate. He witnessed Warden's will, and Bockius witnessed a subsequent codicil. When Warden died in 1895, the Firm handled the estate administration, including the disposition of his Standard Oil stock.

Considering his business successes, Warden must have been tireless on the job. Apparently, he was also tireless at home, since he fathered thirteen children, of whom twelve survived him. A daughter named Sarah married William McLean in 1889. The Firm has represented generations of Wardens and McLeans during the past century. In 1895, William McLean acquired the *Bulletin*, which became a client of the Firm in 1909.

If ever there was a stereotypical Philadelphia institution, it was the *Bulletin*. Billboards proclaimed: "In Philadelphia nearly everybody reads The Bulletin." When the *Bulletin* celebrated its hundredth anniversary in 1947, it had a circulation of 771,300 and was the largest evening newspaper in the Western Hemisphere.[1] A Sunday edition was launched in 1947. Soon its circulation was 630,000. Even when the *Bulletin* ceased publishing in 1982, it still had a daily circulation of 405,000 and a Sunday circulation of 426,000. In its heyday it was the "envy of publishers everywhere."[2]

The *Bulletin's* history goes back to 1847 when its name was the *Cummings Telegraphic Evening Bulletin*. It got off to a good start that year, reporting in its very first edition on April 12 the capture of Vera Cruz by General Winfield Scott during the Mexican War. But it suffered reverses, and when William McLean bought it in 1895 for $17,000, it was the smallest of Philadelphia's thirteen papers, with a circulation of only 6,317 copies. McLean, then forty-three years old, had already been in the newspaper business for twenty-five years, primarily in Pittsburgh. It did not take him long to turn the

Bulletin around. By 1905, it had a circulation of more than 200,000 and was Philadelphia's largest daily newspaper, a distinction it retained until 1980 when it was overtaken by the city's primary morning newspaper, the *Philadelphia Inquirer,* generally called simply the *Inquirer.*

When William McLean died in 1931, he was succeeded as president of the Bulletin by his son Robert, who ran the paper until he retired in 1975. Robert had held the rank of major during World War I, and everyone at the Firm called him Major McLean. The McLeans were fully committed to the newspaper business. William served as a director of the Associated Press from 1896 to 1924, when the major succeeded him. The major also served as president of the Associated Press from 1938 to 1957. The McLeans preached short leads, such as "President Shot Dead," "We're Number One," and "Man's Great Leap." The McLeans also held that a newspaper came into the home as a guest and should therefore be unobtrusive.

Under the McLeans, the *Bulletin* was not only unobtrusive but also conservative and identified with Republican principles. Although it won Pulitzer Prizes in 1964 and 1965, critics found it bland and lacking in depth. Still, it knew how to please the local crowd. An example is the edition (July 30, 1931) reporting William McLean's death. His obituary and a large picture of him were centrally placed on page one. Below the obituary were three other items. One noted the death of the mother of a former Philadelphia magistrate. She was eighty-one and was "felled by heat prostration." The second told of a woman in Atlantic City who suffered cuts and bruises when she stumbled while trying to recover a glove she dropped as she alighted from a trolley car. The third recorded the launching in Wilmington of "a double-ended steel automobile ferry." Hardly world-shaking events for the front page.

Joseph de Maistre observed that "every country has the government it deserves."[3] *Time* magazine quoted critics who applied the rule to newspapers. Parodying the *Bulletin's* slogan, *Time* wrote: "Only in Philadelphia would nearly everybody read the *Bulletin.*"[4]

Newspapers are active clients. They employ bright and well-informed people who are at the cutting edge, know where the bodies are buried, and work under extreme time pressures. They are marvelous sources of information for their law firms which, in turn, they regard as one of their research tools. Fellow pros working together.

But it is often dangerous for a newspaper to print all it knows (or thinks it knows), and one function of a newspaper's law firm is to review sensitive material before it goes to press. When something occasionally slips through or the decision is made to publish regardless of the risk, the resulting libel suit can be even better copy than the original story. The Firm's lawyers who defended libel suits brought against the *Bulletin* were amused at how keenly the *Bulletin* enjoyed publicity about itself, especially when it could righteously invoke the First Amendment.

One such case in 1963 involved contempt proceedings against the *Bulletin's* president and city editor for failing to disclose their sources in response to a subpoena by the then Philadelphia district attorney. He was Arlen Specter, subsequently a United States senator from Pennsylvania. The case was defended for the *Bulletin* by Firm partners Arthur Littleton and John McConnell, assisted by then associate Gregory Harvey. The lower court held the two defendants guilty of contempt, imposed fines, and sentenced them to five days in Philadelphia's county prison. On appeal, the order was reversed and the sentences were vacated.[5] The *Bulletin* reveled in the proceedings.

Like other newspapers, however, the *Bulletin* did not revel in its labor relations problems. Few industries can match publishing in terms of resistance to change by employees. Ultimately, the *Bulletin's* labor costs would be a factor in its demise. Nevertheless, the *Bulletin's* labor problems conferred a fortuitous benefit on the Firm. Today, the Firm is renowned for its extraordinary labor and employment law practice. The seeds of that practice go back to the late 1930s and the *Bulletin*. This is the place to summarize the story, which involves two lawyers, Richard Slocum and Kenneth Souser.

After graduating from Harvard Law School in 1925, Slocum helped form the firm of Saylor, Slocum & Ferguson. In 1930, that firm employed associate Kenneth Souser, just out of Penn Law School. Early in Slocum's practice, he had won a case holding unconstitutional a $10 license fee on delivery wagons operated by bakery companies. Consequently, Slocum came to represent the major commercial bakeries in the Philadelphia area. When the National Labor Relations Act was passed in 1935 and the bakeries had labor problems, they turned to Slocum. So Slocum turned to labor law, as did young Souser. Slocum landed the *Bulletin* as a labor client in 1937. A year later, he was invited to become the *Bulletin's* general manager (a new designation) and subsequently its executive vice-president in charge of operations. Slocum was a powerhouse who found the law too confining. When he gave it up, Souser inherited Slocum's labor practice. That inheritance included the *Bulletin's* labor representation. Meanwhile, the Firm continued as the *Bulletin's* general counsel.

By 1959, Souser's firm (Souser & Kleeb) was the premier management labor boutique in Philadelphia. At the same time, ML&B needed to enhance its labor law capacity. So it approached Souser, whose firm then merged with ML&B, as recounted in Chapter 15. The merger was a coup for both Souser and the Firm. Slocum, who died in 1957, would surely have applauded the combination. In addition to uniting the two lines of the *Bulletin's* representation, the merger gave ML&B the city's strongest labor law arm, which had its roots in Slocum's original labor practice. By the time Souser died in 1970, he could survey a veritable empire of labor law practice at ML&B, which he enjoyed tracing to Slocum when Slocum went to the *Bulletin*.

For many years, the *Bulletin's* publishing plant was at Filbert and Juniper streets, diagonally across from City Hall. Then, in 1955, the paper moved to a stunning new plant it had spent four years planning and constructing. Located west of the Schuylkill and Thirtieth Street Station, the new plant boasted two press lines longer than a football field. It was called the "world's most modern, 'horizontal' newspaper plant [and was] visited by newspaper publishers from all over the world."[6] The *Bulletin* appeared to be riding the crest. Then came the fall.

Applying the *Bulletin's* rule about short leads: TV killed evening newspapers. Although all newspapers were hurt by television, the effect was lethal for many evening papers. During the *Bulletin's* pretelevision heyday, many Philadelphia wage earners arrived home at roughly five in the afternoon. At about the same time, the *Bulletin* was lobbed onto their front steps by so-called paperboys—the *Bulletin* had 7,000 of them. The *Bulletin* was divided into two sections. After dinner, dad read the first section, while the kids worked on the second section, which included three pages of comics. (The *Bulletin* always had the best comics.) After dad finished the first section, he bumped the kids from the second section and dispatched them to do their homework. When mom emerged from doing her kitchen chores, it was her turn to read the paper. As the family's purchasing agent, she also paid special attention to the ads.

This comfortable way of life changed in the 1950s, when Philadelphia moved from an industrial to a service economy. Also, the suburbs grew, making it more costly and time-consuming to deliver a centrally produced newspaper over a wider area through dense rush-hour traffic. But worst of all, there was television. After dinner, the TV went on (if not already on) and did not go off again until bedtime. People had less time for reading, especially about events that happened much earlier in the day and could be seen more dramatically on the tube. Many evening newspapers became extinct.

It was different for morning papers. People still wanted to read about what had taken place during the night. On their way to work, they read on buses, trains, subways, and trolleys. Moreover, a morning newspaper was less subject to deadlines or dependent on home delivery than an evening newspaper. Of the *Bulletin's* circulation, 70 percent was delivered to the home, whereas only 50 percent of the *Inquirer's* morning subscribers had their papers delivered. Obviously this increased the *Bulletin's* costs.

The *Inquirer* is now *the* newspaper in Philadelphia. But it was a marginal enterprise before it and the *Philadelphia Daily News* were sold in 1970 by former Ambassador Walter Annenberg for $55 million to Knight Newspapers, Inc., later Knight-Ridder, Inc. Knight published a chain of newspapers, including the *Detroit Free Press* and the *Miami Herald.* It had the advantage that the *Inquirer* was a morning paper. It also had the resources to improve the *Inquirer* and drive the *Bulletin* to the wall. The *Inquirer* did improve: During the 1970s, it won five Pulitzer Prizes. It also cut its advertising rates when the *Bulletin* could ill afford to reciprocate. The *Bulletin* lost advertising and money. It tried everything, including different formats and local editions. In 1978, it even tried to become a morning paper. But it was too late. The *Inquirer* had the market.

There seemed no way out for the McLeans. They wanted the city to have a second media voice, but the losses were too heavy for the family to sustain indefinitely. One possibility was to utilize a special antitrust exemption that permits joint operating agreements in the case of failing newspapers. A Firm team, led by Brady Bryson and Joseph Hennessy, approached the *Inquirer.* But it did not want to save its rival.

With no alternative in sight, the McLeans reluctantly put the *Bulletin* up for sale. Among possible buyers they approached Rupert Murdoch, then owner of the *New York Post.* (In the late 1980s, some of Murdoch's many media companies would become clients of the Firm, as recounted in Chapter 20.) Murdoch was not interested. The *Bulletin* was finally bought by the Charter Company, a Florida-based oil-insurance-communications conglomerate, in a joint venture with Karl Eller, an Arizona entrepreneur who had made a fortune in outdoor advertising. The transaction, handled by the Firm, closed on April 30, 1980. By selling the paper to buyers with deep pockets, the McLeans hoped to keep Philadelphia a two-newspaper city.

Charter brought in new people. The *Bulletin's* quality improved, and there was even a slight increase in circulation. But advertising continued to decline and losses mounted. Charter issued an ultimatum during the summer of 1981: It would close the paper unless the *Bulletin's* unions granted concessions worth $4.9 million. Unions in the publishing industry elsewhere had rejected such ultimatums. A team of the Firm's lawyers led by Mark Dichter worked tirelessly to sell the package. To everyone's surprise, the unions accepted on August 16, 1981.

But even that did not halt the plunge. Toward the end of 1981, Charter announced that it expected a loss of $21.5 million for the year and would shut down operations in six weeks unless a buyer appeared. Despite frantic efforts, no buyer could be found, and the paper closed on January 29, 1982—but only after there had been a candlelight vigil by employees and their children outside the *Bulletin's* plant, and a local radio station had mounted a "save our *Bulletin*" campaign.

Although publication stopped, the Firm's work continued for several years after the closing, as libel cases dragged on and miscellaneous claims were sorted out and settled. Then, in 1984, the Charter Company, the *Bulletin's* parent corporation, went bankrupt.

Between 1909 and 1984, the Firm had opened 1,421 subfiles for the Bulletin Company. The last of them could now be closed and file Number 1 again retired, this time presumably forever.

CHAPTER 6

WASHING UP

Sir Alastair's floating glass ■ *Competitors on a string* ■ *Licensing diplomacy* ■ *Pilkington becomes a client in 1912* ■ *The drawn-cylinder process* ■ *"Fully shrewd lawyers"* ■ *World War I* ■ *Miles Kirkpatrick dripping wet* ■ *Antidumping proceedings* ■ *Entering the United States by licensing competitors* ■ *Buying a competitor* ■ *A Japanese joint venture* ■ *Caswell Hobbs takes over* ■ *The FTC investigates* ■ *Sir Alastair is surprised* ■ *The long voyage*

In 1826, the Pilkington family began making window glass at Saint Helens, eleven miles east of Liverpool. The area is an ideal location for glassmaking. There are rich coal deposits to provide the fuel, along with plentiful reserves of sand, limestone, and dolomite. More recently, in addition to its enormous facility at Saint Helens, Pilkington has operated plants on five continents and become "the world's leading producer of flat and safety glass."[1] For almost a century and a half after its founding, Pilkington was a family business. It was Britain's largest private company before it went public in 1970.

In the years after World War II, Sir Alastair Pilkington was the company's presiding genius. He made history by inventing float glass. The inspiration for float glass was not unlike the inspiration for the theory of gravity. Both had mundane origins. Sir Isaac Newton was hit on the head by a falling apple, at least according to legend. Sir Alastair got the idea for float glass one night in June 1952 while "doing the washing up." (The Brits "do the washing up" as the Yanks "do the dishes.") Sir Alastair noticed how dishes can float on dishwater.

Years of exhaustive and highly secret experimentation were required before the float-glass process could be implemented. But as finally mastered (the British patent was issued in 1958), it was "about the most important manufacturing change that flat glass has ever undergone during the whole of its history stretching back more than 2,000 years."[2] A *Fortune* magazine article commented: "The moment the process was announced . . . several hundred million dollars' worth of plate-glass-making machinery became obsolete."[3] The article also noted that Pilkington had "every one of its competitors on a string."[4]

The process involved using molten tin as a means for supporting a ribbon of glass still in liquid form as it left the furnace and floated horizontally into a cooling zone. The upper side of the glass smoothed out naturally, while the molten tin provided a frictionless surface and smoothed the lower side. The result was a glass of uniform thickness that could be produced continuously and required no grinding or polishing.

The float-glass process so revolutionized glassmaking that Harvard Business School published a case study about it in 1971. The study debated whether Pilkington should manufacture or license:

> Under the first alternative Pilkington could use its proprietary product and lower manufacturing costs to take over the entire free world market for ¼" plate which is estimated to be $.35B. This would entail building some 15 plants at around $30 million a piece. Due to the lower costs of the float process Pilkington could expect to undersell all other plate manufacturers while still achieving profits of as much as 20% of sales over the life of the patent.[5]

The other approach was to license the technology, which is what Pilkington did. Licensing had become a way of life in the glass industry during the twentieth century, as one manufacturer after another made step-by-step improvements on the prior art.

It was this licensing diplomacy, as the glass industry called it, that first brought Pilkington to the Firm in 1912. The problem involved a 1909 agreement between Pilkington and American Window Glass Company, headquartered in Pittsburgh. That agreement gave Pilkington an exclusive license in Canada and Britain to use an invention called the drawn-cylinder process. The idea was to transform glassmaking from an intermittent to a continuous operation: The glass would be blown by machines into large cylindrical shapes, which would then be cut into smaller lengths, flattened, and annealed. Under their agreement, American Window Glass and Pilkington created a joint venture called Empire Machine Company. Pilkington undertook on Empire's behalf to license the drawn-cylinder process outside Britain, Canada, and the United States.

But the process promised more than it delivered. Although output increased, the glass was of such poor quality that much of it had to be rejected. Pilkington failed to find licensees. American Window

Glass was aggrieved at Pilkington for not finding licensees and for not using the process in Pilkington's Canadian plant. A further complication arose when Pilkington improved the process. The 1909 agreement was unclear as to who owned the improvements.

Pilkington's Toronto counsel, now known as Blake, Cassels & Graydon, referred Pilkington to Morris Bockius. Wires were sent between Toronto and Philadelphia, and an appointment was made for April 8, 1912, in Bockius's office. Pilkington was represented by the future Lord Cozens-Hardy, Third Baron of Letheringsett, whose father was a lord justice of appeal (later to become master of the rolls), and whose sister had married into the Pilkington family. At the meeting, Bockius involved Firm partner Charles E. Morgan III. Called Eldridge Morgan, he was the son of founding partner CEM. Pilkington's records include Cozens-Hardy's cable back to Saint Helens on April 18, 1912, in which he recounts that he stayed at the "Belle Vue" (Bellevue Stratford Hotel) in Philadelphia and "consulted with fully shrewd lawyers." Shrewd is another apt adjective for Bockius.

Bockius and Eldridge Morgan analyzed the documents, the bargaining history, and glassmaking technology. The Firm rendered its "final opinion" on April 23. (As to response time, no grass grew under anyone's feet when Bockius was in charge.) The legal course having been charted, bitter negotiations got underway. They continued until December 16, 1912, when a supplement to the 1909 agreement was executed. By the supplement, Pilkington granted to Empire Machine Company an exclusive license for Pilkington's improvements to the machine, free of royalties in all countries except Britain and Canada. Pilkington also agreed to work the process in Canada to protect the patent there.

Bockius believed in the prompt rendition of bills, and Pilkington apparently believed in their prompt payment. So on January 7, 1913, Pilkington paid the Firm's bill of $2,884.53 by a draft in the amount of £593. (The cover letter set forth the exchange rate of the pound at $4.86, about three times the 1993 figure.) This was a respectable fee for a year when the Firm's gross revenue approximated $135,000.

New problems arose involving the Empire Machine Company. Eldridge Morgan went to Saint Helens to meet with Pilkington officials on July 19, 1914. He arrived exactly three weeks after the assassination of Archduke Francis Ferdinand at Sarajevo, an event that sent Europe careening helplessly toward World War I. Completing his business, Morgan hurriedly left England before the formal outbreak of hostilities on August 4. Although the Firm continued to work with Pilkington during the war and thereafter on aspects of the drawn-cylinder process, that technology was not the answer. Other innovations were pursued, some by Pilkington and some by its competitors, until Sir Alastair's revolutionary invention of float glass more than forty years later.

Pilkington's decision to license its float-glass invention worldwide raised important United States antitrust considerations. So, as ML&B's contacts with Pilkington intensified beginning in 1959, it was fitting that responsibility for the relationship pass to the Firm's then premier antitrust lawyer, Miles Kirkpatrick. He succeeded Arthur Littleton as responsible attorney for Pilkington, just as Littleton had succeeded Eldridge Morgan, who retired in 1944.

Kirkpatrick was a partner from 1955 to 1985 (he chaired the Firm's Executive Committee in 1980), except for 1970 through 1973 when he chaired the Federal Trade Commission (FTC). Early in 1970, Kirkpatrick learned that he might be offered the FTC chairmanship. After careful consideration, he told the inquiring officials he would decline the offer unless it came directly from the President. He thought that would surely put an end to it. But the offer did come, and it caught him off balance and wet. He was in the shower when his wife answered the telephone. She called to him. He shouted back, "Tell them I'm in the shower." She responded, "But it's the President." Dripping wet, Kirkpatrick took the call. He heard Richard Nixon's mellifluous baritone asking him to serve his country, and he heard himself say, "Yes, sir."

But back to 1959 and Kirkpatrick's first Pilkington assignment. It involved antidumping proceedings before the International Tariff Commission. To prepare for the proceedings, Kirkpatrick went to Saint Helens. During a meeting there with Pilkington personnel, old Sir Harry Pilkington entered the room. He sat for twenty minutes listening to the discussion without saying a word. Then he rose and announced, "Kirkpatrick, you will do." And so Kirkpatrick did—for more than two decades.

At almost the same time as the antidumping proceedings, Pilkington took steps to license the float-glass process in the United States. Kirkpatrick was instructed to negotiate licensing agreements with the three major American plate-glass producers, PPG Industries, Libbey-Owens-Ford Co. (LOF), and Ford Motor Company. The agreements contained some novel provisions. PPG wished to be certain they passed muster with the Department of Justice (DOJ). So PPG submitted them to the DOJ. There was concern that

Kirkpatrick had gained advantages for Pilkington the DOJ might find unacceptable. But the DOJ reviewed the agreements favorably, and Pilkington enjoyed several decades of royalties from its American licensees.

In the early 1980s, with its patents approaching expiration and its major competitors growing internationally, Pilkington determined to enter directly into the world's largest glass market, the United States, by acquiring one of its licensees. That licensee was LOF, the number-one United States glass manufacturer. The transaction received intensive antitrust scrutiny.

Such scrutiny was not surprising, considering that Pilkington had created a worldwide network of float-glass manufacturers through its licensing policy. The FTC viewed Pilkington as the key participant in a highly concentrated, almost cartelized industry. Under the circumstances, the FTC would have preferred that Pilkington enter the United States market in its own right and not by acquiring a major competitor. Nevertheless, after a lengthy antitrust investigation, Kirkpatrick achieved a negotiated settlement with the FTC, permitting the LOF transaction to go forward. In 1982, Pilkington acquired 30 percent of LOF, and in 1986 it exchanged that 30 percent for the LOF name and its glassmaking division; its other assets were spun off under a different name.

With LOF as Pilkington's centerpiece, it embarked on a major program to acquire complementary product lines. The Firm served as Pilkington's counsel in these acquisitions. The Firm also helped facilitate a joint venture in the United States by Pilkington with a major Japanese glass manufacturer, Nippon Sheet Glass Co. (NSG). During the 1980s, Japanese automobile manufacturers sharply increased their market share in the United States. They preferred Japanese sources of supply, including NSG. Pilkington wished to enlarge its market share as a supplier of automobile glass through the proposed NSG joint venture. To do so, it offered NSG a 20-percent interest in LOF for $230 million. Again, the United States antitrust authorities expressed concern at what they considered a virtual cartelization of the world's glass manufacturers. Was Pilkington's proposed United States joint venture with NSG just another tightening of the noose? The FTC initiated an extensive investigation.

After Kirkpatrick's retirement from the Firm in 1985, he had been succeeded as responsible attorney for Pilkington by Caswell Hobbs. Prior to joining the Firm in 1973, Hobbs had been Kirkpatrick's executive assistant at the FTC. Hobbs led Pilkington's response to the FTC inquiry, which expanded to five continents, lasted fifteen months, resulted in the production of seventy boxes of corporate documents, and entailed lengthy depositions by Pilkington officials. Before it was over, the investigation took ML&B lawyers to twelve countries, required translations in five languages, and generated an index of documents that alone was 700 pages long. But the result was a victory for Pilkington and the Firm, as the NSG transaction closed in 1990.

Although Hobbs made frequent trips to Saint Helens and became part of Pilkington's extended family, he thought for years that the relationship between the Firm and Pilkington had originated with his mentor Kirkpatrick. Hobbs was surprised to discover that it went back to 1912. He was not alone in his surprise. In 1973, Arthur Littleton sent a copy of J. Tyson Stokes's centennial history of the Firm to Sir Alastair, who replied:

> I was very interested to look up and see when Pilkingtons first became associated with you and was amazed to see that it dated back to as early as 1912. I don't suppose that even your firm has many clients who have been with you for more than 61 years.[6]

The Firm is like a ship on a long voyage with many ports of call. Lawyers embark and disembark en route. They see only segments of the total journey. It began before their time and will continue after they are gone.

CHAPTER 7

McCABE'S
MARKETING MIRACLE

Scott Paper Company becomes a client in 1915 ■ *Thomas McCabe joins Scott a year later* ■ *The Scott brothers in 1879* ■ *A marketing conundrum* ■ *Arthur Scott dies in 1927* ■ *McCabe assumes command* ■ *Bockius brings in Edward Stotesbury and Scott goes public* ■ *FTC proceedings in the 1930s* ■ *McCabe's government service* ■ *William Clarke Mason fills the void* ■ *McCabe's death* ■ *Brascan attempts a takeover* ■ *Eight years of legislation* ■ *The toughest statute in the country* ■ *Hegelian dialectic*

Thy story of the *Bulletin* has already been recounted in Chapter 5. It was a paper meant to be read. Paper produced by another early Firm client had quite a different use—so different that for years it could not even be mentioned in polite society. Its manufacturer was the Scott Paper Company.

What the Firm owes to Morris Rex Bockius, the Scott Paper Company owes to Thomas Bayard McCabe. When he retired in 1971, he had been with the company for fifty-five years, and for forty-one of those years he had been in charge. Scott was a small local enterprise when McCabe joined it in 1916. At his retirement, it was the world's leader in its field.

In 1973, W. James MacIntosh sent McCabe a copy of J. Tyson Stokes's centennial history of the Firm. McCabe acknowledged the book by writing to MacIntosh:

> Mr. Bockius was handling the Scott account when I came with the company, and I remember visiting him at his country place. I also enjoyed reading about Clem Wood, one of my very close friends, and, of course, Bill Mason, who served so long on our Board.[1]

McCabe's recollections match the Firm's file records, which for Scott Paper Company go back to 1915, when the Scott family still ran the company.

The company's origins were modest. It was founded in 1879, six years after the Firm, by brothers Clarence and Irvin Scott. They occupied a storefront property at 27 North Sixth Street in Philadelphia, where they sold bags and wrapping paper. Clarence was the inside man, while Irvin canvassed local merchants for orders. Deliveries were made by pushcart. The brothers took a giant step in 1881 when they acquired a horse and wagon.

Revolutionary breakthroughs of the nineteenth century included the telephone, the electric light, and the automobile. Less heroic but as ubiquitous was the revolution in sanitary plumbing. That revolution emanated from the invention of the flush toilet, allegedly by Thomas Crapper in 1884. With that revolution came toilet tissue. And with toilet tissue came the Scott Paper Company.

But there was a problem. Victorian sensitivities forbade any display of the product. Where it was sold (generally in apothecary shops), it had to be kept behind the counter and out of sight. Nor could it be advertised.

Now here was a product for which there was clearly a demand. But without advertising, brand-name awareness could not be cultivated. How to reach the customer? The Scott brothers had the answer. To use their terminology, they first arranged to have the product made in the form of "parent rolls" by suppliers called "ghost manufacturers." Then the brothers cut the parent rolls into smaller rolls and packaged them with the names of each retailer that was their customer. In this way, each retailer sold its own brand of rolls, all without the benefit of advertising. At the turn of the century, Scott was distributing almost 2,000 different house brands of toilet tissue. The number of brands was imposing. The total volume was not.

Irvin Scott's son Arthur was running the company in 1915 when the Firm became its counsel. Arthur foresaw the day when toilet tissue could be advertised and a brand name promoted. Waldorf was the house brand of one of Scott's customers. In 1902, Arthur arranged for Scott to purchase the name. Eventually, Waldorf toilet tissue would become a best seller all over the world. But that had to await the advent of toilet tissue advertising, which did not become socially acceptable until the 1920s when *Good Housekeeping* and the *Ladies' Home Journal* agreed to some experimental runs of discreet ads for the product.

Until 1910, Scott simply cut and packaged the parent rolls. That year it began to manufacture its own paper. To do so, it issued $100,000 of bonds and used the proceeds to buy and equip a former soap factory located along the Delaware River in Chester, fifteen miles south of Philadelphia. That small brick building was the embryo of what would become Scott's world headquarters. The new manufacturing facility dramatically increased the company's output, and Scott's sales grew to $1 million by 1915 when the Firm and Scott began their association.

McCabe was hired in 1916 as a clerk in the sales office. Paid $10 per week, he was such a phenomenon that Arthur Scott immediately began grooming him as Arthur's successor. McCabe became sales manager in 1920, a company director in 1921, vice-president in 1927, and president and chief executive officer in 1928. He was thirty-four years old. He remained CEO until 1962 and then served as chairman of the board until 1971.

When Arthur Scott died in 1927, the Firm handled his estate. In accordance with Arthur's wishes, his stock was sold to McCabe and other company employees. At that time, the company's annual sales were $5 million, and it had sixty stockholders, most of them employees. McCabe was eager to expand. So Bockius introduced him to Edward Stotesbury. Stotesbury was the senior Philadelphia partner of Drexel & Company. He was a Firm client, and he and Bockius were close friends. Drexel placed a debt offering for Scott. Drexel's imprimatur drew attention to the company. It was time to go public.

The Firm's files show that additional common stock was authorized and issued early in 1929, when ML&B handled the initial listing of Scott's stock on the New York Stock Exchange. The listing was effective July 15, 1929. The timing by McCabe/Bockius/ Stotesbury was impeccable, with the first sale at $62 per share. The market crashed three months later. By 1932, the company's stock reached a low of $18 per share. But Scott did well, considering that the Dow Jones Industrial Average lost 89 percent of its value over the same period. The public had reason to like the company and its management. Moreover, few commodities are less cyclical than toilet tissue.

McCabe once told MacIntosh there was "nothing special" about Scott's products and that "anybody can make them." He said the company's success was due simply to sound management and most of all to effective marketing. Still, during the 1930s, Scott's marketing may have been too effective. Its ads referred to competitive toilet tissue as having inferior attributes. The Firm's files note Federal Trade Commission proceedings commencing in 1931. There was a settlement, and Scott ceased to demean its competitors. These problems did not adversely affect sales during the Depression. Instead, sales increased every year except 1932 and 1933 and amounted to $18 million just before World War II.

During the war years, McCabe devoted himself to public service. Starting in 1941, he spent most of his time in Washington, first as deputy lend-lease administrator, then as deputy director of the Office of Production Management, and finally in 1945 as foreign liquidation commissioner. While in Washington, he continued his contacts with MacIntosh, who was there serving as general counsel to the Renegotiation Division of the War Department and subsequently to the War Contracts Price Adjustment Board. Their friendship deepened, and MacIntosh eventually became one of McCabe's executors and trustees. After the war, McCabe was named chairman of the Board of Governors of the Federal Reserve System and did not return to active duty with Scott until 1951.

With McCabe away for so many years, problems of governance inevitably arose at the company. The Firm played a major role in filling the void, principally through William Clarke Mason and Thomas Ringe. The June/July 1979 issue of the *ScotTissue Broadcast,* a company newsletter, declared:

> During Mr. McCabe's absence, Scott's splendid organization carried on. Scott had an exceptional Board of Directors which assumed many overall duties with William Clarke Mason, general counsel, giving much overtime and effort and counsel to the executive group.[2]

Former Firm partner Orvel Sebring has similar recollections concerning Mason's role:

> In those years when McCabe was away with the government and as chairman of the Federal Reserve, Mason gave those who were running Scott forceful leadership and good counsel which helped fill the gap. Here Mason showed those rare qualities which enabled him to assert strong views without disrupting the attachments of those around him. Mason and McCabe had a great deal in common, although their personalities often reflected different styles, McCabe being more quiet and modest. They were both leaders with a knack for looking ahead and planning accordingly. Courage and strength, loyalty, strong likes, and dislikes—more pronounced in Mason. They liked and respected each other.

During his fifty-five years with Scott, McCabe saw the company's sales grow from $1.4 million in 1916 to almost $1 billion when he retired in 1971. After he died at age eighty-eight on May 27, 1982, the Firm handled his estate. It included 418,514 shares of Scott

Paper Company, then selling at $16 per share.

McCabe was succeeded as Scott's CEO in 1967 by Harrison Dunning who, in turn, was succeeded in 1971 by Charles Dickey, Jr. Dickey ran the company until 1983. Dickey's father had been a partner in Drexel & Co. By putting Drexel and Scott together, Bockius had helped indirectly to provide a successor for McCabe.

■ ■ ■ ■ ■

McCabe's retirement in 1971 meant that he missed the excitement of a hostile takeover attempt by Brascan Limited, a Canadian company controlled by Peter and Edward Bronfman. The 1980s were a time of takeovers, and Scott was an attractive target. Early in 1981, there was unusual trading activity in Scott's stock, and rumors began to circulate about possible predators, several of them Canadian. Then in February, Brascan filed a Schedule 13D with the SEC, revealing that it owned or had the right to acquire more than 11 percent of Scott's outstanding common stock.

Scott's management advised Brascan that it would absolutely oppose any further accumulation of Scott's stock by Brascan. Taking no chances, the company engaged a number of law firms, including ML&B. Several were not Pennsylvania firms. But Scott was a Pennsylvania corporation, so responsibility for its corporate-law strategy devolved upon the Firm. The ML&B corporate team was led by Donald Scott (not related to the founding Scott brothers), who by this time had inherited the Firm's relationship with Scott Paper. In addition, preparations were made for litigation.

Then on March 21, 1981, as suit was about to be filed, Scott's management and Brascan negotiated a standstill agreement by which Brascan obligated itself not to increase its ownership of Scott's stock above 25 percent until December 31, 1985. For its part, Scott agreed that four Brascan representatives would be added to Scott's board, including Brascan's president.

The standstill agreement gave Scott some breathing room. But the situation was unstable. What would Brascan do after the standstill expired? What should Scott do in the meantime? One approach was legislative. Over time, the Brascan takeover attempt would be instrumental in triggering fundamental changes in the corporate laws of Pennsylvania. By 1990, those changes would put Pennsylvania at the top of the list among those states with corporate laws favoring incumbent management. For eight years, the Firm was at the vortex of these controversial changes.

The first step was the Shareholder Protection Act of 1983, which streaked through the legislature in record time and was signed by Governor Richard Thornburgh on December 23, 1983. It provided that in certain cases when a person acquired more than 30 percent of the voting stock of a corporation, the remaining shareholders could demand fair value for their shares from such person, including a premium for control. Another provision authorized boards of directors in evaluating tender offers to consider a number of factors, including the effects of any action upon employees, suppliers, customers, and the communities in which the corporation was located. Thus, social concerns could outweigh quick profits when a board was faced with a takeover attempt. (Another Firm client, Strawbridge & Clothier, would invoke this provision to thwart a hostile tender offer in 1986, as detailed in Chapter 38.)

The 1983 act was a joint campaign by Scott Paper's inside legal counsel, various inside counsel of other major Pennsylvania corporations, the Pennsylvania Chamber of Commerce, and several law firms, including ML&B. It was a significant corporate and political landmark.

Still, the company did not wish to rely entirely upon these legislative changes. So in 1985, it negotiated a repurchase of Brascan's holdings in exchange for approximately $540 million in cash plus warrants to acquire 4 million shares of Scott Paper stock. The agreement contained a fifteen-year standstill provision—an unusually long period. Several law firms, including ML&B, opined to Scott's board in connection with the board's exercise of its business judgment in approving the agreement. Brascan was taken out entirely in 1989 when Scott repurchased the warrants for $200 million. A year later, the last Brascan representative went off the Scott board.

But long before the Scott-Brascan chapter closed, the Pennsylvania legislative initiative, begun in 1983, acquired a life of its own. The group that masterminded the 1983 act continued its efforts. Those efforts produced further legislation in 1986 and 1988. Finally, the initiative culminated in an unprecedented antitakeover law in 1990. Several ML&B partners played important roles in this nationally publicized legislation, including William Zeiter and Gregory Harvey. Zeiter's specialty was drafting legislation, including Pennsylvania's business corporation law and judicial code. Harvey was a litigator with an intimate knowledge of the political scene. While many cooks stirred the broth, Zeiter was the head chef, and Harvey acted as head waiter in steering the bill through the legislature.

The Pennsylvania Senate passed the bill 35 to 4 on December 13, 1989; the House passed it 182 to 10 on April 3, 1990; and Governor Robert Casey signed it on April 27, 1990. Officially known as the Act of April 27, 1990, P.L. 129, No. 36, the legislation also received labor union support because it protected severance payments and fostered the continuation of labor contracts. One lobbyist commented: "How many times does a legislature get to vote for both business and labor?"[3]

In their feeding frenzy, the legislators cited Pennsylvania's loss of Gulf Oil Company in 1984, when T. Boone Pickens drove Gulf into the arms of Chevron Corporation. Then there was the loss in 1989 of Pennwalt Corp. (renamed Atochem North America, Inc.) to white knight Société General Elf Aquitaine in reaction to a hostile takeover attempt by Centaur Partners. And even as the legislators were voting, there was an effort by the Canadian Belzberg family to gain control of Armstrong World Industries in Lancaster, Pennsylvania. The Belzbergs had previously "reaped raider benefits . . . [including] a $134.1 million greenmail payout from Ashland Oil Co. and a $245 million reward for forcing Southland Corp. into a leveraged buyout."[4]

As enacted, the 1990 law was "the toughest statute in the country that protects publicly traded companies from 'corporate raiders.'"[5] It contained three main features. First, it gave a board of directors specific additional grounds for voting against a takeover. Previously, a board could consider the effect of any action on employees, suppliers, customers, and communities in which the corporation was located. Now, it could also consider the long-term interests of the corporation and whether they might be better served by maintaining the corporation's independence.

A second feature of the law denied voting rights to any acquirer of 20 percent of the corporation's voting stock without the approval of the corporation's "disinterested shares." Thus, existing shareholders were given special rights to resist the assumption of control by outsiders. This certainly deterred predators.

Third, the act provided for the disgorgement of greenmail profits. Such profits would belong to the corporation whenever an acquirer of 20 percent of the stock who had not already held it for two years sold it at a profit within eighteen months of reaching the 20-percent mark. This discouraged predators and also slowed the takeover process.

Before its enactment, the bill stirred up a hornet's nest. The *Wall Street Journal* said it constituted "corporate protectionism" and was "an awful piece of legislation."[6] The *New York Times* said it created a "safe haven for executives."[7] SEC Chairman Richard Breeden said it "shield[ed] management from investor oversight."[8] Warming to his work, one dissenter in the Pennsylvania Senate called it the "Fat Cat Protection and Shareholder Ripoff Act of 1990."[9] And a Belzberg lobbyist labeled it "Corporate Stalinism."[10]

On a less emotional level, spokespersons for several state pension funds, including those in California, New York, and South Dakota, questioned whether they could invest in Pennsylvania corporations consistent with "their fiduciary duties to maximize their funds' value."[11] And closer to home, the head of the Pennsylvania State Employees Retirement Fund said simply that the fund would stop investing in Pennsylvania corporations. A study purported to show the measure had cost such corporations $1 billion in market capitalization just during the legislative process and before enactment, with more losses presumably to follow.

As the leading authority in Pennsylvania on the legislation, Zeiter spoke to business groups and lawyers all over the state. He answered the charges:

> The Act doesn't affect proxy contests that do not involve control. And where control is involved, the shareholders are given greater input to determine their destiny. As to greenmail disgorgement, it applies where a person buys shares in a company, puts the company in play, and sells those shares, all within a short period of time. The legislation is a good thing, because it favors the national economy and long-term investors in preference to those who take over companies, saddle them with debt and carve them up.

Another supporter of the legislation was Firm partner David King. In 1990, the press referred to him as "a takeover attorney with Morgan, Lewis & Bockius" and quoted his view: "The essence of the success of our country is . . . corporations being able to manage for long-term interests rather than being forced to respond to quick-buck takeover artists."[12]

Some of the Firm's Philadelphia lawyers were concerned that the Pennsylvania legislature had overreacted to the Gulf and Pennwalt takeovers, as well as to the Brascan threat to Scott and the Belzberg threat to Armstrong. If so, there was always the act's ninety-day opt-out provision. All publicly held Pennsylvania corporations scurried to convene their boards in special session to consider opting out of the act in whole or in part by July 26, 1990. As authorities on the legislation, the Firm's Philadelphia partners were much in demand making presentations and helping boards parse the act. When it was all over, some Firm clients opted out of one or more provisions of the act, including CoreStates Financial Corp; Consolidated Rail Corporation; Pennsylvania Power & Light Company; the Rorer Group, Inc.; Safeguard Scientifics, Inc.; and SEI Corp. Other clients took no action and remained covered by all provisions of the act, including Philadelphia Electric Company and Scott Paper Company.

Always philosophical, Zeiter noted the ebb and flow of legislation. "Abuses generate overkill," he commented, "which itself becomes an abuse." Hegelian dialectic and a source of employment for lawyers.

Thus, the Firm's recent work for Scott Paper Company has included some momentous legislative initiatives. But over a longer period—eight decades—the Firm's assignments for the company have covered the whole spectrum of legal activity. One responsible attorney has succeeded another in looking after the Firm's relationship with the company: Morris Bockius, Clement Wood, William Clarke Mason, Thomas Ringe, Orvel Sebring, and Donald Scott. More than a thousand files have been opened for Scott Paper Company as its sales increased from $1 million to $5 billion. A long journey for a small family enterprise in a former soap factory in Chester that the Firm began representing in 1915.

CHAPTER 8

AN AFFAIR WITH STEAM

The Baldwin Locomotive Works becomes a client in 1917 ■ The world's largest manufacturer of steam locomotives ■ The original Philadelphia plant ■ Relocation to Eddystone ■ Labor relations and unfair labor practice litigation ■ International transactions ■ Reilly, Ace of Spies ■ Eastern Europe after World War I ■ Squealing pigs on the roof ■ Doing business in Poland, Romania, and Mexico ■ The reorganization of 1935-38 ■ Diesels versus steamers ■ An appalling study ■ General Motors captures the market ■ Baldwin after World War II ■ Love affairs in distant places

Morgan, Lewis & Bockius began representing the Baldwin Locomotive Works after the death in 1917 of Baldwin's prior legal counsel, John G. Johnson. Baldwin's significance as a business enterprise cannot be overemphasized. In writing about industrial Philadelphia, Scranton and Licht state: "If any firm could claim that it was principally responsible for Philadelphia's global image as a manufacturing city, it was surely Baldwin Locomotive."[1]

Baldwin was established in 1831 to build "iron horses," as locomotives were then popularly called. Its first such horse, Old Ironsides, began service the following year for the Philadelphia, Germantown & Norristown Railroad, later a branch of the Reading Railroad, and incidentally the line the Firm's name partners would have used to commute from Germantown to Philadelphia. By the beginning of the twentieth century, Baldwin was producing 40 percent of all locomotives used domestically and was "[t]urning out three times as many locomotives as any other concern in the world (1500 a year by 1902), [and] shipping them all over—South America, Russia, Palestine, Australia [and] Japan."[2]

During the first quarter of the twentieth century, Baldwin was by far the largest industrial employer in the Philadelphia area. It reached peak employment and production during World War I, when it employed more than 20,000 workers and built 5,551 locomotives.

Its war production included "cradle-shaped gun carriage[s] . . . for carrying heavy ordnance on railroads," which would later be the subject of a patent infringement suit defended and won for Baldwin by the Firm.[3] By 1928, Baldwin had produced nearly 62,000 locomotives. Its repertoire included every sort of steam locomotive from switching engines to leviathans.

One of Baldwin's larger locomotives can be seen today at the Franklin Institute, another Firm client. It is No. 60000, a 4-10-2 engine weighing 350 tons and measuring 101 feet in length. Baldwin built it in 1926 for heavy-freight service. Before removal to the Franklin Institute in 1933, No. 60000 saw 100,000 miles of duty, including crossing the Donner Pass in California's Sierra Nevada. Reference is made to No. 60000 not only because it was produced by a Firm client and is exhibited by a Firm client, but also because it is more likely than any other moving object to have been boarded and ridden (it is drawn back and forth on a short section of track) by children of the Firm's lawyers in Philadelphia for three generations.

Baldwin's original plant, built starting in 1834, covered almost twenty acres (equal to about as many city blocks) and extended westward from Broad Street (the equivalent in Philadelphia of Fourteenth Street) to as far as Twentieth Street and northward from Pennsylvania Avenue to Spring Garden Street. The Firm's present offices on Logan Square, if they had existed early in the century, would have offered a panoramic view of its once largest client.

But the city's growth stifled expansion of Baldwin's Center City plant. So it was closed in 1928, and the company moved to a 600-acre site at Eddystone, south of Philadelphia and not far from today's Philadelphia International Airport. (Development of the huge Eddystone facility was tragically ill-timed considering economic conditions in the 1930s.) The original Philadelphia plant was not demolished until 1937, except for segments razed beginning in 1924 to make way for the Philadelphia Museum of Art and the Benjamin Franklin Parkway complex.

In addition to its Philadelphia and Eddystone plants, Baldwin had major installations elsewhere in the country and abroad, as well as offices in twelve American cities and thirty-two foreign countries. The company was vertically integrated. It made almost every part of its locomotives, and each locomotive was custom tailored to the specifications of its buyer.

Baldwin was considered a prestigious place to work, and its employees were highly skilled. But all was not paradise. On March

22, 1910, several divisions of Baldwin's night shift petitioned for a Saturday half-holiday and sixty-five hours of pay for sixty hours of work. Baldwin capitulated, but not immediately, lest it show weakness in the face of such outlandish demands. Indeed, it was not until 1937 that an effective organizing campaign was mounted against the company by the United Steelworkers of America, CIO. Baldwin resisted, furtively proffered a company union, engaged Pinkertons to spy on union activities, and discharged union organizers. Unfair labor practice charges against Baldwin were defended by the Firm, with William Clarke Mason leading the effort. The litigation continued until 1942, when the Court of Appeals for the Third Circuit finally affirmed earlier findings for the union, by which time the record in the case had grown to 16,000 pages.[4] Baldwin and Mason were not easy targets.

Many Philadelphia industries had been organized earlier than Baldwin, and by 1940 Philadelphia was a union stronghold. Immediately after World War II, the Philadelphia area was hit by massive and prolonged strikes. These accelerated the relocation of industry to other parts of the country, particularly the South, and helped bring about Philadelphia's shift to a service economy. The Firm's files show that Baldwin suffered a two-month strike by the Steelworkers in 1946. The strike came at an especially bad time, as Baldwin was converting to peacetime production. Moreover, a costly settlement put further pressure on the company's steeply declining net income.

■ ■ ■ ■ ■

The frontispiece of a 1923 history of the Baldwin Locomotive Works lists its directors and officers and then recites "General Counsel, Morgan, Lewis and Bockius, 934 Land Title Building, Philadelphia." In those days, the relationship between a great corporation and its lawyers was more focused and continuous. That relationship generated in excess of a thousand matters handled by the Firm for Baldwin during the first decade of the representation alone. The list of file titles is enough to quicken a lawyer's heartbeat: "Chinese Notes," "National Railways of Mexico," "Polish Bond Issue," "Belgium Contract," "Persian Loan," "Contract with Peru," "Egyptian State Railway," "Contract with Romania," "Cuba Company," "Lease to Argentine Republics," "Portuguese East Africa," "Philippine Agency," "Germany—War Insurance," "His Britannic Majesty's Lease," "Claim of Sidney G. Reilly," and so on.

The last item, Claim of Sidney G. Reilly, will titillate those who read the book *Reilly: Ace of Spies*[5] or watched its adaptation in a 1980s public television series. Formally named Sigmund Georgjevich Rosenblum, Reilly was born near Odessa in 1874, spoke seven languages, and was said to "possess eleven passports and a wife to go with each."[6] Suave, fearless, ruthless, and mercurial, he not only engaged in espionage but also made and lost fortunes as an arms dealer. Before World War I, he functioned in Saint Petersburg simultaneously as a spy for the British and a purchasing agent for the Russians. When the war came, he successfully infiltrated the German General Staff for the British while continuing to arrange munitions purchases for the Russians.

Reilly brought suit in 1920 against Baldwin and related defendants for $543,000 in commissions which he claimed from sales by the defendants of 2.3 million field artillery shells to the Russian army.[7] Exposing a nether world of espionage and double-dealing, the suit alleged contracts with the czarist and British governments, phony guarantees by third parties, and betrayal by the defendants as they cheated Reilly of his just deserts.

After 1917, Reilly was obsessed with toppling the Bolshevik government, which he loathed. Nevertheless, he appeared in 1924 at the Baldwin trial in New York. He may have been a fantastic spy, but he was a terrible witness. He was so embittered and emotional that "he literally foamed at the mouth" as he testified.[8] The jury was probably fascinated. But it was also incredulous and returned a verdict for the defendants. A year later, Reilly reentered the Soviet Union, was captured by Dzerjinsky's operatives, tortured in the Loubianka prison, and executed on Stalin's orders in a snowy pine forest outside Moscow. At least that is one story. Another version has it that he never reached Moscow and was shot while crossing the Finnish border. A third possibility is that he survived capture and either defected to the Soviets or simply disappeared—a man of mystery to the end.

■ ■ ■ ■

Admittedly, all matters for Baldwin were not so intriguing as the Reilly case. But they were voluminous and required the attention of every one of the Firm's lawyers at some time or other. Bockius was at the vortex. In the 1920s, he made trips for Baldwin across Europe and especially to Poland and Romania. Other trips took him to Mexico and South America. He usually accompanied the colorful Baldwin CEO, Samuel M. Vauclain, who presided over the company from 1919 to 1929. Vauclain would sell locomotives to the governments that owned the railroads, and Bockius would document the transactions and their financing.

Vauclain kept a minute-by-minute report of one such trip he and Bockius took in the spring of 1920. Starting in Paris, they went through Switzerland, Austria, and Czechoslovakia to Poland, then down into Romania and finally back through Yugoslavia (as it was later called), Italy, and Switzerland to Paris. Before leaving Paris, they had rented a private car from Wagon-Lits for their party of six.

It was well they did, because when they got to Eastern Europe, they found not only postwar devastation but also hordes of refugees on the move. Many were coming out of the nascent Soviet Union to escape famine and civil war, as the Red and White factions laid waste to the countryside and each other. The Vauclain/Bockius private car was drawn by regular trains packed with humanity not only in the cars themselves but on their roofs as well. During much of the trip from Warsaw to Bucharest, which took several days, the roof of the Vauclain/Bockius car was occupied by refugees and their livestock. (Squealing pigs were the most vocal.) The Baldwin party had to spend ten consecutive nights in their car because of the absence of hotel accommodations. Not a pleasure trip.

Baldwin had previously sold locomotives to Poland. They had been sent by boat from Eddystone to the great shipyard at Danzig, where they were then being unloaded and assembled. Assembly was taking place very close to the water's edge, and Vauclain was afraid workers and parts would fall off the wharves into the water. When the Baldwin party arrived, Danzig, previously German, was under British occupation before being turned over to the Poles, who would administer it as a free city under League of Nations supervision.[9]

Payment for the locomotives was to be made by notes issued by the new Polish government. Bockius prepared the notes, which were numerous and had to be signed individually by the finance minister. The minister was efficient and timed himself as he signed one every four seconds. The notes were then delivered to the Baldwin party and placed in a sealed diplomatic pouch consigned by the Polish Ministry to its embassy in Paris. Thus, the notes were immunized from examination and confiscation by customs officials on the train trip back to Paris.

The Polish government was not exactly a good credit, as bankers say. Still, the situation in Romania was far worse. The Romanians had been at war first with the Austro-Hungarians, the Germans, the Bulgarians, and the Turks, and subsequently with the Russians, their former allies. Their country was in ruins. A more imaginative means of payment would have to be devised for the Romanians. As the contract was finally negotiated, it permitted the Romanians to pay for their order of fifty locomotives over a period of five years in either dollars or oil. The agreement had to be authorized by the prime minister, executed by the finance minister, and approved by King Ferdinand I, with whom Vauclain and Bockius had lunch. Bockius drafted the instruments, which were then translated and printed. Again, the executed notes were carried by diplomatic pouch back to Paris. Vauclain commented that Bockius was "exceedingly busy . . . [and] worked harder than he had ever done in Philadelphia."[10]

Bockius's trips on Baldwin business took him out of the office for long periods. For example, the 1920 trip lasted two months—a month getting there and back, and a month doing business. It was not until 1939, just two months after Bockius's death, that Pan American Airlines—a Firm labor client from 1969 to 1992—inaugurated its commercial trans-Atlantic service by "flight boats" between Port Washington, New York, and Marseilles, France. The trip one-way took forty-two hours. Today, the Concorde does a similar run in four.

Traveling with a client for several months at a stretch certainly tests a lawyer's mettle. Perhaps one way Bockius and Vauclain managed was through the utmost formality. Despite their many years of close contact, they always called each other "Mr. Vauclain" and "Mr. Bockius." Thus, they were like partners in some French and German law firms who do not *tutoyer* or *duzen* each other, despite years of close association.

■ ■ ■ ■ ■

The Firm continued to represent Baldwin as the locomotive giant died a lingering death during the 1930s. Orders fell, starting in the late 1920s. Then came the Depression. Locomotives represent major capital commitments, which in bad times are postponed or canceled. By 1933, Baldwin's production had fallen to 1850 levels, and 80 percent of its work force had been laid off. Two years later, the company could not service its long-term debt. On February 25, 1935, a petition for reorganization was filed on behalf of the company by William Clarke Mason and Francis Bracken. The affidavit recited:

> The company has passed through four years of deep depression during which entire period its locomotive business has aggregated less than six months' normal volume.

The reorganization lasted three and a half years. It was expensive.

Only those who live through such proceedings comprehend why they are so expensive. But even some who live through them are uncomprehending. Judges sometimes fall into that category. District Court Judge Oliver Dickinson presided over the Baldwin reorganization. On February 3, 1938, the *New York Times* carried an ominous headline: "Court Decries 77-B Fees." According to the article, the judge "commented on the 'lengthy and oppressively expensive' method of administering justice . . . in the reorganization of the Baldwin Locomotive Works. Claims for $890,000 were filed by attorneys, banking interests and various stockholders' committees." Among them was the Firm's petition for a fee of $150,000, worth $1,542,553 in 1993. Signed by Morris Bockius, the petition detailed the services rendered over a thirty-four-month period "during both the daytime hours and the night-time [as] required."[11]

How did the Firm do? Very well is the answer. The court allowed the Firm's request in full, although most other claimants suffered reductions. Some appealed and did better.[12] In those days, lawyers did not keep time records, and the compensation of each claimant depended upon its contribution to the outcome, about which reasonable men could differ—including judges.

There was a renewed demand for locomotives just as Baldwin emerged from its reorganization. Some of that demand was for steam locomotives, but mostly it was for electric and diesel locomotives.[13] In 1935, the Pennsylvania Railroad had commenced electrified service between New York and Washington. The best steam locomotives needed more than four hours for the run, whereas today's electrified Metroliners do it in two hours and fifty-five minutes.

But diesels led the way. Invented toward the turn of the nineteenth century, some diesel locomotives had actually been produced by Baldwin on an experimental basis during the 1920s, a time when the Central Railroad of New Jersey, another Firm client, was also testing diesel prototypes on its tracks. Still, it was not until the 1930s that railroads took a serious interest in diesels. The diesels got four times as much work out of a pound of fuel and were faster off the mark than the old steamers. General Motors seized the opportunity. Its Electro-Motive Corporation entered the diesel switcher market in 1935 with a low-cost, standardized product. By 1938, railroads in the United States were placing more orders for diesels than steamers.

The time had clearly come for Baldwin to move aggressively into the diesel and electric fields. It had the plant, the equipment, the reservoir of skilled workers, the name, and a worldwide sales organization. Had Baldwin embraced the new technology, the Firm might presently number among its clients the world's largest manufacturer of diesel and electric locomotives. Baldwin's failure to do so recalls the *Bulletin's* belated move from an evening to a morning paper, as discussed in Chapter 5. Both companies could have maintained their hegemony if they had not resisted change.

Baldwin's management commissioned a study on the diesel question. Normally, a study can be a valuable tool in decision-making. But conductors of studies should not be motivated either by their own bias or by the perceived bias of those to whom they are addressing their findings. Sadly, it was otherwise with the Baldwin study, *The Motive Power Situation of American Railroads*. Dated September 10, 1937, it contained seventy pages of analysis, statistics, and engineering calculations. It concluded:

> The inherent nature of the Diesel locomotive and its accompanying electrical equipment in the present state of development debar it from high speed road service because of the physical characteristics of the power itself, its excessive capital cost, and its probable high maintenance costs. . . .

> Present fuel economies of the Diesel locomotive are real, but their continued repetition in the distant future is uncertain; and it appears more likely that Diesel oil will increase in price than that coal will do so.[14]

Since the handwriting was already on the wall, there can be no excuse for the appalling Baldwin diesel study. It simply echoed the prejudices of the company's senior executives, according to W. James MacIntosh. As children, they had heard the distant cry of steam locomotives in the night. As adults, they had made those locomotives more efficient, more powerful, and more beautiful. They could not shake off their love affair with steam.

Baldwin did profitable defense work during World War II, subject to mandatory renegotiation. In 1945, the year the war ended, Baldwin received orders for 691 steam locomotives, some from as far away as India and Thailand. It also received orders for 187 diesel electric locomotives. Among its postwar customers was client Reading Railroad, which was effectively dieselized by 1953. But as a late entrant, Baldwin could not compete in the diesel field. During the war, General Motors had concentrated on diesel locomotives. With its expertise and track record, it effectively captured the postwar diesel market. Baldwin's once-proud products became museum pieces.

In order to continue operations, Baldwin turned to nonrailroad machinery. It merged in 1950 with the Lima-Hamilton Corporation, which produced heavy construction equipment. The Firm handled the merger, as it did a second merger in 1965, when Baldwin-Lima-Hamilton Corporation disappeared into Armour & Co., which auctioned off the remaining Baldwin equipment at the Eddystone plant in 1972. That was also the year the Firm opened its last Baldwin file.

During the 1980s, a television series called *Great Railway Journeys of the World* took viewers to distant places where steam locomotives are still in use. Occasional close-ups revealed Baldwin locomotives, more than fifty years old and clearly the worse for wear, still laboring on mountainsides and through jungles. In those far climes, the affair with steam continues even today.

CHAPTER 9

IMMORTAL SOUNDS

Ferries to Camden ■ *A terrier named Nipper* ■ *Bleating like a sheep* ■ *Opera's golden age* ■ *Contracts for Fritz Kreisler and Victor Herbert* ■ *Everything goes wrong in 1924* ■ *The passing of the acoustical process* ■ *The advent of electrical recordings* ■ *Race to the market* ■ *Litigation with Brunswick* ■ *The company is sold* ■ *Priceless Americana bargained away*

Ferries plied the Delaware River between Philadelphia and Camden starting in 1688. Before the Benjamin Franklin Bridge was built in 1926, they carried as many as one hundred thousand passengers a day with departures from each side of the river every three minutes during the rush hour. The service was discontinued in 1952 but reinstated in 1992 with the opening of the New Jersey State Aquarium in Camden.

Ferries offer unusual sounds and views. There are the sounds of horns, of ropes straining, and of bows (ferries seem to have only bows) scrapping against landing berths. And there are views of skylines. For much of the twentieth century, one of Camden's buildings attracted special attention. Located at Front and Market streets, it included a tower showing on each of its four sides a giant stained-glass reproduction of the world's most famous canine trade-mark. The terrier listening to His Master's Voice was Nipper, painted by English artist Francis Barraud. The building, tower, and stained-glassed terrier belonged to what was known between 1901 and 1929 as the Victor Talking Machine Company. The company occupied 2.5 million square feet of plant space in thirty-one buildings on fifty-eight acres of Camden's waterfront.

The Firm's relationship with Victor lasted only from 1920 to early in 1927, when the company was sold to New York investment bankers. But what exciting years they were for the company, not to mention for sound reproduction generally, as the old acoustical process of recording yielded to electricity and as radios made their way into millions of homes.

The cylinder phonograph was invented by Thomas Edison in 1877. A decade later, Emile Berliner developed a flat disc record and a hand-cranked player—the very one shown in the Nipper painting. But it was Eldridge Johnson who made the phonograph commercially feasible in 1896 by perfecting a spring motor drive. When wound up, it maintained a constant pitch until it wound down, bleating like a sheep. Johnson formed the Victor Talking Machine Company in 1901. The Johnson and Berliner patents were consolidated in the new company. It built its first plant in Camden, and over the years everybody came there to record.

Enrico Caruso, the century's most celebrated tenor, led the way. He traveled to the United States in 1903 and the next year made his first Victor records. They made him famous. They also made Victor famous. Other performing artists, previously skeptical of the process, followed suit. Included were many voices of opera's golden age: Patti, Eames, Ferrar, Melba, McCormack, Sembrich, Scotti, Schumann-Heink, and Homer. Instrumentalists were also memorialized on Victor records, including Rachmaninoff, Paderewski, and Elman. Another renowned Victor instrumentalist was Austrian violin virtuoso Fritz Kreisler. One of the Firm's first assignments for Victor involved his recording contract.

Records were made by the acoustic process until 1925. With a small orchestra crammed on risers to the rear, soloists sang or played into a horn. For a crescendo, they advanced closer to the horn; for a diminuendo, they retreated a few steps. Large orchestras were more difficult to record by the acoustic process. But Victor engaged the Boston Symphony and the Philadelphia Orchestra. The latter took the ferry ride across the Delaware River to Camden and made its first recordings in 1918. Smaller orchestras fit the bill better. One was Victor Herbert's Orchestra. The Firm represented the company in documenting Herbert's recording contracts in the early 1920s. For many years until his death in 1924, Herbert was part of the Philadelphia scene, conducting his orchestra at Willow Grove Park.[1]

Having recorded everybody and everything from 1901 until the mid-1920s, Victor certainly had a vested interest in acoustic recordings. In addition, the company produced the machines that played the records: open-horn phonographs, table Victrolas, and massive cabinet Victrolas—almost six million of them in the first quarter century. They were expensive pieces of furniture made of fine wood by skilled artisans at the Camden plant.

Then, in 1924, everything went wrong for the company. Sales fell as the world seemed sated with acoustic recordings and Victrolas. Their sound no longer satisfied. Moreover, starting in about 1921, radio receivers had ceased to be a mere curiosity and were evolving from the wound-coil, cat's-whisker stage to commercially practicable instruments. By 1925, five-tube sets were on the market for between $150 and $250. They were new, they produced their sounds electrically, and the entertainment they provided was free: No records had to be purchased.

Victor faced another problem: The company had lost its leadership. Johnson was still in control, but he had been relatively inactive in management since 1917. The company was at a crossroads, leading to endless analysis. Morris Bockius wrote to William Clarke Mason, then on vacation, that one evening he gathered up some of Victor's executives and took them to his home for dinner, after which the deliberations continued into the night. Could the recording industry survive in the new age of radio?

Victor seemed paralyzed. But General Electric (GE), Radio Corporation of America (RCA), Westinghouse, and Bell Telephone Laboratories were all working on devices for electrical sound reproduction. Victor awakened just in time, got the rights to the new devices, and developed an early form of electrical recording called the Orthophonic process. Records demonstrating that process were made by Paul Whiteman, the Philadelphia Orchestra, and Fritz Kreisler, among others. Turning its back on its priceless library of acoustic records, Victor saved itself by a combination of electrical recording and electrically amplified reproduction. Would it have to record everything again? In some cases, that would be impossible: Caruso, Victor's best-selling artist, had died in 1921.

Then, an unexpected problem arose in which the Firm was involved. The Brunswick-Balke-Collender Company boasted it had developed a "light ray" electrical recording process superior to Victor's Orthophonic process. There were charges and countercharges. The Firm represented Victor in litigation with Brunswick. Victor introduced its Electrola; and Brunswick introduced its Panatrope, which it demonstrated at Carnegie Hall. Whatever the virtues of the Brunswick process, Victor got into production first. Brunswick's product never reached the market. The litigation wound down, and recording entered a new era with Victor still supreme.

But could Victor raise the capital demanded by the new era? And how about Eldridge Johnson? He was in ill health and simply wanted to dispose of the company. So in the fall of 1926, he agreed to sell his stock to New York investment bankers Speyer & Co. and J. W. Seligman, on condition that his colleagues receive the same opportunity. The offer was made, and his colleagues, some of them advised by the Firm, reluctantly agreed.

A further crisis arose as the old Berliner interests threatened to scuttle the transaction. (Their interests derived from the 1901 consolidation by which Victor had acquired licenses to use their patents.) Mason was dispatched to deal with them. They were placated, and the transaction closed on January 6, 1927. The purchase price—an enormous one for its day—was $53 million, of which Johnson received $28 million. The Firm's archives contain Mason's congratulatory letter to Edward E. Shumaker, whom the bankers had, as Mason put it, "so wisely chosen [as] the new President."

After that, no new Victor matters came to the Firm, and contact with the company ceased. Shumaker lasted only two years as president of Victor before it was acquired by RCA in 1929. Previously formed by GE in 1919, RCA was spun off in 1932 and subsequently reacquired by GE in 1986. Later that year, the record division of RCA with its unique collection of sounds from a vanished age was sold by GE to Bertlesmann AG, a German publishing conglomerate. In such a casual manner was priceless Americana bargained away.

Looking back, Eldridge Johnson may have been right to sell out in 1927. Although the product was famous the world over, the company might not have survived the Depression, especially considering the capital demanded by the new technology. All the same, Bockius and Mason were surely unhappy about the disposition, as a client was lost and control of a leading local enterprise moved elsewhere. In those days, elsewhere meant New York. Today, elsewhere means Japan. Its manufacturers produce the present-day equivalents of yesterday's Victrolas.[2]

Over the years, the wrecker's ball has claimed much of Victor's once sprawling Camden plant. The original stained-glass windows picturing the terrier and the horn were replaced in 1969. One of them is now in the Smithsonian Institution. But the immortal sounds captured at Victor's Camden plant early in the century are still being heard today, reissued on compact discs.

CHAPTER 10

BLACK DIAMONDS

William Clarke Mason and early FELA cases ■ *The Central Railroad of New Jersey* ■ *Black diamonds in Schuylkill County* ■ *Stephen Girard again* ■ *Canals and railroads* ■ *The Reading's hubris and J. P. Morgan* ■ *The* Crusader *and the morning meeting* ■ *The Philadelphia & Reading Coal & Iron Company* ■ *Its reorganization* ■ *The Firm does not keep time records* ■ *The Reading's ghastly labor relations* ■ *The Molly Maguires* ■ *Management by divine right* ■ *Noerr Motor Freight* ■ *The last bankruptcy* ■ *From beyond the grave*

Railroads have historically been among a law firm's most coveted clients, according to the senior partner of another firm quoted in Chapter 4. Recently, in 1990-92, Morgan, Lewis & Bockius advised the National Railway Labor Conference in unprecedented collective bargaining that precipitated two special acts of Congress and achieved a breakthrough in reduced crew sizes. (More about this in Chapter 20.) And earlier, during most of the twentieth century, the Firm was general counsel to the Reading Company, whose distinctions included being one of four railroads on the *Monopoly* board.

When William Clarke Mason joined the Firm in 1922, he had already represented the Reading for almost twenty years. That representation went back to 1903, the year Mason graduated from Penn Law School and rented space from Gavin W. Hart in the Franklin Building at 131-33 South Twelfth Street. Hart was a litigator with such an overflow of Reading cases that he let young Mason work on some. Mason soon began taking them to court. By the time Hart died in 1909, the twenty-eight-year-old Mason had so impressed the Reading that he succeeded Hart as the Reading's chief trial counsel. Later, he would become general solicitor of the Reading and in 1929 its general attorney. Few lawyers know the joy of representing a client for fifty-four years as Mason did the Reading. The relationship began in his first year at the bar and lasted until his death in 1957.

The Federal Employers' Liability Act (FELA) was passed in 1908.[1] It gave railroad employees the right to sue their employers in federal court for injuries sustained on the job. Under FELA, contributory negligence might reduce but not necessarily bar recovery. Nor were benefits subject to any formula. Consequently, railroad employees enjoyed advantages under FELA not available at common law or by workers compensation statutes. Over the years, such employees have asserted literally hundreds of thousands of FELA claims, of which ML&B has handled several thousand, most of them for the Reading and its sometime affiliate the Central Railroad of New Jersey (CNJ). Before 1916, when Mason was still only thirty-five, he had already argued four Reading FELA cases in the United States Supreme Court and won all of them.[2]

After Mason came to ML&B in 1922 and succeeded to other responsibilities for the Reading, waves of later ML&B lawyers took over the railroad's FELA cases. One such lawyer was Henry Heebner, who became a partner in 1932 and retired in 1967. He tried FELA cases almost exclusively, as can be seen from listings forty years ago in *The Legal Intelligencer*.[3] His name was regularly on dozens of FELA cases awaiting trial, whether they were tried by him or by other ML&B partners. Over the years, those partners included John McConnell, Richard Brown, Thomas Masterson,[4] William Taylor, John Lewis, E. Barclay Cale, Denis Brenan, Jay (Jerry) Calvert, Raymond Cullen, Thomas (Tim) Kittredge, Marc Sonnenfeld, Joseph Torregrossa, and Kell Damsgaard.

Cale remembers regular Saturday morning conferences in the 1960s at which the Firm's railroad trial team reviewed their FELA cases. Each case would be exhaustively presented and evaluated, with the most junior lawyer required to go first. As positions were critiqued and theses defended, the team came to understand the strengths and weaknesses of each case, as well as its likely cost in settlement or at trial. Generations of ML&B litigators cut their teeth on the Firm's FELA litigation.

■ ■ ■ ■ ■

The raison d'etre for the Reading Railroad was anthracite coal, a fact the Reading acknowledged in 1906 by adopting the Black Diamond as its trade name and logo. The country's largest anthracite fields are located in five Pennsylvania counties, with the richest fields in Schuylkill County. Endless carloads of coal brought from those fields by the Reading to Philadelphia helped make that city the "Workshop of the World" after the Civil War.

Earlier, Stephen Girard saw the opportunity. The First Bank of the United States had foreclosed on coal lands in Schuylkill County owned by Robert Morris, a signer of the Declaration of Independence. (Often called the financier of the American Revolution, Morris later went bankrupt through real estate speculation, a familiar phenomenon still today.) After the First Bank dissolved in 1811, Girard bought most of its assets, including the former Morris properties, which comprised 17,000 acres of coal lands. Following Girard's death, they would turn out to be the most valuable asset of his estate. For more than a century, their output of coal supported Girard College, whose trustees the Firm would represent in landmark litigation during the 1950s and 1960s, as recounted in Chapter 16.

Since coal at the mine head is of little use, a means had to be found to transport it to the market. Initially, canals were the means. The Schuylkill Canal was completed in 1825, the same year as the more celebrated Erie Canal. By 1832, more than 200,000 tons of anthracite were moving down the Schuylkill Canal annually to Philadelphia. But canals quickly yielded to railroads, including the Reading, which was established in 1833. Its tracks fanned out like fingers over southeastern Pennsylvania. By 1844, it was hauling more coal than the canal, which fell into disuse and was acquired by the Reading in 1870.

Three decades after its founding, the Reading became the first American railroad to carry 1 million tons of freight a year. Eventually, the Reading would operate not only a railroad but also sixty-three anthracite mines and ten ocean-going colliers. Along its tracks would be located 15,000 industries. It would manufacture 627 locomotives in its own shops, maintain 79 freight interchange junctions with other railroads, and serve 22 million passengers a year at its Twelfth and Market streets terminal in Philadelphia. But the Reading was also notorious for its volatility: It went bankrupt four times—in 1880, 1884, 1897, and finally in 1971.

The Reading's earlier bankruptcies were caused by overweening ambition: It aspired to reach beyond its natural territory and become a trunk-line carrier. In 1883, it even challenged the Pennsylvania Railroad. With the backing of William Vanderbilt, Andrew Carnegie, Henry Clay Frick, and John D. Rockefeller, it began constructing a line from Harrisburg to Pittsburgh. But J. P. Morgan thought it wasteful for railroads to parallel and compete with one another. When he torpedoed the project in 1885, the new road was 60 percent finished, including seven tunnels bored through the mountains. Judged an engineering marvel, 160 miles of it were later adopted as the bed of the Pennsylvania Turnpike from Carlisle to Irwin (near Pittsburgh) that opened in 1940.

In another dramatic gesture, the Reading leased the Central New England Railroad and got control of the Boston & Maine Railroad in the 1890s. Using owned and leased lines, it thus extended throughout New England to the Canadian border. But again J. P. Morgan stepped in, the acquisitions were reversed, and the runaway railroad was humbled. Following J. P.'s death in 1913, the House of Morgan's man on the Reading board from 1914 to 1938 was Edward Stotesbury, whose story is told in Chapter 11. He was a Firm client, a close friend of Morris Bockius, and the Philadelphia senior partner of Drexel & Company.

The Reading was an outstanding passenger carrier as well as a freight hauler. Between 1938 and 1952, ML&B lawyers heading for Wall Street could walk four blocks from the Fidelity Building to Reading Terminal and board the *Crusader*, then the pride of the Reading fleet. Between its four reserved-seat parlor cars was a deluxe dining car where delicious food was served by white-glove attendants. Although the *Crusader* was sleek and streamlined, its stainless steel mantle concealed a steam locomotive: The Reading was electrified only as far as West Trenton. The *Crusader* operated on Reading tracks until it reached Bound Brook, New Jersey. From that point, it proceeded on CNJ tracks to Jersey City. There, passengers disembarked and took the ferry across the Hudson River to CNJ's Manhattan terminal at Liberty Street, just southwest of today's World Trade Center.[5] When service began in 1938, the trip took an hour and forty-five minutes and cost $1.80 one way. Since the train left Reading Terminal at 7:40 a.m., ML&B partners on board missed the Firm's morning meeting.

■ ■ ■ ■ ■

ML&B also represented the Reading's most prominent subsidiary, the Philadelphia & Reading Coal & Iron Company (C&I). C&I had been created by the Reading in 1871 to mine coal for the railroad to haul. Only nine years after its founding, it was the world's largest anthracite mining entity, with 170,000 acres estimated to contain 1.7 billion tons of recoverable coal. At its peak in 1927, C&I employed 15,000 miners and 1,200 salaried workers. But the Depression and the advent of oil for home heating brought C&I to its knees. The Firm represented C&I as debtor-in-possession after it filed for bankruptcy in 1937. During the ensuing eight-year reorganization, C&I restructured its debt and gave up 125,000 acres of its coal lands. Its reorganization also generated litigation that involved the Firm in three appeals to the Court of Appeals for the Third Circuit.[6]

When C&I's reorganization ended, the district court considered fee applications. They totaled $1.5 million, of which the Firm requested $300,000, worth $2.4 million in 1993. While some of the applicants fared badly, ML&B was paid in full. The court noted:

> The firm [ML&B] does not keep hourly timesheets but the Securities and Exchange Commission, in accordance with a method of its own, estimated from the records and counsel's statements that the firm spent approximately 41,000 hours on reorganization work. The Commission doubts the accuracy of its estimate and believes that the time actually spent was much less. However, even if it be assumed that the estimate is as much as 25 percent too high, the request would be at the rate of $10 an hour, which can hardly be called excessive in an employment involving as much responsibility as this. If the estimate is anywhere nearly correct the claim would be on the basis of $7.50 or $8 an hour. I see no reason to reduce this allowance below the amount requested and it will be approved in the total amount of $300,000.[7]

Although C&I came out of reorganization in 1945, its glory days were over. In 1955, it shut down what was still "the biggest anthracite mine in the world"[8] and parceled off its properties to smaller operators. By that year, when the Firm opened its last C&I file, the company had mined at least 1 billion tons of anthracite coal during its eighty-five-year life.

■ ■ ■ ■ ■

Many matters handled by the Firm for C&I and the Reading were in the labor field, with file titles including: "Takeover by United States Government—General Strike," "Injunction Proceedings Against Teamsters Union," "Picketing by International Organization of Master Mates and Pilots of America," "Injunction Against Teamsters 107," "Injunction Against Brotherhood of Locomotive Engineers," and "Strike by Railway, Airline & Steamship Clerks, Freight Handlers, Express and Station Employees." Books have been written about the Reading's ghastly labor relations, and especially about the fabled Molly Maguires.

The Molly Maguires were Irish immigrants, some of whom had fled the potato famines in the mid-1840s. They tried to unionize the Reading and the mines. In 1864, there was a strike by the Brotherhood of the Footboard, later renamed the Brotherhood of Locomotive Engineers. President Lincoln ordered the Reading seized and operated by the army for several days until the strikers capitulated. The movement then went underground and spawned an organization called the Workingmen's Benevolent Association. A decade of terrorism followed, during which in Schuylkill County alone there were 142 unsolved murders, with Reading supervisors among the victims. The Reading hired the recently formed Pinkerton Detective Agency to infiltrate the Mollies. Ultimately, the movement was crushed, about twenty reputed Mollies were tried and convicted, and there were mass hangings in 1875-77. The Reading's then president was Franklin Gowen, a spellbinding orator and former Schuylkill County prosecutor. Although in the private sector, he masterminded the prosecutions, often making opening arguments, questioning witnesses, and summing up. Such was the power of the Reading in its heyday.

But power cuts both ways, as one of Gowen's successors, George Baer, discovered. He was also a lawyer and the Reading's president from 1901 to 1914. In 1902, 147,000 miners walked off their jobs, demanding recognition of their union, the United Mine Workers of America (UMW). The governor of Pennsylvania called out the 9,000-member National Guard. When they could not restore order, President Theodore Roosevelt prepared to send federal troops. Once again J. P. Morgan intervened. Speaking for the Reading, he agreed to an investigation, during which work resumed. The investigation was held in Philadelphia at the old federal courthouse on South Ninth Street where 500 witnesses testified. The UMW was represented by Clarence Darrow, the Reading by George Baer. Baer's position was already of record. In a letter leaked by its addressee to the press, Baer had stated:

> The rights and interests of the laboring man will be protected and cared for—not by the labor agitators, but by the Christian men to whom God in His infinite wisdom has given the control of the property interests of the country.[9]

During the hearings, Baer did not retreat from his claim of divine right. Instead, when Darrow deplored the sufferings of working men, Baer retorted: "They don't suffer. Why, they can't even speak English."[10] Baer's public-relations debacle led William Randolph Hearst to attack the "coal barons" and demand dissolution of the anthracite combines.

The combines were dissolved. But the process would take twenty years. By then William Clarke Mason was representing the Reading interests. That was in 1922, when the United States Supreme Court approved decrees separating the Reading, CNJ, and C&I.[11] After their separation, all three remained ML&B clients just the same.

■ ■ ■ ■ ■

The Reading was haunted by its labor-relations history well into the twentieth century. It was also hurt as coal lost out to oil, and trucks supplanted railroads. To beat the truckers, the railroads mounted a desperate offensive in the early 1950s. Through a public-relations agency, the railroads combined to conduct campaigns against the trucking industry. The campaigns were designed to limit truck tariffs, raise taxes on trucks, and encourage the rigid enforcement of state laws regulating trucking. The truckers fought back in what became the leading case of *Noerr Motor Freight, Inc. v. Eastern Railroad Presidents Conference.*[12]

In the *Noerr* case, forty-one long-distance trucking companies and their trade association sued twenty-four major railroads, the Eastern Railroad Presidents Conference, and a public-relations agency engaged by the conference. The Firm, with Arthur Littleton at the laboring oar, represented the Reading, the Chesapeake & Ohio, and four smaller railroads. Following a four-month trial in 1956, the District Court for the Eastern District of Pennsylvania found for the truckers, and the Court of Appeals for the Third Circuit affirmed. But the Supreme Court reversed, holding that collective efforts to influence governmental action, despite an anticompetitive purpose, did not violate the Sherman Act. The *Noerr* case was not only a victory for the railroads, it also helped the Firm achieve the reversal twenty-eight years later of an $844.2-million judgment against client Kansas City Southern Industries, Inc. (More about this in Chapter 39.)

Although the railroads won the *Noerr* case, the tide did not turn. Instead, the truckers only increased their loadings. Moreover, there was less to load, as a worsening industrial blight afflicted the Northeast after World War II. In the 1960s, the area's railroads began going into bankruptcy. The CNJ filed in 1967. The Penn Central followed three years later in what was then America's biggest bankruptcy. And in 1971, the Reading filed for the fourth and final time. Trustees were appointed. Initially, they were Richardson Dilworth, formerly a mayor of Philadelphia, and Drew Lewis, a once and future client of the Firm. With the approval of the district court, the Firm continued "as special counsel to handle the same types of litigation . . . [it] had previously conducted for the railroad."[13]

During the Reading's ten years in reorganization (it emerged on January 1, 1981), new interests took control of it in 1973, and

Conrail absorbed its railroad operations in 1976. By that time, ML&B's assignments had dwindled to FELA cases and tax matters. Consequently, the Firm was free to represent the Penn Central in its valuation claim against the United States for the taking of its railroad properties by Conrail, a claim settled in 1981 for $2 billion, as detailed in Chapter 35. Others handled the Reading's claim, ultimately settled for approximately $160 million.

Shorn of its railroad, the reorganized Reading's assets included substantial net operating loss carryovers (NOLs). To utilize its NOLs, the Reading cast about to acquire an operating business. It found what it wanted in the industrial products group of Gould, Inc. Once again it turned to the Firm. The resulting $355-million Reading-Gould acquisition in 1981 was the largest transaction handled up to that point by the Firm's New York office. From the grave, the Reading was again a client, but for the last time.

■ ■ ■ ■ ■

The Reading story deserves a postscript. In addition to its NOLs and its claim against the government, the Reading emerged from its last bankruptcy with a miscellany of properties. That miscellany included the massive Reading Terminal train shed spanning thirteen rows of tracks. The shed became obsolete in 1984 with the construction of the Center City Commuter Tunnel connecting the former Reading and Pennsylvania lines. With the trains gone from the shed, its tracks were removed, and grass grew in its roadbeds. But the shed was destined to enjoy a renaissance when rehabilitated in the 1990s as the "crown jewel" of Philadelphia's half-billion dollar convention center.[14]

The Reading's postreorganization miscellany of properties also included the eight-story pink granite Reading Terminal headhouse opened in 1893, vacated in 1985, and acquired by the city in 1993 as the convention center's gateway. In that historically certified structure, generations of ML&B lawyers held hundreds of meetings with Reading officials over the years. At the highest level, some of those meetings took place on the southwest corner of the fourth floor, where an apse-like projection was part of the luxurious suite of the Black Diamond's CEO. From there he once ruled the Reading empire by divine right.

CHAPTER 11

DREXEL AND STOTESBURY

The collapse of Drexel Burnham Lambert ■ *Representing Drexel in the 1920s* ■ *Drexel's pedigree* ■ *Stotesbury as a client and friend of Bockius* ■ *German hyperinflation in 1923* ■ *The Versailles of America* ■ *Lifestyle before the Crash* ■ *A bomb threat* ■ *The Stotesburys leave Bockius in charge* ■ *"The richest man at Morgan's"* ■ *Stotesbury's death and estate* ■ *The disappearance of wealth* ■ *The great hall is demolished* ■ *An era ends*

Shortly before midnight on February 13, 1990, at the home of the clerk of the United States Bankruptcy Court for the Southern District of New York, Drexel Burnham Lambert filed for reorganization under Chapter 11 of the bankruptcy laws. Twenty years earlier, Drexel had employed a young Wharton School graduate named Michael Milken. Due primarily to the market Milken created for junk bonds, Drexel had become the country's most profitable and feared force in investment banking by the mid-1980s.

But as new depths of avarice and arrogance were plumbed, it was inevitable, as in Greek tragedy, that the hubris of the protagonists would bring them down. Drexel's liabilities were short. Its assets, comprising primarily junk bonds, were long. No respectable financial analyst would condone such a classic mismatch. When the junk-bond market collapsed, Drexel's balance sheet was so debilitated that it could not roll over its short-term debt. It had made obscene riches by marketing petards. Now it was hoist with its own.[1]

Earlier, in December 1988, Drexel had agreed to plead guilty to six felony counts of mail and securities fraud. The guilty plea became part of a settlement with the SEC. By that settlement, Drexel undertook to pay $650 million in fines and restitution—then by far the largest settlement in securities-law history—and to cooperate with the SEC in its ongoing investigation. As part of that cooperation, Drexel consented to the engagement of an independent consultant to review and report to the SEC concerning Drexel's compliance with federal securities laws. There was a beauty contest for the appointment of the independent consultant. The Firm won, and its selection in June 1989 was given wide media attention. Unfortunately, Drexel's bankruptcy the following February cut short the assignment only five months after the Firm began its work, as noted in Chapter 22.

■ ■ ■ ■ ■

Drexel Burnham Lambert had a remarkable pedigree. Before Drexel Burnham Lambert there was Drexel Burnham (1973-76); before that, Drexel Firestone & Co. (1970-73); before that, Drexel Harriman Ripley (1966-1970); and before that, simply Drexel & Co. (1838-1966). For most of its long life, Drexel was a Philadelphia institution. It was not until the early 1970s that Drexel moved the center of its operations to New York.

Although the Firm did not represent Drexel & Co. as general counsel, it acted for the company in the 1920s as underwriter in many debt offerings, particularly by utilities (again evidencing the Firm's special expertise in that field), railroads, and municipalities. Among those offerings were literally dozens in which the borrower was the city of Philadelphia. Some issues were substantial, including one in 1921 by the Commonwealth of Pennsylvania in the amount of $50 million, the equivalent of $450 million in 1993.

Drexel & Co. was founded in 1838 by Francis Martin Drexel, an Austrian immigrant. Five years earlier, President Andrew Jackson had effectively won his war against the Second Bank of the United States by draining it of government deposits. These deposits were then transferred to state-chartered banks, which multiplied like rabbits and funded themselves by issuing notes—the antecedents of today's certificates of deposit. The notes were only as good as their obligors, whose strengths varied widely, so a lively market developed in bank paper. At the outset, that market was Drexel's forte. Then, within a decade, Drexel broadened its activities and became a multifaceted private bank. During the Mexican War (1846-1848), it marketed almost $50 million of United States Treasury Bonds. It expanded to New York in 1855 and to Paris in 1867.

But the Drexel principals were dissatisfied with their New York colleagues. So, in 1871, they approached a banker named John Pierpont Morgan, then thirty-four years old. Morgan was employed by Dabney, Morgan & Co., the New York arm of J. S. Morgan & Co. The J. S. stood for Junius Spencer, who was J. P.'s father. Junius operated in London, where he channeled British capital into the

United States. Drexel approached J. P. at both a good and a bad time: good, because Junius and J. P. were also unhappy with their partners in New York; bad, because young J. P. was ill and about to abandon investment banking entirely.

In May 1871, J. P. Morgan and Anthony J. Drexel—then senior partner of Drexel and Co. and son of founder Francis Drexel—met for dinner at Drexel's Philadelphia home. Drexel proposed that his firm and Morgan create a New York partnership to be known as Drexel, Morgan & Co., with an equal division of profits and losses. Morgan protested that he was ill. Drexel kept after him. Finally, a deal was struck. The firm of Drexel, Morgan & Co. would open on July 1, 1871, as the New York arm of Drexel & Co. Meanwhile, Morgan would take an extended vacation (which lasted fifteen months) and would report to work when he was fit. After dinner, Drexel scribbled the terms of the agreement on the back of a used envelope in his library. These scribblings constituted the First Articles of Partnership of Drexel, Morgan & Co. At that moment was born the direct antecedent of today's Morgan Stanley & Co., Inc., as well as of J. P. Morgan & Co., Incorporated, and its subsidiary, Morgan Guaranty Trust Company.

It went exactly as planned. There was J. S. Morgan & Co. in London, run by Junius, who died in 1890. This firm became Morgan Grenfell & Co. in 1910.[2] There was Drexel, Harjes & Co. in Paris, which had been established in 1867 and changed its name to Morgan & Cie. in 1926. There was Drexel, Morgan & Co. in New York, which changed its name to J. P. Morgan & Co. in 1895. And there was Drexel & Co. in Philadelphia, of which J. P. Morgan became the senior partner following the death of Anthony J. Drexel in 1893.

When Morgan died in 1913, his son, J. P. Morgan, Jr., generally called Jack, succeeded him as the ranking partner of both J. P. Morgan & Co. (New York) and Drexel & Co. (Philadelphia). Jack lived until 1943. In 1924, he dedicated the Pierpont Morgan Library on Thirty-sixth Street between Park and Madison avenues, a short walk from the Firm's New York office today. Jack also continued to have an interest in Drexel until 1940.

The Glass-Steagall Act of 1933 required that banks choose between commercial and investment banking. Both J. P. Morgan & Co. and Drexel & Co. chose commercial banking. This choice did not sit well with a minority of the firms' principals. In 1935, they left to form Morgan Stanley & Co. and engage in investment banking, although the September 6, 1935, *New York Times* noted their confession that "at the present time there was not a great deal of security business."

Both Morgan and Drexel remained private commercial banks until 1940. In that year, the New York partners withdrew from the Philadelphia partnership, and the Philadelphia partners withdrew from the New York partnership, which incorporated. The entities went their separate ways. The Philadelphians, Drexel & Co., again became an investment bank; the New Yorkers, J. P. Morgan & Co., Inc., continued as a commercial bank. In 1959, J. P. Morgan & Co., Inc., merged with Guaranty Trust Company of New York, a public company, to form Morgan Guaranty Trust Company of New York. Then, a holding company was created in 1969 for the stock of Morgan Guaranty Trust Company. Reflecting its lineage, that holding company was named J. P. Morgan & Co., Incorporated.

■ ■ ■ ■ ■

But back to the early days. By 1895, J. P. Morgan had sole authority to determine the shares of each partner in the New York, Philadelphia, London, and Paris entities. The various interests of the ten partners were the same in both the New York and Philadelphia partnerships, a condition that prevailed until 1940. Morgan had a 35-percent interest, followed by Edward Townsend Stotesbury, whose share was 14 percent. Considering Stotesbury's interests in the New York and Philadelphia partnerships, it is not surprising that he became so fantastically wealthy. He also became an important client of the Firm.

Stotesbury was the son of a Philadelphia sugar refiner. After graduating from Friends Central School, he became a Drexel office boy in 1866 at age seventeen. He worked a six-day week for an annual salary of $200. Advancing through the ranks, he became a Drexel partner in 1882, and by the early 1890s, he was second only to J. P. Morgan in the two firms. In 1905, he became the resident senior partner in Philadelphia.

Stotesbury, called Ned by his friends, was a small, dapper man of inexhaustible energy. Perhaps because he never sat down for more than a few minutes, it was said that "he never read a book."[3] As Drexel's resident senior partner, he was the main source of financing for many businesses located in Philadelphia and to the west. His numerous board memberships included UGI, Baldwin Locomotive Works, Fidelity Trust Company, and Reading Company, all clients of the Firm. Also, between 1896 and 1904, he and the Firm were physically close to each other when the Firm and Drexel were both located in the Drexel Building.[4]

Stotesbury's extensive 1938 obituary (which occupied much of the *Bulletin's* first page) said he was "lightning-like in his decisions, and as there was no appeal from the Stotesbury court the arguments were swift and the business was dispatched with an amazing quickness, considering the enormous amounts involved."[5]

The mutual client dealings of Morris Bockius and Edward Stotesbury occasionally took them abroad. In 1922, Samuel Vauclain, CEO of the Baldwin Locomotive Works, and Bockius, Baldwin's counsel, picked up Stotesbury in Paris. Vauclain and Bockius were making a second trip to Poland and Romania. Stotesbury accompanied them in their private railroad car as far as Berlin. In that city, according to J. Tyson Stokes, they experienced the first ravages of German hyperinflation and "Stotesbury took great delight in finding an error of two million marks in the bill for their hotel breakfast."[6] By November 1923, the official exchange rate reached an astronomical 4.2 trillion marks to the dollar and the black market rate, 11 trillion marks—a distinction without a difference. In a historical coincidence, twenty-two years later at the Nuremberg trials, Firm partner Brady Bryson would prosecute Hjalmar Schacht, the financial wizard who wrestled with Germany's money problems in the 1920s and rehabilitated its currency. (More about this in Chapter 18.)

Considering Bockius's many contacts with Stotesbury, it is not surprising that they enjoyed an unusually close personal and professional relationship. Together, they went through the fabulous 1920s, followed by the catastrophic 1930s. After Stotesbury died in 1938, Bockius was his executor and trustee, along with Lucretia Bishop Roberts Cromwell Stotesbury (she insisted that everyone call her Eva) and Charles Dickey, a Drexel partner and father of a future Scott Paper president.

President William Howard Taft was among the wedding guests when Stotesbury married Eva Cromwell, a widow, in 1912. The groom was sixty-two; the bride, forty-seven. She had been prominent in Washington and New York society, and following their marriage they embarked upon a lifestyle so lavish as to seem embarrassing today. One of their three main residences was El Mirasol in Palm Beach. It was designed as a reproduction, at least externally, of an old convent near Burgos, Spain. Built around a patio with a fountain in the center, its rooms had ceiling heights of twenty-five feet, and its amenities included a complete motion-picture theater. Bockius visited Stotesbury there.

But El Mirasol was as nothing compared with Whitemarsh Hall. That Palladian palace, which beggared the Gilded Age homes at

Newport, was constructed over a five-year period and had its grand opening in 1921. The gate house that marked the main entrance was on Willow Grove Avenue east of Chestnut Hill. A mile-long drive extended through its grounds to a statued forecourt north of the main building. The gardens were by Jacques Gréber who laid out Philadelphia's Parkway. The house was by architect Horace Trumbauer, several of whose commissions are visible from the Firm's Logan Square offices, including the Free Library and the Philadelphia Museum of Art.

Whitemarsh Hall comprised six stories, three above ground and three below, containing 147 rooms (including forty-five baths) and totaling 100,000 square feet of floor space. Besides the main house, there were twenty-two other buildings on the 305-acre site, including twelve dwellings, garages, greenhouses, stables, and gate houses. The estate, often called the Versailles of America, was arguably superior to its namesake in one respect: It afforded a panoramic view of its main building and gardens from almost a mile away, which is not possible at Versailles itself.[7]

Social life at Whitemarsh Hall was nonstop, skillfully orchestrated by Eva, but appreciated equally by Ned. Evidently, she "taught him, as they say, to 'play.' "[8] Celebrities enjoyed visiting. One of them, Henry Ford, reportedly remarked: "It's a great experience to see how the rich live."[9] Bockius was on the scene frequently. In fact, he was one of a few visitors Stotesbury's footmen had standing orders to admit anytime.[10]

■ ■ ■ ■ ■

Before the Crash, Stotesbury "had counted his fortune . . . at $200,000,000."[11] During the Depression, the Stotesbury way of life became an anachronism. More than that, it became a target for public outrage, which went beyond mere verbal abuse. In the spring of 1932, radio commentator Boake Carter urged that the Stotesbury home be bombed. Would a mob attack Whitemarsh Hall as another mob had attacked the real Versailles in 1789? If so, it was unlikely that Whitemarsh Hall would be better defended by Stotesbury's staff of 150 than was Versailles by the Swiss guards, several of whose heads were severed and mounted on pikes, as Louis XVI and Marie Antoinette were marched to a Paris prison and later to the guillotine.

With the Stotesburys in peril, plans were made for their evacuation. Fiske Kimball, one-time curator of the Philadelphia Museum of Art, has written about the arrangements:

One day that May [1932], Morris Bockius, Stotesbury's old and trusted legal counsel, called to ask me if I could go out to the house that afternoon, with a view to taking care of the works of art at the Museum that summer. He said, "It might influence the disposition of the collection." The Stotesburys were to close the house, disband the servants and go abroad.

Both Mr. and Mrs. Stotesbury were there. She was all graciousness, saying, "We consider ourselves only trustees of our collection for the public." "What's that? What's that?" [Stotesbury] asked, rousing momentarily from the deep lethargy in which he sat. Beyond the loggia the parterre danced purple in the sunlight. "Well, Morris," said Mrs. Stotesbury to Bockius with a spirit which one could not fail to admire, "if we never come back, we've had ten wonderful years of it."[12]

Representatives of the museum went to Whitemarsh Hall and inventoried the collection that famed art dealer Joseph Duveen had amassed for Stotesbury. Arrangements were made to have the collection removed after the couple departed. Ned and Eva did leave safely and made it to Europe. With the Stotesburys gone, Bockius was in charge of the legal details. As agreed, the art collection was moved to the museum, where it filled five galleries.

But there was a change in the public's confidence factor during the summer of 1932. People really believed the worst was over. Of course, they were wrong. Still, the rabble-rousers ceased their clamor, and by fall it was safe for the Stotesburys to come home. Over time, the plan to give the art collection to the museum was abandoned. Instead, it was determined that the collection would ultimately have to be sold to fund estate taxes. Bockius changed the will accordingly. After Stotesbury's death in 1938, some pieces of sculpture that were left to Eva did eventually reach the museum. The rest of the collection was auctioned and scattered. The wonderful English portraits and fine furniture "realized little more than ten cents on the dollar" in what Kimball called "a butchery."[13]

Bockius died a year after Stotesbury and was succeeded by William Clarke Mason as co-executor and co-trustee of the Stotesbury estate. The executors' account in 1941 showed assets of only $10 million. Was Stotesbury really worth $200 million before the Crash in 1929? If so, some of his possessions had certainly lost their values, or at least their perceived values.

One example is the tragic fate of Whitemarsh Hall. During World War II, it became a warehouse, as the prospect of German bombs led several museums, including the Metropolitan Museum, to store hundreds of paintings and other art objects in its cavernous basements for the duration.[14] The duration ended when the tide of battle turned in Europe, and the treasures went back to their normal repositories by the spring of 1944. Some months earlier, in October 1943, Whitemarsh Hall was sold to the Pennsylvania Salt Manufacturing Company (later Pennwalt Corporation and still later Atochem North America, Inc.) as a research laboratory for $167,000. Seventeen years later, the company vacated the property. Despoiled by vandals, Whitemarsh Hall was sold for demolition and development in 1982. In a final irony, the developers were reported to have lost money when demolition costs exceeded their estimates.

In addition to assets that lost their value, some of Stotesbury's wealth was consumed in a brave effort to continue his old lifestyle through the 1930s. He had been "the richest man at Morgan's," but he "withdrew $55,000,000 from his account [there] between 1933 and his death—a rate of withdrawal of more than $10,000,000 a year!"[15] Although he remained active in business until the end—he was stricken while returning from a meeting of the Reading Company board—he seems never to have comprehended the meaning of the Depression. For a man in his eighties this might be asking too much. It also might be asking too much for a man in his seventies, as was Bockius. After all, the Great Precipitator had emerged from law school during the Gilded 1880s, and his career had reached its apogee during the Roaring 1920s. The 1930s were such a repudiation of what he and Stotesbury had experienced earlier.

■ ■ ■ ■ ■

Miss Rebecca Conover was Bockius's long-time secretary. She had come to the Firm as a relatively young woman and remained until he died. She never answered back, and she never commented to anyone about her years of service with the Firm. When Miss Conover was occasionally absent in the late 1930s, Bockius would go looking for another secretary to take his dictation. He would pick an older woman, one with whom he felt comfortable. Such a person was Margaret Johnson Robinson, whose letter about Bockius's declining years is in the Firm's archives. She noted that as the old man dictated in his last years, he sometimes dozed off. She would wait patiently until he resumed.

The Great Precipitator remained titular head of the Firm until his death in 1939. But by the mid-1930s, an era had unquestionably ended, and the Firm's effective management was in the hands of William Clarke Mason.

CHAPTER 12

THE MAN IN
THE BATTERED HAT

Bockius and Mason compared ■ *An arresting baroque figure* ■ *Rare ducks* ■ *Mason is lured from his own firm* ■ *Philadelphia trial lawyers of the 1920s* ■ *Mason leads ML&B from 1939 to 1957* ■ *Francis Bracken misses morning meetings* ■ *Mason's bar association activities and versatility* ■ *Seashells and islands* ■ *A lion in winter* ■ *All the business the Firm needs* ■ *A guardian angel in the prompter's box*

New lawyers who join Morgan, Lewis & Bockius each year are encouraged to visit the Firm's main Philadelphia boardroom on the twentieth floor of One Logan Square and there contemplate the portraits of Morris Rex Bockius and William Clarke Mason. On the east wall is the portrait of Bockius. He is serene and imperious. There is no hint of humor in his glacial eyes. He is carved in granite. On the opposite wall is Mason. How different he is, with his projecting jaw and unruly hair. He sports a floppy bow tie with polka dots, and there is a carnation in his buttonhole. While Bockius dominates merely by existing, Mason radiates compressed energy as if ready to rise and pummel the viewer. Those who knew Mason said he was always spoiling for a good fight. He was born to be a trial lawyer.

The boutonniere in Mason's portrait was part of his attire. He regularly wore carnations, often from his garden. They numbered among his eccentricities, of which he cultivated many. For example, in cold weather he wore a raglan coat and a battered felt hat. Everyone thought Mason had just one favorite felt hat that he wore year after year, although by the usual sartorial standards it had clearly seen better days. Anyway, he was a busy man and could be excused for not taking time to go hat shopping. But such was not the case. Benjamin Quigg tells of visiting Mason at his Chestnut Hill home. Quigg opened the door to Mason's hall closet. Inside, there must have been a dozen felt hats, and each was carefully battered.

Mason's striking mien was the subject of comment. One lawyer wrote that Mason was "an arresting baroque figure . . . [with] an amiable ferocity of appearance that was irresistible."[1] Even the slightest contact with Mason made an impression. As another lawyer recounted: "An unhurried courteous bow Mr. Mason gave me some twenty years ago as I was sitting in your reception area . . . [when] he walked through made such an impression on me that my behavior has been improved ever since."[2]

Mason's character was consistent with his portrait. He was commanding, down-to-earth, forceful, outspoken, and not economical in his use of expletives. According to Orvel Sebring, Mason had two sides—tough and gentle. As he aged, his gentle side won out. If a lawyer's child was sick, Mason would be concerned. The lawyer would get a call from him every night.

But in Mason's tough moods, he was dogmatic and utterly intractable. In the early 1950s, when the Philadelphia Electric Company asked for information about the hourly rates of ML&B lawyers working on the company's matters, Mason responded: "You run your business and I'll run mine." Only Mason could get away with such hauteur. It even extended to cooking. Ducks bagged at Mason's shooting club in South Carolina were sent back and prepared at the Midday Club, an eating place frequented by the Firm's partners on the top floor of the Fidelity Building. Mason went in person to the kitchen and told the chef exactly how to prepare the ducks. Mason liked his ducks extremely rare, some said raw. Everybody had to eat them as Mason liked them.

■ ■ ■ ■ ■

William Clarke Mason was born in Philadelphia on April 26, 1881. He was educated in the Philadelphia public schools, including Central High School, from which he graduated in 1900. He was president of his class and its valedictorian. Central, founded in 1836 and then located at Broad and Green streets, was one of only two high schools in the country authorized to grant bachelor's degrees.

Following high school, Mason went directly to the University of Pennsylvania Law School, where he was a member of the class of 1903. The Firm's archives include a photograph of that class showing young Mason seated at one end of the front row and looking especially jaunty. The picture was taken outside the new law school building at Thirty-fourth and Chestnut streets. It had been completed just two years earlier and was named Lewis Hall in honor of William Draper Lewis, the school's then dean and only full-time faculty member. (In those days, most law schools considered practicing attorneys better teachers than academicians.) He was a relative of Francis Draper Lewis, a founding partner of the Firm.

After graduation, Mason rented office space from Gavin W. Hart in the Franklin Building at 131-33 South Twelfth Street. The following year, Mason was joined by his law school classmate, Franklin Spencer Edmonds. They formed the firm of Mason & Edmonds. After Mason joined ML&B in 1922, his old firm became Edmonds & Obermayer. Still later, it became Obermayer, Rebmann, Maxwell & Hippel, which remains its name today. Mason's landlord, Gavin Hart, was a busy trial lawyer whose main client was the Reading Railroad. Mason assisted Hart with his Reading cases and in 1909, after Hart's death, succeeded him as Reading's chief trial counsel.

The outstanding trial lawyers operating in Philadelphia during the 1920s included William Clarke Mason of ML&B; Robert T. McCracken of the firm known today as Montgomery, McCracken, Walker & Rhoads; George Wharton Pepper, a founding partner of today's Pepper, Hamilton & Scheetz and a United States senator from 1922 to 1927; and Ralph Evans, a protégé of John G. Johnson and a founding partner of Evans, Bayard & Frick, which merged with Pepper, Hamilton & Scheetz in 1954.

In addition, the list should include Owen J. Roberts, also of the firm known today as Montgomery, McCracken, Walker & Rhoads. Roberts was appointed in 1924 by President Calvin Coolidge to prosecute the Tea Pot Dome bribery cases, in which Roberts obtained the conviction of President Warren Harding's Secretary of the Interior, Albert B. Fall. In 1930, President Herbert Hoover appointed Roberts to the United States Supreme Court, on which he served until 1945. (More about Roberts in Chapter 13.)

Some trial lawyers are at ease with juries and try their cases to them. Others harbor suspicions of juries and try their cases to the record. The first group has a better chance of winning at the outset. The second group has its eye fixed on the appeal: Trial court victories are pleasant, but ultimately appellate courts set things straight. Mason was clearly in the first category. He was fascinated by the way ordinary people thought and by how he could influence their thinking. There was something of the Horace Rumpole in him.[3] In an American Bar Association tribute to Mason dated March 11, 1958, Vincent P. McDevitt (long-time general counsel of the Philadelphia Electric Company) wrote: "Even the most experienced attorney found it quite profitable to observe William Clarke Mason plead a case."

One of Mason's constant courtroom competitors was Robert T. McCracken, who had been a classmate of Mason's at Central High School. In a May 1952 profile of Mason in *The Shingle*,[4] McCracken wrote:

> [Mason] tried all kinds of cases in the civil courts, State and Federal. He tried them fearlessly, tenaciously, ingeniously. No point on which the slightest reliance might be placed escaped his attention. No Court was too remote for him to endeavor to invoke its assistance. In his eyes, his client was always right. Sometimes the jury, and not infrequently the Court, disagreed with him. He was saddened by those disagreements, but seldom convinced.[5]

■ ■ ■ ■ ■

Considering Mason's qualifications as a litigator, it is not surprising that Bockius approached him in 1922, following the death of the Firm's leading trial lawyer, R. Stuart Smith. More surprising is the fact that Mason left Mason & Edmonds, which then comprised at least four lawyers, to join MLB. He was forty-one years old. Maybe he was tired of managing his own firm. Maybe he wished to play on a bigger stage. Or maybe Bockius made him an offer he simply could not refuse.

According to received wisdom, Bockius knew in 1922 when he attracted Mason that he was consciously determining his successor as ML&B's next senior partner; and, indeed, Mason did succeed Bockius in 1939. However, in 1922, the Firm already had among its partners at least two distinguished lawyers whose prior service with the Firm ostensibly favored them over Mason. One was Clement Wood, a partner from 1910 until he died in 1940, whose son, William Wood, was a partner from 1964 to 1991. The other was Francis Bracken, a partner from 1918 until he died in 1937, whose nephew, John Bracken, was a partner from 1955 to 1977. (More about John Bracken in Chapter 18.)

Francis Bracken was a more forceful lawyer than Clement Wood, and was clearly one of the best technicians in the Firm's history. Bracken was also a trial lawyer, although very different from Mason. Bracken was one of those who harbored suspicions of juries. He tried his cases to the record. (Chapter 13.)

Bracken was well respected by members of the legal profession and served as chancellor of the Philadelphia Bar Association in 1936. But Bracken and Bockius did not always see eye to eye. For example, Bracken's attendance at the morning meeting in Bockius's office was grudging and sporadic. He felt he could use his time more productively elsewhere. An inexhaustible worker, he was also something of a loner and not given to levity. His stern portrait hangs in the Firm's Philadelphia office.

Sebring tells this characteristic story about "Frank" Bracken:

> One morning I was in Mr. Bracken's room reviewing with him a research memo in preparation for a day in court. Mr. Mason appeared in the doorway. Mr. Bracken looked up and growled, annoyed at being interrupted, even by his good friend, Will Mason.
>
> "Frank, Morris would like us in his office to settle the billing in that estate matter."
>
> "Who will be there?"
>
> "Just you, Morris, Clem and I."
>
> At that, Mr. Bracken threw down his pencil. Those penetrating blue eyes shot fire.
>
> "You'll never get anything done with a goddamn town meeting!"

According to J. Tyson Stokes, Bracken's office was always as isolated as possible and he was handled charily by Bockius. So received wisdom may be correct that from the beginning Bockius viewed Mason and not Bracken as Bockius's successor. Moreover, there is evidence of this in the archives. In a letter dated August 13, 1925, Bockius, then about to go abroad, asked Mason to renegotiate the office lease in the Land Title Building. Why not Bracken? He was the senior lawyer, had the negotiating skills, and was probably a better real estate technician than Mason. The answer is that Mason had the charisma.

Mason was not only an absolutely topnotch trial lawyer, he was also an excellent business lawyer. He believed that lawyers should be generalists, and he displayed his versatility by handling acquisitions, reorganizations, securities issues, and estate administrations. Like Bockius before him, Mason held some of Philadelphia's choicest directorships, serving on the boards of the Philadelphia National Bank, Scott Paper Company, and the Baldwin Locomotive Works.

Bockius was in a position to cultivate Mason for board memberships. But Bockius was in no position to advance Mason's standing with the organized bar, which Bockius considered a waste of time. Mason thought differently, and over the years he held top positions in the Philadelphia and Pennsylvania bar associations. He was chancellor of the Philadelphia Bar Association in 1940 and president of the Pennsylvania Bar Association in 1943. For many years, he was also a member of the American Bar Association's house of delegates and board of governors. He would probably have capped his career by serving as the association's president, but for failing health toward the end of his life. Tyson Stokes recounts that "[a]t one time a delegation from the American Bar Association called on Arthur Littleton to see if Mason could be persuaded to be nominated. . . . Their efforts proved unavailing."[6]

Although Mason never reached the ABA's pinnacle, John Bracken has pointed out that few people are more venerated in its annals than Mason. This is primarily due to the extraordinary role he played in enhancing the American Bar Endowment. During the 1950s, Mason conceived an idea that would generate more than $100 million for the endowment. The idea called for the ABA to sponsor a group life insurance program for its members. Dividends from the program would be payable by the insurance company to the endowment to further its purposes: "the advancement of jurisprudence . . . through education and scientific research." But at first the ABA's board of governors was cool to the concept and rebuffed Mason when he requested an appropriation of $5,000 for actuarial studies. So he asked the board to let him furnish the studies at his own expense. Ultimately, the board embraced the plan, and the American Bar Association in one of its brochures states: "Mason is rightfully recognized as the father of the insurance program."

In 1958, a wing of the American Bar Association Center in Chicago was named for Mason. It includes the William Clarke Mason Conference Room, in which hangs a portrait similar to the one in the Firm's Philadelphia boardroom. Both are the works of Alice Kent Stoddard. The boardroom portrait was painted from life. Using the boardroom portrait and the artist's recollections of her subject, the ABA portrait was painted after Mason's death. It shows Mason leaning forward and even more ready to rise and pummel the viewer. On July 15, 1957, just four months before Mason died, he was awarded the American Bar Association Medal for "Conspicuous Service to the Cause of American Jurisprudence." Stokes commented that "[n]one of [Mason's] numerous honors pleased him half so much."[7]

■ ■ ■ ■ ■

Unlike Bockius, Mason balanced his professional life with a warm and rewarding home life. In 1909, he married Mary Townsend, who was an accomplished painter. Starting in the 1930s, the walls of the Firm's offices in the Fidelity Building were adorned with her oils and watercolors. Mason's interest in art stemmed from his wife's avocation. He served on the board of the Pennsylvania Academy of the Fine Arts, where his wife had been a student.

It was characteristic of Mason that he considered himself an authority on many subjects, even seashells. He collected rare specimens by the hundreds, largely from the Gulf Coast of Florida. During the Mason years and until the Firm's move to Logan Square, vitrines of shells were placed about the office as decorations. Those who did not know of Mason's interest must have been puzzled by these objects.

Another of Mason's avocations was hunting. As mentioned earlier, he was a member of a shooting club in South Carolina, where he vacationed a week or two every winter. He also owned three small islands off the coast of Maine. They were uninhabited except that his family spent part of every summer on one. On another he proposed to raise Icelandic ponies. Still another island was intended as a communal summer vacation site for Firm lawyers and their families. Mason considered it a great idea. Whatever the feelings of the lawyers, the program was vetoed by their wives. Too much propinquity. The islands were sold just before Mason's death.

The Masons enjoyed music. They had a box at the opera and rarely missed a performance, according to Stokes. At that time, the Metropolitan Opera often performed on Tuesdays in Philadelphia. The house in New York was dark those nights, and the sets, less elaborate than today, were transported and adapted to the stage of the Academy of Music. The casts were the same as in New York, and the Philadelphia performances were regarded as part of the Met's regular schedule.

Mason had a meandering home, still called "the Mason house," in Chestnut Hill. It was as if five stone farmhouses had been stuck together at right angles to form a zigzag. Located in a glen, the Mason property included a stream, a pond, resident geese, and a spring house. As McCracken recounts:

> [P]erhaps [Mason's] principal love is his beautiful garden, surrounding his stately and comfortable residence in Chestnut Hill. It is definitely *his* garden. He planned it, laid it out, and watches over it with constant care.[8]

Mason's many interests in subjects other than the law set him apart from Bockius. Also, there seems to have been a difference between the Firm's management during the Bockius and Mason years. Everyone agrees that Mason was a superlative litigator, a fine general practitioner, a charismatic figure, and a tough guy. But he does not seem to have had the unique capacity for administration and firm building that belonged to Bockius, even though Mason was probably the better all-around lawyer.

Perhaps Mason did not relish the leading role and was happier in earlier times when Bockius was in charge. If so, his unhappiness may have been aggravated by the deaths of his two near contemporaries, Francis Bracken in 1937 and Clement Wood in 1940. There was a sizable age gap between Mason and the remaining partners. (Succeeding senior partners Littleton and MacIntosh were fourteen and twenty years younger than Mason respectively.) From the late 1940s until Mason's death in 1957, although he clearly led the Firm, his main interest was in thrusting the younger lawyers into the limelight. While often excoriating them to their faces, he asserted their infallibility to the outside world. According to John Bracken, Mason would say that they did all the driving and that he was only along for the ride.

During his last years, Mason also withdrew from the courtroom. He was in his seventies and had suffered the eighteen-year ordeal of UGI's dismemberment, to be recounted in Chapter 14. Still, a trial lawyer out of the courtroom is a lion in winter. Robert Young remembers Mason as "detached and running the Firm on automatic pilot" during the last ten years of his life. Young also recalls Mason's repeated statements to the partners that they should not look for new business since the Firm had all the business it wanted or needed. Bockius would never have said that. But then rainmaking was Bockius's hallmark.

A change in the duration of vacations attests to the relative detachment of the Mason years compared with the intensity of the Bockius period. In earlier times, three or four weeks were the standard vacation, even for senior lawyers. But after World War II, six weeks of vacation for partners and four weeks for associates became the custom. The partners split theirs—four weeks in the summer and two in the winter. The associates took their four weeks in the summer, normally avoiding August when the partners took theirs. But lengthier vacations were a temporary respite. It would be unusual today to find a partner taking six weeks of vacation. The average number is again closer to the Bockius regimen. (The vacation question will be considered again in Chapter 42.)

Mason remained active with the Firm until the very end, when he died at his desk on November 19, 1957. He had presided over the morning meeting of partners in the twenty-first-floor Fidelity Building boardroom. He then went to his office to prepare for a meeting of the board of directors of the Philadelphia National Bank, of which he and Arthur Littleton were both members. When Littleton stopped at Mason's office, Mason was unconscious.

Mason left his mark on clients and other lawyers. One client was Robert McLean of the Bulletin Company. McLean wrote to Stokes:

> Not only did [Mason] counsel me in the law but I had the feeling that he dedicated himself to the proposition that my life should be as free of error as our close association would permit. Though I did not always do what he said, I felt I had a guardian angel in the prompter's box.[9]

Leon Obermayer, who knew Mason professionally longer than anyone, wrote to Stokes in 1973: " [A]ll the 'good law' I know I learned from Mr. Mason between 1905 and 1922." Obermayer also noted that when he became president of the Board of Public Education in Philadelphia, Mason "did not write me a letter or telephone to congratulate me, but came over to my office to see me because he wanted to shake my hand in person."[10]

Finally, there is McCracken's May 1952 tribute to Mason in *The Shingle*:

> [N]o man, at this or any Bar, has exhibited a higher sense or a more rigid observance not only of the ethics, but of the utmost proprieties of this, the greatest of all professions, than has William Clarke Mason.

CHAPTER 13

THE DEPRESSION YEARS

Baseball and unemployment ■ The stock market plunges ■ The Firm is busier than ever ■ Mortgage foreclosures ■ Private charities ■ Hoover at the end of the string ■ Roosevelt closes the banks ■ New Deal legislation ■ The Supreme Court yields ■ The NLRB and the SEC ■ A pioneer securities offering ■ The underliers and the PRT re-organization ■ Trying cases to the record ■ New doors open ■ "The biggest, richest and most active [law firm] in the city"

It is said simplistically that the Depression began in 1929 and lasted about ten years until World War II finally spurred an economic revival. But for lovers of baseball in Philadelphia, the depression years did not begin so badly. The Philadelphia Athletics (the As) won the World Series in 1929 and 1930, and the American League championship in 1931. Managed by Cornelius McGillicuddy, a/k/a Connie Mack, the As included Jimmy Foxx, Lefty Grove, and Eddie Rommel. Some aficionados consider it the greatest baseball club of all times.[1]

Successes in baseball may have diverted Philadelphians from the fact that even in 1929 the city had a 10-percent unemployment rate. Despite the pennants, that rate increased the next year to 15 percent and the following year to 20 percent. When nineteen major cities were canvassed by a federal census of unemployment, "only Detroit and Cleveland were found to have more people out of work in proportion to population than Philadelphia."[2] At its worst, unemployment in Philadelphia probably reached 30 percent by 1932-33. An extreme case was client Baldwin Locomotive Works. Once Philadelphia's largest private employer, it had laid off 80 percent of its work force by 1933.

Economists quip that the stock market has accurately predicted ten of the last four recessions. The point is that the market often declines, even if the economy does not necessarily follow. But they paralleled each other between 1929 and 1932, when the market plummeted as never before or since. The thirty stocks then comprising the Dow Jones Industrial Average reached a high of 381.17 on September 3, 1929, a level not regained for twenty-five years. From that high the indicator fell until it registered 41.22 on July 8, 1932. The descent was exacerbated by margin trading. Of 2 million to 3 million investors (the country's total population was 122 million), 600,000 had margin accounts. They could buy stocks by paying as little as 10 percent and borrowing the rest—a wonderful vehicle for leverage in an *up* market. But in a *down* market, they were forced to sell to cover their margin calls. As they dumped their holdings, the roller coaster accelerated.

The ride up had been delightful. For example, on a single day, March 6, 1929, the stock of client Philadelphia National Bank (PNB) jumped 15 percent. And in the first eight months of 1929, client UGI's stock more than doubled. According to W. James MacIntosh, many people were wary, but they hated to miss out. Maybe the rules had changed and this was a new era. They had forgotten that bulls win sometimes and bears win sometimes, but pigs always get slaughtered. Some investors remembered and folded their tents. Among them were park-bench sage Bernard Baruch and Joseph P. Kennedy, who became the first chairman of the SEC and fathered a president. Kennedy knew that time was up when his bootblack began giving him stock tips.

Black Tuesday was on October 29, 1929. A banking pool of $240 million was formed to support the market. Richard Whitney, then vice-president (later president) of the New York Stock Exchange, announced that he was using the pool to buy large blocks of stocks and that everything was fine. But Whitney was playing King Canute. He could not control the tides. Moreover, he would later be convicted of fraud and sent to Sing Sing, where he was said to be the only inmate ever called Mister by his fellow prisoners and the warden.

From September through November of 1929, General Motors dropped from $72 to $36, Union Carbide from $137 to $59, and Electric Bond & Share from $186 to $50. And that was just the beginning. The carnage went on for three years. Between 1929 and 1932, PNB dropped from a high of $232 to $43, UGI from $60 to $9, Baldwin Locomotive from $67 to $2, and Scott Paper from $62 to $18. MacIntosh said Thomas McCabe, Scott's CEO, considered Scott depression-proof. Relatively speaking, McCabe was right.

■ ■ ■ ■

The Firm's revenue fell 32 percent between 1930 and 1935 (the low point), and net income per partner decreased 46 percent.

But deflation during that period offset some of the loss. It increased purchasing power by 25 percent.

Still, law firms may be even more depression-proof than manufacturers of toilet tissue. MacIntosh frequently remarked that the Firm's lawyers, instead of being unemployed, worked harder during the Depression than at any other time in his memory. In 1930, the Firm had eleven partners and four associates. By 1940, the numbers were thirteen and eleven. Instead of layoffs, the tremendous pressure of work required the hiring of additional lawyers—some of them laterally, including Frederick Knight in 1933 and Thomas B. K. Ringe in 1938. But it was also during this decade that the Firm lost through death three of its powerhouses: Francis Bracken in 1937, Morris Bockius in 1939, and Clement Wood in 1940.

While stocks were in a free-fall on Wall Street, the problem on Main Street was just making ends meet. As employment decreased, consumption also decreased. And as consumption decreased, employment decreased further. It was a vicious circle. Tradespeople went unpaid and debt went unserviced. The banks got it both ways. Depositors withdrew and borrowers defaulted.

Morgan, Lewis & Bockius was *the* Philadelphia law firm for banks. As noted in Chapter 4, the Firm represented the largest commercial bank in the city (PNB) and the largest trust company (Fidelity-Philadelphia Trust Company). Bockius was on both boards. PNB's CEO was Joseph Wayne, Jr., Bockius's long-time friend and client. Fidelity's CEO was William P. Gest. The Firm's offices were a central meeting place where these two banking leaders (often joined by C. Stevenson Newhall, later president and chairman of the Pennsylvania Company) agonized over questions of policy. Among those questions was whether the stronger banks could and should prevent the weaker Philadelphia banks from failing.

The first to fail was United Strength Bank & Trust Company at Fourth and Market streets. It closed on Christmas Eve 1929. Its problem was simply illiquidity, and no effort was made to save it. Its closing was a harbinger. From 1930 through 1932, there would be more than 9,000 bank failures nationwide, including 50 in Philadelphia.

The most serious of the 1930 failures in Philadelphia was Bankers Trust Company. That bank was the creation of Albert M. Greenfield, of whom more later. Bankers Trust had become a sizable institution by ingesting small marginal banks. When it failed, it had more than

100,000 depositors and $35 million in deposits. The Firm's banking team, led by Francis Bracken and Arthur Littleton, worked with Wayne and Newhall to keep Bankers Trust alive. At first Wayne and Newhall staked it. But then they decided it could not be saved. It closed its doors on December 22, 1930. There were recriminations that the major banks should have done more to support it. There were also charges of anti-Semitism. Greenfield was Jewish.

Actually, Wayne did all he could to keep Philadelphia's banks open. After the Bankers Trust failure, the Franklin Trust Company was believed to be in a precarious condition. Customers were storming it to withdraw their deposits. Wayne "entered the [bank] and mounting a table in the center of its lobby, dramatically stemmed the tide by telling depositors that the bank was sound and to 'go home and stop worrying,' "[3] Wayne was right that runs on banks cause failures. But he was wrong about the Franklin Trust Company. Despite his swashbuckling effort as Mr. Philadelphia Banker, the Franklin Trust failed ten months later. Those who took his advice lost their savings.

The Firm's records show that it handled hundreds of mortgage foreclosures for its clients during the 1930s. On a citywide basis, there were 19,000 foreclosures in 1932 alone. Most of them were by building and loan associations, about half of which also failed during the 1930s.

There were periods when two of the Firm's young lawyers, Howard Rapp and William Lingelbach, spent most of their time foreclosing mortgages on real estate. Rapp came to the Firm in 1929 and was a partner from 1941 to 1974. Lingelbach arrived in 1930 and was a partner from 1938 to 1975. Their tasks were rendered more onerous by Bockius's distrust of title insurance companies. He had started his career as a conveyancer and believed that the primary sources should be examined. Consequently, no mortgage was foreclosed until Lingelbach or Rapp did a thorough title search at the appropriate recorder of deeds office.

Compounding the situation was the Unemployed Citizens League, which was organized in May 1932 to stop foreclosures and prevent the shutting off of gas and electric service to the homes of the jobless. The Firm's position was unenviable. It represented not only the banks but also the utilities, Philadelphia Electric Company and Philadelphia Gas Works. Stokes commented that young lawyers became "hardened to . . . suffering."[4]

Some compassion was manifest through private charities. During the winter of 1930-31, John E. Zimmerman, chairman of UGI, headed a subcommittee that employed a maximum of 14,000 heads of families in specially created jobs three days a week at a base wage of $4 a day. And one of Drexel's partners, Horatio Gates Lloyd, chaired a committee on unemployment relief that raised $3.8 million. The committee funded a shelter for homeless men in an unused eight-story loft building formerly part of Baldwin Locomotive's plant in Center City. The shelter cared for 12,000 men before funds ran out.

But no one had any real idea how to deal with the city's unprecedented problems, much less those of the nation. Nor at first was there a clear conviction that anything should be done, except through private charity. The mayor of Philadelphia, J. Hampton Moore, made an inspection tour of the city and pronounced everything in good order, despite reported cases of starvation. (He did not wish to give ammunition to the Democrats.) The city did little; the state, not much more. The country had always weathered depressions and panics in the past.

Perhaps prosperity was just around the corner. The confidence factor rose during the summer of 1932. But it was false optimism: The economy really did not improve. As his term expired, President Herbert Hoover summarized the situation: "We are at the end of our string. There is nothing more we can do."[5] Drastic measures were required. They took the form of the New Deal. Whatever else may be said of the New Deal, it certainly revolutionized the practice of law in the United States.

■ ■ ■ ■ ■

Franklin Delano Roosevelt was elected President on November 8, 1932.[6] He took office on Saturday, March 4, 1933, but did not attend his inaugural ball. He was too busy working on measures relating to banks and the currency. Business was literally at a standstill. Banks were closing all around as depositors demanded their deposits. And they did not simply want paper. They wanted gold.

To stem the tide, Roosevelt ordered all the banks closed effective March 6. A number of states had previously taken the same action. Pennsylvania joined them when Governor Gifford Pinchot declared a bank holiday, effective Saturday, March 4, two days before Roosevelt acted. Holidays in one state precipitated runs on banks in other states. Roosevelt was simply applying the closure across the board.[7]

During the bank holiday, there would be no access either to gold or to the country's currency then backed by gold. So an alternate means of exchange had to be found. Scrip was the answer. It would be issued in denominations of $5, $10, $20, and $50 by bank clearing house associations and backed by their members' collateral instead of by gold. PNB president Joseph Wayne was also president of the Philadelphia Clearing House. On Sunday, March 5, anticipating Roosevelt's announcement, the Firm's lawyers and major banking clients worked through the problem. One question troubling those at the meeting was whether the scrip would be accepted at places distant from the clearing house issuing it. It was reminiscent of the nation's early days when each bank issued its own notes.

According to MacIntosh, the Firm's lawyers labored on the scrip problem virtually without sleep for several days. But when the banks reopened four days later, it became academic. In short order, the export of gold was embargoed; and on April 5, gold coins were called in. Despite Roosevelt's assurances to the contrary, the country effectively went off the gold standard.

New Deal legislation vitally affected the Firm's banking practice and its numerous banking clients. The Banking Act of 1933 (approved June 16, 1933) extended the Federal Reserve's open-market activities, created the Federal Deposit Insurance Corporation (FDIC), and effected the separation of commercial and investment banks. The Bank Deposit Insurance Act (approved July 19, 1934) provided $5,000 of insurance on each bank deposit. Counterpart legislation created the Federal Savings and Loan Insurance Corporation (FSLIC) to insure deposits in thrift institutions.[8]

Other New Deal legislation of importance to the Firm included the Securities Act of 1933 (approved May 27, 1933), setting procedures and disclosure requirements for the issuance of securities; the Securities Exchange Act (approved June 6, 1934), providing for securities regulation and the establishment of the Securities and Exchange Commission (SEC); and the National Labor Relations Act (approved July 5, 1935), protecting the rights of employees to organize, encouraging collective bargaining, and conferring authority on the National Labor Relations Board (NLRB). Finally, the Public Utility Holding Company Act (approved August 26, 1935) included provisions that would dismember the great public utility holding companies.

■ ■ ■ ■ ■

Roosevelt and the New Deal were not universally popular, despite the devastation of the Depression. Business interests regarded regulation as fundamentally contrary to the free enterprise system. Also, a respectable segment of the population feared Roosevelt and foresaw dictatorship. Still others were lawyers trained in strict construction. They found no warrant for the New Deal in the American constitutional system.

Such a person was Owen J. Roberts, an outstanding litigator in Philadelphia during the 1920s. Between 1930 and 1945, he was a Justice of the United States Supreme Court. Subsequently, he served from 1948 to 1951 as dean of the University of Pennsylvania Law School. His seminar there on constitutional law gave an insider's view of what a wrenching experience the New Deal was for the Court. Precedents had to be sacrificed for the nation's survival. Justice Roberts was the swing man on the Court.

At first, Justice Roberts sided with the conservatives, giving them the majority they needed in a series of five-to-four decisions to block Roosevelt's program. He told his seminar students (including the author) how he "pushed a pen on Christmas Eve of 1935," writing the majority opinion in *United States v. Butler*,[9] that struck down the Agricultural Adjustment Act. But with Roosevelt's landslide reelection in November 1936 and his threats in February 1937 to pack the Court, Justice Roberts deserted the conservatives and made a liberal majority possible. On April 12, 1937, the National Labor Relations Act was held constitutional in *NLRB v. Jones & Laughlin Steel Corp.*[10] Six weeks later, *Steward Machine Company v. Davis*[11] effectively overruled the *Butler* case. The New Deal was in business, and business would never be the same. Scholars have offered sophisticated rationales for why the Court did such an about-face. But the explanation Roberts gave in the privacy of his seminar was the most trenchant. He said simply: "We weren't dunces."

Of the New Deal legislation mentioned above, certain provisions of the Public Utility Holding Company Act had the shortest effective life, being designed to achieve a specific one-time purpose. Under them, UGI, the Firm's oldest major client, was broken up during the 1940s and finally ceased being a holding company in 1953, as detailed in Chapter 14.

Several other areas of New Deal legislation had enormous consequences for the Firm. One area was labor law. The labor problems of the 1930s that led to the passage of the National Labor Relations Act also caused the Firm to the hire Frederick Knight as its first lawyer designated to spend significant time doing labor work.

Knight arrived in 1933 from the business world; he had been treasurer of Susquehanna Silk Mills in New York. Sixty years later, more than 100 ML&B lawyers would be engaged full time in the practice of labor law.

Another area was securities regulation. In 1934, it seemed sensible for a small group of people to keep an eye out for abuses in an area like securities issuance and trading. But before long, that small group, called the SEC, became an army issuing edicts and instilling greater fear than the governments of most nations. Whole generations of the Firm's lawyers have been nurtured on SEC law. But in the beginning, there was just confusion. Orvel Sebring tells the story:

> We represented Clarence Geist. He had built an empire of gas and water utilities. One of his entities was Indianapolis Water Company. It was issuing $16.5 million of first mortgage bonds and had to file under the 1933 Act. No one had done this before, because Wall Street was on strike against the new act. Wall Street simply did not know what its liabilities might be. Morgan Stanley had been formed the year before and it underwrote the issue in what I believe was the largest utility financing in 1936. We were breaking ground. The issue was a success, and it wasn't long before Geist named us as counsel for one of his other companies, the Philadelphia Suburban Water Company, which is still a client today.

■ ■ ■ ■ ■

In addition to the challenges posed by New Deal legislation, the Firm's Depression work included some major reorganizations. As already noted in Chapters 8 and 10, ML&B represented the Baldwin Locomotive Works and Philadelphia & Reading Coal & Iron Company as debtors-in-possession in two of Philadelphia's most massive reorganizations. A third celebrated reorganization of the 1930s involved the great transportation system serving Philadelphia and its suburbs. It was then called the Philadelphia Rapid Transit Company (PRT). In 1934, it went into bankruptcy, emerging in 1940 as the Philadelphia Transportation Company (PTC). It was acquired by the Southeastern Pennsylvania Transportation Authority (SEPTA) in 1968. (More in Chapter 16 about the Firm's representation of PTC before its acquisition by SEPTA.)

In the PRT bankruptcy, the Firm represented the Philadelphia Traction Company, the largest of the system's so-called "underliers." They were the creation of traction magnates Peter A. B. Widener and William Elkins, who also helped form UGI and Philadelphia Electric Company. The underliers functioned like Matryoshka dolls, one within the other. Fortunes could be made by consolidating them.[12]

Here is how the underliers worked. Beginning in the 1850s, Philadelphia granted perpetual licenses to use the city's streets for traction purposes (first horse cars and then trolleys), conditioned upon the licensee's laying the tracks. The licensee paid nothing for the license. The licensee laid the tracks, competed with other licensees, and often lost money. Along came the consolidators. At little cost, they bought up the licensee companies, thereafter called the underliers. The consolidators then created new companies which, in effect, leased the underliers.[13]

The 999-year leases between the underliers and their newly created parent companies guaranteed the underliers a fixed rental. The fixed rental gave value to the underliers' stock, which the consolidators then sold. The same process could be repeated one or more times in ever bigger units (the Matryoshka dolls) before the entire system was consolidated at the operating level. The effect was

> an accumulation of fixed charges probably never paralleled in the history of street railway exploitation, all of which had now become the direct obligation of the operating company. These charges, not including taxes, amounted in the first year of [PRT's] operation [1902] to 44½% of the gross receipts, viz.:—$6,805,089.81 out of gross receipts from passengers of $15,277,806.58.[14]

In short, the consolidators had placed in the hands of the public $54 million of securities for something that had cost the consolidators very little, apart from their efforts in putting the system together. The securities were supported by annual rentals paid by the operating company. In 1934, immediately prior to PRT's bankruptcy, these annual rentals amounted to $7.3 million.

The wonder is that the system survived for so long under such a crushing burden. But between 1929 and 1934, the Depression reduced the system's revenue by more than 40 percent, so that bankruptcy became unavoidable. In the ensuing reorganization proceedings, the Firm took the lead in representing the underliers— another unenviable assignment, since the underliers were a millstone around the neck of the system. On the other hand, the underliers' securities were by this time in the hands of innocent parties, the consolidators having long since departed with their profits.

The PRT reorganization was a free-for-all. People swarmed about the courtroom. Everyone was aggrieved, and it seemed that every lawyer in town had a client who wanted to intervene. Francis

Bracken took charge of the matter for the Firm. He did not like crowds. Federal District Court Judge George A. Welsh liked crowds and played to them. On one occasion when some obscure complainants tried to intervene, Bracken moved to dismiss their petition on grounds that they had no standing. The judge asked Bracken if he would have the court take a "public-be-dammed attitude." "No, Your Honor," said Bracken, "I just want you to take a *judicial* attitude."[15] Fortunately, Judge Welsh appointed Albert M. Greenfield as trustee. Greenfield, who previously headed the Bankers Trust Company (which Wayne and Newhall failed to save in 1930), was a savvy businessman. He assumed a major role in engineering the emergence of the PTC from the ashes of the PRT.

When it was all over, Bracken struck a deal for the underliers by which they received roughly $32 million of the reorganized company's bonds, even though they surrendered leases that had brought them annual rentals of some $7 million. The bonds guaranteed a 3-percent return, plus an additional 3 percent if earned. The underliers also got $12 million of preferred stock. The settlement was amazing, considering that the underliers were a scourge throughout the proceedings. Bracken had held the line against every effort to wring the water out of the system. But he did not live to see the settlement implemented. He died at his desk while working late on the night of February 1, 1937.

When the Pennsylvania Public Utility Commission (PUC) held hearings on the PRT reorganization plan, Bracken's place was taken by John Russell. (Russell came to the Firm in 1921, became a partner in 1929, and retired in 1974.) A divided PUC approved the plan. The dissenting opinion argued that the Commission was "approving $20,000,000 of water upon which a return must be allowed."[16] The dissent was correct. Serving its client well, the Firm had kept the millstone around the neck of the system. In 1962, its full weight would be felt in an enforcement action brought by the Firm against PTC, as recounted in Chapter 16.

Another story, courtesy of Sebring, should be told about Francis Bracken. As Philadelphia's leading surety lawyer, Bracken numbered among his clients Fidelity & Deposit Company of Maryland (F&D). In 1933, the Pennsylvania Railroad sued F&D for more than $5 million, an extraordinary sum in those days. The suit was based on the failure of Pennsylvania Dock & Warehouse Company (Penn Dock) to complete construction of an $8-million warehouse and cold-storage plant on property owned by the railroad in Jersey City. F&D was Penn Dock's surety.

Penn Dock's contract with the Pennsylvania Railroad antedated the stock-market crash. After the crash, Penn Dock was unable to get financing for the project. It defaulted and went into bankruptcy. The railroad completed construction and looked to F&D. The railroad was represented by Robert T. McCracken, William Clarke Mason's Central High School classmate. The case was so important to F&D that it wanted both Bracken and Mason in the courtroom, with Bracken as lead counsel. He defended primarily on grounds that Penn Dock and the railroad had materially changed the terms of their contract without the knowledge and consent of F&D as surety.

As Sebring tells the story, the proceedings were vintage Bracken. He tried his case to the record with total disregard for the jury, "mumbling so the jury could not possibly have heard him over the noise and traffic outside at Ninth and Chestnut streets."[17] Mason, a superb jury trial lawyer, must have been appalled as he sat at the counsel table day after day. But he nodded approvingly, for appearances' sake. Ultimately, the judge took most of the claims away from the jury, as Bracken intended. But some of the claims remained, and the jury showed its disaffection for Bracken by returning a verdict of $748,000, said to be the largest verdict ever returned by a jury in the Eastern District up to that time. Still, Bracken had made such a perfect record that the railroad ultimately settled for much less to avoid a likely loss on appeal.

■ ■ ■ ■ ■

During the Depression, the Firm sadly witnessed the demise of some of its clients and the reorganization of others, including the Baldwin Locomotive Works and Philadelphia & Reading Coal & Iron Company. But as future partner Kenneth Souser would remark, when some doors close, other doors open. Among the doors that opened during the 1930s were Esso Standard Oil Company; Janney Montgomery Scott Inc.; W. Atlee Burpee Co.; Independence Blue Cross; Philadelphia Suburban Water Company; and Strawbridge & Clothier.

Esso Standard Oil Company was a subsidiary of Standard Oil Company of New Jersey (now Exxon Corp.), whose inside general counsel had been Clement Wood's classmate at Harvard Law School. The Firm's activity for Esso started in 1935 and primarily involved the acquisition of sites for gas stations all over Pennsylvania. These assignments continued through the 1950s, by which time Pennsylvania was sated with Esso stations. On December 31, 1959, Esso merged into Humble Oil & Refining Company, another Standard Oil

Company of New Jersey subsidiary. Pennsylvania's Department of Revenue asserted that the merger triggered realty transfer taxes on hundreds of Esso stations scattered throughout the state. The tax liability would have been formidable. But the Firm won the case in the Pennsylvania Supreme Court, which held that title to the stations passed by operation of law without a taxable event under the statute.[18]

Janney Montgomery Scott Inc. is presently the largest securities brokerage house headquartered in Philadelphia. It became a Firm client in 1936 when Sebring began representing Janney Dulles & Co. Later that company became Janney Dulles & Battles; then Janney, Battles & E. W. Clark, Inc.; and finally, in 1971, Janney Montgomery Scott Inc. The company was acquired by the Penn Mutual Life Insurance Company in 1982. It remains an active client today.

W. Atlee Burpee Co. was founded in 1876. The Firm represented the company from 1937 until it was acquired by General Foods Corp. in 1970, by which time it had become the world's largest seed producer and was selling 21 million packets of seeds annually to 4 million customers. Burpee's presiding genius from 1915 to 1970 was the founder's son, David Burpee. He was not only a horticulturist but also a promoter who lobbied Congress endlessly (and unsuccessfully) to make the marigold the national flower. Another of his projects aimed to deodorize the marigold. But rabbits liked deodorized marigolds, and customers complained about rabbits. So the company carried two lines of marigolds, the odoriferous as well as the deodorized.[19]

David Burpee's philosophy was succinct: "If you want to be happy for an hour, get drunk. If you want to be happy for a weekend, get married. If you want to be happy for a whole week, kill your pig and eat it. But if you want to be happy all of your life, become a gardener."[20] Through the 1960s, packets of Burpee seeds were distributed free each spring by the company to the Firm's lawyers, many of whom planted and nurtured them. Lifetime happiness presumably ensued.

Independence Blue Cross is today the second-largest health care organization of its kind in the United States and a major Firm client. It was formed by ML&B in 1937 and was capitalized by a loan of $25,000 from the United Fund. Mason asked Lingelbach, then an associate, "What do you know about insurance?" Lingelbach replied: "A little." Mason commented: "Well, you will learn more." Lingelbach learned a lot more, as have subsequent generations of Firm lawyers assigned to Blue Cross matters. After his retirement from the Firm in 1991, Robert Young became chairman of Independence Blue Cross.

Philadelphia Suburban Water Company (Philly Suburban) was added to the Firm's list of utility clients in 1936. That was after the Firm's successful handling of an SEC registration for Indianapolis Water Company, both companies being owned by Clarence Geist. In the late 1960s, Philly Suburban grew tired of being just a utility. So it went into paint contracting, fire prevention, and oil-field service operations. These operations were spun off in 1981 to the shareholders of Philly Suburban as Enterra Corporation. The next year, a group of investors accumulated a substantial position in Enterra. With the sharp downturn in the energy sector that followed, the group attempted to take control of Enterra. However, they lost a decisive court battle in 1985[21] and sold their interests a year later to Shamrock Holdings, Inc., the investment vehicle of the Roy E. Disney family. The Firm continues to represent both Philly Suburban and Enterra.

Strawbridge & Clothier (S&C) became a Firm client in 1937. At first, the Firm's contacts with S&C were sporadic. But in 1941, they culminated in a major reorganization of that company and a relationship that has endured for more than fifty years. (More about S&C in Chapters 14 and 38.) The addition of S&C as a client permits a reference to Chapter 4 and the senior partner (of another firm) who said that a truly great law firm had to represent a bank, a railroad, and a department store. ML&B now met that test, the only firm in the city to do so.

But rough tests aside, a more subtle transformation was evident: ML&B had evolved from a collection of individual practitioners into an institution—a consummation actually achieved by relatively few law firms. Deeply shared values, long traditions, and superior leadership are requisites. By the waning years of the Depression, those attributes were unmistakable at the Firm. It was no longer solely the creation of Messrs. Morgan and Lewis, which Bockius had shaped and raised to such prominence. Rather, it had become a discrete institution with an identity separate and apart from the lawyers who practiced under its name.

Edwin Wolf, scholar and long-time librarian of the Library Company of Philadelphia, noted the phenomenon. In *Philadelphia, Portrait of an American City*, he described how the Depression altered the city's makeup:

> [I]nstead of the man giving lustre to the institution, it was the

corporation which gave position to the man. . . .

Nowhere was the change more clearly seen than in the legal profession, long the pride of Philadelphia and the reservoir whence many of its leaders came. . . . As the period drew to a close no Morgan, Lewis or Bockius was renowned as an individual, but the firm was the biggest, richest, and most active in the city.[22]

CHAPTER 14

WORLD WAR II

No peace in our time ■ *De Gaulle at 4 Carlton Gardens* ■ *Wartime regulations* ■ *Lawyers in the service* ■ *Strawbridge & Clothier recapitalizes* ■ *Mason wrestles with UGI's death sentence* ■ *Insull's empire and ordeal* ■ *The SEC plays a waiting game* ■ *Cutting the Gordian knot* ■ *All arguments are rejected* ■ *UGI's dismemberment* ■ *Napoleon and Marshal Ney* ■ *The New Deal was anathema to Will Mason*

While the global Depression continued, Europe was lurching toward war. Germany reacquired the Saar after a plebescite in 1935 and reoccupied the Rhineland in 1936. There followed a series of demands by Adolf Hitler. Each would be his last, he said, and each time he was placated. In 1938, Austria was annexed and the Sudetenland ceded by Czechoslovakia. Apologists who had not read *Mein Kampf* maintained that Hitler was simply reuniting pockets of German-speaking peoples with the Fatherland. Their delusions were echoed in September 1938 by Neville Chamberlain, the British prime minister. Returning home from the ignominious Munich conference, he proclaimed "peace in our time." Surely a repetition of 1914-18 was unthinkable.

But Hitler was insatiable, and on September 1, 1939, the German blitzkrieg struck Poland, followed the next spring by Denmark, Norway, the Benelux countries, and France. They succumbed after hostilities of less than two months. On June 10, 1940, General Charles de Gaulle, having fled France, established the *quartier-general* of the Free French at 4 Carlton Gardens, which in 1981 became the Firm's location in London.[1]

There was a short lull before what Churchill called the "Battle of Britain." It raged from July until October 1940, as the Royal Air Force fought off the Luftwaffe and frustrated a German invasion. Nine months later, the Germans launched Operation Barbarossa, wheeling east to invade the Soviet Union on June 22, 1941. They wore their summer uniforms for a short campaign, only to be swallowed up by the Russian winter. It was *Die Götterdämmerung*: Hitler had spurned the advice of his generals and ignored the debacles of Napoleon and the Kaiser. Next, on December 7, 1941, "a date which will live in infamy," as Roosevelt told Congress, the Japanese bombed Pearl Harbor. The world was in flames.

■ ■ ■ ■ ■

Everything is regulated in a wartime economy. Consumer goods yield to armaments. There are shortages. There is rationing. The economy overheats. Excess demands and inadequate supplies trigger inflation. So wage and price controls are imposed. Excess purchasing power must be absorbed, and the war must be funded. So taxes are raised, and government securities are sold on a vast scale. Defense contracts are let and then renegotiated to mitigate profiteering. Lawyers scramble to master the new rules and keep their clients informed.

During the war, one of the Firm's partners switched to the client side, as J. Tyson Stokes became vice-president and general counsel of the Baldwin Locomotive Works. Baldwin, in turn, became a major manufacturer of guns, shell forgings, armor plate, and especially tanks. Some of Baldwin's output went to the Soviet Union during World War II, just as it had gone to Russia during World War I.

Even before the war, Baldwin sold heavy equipment to Amtorg, the Soviet trading company. Stokes handled the endless and tedious negotiations. Although some of the Russians spoke rudimentary English, none of the Baldwin team spoke any Russian. The Russians were in bureaucratic disarray. Week after week they argued among themselves, in Russian of course, while the Baldwin team sat by. Finally, according to Orvel Sebring, Stokes could stand it no longer. He slammed his fist on the table and bellowed, "Damn it all, I don't believe a word of it." A stunned silence followed. In fact, Stokes spoke no Russian, but his performance seemed to have a cathartic effect. The bargaining proceeded, and Baldwin got the orders it wanted.

While Stokes moved in-house, W. James MacIntosh joined the public sector. He went to Washington in 1943 as general counsel to the Renegotiation Division of the War Department and subsequently to the War Contracts Price Adjustment Board. At the end of his government service, he received a citation that spoke of "his tireless efforts, his integrity, his sound judgment and knowledge of business problems and his practical foresight and persuasiveness . . . [as well as] his consummate charm . . . [and] his eminent fairness."[2] An apt description of MacIntosh.

Other Firm lawyers went into the armed services. In fact, the Firm's stationery neatly reflected the division between those in mufti and those in uniform. On the left side of the letterhead was the home team, numbering twenty. On the right were thirteen lawyers listed as "Absent with the Armed Forces of the United States."

Those who remained civilians felt an obligation to give their all. Orvel Sebring tells how one day at 4 a.m., Thomas Ringe and William Lingelbach converged at the Fidelity Building's sign-in/sign-out desk. Ringe was coming to work, and Lingelbach was going home.

ML&B's army contingent included Oscar Hansen, Anthony Whitaker, and Howard Kellogg. Hansen was a lieutenant colonel in the Office of the Chief of Ordnance for the War Department in Washington, D.C. Whitaker and Kellogg were in the Army Air Corps. Whitaker was a lieutenant colonel; Kellogg was a first lieutenant. Whitaker was chief of aircraft procurement at Wright Field, Ohio. Kellogg taught military law to officer candidates at Camp Barkeley, Texas, and subsequently at Wright Field.

The navy claimed the lion's share of ML&B lawyers, including John Bracken, Brady Bryson, John McConnell, Martin Snyder, Howard Taylor, and Ernest von Starck. Of these, Lieutenant Commander Bracken served the longest, about six and a half years, in both the Atlantic and Pacific theaters, and as a member of the staff of Justice Robert Jackson, chief counsel for the United States at the Nuremberg War Crimes trials.

Bryson also served on Jackson's staff at Nuremberg as a lieutenant (j.g.). Earlier, he received his commission as an ensign after attending officers training school at Fort Schuyler, New York. Subsequently, he studied naval communications at Harvard and was transferred to Naval Intelligence at the University of Colorado, where he studied Russian before being sent to Washington to assist in breaking Russian language codes for the navy.

Among the other naval officers, McConnell served as a lieutenant in the Atlantic, where he commanded the gun crews of a Liberty ship and a tanker in the early days of the battle of the Atlantic. He also saw action on an ammunition ship in the Mediterranean. Later, in the Pacific, he was a gunnery officer, navigator, and executive officer on several naval vessels.

Snyder was a versatile lieutenant with a broad geographical reach.

He started with the Office of Naval Procurement in Los Angeles, was transferred to Chicago, then to Plattsburg, New York, and thereafter to Pearl Harbor. Finally, he served as a legal officer in courts martial on Saipan. There, he saw hundreds of B-29s take off from the island's air strips to fly missions up "Hirohito's Highway." These included the incendiary bombings of March 1945 that devastated huge portions of Japan's major cities and accelerated the fall of the Rising Sun.[3]

Taylor was a lieutenant commander who taught advanced air navigation to navy pilots in Peru, Indiana, then in Hollywood, Florida, and finally at the Naval War College in Rhode Island. Bodie, as he was called at the Firm, repeatedly requested sea duty, but he was considered too good a teacher. Assuming that he then clarified navigation as well as he later clarified SEC regulations, the navy had a point.

Von Starck was a lieutenant in the Pacific theater, where he captained an LST across the Pacific on a tour of duty that took him to the Marshall Islands, Guam, Saipan, Okinawa, Iwo Jima, and eventually to Yokohama. (More about von Starck's sea duty in Chapter 18.)

Fortunately, there were no casualties among the Firm's lawyers in the service. In due course, they all returned home and resumed civilian life. They had experienced hardship, danger, boredom, and occasionally heroism. The Firm stayed in touch with them. There were sporadic editions of the *Morlebock Bulletin,* recording who was stationed where and doing what. It also reported about home-front victory gardens and air-raid drills, as well as the workload at the Firm. Those who carried on at home missed the excitement. Lieutenant Kellogg received a letter from Ringe expressing his envy of the Firm's lawyers in the service. But there was little time to be envious. The Firm's home-front lawyers were stretched. Client problems were more varied than ever, considering wartime conditions.

■ ■ ■ ■ ■

Strawbridge & Clothier (S&C) noted an extraordinary increase in the difficulties of doing business during the war—a claim supported by the Firm's files. It was during the war years that S&C became a major client of the Firm. Today, it employs 12,700 people, enjoys annual sales of almost $1 billion, maintains its flagship store in Center City, and has twelve branch department stores in three states, plus twenty-five Clover discount stores.

Philadelphia department stores rarely branched until after World War II. Instead, customers came to Center City to shop, appropriately enough to Market Street. Along its seven blocks from Seventh to Broad streets, they had their choice of Lit Brothers, S&C, Gimbel Brothers, N. Snellenburg, Frank & Seder, Sterns, and John Wanamaker. Only two remain: John Wanamaker, which has been sold and resold, and S&C, which has prospered and, although a public company, is still operated by descendants of its founders.

Those founders were Justus C. Strawbridge and Isaac H. Clothier, both Quakers and thirty years old in 1868 when they opened their store. Its original location, where its main store remains today, was at Eighth and Market streets. Three quarters of a century earlier, the building on that corner had been occupied by the United States Department of State. Today, a plaque commemorates the fact that between 1790 and 1793, the country's first secretary of state, Thomas Jefferson, had his office where the store now stands.

S&C's founders were indefatigable workers, as well as men of principle. Their motto was, "Small Profits, At One Price and For Cash Only." From the very beginning, their enterprise was a success. It soon became the city's largest retail dry-goods store.

Before there were cash registers, there were "cash boys." When a sale was made, a salesclerk rang a hand bell. Dashing to the location of the sale, a cash boy took the payment and the merchandise to the cashier's office. The merchandise was wrapped, and the cash boy returned with any change, a receipt, and the wrapped goods. In 1892, one such S&C cash boy was thirteen-year-old William Claude Dukenfield. He may have foreseen the advent of pneumatic tubes and the redundancy of cash boys, so he turned to other pursuits as comedian W. C. Fields.

S&C was among the first businesses in Philadelphia to provide disability benefits for its employees, as well as pension benefits, vacation facilities, a medical department, on-premises education, and even a chorus that gave concerts at the Academy of Music and Willow Grove Park. Management still refers to "the store family," and few other organizations can point with such pride to the loyalty and long service of their employees. Much of the same goodwill exists on the part of S&C's shareholders and Philadelphia's buying public. S&C would draw on this goodwill in 1986, when faced with a hostile tender offer, as recounted in Chapter 38.

S&C was a partnership until 1922. When it incorporated in that year, various Strawbridges got most of the nonvoting preferred stock, and various Clothiers got most of the voting common stock. The division was based on preexisting partnership interests and the extent to which family members then participated in management. At that point, the Clothiers were in charge and the Strawbridges less active.

Starting in January 1929, S&C's old store at Eighth and Market streets was demolished, and a new store was constructed on the site. But the new building was built at just the wrong time. Faced with the building's carrying costs, as well as shrinking sales due to the Depression, S&C could not pay cumulative dividends on its nonvoting preferred stock. The company's default gave voting rights to the preferred shareholders. The Strawbridge family took over. The situation cried out for a reorganization. Between 1937 and 1941, various reorganization plans were proposed before a consensus was reached. William Lingelbach had married a Strawbridge and was consulted by family members, as were Arthur Littleton, W. James MacIntosh, and Orvel Sebring.

In its final form, the 1941 recapitalization provided that the old preferred shareholders exchange their shares for new preferred shares plus two shares of common stock. The dividend arrearages were wiped out. As a result, the Strawbridge family emerged with 53 percent of the common stock; the Clothiers got 22 percent. The balance went to the public, which previously held some of the old preferred stock. It speaks well for the parties and their advisers that the restructure satisfied everyone.

Following the restructure, S&C became an active and valued client of the Firm during the war years, when its operations were subject to every possible kind of regulation, and thereafter during the great postwar boom. Today, third-, fourth- and fifth-generation family members sit on the board and/or work in the stores. Long family traditions are unusual in American business. S&C is an extraordinary case history.[4]

■ ■ ■ ■ ■

The Firm's work for S&C proliferated as the client grew. But in the case of UGI, the Firm's work proliferated as the client shrank, and shrank dramatically. The Firm's assignment to dismember UGI began with the passage in 1935 of the Public Utility Holding Company Act (PUHCA) and did not end until 1953. It was an enormous undertaking involving many ML&B lawyers, with William Clarke Mason in the spotlight. The eighteen-year effort was given file No. 1520-106. Fifteen single-spaced pages were required just to list the subfile titles. Since the greatest shrinkage took place during World War II, the story is appropriate for telling at this point.

UGI, which became a client of the Firm immediately after the company's founding in 1882, was the country's largest gas and electric holding company at the end of the nineteenth century. By 1930, it had controlling interests in twenty-seven major companies, most of them utilities. These companies in turn controlled forty-four other companies. In addition, it had less than controlling interests in another twelve utilities, which in turn controlled twelve operating companies. One of UGI's acquisitions was the Philadelphia Electric Company in 1928. That acquisition produced "the largest consolidation of public utility enterprises yet attempted in the United States."[5]

UGI, with PE as its major subsidiary, was regarded by financial analysts and consumers alike as a well-managed, progressive, and efficient enterprise—a good utility holding company. But to politicians a good utility holding company was an oxymoron. Gifford Pinchot, who became governor of Pennsylvania in 1930, waged constant war against utility holding companies. Senator George Norris of Nebraska felt about utility holding companies as Cato the Elder felt about Carthage: Only destruction would suffice. Norris called the power trusts "the most disgraceful and far-reaching and shameful combination that has ever been organized by man."[6] And Rexford Tugwell, one of Roosevelt's brain trusters, commented: "Until totalitarianism, incarnated by Hitler, turned up, power was the most satisfactory of all Franklin's political *bêtes noires*."[7] Even humorist Will Rogers joined in, saying "[a] Holding Company is a thing where you hand an accomplice the goods while the policeman searches you."[8]

The business leader who bore the special brunt of it was Samuel Insull. He died in 1938 at age seventy-eight as a self-imposed exile in Paris. His body was found on the platform of the Tuileries Metro station near the Place de la Concorde; on his person were seven francs and seven centimes. But in his heyday he controlled a light and power empire worth almost $3 billion and had a personal fortune of $150 million. One million people had invested in his hundreds of corporations. Insull was "president of 11 companies, was board chairman of 65 companies and sat on the boards of 85 companies. He controlled 6,000 power plants in thirty-nine states. He manufactured more than 10 percent of this nation's power and sold it to 20,000,000 customers. He employed more than 150,000 workers."[9]

Insull was born in a lower-class London neighborhood in 1859. At twenty-one, he became Thomas Edison's private secretary. He learned the electric industry almost overnight, and by 1892 he was president of Chicago Edison Company. He consorted with American presidents (before Roosevelt), and at his pinnacle he was the prime mover and financier in the building of the Chicago Civic Opera House. It opened on November 4, 1929. Exquisite timing.

When the bubble burst, the collapse of Insull's empire was "the biggest business failure in the entire history of the United States."[10] Insull was indicted on charges of embezzlement and larceny. He fled to Europe. Extradition proceedings were begun in Greece. The United States Senate even ratified a long-pending extradition treaty with Greece, hoping to get him back. But the Greek authorities held the evidence insufficient. Insull left Greece for Turkey, from which he was extradited without the niceties of a treaty. When tried in Chicago, he took the witness stand and wove a spell as he told his rags-to-riches story. The prosecution objected to the monologue, but the judge seemed mesmerized and overruled the objection. The jury deliberated for five minutes and acquitted the old man.

Despite the acquittal, Insull had in fact built an evil empire, and his investors had lost up to a billion dollars. How did it all happen? In essence, Insull dealt in electric utilities as Widener had dealt in the underliers. Both men perceived utilities as natural monopolies. Since no one could compete with them, they could theoretically raise their rates indefinitely. And if rates could be raised indefinitely, so could capital. As corporate structures pyramided, everyone got rich, especially the promoters.

It actually worked that way for a while. Utility holding companies—including Electric Bond & Share Company, Standard Power & Light Corporation, and Commonwealth & Southern Corporation—listed their assets in the billions. They could always acquire more utilities by issuing more securities. One reason for the acquisition by UGI of Philadelphia Electric Company in 1928 was the concern of UGI's investment banker, Drexel & Company, that Insull was expanding his operations eastward. As Wainwright pointed out in his *History of the Philadelphia Electric Company 1881-1961*: "Without any regard to geographical unity, [Insull] was purchasing companies all over the country, and was paying too much for them. These inflated values went into his holding company structures."[11]

The ratepayers were the victims. They had no representation, since state regulatory agencies were generally controlled by the utilities. But little people were of no concern to Insull. Little people included the unemployed, of whom he said: "My experience is that the greatest aid to efficiency of labor is a long line of men waiting at the gate."[12]

Still, in fairness, the ratepayers enjoyed some benefits. Wainwright noted that "while the cost of living in 1931 was 50 percent higher than in 1913, the average cost of electricity to the consumer had shrunk 31% during that period."[13] The miracle of electrification had benefited everybody and permitted the excesses of holding companies and promoters like Insull.

By 1929, subsidiaries of utility holding companies accounted for more than 82 percent of the total electricity generated in the United States. But between 1929 and 1935, the stock market capitalizations of the twenty-five leading utility holding companies plunged from $19.2 billion to $2.3 billion. Insull's company collapsed completely in April 1932. Since almost everyone was a ratepayer and since so many investors had lost their savings, it was natural that utility holding companies figured prominently in the election that year. Good and bad alike, they were irresistible political targets.

In his 1932 campaign, Roosevelt pledged to destroy the holding companies. They fought back with a tremendous lobbying effort. Roosevelt called it the most daring lobby ever to function in Washington.

UGI and Philadelphia Electric were in bad company and knew it. They resigned from the National Electric Light Association, which was identified with the Insull interests, and they helped form the Edison Electric Institute (EEI) in 1933. Later, Charles W. Kellogg became president of EEI. As an engineer with Stone & Webster, he had worked with Bockius and Mason in building a number of Philadelphia Electric power stations, including Conowingo. He was the father of Howard Kellogg who became a Firm partner in 1956 and retired in 1978. With EEI, some utilities now had a fresh face. But they could not hold back the onslaught.

The Wheeler-Rayburn bills, which became PUHCA, moved relentlessly toward passage. The only question was how adverse the law would be to the utility holding companies. Would they merely be regulated? Or would they be dismantled by what came to be called the "death sentence"? The Senate version of the bill contained the death sentence. The House version did not. The Conference Committee Report, drafted by Felix Frankfurter, preserved the death sentence. That Frankfurter personally favored the death sentence did not then seem so important. It would become more important in

1939 when he became a Justice of the Supreme Court. Another antagonist of the utilities was William O. Douglas. It was bad enough that in 1937 he became chairman of the Securities and Exchange Commission, which was charged with implementing PUHCA. It was worse that he also went on the Court in 1939.

After one of the most politically contested struggles of the New Deal, PUHCA became law on August 26, 1935. The Federal Power Commission was given the authority to regulate the business of public utilities, much as the Interstate Commerce Commission regulated the business of railroads. The act also provided that utility systems containing more than three tiers of companies would be abolished completely and that the SEC would move to limit the rest to a single, integrated public utility system as soon as practicable after January 1, 1938. Exceptions might be made in the interest of efficient operations or if simplification would mean the loss of substantial economies.

What made PUHCA remarkable was that it punished a structure. Companies had been dismembered in the past when they were guilty of improper conduct. Now they would be dismembered simply because of their configuration. This was confiscation, and confiscation was unconstitutional. The utilities dug in.

■ ■ ■ ■ ■

The Firm delivered its opinion to UGI that PUHCA's death-sentence provisions were unconstitutional. This view was shared by counsel for most other utility holding companies. But unlike the others that did nothing, UGI wanted to test the question. On November 20, 1935, the Firm filed for an injunction in the District Court for the Eastern District of Pennsylvania. The complaint sought to have the act declared unconstitutional and restrain the SEC and other government agencies from enforcing its provisions. The suit made the first page of the *New York Times* the next day. Mason and Francis Bracken were featured, and the averments of the complaint were set forth in detail.

Editorial comment at the time suggested that UGI was a respectable banner carrier for the industry and was doing the honorable thing by taking the matter to court instead of simply ignoring the law. But the injunction did not issue, and the act was not struck down. Instead, the court agreed with the government's contention that the suit was premature, since no irreparable damage could be established, at least until registration had been effected and the Commission had acted adversely to UGI. That would be years in the future.

The matter had a different posture when PUHCA reached the Supreme Court in 1938. This time, the SEC was the plaintiff and had selected as its defendant the most notorious public utility holding company of all, Electric Bond & Share Company. The SEC brought its action in response to the utility's failure to register. The remedy desired was that the utility be banned from using the mails or other facilities of interstate commerce, as provided by the act. The SEC got its injunction, and the Supreme Court affirmed. The Court held that the registration provisions were severable from the regulatory provisions and as such were enforceable.

Thus, the constitutionality of the "death sentence" was not decided by *Electric Bond & Share Company v. SEC*.[14] Instead, by deferring the question, the Court permitted the SEC to nibble away at the utilities. If the Court was not sympathetic in 1938, it would be even less so after 1939 when joined by Frankfurter and Douglas.

The result might have been different if the issue had been adjudicated immediately after passage of PUHCA in 1935, something the Firm sought to do for UGI. The Court was differently constituted then, and even the act's proponents had grave concerns about the validity of the death sentence. But the three-year postponement for registration worked for Roosevelt. By 1938, the climate at the Court had changed.

There was no alternative but to register. The Firm filed UGI's registration papers with the SEC on March 29, 1938, one day after the decision in *Electric Bond & Share*. Douglas, then chairman of the SEC, welcomed the filing and invited other utilities to come forward and comply with the act. But, despite his smiling face, Douglas was on record that he considered the death sentence "misnamed," saying that "its basic threat is not to investors but to certain types of management essentially concerned with retaining economic power."[15]

Registration was just an opening formality. The main event would involve the SEC's view of a "single, public utility system." Many arguments were available, and Mason would make them all for UGI during the years that followed. First, he would contend that a holding company should not be dismembered if it had come about naturally and operated efficiently. Second, a holding company should not have to divest minority investment interests in utility subsidiaries if it did not seek to control their operation. Third, some investments by holding companies should be grandfathered, since the SEC had signaled that it would permit the retention of miscellaneous interests in coal, water, railway, bus, and bridge companies, as an inheritance from an earlier age. Fourth, a holding company that operated electric and gas utilities in a particular area should not be required to divest one or the other.

The first two arguments were viewed by commentators as clear losers, the second two as possible winners. Mason viewed them all as winners. As Robert McCracken said: "In [Mason's] eyes, his client was always right."[16]

The lines were drawn in 1938, but the SEC was apparently unwilling to do battle: Not until 1940 did hearings begin. But in the interim, the SEC asked the utilities to submit plans showing how they would comply with the law. It was a clever strategy. The utilities would submit their plans, and the SEC would reject them. The utilities were being asked to bid against themselves. Meanwhile, the SEC would take no position that would give the utilities any basis for a court test concerning the constitutionality of the death sentence.

UGI again took the high road, and Mason again made a *New York Times* headline on April 25, 1940: "W. C. Mason Reads a New Meaning Into the 'Death Sentence' Section of the Law." Complaining that "we are all groping around in the dark," Mason said the SEC should tell the utilities what it had in mind instead of asking them to guess. He argued that the act required the SEC to "examine the holding companies . . . [as] a condition precedent to starting proceedings." There had been no examinations, and there were no proceedings. The trial lawyer in Mason was itching to get started.

Mason prevailed. Late in May 1940, the SEC "in a surprise move . . . embarked on a major change in policy."[17] It would do as Mason urged. It would promulgate an integration plan for each major public utility system. Mason had cut the Gordian knot. The SEC would show its hand, and Mason would grapple furiously with the agency every step of the way. He would go twice to the Third Circuit and petition twice for certiorari to the Supreme Court.

But to no avail. The SEC, at first uncertain of its position, gained confidence as it went along. And with every sign that the courts would not interfere, that confidence turned to arrogance. No, UGI's history and operating efficiency would not be considered. No, UGI could not maintain small, nonoperating investments in other utilities. No, UGI could not retain its inheritance from an earlier age. And no, UGI could not keep both its gas and electric holdings in a single area.

Dismemberment began. UGI divested itself of its 28-percent interest in Public Service Corporation of New Jersey and its sizable holdings in Arizona, Kansas, Tennessee, Connecticut, and New Hampshire. It also disposed of its inheritance from an earlier age. And its biggest holding, Philadelphia Electric Company, was spun off by UGI to its shareholders.

The legal work was intensive. In a single decade, ML&B lawyers disposed of what their predecessors had helped UGI acquire over five decades. When it was finally over in 1953, UGI ceased to be a holding company and became an operating company, essentially in eastern Pennsylvania. It had divested two-thirds of its almost $1 billion in assets.

UGI played a leading role in PUHCA history from 1935 to 1953. This was not because UGI was then the country's largest public utility holding company: By the 1930s, UGI had been overtaken in size by at least five other holding companies that had burgeoned through their indiscriminate marketing of securities and their acquisition of utilities everywhere. Instead, UGI's leading role derived from its character and relationships. First, its securities were not watered. Its growth had been based on sharing technological innovation and management skills. It was a respectable front-runner in litigation. Second, from UGI's inception in 1882, it and its law firm functioned virtually as one. (During the SEC hearings in the early 1940s, UGI's CEO was William Warden Bodine who had started his career as an ML&B associate.) In legal matters, it was natural for UGI to point the way. Third, there was Mason. He was a fighter brought to fever pitch by what he perceived as the outrages of PUHCA.[18]

Mason always preferred the offensive. Much better to play Napoleon moving forward than Marshal Ney conducting a rearguard action. But even outside his accustomed role, Mason outdid Ney. For despite Ney's legendary efforts, his retreat from Moscow in 1812 lasted only two months and cost Napoleon 85 percent of his army. By comparison, Mason's rearguard action for UGI consumed almost eighteen years—he was fifty-three when it began and seventy-one when it ended—and UGI lost two-thirds of its assets. But half of those lost assets comprised Philadelphia Electric Company, which was spun off to UGI's shareholders.

■ ■ ■ ■ ■

Mason continued fighting even after the war was lost. In 1953, the SEC had to mandamus the Firm—all partners were listed as defendants—to register under PUHCA, alleging that the Firm was "represent[ing] a registered public utility holding company in matters pending before the Commission." Mason was unreconciled. He argued that only lobbyists had to register, not lawyers. Lawyers answered only to the courts—and to God. As the court of appeals opinion acknowledged: "The integrity of the defendants is unquestioned and there is not the slightest suggestion that the issues which they raise are not raised in perfect good faith." Nevertheless, the court held that Mason's arguments were "without merit" and the statutory language "so clear and unambiguous as to need no construction."[19]

This final act of defiance highlights Mason's fierce tenacity. It shows him as hostile to the SEC as he had been earlier to the NLRB in the Baldwin Locomotive/Steelworkers litigation. As detailed in Chapter 8, a 16,000-page record was generated in that case over a three-and-a-half-year period before the company appealed unsuccessfully to the Court of Appeals for the Third Circuit and finally succumbed to the NLRB's unfair labor practice charges.

Those who knew Mason say he was adamant in his opposition to government regulation in any form, and even more so to the regulators themselves. He had nothing but contempt for bureaucrats. He railed that they were intermeddlers who knew nothing about meeting payrolls, while anointing themselves to redistribute other people's wealth. As Sebring put it, "Until the very end, the New Deal was anathema to Will Mason."

The period of UGI's ordeal from 1935 to 1953 witnessed depression, war, and then peace. It also witnessed a revolution in the practice of law. The age of specialization had begun.

CHAPTER 15

THE AGE
OF SPECIALIZATION

A cataclysmic struggle ends ■ *Reform and renaissance in Philadelphia* ■ *D'Artagnan in a double-breasted suit* ■ *An ancient galleon on an alien beach* ■ *Specialties and de facto sections* ■ *Soaked by taxes* ■ *Thomas Ringe's fantastic work habits* ■ *Kenneth Souser's extraordinary legacy* ■ *Troubles at Philco* ■ *Railroads and Sherlock Holmes* ■ *Other boutiques* ■ *Harold Shertz and the trucking industry* ■ *Lawyers become hedgehogs* ■ *The stage is set for national practice*

The turning points of World War II came in 1942 with Midway, El Alamein, and Stalingrad, as the Allies began their long trek to victory. By 1945, history was moving at a gallop. President Roosevelt died on April 12. Germany surrendered on May 7. On August 6, a solitary B-29 dropped a "nuclear device" on Hiroshima, killing 80,000 civilians almost instantly. When there was no response, a second such device (only two existed) was exploded over Nagasaki on August 9. This time a response came, leading to the September 2 signing of a formal capitulation by Japan on board the USS *Missouri* in Tokyo Bay. Six years and one day after Hitler invaded Poland, the most cataclysmic struggle in human history was over.

The postwar era brought reform and renaissance to Philadelphia. Joseph Clark was elected mayor in 1951, the first Democrat to hold that office in almost seventy years. Clark, a patrician lawyer from Chestnut Hill, had been a name partner in the firm then called Barnes, Dechert, Price, Myers & Clark (now Dechert Price & Rhoads). He was mayor for just one term before moving on to the United States Senate, where he served from 1957 to 1968.

Clark's running mate as district attorney was Richardson Dilworth. Following law school, Dilworth had joined Evans, Bayard & Frick, a firm created by former John G. Johnson associates, before helping found in 1938 the firm known today as Dilworth, Paxson, Kalish & Kauffman. A marine in both world wars, he was a fearless trial lawyer—some said an unprincipled one. But he had a vision of Philadelphia, and he knew how to inspire those who worked with him. He was Hollywood handsome and boundlessly energetic. Clark called Dilworth "D'Artagnan in long pants and a double breasted suit."[1]

Dilworth succeeded Clark as mayor in 1956. He served until 1962 when he resigned and ran unsuccessfully for governor of Pennsylvania. (Following his defeat, ML&B lost the Philadelphia Gas Works as a client, when Dilworth's firm was appointed its counsel "as a consolation prize," according to W. James MacIntosh.) Clark and Dilworth had taken to the streets to overthrow almost single-handedly "the nation's most entrenched and incredibly corrupt political machine."[2] These two lawyers gave Philadelphia its own brief Camelot before the city sank again into its old ways.[3]

With a new city charter, the reformers changed the way the city was governed. And during their administration the city changed its face as well. The Independence National Historical Park project got underway in 1952. Razed for blocks around were the Victorian buildings that crowded Independence Hall. Nearby, Society Hill emerged, as colonial and federalist buildings were lovingly restored. In the course of rebuilding the old city, three structures in which the Firm's offices had been located during the nineteenth century were demolished, including the Drexel Building.

West of City Hall, Philadelphia went through an even more ambitious transformation. On April 28, 1952, the last train pulled out of the Pennsylvania Railroad's Broad Street Station before demolition began. In describing the demise of that landmark, one writer commented that Philadelphia, "that once had the world's largest railroad station and the world's largest locomotive works, only half a mile apart, now had neither."[4]

Sixteen tracks had funneled into the great train shed adjoining Broad Street Station at Fifteenth and Market streets. The tracks were supported by the so-called Chinese Wall that ran west to the Schuylkill between Market Street and present-day John F. Kennedy Boulevard. Demolition of the station and the wall opened up the northwest quadrant (measured from City Hall) of the city's center and made possible the construction of many blocks of office buildings called Penn Center. Ultimately, that construction would continue northward to the Parkway and include One Logan Square, to which the Firm moved in 1983.

Major new highways, especially the Schuylkill Expressway, made the city more accessible to traffic from its suburbs. The demographic effects were pervasive. There was an exodus from the city to new residential developments beyond its borders. Some people commuted back, while others went to work at industrial parks springing up in adjacent counties. Meanwhile, gentrification in Center City, together with an exploding low-income population, put pressure on once-stable neighborhoods. One such neighborhood was Germantown where two of the Firm's three name partners had lived. CEM's stately Victorian residence had already disappeared in 1926. Although the Bockius home remains today, it stands like an ancient galleon marooned on an alien beach.

■ ■ ■ ■ ■

The Firm's 1944 stationery showed only twenty lawyers in the office, with thirteen listed as "Absent with the Armed Forces." By 1947, the Firm comprised thirty-seven lawyers, and they were all in the office.

While lawyers everywhere had long concentrated on some kinds of matters in preference to others, they still remained competent generalists in most fields of law. This changed in large American firms after World War II. ML&B was no exception. What happened was the de facto evolution of the Firm's practice into something like the sections existing today, although at that time with much overlap. They were: litigation, corporate, real estate, estates, utilities, labor, tax, and trade regulation. (International was not added until 1972. See Chapter 24.)

The responsibility for litigation, which had been William Clarke Mason's bailiwick, increasingly devolved on Arthur Littleton and Thomas Ringe, as well as on Henry Heebner. Heebner endured a steady diet of Federal Employers' Liability Act (FELA) cases, which he defended on behalf of the Reading Company and the Central Railroad of New Jersey.

In addition to the four senior trail lawyers, there was John McConnell, about whom a former president judge of Philadelphia's Court of Common Pleas once commented to the author: "McConnell tries his cases perfectly by the book." McConnell tried his cases so perfectly that, starting in 1969 and for more than twenty years, he gave a clinical course at Temple University Law School on the preparation and trial of cases. He represented the defendant's point of view, while a leading Philadelphia plaintiff's lawyer presented the other side. Generations of Philadelphia trial lawyers grew up under the influence of this celebrated course. McConnell was also chancellor of the Philadelphia Bar Association in 1971.

Naturally, the Firm's corporate section was the largest. It included William Clarke Mason, Arthur Littleton, W. James MacIntosh, Thomas Ringe, A. Allen Woodruff (who died in 1949), Orvel Sebring, Anthony Whitaker, Martin Snyder, John Schaeffer, Howard Taylor, Oscar Hansen, John Bracken, and Benjamin Quigg.

Related to the corporate section was the real estate practice. That specialty had grown out of the intensive mortgage foreclosures of the Depression. It was the domain of Howard Rapp and William Lingelbach, assisted by Howard Kellogg.

Next, there was the estate practice. Mason, MacIntosh, and Ringe all had their important estate clients. But after the death of Clement Wood in 1940, John Russell, Jr., became the Firm's expert in estate work.

Utility law had been a specialty in the Firm going back to the 1880s with clients UGI and the Philadelphia Electric Company. Before World War II, Mason had handled utility matters along with everything else. After MacIntosh returned from Washington in 1945, he was responsible for many new utility clients, including American Water Works Company, Penn Fuel Gas, and briefly Bell Telephone Company of Pennsylvania. MacIntosh was assisted by Ernest von Starck. The practice so flowered that in 1948 the Firm hired Robert Young just to do utility work.

Labor law was a specialty spawned by the Depression. Frederick Knight had been hired in 1933 to attend to the Firm's needs in that area. After World War II, he was assisted by Miles Kirkpatrick and Norman Dutton. The practice grew exponentially with the acquisition of Souser & Kleeb in 1959.

Taxation was another specialty stimulated by the Depression, as business decisions were increasingly driven by tax considerations. It all started innocently enough. In 1913, the Sixteenth Amendment was adopted, permitting the imposition of an income tax. At first the rate was 1 percent on income over $20,000, reaching 6 percent at $500,000. There was grumbling—more on grounds of principle than money. Then rates climbed. By the late 1930s, the highest marginal rate was 79 percent, and during World War II it reached 91 percent. At that point, the grumbling was definitely about the money. What once had soaked only the rich soon soaked everybody.

The Firm's first full-time tax lawyer was Brady Bryson, who

arrived in 1941 as an associate. He left in 1943 but returned in 1955 as a partner. On his return he brought with him Thomas Lefevre. Both Bryson and Lefevre were superb tax lawyers. They joined Alfred McDowell, a tax lawyer who came to the Firm in 1946, became a partner in 1951, and retired in 1973. McDowell was a tireless worker, perennially practical and pleasant, and eternally youthful.

Finally, there was the trade regulation section, comprising Ringe, Kirkpatrick, and Quigg.

During the decade after World War II, the Firm's four leading partners were Mason, Littleton, MacIntosh, and Ringe. Mason received attention in Chapter 12. Littleton and MacIntosh will be covered in Chapter 17. Here is the place to consider Ringe.

■ ■ ■ ■ ■

Thomas Biddle Kenilworth Ringe came to ML&B in 1937 and became a partner the next year. He spent roughly two years at the Firm before Bockius died. He must have brought joy to the old man's heart, for Ringe was the most fantastic worker of them all. He was the only lawyer during his tenure at the Firm who required the services of two full-time secretaries. His work habits extended to summer weekends: From morning to evening he dictated and marked up documents while sitting on the porch of his seashore home.

In addition to dictating machines in his office, at home, and at the seashore, Ringe also had one in his car. Simple? Not in those days. Dictating machines of that vintage used large black cylinders. Thomas Edison would have recognized them instantly. The machines could not be stuffed into briefcases; they were pieces of furniture to be rolled from place to place. The user spoke into something resembling a World War I gas mask. Ringe maintained such a piece of furniture in the back of his car, with the gas mask extending from back seat to front seat. Every day he would arrive at the office, frequently before dawn, with cylinders for transcription by his two secretaries.[5]

Ringe was born in Three Tuns, Pennsylvania, on January 2, 1902, about eight months after MacIntosh. He and MacIntosh were classmates at the University of Pennsylvania Law School. When MacIntosh was elected editor-in-chief of Penn's law review, he arranged for Ringe to become its business manager. It was typical of these two energetic young men that they increased the publication's output from four to eight issues per year and doubled its circulation. One of their associate editors was classmate Joseph Clark, later a mayor of Philadelphia and United States senator.

After graduation from law school, Ringe practiced with his older brother. While doing so, he also served as a trial lawyer for the Philadelphia Rapid Transit Company from 1928 to 1936 and as an assistant city solicitor from 1930 to 1936. No labor was too herculean for him.

Ringe was drawn to the Firm by his classmate MacIntosh. Like Mason, Ringe is an example of a lateral entrant recruited to fill a specific need as he plunged into the litigation bred by the reorganizations of the Depression years. He was a lawyer who relished detail and believed in total preparation. So he was ideal for major cases, especially in the trade regulation area. While with the Firm, he handled important trials for the Philadelphia Electric Company, the Pennsylvania Newspaper Publishing Association, UGI, and Scott Paper Company. He also became Scott's lawyer of choice, as Mason, who had served so long on Scott's board, neared the end of his career.

Ringe was a born leader. He was the perennial president of his class at Episcopal Academy, president of his undergraduate class at the University of Pennsylvania, a member of the Philadelphia Charter Commission (he worked closely with Clark and Dilworth), chairman of the United War Chest, chancellor of the Pennsylvania Diocese of the Episcopal Church, and a member of the Board of City Trusts. Many years earlier, CEM had also served on the Board of City Trusts, which administers the Girard estate. (More about the board, the Girard estate, and litigation involving Girard College in Chapter 16.)

The author recalls observing Ringe try an antitrust case in federal court in 1950. Ringe was representing UGI. Each of the several defendants had as counsel a luminary of the Philadelphia trial bar. One such luminary was Morris Wolf, a founding partner in 1903 of what is presently Wolf, Block, Schorr & Solis-Cohen. Despite his years, Wolf knew exactly what he was about and absolutely charmed the jury. His closing speech contained many homey analogies. He likened the plaintiff's case to a toy train used by children on a Christmas platform. But he said the little engine was not powerful enough. Nor did the tracks extend far enough. Only a real train could win the case. According to Wolf, the plaintiff did not have a real train. The jurors nodded and smiled. By comparison, Ringe was more in the Francis Bracken mold—not as severe but still a lawyer working for the record. No homey analogies for him.

Ringe suffered a stroke when he arrived at the office the morning of January 21, 1957. Death came at University Hospital later in the day. His loss at fifty-five was a heavy blow to ML&B and the many client relationships he had so assiduously cultivated. (Nine months later, the Firm would suffer another loss with Mason's death.) Ringe's obituary in the Philadelphia *Evening Bulletin* quoted one Firm partner as saying that Ringe had put "many more than 55 years" into his life.[6] A fitting description for someone who was all business and always in a hurry.

■ ■ ■ ■ ■

Two years after Ringe's death, a very different kind of lawyer came to the Firm. He would spend only eleven years there, but his legacy was extraordinary. He was Kenneth Souser.[7] He had been the senior partner of a Philadelphia labor law boutique named Souser & Kleeb. It comprised three partners (Kenneth Souser, Robert Kleeb, and Kenneth's younger brother, Ronald Souser) and two associates (Jackson Bonney and James Matthews). The growth of ML&B's labor practice in the 1950s, as well as the death of labor partner Norman Dutton, led the Firm to approach Souser and acquire his firm by merger on April 1, 1959. ML&B thereby became the preeminent management-oriented labor law firm in Philadelphia at a time when other major firms usually had only one labor lawyer, if they had any.

Souser graduated from the University of Pennsylvania Law School in 1930 and went to work for Richard Slocum. After passage of the National Labor Relations Act in 1935, Slocum turned to labor law, as did young Souser. When Slocum became general manager of the Bulletin in 1937, Souser inherited Slocum's labor practice. By 1959, the Souser firm's labor clients included the bakeries (a legacy from Slocum), the laundries, the meatpackers, Mobil Oil (then Socony Mobil Oil), Vanity Fair Mills, A&P, the Bulletin Company, and Philco Corporation.

Philco was Souser's most active client during the 1950s. It was a major manufacturer of radio and television sets, refrigerators, home freezers, and air conditioners. The company sold its products worldwide, was a household name, and was then the largest industrial employer in the Philadelphia area, just as another Firm client, the Baldwin Locomotive Works, had been thirty years earlier.

At the time of the Souser-ML&B merger, Philco employed some 26,000 workers. Five of its twelve plants were in the Philadelphia area, and its production employees were members of Locals 101 and 102 of the International Union of Electrical Workers (IUE). The IUE was confrontational. It was characteristic of Souser that he would try to "blunt the spears," as he put it, of a hostile union. But the IUE never responded to Souser's blunting efforts. Philco and the IUE did not even start bargaining without first going into mediation. And at the end of their bargaining, they rarely succeeded in fully reducing their agreements to writing. Consequently, only Souser and his union counterpart knew what had been agreed, or thought they knew. Nor would the union negotiate contracts exceeding one year in duration. Moreover, there were constant work stoppages and threats of stoppages, as well as grievances and arbitrations.

The author remembers a forty-five-day Philco strike in 1954. Souser continued to bargain at the Federal Mediation and Conciliation Service, while Kleeb sought an injunction in the state court to restrain mass picketing at Philco's plants. For two days, Kleeb carefully adduced testimony from management about the picketing by hundreds of strikers. The union had a different view, claiming just a few employees were on the job sites politely exercising their right of free speech.

On the third day of the trial, Common Pleas Judge Gerald Flood opened the proceedings by declaring: "I have just visited the plants. There is mass picketing. I will grant the injunction." But even that was not a solution, since the union spurned the injunction, and 500 policemen had to open paths through the picket lines for nonstriking employees. It is easy to see how Souser and his colleagues were kept busy with Philco's labor work.

Philco's unfortunate labor history was one reason the company sold out to the Ford Motor Company late in 1961. Ford wanted to extend its electronics capacity, as well as acquire a counterpart to General Motors' Frigidaire division. Philco-Ford was run briefly by some of Ford's celebrated whiz kids. But it was hopeless, and today Philco is simply a name. For audiovisual products, the Philco name is owned by Philips Gloeilampenfabrieken N.V. For household appliances, the Philco name is owned by White Consolidated Industries, a United States subsidiary of Swedish conglomerate Electrolux AB. A strange odyssey.

Souser's portrait graces the Firm's labor section conference room on the twenty-fifth floor of One Logan Square. He is wearing half glasses and a cherubic smile. If, by reference to their portraits, Morris Bockius was majestic, William Clarke Mason was vital, and Francis Bracken was grave, then Kenneth Souser was whimsical. Eccentricities, which Mason labored to cultivate, came naturally to Souser.

Souser commuted to Philadelphia on the Paoli local from Berwyn, where he maintained a thirty-six-acre farm. But he did not farm it. He operated a railroad on it. It was called the Paoli, Leopardtown & Sugartown Railroad. It ran through his apple orchard, and its gauge was sufficiently broad that children could ride the rails behind small locomotives powered by live steam. The farm included a large barn for the storage of equipment, as well as a machine shop where Souser and other railroad buffs lovingly crafted their rolling stock. As railroad operations expanded, the machine shop overflowed. Lathes and drill presses infiltrated Mrs. Souser's laundry room and pantry. Her protests were in vain.

Souser was born on October 21, 1905, in Somerset County, Pennsylvania. The day of his birth coincided with the 100th anniversary of the Battle of Trafalgar, a fact Souser said made it easier for him to remember his age. He spent his childhood by the tracks of the Baltimore and Ohio Railroad, which employed his father as a telegrapher. When Souser died in 1970, a codicil to his will instructed that there be no religious services of any kind, that his body be cremated, and that his ashes be "strewn along the right-of-way of the Somerset and Cambria Branch of the Baltimore and Ohio Railroad, approximately half way between RW Tower and RX Tower."[8] These instructions were dutifully carried out by his brother Ronald.

Souser had an encyclopedic knowledge of just about every steam locomotive that had ever done service in the United States. His fixation with railroads led him to install a former Central Railroad of New Jersey caboose on a short section of track adjoining the swimming pool at his Berwyn farm. The caboose was renovated to function as a cabana. Although Mrs. Souser was resigned to her husband's passion for railroads, she really had marginal enthusiasm for the caboose, the lower berth he installed in their bedroom, and his choice of handkerchiefs. They were huge and red like those carried by railroad engineers.

In 1966, Souser and some friends purchased from the Reading Company 17.6 miles of track running southwest from New Hope to Ivyland in Bucks County north of Philadelphia. They added rolling stock, including a 1925 Baldwin 2-8-0 steam locomotive called No. 40, and christened their prize the New Hope & Ivyland Railroad. The route included the famous *Perils of Pauline* trestle, scene of the 1914 silent-movie classic. As a tourist attraction, the railroad brought joy to children of all ages, and especially to Souser. In altered form the attraction remains today.[9]

Souser's avocations were not limited to railroads. He collected first editions of works by Joseph Conrad and Arthur Conan Doyle. He was a Baker Street Irregular and a Son of the Copper Beeches. When he attended the Academy Ball (a Philadelphia social event), he wore a deerstalker and a black cape. Combining his avocations, he numbered/named his caboose/cabana 221B in honor of Sherlock Holmes's address on Baker Street.

Today, labor law comprehends many subspecialties, including the whole field of discrimination litigation. The practice was simpler in Souser's day. There were certification and unfair labor practice proceedings before the National Labor Relations Board, arbitrations, pension matters, and litigation relating to strikes. But for Souser, collective bargaining was the pièce de résistance. He was the quintessential poker player. He never raised his voice, and he looked like a wise old owl as he slouched at the bargaining table. No matter what the level of emotional intensity around him, it washed over him. He just could not be provoked.

Souser had a sixth sense for how a dispute would play out. Often the indispensable ingredient was simply the passage of time. Once, after a week of around-the-clock negotiations, the author, who was working with Souser, commented wearily to him: "Ken, we haven't accomplished a thing." Souser, looking a bit hurt, replied, "But we haven't lost anything." Like Fabius Maximus, the great Roman general called Cunctator for his delaying tactics, Souser avoided all-out battle and prevailed simply by outlasting his foes. It was an education to watch him bargain.

Souser was just short of sixty-five when he died. He had taken the day off and was stricken at home while preparing his lunch. By the time of his death, the Firm's labor section numbered twenty lawyers. It was Souser's legacy. If he had lived twenty years longer, he would have seen his protégé William Curtin give labor law advice to the entire railroad industry in 1990-92. Imagine the joy Souser would have felt in witnessing a combination of the section he created (which by 1993 numbered more than one hundred lawyers) and his beloved railroads.

■ ■ ■ ■

The merger of Souser & Kleeb and ML&B was a marriage made in heaven. Perhaps other boutique law firms could be found that would generate similar synergy. MacIntosh thought one such boutique might be Shertz, Barnes & Shertz. It had a lock on the legal work of the motor trucking industry in the Philadelphia area. It was also counsel to the Pennsylvania Motor Truck Association. The Shertz firm merged with ML&B in 1961.

Shertz, Barnes & Shertz comprised two partners and an associate. The two partners were Shertz *père* and Shertz *fils*. (Barnes had just died.) As it turned out, Shertz *fils* was an ML&B partner less than a year before leaving to head E. Brooke Matlack, Inc., a Firm client. That left Shertz *père* and associate Baker Smith. Appropriately, Shertz *père* was called "Pop" by everyone. (His given name was Harold.) Pop became counsel to the Firm, even though he was then seventy-eight years old. Despite his age, he was as strong as a bull with a voice to match. Young lawyers marveled at how he could talk (or roar) into a telephone while clenching between his teeth a lighted cigar that his lips never touched. This exercise served him well. He continued to practice until 1969, when he was eighty-six, and his name remained on the Firm's letterhead until 1972. In 1979, Pop died at ninety-seven.

Although the Shertz acquisition had merit in theory, it did not work out as MacIntosh hoped. Pop was venerated by the trucking industry. But he was in the twilight of his career. And Smith, who was well liked, died in 1975 after a long battle with cancer. Also, it was found that truckers were not always respectful of legal advice, had frequent cash-flow problems, and could be cavalier in paying their bills. Finally, deregulation of the trucking industry swept away much of the need for the Shertz expertise. It also swept away many truckers.

The Shertz experience taught that a practice and the lawyers who run it are inseparable: One cannot be acquired without the other. In addition, all businesses are not created equal as law clients. The Souser success and Shertz failure became case studies often cited by the Firm's management when ML&B went national during the 1970s.

■ ■ ■ ■ ■

As specialization increased, the generalist became a dinosaur. While some lawyers managed more than one specialty, they were exceptions. It was hard enough to keep up with one field of law and almost impossible to keep up with two or three. "The fox knows many tricks," wrote Archilochus, "but the hedgehog one great one."[10] Formerly foxes, lawyers were becoming hedgehogs.

Moreover, specialization itself became specialized. A corporate lawyer might handle only banking work. Another might handle just bank regulatory work and not even lending transactions. Or a tax lawyer might handle only employee-benefit work and know little about Subchapter C. It was a case of knowing more and more about less and less, while avoiding the *reductio ad absurdum* of knowing everything about nothing. Yes, lawyers were sure-footed in their subspecialties. Adam Smith would have been pleased with their efficiency. But they seldom got to see the whole picture. And they sometimes wondered if they were really lawyers.

With specialization by lawyers came selectivity by clients. One firm might advise a client regarding environmental law, while another firm handled its financings, and still another its employee-benefit work. Institutional relationships gave way to transactional relationships. As responsibilities multiplied, it became unclear whether any firm represented the whole client. This enabled in-house lawyers to function as general counsel in fact as well as name. Sometimes they seemed to encourage the multiplication to achieve the distinction.

In the new order of things, a client's ties with its law firm would seldom match the relationships ML&B had enjoyed earlier with UGI, Philadelphia Electric Company, Philadelphia National Bank, and Scott Paper Company. Legal services were increasingly sold by law firms and bought by clients like lengths of wire from a reel, as the client stood by with clippers to make sure the wire was snipped immediately on the completion of each task. The client might return for something else, or it might make its next purchase at another firm down the street.

Still, the Firm adapted smoothly to the twin challenges of specialization and selectivity, despite their erosion of relationships. In the decades after World War II, ML&B was among the first firms to attract clients by reason of its specialties in utility law, tax law, securities law, and especially labor law. On balance, the Firm gained more than it lost. Its ability to serve clients on a specialized basis in multiple markets facilitated its success as a pioneer in national practice. And this was at a time when other law firms had yet even to consider venturing outside their home turfs.

CHAPTER 16

CHANGING TIMES
IN PHILADELPHIA

Two Guys ■ *The "blue laws" are ignored* ■ *Even Strawbridge & Clothier opens on Sundays* ■ *The courts give up* ■ *The city tries to buy the PTC* ■ *Enforcing the trust indenture* ■ *A dead duck is resuscitated* ■ *SEPTA in the driver's seat* ■ *The old era all over again* ■ *Girard College* ■ *Poor male white orphans* ■ Brown v. Board of Education ■ *Private trustees are appointed* ■ *Certiorari is denied* ■ *A school under siege* ■ *Cecil Moore and Martin Luther King* ■ *The walls come tumbling down* ■ *Alone on the stage* ■ *The lawyer's duty*

During the years following World War II, ML&B's lawyers in Philadelphia took part in some high-profile matters on the local scene. Three stories will be recounted here. The first concerns the "blue laws" litigation, testing whether Pennsylvania could prohibit its merchants from opening for business on Sundays. The second deals with the Firm's representation of the Philadelphia Transportation Company (PTC), then the nation's largest privately owned local transportation system, as it continued its battle with the city before ultimately being acquired by a public authority. And the third pertains to the celebrated Girard College case with its collision of civil rights and probate law.

■ ■ ■ ■ ■

Since colonial times, Pennsylvanians had kept Sunday more or less holy. Quakers went to their meeting houses. Others went to their churches. Businesses did not open. Then, starting in the late 1940s, this relaxed way of life yielded to the explosive growth of suburbia and the advent of shopping centers and malls. They often occupied the geographical hubs of their communities and provided, in a secular society, many occasions for civic interaction that had been the special province of churches in earlier times. Another sociological innovation after World War II was the number of women in the workplace. Drawn into the labor force during the war, they continued to work after the war. For some of them Sunday was their only shopping day.

Aggressive retailers seized the obvious opportunity. Among them were Two Guys from Harrison-Allentown, Inc., called Two Guys for short. They operated discount department stores, another postwar phenomenon. One such store, located in Lehigh County, opened on Sundays and did one-third of its weekly business on that day. Monumental traffic jams were triggered by customers who came from scores of miles away. Two Guys certainly seemed to be violating the blue laws, which imposed fines and imprisonment upon "[w]hoever engages on Sunday in the business of selling, or sells, or offers for sale, on such day, at retail [certain enumerated property]."[1] But were the blue laws constitutional?

Pennsylvania retailers had three choices. First, they could lobby for repeal of the blue laws and all open on Sunday, contrary to their practice since colonial times. Second, they could simply ignore Two Guys and suffer a loss of market share. Or third, they could join together in supporting the prosecution of Two Guys, which is what they did.

The Pennsylvania Retailers Association engaged the Firm. The effort was led by W. James MacIntosh and Benjamin Quigg, who were charged with providing firepower for the local district attorney. A statutory three-judge federal court was convened, and in 1959 a scholarly opinion by Court of Appeals Judge William Hastie held that the Pennsylvania blue laws were constitutional.[2] Two years later, the United States Supreme Court affirmed, deciding that the Pennsylvania legislation did not violate the equal protection clause of the Fourteenth Amendment or the First Amendment prohibition against any "law respecting an establishment of religion."[3]

Chief Justice Earl Warren's opinion recounted the history of legislation intended to punish those who "profane the Lord's day." But whatever the purpose of such legislation in years past, Warren concluded that the contemporary focus was not so much religious as economic. He cited a statement by a Pennsylvania legislator:

> As I read this bill, I find nothing in it which is of a religious nature. The bill was prompted by the thousands of letters that we have all received in the Senate of Pennsylvania, asking us to do something for the men and women who work in the department stores. These people are not asking to go to church; they are asking for a day of rest.[4]

In 1962, a year after *Two Guys*, there was another ruling on the blue laws. This time it was at the state court level and involved a

Philadelphia store. Again, the Firm provided firepower, which took the form of an amicus curiae brief and oral argument by Arthur Littleton. The store tried to knock out the blue laws on grounds that they were "special legislation" in violation of the Pennsylvania constitution because they did not forbid all sales on Sunday but merely sales of specified commodities. But in *Bargain City U.S.A., Inc. v. Dilworth* the Pennsylvania Supreme Court rejected the store's argument, holding the classifications reasonable and the blue laws constitutional.[5]

Having won their cases in both the federal and state courts, surely Pennsylvania's retailers could now settle back secure in the knowledge that no stores would henceforth open on Sundays. But such was not the case. In fact, there was an increase in store openings on Sundays and a decrease in enforcement actions.

Take client Strawbridge & Clothier (S&C) for example. In 1961, S&C initiated the first large covered mall in the eastern United States. Located in Cherry Hill, New Jersey, the mall featured a 215,000-square-foot S&C store. From the outset, that store opened on Sundays between noon and 5 p.m, despite S&C's conservatism and pious traditions. According to Frank Veale, a former S&C executive vice-president, Sunday openings at Cherry Hill "gave us a taste of what Sundays could do for us." Nevertheless, until a decade later, no S&C store would open in Pennsylvania on Sundays.

During the 1960s, discount chains were the most active Sunday retailers in Pennsylvania. S&C's answer to the discount chains was its Clover stores. S&C's first Clover store in Pennsylvania was constructed in Morrisville, north of Philadelphia. It commenced business in 1972 and was open on Sundays from noon to 5 p.m. This pattern was followed as each new Clover store came on line. By 1977, Sunday openings had become the rule for all S&C stores in Pennsylvania. That year even the flagship store at Eighth and Market streets capitulated and opened on Sundays as part of the multistore Gallery development.

By 1978, just about every sizable retailer in Pennsylvania was open on Sundays. With the blue laws still on the books, everyone was operating illegally. What was the law to do? It had to protect its dignity. If its constituents would not follow it, then it would have to follow its constituents. Such was the case in *Kroger Co. v. O'Hara Township*,[6] where the Pennsylvania Supreme Court enjoined further enforcement of the Sunday closing laws, saying they had become such an irrational patchwork of exemptions as to violate Pennsylvania's constitutional prohibition against any "local or special law . . . [r]egulating . . . trade."[7] The argument that failed in *Bargain City* in 1962 succeeded in *Kroger* in 1978.

The Firm took no part in *Kroger*. To do so, it would have had to switch sides, since by that time its clients were all open on Sunday. When customs change, so do laws.

■ ■ ■ ■ ■

A second high-profile event during the postwar era was the takeover by a public authority of the Philadelphia Transportation Company, which the Firm represented in 1964-65.

The transit system's history has already been traced in Chapter 13: its antecedents going back to the second half of the nineteenth century; the structuring of its underliers by Peter A. B. Widener; its consolidation as the PRT in 1902; its Depression reorganization in which the Firm played a major role; and its emergence as the Philadelphia Transportation Company in 1940.

The Depression reorganization permitted the system's continued operation but did not solve its fundamental problems. Its securities remained watered, thanks to Francis Bracken. Also, it paid rentals to the city of Philadelphia, whereas other transportation systems were subsidized by their cities. And along with all municipal transportation systems, the PTC suffered from constantly increasing labor and equipment costs. Such increased costs triggered fare boosts. But revenue did not increase proportionately, because with every fare boost the system lost some of its riders. Compounding its problems, the PTC was unwilling or unable to make the huge capital expenditures necessary for the system's maintenance, not to mention its improvement. Finally, being privately owned, the PTC was a convenient whipping boy.

The PTC cut every possible corner. It made no contributions to its pension funds, nor did it accrue its pension obligations on its financial statements. Also, it took liberties in servicing the additional interest feature of the bonds that Francis Bracken had caused it to issue to debt holders of the former underliers. The indenture trustee for the bonds was the Fidelity-Philadelphia Trust Company (later the Fidelity Bank), which engaged the Firm to enforce the obligation. Whether the PTC had to pay additional interest on its bonds turned largely on accounting questions, including depreciation, amortization, and obsolescence. Ernest von Starck was an expert in such matters as a result of his rate-making practice before the Pennsylvania Public Utility Commission. In 1962, he beat the

PTC and won the case for the bondholders.[8]

The next year, the PTC approached von Starck and asked if the Firm would represent the PTC in ongoing negotiations with the city regarding the possible purchase of the system by the city. Few compliments are as gratifying as when a former adversary, having been well and truly trounced, asks its one-time foe to become its advocate. The Firm took on the assignment.

Those were tense times for the PTC. As part of Philadelphia's renaissance, Mayor Richardson Dilworth had proposed in 1956 that the city buy the giant transportation system. His proposal touched off eight years of desultory negotiations with everyone in the act: the mayor, the city council (almost always at odds with the mayor), the PTC's management, the PTC's shareholders (frequently at odds with its management), the Transport Workers Union (sometimes at odds with its membership), the system's riders, and the media.

How much should the city pay for the system? The city first offered $40 million. After six years, its offer reached $75 million. The PTC rejected the city's offers, noting that the cost of duplicating the system would run into the billions of dollars. Alternatively, it argued that the system, if taken by eminent domain, would cost the city at least $200 million. Even for rate-making purposes, the Public Utility Commission had valued the system at $92 million in 1959.

But the deck contained a wild card, which the city held. In 1907, the city and the Philadelphia Rapid Transit Company (PRT), prede-cessor of the PTC, had entered into an agreement giving the city the right to acquire the system. The 1907 agreement contained a formula by which the system would be valued for buy-sell purposes. Applying the formula, the PTC's shareholders would be subject to some heavy charges, including $17.6 million representing the PTC's unfunded pension liabilities. Thus, the shareholders would receive much less than the purchase prices then being discussed. But was the 1907 agreement still in force, considering the PRT's reorganiza-tion in the 1930s? No one was sure.

The only sure thing was that the parties were far apart in negotiations that were going nowhere. Also, the times had changed. By 1962, Dilworth was no longer mayor. The new mayor, James H. J. Tate, said the city was not interested in the system and the whole affair was a "dead duck."[9]

Two years later, the duck was resuscitated. Pursuant to the Metropolitan Transportation Authorities Act of 1963,[10] the Southeastern Pennsylvania Transportation Authority (SEPTA) was formed on February 17, 1964. SEPTA was a nonprofit public authority designed to assemble and operate a consolidated transit system in the Philadelphia area. As consolidated, the system would eventually include the PTC, the commuter railroad lines, and peripheral feeders.

SEPTA moved quickly after its founding. It took over the extensive network of commuter rail lines in the Philadelphia area. For years, these lines had been a drain on the Pennsylvania and Reading railroads. Henceforth, the railroads would operate them for SEPTA on a reimbursement basis. New equipment was acquired and service improved. SEPTA was off to a good start.[11]

The next step was for SEPTA to acquire the PTC. To do so, it determined to play the wild card. On June 8, 1965, SEPTA took an assignment of the city's purported rights under the 1907 agreement. SEPTA then notified the PTC of its intention to purchase the system in accordance with the agreement. Three days later, SEPTA offered the PTC $43 million. That figure reflected SEPTA's application of the formula and its position that the PTC's financial statements overstated its assets and understated its liabilities, including its unfunded pension obligations. A week later, SEPTA commenced a declaratory judgment action in which it sought a determination that it could acquire the system for $43 million under the 1907 agreement.

Since SEPTA's creation in 1964, it had become obvious that the PTC would have to sell. Only the price remained at issue. As negotiations intensified, the last thing the PTC wanted was a declaratory judgment that the 1907 agreement was alive and applicable. The PTC desperately needed time.

The Firm filed objections to SEPTA's complaint, arguing that the matter was inappropriate for declaratory judgment. The lower court dismissed the objections and directed the PTC to file an answer. The Firm appealed to the Pennsylvania Supreme Court. The matter was argued before that court on October 12, 1965, by Littleton and von Starck. They contended that the case was too socially significant and factually complex to be dealt with by a declaratory judgment, that the 1907 agreement was no longer in force, and that in any event the agreement was not assignable by the city to SEPTA. One Philadelphia newspaper, reporting on the oral argument, noted that the Firm's lawyers "cautioned the Supreme Court against making a hasty decision," saying it would be a "travesty of justice . . . [to conduct the litigation] as though it were a foot race."[12] But the Supreme Court rejected the Firm's arguments and remanded the case to the trial court.[13] Nevertheless, the PTC got what it wanted: time for further negotiations.

Actually, the Pennsylvania Supreme Court did not decide the case on its merits until almost two years later, when a four-to-three decision on July 27, 1967, upheld a lower court ruling that the 1907 agreement was still in effect and that PTC's shareholders would have to bear the accrued pension costs.[14] However, at that juncture the parties were far along in their negotiations, SEPTA was under intense public pressure to stop dickering and actually take over the system, and the PTC had changed legal counsel once again. So ML&B did not lose the case!

By that time, the case really did not matter because the PTC, while losing the battle, had won the war. In the bargaining, SEPTA had agreed to shoulder the pension liability, and the PTC had gotten an acceptable price. SEPTA took over the system and commenced operations on October 1, 1968. Mayor Tate proclaimed "a new era for the people of this area."[15]

Tate was wrong. It was the old era all over again. There would be the usual strikes and threats of strikes, followed by the customary wage concessions. And once again, increases in rates would depress the number of riders. No money would be available to maintain the system, much less improve it. By 1990, it was estimated that $5 billion might be required for its rejuvenation. Moreover, SEPTA would become an even more notorious political football than the PTC. The legislature, the city, and the surrounding counties would all disagree concerning SEPTA's operations. In 1990, the *Wall Street Journal* printed a letter to the editor advocating that the system again be privatized![16]

None of this should have come as any surprise. The author recalls how it was all predicted in uncanny detail by Albert Lyons, the PTC's CEO, at an informal meeting with a number of the Firm's partners in 1965. Government ownership is generally a mistake. And even when it is inevitable, it is rarely a solution.

Francis Bracken would have been amused by one aspect of the SEPTA takeover: The 100-year bonds maturing in 2039 that he caused the underliers to receive in the Depression reorganization were redeemed at their face value by SEPTA in 1968. But they were redeemed with proceeds from new bonds issued by SEPTA. So there was a change of obligor and obligee, but the water remained.

■ ■ ■ ■ ■

While SEPTA was taking over the PTC, the Firm was also engaged in a bitter collision between probate law and civil rights law. That collision generated fifteen years of litigation and a third story. It concerns a Frenchman who ran away to sea when he was fourteen, became a ship captain, settled in Philadelphia in 1776 just before the Declaration of Independence, achieved spectacular success as a merchant and banker, and may have been the richest man in America when he died in 1831. The story also involves a will contest led by Daniel Webster; a nationally known school with almost 20,000 graduates since its founding; picketing and violence; political posturing; and endless court battles.

Stephen Girard left a will of thirty-five pages and an estate of $6 million, including rich coal lands in Schuylkill County. The residuary estate, which grew to $100 million by 1960 (and exceeded $200 million by 1990), was to be administered by the city of Philadelphia to create a "college" for "poor male white orphans, between the age of six and ten years."[17] Girard was precise about the objects of his charity, as well as other aspects of the bequest. His will provided that the school, later called Girard College, was to be located on forty-three acres of farmland owned by him not far northwest of where City Hall stands today. The buildings were to be constructed of stone, and the campus was to be "enclosed with a solid wall, at least fourteen inches thick and ten feet high, capped with marble and guarded with irons on the top, so as to prevent persons from getting over."[18]

The Girard College bequest gave rise to the most celebrated will contest in American history. It also gave rise to the longest argument in the history of the United States Supreme Court. In its early days, the Court was not busy. It had the luxury of permitting argument until it was satisfied, a tradition in the English law courts. In *Vidal v. Girard's Executors*,[19] the Court heard argument for ten days in 1844. Considering how the Court now operates, this record will never be broken. It attests to the importance of the *Girard* case that *McCulloch v. Maryland* took only nine days, that *Gibbons v. Ogden* took five days, and that the *Dartmouth College* case got only three days.

At Girard's death, his sole relatives were a mercurial brother— whom Girard was forever rescuing from scrapes—and three nieces in France. Two of these relatives retained Daniel Webster to break the will. Webster argued that Philadelphia did not have the capacity to serve as trustee of a charitable bequest. He also argued that the bequest was void as contrary to the laws of Pennsylvania, since it was "hostile to the Christian religion": Clergymen were not allowed on the campus.

Webster lost the case, and the school was built and operated as specified. Today, surrounded by its wall, it is a beautiful oasis in North Philadelphia. Founder's Hall, a handsome Corinthian temple, makes Girard College easy to identify when looking north from the Firm's Logan Square offices.

The city implemented the provisions of Girard's will until 1869, when the Pennsylvania legislature created the Board of City Trusts to administer the Girard bequest, as well as other lesser estates that had been left to the city. Firm founding partner CEM was a member of the Board of City Trusts. Later, in the 1950s, Thomas Ringe was a board member. The Firm did work for the board, and Ringe was the responsible attorney.

On July 17, 1953, Ringe opened file No. 2108-412-4-e, entitled "Girard College—Admission of Non-White Boys." The file was a response to arguments by Raymond Pace Alexander that two black boys should be admitted to the college. Alexander was a distinguished black lawyer and a member of Philadelphia's city council. He argued that Girard College should not enjoy tax exemption as a public charity if it continued to exclude "non-white" boys. But since many charities restricted their beneficiaries and still enjoyed tax exemption, little credence was given to Alexander's arguments.

The next year, the United States Supreme Court handed down its landmark decision in *Brown v. Board of Education of Topeka*.[20] By that decision, racial segregation in public schools was held unconstitutional. Was Girard College a public school? Clearly, it derived its revenue from the Girard bequest and not from taxes. On the other hand, it was administered by a governmentally appointed board. The question was whether the college could remain a hybrid or, if not, which of the will's provisions should yield.

Mayor Joseph Clark thought the exclusionary provision should yield and that non-white boys should be admitted. But John A. Diemand, president of the Board of City Trusts, insisted that the will be carried out exactly as written. Diemand was an active Girard College alumnus, CEO of the Insurance Company of North America, and a powerful figure in the community. The board rejected the applications of the two black orphans whom Alexander had proposed, and the matter went to court.

The Philadelphia Orphans' Court endorsed the position of the board.[21] The Supreme Court of Pennsylvania affirmed,[22] holding that, through the board, the city was merely administering a private bequest and not a municipal school system. As to that bequest, "a man's prejudices are part of his liberty," said the Pennsylvania Supreme Court.[23]

But that did not end the matter. On April 29, 1957, in response to a petition for certiorari, the United States Supreme Court held without oral argument that the board was operating Girard College as "an agency of the State of Pennsylvania," so that "its refusal to admit . . . Negroes was discrimination by the State." The Court "remanded for further proceedings not inconsistent with this opinion."[24]

The Court's words were cryptic. Did it mean that the black applicants should be admitted, or that the city should cease administering the trust? The latter construction was adopted by the Orphans' Court, which removed the board and appointed thirteen private trustees, six of whom were also members of the board. The Firm, which had not handled the litigation up to that point, was then retained by the private trustees. Arthur Littleton led the ML&B team.

By appointing private trustees, the Orphans' Court said it was simply applying a time-honored principle of trust law: If a trustee becomes disqualified to carry out the terms of a trust, another trustee will be appointed in its place.[25] Responding to Daniel Webster, the United States Supreme Court had said as much in 1844. Webster had hoped to knock out the bequest by arguing that the city did not have the capacity to serve. The Court held that the city *did* have the capacity. But even if it lacked the capacity, the opinion noted that an equity court could appoint a trustee who did.

There was an appeal from the Orphans' Court decision substituting private trustees for the board. Littleton argued in support of the decision, and the Pennsylvania Supreme Court affirmed.[26] Significantly, the United States Supreme Court denied certiorari.[27] Surely the matter was now in repose.

But whatever the state of the law, the civil rights movement was not in repose. There were charges that the appointment of private trustees was a subterfuge. Moreover, by the 1950s, the farmlands once surrounding the school were long gone and Girard College was "in the middle of North Philadelphia, the city's darkest Negro ghetto."[28]

Demonstrations began, and ultimately the school was placed under siege. Incident followed incident until August 1964, when

Philadelphia endured its longest, hottest summer. The ghetto exploded. There were nights of fire and looting. The police barricaded the area and slowly battled their way back to control. By that time, Raymond Pace Alexander was a judge of the Common Pleas Court. He pleaded for moderation.

But Alexander was called an "Uncle Tom"[29] by Cecil Moore, the feisty president of the local branch of the National Association for the Advancement of Colored People. Firm partner Gerald Brawner remembers Moore as "an even-handed agitator who regularly denounced friend and foe alike regardless of color." A former marine, Moore was by that time a flamboyant criminal lawyer and bon vivant. Later, in 1976, he was elected to Philadelphia's city council and served for four years. In a sense he served without pay, since the IRS always attached his salary to cover back taxes. Philadelphia City Council renamed Columbia Avenue near Girard College for Cecil Moore in 1986.[30]

Martin Luther King, Jr., visited Girard College in the summer of 1965 and stood with Moore on a flatbed trailer outside the wall. With stirring eloquence, King declared that Girard's white students were "slaves" of the "festering sore of segregation." "[T]he city . . . has a kind of Berlin Wall to keep God's colored children out."[31] Invoking a biblical parallel, King also prophesied that the "[w]alls of segregation will come tumbling down."[32]

Moore declared that he was not interested in a court battle and that Girard College would "either integrate or disintegrate."[33] Moore's militia turned out with ladders and other equipment to scale the wall. The city increased an around-the-clock police guard. Moore boasted that he had already cost the city $2 million to protect the school and that he was just starting his campaign.

Something had to be done. Civil rights activists wanted the question resolved their way, while strict constructionists wanted to hold the line. Politicians were more flexible: They simply wanted the problem to go away. There were countless meetings of city and state representatives with the Girard trustees. But the trustees pointed to the will and the court decisions. They said their hands were tied.

Governor William Scranton decided to force the issue. If the times had changed, the legal question should be revisited. On September 23, 1965, the governor appointed William T. Coleman, Jr., and Charles J. Biddle as special counsel. Coleman was black, Biddle white. (Coleman would later serve as Secretary of the United States Department of Transportation from 1975 to 1977.) Special counsel filed suit alleging violations inter alia of the Fourteenth Amendment and the Pennsylvania Public Accommodations Act.

With Littleton's health failing, von Starck led the defense, assisted by John Russell and Richard Brown. A motion to dismiss was filed. The motion asserted that the constitutional questions were res judicata by reason of the prior related proceedings, and that the Pennsylvania Public Accommodations Act had been dealt with in the earlier state court litigation that had resolved the issue against the plaintiffs.

District Court Judge Joseph Lord apparently wished to skirt the broader constitutional inquiry and the res judicata question. So he addressed only the public accommodations issue. He said it had not been dealt with previously, held the trustees in violation of the act, and gave the college two weeks to integrate.[34]

The Court of Appeals for the Third Circuit granted a stay, and a six-judge court heard argument late in 1966. By this time, nerves were frayed all around. Richard Brown recalls how von Starck, Coleman, and Biddle went at one another during the extended oral arguments. With rising emotion, Coleman denounced the historic *Dred Scott* decision, which the court said did not advance the inquiry. Coleman also questioned if the trustees were "civilized, responsible human beings." Von Starck asked that Coleman withdraw the accusation. It was not withdrawn. The newspapers duly reported these recriminations.[35]

The appeals court vacated the order of the district court, saying the Pennsylvania courts had already held the Public Accommodations Act inapplicable to Girard College. The appeals court then remanded the case to the district court to pursue further the fundamental constitutional issues. With this mandate, the district court flatly held that the trustees' refusal to admit non-white boys violated the Fourteenth Amendment. By its decree of July 5, 1967, the district court enjoined the college from denying admission to non-white applicants.[36]

The trustees appealed once more, but the Court of Appeals for the Third Circuit affirmed. First, the opinion noted that no inference could be drawn from the Supreme Court's denial of certiorari almost ten years earlier when the private trustees were appointed. Then, the court pointed to the "close, indispensable relationship between the College, the City of Philadelphia and the Commonwealth of Pennsylvania intended by Mr. Girard." The court also noted that, "[t]he Commonwealth's Orphans' Court, through its assumed power of appointment and reappointment of the Trustees, is significantly concerned with the current administration of the college." Thus, at all times there was "state action," which the will required in the operation of the institution. Moreover, state action included the appointment of the private trustees, which itself was a violation of the Fourteenth Amendment.[37]

The trustees petitioned the United States Supreme Court for certiorari, which was denied on May 20, 1968.[38] The trustees and the Firm had reached the end of the line. After 1968, black boys were admitted to Girard College; and by 1990, three-quarters of its students were African Americans. Starting in 1984, girls (Girard's will made no mention of them) were also admitted; and by 1990, they comprised one-third of the student body.

The lengthy *Girard* litigation generated much debate around the Firm. First, what was the thinking behind the Supreme Court's cryptic order in 1957 remanding the case and noting that the state could not discriminate? By its remand, did the Court really intend to give the state courts the option of substituting private trustees for a public trustee? If not, why the peculiar language of the Court's order? Second, if the Court had wanted to outlaw discrimination at the college, why did it deny certiorari when the private trustees were appointed? Third, would the result have been different if Daniel Webster's argument had prevailed in 1844 that the city could not serve, in which case private trustees would have operated the school from the outset? Fourth, would the case ever have become a cause célèbre if Girard College had been situated in an outlying area instead of in what had become a ghetto neighborhood? As Cecil Moore said, "this school is located in the heart of an area where it is a perpetual red flag."[39]

Finally, what did Stephen Girard really intend? Throughout the litigation, everyone purported to speak for the testator from the great beyond. He was a kind and wise man. Surely he did not mean what he said. Or if he had lived in a later age, he would have said something different. On the other hand, it was noted that Girard had owned many slaves during his business career, including thirty at his death. Only one of them had ever been freed by him, and she was the daughter of Girard's irresponsible brother and another of Girard's slaves taken by the brother as a mistress.[40]

At the end of the case, von Starck stood virtually alone on the stage. Only the well-organized Girard College Alumni Association wanted to preserve the school exactly as its graduates knew and loved it. Others, even some of the trustees, had become ambivalent if not antagonistic. Few were interested any longer in rigorous legal analysis, except to find a way around it. Von Starck had to contend with the city, the state, the pickets, and the media. What had been a generally acceptable position in 1953 had become repugnant by the mid-1960s.

Von Starck hated the case. So did almost all the Firm's lawyers. They often had to remind themselves of their duty that a client be served loyally and effectively, regardless of their personal beliefs concerning the merits of the client's cause.

■ ■ ■ ■ ■

The Sunday closing cases, the PTC takeover, and the Girard controversy were all generation-defining events. They epitomized the post-World War II spirit. The Firm played its role as tradition yielded to changing times.

CHAPTER 17

A SAINTLY MAN
AND MAC THE KNIFE

Arthur Littleton and W. James MacIntosh run the Firm from 1957 to 1971 ■ A study in symbiosis ■ The era of the first name ■ The law as life itself ■ The inevitable word ■ The philosopher king ■ The Firm's culture ■ Mai tais ■ The resurrection of the body ■ Opting for chaos ■ The suit or the overcoat ■ Dictaphones and disgrace ■ Dividing the profits ■ Working like the devil ■ Water law ■ Clients and friends ■ Also thieves ■ Taking risks ■ Law firms should be everywhere ■ Buy consols

Morgan, Lewis & Bockius was dominated both de jure and de facto by a single senior partner during most of its first century. There was CEM from 1873 until 1908, Morris Bockius from 1908 until 1939, and William Clarke Mason from 1939 until 1957. These three senior partners reigned for thirty-five, thirty-one, and eighteen years respectively. They were followed by Arthur Littleton from 1957 through 1966 and W. James MacIntosh from 1967 to 1971. Littleton and MacIntosh will be considered together because their reigns were short and because for the first time in the Firm's history the burdens of Firm governance were borne simultaneously to some extent by more than one senior partner.

Littleton and MacIntosh were both brilliant and versatile lawyers, but otherwise they were quite different. Littleton was gentle and kind, like the old-fashioned family doctor who made house calls. He was also eloquent, probably the most eloquent lawyer in the Firm's history. He was a venerable man and a giant at the bar. He seemed almost otherworldly.

By contrast, MacIntosh was very much of this world. He had street sense and was a politician—not only figuratively but also for many years as counsel to the Pennsylvania Republican State Committee. He also had a head for business. While Littleton agonized over important business decisions and often reached them through prayer (he was deeply religious), MacIntosh's approach was secular;

his judgments were instinctive, immediate, and irrevocable. Littleton felt anguish over distasteful personnel problems, like asking a superannuated partner to retire. MacIntosh felt no such anguish. Actually, he seemed to enjoy administering strong medicine. Working together, the Saintly Man and Mac the Knife were a study in symbiosis.

With Littleton and MacIntosh, the Firm reached the era of the first name. There is no suggestion that CEM was called Charlie by his colleagues. Nor was Bockius called Morrie or even Morris by anyone except Mason, Francis Bracken, Clement Wood, and the founding partners. And while Mason was often called Bill (or Will) behind his back, he was called Mr. Mason to his face, except by a few of his older colleagues. But Littleton was called Arthur by almost all of his partners, and MacIntosh was called Jim even by associates.[1]

■ ■ ■ ■ ■

Arthur Littleton was born in Rutledge, Pennsylvania, on October 26, 1895. He was the son of a lawyer, and he married the daughter of a lawyer. The marriage produced three sons, all of whom became lawyers. For him the law was life itself.

Littleton received his first bachelor's degree from Philadelphia's Central High School, where William Clarke Mason had received his. He received his second bachelor's degree from the University of Pennsylvania, where he was elected to Phi Beta Kappa and rowed on the crew. It was the golden age of Penn's English Department, with legendary professors Felix Schelling, Clarence Child, Cornelius Weygandt, Arthur Hobson Quinn, George McClelland, and William Page Harbeson. From Quinn, Littleton learned to pursue "the inevitable word." Only one word fits perfectly. Finding it is the trick. All his life, Littleton kept a thesaurus at hand. With his classical education (he was a dedicated student of Greek and Latin) and his literary training, he was intoxicated by the beauty of language.

Littleton entered Penn Law School in 1916. His studies were interrupted for two years by military service during World War I as a lieutenant (j. g.) in the navy. In 1920, he graduated from law school, where he was an associate editor of the law review. He joined the Firm immediately following graduation and became a partner in 1926.

In those days, most lawyers were generalists; they did almost everything. Littleton was no exception. But he was especially active as a litigator and a business lawyer with a subspecialty in banking law. Today, it would be remarkable for a lawyer to be simultaneously a fellow of the American College of Trial Lawyers and a member of the Editorial Board of the Uniform Commercial Code. Littleton was both.

His versatility led to service on the boards of Philadelphia National Bank, the Philadelphia and Reading Corporation, Fidelity Building Corporation, Acme Markets, Fidelity and Deposit Company of Maryland, and Baldwin-Lima-Hamilton Corporation. He was also a trustee of the University of Pennsylvania and a director of the Philadelphia Orchestra. His interest in the orchestra was not just one of stewardship: He loved classical music and regularly attended concerts.

Littleton's role as a litigator in the Sunday blue laws, PTC, and Girard College cases has already been noted. He also appeared at the appellate level for such clients as the Bulletin Company, Philadelphia Gas Works, Fidelity Bank, Reading Eagle Company, Dauphin Deposit Trust Company, Glen Alden Corporation, Presbyterian Hospital of Philadelphia, Philadelphia & Reading Coal & Iron Company, Fidelity & Deposit Company of Maryland, Provident Trust Company, Southern Pennsylvania Traction Company, Southern Surety Company, Globe Indemnity Company, American Surety Company, American Container Company, and the Insurance Company of North America.

Like Mason, but unlike Bockius, Littleton was active in bar association affairs. He was chancellor of the Philadelphia Bar Association from 1950 to 1952 and president of the Pennsylvania Bar Association from 1956 to 1958. He was also a member of the House of Delegates of the American Bar Association.

Littleton's distinguished service with bar associations gave him the opportunity to shape the policy and sound the tone of those organizations. No one who heard him speak on important bar occasions ever forgot either what he said or how he said it. In 1952, when the Philadelphia bar celebrated its 150th anniversary, the ceremonies were held at the Academy of Music, with Littleton as chancellor opening the proceedings. Capturing the cadence of the King James Version, he began:[2]

> Let us now praise famous men and our fathers that begot us. . . . men renowned for their power, giving counsel by their understanding, leaders of the people by their counsels, and by their knowledge of learning meet for the people, wise and eloquent in their instructions. . . . These were honored in their generations, and were the glory of their times.[3]

When the American Bar Association met in London in 1957, the eloquence of the barristers convened at Lincoln's Inn Hall was dazzling. But no one outdid Littleton, as one inevitable word followed another without a written note. His technique was to write down his thoughts, polish the words, and commit the finished product to memory. He did not believe in using notes. (In this he was like musicians who say the notes are not in your head if your head is in the notes.) His delivery was smooth, clear, and compelling. He had a beautiful voice, which he never raised, but which, in Wordsworth's phrase, was "of ample power to chasten and subdue." As he spoke, he evoked the image of a father, patiently correcting his children's errors and reminding them of their higher duties.

Littleton did not so much attract clients to the Firm as he attracted cases. Especially during the last several decades of his career, litigants felt their chances enhanced by engaging a lawyer of his stature and persuasiveness. In this respect, he was not unlike John G. Johnson a half century earlier.

It is doubtful if running the Firm was something Littleton ever coveted. Surely his highest and best use was not as a manager. But he was so inured to doing his duty that doing otherwise would never have occurred to him. Consequently, when Mason died in 1957, Littleton quietly assumed the Firm's leadership. He was the good shepherd looking after his flock, a latter-day Marcus Aurelius leading his troops into battle while preferring the serenity of scholarship. Littleton and the philosopher king were both fated to rule, and with stoic resolve they fulfilled their destinies.

Consistent with his modesty, Littleton kept his desk well away from the spot where the senior partner could look down the long hall and monitor traffic, as had Bockius. Littleton simply assumed every member of the Firm family would do his or her duty at all times and without oversight. When MacIntosh succeeded Littleton, the desk was moved back to its position of prominence and surveillance.

In those days before the era of the Allocation Committee, the senior partner set the compensations of all the partners at the end of each year. Bockius had done it without the slightest hesitation. It was natural for him. Mason did it, at first apologetically, then warming to his task. But Littleton never felt at ease with such a burden. Monetary distinctions among his partners were difficult for him to draw. Every year, the eagerly awaited compensation sheet would be accompanied by a cover memorandum from him protesting his inadequacy. He would say he had reached his conclusions prayerfully. The law was a higher calling, as he reminded the partners on the occasion when he first set their allocations (for 1958):

> Ours is the "obligation of the impossible." Perhaps we say we "practice" law because we never can attain that perfection for which we, nevertheless, must strive. And, in this profession, the man who thinks he has arrived, is already beginning to slip.[4]

Littleton was the quintessential team player. He once wrote: "[T]here is no limit to what can be accomplished if it makes no difference who receives the credit."[5] During the summer of 1990, a reporter for the *American Lawyer* interviewed a number of the Firm's partners. So many of them, independently of one another and a generation after the fact, quoted Littleton's words that the reporter cited them in an article about the Firm published in September 1990. Yes, Littleton's epigram has a seductive symmetry, but what does it mean?

It is fundamental to ML&B's culture that individual egos are subsumed in the Firm's collective goals. For example, the Firm encourages the use of the first-person plural and views with disapproval a lawyer who speaks of "my client" or "my case": There is no letter "I" in the word "team"—as coaches like to tell novice athletes. Some people suffer from first-person-singular syndrome. General Douglas MacArthur was an example. Following his evacuation from Corregidor to Australia in 1942, he insisted on announcing "*I* shall return," even though the War Department entreated him to say "*We* shall return." Swollen egos and the first-person singular may be appropriate for military command but not for ML&B.

The Firm's special culture is invariably noted with surprise and delight by lateral-entry partners. In a position to draw comparisons, they discover and remark how the Firm's lawyers are so extraordinarily respectful and deferential to one another. They cooperate rather than compete with each other. And they interrupt what they are doing for their own clients in order to help a colleague, perhaps one barely known to them from another of the Firm's offices. Thus, there is in the Firm a kind of familial concern rarely found elsewhere that contravenes the stereotype of lawyers as combative, unyielding, and self-centered. Over the years, only a few iconoclastic partners have rejected this culture. Eventually, they have recognized their incompatibility and gone elsewhere.

How is it that ML&B lawyers, who can be tigers in the courtroom and at the bargaining table, are so gracious in their relationships with one another? It is hard to account for this extraordinary civility. It is a blessing that seems to pass by inheritance, as it continues in remarkable measure today even though the Firm has grown large and increasingly depersonalized. No ML&B partner ever embodied this phenomenon more than Arthur Littleton.

Describing Littleton, a piece in *The Shingle* for December 1949 said:

> Arthur Littleton in a unique way tempers a brilliant mind and a tremendous energy with the dignity of a quiet simplicity. He has a wide acquaintance at the Bar. The appraisal of these men who know him well stamps him as a public spirited citizen, able administrator, sound lawyer, staunch friend, and—in the best sense—a good man.

The goodness of some people is more apparent than real: Hypocrisy masks truth. But with Littleton there was no difference. As Benjamin Quigg put it succinctly: "Arthur Littleton was as good as he seemed." Writing about goodness is difficult, as Dante presumably found when he reached the *Paradiso* after the orgy of inspiration that drove the *Inferno* and the *Purgatorio*. How can a man be described in whose presence it was virtually impossible even to say "damn"?

Richard Brown liked to recount one Littleton exposé that went about as far as possible. It pertained to the consumption of alcoholic beverages. Littleton normally eschewed them, although later in life he discovered wines and became a connoisseur. (He regarded his interest in wines as an intellectual pursuit.) But on his travels, he happened upon mai tais, which he exempted from his code of abstinence. Mrs. Littleton would buy packaged mai tai ingredients and add rum. Once when Brown was in Hawaii, he brought back for Littleton a bottle of premixed mai tais. Unlike the usual packaged ingredients, Brown's offering included the rum. Nevertheless, in accordance with her custom, Mrs. Littleton added rum, thus doubling its content. Always meticulous to acknowledge a courtesy, Littleton telephoned Brown, saying that the mai tais were the best he had ever tested. Brown noticed that Littleton, whose diction was normally impeccable, was "thick of tongue." The partners enjoyed the story, delighting in any "falling from grace however slight," as Brown put it, of so saintly a man.

In the early 1960s, while still in his sixties, Littleton's health began to fail. He was at the zenith of his professional powers and reputation. His coworkers watched sadly as this once-mighty man grew weaker. He had prayed for the Firm. Now it was the Firm's turn to pray for him. Something had to be done to ease the Firm's burdens from his shoulders. But it had to be done without offending his dignity and sense of duty.

On July 13, 1966, J. Tyson Stokes and Littleton had lunch at the Union League. Hesitantly, Stokes suggested that Littleton "move to counsel status" at the Firm. It was a difficult moment for Stokes. But Littleton jumped at the suggestion. According to Stokes, Littleton "repeated over and over again that this was the happiest day of his life and that he would now be able to sleep through the night."[6] The change was effective January 1, 1967. Thereafter, as the years passed, Littleton came to the office only infrequently, then not at all.

In March 1973, the Firm held its 100th anniversary dinner at the Bellevue Stratford Hotel. Considering his health, it was uncertain if Littleton would attend. But he was finally persuaded. Seated in a wheelchair, he said he wished to remain unobtrusive, adding that he was "embarrassed to be there in such a condition." His modesty kept him from fully appreciating the love his partners felt for him.

Littleton died nine months later on December 19, 1973. The *Bulletin* devoted an editorial to his achievements and renown.

ARTHUR LITTLETON, LAWYER

Arthur Littleton, who died yesterday was a "Philadelphia Lawyer" in the finest meaning of that term.

Mr. Littleton was a man of awesome legal learning and was a brilliant and effective advocate. But no matter how tension-filled the case, no matter how great the courtroom pressures, he was unfailingly courteous, thoughtful and considerate of others. This was his special mark.

Mr. Littleton was an unswerving servant of the law. He believed in it as devotedly as he practiced it. His service as chancellor of the Philadelphia Bar Association, as president of the Pennsylvania Bar Association and as a member of the House of Delegates of the American Bar Association gives testimony to this special dedication.

He also gave of his time and his talents to charitable and educational matters and to the Presbyterian Church. The high standard he set in his professional career and in his personal works is Arthur Littleton's legacy to his community.[7]

A memorial service for Littleton was held at the First Presbyterian Church at Twenty-first and Walnut streets. It is a large church, and it was packed to overflowing. The eulogy was delivered by Dr. Ernest Somerville, a Scottish Presbyterian minister whose eloquence was in a class with Littleton's. Somerville and Littleton had known each other well. In his eulogy, Somerville described Littleton's ascent in the hierarchy of Presbyterian laity. Still, he had steadfastly declined the highest honor, which was to be an elder. Since he was eminently qualified, Somerville pressed him repeatedly until at last the truth came out. Littleton said that to be an elder he would have to believe in the resurrection of the body. He confessed that he had never been able to do so. In this he was again like the philosopher king, who was convinced of the soul's survival but resigned to the body's dissolution. Somerville addressed Littleton's concern. After counseling by Somerville, Littleton embraced the doctrine of physical resurrection and became an elder. Others would have glossed over the problem. Littleton's unshakable integrity never permitted glossing.

Donald Scott remembers a reporter's characterization of Littleton, that he was so conservative he would have opted for chaos if he had been present at the Creation, in order to preserve the status quo. His values were traditional and exemplary; he was a singularly good man; and of all the Firm's senior partners, he was the most intellectual. But he was not a risk taker: The Saintly Man did not live dangerously. By comparison, MacIntosh enjoyed the dangerous life. He would advocate the risks that revolutionized the Firm from the 1970s forward.

■ ■ ■ ■ ■

William James MacIntosh was born in Glens Falls, New York, on May 12, 1901. He rarely referred to his father, a shadowy figure who may have suffered business reverses, possibly including bankruptcy. But he liked to tell stories about his mother and sister. During the summer of 1914, the three arrived in Philadelphia, which his mother had been told then offered the country's best public school system. Disembarking at the old Broad Street Station, they made their way to the nearby Central YMCA. There they heard about the newly opened West Philadelphia High School. So they located in West Philadelphia, where MacIntosh attended school, graduating in 1918 at the head of his class. He then received a scholarship to the Wharton School, from which he graduated in 1922 with every possible honor.

For financial reasons, MacIntosh did not attend law school immediately after college. Instead, he spent a year selling bonds for the Guaranty Company of New York (later Morgan Guaranty Trust Company). After suitable training, he was turned loose during the winter of 1922-23 to make customer calls in Philadelphia and southern New Jersey. This posed a problem, since he had neither a suit nor an overcoat befitting a bond salesman. He had just enough money for one but not both. Which should he choose, the suit or the overcoat? MacIntosh liked to recount how he opted for the overcoat. His theory was that he could keep it on while making his sales pitch and writing up an order. If a customer insisted that he take it off and stay awhile, his ragged suit underneath would make no difference, since he had already made the sale.

He entered the University of Pennsylvania Law School in the fall of 1923 on a tuition-free basis as a part-time instructor in finance at the Wharton School. There he taught 120 students in five sections from 8 to 9 in the morning and 2 to 4 in the afternoon. (Law School classes were held in the morning from 9 to 12.) During his second and third years, he also taught at Wharton's extension schools in Harrisburg, Wilkes-Barre, and Scranton, as well as its evening school in Philadelphia. Despite this hectic schedule, he served as editor-in-chief of the law review and doubled both its number of issues and circulation.

MacIntosh brought to his choice of law firm the same common sense he had applied in opting for the overcoat. He studied each major Philadelphia firm in terms of its clientele and the opportunities it afforded. He rejected firms that had recently employed those of his schoolmates who were socially well connected. He had no connections, and he was concerned that ability alone might not suffice. A faculty member referred MacIntosh to Littleton. Littleton was impressed and agreed to introduce MacIntosh to Bockius. MacIntosh recalled his interview with Bockius:

> Q: Why do you want to come to this Firm?
>
> A: Because it is the best in the city.
>
> Q: What kind of law do you want to practice?
>
> A: Whatever you need most for me to do.
>
> Q: What salary do you expect?
>
> A: The starting salary is not important. I want an opportunity with a firm that will make the greatest demands on me. In my last position, selling bonds, I was making $2,500 per year, but I understand starting salaries for lawyers in Philadelphia are lower.

That about ended the interview. Littleton advised MacIntosh later in the day that he had been hired and that he would start at $2,500, even though the prevailing salary for starting lawyers in 1926 was $1,200. As usual, Bockius knew what he was doing.

But Bockius was not always impressed by young MacIntosh. In later years, MacIntosh was sometimes called Sunny Jim because he smiled frequently and apparently had an amiable disposition. Bockius sensed some inconsistency between smiling and being a lawyer. Of MacIntosh he asked, "Why can't that young man stop grinning?"

Another of MacIntosh's favorite stories relates to his efforts during his first year as an associate to get secretarial help. The Firm's secretaries were quite conscious of their pecking order, which derived from the standings of the lawyers whom they served. It was demeaning to take dictation from a grinning kid. MacIntosh was working every waking hour and was frustrated by his inability to turn out enough work product in typed form.

One day a dictaphone salesman stopped at the office. It was then the custom for the receptionist to refer any inquiry outside her jurisdiction to the youngest lawyer in the office. Since she had never heard of a dictaphone, the inquiry seemed outside her jurisdiction. And since MacIntosh was the youngest lawyer, it was referred to him. He immediately saw the possibilities.

MacIntosh interviewed the dictaphone salesman. As he did so, word spread, and some of the secretaries congregated to speak into the machine and hear the playback of their voices. What excitement! Several days later, Bockius learned of the incident. MacIntosh was summoned. Bockius lost no time. He said: "Young man, when I want you to run this office, I will let you know." MacIntosh was in such disgrace with Bockius that Mason had to intervene. He pacified Bockius, and in due course a secretary was hired for MacIntosh.

MacIntosh had underestimated Bockius's involvement in every detail of the Firm's operation—even the purchase of office equipment. But as the years went on, MacIntosh understood and was fascinated by the way Bockius ran the Firm. Next to Bockius's office was a small cubicle housing his secretary, Rebecca Conover, and the Firm's cashier, Louis Troelsch. If the Firm needed money to pay its bills, Troelsch would tell Bockius, and Bockius would advance his own funds. Only to Bockius did Troelsch render financial reports. Nevertheless, MacIntosh managed to find out how the Firm's profits were divided. In 1920, according to MacIntosh, Bockius received 40 percent, four other senior partners each got 12½ percent and the remaining partners divided the 10-percent balance. If MacIntosh's recollection is correct, Bockius would have made $147,262 that year, worth $1,070,000 in 1993. By 1926, MacIntosh's first year with the Firm, Bockius had reduced his share to 25 percent and raised his four senior colleagues to 17 percent each, leaving 7 percent for the other partners. Bockius's distribution that year was $103,744, worth $850,000 in 1993.

MacIntosh soon concluded that "working like the devil," as he put it, was not enough. Lawyers had to have clients. So he generated some. By 1931, he was supplementing his annual salary by $10,000 to $15,000 in fees, which in those days were kept in full by the associates. He attributed his early partnership (in 1932) to the fact that he was already earning considerably more as an associate than some of the partners.

MacIntosh's expertise in finance made him an ideal assistant for Francis Bracken in the reorganizations of the 1930s, including the Baldwin Locomotive Works and Philadelphia Rapid Transit Company. MacIntosh also participated in work for the Firm's utility clients. One major case for Philadelphia Electric Company posed the question whether PE or the city would bear the expense of relocating PE's voluminous conduits under Broad Street, as the city built the Broad Street subway during the 1920s.[8]

Another utility assignment involved Philadelphia Suburban Water Company. Its company history tells the story:

> In the mid '30s, Pennsylvania's Governor George H. Earle held proceedings to ask for rate reductions by several utilities. In 1936, W. James MacIntosh, a young lawyer with Morgan, Lewis & Bockius, was called upon to represent Philadelphia Suburban Water Company. Because Geist owned other utilities in addition to Philadelphia Suburban Water Company, the outcome was especially critical. In the end, the proceedings' decision favored the Company, and MacIntosh became a member of the Philadelphia Suburban Water Company's board.[9]

MacIntosh acquired such expertise in water law and the regulation of water companies that when the American Water Works Company became a client, he managed its relationship with the Firm and was named a director of the company. Its company history recites:

> In the early summer of 1947 a man named John Ware, Jr., telephoned the prestigious Philadelphia law firm of Morgan, Lewis & Bockius and asked for an appointment to see William Clarke

Mason, the senior partner.

The John Ware who arrived to keep the appointment hardly seemed to fit the elegant surroundings of Philadelphia's leading law firm. Plain in appearance, unassuming, almost diffident in manner, he lacked the presence, the elegant tailoring, of the lawyers at Morgan, Lewis. . . .

Appearances notwithstanding, John Ware . . . was a relatively small millionaire . . . So Mr. Mason was more than willing to find out what was on John Ware's mind. After they had talked for a few minutes, Mason invited W. James MacIntosh, another partner in the firm and a specialist in public utility law, to join them.

What was on John Ware's mind became clear almost from the moment he sat down. He wanted to buy an entity called the American Water Works Company, which was then being created as a result of the breakup of a public utility empire, and was asking the help of Morgan, Lewis in accomplishing that purpose.[10]

Ware and MacIntosh realized their objective, and the Ware family came to control a "$2 billion enterprise, the American Water Works Company, which . . . [became] the largest investor-owned supplier of water in the United States."[11]

The manner in which MacIntosh combined law and business was reminiscent of Bockius. He sought people out, made them his friends, and then made them his clients. Speaking to the Firm's young lawyers, he frequently said, "All of my friends are clients, and all of my clients are friends." As a result, MacIntosh was much in demand for membership on boards of directors. In addition to Philadelphia Suburban Water Company and the American Water Works Company, he served at various times on the boards of the Fidelity Bank; Norcross, Inc.; and Better Materials Corp. He was also active in the American Bar Association's Public Utility Law Section, which he chaired in 1964-65.

Before expansionism became fashionable, MacIntosh could foresee the law firm of the future. His government service in Washington during World War II, together with his public utility specialty, led him to champion the idea that the Firm should have a Washington office. (That office opened in 1947, as described in Chapter 20.) Other aspects of his character and experience also played a role. First, there was his exuberance, which generated endless ideas. If one was rejected, he was not affronted; he had three more waiting. Then there was his vision. As a businessman, he could not accept geographical limitations on law firms. He was one of the first lawyers to assert the then revolutionary idea that law firms would ultimately travel the road of major accounting firms and have offices "everywhere," as he put it. In this respect, he was very different from Littleton, who had difficulty reconciling the intimacy of attorney-client relationships with law practices that were nationwide, not to mention international. MacIntosh would also take risks that Littleton found intolerable. Of course, they were both right: Littleton in the ideal world and MacIntosh in the real one. MacIntosh was the perfect leader for the real world at a crucial time in the Firm's history.

From modest beginnings, MacIntosh had made his way into Philadelphia's business and social circles. His beautiful home in Gladwyne featured formal gardens and manicured lawns and shrubs. He entertained constantly. He was comfortable in every kind of social setting from the Academy Ball to his poker group. That group included John T. Dorrance, Jr., Walter Annenberg, and Stuart Saunders. (Dorrance, a client who was synonymous for many years with the Campbell Soup Company, will be considered in Chapter 31.) Unlike Dorrance, Annenberg and Saunders were not clients, and therefore exceptions to MacIntosh's rule that all his friends were clients. Annenberg was the United States ambassador to the Court of St. James from 1969 to 1974. His fortune derived from the *Philadelphia Inquirer*, which he sold to Knight Newspapers, Inc., in 1970; and even more from Triangle Publications Inc., which he sold to a subsidiary of client News Corporation Limited in 1988. Saunders was CEO of the Pennsylvania Railroad and subsequently of the Penn Central Transportation Company from 1964 to 1970.

As MacIntosh worked hard, so he played hard, with extended vacations in Barbados. But for him vacations were not a time of surcease and contemplation. Instead, he surrounded himself with friends. In accordance with his maxim, they were also clients. There was much of the politician in the way he cultivated relationships.

This extended even to his adversaries. On one occasion, it became clear that a prominent party to an important transaction was untrustworthy. MacIntosh put it more strongly, saying, "He's a crook." As MacIntosh uttered those words, his secretary signaled that "the crook" was on the telephone. MacIntosh changed completely. Picking up the receiver, he gave his distinctive "Hello" (the "hel" was always four full tones higher than the "lo"), and the saccharine conversation that followed was literally a love feast. It seemed as if MacIntosh was speaking with his dearest friend. When the call ended, MacIntosh put down the receiver, changed again and repeated, "He's a crook." MacIntosh had strong personal opinions, but he never let them interfere with getting the job done.

MacIntosh was the Firm's senior partner for less than five years. His extraordinary gesture in relinquishing power will be covered in Chapter 18. Although he relinquished it, he remained on the scene to make sure the Firm was governed to his satisfaction. Occasionally, when he thought it was not, he would announce that he was "stepping back in." This produced the desired effect, and he never had to step back in.

In 1979, when MacIntosh was seventy-eight years old, he retired as a partner, but he remained counsel to the Firm until he died on May 15, 1989, at age eighty-eight. During his years as counsel, he came to the office almost every day, followed every detail of the Firm's operations, and continued to cultivate clients and manage transactions. Even at the very end, when in the hospital and only a shadow of himself, he inquired of a visiting partner about the Firm's receivables, saying he had recently reviewed them and was troubled by some of them. In this respect, he was not unlike Uncle Timothy in Galsworthy's *Forsyte Saga* who, on his deathbed at age 101, was still preoccupied with whether the family should invest in consols.[12]

One final point. Did MacIntosh know he was sometimes called Mac the Knife? Yes, he did. Did he mind? No, he liked playing the tough guy—with a smile, of course.

■ ■ ■ ■ ■

From 1957 to 1971, the Firm was blessed by having at its helm two such different lawyers as a Saintly Man and Mac the Knife. Who could possibly succeed them?

CHAPTER 18

THE OLD ORDER YIELDS

Speculation at the Colonnade ■ *Augustus in search of a Caesar* ■ *John Bracken* ■ *Submarine warfare* ■ *Judgment at Nuremberg I* ■ *Managing the Firm* ■ *Brady Bryson* ■ *The tax specialty* ■ *Financing the Third Reich* ■ *Judgment at Nuremberg II* ■ *Ernest von Starck* ■ *Captain and mentor* ■ *High-profile and unpopular cases* ■ *An overworked lawyer* ■ *MacIntosh breaks tradition* ■ *Young Turks on the march* ■ *Demise of the deity system* ■ *Improved ratios and compulsory retirement* ■ *Montesquieu and Voltaire* ■ *The wheel loses its hub*

Starting in the late 1960s, the topic of the Firm's succession was much discussed during the lunch break. In those days, some ML&B lawyers in Philadelphia ate at the Colonnade. It occupied the basement of the Bankers Securities Building at Juniper and Walnut streets just behind the Fidelity Building. The Colonnade food was good and, being a cafeteria, the service was as efficient as the customer made it. The menu was cyclical, with chicken pot pie as one of the Saturday specialties. Kenneth Souser was, as he said, "partial to chicken pot pie." So back when Saturday was a half-workday, Souser would organize junkets to the Colonnade.

Colonnade conversations were exciting. Deals and cases competed with sports and current events. And they all competed with the Firm's future. As the 1960s ended, the rumor was rife that W. James MacIntosh was not in good health. In retrospect, there was no cause for concern: He was then only sixty-nine, and he would live to be eighty-eight. But no one knows how it will turn out until it turns out, so there was concern just the same.

The veteran lawyers who constituted the Firm's Old Guard spoke about the seamless transfer of power from Morris Bockius to William Clarke Mason, from Mason to Arthur Littleton, and from Littleton to MacIntosh. Another seamless transfer would again vest all power in a senior partner, since that was how the Firm had always been governed. No one thought it would ever be otherwise. Benevolent despotism was a good thing.

Speculation centered on John Bracken, Brady Bryson, and Ernest von Starck, to name them alphabetically. In 1970, Bracken and von Starck were both fifty-eight years old, and Bryson was fifty-five. Each had a commanding personality, presence, and charisma. But they differed sharply in their strengths and weaknesses. Hence the endless speculation. ML&B lawyers knew the choice would determine the Firm's destiny. They also knew the choice lay with MacIntosh. He would adopt his successor in the same manner as the Five Good Emperors during Rome's heyday (96 A. D.-180 A. D.) had adopted theirs. Each of them, called an Augustus, designated an heir, called a Caesar. As an Augustus died, the designated Caesar took his place, and the process began again. (The system worked well until the last of the five designated his natural son.) Whom would MacIntosh as Augustus designate as Caesar?

Bracken seemed to have an inside track. He had been the managing partner since 1958. (His predecessor was J. Tyson Stokes, for whom the office of managing partner had been created in 1946.) Thus, Bracken had served as commander of the Praetorian Guard under both Littleton and MacIntosh. He occupied the office next to the senior partner's office. A special door gave him a shortcut into that office. Obvious symbolism.

■ ■ ■ ■ ■

John Paul Bracken was born in Carnegie, Pennsylvania, on June 10, 1912. He received his undergraduate degree from the University of Pittsburgh in 1934. Before going to law school, he spent several years in Washington as administrative assistant to Homer S. Cummings, then attorney general of the United States. On January 8, 1935, Bracken answered Cummings's phone. The caller's voice was unmistakable. It was FDR. Bracken told the President the attorney general had just left for the Supreme Court to argue the government's position in the so-called *Gold Clause* cases. Roosevelt was calling to wish Cummings luck.[1]

Bracken next attended the University of Pennsylvania Law School, graduating in 1939. As a favorite nephew of Francis Bracken, it was always assumed that Jack, as he was called, would join his uncle's firm. After Francis died in 1937, Jack was taken under the professional wing of William Clarke Mason, whom Jack adored. Mason urged Jack to sit for the bar examination in the District of Columbia as well as in Pennsylvania, which suggests that even then

Mason may have been considering the possibility of a Washington office.

After he was admitted to the bar, Bracken worked for the Firm early in 1940 before starting his military service, which lasted until late in 1945. During active duty in both World War II and the Korean War, he rose to the rank of lieutenant commander, before finally retiring from the navy in 1956 as a captain. He served with the Pacific Fleet on the USS *Marblehead* (1941-42); in the Caribbean on antisubmarine and convoy operations (1942-44); as executive officer of the USS *Bailey*, and finally as commanding officer of the USS *Overton* on underwater demolition and antisubmarine operations in the Philippines, at Iwo Jima and Okinawa (1944-45).[2]

Both Bracken and Bryson took part in the most celebrated judicial proceedings of the century: the war crimes trials of twenty-four German leaders held in Nuremberg in 1945-46. Bracken's role involved Karl Doenitz. Doenitz had been grand admiral of the German navy. After Hitler's suicide on April 30, 1945, Doenitz was designated by Hitler's will as his successor to head the German state. It was Doenitz who surrendered Germany to the Allies on May 7, 1945.

Most of the Nuremberg defendants were opportunists, psychopaths, sadists, and fanatics. But among them were some career military officers doing their duty, as they saw it, and serving their country. Doenitz was such a person. He had spent his life in the German navy, where his special genius was the U-boat. He absolutely worshiped Hitler and took no notice of the ongoing genocide (which he later blamed on Himmler) or of Hitler's military blunders. Those blunders generally resulted from Hitler's constant meddling with army and air force strategies—something he never did with his navy. Doenitz had a free hand.

The chief American prosecutor at Nuremberg was United States Supreme Court Justice Robert Jackson, who designated Bracken to a special post. His orders named him "liaison officer with the United States Navy and with the [British] Admiralty [to] have exclusive charge of administrative matters of a naval nature and be generally in charge of . . . the interrogation of witnesses in naval custody." The investigation went slowly. The Germans resisted on grounds that their alleged crimes had been invented by the Allies ex post facto.

Doenitz further objected to being interrogated by army officers. He insisted that he would deal only with a naval officer familiar with submarine warfare. He knew of Bracken from a prior interrogation, and it was to Bracken that he made his statement. He did so in English, after which Bracken conducted the interrogation.

One of the charges against Doenitz was that he had given orders instructing German U-boats not to rescue survivors after submarine attacks. Fleet Admiral Chester Nimitz, commander of the American naval forces in the Pacific, had given similar orders. Bracken had served under Nimitz.[3] Doenitz appealed to Bracken as a naval officer. Surely Bracken understood the difficulties that faced a submarine attempting rescue operations and its vulnerability to attack after a torpedoing. Doenitz cited the *Laconia* affair. It gave rise to the infamous *Laconia* order, in which Doenitz had declared that "rescue runs counter to the elementary demands of warfare for the destruction of enemy ships and crews."[4]

Bracken's lengthy interrogation of Doenitz took place before an assemblage of prosecutors, as well as General William Donovan, chief of the United States Office of Strategic Services. Bracken believes it was the first time a Nuremberg defendant gave chapter and verse to explain his conduct. Impressed by Doenitz's explanation, Bracken recommended to Donovan and Jackson that the submarine allegations against Doenitz be dropped. According to Bracken, they agreed but said the Soviets would never permit any allegations against Doenitz to be dropped, since he had prolonged the war in order to allow as many German forces as possible to escape to the West and avoid capture by the Soviets.[5]

At the trial, the Doenitz plea of *tu quoque* was accepted and the tribunal found him not guilty of the submarine allegations. Bracken's advice to Donovan and Jackson had been correct. But Doenitz was found guilty of other war crimes. He was sentenced to ten years' imprisonment at Spandau, his dedication to Hitler and the Third Reich unabated. While in prison, Doenitz received dozens of letters from senior American naval officers supporting his conduct in the war and deploring the verdict. Some said they had done exactly what he had done.[6]

Bracken had scarcely returned to Philadelphia when he was asked by Mason and MacIntosh to take part in establishing the Firm's Washington office in 1947. He remained in Washington until August 1950, when he was recalled to active duty with the navy during the Korean conflict. He finally returned to Philadelphia in 1953, became a partner in 1955, served as managing partner from 1958 to 1972, and retired in 1977.

In addition to administering the Firm, Bracken found time for a wide variety of other activities. He served as president of the American Bar Endowment in 1973-74, and as chairman of the House of Delegates and a member of the Board of Governors of the American Bar Association in 1974-76. Reflecting his interests abroad, he served as secretary general of the International Bar Association (1976-80). He was also a director of the Philadelphia National Bank (1969-82), president of the Greater Philadelphia Chamber of Commerce (1968-70), and recipient in 1972 of the William Penn Award for Distinguished Professional and Civic Leadership Given to the Nation and Greater Philadelphia.

By his presence, Bracken dominated every business and social situation. Six feet four inches tall and with prematurely white hair, he was often called "the Admiral" by lawyers at the Firm. Like his mentor, William Clarke Mason, Bracken looked the part he played.

■ ■ ■ ■ ■

Brady Oliver Bryson was born in Overton, Nebraska, on March 14, 1915. He received his undergraduate degree from Western Maryland College in 1935 and his law degree from Columbia University in 1938. He was an outstanding student at Columbia, served on its law review, and was at various times a Kent and Stone scholar.

Between 1938 and 1941, Bryson practiced in Washington with a small firm handling matters before administrative agencies, including the Internal Revenue Service (then the Bureau of Internal Revenue). When ML&B decided to look for a tax lawyer, Frederick Knight spoke with a Columbia Law School professor who recommended Bryson. Bryson arrived at the Firm as an associate in 1941, just before its tax practice exploded with the passage of the Revenue Act of 1942 and the wartime Excess Profits Tax Act. He was then the Firm's only full-time tax lawyer.[7]

In 1943, Bryson grew tired of practicing tax law alone and rejoined his former firm. By then, it had opened an office in New York, and he went back as a partner. Nevertheless, his relationship with ML&B continued, and for some months he was paid a retainer to do the Firm's tax work.

Bryson volunteered for the navy in 1944. He was sent to the University of Colorado to study Russian and then to Washington to serve in a unit that specialized in breaking Russian-language codes used for naval intelligence. From there he was sent to Nuremberg as a liaison officer (he was a lieutenant j. g.) between the American and

Soviet legal staffs.

Bryson tried to befriend the Soviets and perform his duties. But they isolated themselves and would not fraternize: The Cold War had already begun. So he joined Chief Prosecutor Jackson's group and was designated to handle the Allies' case against Hjalmar Schacht. Telford Taylor, who assisted and succeeded Jackson at Nuremberg, "was surprised that [Jackson] did not handle the presentation, . . . [since he] had his heart set on [Schacht's] conviction. Nothing was lost, however, as Bryson made a poised and well-organized presentation."[8]

At thirty, Bryson may have been the youngest American officer responsible for a case against any of the twenty-four Nuremberg defendants. The *New York Times* took note of Bryson's role:

> In summing up the case against Schacht, Lieutenant Bryson declared it proved that Schacht's work had been indispensable to Adolf Hitler's rise to power and the rearmament of Germany: that the banker had known that Hitler planned an aggressive war and approved, and that he had withdrawn from the conspiracy because of a jurisdictional row with Hermann Goering and not because of any disagreement with Hitler's policy.[9]

Horace Greeley Hjalmar Schacht[10] had studied medicine, philology, political science, and economics. While still in his thirties, he had become a top official of Dresdner Bank. He had the highest IQ of any Nuremberg defendant and was a financial wizard. He was mainly responsible in the 1920s for solving the problem of German hyperinflation, the beginnings of which had been experienced in Berlin by Bockius, Stotesbury, and Vauclain, as recounted in Chapter 11.

Schacht was president of the Reichsbank from 1923 to 1930 and was reappointed by Hitler to serve again from 1933 to 1939. In the role of international banker, he was well known in London, New York, and Washington, where he visited Roosevelt, Sumner Wells, and Cordell Hull. He spoke fluent English, which he used during the early 1930s to assure American audiences that Hitler was not a dictator and that the rights of Jews would be respected. He was not a member of the Nazi party: Hitler considered him more valuable outside the party.

As a conservative economist, Schacht worked closely with Hitler on the premise that only Hitler could end German anarchy and rebuild the nation's economy. He backed Hitler's program of public works and *limited* rearmament. But he opposed *excessive* rearmament, because it would lead to war, and war was uneconomical! Quarreling incessantly with Goering, Schacht was dismissed by Hitler in 1939 when he refused further credit to the government, which he said was bankrupt. He continued as an irritant to the Nazis; and on July 21, 1944, the day after the attempt on Hitler's life, he was rounded up by the SS and sent to a concentration camp. He remained there until the Americans took him into custody.

Bryson reported that Schacht disdained earphones at the Nuremberg trials and followed the proceedings in English. Schacht also disdained the one-hour nightmare to which the defendants were subjected when motion pictures of the ghastly concentration camps were shown in the courtroom. Most of the defendants followed the gruesome scenes with rapt attention, craning their necks to get a better view. Schacht turned his back and stared into space.

Schacht was one of three Nuremberg defendants who were acquitted. But the Soviet judge dissented, producing what Bryson considered a "better-written opinion than the others."[11] Justice Jackson, Bryson's boss, commented: "Our argument for . . . [his] conviction, which seemed so convincing to all of us prosecutors, seems not to have made a similar impression on the tribunal."[12]

Bryson returned to law practice in New York, forming a two-lawyer firm—later expanded as Chapman, Bryson, Walsh & O'Connell, with which he spent six years until 1954. That year, Frederick Knight came calling again, saying that Mason wanted Bryson back, not only to enhance the Firm's tax practice but also to play a role in developing the Philadelphia-Washington axis. Bryson returned to the Firm in 1955 as a partner.

After rejoining ML&B, one of Bryson's first victories in a major tax case was for long-time client UGI. The case had been lost in the Tax Court, and the client felt an appeal would be futile. Bryson urged an appeal and persuaded the Firm to take the matter on a contingent basis—then an innovative idea for ML&B, especially in the tax field. Bryson rethought the case, recharacterized a capital loss as an ordinary loss, and won in the Court of Appeals for the Third Circuit. The client was delighted, and the Firm received an unusually substantial fee.[13]

The UGI case typifies what Bryson could do when he wanted to. It is doubtful if any Firm partner ever had a more penetrating intellect. Some years ago, while traveling abroad, the author met a law school classmate of Bryson's who commented, "Brady could have done anything." Hearing the story, Bryson amended the comment, "I could have done anything I wanted to do." Bryson did not want to do everything. He was even ambivalent about tax law. He was at his best with blinding insights. He would attend a meeting, say nothing for half an hour, and finally, in tones barely audible and a bit reedy, he would brilliantly summarize the problem and outline a stunning solution that had occurred to no one. To implement Bryson's solution, all hands would then descend to the boiler room, except Bryson who would ascend to the bridge. There he would await another challenge befitting his extraordinary analytical skills.

Bryson retired in 1980 to his 100-acre farm in Westminster, Maryland. Since his retirement, he has ridden to the hounds, read and traveled widely, opened a wine and antique shop, and written extensively on wines and current events.

Bryson always did exactly what he wanted to do. And he did it superbly. Drudge work occupies so many in the practice of law. It was not for him.

■ ■ ■ ■ ■

Such distinctions were not drawn by Ernest Frederick Rudolph von Starck, who was a practicing lawyer in the fullest sense. He was committed, tireless, and uncomplaining. In the courtroom he was especially impressive, with an avuncular voice that resounded an octave below anyone else's.

Von Starck was born on February 5, 1912, in Princeton, New Jersey. He attended the Lawrenceville School and then Princeton University, from which he graduated in 1934. He served on the law review at the University of Pennsylvania Law School, receiving his LL.B. in 1937. He became an associate at ML&B in 1938 and was made a partner in 1948.

Von Starck spent more than three years in the navy, rose to the rank of lieutenant and commanded his own ship. It was Landing Ship Tank (LST) No. 1085—327 feet long and 27 feet wide with a 200-ton displacement. The vessel was built by the American Bridge Shipyard in Pittsburgh, Pennsylvania, where von Starck and his crew took possession of it. They made their way via the Ohio and Mississippi rivers to the Gulf of Mexico, down through the Panama Canal, and then across the Pacific on a tour of duty that included the Marshall Islands, Guam, Saipan, and Okinawa, as well as shuttling troops from Iwo Jima to Yokohama in support of MacArthur's occupation of Japan.

Von Starck's crew consisted of 9 officers and 120 enlisted men. One of the officers was George J. Miller, who has provided a moving account of his service under Captain von Starck. Von Starck was an enormous influence on Miller—to such a degree that Miller gave up a career in engineering, graduated from Penn Law School in 1951, and went on to form his own firm in Pittsburgh. Let Miller tell the story:

> We had no encounters with the enemy, but we had plenty with the elements. As that little ship crossed the Pacific, the storms were often wild. We would drop like a matchstick from the crest of one wave to the valley between.
>
> Ernie led us by example. He did not have to order us around. We knew how to behave just by watching him. He was a father figure who brought out the best in all of us. We held him in awe and wanted to be worthy of him.
>
> He was every inch the captain—in demeanor and bearing, in his competence and in the way he exercised command. We knew that no matter what the hazards of war, he would get us through.
>
> No man has ever influenced me so totally as Ernie did. Out of profound respect and admiration, I issue an eternal salute to my captain, mentor and friend.[14]

After von Starck returned to the Firm, he plunged into utility work under MacIntosh. Over the years, he also litigated cases in many other fields of law: corporate governance, suretyship, municipal contracts, trusts, admiralty, patent infringement, securities regulation, railroad mergers, and trade regulation.

During the late 1960s and early 1970s, von Starck spent much of his time in major rate cases for the Philadelphia Electric Company. These involved hundreds of millions of dollars. They were driven by population growth and increased power consumption in the Philadelphia area, as well as by inflation and the advent of nuclear energy. They were not popular cases. In allowing rate increases, regulatory agencies were dealing blows to consumers. Some consumers fought back by participating in the proceedings and organizing demonstrations. The cases took years to develop, present, and appeal. They involved engineering, accounting, demographics, economic forecasting, and politics. They also claimed much media attention. Von Starck handled them with the same demeanor and competence he applied, according to Miller, in crossing the Pacific.

Von Starck had more than his share of high-profile and disagreeable cases, including the PTC and Girard College cases. He was an overworked lawyer, and he sometimes showed signs of strain. Unlike Bryson who did what he wanted to do, von Starck did what had to be done. He was stoic, dedicated, deliberate, and totally prepared, as well as straightforward in his dealings.

Von Starck had his lighter side. He loved the outdoors and was an avid hunter and fisherman. He also fancied foreign sports cars at a time when they were rare in the United States. He progressed from an MG, through an Aston Martin (with a Ford V-8 engine) to a Maserati. No one for miles around had such a toy.

After an extended illness, von Starck died on May 19, 1978. Just as he influenced George Miller, so he set an example for many lawyers in the Firm.

■ ■ ■ ■ ■

Now back to the speculations that raged at the Colonnade and elsewhere. Would MacIntosh, in his role as Roman emperor, adopt Bracken, Bryson, or von Starck as his successor? Actually, those who speculated were theorizing in vain. For despite their qualifications, none of the three was anointed, and MacIntosh became the last senior partner to rule the Firm as his four predecessors had done during its first century.

What explanation did MacIntosh give for breaking tradition? At the time, he spoke of his concern that the Firm had grown too large to be run by a single senior partner. (There were then 125 lawyers in Philadelphia, Washington, and Harrisburg.) Later, he would lament that the best qualities of the three heirs-apparent were not combined in one: Bracken's administrative ability, Bryson's extraordinary mind, and von Starck's fierce commitment to the practice. But even that hypothetical combination might not have satisfied MacIntosh. He had been raised in the rainmaking tradition of Bockius. None of the three was a substantial rainmaker, much less a rainmaker in that tradition.

But if the senior partner system were abandoned, what would take its place? On April 21, 1971, MacIntosh appointed a Management Review Committee with a broad mandate: It was to analyze the Firm's structures, objectives, and operations. The main committee was divided into three subcommittees: management and administration, allocation of profits, and long range planning.

The subcommittee on management and administration had some small precedent on which to build: An executive committee of sorts had existed at the Firm since 1949. But its function was advisory and its purview limited. It had been formed by Mason to consider problems relating to personnel, office arrangements, and administrative operations. Its original members were Mason, Arthur Littleton, John Russell, W. James MacIntosh, Thomas Ringe, and J. Tyson Stokes. The Firm's archives include minutes of their meetings. It was coffee-klatch conversation: Who was going on vacation; what should be the color of the new carpet; Mason's forthcoming garden party; which associates were doing well enough to warrant raising their annual compensations from $5,500 to $6,000; and should the Firm provide oversized briefcases for transporting voluminous documents to court. Apparently, the old executive committee kept a discreet distance from questions of policy. These were the domain of the senior partner.

The second subcommittee of the newly appointed Management Review Committee would deal with the allocation of profits. Although there was some small precedent for an executive committee, there was none whatever for an allocation committee or any other vehicle for melon cutting. Every year, the senior partner had simply produced the crucial list allocating the Firm's profits among its partners. The *American Lawyer* (September 1990) quoted the terse comment of a former Firm partner: "If MacIntosh said you made a thousand bucks, you made a thousand bucks." No longer would this be the case. But who would now set the allocations, and what criteria would be applied? The planners were in uncharted waters.

The third subcommittee, on long range planning, was asked to look ahead ten or fifteen years and speculate about the world in general and law practice in particular. That subcommittee could fantasize extravagantly: No one would ever mistake its musings for sacred canon. Its report, dated December 15, 1971, prophesied a service economy (accurate), more women in the workplace (accurate), automation (accurate), a twenty-five hour workweek by 1985 (the trend went the other way), a $3-trillion gross national product by the year 2000 (actually achieved in 1981), less emphasis on profits and more on the betterment of society (both would be emphasized), and 286 lawyers at the Firm by 1985 (the actual number was 425). It also forecast that labor, environmental, and international law would become increasingly busy areas of practice in future years. Even the most pedestrian soothsayers are right some of the time.

Significantly, there was some precedent for the 1971 long range planning subcommittee. Nine years earlier, on September 28, 1962, a report had been delivered to the senior partner by Richard Brown,

Thomas Lefevre, Robert Young, and Howard Taylor. Somehow these Young Turks had gotten leave to critique the Firm's professional personnel policies. In doing so, they noted the then prevailing ratio of associates to partners. ML&B had forty-three partners and only thirty-three associates in 1961. Hamlet would have dubbed such a ratio "flat and unprofitable." Not only were too many associates becoming partners, but also too many partners were staying on indefinitely in the absence of any policy requiring that they retire. Whatever its strengths, the Firm was on a financial plateau.

The Young Turks then proceeded with the subtlety of a battering ram. Their 1962 report recommended "immediate adoption of policies . . . including more selective admissions to partnership, improved procedures for evaluation of associates and a retirement plan for professional personnel." How was their report received? According to Lefevre, it "went over like a lead balloon at a levitation contest." It blatantly questioned some hallowed traditions. One was the apprentice system whereby competent associates who had committed no heinous crimes and had served their terms became partners. Another was that partners could continue to practice and be well paid as long as they could drag themselves to the office.

The 1962 report of the Young Turks was understandably considered heretical by their elders. But only two years later, one of their ideas—that the Firm should have a retirement policy—was accepted, albeit without attribution to them. An HR-10 Plan was installed in 1964. Under it, as the tax law then stood, partners could make deductible contributions of $2,500 each year to fund their retirements. Considering that modest sum, no partner could afford to retire on an HR-10 account. Something more was required.

The solution was the Partners Unfunded Pension Plan (PUPP), also adopted in 1964. The PUPP supplemented the HR-10 benefits and provided for normal retirement at age sixty-five. Actually, the retirement provision was then more theoretical than real, since partners who wished to remain active could do so indefinitely by mutual consent from year to year. It was not until 1973 that the PUPP was amended to provide for a maximum of five annual extensions after age sixty-five, followed by mandatory retirement at age seventy. Even then, some partners were grandfathered and continued with the Firm beyond age seventy. MacIntosh was among them.

The Firm's lawyers now fully accept the idea that older partners should retire on adequate pensions to make way for fresh blood. But the issue was still novel and controversial during the 1960s. By their nature, lawyers are not a retiring lot; and during ML&B's first century, partners generally left the partnership only as and when they desired. It was a wrenching experience for the Firm's older partners to realize that someday they would no longer come to the office.

Although the 1962 report was ahead of its time, the ideas it espoused acquired respectability during the following decade. So much so that when MacIntosh appointed the Management Review Committee in 1971, he did not name the Old Guard to head its subcommittees. Instead, he reached down to the Young Turks for the innovations that would dramatically change the Firm's governance during its second century. Thus, he named Lefevre to head the subcommittee on management and administration and Young to head the subcommittee on the allocation of profits. To head the long range planning subcommittee, he named Brown—an exceptional litigator who came to the Firm in 1948, became a partner in 1956, and retired in 1988.

While Brown's subcommittee took its time forecasting the future, Lefevre and Young were quick to convene their subcommittees and report back to the committee as a whole. That committee endorsed the subcommittees' recommendations, which then went to MacIntosh. Losing no time, MacIntosh called a meeting of the entire partnership for Saturday, September 25, 1971, to receive and adopt the proposals of the subcommittees on management and the allocation of profits. The proposals were adopted, although some partners recall being stunned by the pace of events, not to mention the changes themselves.

Never a man of half measures, MacIntosh proceeded at full throttle. It had originally been contemplated that the new structure would become effective on January 1, 1972. But MacIntosh did not wait. He appointed a committee that made nominations to the Executive and Allocation committees. The nominees were elected, and the new Executive Committee held its first meeting on October 19, 1971. It was even agreed that the nascent Allocation Committee would divide the Firm's profits for the fiscal year ended September 30, 1971, thus relieving MacIntosh of the task.

The constitutional convention was clearly a watershed event in the Firm's history, and the proposals adopted there were revolutionary. In lieu of the senior partner system (Lefevre called it the "deity system"), a six-lawyer Executive Committee would run the Firm, and a three-lawyer Allocation Committee would divide its profits. Entrenchment would be avoided by a provision that committee members could not succeed themselves for one year after serving a three-year term, although they could move from one committee to the other and back again without a break. Henceforth, there would be continuity without perpetuity.

Another striking feature of the new system was its separation of the management and allocation functions, thus discouraging service on the Executive Committee as a vehicle for financial self-aggrandizement. But how could that problem be avoided with respect to the Allocation Committee? Would partners vie for service on that committee to reward themselves? The solution would have charmed Montesquieu: The three allocators would set the allocations of all partners, including members of the Executive Committee, but would not set their own allocations; these would be set by the Executive Committee.

Finally, a new body would be created called the Senior Council, comprising the top one-third of the partners as measured by their allocations. It would elect the Executive and Allocation committees, based on nominations received from all the partners. Thus, democracy was tempered by plutocracy and vice versa.

The Firm's constitution is now regarded as a given. But it was a close question in 1971. Was the Management Review Committee engaged in an academic exercise? Such were the senior partner's powers that he might have received the proposals only to trash them. But MacIntosh embraced them, and by that embrace, they were adopted.

So far during the Firm's second century, the 1971 constitution as amended has served it well. It was an extraordinary document for its time. Even more than twenty years later, it is a revelation to the managements of other law firms as they discover and understand its provisions. Its checks and balances paralleled in microcosm the work of the Founding Fathers during that stifling summer in Philadelphia some 184 years earlier. And like their product, it was specific enough to be workable yet general enough to be durable.

An advantage of monarchy, Voltaire observed, is that a reformer need convince only one person. After 1971, that convenience was lost to the Firm. When MacIntosh relinquished the senior partner's traditional powers, the person behind Bockius's old desk looking down the long hall ceased to be the centerpiece of it all. No longer could a lawyer simply stop at that desk and deliver an important message, knowing that by doing so, everyone had been told who needed telling. The wheel had lost its hub.

CHAPTER 19

THE QUADRIVIRI

The Old Guard and the Young Turks ▪ The Gang of Four ▪ Thomas Lefevre ▪ Robert Young ▪ Park Dilks ▪ William Curtin ▪ They divide areas of governance ▪ They appear to agree ▪ Differences in their personalities ▪ Their management techniques ▪ The Firm expands five-fold between 1971 and 1988 ▪ National and international practice ▪ Exporting the Firm's culture

A perfect institutional structure is useless unless it is implemented effectively. So W. James MacIntosh made certain the right mix of partners constituted the newly formed Executive and Allocation committees. At first, there were three representatives of the Old Guard. John Bracken spent two years on the Executive Committee (chairing it in 1973), then three years on the Allocation Committee. Ernest von Starck spent a total of four years on the Executive Committee (chairing it in 1974), and Brady Bryson spent three years on the Allocation Committee. After that, the three ceased to play roles in the Firm's management.

As to new blood, MacIntosh arranged for Thomas Lefevre to go on the first Executive Committee and for Robert Young to go on the first Allocation Committee—entirely fitting, since they had been the architects of their respective committees. In addition, Richard Brown, who chaired the Long Range Planning Subcommittee, and Park Dilks, who had worked with Brown on that subcommittee's report, were both named to the first Executive Committee. The following year, William Curtin was also named to that committee.

It is significant that Lefevre was elected chairman of the first Executive Committee in 1971, and that Dilks was elected chairman in 1975, Young in 1976, and Curtin in 1977. During only five of the first eighteen years of that committee's existence was it chaired by someone other than Lefevre, Young, Dilks, and Curtin.[1] And during that entire period, the four served without a break on either the Executive Committee or the Allocation Committee, until Lefevre retired in 1979 (to head UGI), and Young and Dilks stepped down from the Firm's management in 1988.

The *American Lawyer* put it bluntly:

> In 1971 MacIntosh turned the Firm over to a Gang of Four—Curtin in Washington and three Philadelphia partners: utilities lawyer Robert Young, corporate and international lawyer Park Dilks, Jr., and tax specialist Thomas Lefevre—who proceeded to implement his vision of expansion.[2]

ML&B's new structure surely did not contemplate a Gang of Four, or any kind of gang for that matter. Some partners commented that the four were running the Firm from whatever positions they happened to occupy, either on the Executive Committee or the Allocation Committee—a kind of shadow government, except that it was in office even when out. Perhaps the Firm had gone from one benevolent despot to four. Still, the 1970s and 1980s were heady times for ML&B in terms of prominence and prosperity. Success mutes criticism.

The title used by the *American Lawyer*, a Gang of Four, suggests heavy-handedness. The title is misplaced. The four knew that their powers were more de facto than de jure, and that they could not succeed by compulsion but only by persuasion. So for present purposes, a description will be used that is neutral, without over-tones: Quadriviri—four men—will serve.

In a profession run historically by elder statesmen, one attribute of the Quadriviri was their relative youth. As 1971 ended, Lefevre was fifty-three; Young, fifty; Dilks, forty-three; and Curtin, forty. They will be discussed in that order.

■ ■ ■ ■ ■

Thomas Vernon Lefevre was born in Dallas, Texas, on December 5, 1918. His mother, whom he describes as "heroic, tireless and selfless," was raised on a Kansas farm. His father, a restless and rebellious young man, had separated himself from his wealthy French antecedents and emigrated to the United States. His restlessness persisted, and he also separated himself from Lefevre's mother. Lefevre was then six years old and had three older siblings. The stranded family lived in Saint Petersburg, Florida.

During the Depression, Lefevre recalls "earning spending money by an array of poor-boy jobs, such as peddling mangoes and avocados from a wagon, selling the *Saturday Evening Post*, working as an early-morning janitor and clerking in grocery stores." None of these activities, he says, interfered with a happy childhood. He was an excellent student, graduating from high school at sixteen. While continuing his many jobs, he received his B.A. from the University of Florida in 1939 and his law degree from the same university in 1942. He was first in his class.

Lefevre enlisted in the marine corps, received a commission, and participated in landings at Kwajalein, Saipan, Tinian, and Iwo Jima. He was promoted to captain and later retired as a major. He saw more bloody combat than any other Firm partner. But despite heavy casualties all around him, he emerged without injury in October 1945.

To "absorb a little Eastern culture," as he put it, and to further his objective of becoming a Wall Street lawyer, he attended Harvard Law School and received an LL.M. degree in October 1946. With his law school and marine credentials, he went to work for Sullivan & Cromwell. Given a choice between tax law and litigation, he chose litigation, thinking that every young lawyer should know how to try a case. He was assigned only one case, and it was not tried until five years after he left the firm. Discovery, that bottomless pit of the trial lawyer's trade, did not even commence while he was still there. Consequently, he was bored at Sullivan & Cromwell and "disillusioned about the lifestyle of Wall Street lawyers." He left the firm after two years.

In order to pursue a tax career, Lefevre took a job with the Internal Revenue Service, moved to Detroit, and spent two years actually trying tax cases. There, he got the litigation experience he wanted. He also got tax experience. But he had inherited something of his father's restlessness. Government service was not the answer.

Leaving the government, Lefevre joined—initially as an associate and shortly as a partner—a firm created in Washington by Claude Pepper. Pepper had just been defeated as a United States senator from Florida. He was a skillful politician and a superb orator. But he was not, according to Lefevre, much of a businessman. He attracted a variety of cases from people who wanted their problems solved at a political level. Moreover, the only tax matters that arrived were fraud cases. Pepper's firm dissolved after two years, and Lefevre moved again, this time becoming an associate in the Washington office of Paul, Weiss, Rifkind, Wharton & Garrison. There, he devoted himself full time to tax practice.

After only a year or so, Lefevre made another change when he became an associate in the Washington office of Chapman, Bryson, Walsh & O'Connell, where he formed his working relationship with Bryson. The firm attracted a desirable clientele, but its senior partner's work habits were eccentric, according to Lefevre. Bryson was uneasy about the firm's future. Shortly before Bryson announced his departure from the firm and his return to ML&B, he invited Lefevre for a Sunday visit to his farm in Westminster, Maryland. Lefevre recalls how he and Bryson went out in a field and sat on a log as Bryson proposed that Lefevre follow Bryson by leaving their firm to join ML&B. For Bryson it would be a homecoming. For Lefevre it would be another move—this time, he hoped, to a more stable environment.

Lefevre decided to explore Philadelphia. As he put it, he "found the Bellevue lobby full of scaffolding, the downtown at night positively spooky, and Germantown Avenue teeth-rattling." Nevertheless, he joined Bryson in accepting the Firm's offer and came to work as an associate in 1955, followed by a partnership in 1956.

The tax law held no terrors for Lefevre's steel-trap mind. Moreover, with his gift for clarification, he could make its intricacies intelligible to others. So when Bryson adopted a personal agenda that rendered him less accessible to his partners and clients, Lefevre became the Firm's "show" tax lawyer. He and tax partner Alfred McDowell attracted bright young associates and did tax work for many of the Firm's mainstay clients: Scott Paper Company; the Bulletin Company; Philadelphia National Bank; American Stores (Acme Markets); Strawbridge & Clothier; Philadelphia Suburban Corporation; Alan Wood Steel Company; International Utilities; and Standard Oil of New Jersey (later Exxon).

Lefevre also helped develop a strain of tax law that would have significant consequences for the Firm. It is called leveraged leasing. Leveraged-lease transactions are viewed by practitioners of the art with an almost religious ecstasy. Such transactions frequently involve big-ticket items, including aircraft, ships, and electric generating plants. Through limited recourse borrowing, a lessor can minimize its outlay and risk, while maximizing its tax benefits. The lessor passes on some of those tax benefits to its lessee, who thereby obtains off-balance-sheet financing at favorable rates. Everyone benefits, except the taxing authorities, from the Archimedean principle of leverage.

In the 1960s, the Firm was approached by some financing specialists who were pioneers in the leveraged-leasing field. They foresaw the possibilities of syndicating limited-partnership interests in the leased property. Benefiting from Lefevre's counsel, the pioneers prospered. They also employed apprentices who learned the trade and spun off to create similar enterprises. The former apprentices, now entrepreneurs in their own right, often engaged the Firm. Thus, clients multiplied along with transactions. In no time, leveraged leasing became an ML&B specialty and one reason for the creation of the Firm's New York office in 1972, as detailed in Chapter 21.

Immediately after Lefevre arrived at the Firm in 1955, he and Young became allies. They were soon named to the newly formed Professional Personnel Committee with jurisdiction over recruiting and training associates. It had no mandate to deal with partnership admissions or retirements. Nevertheless, Lefevre and Young united to study both questions, thereby producing the notorious 1962 "lead balloon" report. For their audacity, they were dismissed from the Professional Personnel Committee, control of which was revested in the safe hands of J. Tyson Stokes. But as a consequence of their recommendations, they were later called upon to play major roles in the Firm's 1971 reorganization.

Lefevre served on the Executive Committee from 1971 through 1974 and again from 1977 through 1979, chairing it in 1971-72 and 1978. During 1975 and 1976, he served on the Allocation Committee. Thus, he helped shape the manner in which both committees functioned in their early years.

Having accomplished his objectives at the Firm by late 1979, Lefevre answered the siren's song of business and took early retirement to become president of Firm client UGI. A restless, incisive and dominating man.

■ ■ ■ ■ ■

Robert Hugh Young was equally dominating, perhaps less incisive, and certainly not as restless. Unlike Lefevre, Young spent his entire professional career at the Firm. But for the retirement policy which he helped shape, he could have remained at the Firm indefinitely. He would have been encouraged by his partners to do so, for no partner since MacIntosh made the Firm so completely his life.

Young was born in Pittsburgh, Pennsylvania, on March 31, 1921. His mother was a school teacher and his father a credit manager for Carnegie Steel, a United States Steel subsidiary. In 1927, the family moved to Bethlehem, Pennsylvania, where Young's father took a similar job with Bethlehem Steel Company. In those days, Bethlehem

Steel took good care of its own, even during the Depression, and Young learned to swim and play golf and tennis at the local country club. He attended public schools in Bethlehem before spending his last two years of secondary school at Andover. The transition was a challenge. Andover was demanding; public school was not. But Young always responded superbly to challenges. He did well at Andover, except in foreign language studies for which he professed "a congenital deficiency."

Young played varsity soccer at Andover and later made the freshman team at Princeton. During a Princeton/Haverford game in the fall of 1938, he tore ligaments in his left knee. He would be plagued all his life by the consequences of that injury.

At Princeton, he took most of his studies in the School of Public and International Affairs. A fellow student was George P. Shultz.[3] Young and Shultz played squash and tennis together. On the eve of World War II, they debated with classmates whether the United States should enter the war. Young and Shultz were among the hawks. Others were doves, feeling that the country's interests were better served by continued isolation. Then came Pearl Harbor.

Shultz joined the marines, was commissioned, and fought at Okinawa. Young's knee problem kept him from getting a commission. After graduating from Princeton in June 1942, he went immediately to Harvard Law School, then functioning on a year-round basis. He completed two semesters before entering the service.

Young recalls that during the war Harvard Law School resembled a ghost town. There were only about twenty students to a class. The younger professors had gone off to do their patriotic duty, leaving the teaching to legends like Roscoe Pound, Warren Seavey, Ralph Morgan, and Edward Henry "Bull" Warren. According to Young, "the scare tactics Warren had used on generations of regular students did not work on small classes of draft bait." So Warren simply declared that Young and his classmates were "dregs" and stalked out of the classroom. Such picturesque stories have a luster in retrospect they probably lacked at the time.

Young finally did enter the service in February 1943 as a private in the army. He trained in army finance at Fort Harrison and the Army Fiscal Policy School at Duke University. Next, he went to Ordnance Officers Training School at Aberdeen, Maryland, from which he graduated as a second lieutenant. He was then sent to the army's Special Education and Information School in Lexington,

Virginia, after which he was assigned to an engineering regiment as an information officer and later as regimental adjutant. The regiment was sent to England to build POW camps for Germans. But the war in Europe ended in May 1945, so Young's unit was immediately transshipped to Clark Air Force Base in the Philippines. The voyage from Europe through the Panama Canal and across the Pacific Ocean lasted forty-eight days. Then the war in the Pacific ended in August 1945, so the regiment was ordered to Japan to build landing strips for B-29s. Young finally had enough points to be mustered out as a captain in June 1946.

Young returned to Harvard Law School and graduated in January 1948. He interviewed at a number of Philadelphia firms but found most of them interested in the sons of their partners or of senior officials of their major clients. Young was neither. He received an offer from ML&B on the understanding that he would do public utility work, which was apparently not regarded as an inducement. In April 1948, he became an ML&B associate at an annual salary of $3,300, the highest rate then being paid in Philadelphia for starting lawyers.

Just as von Starck had plunged into utility work under MacIntosh in 1945, so Young took the same plunge in 1948 under von Starck. Young is critical of his early efforts at legal writing and full of praise for von Starck's patience. Night after night and paragraph after paragraph, they rewrote Young's drafts until von Starck was satisfied. Young looks back on the training he received from von Starck as exhausting, exacting, and invaluable.

In the early 1950s, American Water Works was impressed by Young's performance and offered him a position as its inside counsel. He turned down the offer, but to good effect. That year, instead of the usual several-hundred-dollar annual increase in compensation from the Firm, Young received an extraordinary increase of $1,500. He was made a partner in 1956, the same year as Lefevre, Quigg, and Brown.

In Young's early years of partnership, matters for American Water Works were pervasive. Cases sitused in Pennsylvania and New Jersey were routinely assigned to him. In no time, he became an expert on the water problems of such communities as Keene, Butler, New Castle, Phillipsburg, Montrose, and Clarks Summit, to cite a few. It was also through water-law assignments that Young played an active role with the Public Utility Law Section of the American Bar Association (ABA), chairing that section in 1971. Contacts with potential clients were developed through that section by MacIntosh and later by Young. The Associated Gas Distributors became a client in Washington; then Peoples Natural Gas, a large Pittsburgh utility; and finally its parent, Consolidated Natural Gas Company.

In addition, through ABA section activities, Young came to represent Buckeye Pipe Line Company. It was a third-tier subsidiary of the Penn Central Transportation Company, which the Firm also represented in a $2-billion valuation case after the railroad was taken over by the government. Later, Young added General Battery Corporation (Exide) as a client. In the 1970s, he succeeded von Starck as responsible attorney for Philadelphia Electric Company. He also took charge of the Firm's long-time relationship with Independence Blue Cross, chairing its board starting in 1991.

Young was an exceptionally responsive and common-sense lawyer. For him the law was no metaphysical ritual but simply a means by which everyday problems were solved quickly and rationally. Clients liked that.

As already mentioned, Young and Lefevre worked hand in hand on the infamous 1962 report that led to the famous 1971 report. As architect of the Allocation Committee, Young served on that committee in 1972 and 1973. He had also served in 1971, because MacIntosh was in such a hurry to implement the new constitution that he asked the nascent Allocation Committee to divide that year's profits as well, thus relieving him of the task.

The Allocation Committee was a completely new vehicle that could have foundered. Merit was suddenly more important than seniority. But what was merit? There were some newly adopted criteria, but they were as vague as they were lengthy and elegant. Young had to apply them, sometimes over the objections of the Old Guard. He was always an excellent allocator, returning to the Allocation Committee twice: in 1977, and again from 1981 through 1983.

Young also served on the Executive Committee from 1974 through 1976, from 1978 through 1980, from 1984 through 1986, and again in 1987. He chaired that committee in 1976, 1979, 1984, 1986, and 1987. Throughout the 1970s and 1980s, he also headed the Firm's Professional Personnel Committee. In that capacity, he fashioned the Firm's associate evaluation procedures, partner admission criteria, and partner lateral-entry processes. These were of critical importance to the Firm during its years of extraordinary expansion, particularly in New York and Los Angeles.

Young retired in 1991, a youthful seventy years old. He is

remembered as uncomplicated, a man of genuine goodwill, outgoing and accessible. Everyone knew him, admired him, and truly liked him.

■ ■ ■ ■ ■

Park Bankert Dilks, Jr., was more complicated and less accessible. He combined some of Bryson's insights with von Starck's diligence, and like them he was something of a loner.

Dilks was born in Philadelphia on March 25, 1928. His father's ancestors were Quakers who came from England to southern New Jersey in 1709. From them Dilks got his frugality, number skills, and work ethic. His mother's ancestors, also from England, arrived 150 years later. From them he got his interest in the classics, history, and music.

After attending public elementary school in Philadelphia, Dilks spent four years at George School. That Quaker school's unusual emphasis on international affairs drew students from all over the world. Some of Dilks's classmates had fled the Nazis under pressure or in protest, and Dilks learned German while at school. He also played soccer and was on the track team.

Dilks received his undergraduate degree from the University of Pennsylvania in 1948. He completed college in three years, majored in philosophy, learned French, and was elected to Phi Beta Kappa in his junior year. In 1951, he graduated from Penn's law school, opting for moot courts instead of law review and winning in his second and third years all the elimination cases and the school championship (Keedy Cup), as well as representing Penn in the national moot court competition. He wanted to be a trial lawyer.

Dilks came to the bar in Philadelphia just as the Democrats were sweeping the Republicans out of office after sixty-seven years. In 1951, Joseph Clark was elected mayor and Richardson Dilworth district attorney. Although Dilks was only twenty-three and a registered Republican, Dilworth hired him as an assistant district attorney. His friends called him "the boy D.A." The job paid $4,500, about $700 more than prevailing salaries at top Philadelphia law firms, and provided excellent experience for an aspiring litigator.

But the Korean War was continuing, and Dilks was called to active duty as a first lieutenant in the Judge Advocate General's Corps. After attending the JAG School at the University of Virginia, he was assigned to the Defense Appellate Division in the Pentagon, where he handled cases before Boards of Review and the Court of Military Appeals. When his father died suddenly, Dilks was released from active duty to support his mother and younger sister by operating his family's insurance business. It was an around-the-clock job, leaving little time for law practice. But it provided a mini-crash course in marketing, management, and accounting.

When the insurance business could be turned over to others, Dilks practiced law part time and then full time with Kenneth Souser's nine-lawyer firm. That firm split up, and its labor lawyers merged with ML&B in 1959. Although Dilks did some labor work, he spent more time in litigation, business law, and taxation. So he was not part of the merger. Nevertheless, he maintained a filial relationship with Souser, who suggested in 1961 that he join ML&B.

As a generalist, Dilks was of little interest to ML&B and would have to be "recycled," as Souser put it. Aware that the Firm was looking for a state and local tax lawyer, he told Dilks: "For purposes of your interview, that is what you are." Dilks was interviewed by Lefevre and von Starck, tackled the role in which Souser cast him, probably fooled no one, but was hired anyway.

Making a virtue of necessity, Dilks immersed himself in the Firm's state and local tax practice. His objective was to convert it into a litigation practice, in line with his earlier experience. This he did in cases involving Strawbridge & Clothier; Finance Company of Pennsylvania; Alan Wood Steel Company; Heinz Investment Company; Humble Oil and Refining Company; the Eastern Conference of Water Companies; the Philadelphia Chamber of Commerce; and the Henry Houston estate. Most of these cases reached the Pennsylvania Supreme Court (one went on to certiorari proceedings in the United States Supreme Court), and Dilks acquired an unsought reputation as a state and local tax expert. He worked in other areas as well: The Firm's tables of organization in the 1960s show him as a member of the litigation, tax, labor, and business and finance sections—with the international section to follow.

Dilks brought with him a sizable practice from his pre-ML&B days. At that time, associates kept all their personal fees. Consequently, his compensation as an associate exceeded that of some partners. When he became a partner in 1964, his compensation was "normalized," as Bracken put it, by being reduced. Status superseded remuneration.

Dilks's knack for generating clients appealed to the rainmaker in MacIntosh, with whom Dilks enjoyed an especially warm working relationship. MacIntosh complained that so few of the Firm's lawyers "thought like businessmen." Dilks did, or at least so MacIntosh said. MacIntosh thrust Dilks forward.

When the General Building Contractors Association became a major client of the Firm in the 1960s, it wanted its matters managed by a lawyer familiar with labor law, corporate law, and tax law. MacIntosh designated Dilks. Later, in 1969, when MacIntosh wanted to restructure the personal law section, he approached Dilks to be its chairman. Dilks demurred: He was preoccupied with securities offerings at a time when every business seemed to be going public. Still later, when the Management Review Committee was formed in 1971, MacIntosh appointed Dilks to the Long Range Planning Subcommittee and made certain that he went on the first Executive Committee. Dilks subsequently headed the Firm's banking subsection, attracting Citibank as a leading client and inheriting responsibility for the Firm's long-time relationship with Philadelphia National Bank. During the 1970s, he spent much time abroad after founding the international section and becoming its chairman in 1972, as detailed in Chapter 24.

Dilks served on the Executive Committee from 1971 through 1976, from 1980 through 1982, and from 1986 through 1987. He chaired it in 1975 and again in 1981. He served on the Allocation Committee from 1977 through 1979 and again from 1983 through 1985.

After Lefevre retired in 1979, Dilks also chaired the Finance Committee, managing the Firm's financial operations into the 1990s. Revenue and expenses were painstakingly forecast, variances were noted and acted upon, and targets were regularly achieved or exceeded. He introduced such concepts, later standard procedure, as the APA (a formula for determining the profitability of the Firm from the individual partner's viewpoint), the Countdown (a procedure for getting bills out and collecting receivables at year-end) and the billing factor (a calculation for determining the profitability of a given hour of time booked). He was conservative—some said parsimonious—and debt-averse, believing that law firms should generate their capital internally. His Quaker ancestors would have approved a headline to the *American Lawyer's* article about the Firm that appeared in September 1990: "Says one former partner: 'It is the strong Philadelphia, conservative Quaker management that really knows what it is doing fiscally.'"

With Lefevre gone and Young nearing retirement, it was Dilks who suggested the time had come for a transition to new managers.

When Young and Dilks laid down their management responsibilities in 1988, only Curtin remained of the Quadriviri.

■ ■ ■ ■ ■

William Joseph Curtin was born on March 9, 1931, in Auburn, New York. Auburn, which then had a population of 35,000, is the county seat of Cayuga County in the Finger Lakes district. Curtin's mother was a registered nurse; his father, an insurance broker.

Love of the law ran in Curtin's family. His father had attended St. John's Law School until the Depression forced him to withdraw. Curtin's Uncle Bill, a family hero, was a prominent trial lawyer in Buffalo. By becoming lawyers, both Curtin and his younger brother emulated their uncle and achieved what lay beyond their father's reach.

Curtin was a good student and a popular one. In high school, he won a New York State Regents Scholarship and was president of the student body. He was also a fine athlete, winning more varsity letters (for football, basketball, tennis and track) than anyone in his class. He was offered football scholarships to Cornell, Dartmouth, and Georgetown.

He wanted exposure to a larger community, so he chose Georgetown. Although Georgetown dropped football as an intercollegiate sport in Curtin's sophomore year, it continued to provide him with free room and board for acting as a student counselor. Always reliable, well organized and a leader, Curtin served as president of his class and of Georgetown's Collegiate Club.

Next he went to Georgetown Law School, from which he graduated in 1956. Unlike lawyers who do not identify their specialties until they have practiced for some years, Curtin was drawn to labor law while still in law school. Later, he would say, "The only course in law school I really enjoyed related to labor law." So he continued at Georgetown and took an LL.M. in labor law in 1957. Over the years, Curtin would maintain a close relationship with his alma mater, ultimately becoming chair of the Georgetown University board of directors in 1992.

While working for his LL.M., Curtin clerked at the Washington firm of Hogan & Hartson. In February 1956, he became an associate in that firm's trial department at a starting salary of $3,600 per year. Still, his objective was labor work.

When labor work at Hogan & Hartson failed to materialize, a labor law professor at Georgetown proposed Curtin as house counsel and assistant to the chairman of the Eastern Conference of Teamsters, headquartered in Washington. Curtin had never identified with organized labor, much less the International Brotherhood of Teamsters (IBT). But whatever the problems of the IBT, the Eastern Conference was regarded as clean, incorrupt, and without mob connections. Moreover, the job would triple Curtin's salary. He said yes.

Then in the fall of 1956, the Senate's Permanent Subcommittee on Investigations began looking into teamster corruption. A Special Committee on Labor Rackets was set up under the chairmanship of Senator John McClellan of Arkansas. Counsel to the committee was Robert F. Kennedy, the younger brother of Senator John F. Kennedy from Massachusetts. Curtin says that Bobby, as everyone called him, was "painfully shy, but he became an incredibly aggressive investigator for the committee." The committee's targets were Dave Beck, president of the IBT, and Jimmy Hoffa, who succeeded Beck as president in 1957, the year the IBT was expelled from the AFL-CIO.

By 1957, the IBT and its leaders were under siege. They needed all the good legal advice they could get. Hoffa's lawyer, Edward Bennett Williams, recommended that Curtin be hired as house counsel to the IBT. While flattering, the offer came at a bad time. Hoffa was furious at the AFL-CIO for expelling the Teamsters. He wanted revenge. One facet of his revenge was having teamsters cross legally constituted AFL-CIO picket lines. Hoffa insisted he had no choice as a matter of law. Curtin opined otherwise, incurred Hoffa's displeasure, and remained with the Eastern Conference.

A group of trucking companies approached the Eastern Conference in 1959 to negotiate an East Coast cement hauling agreement. The truckers wanted to take on the railroads. To do this they needed a competitive labor agreement. In his three years with the Eastern Conference, Curtin had become an expert on area-wide contracts. He was designated to lead the negotiations for the Eastern Conference. The truckers had no comparable experience with such contracts. One trucking company was represented by ML&B associate John (Jay) Peet.[4] He was a quick study, spoke publicly for the group, and worked with Curtin to produce a prototype for area labor contracts still in use in the eastern and midwestern United States.

As the government and the media bore down on the IBT, Curtin decided that the Eastern Conference, despite its respectability, was not his long-term career choice. So he accepted Peet's invitation and came to Philadelphia in September 1959 to meet with Kenneth Souser and Arthur Littleton. They offered him a job as an associate in Philadelphia. Impressed as he was by them, his interests were in Washington, so he declined.

But Souser and Littleton really wanted Curtin. They rethought their offer. The Firm had a four-lawyer office in Washington but only one labor client. Would Curtin be interested in joining such a small "branch office" with the understanding that he would practice administrative law while he and the Firm tried to develop a full-time labor practice in Washington?

Curtin accepted the offer and joined the Firm on January 1, 1960. He did not have to practice administrative law very long. By the summer of 1960, the Firm had a full-time labor practice in Washington. In his early years with the Firm, Curtin specialized in representing groups of truckers in their relationships with the teamsters.

A breakthrough came for Curtin in 1964 when the leading grocery chains (A&P, Acme, Food Fair, Grand Union, Giant, and Safeway, among others) retained him to bargain with the Retail Clerks Union (now the United Food and Commercial Workers), which had struck one of the chains, thus triggering a "defensive lockout" by the other chains. The dispute, which originated in Baltimore, intensified and spread to the Washington area, where it attracted national attention.

That attention was such that in 1965 five major airlines (Eastern, National, Northwest, TWA, and United) retained Curtin to negotiate a multicarrier agreement with the International Association of Machinists. It was the airlines' first experience with joint bargaining. A forty-two-day strike lasted until August 19, 1966, received front-page attention, and brought Curtin into contact with Secretary of Labor Willard Wirtz and President Lyndon Johnson. From there, Curtin attracted one major client after another, including Walt Disney World in 1968; the Trans-Alaska pipeline in 1971; the Department of Transportation (the air traffic controllers strike) in 1981; the National Football League in 1982; and the National Railway Labor Conference in 1990.

But it almost did not happen. When Curtin became a partner on January 1, 1965, Littleton was still the senior partner. Increases in partner allocations moved by hoary custom at glacial speed. Merit had yet to supplant seniority. Curtin was vulnerable to outside offers. His old firm, Hogan & Hartson, had watched him develop and liked what it saw. It pursued him in 1967 and again in 1968. It offered to pay him 30 percent more than he was receiving from the Firm. In addition, it offered a full-service Washington office, instead of what Curtin called the Firm's "gas and labor boutique." By April 1968, he had made up his mind to leave ML&B and had actually accepted Hogan & Hartson's offer. When word reached the Philadelphia office, there was consternation. Would he please meet immediately with MacIntosh, Souser, Bryson, and Bracken?

Curtin came to Philadelphia never thinking he would reconsider. He was not a person who made rash decisions, and his election to return to Hogan & Hartson was final. But, as he tells the story, he did change his mind, for two reasons. First, during the hour he spent with Souser at the Union League before catching the train back to Washington, he found Souser's "charm and warm friendship irresistible." Second, at his meeting with MacIntosh, Souser, Bryson, and Bracken, the concept of the Washington office as it exists today was born. When Curtin told his Philadelphia colleagues that he longed for a broader practice base in Washington, they informed him, to his surprise, that they agreed and that they were in fact developing plans to make Washington a full-service office.

Today, the Firm takes for granted its Washington office as a broad-based entity in its own right. It stands alone and is certainly not a branch of Philadelphia. But in 1968, the idea that a law firm could have more than one major office was novel and dubious.

If there is any watershed date when the Firm went national, it is that time in April 1968 when four senior lawyers met with Curtin to dissuade him from leaving. As Curtin puts it:

> ML&B was then the first law firm of its kind to conceive of the development of offices other than its founding office to a full-service capacity and to implement the strategy of planning and developing a national law firm.

After Souser died in September 1970, MacIntosh became Curtin's contact in Philadelphia. MacIntosh was not only Washington's staunchest rooter, he was also Curtin's champion. He recognized in Curtin many of his own qualities: commitment, tirelessness, attention to detail, leadership, and an extraordinary talent for attracting clients. It was MacIntosh who arranged that Curtin go on the Executive Committee during its second year in 1973. He was elected for a two-year term and subsequently reelected for a three-year term, thus serving from 1973 through 1977. He also served on that committee in 1981 through 1983, and again from 1986 through

1991, after which the Firm's management structure was reconstituted. He was chairman in 1977, 1982, 1988, and 1989. He served on the Allocation Committee from 1978 through 1980 and from 1984 through 1986.

Curtin brought his labor negotiating techniques to Executive Committee deliberations. Preparations were total, presentations were comprehensive, and debates were endless. When Curtin considered a question ripe for decision, all aspects of it were exhaustively analyzed, and the focus was sharp. But he also had a unique ability for keeping out of focus an issue he considered unripe for disposition. During the Quadriviri years, no one matched Curtin's facility for orchestrating debate, for inducing warring factions to lay down their arms, and for building consensus.

■ ■ ■ ■ ■

In the Firm's first century, its senior partners had transferred power like those Roman emperors who adopted their successors. But before the empire, Rome had functioned as a republic with constant turmoil and several triumvirates. They were notoriously unstable. Inevitably, the triumviri fought it out and civil wars ensued. If triumvirates are unstable, quadrivirates should be even more unstable—unless, by some miracle, all four leaders thought alike. Did they?

Michael Klowden, who headed the Firm's Los Angeles office, was fascinated that Lefevre, Young, Dilks, and Curtin apparently thought alike. He said he had come from a firm where the senior partners literally shouted at one another in the halls. He was amazed by the contrast.

In fact, the Quadriviri did not think alike. But they agreed that the Firm's interests took precedence over sectional, geographical, and individual interests. They also agreed not to compete with one another or to air their differences publicly. So they appeared monolithic.

Only once was there a visible chink in the leadership's armor. In 1986, one of the Firm's offices wanted to acquire by merger a firm of several hundred lawyers. Young found the prospect exciting and urged that it be pursued. Dilks generated financial models that gave him pause; nevertheless, he thought the discussions should continue. Curtin, on the other hand, saw conflicts with existing clients and was deeply concerned about diluting the Firm's culture. Tensions ran high as word spread that the Firm's leaders were in disagreement, apparently for the first time. In the absence of a consensus, the transaction did not move forward. Some partners were disappointed. Most were relieved.

The Quadriviri were quite different in personality and style. Lefevre, for example, was exceptionally impatient. He placed a particularly uncomfortable chair opposite his desk so that no visitor would tarry too long. He spoke in conclusions, leaving the listener to plug the gaps in his reasoning. He laced his pronouncements with humor to camouflage their severity. He wielded the scalpel with a smile.

If Dilks was similarly impatient, it rarely showed. Of the four, he spoke least and listened most. He had been raised in the Souser school, which regarded listening as a fine art and taught that the other party, by talking long enough, just might reach the right conclusion.

Young's patience appeared to be infinite. Every day he held endless conversations with lawyers from all over the Firm. He would, in his words, "tune in" with them. In his case, the medium was the message. The tuning technique made them feel, as he put it, "part of the process."

Young's tuning technique also reflected his inexhaustible energy. He always seemed the best prepared and fastest off the starting blocks. For example, within minutes of a meeting, Young's secretary would deliver to the participants his memo reciting what had just been decided. Sometimes what had just been decided was what *he* had decided. To influence the course of history, be first to write it down.

Curtin had a similar approach. His technique was to envelop the other party in his words. They were pleasant words, always sympathetic, sometimes seductive. Before a discussion, he would ask leave to provide what he called "background." He would then put the matter in context, his context. Inevitably, others ended up playing on Curtin's field, and agreement often followed. Curtin never went for the jugular. He circled the central point and reached it only after all subsidiary points had been resolved. This technique helped make him one of the nation's outstanding collective bargainers.

Based on long association, each of the Quadriviri could anticipate how the others would react to any given question. They could also predict what would finally be the consensus. It was a balancing act.

Lefevre visualized, Young energized, Dilks analyzed, and Curtin humanized. Lefevre and Young played offense; Dilks and Curtin, defense.

For some years the Quadriviri were the Firm's top rainmakers, a fact that buttressed their authority. They also generated goodwill by regularly turning over client responsibilities to younger lawyers. And it was characteristic of them that, while they received the highest allocations, their concern was to minimize the spreads between their allocations and those of other leading partners.[5]

At no time were all of the Quadriviri on the Executive Committee together. Those not on that committee were on the Allocation Committee. How did they manage the Firm? Of course, they were in touch with one another almost daily by telephone. But they needed a formal vehicle to bring them together.

That vehicle was the Firm Practice Committee, created in 1976. The committee originally comprised the Quadriviri plus von Starck. For the first time, a group of partners surveyed the Firm's practice and studied how to enhance it. The age of marketing for lawyers had arrived. Dilks chaired the committee until 1980, when Curtin took over, as Dilks assumed Lefevre's job as chief financial partner. By this time, the three remaining Firm leaders each had his specialty: For Young it had always been personnel, for Dilks it was finance, and for Curtin it was practice development. The three committees they evolved continue today in altered form as pillars of the Firm's structure.

From what the partners saw, it all worked very smoothly, as the Quadriviri imperceptibly ran the Firm. Many partners joined and left the Executive Committee. They took part, satisfied themselves about the Firm's operations, and went back to practicing law. The Quadriviri carried on.

The 1970s and the 1980s were exhilarating for the Firm. Not since Bockius's pre-Depression heyday did ML&B take such strides. It pioneered in national practice. It went abroad. Its size increased dramatically from 125 lawyers in 1970 to 627 lawyers in 1989. So striking was the Firm's growth during the first Quadriviri decade that with 374 lawyers in 1982 ML&B was listed by the *American Lawyer* as the country's second-largest law firm, preceded only by Baker & McKenzie.[6]

All the while, the Firm maintained its sound financial and collegial underpinnings. And most amazing, it was able to export its culture. In writing about the ties among ML&B's lawyers in many locations, the *American Lawyer* (September 1990) quoted a senior partner at another Philadelphia firm: "These people are really bound to them . . . I think they've been very successful. They've been able to inject their culture into the other offices."

Remarkably, those who "injected their culture" were not born to it. Only Young was homegrown. The other three were lateral entrants. In Chaucer's phrase, "gladly . . . [did they] lerne, and gladly teche."[7]

CHAPTER 20

IN THE NATION'S CAPITAL

Power shifts from Wall Street to Washington ■ *Oppressive taxes* ■ *Natural gas after World War II* ■ *Innovation in 1947* ■ *A toy for its proponents* ■ *The dawn of Camelot* ■ *Defections and renaissance* ■ *A national labor practice* ■ *A watershed event in 1968* ■ *Ocean shipping* ■ *Slow off the mark* ■ *A. A. Sommer and the SEC* ■ *Sheldon Cohen and the IRS* ■ *John Shenefield and antitrust* ■ *Sunglasses and Santa Claus* ■ *John Quarles and the environment* ■ *Government contracts and international practice* ■ *Impossible missions* ■ *Strategic plans versus real life*

There were at least five reasons why ML&B opened a small branch office in Washington, D.C., on February 1, 1947: William Clarke Mason's appearances before the Federal Power Commission (FPC) from 1936 to 1939; the government service of W. James MacIntosh during World War II; the expansion of the Firm's tax practice during the war; the postwar interest of the Firm's clients in natural gas; and the availability of John Bracken as a member of the District of Columbia bar.

Although the New Deal and governmental agencies "were anathema to Will Mason,"[1] they occupied much of his time from the mid-1930s onward. Mason fought high-profile battles with the Securities and Exchange Commission (SEC) over the dismemberment of UGI. He took part in protracted litigation with the National Labor Relations Board (NLRB) involving the Baldwin Locomotive Works. And he led lengthy proceedings at the FPC for the Philadelphia Electric Company. Tyson Stokes described those proceedings:

> The hearings [to value PE's Conowingo hydroelectric power plant] were held in Washington and an entire floor of the Mayflower Hotel was engaged throughout the winter of 1938 in order to accommodate the technical staff testifying for the Company and to hold the truckloads of physical records that were introduced in evidence. Mason and [partner A. Allen] Woodruff carried the legal burden,

appearing before the Examiner, on Mondays through Fridays and working in the hotel each evening to prepare the witnesses and documents for the next day's testimony.[2]

Bracken would later wonder if Mason already had a Washington office in mind when he asked Bracken to take the District of Columbia bar examination in 1939. Bracken did so and was admitted the following year. The Washington scene was familiar to him. From 1934 to 1937, between college and law school, he had been on the staff of the Department of Justice, serving as an aide to Attorney General Homer Cummings, as recounted in Chapter 18.

MacIntosh also knew the scene in 1943-44 as general counsel to the Renegotiation Division of the War Department and subsequently to the War Contracts Price Adjustment Board. Reference has already been made in Chapters 14 and 17 to his government experiences and expansionist philosophy.

As the New Deal and then World War II shifted the center of power from Wall Street to the nation's capital, Mason and MacIntosh concluded that the Firm's clients needed direct access to federal agencies. This was especially true of the Bureau of Internal Revenue, renamed the Internal Revenue Service in 1953. During World War II, individual income tax rates had reached 91 percent, and corporate rates 40 percent plus a 90-percent excess-profits levy. Not only were taxes oppressive, but also their collection was highly centralized. Approximately 200 field offices reported directly to the bureau's headquarters in Washington, where all decisions were made. This would change completely in 1952 when the bureau was reorganized and decentralized.[3] After that, an office in Washington was hardly necessary from the tax viewpoint. But by then, the Firm had made its commitment to the nation's capital, with tax law as an urgent consideration.

Less urgent at the outset was natural gas regulation. The Firm's interest in gas derived from its representation of UGI going back to 1882, as well as the Philadelphia Gas Works (PGW) that UGI had operated for the city since 1897. Through World War II, both UGI and PGW manufactured their gas. During the war, pipelines had been built to move crude oil from Texas to refineries up north, as German U-boats sank an average of two ships a day off America's East and Gulf coasts. After the war, those pipelines were converted for use in transmitting natural gas, which up to that time had simply been a nuisance by-product of oil production. The availability of the pipelines spurred the production of natural gas in the Southwest, independently of oil. Best of all, natural gas was cheaper than manufactured gas. So it was in great demand, with distribution companies fighting for their shares of the available supply. As major distributors of gas, UGI and PGW were among them.

■ ■ ■ ■ ■

Such was the situation in 1947 when ML&B set up in Washington, with Mason and MacIntosh sparking the drive. Bracken, then a young associate recently back in Philadelphia from service in the navy and at the Nuremberg trials, was dispatched to the capital. Another associate, in this case a superannuated one, was hired. He was J. Louis Monarch, who brought the desired tax background and experience. A member of the bar since 1912, Monarch handled appellate litigation in the tax field for the Department of Justice from 1926 to 1947. He took early retirement from the government to join the Firm in 1947 and remained an associate until he retired a second time in 1963. With his intimate understanding of the Washington scene, he opposed Mason's plan that the Firm rent space in the Mayflower Hotel. According to Monarch, lobbyists operated from hotel suites. Surely ML&B did not wish to be so identified. Mason yielded.[4]

A space search was conducted by Tyson Stokes, who had just been named the Firm's first managing partner. He chose suite 506 in the Insurance Building at Fifteenth and I streets, owned and primarily occupied by the United Mine Workers of America. On February 1, 1947, ML&B took possession of its first space outside Philadelphia, and Stokes issued a memo to all ML&B lawyers:

> All requests of a general service nature involving the obtaining of information from Government Bureaus, publications, documents, etc. should be addressed to Mr. Bracken. All matters relating to taxes should be addressed to Mr. Monarch.

During those early years, Monarch was definitely not busy with tax work, and he was even less busy after the IRS decentralized in 1952. As it turned out, Bracken was more fully engaged. Although not a public utility lawyer, he was thrust immediately into the natural gas wars. With supervision from Philadelphia by Thomas Ringe, Bracken represented UGI and PGW in two major cases before the FPC. They involved filings by Texas Eastern Transmission Company and TransContinental Gas Pipeline Corporation to bring natural gas through pipelines to New York from Texas and Louisiana. The Firm's clients needed rights to take gas from those lines as they passed through Pennsylvania. After protracted multiparty proceedings, Ringe and Bracken secured such rights, which are still used today to deliver natural gas to southeastern Pennsylvania.

Bracken's gas work introduced him to J. David Mann, assistant to then FPC Chairman Nelson Lee Smith. So when Bracken was recalled to the navy in August 1950 during the Korean conflict, he recommended that the Firm hire Mann as his successor to monitor the gas regulatory scene for UGI and PGW. But Mann had other plans. He had been with the government for three years and wanted to return home to local practice. Stokes was sent to recruit him. According to Mann:

> I told Stokes that Nashville [Illinois] was a very pleasant place and I thought I might enjoy living there. He didn't try to dissuade me, pointing out that there were many advantages to living in a small town, but suggested that I might find working with Morgan, Lewis & Bockius more exciting than foreclosing mortgages on cows.

Mann opted not to foreclose mortgages on cows, became an associate late in 1950, was made a partner in 1956, and retired in 1983. By the time he arrived, the Firm had relocated on December 1, 1949, to 729 Fifteenth Street. There, Mann, Monarch, and a secretary celebrated their first Christmas together in 1950 by sharing a drink with their landlord, a self-made Greek immigrant, who brought with him a paper quart container of eggnog. According to Mann, "the celebratory space bore the title 'conference room' and overlooked an alley through very dingy windows."

It is Mann's recollection that the Washington office did not break even until 1955. Whether true or not, Washington was certainly *perceived* as a loser. Orvel Sebring recalls the grousings of Philadelphia partners who wanted the office closed. It was regarded as a toy for its proponents, Mason and MacIntosh. (Considering the prominence of its proponents, the grousings were sotto voce.) Ironically, some Washington partners would later take a similar disapproving view as the Firm opened offices in other cities, and one group would actually leave the Firm in part because of its expansionist policy.

During the early years, Washington operated on a tight budget— not surprising since Philadelphia viewed it as a drain and controlled its purse strings. Even after the office was well established and Philadelphia more indulgent, Mann remembers that he could not compete in the local secretarial market, which was buoyed by high governmental salaries. So he advertised in London. An English girl (she would be called a woman today) was hired and arrived sporting a miniskirt. When told that her attire did not comport with the Firm's image, she explained tearfully that her luggage had been lost in transit. So, according to Mann, she "let out such hem as existed until her other clothes arrived and she was able to fit herself out properly."

Prior to 1952, the Washington office handled only matters sent by Philadelphia. In that year, it landed its first direct client: a sprinkling of towns in the state of Washington. They wanted to acquire natural gas from pipelines and construct their own distribution facilities. So they engaged Mann to intervene in FPC proceedings involving a proposal by Pacific Northwest Pipeline Company to deliver gas from the Southwest to Seattle and Portland. The towns' intervention was contested by the Washington Natural Gas Company, which then served Seattle. But Mann prevailed on behalf of the towns, and Philadelphia was impressed that Washington could attract a client on its own.

Another breakthrough occurred after the Supreme Court ruled in 1954 that the FPC had jurisdiction over prices charged by natural gas producers marketing their products through interstate pipelines.[5] But the Commission had inadequate personnel to exercise its new-found jurisdiction. So the private sector filled the breech, especially a group of East Coast distributors organized by PGW personnel. They set about developing a regulatory program to present to the FPC as a basis for fixing the field prices of natural gas—a program that was followed until prices were deregulated in the 1980s.

The group's members included PE, Consolidated Edison Company, Brooklyn Union Gas Company, Long Island Lighting Company, and Public Service Electric & Gas Company. The Firm represented the group, called Associated Gas Distributors (AGD), during twelve years of regulatory proceedings and litigation. The proceedings focused attention on ML&B in the gas regulatory field, triggering an expansion of its Washington office as the Firm became a prominent advocate for gas distributors before the FPC. In those days, ML&B lawyers could sometimes be found in three or four FPC hearings simultaneously.

■ ■ ■ ■

During that early period, two lawyers joined the Washington office who played important roles in developing its practice. John Holtzinger arrived in 1956, became a partner in 1964, cultivated ML&B's utility practice, and left the Firm in 1983. William Curtin arrived in 1960, became a partner in 1965, achieved national standing as a labor lawyer, built one of the Firm's largest practices, and led the Firm as one of the Quadriviri.

By the time Holtzinger and Curtin became associates, the Firm's Washington office had moved again, on July 1, 1955, to the eleventh floor of the Pennsylvania Building at the corner of Thirteenth Street and Pennsylvania Avenue. Although off the beaten track by the standards of Washington lawyers, it offered a splendid view of John F. Kennedy's inaugural parade on January 20, 1961. Mann, who was the only partner, and the four associates[6] invited their clients to enjoy the spectacle below on Pennsylvania Avenue, which glistened with a backdrop of newly cleared snow. It was the dawn of Camelot.

But spectacles aside, the Firm was already bifurcated in the Pennsylvania Building and could not expand. So it moved still again on February 17, 1961, to the Bender Building at 1120 Connecticut Avenue, where it leased the eleventh floor and part of the twelfth floor. Mason, who died four years earlier, would have approved, since the Firm's offices were now opposite his 1938 stamping grounds, the Mayflower Hotel. Duke Ziebert's, a famed Washington watering hole (stronger beverages also available) was just a few steps away. Even better, the Firm's new location featured a basement restaurant named Paul Young's. It became ML&B's unofficial luncheon club in a city renowned for power lunches.

The Firm continued to expand in the Bender Building until it ran out of space and moved reluctantly on February 1, 1969, just three doors up the block to 1140 Connecticut Avenue, where it occupied the eleventh floor and two-thirds of the twelfth floor. It was a time of seething unrest in Washington, peaking with the 1971 May Day demonstrations against the Vietnam war. As one partner noted, Pierre L'Enfant's eighteenth-century city plan could at last be put to its intended use, as military emplacements were set up in circular parks commanding 360-degree views of the city's broad avenues. One such emplacement was two blocks north of the office at Dupont Circle, which was ringed with troops. How quickly history changes course: Only ten years had passed since the dawn of Camelot.[7]

To complete the space story, the Firm moved again on June 1, 1975, to Eighteenth and M streets. There it occupied 60,000 square feet on the seventh and eighth floors. In 1987, the Eighteenth and M street lease was extended to the year 2002, and the Firm took floors six through ten, plus options in an adjoining tower. A state-of-the-art conference center was constructed on the tenth floor. Its five conference rooms could seat up to 200 persons, forty-four of them around a huge conference table in the main boardroom. Altogether, the Firm occupied 150,000 square feet of space in the building by 1993.

Returning to the late 1960s through early 1980s, they were exciting years for the Firm's gas and labor practices in Washington, due especially to the efforts of Holtzinger and Curtin. Although the two men dominated their respective fields, they were otherwise quite dissimilar. Holtzinger was informal, projecting genial disarray. He was stubbornly nonhierarchal and committed to decentralization, with each energy practitioner functioning independently. He had little interest in the law outside his chosen field, held that a boutique was the ideal form of law firm, and resisted national practice. He was, as Thomas Lefevre remarked, "the quintessential iconoclast."

By contrast, Curtin believed in total organization and a clear chain of command. No detail escaped his attention, a condition that persisted even after the labor section numbered more than 100 lawyers. Although conservative by nature, he was fully committed to national practice and the Firm's expansion program. Both Holtzinger and Curtin were natural leaders who inspired the devotion of their co-workers. But their styles and objectives were in such constant conflict that it was not surprising, although sad, that Holtzinger left the Firm on December 9, 1983, taking with him six other energy partners[8] to help form the firm of Newman & Holtzinger. Since Mann had retired two months earlier, the only energy partner then remaining was Frank Saponaro, who had joined the Firm laterally in 1973 and would withdraw in 1989.

In its heyday, the Washington energy practice boasted such clients as Consolidated Natural Gas Company; Laclede Gas Company; Pacific Lighting Companies; Houston Natural Gas Corp.; Nebraska Public Power District; Public Service of New Mexico; Midwest Industrial Gas Consumers; Missouri Natural Gas Company; South Carolina Electric and Gas Company; Atlanta Gas Light Company; and Florida Power Corporation. This extraordinary clientele had its roots in the original Philadelphia gas practice, as supplemented over the years by Mann and subsequently by Holtzinger and his colleagues. It was lost to the Firm with the 1983 schism.

An earlier casualty was AGD. Referred to above, it was a collection of some twenty-four Mid-Atlantic and New England gas distributing companies that took positions in producer rate cases before the FPC. By 1978, AGD was a significant force in the industry and an important client of the Firm. It had become the responsibility of Frederick Moring, who came to the Firm in 1961, was made a partner in 1969, and left the Firm in 1978, largely over disagreements with

Holtzinger. Moring took AGD with him and in 1979 helped create the firm of Crowell & Moring. The defections of Moring and Holtzinger were blows to MacIntosh. As their mentor, he had spent two generations pioneering the idea of a Washington office and developing its public utility practice.

But there would be a renaissance in the Firm's Washington energy practice with the arrival of lateral entrants Mary Baluss in 1986 and Roberta Halladay in 1987. They came to the Firm as gas entered an era of deregulation. Previously, sales of gas were made by pipelines to distributors, the Firm's traditional clients. Now distributors would increasingly purchase their gas directly from the producers and contract separately for its transportation by the pipelines. All this spelled a decline in rate cases, once the mainstay of ML&B's utility practice in Washington.

Baluss and Halladay continued to act for some of the Firm's original utility clients: PE, UGI, and PGW. They also introduced their own clients. In the case of Baluss, those clients included Northwestern Minnesota Utilities; Westcoast Energy, Inc.; Connecticut Natural Gas; and Central Gas Manitoba. Halladay's main client was United Distribution Companies (UDC), whose forty members served 13.5 million gas consumers in eighteen states.[9]

Reflecting Halladay's stature in her specialty, she was chosen by UDC to argue before the Supreme Court a 1991 landmark case concerning the pricing of natural gas.[10] Never in the history of natural gas regulation had such an array of parties—interstate pipelines, local distribution companies, state regulatory commissions, state consumer advocates, national trade associations, and consumer interest groups—joined in opposition to a natural gas pricing rule. The Court worried aloud during argument whether the Federal Energy Regulatory Commission (FERC) had exceeded its authority, as the Court of Appeals for the Fifth Circuit had opined. The courtroom was crowded as the justices bombarded Halladay with questions until the red light signaled the end of her time. But anticipating the prospect of endless litigation over contractual changes effectuated under the rule, the Court reversed, holding that FERC had the requisite authority to prescribe price increases for "old natural gas."

■ ■ ■ ■ ■

Unlike ML&B's energy specialty, its Washington labor practice suffered no interruptions and soared. Starting with Curtin's arrival in 1960 and building on Kenneth Souser's base in Philadelphia, the practice went national. By 1993, there were more than 100 labor lawyers spread among all the Firm's domestic offices. Chapters 19 and 25 through 28 chronicle the Curtin story. So it remains here to deal with ten other prominent labor lawyers in ML&B's Washington office. In many instances, their practices derived from Curtin, for no lawyer in the Firm's history except Morris Bockius turned over so many clients to other partners.

Curtin's earliest labor colleague in Washington was Richard Hotvedt, who came to the Firm in 1962 from the General Counsel's Advice Branch of the NLRB and became a partner in 1969. Hotvedt received his baptism by fire working under Curtin in connection with strikes against the food chains in 1964 and the airlines in 1966, to be detailed in Chapter 25. Two years later, East Texas Motor Freight (ETMF), one of Hotvedt's clients, was confronted with disputes between the Teamsters union and the Equal Employment Opportunity Commission (EEOC) over the rights of minority truck drivers. Hotvedt vividly recalls that his negotiations with the EEOC in Memphis were interrupted by rioting on March 27, 1968. Martin Luther King, Jr., had organized a parade to protest the treatment of sanitation workers. The protesters were beaten back by the police. There was an eerie calm as Tennessee National Guardsmen stood watch amid broken glass and other debris. With martial law in effect, Hotvedt and his client wondered if they could make their way through the area to leave town. They got out by "just driving slowly, nodding, and returning [the guardsmen's] salute," according to Hotvedt. After they left, King continued his protests in Memphis, where he was tragically assassinated eight days later.

Various ETMF discrimination cases went on for nine years, with one reaching the Supreme Court. After Hotvedt delivered his argument there, he recalls that his opponent, a lawyer for the Mexican American Legal Defense Fund, began her presentation. She was diminutive and hidden by the lectern. Chief Justice Warren Burger said, "We can hear you, but we can't see you. If you will press the button, the lectern will go down." Pressing the button and coming into view, the lawyer said, "I didn't know that was possible." Ever gracious, the Chief Justice replied, "My dear, everything is possible here." Despite that encouragement, the Court unanimously reversed the Fifth Circuit and embraced Hotvedt's position. As Hotvedt's accomplishments attracted attention, he was engaged by the *Washington Post* to handle its labor work from 1977 through 1988. Subsequently, he represented PPG Industries Inc.; Safeway, Inc.; and Bell Atlantic Corp. He also served several terms on the Firm's Executive and Allocation committees.

Two other Curtin lieutenants, Charles O'Connor and Harry Rissetto, arrived in 1968 and 1970 respectively, becoming partners in 1971 and 1975. Both eventually served on the Firm's Executive Committee. Like Hotvedt, O'Connor came from the General Counsel's Advice Branch of the NLRB, whereas Rissetto served clerkships with Judge John Sirica and Chief Justice Burger. O'Connor's career and especially his involvement with major league baseball are covered in Chapter 29. Rissetto made his mark in connection with the Railway Labor Act, becoming by the 1990s the nation's leading authority on its intricacies and peculiarities.

Since the Railway Labor Act covers not only railroads but also airlines, Rissetto worked extensively for American Airlines, USAir, and the ill-fated Pan American Airlines. But most of all, he applied his expertise to representing railroads, especially Consolidated Rail Corporation (Conrail). In 1976, Conrail took over the six bankrupt railroads in the Northeast. It was Rissetto's assignment to rationalize the scores of labor agreements Conrail thereby inherited. He devised a novel interpretation of the Regional Rail Reorganization Act, arguing that Conrail could not be required to have more than one agreement for each class of employees. He prevailed in this contention, which received legislative sanction in the Staggers Rail Act of 1980.[11]

Separately, to render Conrail viable, Congress had modified provisions in Conrail's labor agreements and eliminated certain windfall payments to employees. The constitutionality of this legislation was attacked by the unions, defended by Rissetto on behalf of Conrail, and upheld by a special three-judge United States district court established under the Regional Rail Reorganization Act.[12] The $5 billion invested by the federal government in Conrail ultimately created self-sufficient and reliable rail service in the Northeast—a success story for the public, Conrail, the Firm, and Rissetto. (More about Conrail in Chapter 35.)

Curtin's Washington labor team also included Kenneth Hickey, Carl Uehlein, Robert Smith, Harry Burton, James Kelley, Thomas Wotring, and Robert Dufek. Hickey came to the Firm in 1968, became a partner in 1973, and left in 1992 to become general counsel of the Bakery and Confectionery Health Benefit and Pension Trust Funds, a client originated by Souser, subsequently managed by Curtin and then by Hickey. Uehlein came to the Firm in 1968, left in 1971 to serve as executive assistant to the Secretary of Labor, and returned as a partner in 1973. He handled the Firm's labor representation of Washington Gas Light Company and Potomac Electric Power Company. But his main commitment was to the construction industry, for which he negotiated and helped implement project labor agreements from Florida to Alaska. One such agreement was entered into by client Kaiser Engineers, Inc., with the Building and Construction Trades Council to accomplish the $6.1-billion cleanup of Boston harbor by the Massachusetts Water Resources Authority. The agreement was attacked but held enforceable by the Supreme Court.[13] (More in Chapters 26 and 27 about ML&B's special expertise with project labor agreements for Walt Disney World and the Alyeska pipeline.)

Smith, who had been a personnel executive with Texas Instruments Inc. before going to law school, joined the Firm in 1972 and became a partner in 1979. As an expert in discrimination law, he took charge of major cases for clients Martin-Marietta Corp; the American Red Cross; Communications Satellite Corporation; Walt Disney World; and MCI Communications Corporation. Kelley, who arrived in 1974 and was made a partner in 1980, represented Grumman Corp. and the Washington Metropolitan Area Transit Authority. Wotring, who came to the Firm in 1975 and became a partner in 1982, handled trucking and maritime labor relations, as well as pension litigation. Burton, who arrived in 1975 and was made a partner in 1982, became an authority on pension law. And Dufek, who arrived in 1976 and was named a partner in 1983, became lead counsel to the Bituminous Coal Operators Association in negotiating labor contracts with the United Mine Workers of America. Those contracts covered 60,000 coal miners and provided benefits for an additional 120,000 retirees and their beneficiaries through the United Mine Workers of America Health and Retirement Funds, which with $5 billion in assets were the third-largest jointly trusteed funds in the United States.

■ ■ ■ ■ ■

Chapter 19 recounted a watershed event in April 1968 when Curtin changed his mind about leaving ML&B. That was when MacIntosh, Souser, Bracken, and Brady Bryson told him they were working on plans to convert the Washington office from a "gas and labor boutique" into a full-service office, although one reflecting the regulatory specialties unique to the Washington scene. An extraordinary idea for its time, it would take twenty years to implement incrementally. First, a small firm with mixed expertise was acquired in 1968, followed shortly by nuclear and maritime specialists. Then, a corporate and SEC specialist as well as a tax lawyer joined the Firm in 1969. Antitrust and trade regulation lawyers arrived starting in 1973. The first litigation lawyer came in 1974; environmental lawyers, starting in 1977; banking lawyers as well as government contracts specialists, starting in 1980; international lawyers, in 1986; and a government relations lawyer, in 1989.

The first step toward achieving Washington's full-service objective was the acquisition in 1968 of the small firm of Pehle, Luxford, Schlezinger & Naiden. Its partners brought a diversity of practice and a rich background of government service. John Pehle, who had been with the Treasury Department from 1934 to 1946, had a clientele that included American Security Bank, later subsumed into Maryland National Financial Corp. He was courtly and considerate. Appointed administrative head of ML&B's Washington office in 1972, he dispatched limousines to pick up Philadelphia members of the Firm's newly created Executive Committee as they arrived at Union Station, until he was told that the frugal Philadelphians were embarrassed by such extravagance.

Ansel Luxford, who spent three years with the Firm before he died in 1971, had been with the Treasury Department and later the World Bank from 1935 to 1951. He brought the Scotch Whiskey Association, which remains a client today. Julius Schlezinger, whose government service was with the Department of Justice, brought Knoll Fine Chemicals, a division of BASF AG. The Firm's Food and Drug Administration (FDA) practice can be traced to Schlezinger and that client. Today, that practice is directed by Stephen Mahinka and Kathryn Gleason, who came to the Firm in 1975 and 1981 respectively, becoming partners in 1981 and 1989. Their specialty ultimately reached all major areas of FDA regulation, including pharmaceuticals, medical devices, food, and food additives. By 1993, Mahinka and Gleason numbered among their clients Sandos Pharmaceuticals; the Upjohn Company; Theratronics, Ltd.; Graco Children's Products; Ueno Fine Chemicals, Inc.; and Otsuka Pharmaceutical. Mahinka was an honored guest at the opening in 1983 of Otsuka's first United States facility, located at Gaithersburg, Maryland. To celebrate the event, Otsuka arranged to fly in from Japan a Shinto priest, Kabuki performers, and the very best sushi.

Neil Naiden, who also came with the Pehle group, formerly served as general counsel to the Atomic Energy Commission (AEC). He brought Simmonds Precision Products, Inc., and expertise in atomic energy and government contracts law. These capacities were enhanced when Loren Olson joined the Firm as a partner in 1970, followed by Oris (Sparks) Hiestand, who came as an associate in 1973 and was made a partner in 1978. Both had been with the AEC, Hiestand as a legal officer and Olson as a commissioner. Other early efforts to gather up federal agency practice included the addition of Edward Schmeltzer, a former managing director of the Federal

Maritime Commission (FMC), who came to the Firm in 1969 and became a partner a year later. In 1970, he was joined by Edward Aptaker, who was made a partner in 1971. Although both left in 1976,[14] it was during their stay that ML&B handled one of the largest proceedings in the FMC's history: the merger of United States Lines with Sealand Service, Inc., the two main United States flag carriers at that time.

Another major engagement in the maritime area was for the Commonwealth of Puerto Rico, a client generated by Mario Escudero, who came to the Firm in 1965 and became a partner in 1970. As an island, Puerto Rico was obviously dependent upon ocean transportation and sensitive to increases in shipping costs. According to Escudero's testimony before the Puerto Rican legislature, such costs could be contained if Puerto Rico acquired the major shipping companies that served it. In 1974, his recommendations were accepted, and ML&B was retained to negotiate the acquisition of three carriers controlling 90 percent of Puerto Rico's shipping trade. To take title and operate the lines, the Firm created the Puerto Rico Maritime Shipping Authority (PRMSA).

The PRMSA acquisitions closed in September and October of 1974. They covered assets valued at more than $400 million, including vessels and terminals both in Puerto Rico and on the mainland. Escudero recalls that the final closing in New York lasted forty-five hours around-the-clock and was followed by an all-afternoon festive lunch at the "21" Club. PRMSA was Washington's first large multidisciplinary, multioffice transaction: Miles Kirkpatrick obtained favorable rulings from the Justice Department in the antitrust field; Kenneth Hickey negotiated labor contracts with six shipboard and land-based unions; Philadelphia partners William Goldstein, Howard Shecter, and Edward Cloues led the corporate team; and Dennis Barnes worked with Escudero on the maritime aspects of the transaction.[15]

A subsequent maritime representation involved the Transpacific Stabilization Agreement (TSA), a matter attracted in 1988 by Robert Peavy, who came to the Firm in 1966 and became a partner in 1971. TSA was another multioffice representation, with segments handled in Tokyo and Brussels. Peavy noted:

> The client's name is indeed an "agreement," reflecting the structure of the United States shipping laws dating back more than seventy-five years which permit certain agreements among ocean common carriers to be filed with the Federal Maritime Commission and, subject to restrictions, to obtain exemptions from United States antitrust laws for price fixing, capacity controls and other

collective actions.

TSA applied this OPEC-type approach to international carriers with roughly 85 percent of the market share in the world's busiest container shipping lanes, from Asia to North America. The original filing, in which six of the Firm's antitrust lawyers participated, was effective in 1989 and became a paradigm for the industry. Named TSA's counsel and "administrator," Peavy found himself a frequent flier to Asia, sometimes making the trip twice a month.

■ ■ ■ ■ ■

Despite ML&B's 1968 decision that its Washington office would go full service, it moved slowly in areas beyond gas, labor, and transportation. Monarch had not been busy as a tax lawyer prior to his retirement in 1963. Not much busier was Stanley Weiss, a tax lawyer who arrived in 1969, became a partner in 1970, and left the Firm in 1977. The same was true of Edwin Kronfeld in the corporate field. He joined the Firm as a partner in 1969 and left in 1979. Kronfeld was a fine SEC practitioner, a careful craftsman, and a good colleague. But the Firm generated little corporate practice in Washington, either in the securities or transactional areas.

All this changed in 1979 with the arrival of two high-profile lawyers, A. A. Sommer in the corporate field and Donald Alexander in the tax area. But Alexander, an encyclopedic tax lawyer and a commissioner of the IRS from 1973 to 1977, had difficulty adjusting to the Firm's deferential culture. He left in 1985, shortly after ML&B attracted another former IRS commissioner, Sheldon Cohen, as a partner. Both Sommer and Cohen became valued members of the Firm family.

Few people have been as prominent in the field of securities law for as long as A. A. Sommer. As an SEC commissioner from 1973 to 1976, he led a review of the entire corporate disclosure program, promoted the idea of internal investigations by companies with improper payment problems, and spearheaded a campaign that abolished fixed brokerage commissions effective May 1, 1975. That abolition revolutionized retail investment banking, resulted in major reshufflings of brokerage firms, and begat discount brokerage. Sommer became such an authority on brokerage competition that in 1983 he was retained by the Office of Fair Trading of the United Kingdom to advise on the elimination of fixed commissions by the London Stock Exchange, which resulted in the "Big Bang," effective October 27, 1986.

After service with the SEC, Sommer returned to the private sector for three years before joining ML&B "to build virtually from scratch a business and finance practice in Washington with heavy emphasis upon the securities aspects." Encouraged to implement his vision, Sommer drew outstanding lawyers from the SEC, including Lloyd Feller, George Yearsich, Linda Griggs, and Kathryn McGrath. Feller, who arrived in 1979 and became a partner in 1981, had been Sommer's legal assistant at the SEC. Earlier, he had been chief counsel to the chief accountant; and when he left the commission, he was associate director of its division of market regulation. While Sommer operated at the policy level, no one outdid Feller in understanding and construing the esoterica of SEC regulations. Yearsich, who came to the Firm in 1981 and became a partner in 1984, had served as special counsel to SEC Chairman Harold Williams. Griggs, who arrived in 1984 and was made a partner in 1987, had been chief counsel to the chief accountant. Finally, McGrath, who joined the Firm laterally as a partner in 1990, had been the SEC's director of investment management. This handpicked and powerful team served all the Firm's offices in securities regulation.

Sommer also maintained a high profile by virtue of his representation of the Business Round Table, as well as his appointment to the American Institute of Certified Public Accountants' Public Oversight Board, of which he became chairman in 1986. In addition, he campaigned in 1982 to repeal the Public Utility Holding Company Act, a consummation William Clarke Mason would devoutly have wished forty years earlier. Sommer all but succeeded in the Senate when the effort ran aground in the House. Yielding to his persuasiveness, even the commissioners and staff of the SEC had supported repeal.

Corporate lawyers not directly associated with the securities field were also added in the 1980s. They were Frank Skillern, Kathleen Topelius, Allen Raiken, and Frank Goldstein. The first three were banking specialists. Skillern came to the Firm in 1981 as a partner, having formerly been general counsel to the Federal Deposit Insurance Corporation. Exceptionally efficient and well regarded, he left the Firm two years later to become general counsel of Investors Diversified Services in Minneapolis. His protégé, Topelius, came from the National Savings & Loan League and before that the Federal Home Loan Bank. She arrived in 1982, became a partner in 1985, and left the Firm in 1993. Raiken, who had served as acting general counsel of the Federal Reserve Board, joined the Firm as a partner in 1988. Goldstein, previously managing partner of Piper & Marbury's Washington office, arrived a year later.

Just as Sommer grew the business and finance practice in Washington, so Cohen developed its tax practice. But unlike Sommer, Cohen took a shortcut: He merged with ML&B his entire firm, then known as Cohen and Uretz.[16]

After graduating from law school in 1952, Cohen spent several years with the IRS helping draft the Revenue Code of 1954, a good start for a young tax lawyer. Next, as an associate in private practice, he did personal tax work for then Majority Leader and subsequently Vice-President Lyndon Johnson, as well as for Mrs. Johnson. Immediately after President Kennedy's assassination on November 22, 1963, Cohen was instructed to put President Johnson's personal affairs in order from the tax viewpoint. Cohen drafted a blind trust to which he transferred control of Johnson's assets, including his ranch and cattle properties. Six weeks later, Johnson named Cohen as chief counsel of the IRS and promoted him to commissioner a year later. Cohen was only thirty-seven.

Looking back, Cohen recalls that Johnson never asked him whether he wanted the commissioner's job. The President simply telephoned and said he was sending Cohen's name to the Senate for confirmation. With Nixon's election in 1968, Cohen was asked to remain commissioner for six months or so. He responded that he wished to resign to the man who had appointed him, not to Nixon. After Cohen joined ML&B in 1985, he rapidly assumed effective leadership of the tax section, becoming its chairman in 1989. He was a tax generalist: No tax question was beyond his purview.

While with ML&B, Cohen handled matters for Subaru of America, Inc.; Aoki American, Inc.; the estate of Edward Bennett Williams; and the governments of Israel and Mexico. For the Williams estate, Cohen took part in selling the Baltimore Orioles, the biggest single asset of the renowned trial lawyer's $100-million estate. For the Mexican government, Cohen helped draft a tax law aimed at plants along the Mexican border. Owned by American interests, the plants assembled and shipped their products back north, seemingly without ever making a profit. Since Mexico lacked the expertise to exact income taxes by applying transfer pricing concepts, a simpler approach was needed. Cohen recommended an asset tax on the plants themselves. Naturally, the plants abhorred the asset tax, since it was ineligible for foreign tax credit in the United States. But the Mexican income tax qualified for such credit. So Cohen provided that the asset tax could be offset by the income tax. As if by magic, the plants began operating profitably, and Mexico got the income taxes it wanted, all as Cohen had predicted.

Less than three months before the Cohen group arrived, tax lawyer B. John Williams came to the Firm as a lateral partner. He had served earlier as special assistant to the IRS's chief counsel and then as a deputy assistant attorney general in the Justice Department's Tax Division. After only a year with the Firm, he was appointed a judge on the United States Tax Court. There, his achievements included a celebrated sixty-page opinion adjudicating a billion-dollar estate tax dispute between the Newhouse publishing family and the IRS.[17]

But Williams's fortune in the public sector did not match his fame. He was, as he put it, "frustrated with having Congress as his allocation committee." So he returned to ML&B in 1990. His Tax Court reputation led Shell Oil Company to engage him as a judge to conduct a mock trial of an important pending tax dispute. Shell was so impressed by Williams's performance that it retained him as lead outside counsel in major tax litigation involving the characterization of tar-sand oil for tax credit purposes. Williams's retention by Shell especially pleased those ML&B New York partners who had been members of Wickes, Riddel, Jacobi & McGuire. That firm merged with ML&B in 1979, as described in Chapter 21. It had represented Shell between 1922 and 1971.

■ ■ ■ ■ ■

From the 1920s to the 1980s, antitrust and trade regulation matters were handled in Philadelphia by William Clarke Mason, Francis Bracken, Thomas Ringe, Arthur Littleton, Benjamin Quigg, and Miles Kirkpatrick. Starting in 1973, when Kirkpatrick returned to the Firm after three years as chairman of the Federal Trade Commission (FTC), he devoted himself mostly to ML&B's Washington office. The antitrust section of the Washington office was born that year, when Kirkpatrick also attracted to the Firm his assistant at the FTC, Caswell Hobbs.

Kirkpatrick was one of the country's leading authorities in his field. Two years before his retirement in 1983, a search began for a successor with similar credentials. The obvious choice was John Shenefield, who was leaving the government after serving as associate attorney general of the United States.[18] But talks with Shenefield hit a snag due to the Penn Central valuation case, discussed in Chapter 35. In 1980, the Firm had helped negotiate a $2-billion settlement for Penn Central, arising from the taking of its railroad properties by Conrail four years earlier. Shenefield, who supervised the government's legal team, discovered the Firm's involvement, discontinued the talks to avoid any appearance of impropriety, and went elsewhere after leaving the government in 1981.

But Shenefield was pursued by Hobbs, who made sure he was regularly beaten by Shenefield at tennis. Shenefield recalls that Hobbs suffered a five-year losing streak before Shenefield finally joined the Firm in 1986, after which Hobbs's game enjoyed an uncanny resuscitation. Shenefield brought with him as a partner Peter Halle, a former assistant chief and trial lawyer in the Antitrust Division.

During Shenefield's four years in the Carter administration, two landmark cases had especially claimed his attention. One was the AT&T dismemberment, while the other was endless litigation over the proposed IBM breakup. In 1982, after Shenefield left the government, AT&T capitulated, and the Justice Department abandoned its pursuit of IBM. Interviewed by the *New Yorker* in 1993, Shenefield noted that AT&T and the Baby Bells went from strength to strength after their defeat and dismemberment, whereas victorious IBM withdrew into its mainframe business, ignored customer demand for compatible equipment, and suffered staggering losses by the 1990s. "History has now proclaimed a verdict," said Shenefield.[19]

In 1983, before Shenefield arrived at the Firm, the ongoing AT&T breakup posed a challenge regarding the extremely valuable Bell trademark. AT&T wanted to use it. So did the Baby Bells, including ML&B client Bell Atlantic, as it would later be called. The Justice Department favored AT&T, arguing that otherwise the proper use of the name would have to be policed by a central licensing agency operated by the Baby Bells, and this might lead to cooperation and collusion among them. An obvious solution, but only in retrospect, was proposed by intellectual property lawyers Michael Kelly and Michael Clayton, who came to the Firm in 1974 and 1980 respectively and became partners in 1981 and 1988. To avoid a central licensing agency, they argued that any regional operating company should be permitted to use the word "Bell" by simply attaching a geographic modifier, thus giving rise to Bell Atlantic, BellSouth, and Southwestern Bell. In this way, Kelly and Clayton helped name some of the world's largest corporations.

After Shenefield's arrival in 1986, the Firm handled antitrust matters for Hallmark Cards, Inc.; McCaw Cellular Communications, Inc.; Southdown, Inc.; and Kansas City Southern Railway Co. (More about Kansas City Southern in Chapter 39.)

Starting in the late 1980s, one of Shenefield's most active clients was News Corporation Limited, a holding company for Rupert

Murdoch's interests and the largest publisher of English-language newspapers in the world. Its acquisitions and dispositions often posed novel antitrust questions in the fast-changing media world. One involved the sale of the *Star* to the *National Enquirer*, requiring a market definition of "impulse buying at the supermarket checkout counter." Persuaded by the Firm's arguments, the Justice Department did not attack the transaction. Another, in 1988, stemmed from Murdoch's $2.8-billion purchase of Triangle Publications (publisher of *TV Guide*) from Walter Annenberg, a previous owner of the *Philadelphia Inquirer*. In still another case, the Rank Organization, the British film producer, tried to buy the film-processing division of Twentieth Century Fox Film Corporation, a part of the Murdoch corporate family. After the transaction was challenged by the Justice Department, a trial was held in Los Angeles, commencing every evening at 6:30 and ending at approximately midnight. The judge was not available during the day: He was trying a major cocaine case he said was "worth far more" than the antitrust case. Shenefield and his team were perplexed by the judge's priorities but acquiesced in his schedule. They also won the case.

Another major matter for the Murdoch interests involved media policy in the United Kingdom. With the introduction of satellite television, the question arose whether joint ownership of newspapers and television networks should be prohibited, as in the United States. Economic analyses and position papers were amassed, and Shenefield appeared as an unsworn expert before the Special Enquiry on Broadcasting (Sadler Enquiry), arguing that a country with eleven daily national newspapers and eleven Sunday national newspapers had adequate diversity in its media, unlike the United States where the norm was one newspaper per city. Such arguments enabled the Thatcher government to block parliamentary calls for a breakup of Murdoch's interests in the United Kingdom. Ultimately, broad legislation acceptable to the client was passed regulating the broadcasting and television industries. For the first time, the Firm found itself behind the scenes in Westminster.

■ ■ ■ ■ ■

Just as the antitrust section of the Washington office was founded by Kirkpatrick after he completed his government service in 1973, so its litigation section was created by Fred Fielding when he emerged from the White House and became an ML&B partner in 1974. Previously an associate in Philadelphia from 1964 to 1970, Fielding served as assistant counsel to the President in 1970-72 and as deputy counsel in 1972-74. Thus, he was on the staff of presidential counsel John Dean, Nixon's bête noire, during the

Watergate affair involving the celebrated burglary of the Democratic Party headquarters in September 1972. Seven persons were implicated, including two former White House aides. Fielding was one of several Nixon officials (others included Alexander Haig and L. Patrick Gray, Jr.) alleged to be "Deep Throat," the senior Nixon administration official who furnished information to *Washington Post* reporters Bob Woodward and Carl Bernstein for use in their Watergate exposé.[20] Although rumors persist to this day, Fielding's passport and a photograph taken in Bolivia show that he was actually out of the country when one important contact between Deep Throat and the reporters took place.

As a Firm partner in Washington from 1974 to 1981, Fielding tried important cases for CBS and Comsat. But with the election of Ronald Reagan, he returned to the White House to serve as counsel to the President between 1981 and 1986, before resuming private practice, this time as a name partner in Wiley, Rein & Fielding.

With Fielding gone, the Washington litigation section really consisted of Howard Weir, who arrived in 1978 and became a partner in 1986. The section remained in limbo until the arrival of William Gardner, who joined the Firm as a partner in 1984. A knowledgeable trial lawyer, Gardner built the section, adding Peter Buscemi in 1986 (he became a partner in 1987) and Ralph Albright, who arrived as a lateral partner in 1987, as well as Grace Speights, who became a partner in 1991. While the five comprised the nucleus of the Washington litigation section, scores of other Washington lawyers were active on a routine basis before their respective agencies and in the courts. Because of the nature of federal practice, there was never a shortage of litigation talent in Washington, with its focus on regulatory specialties.

Gardner and his team handled litigation for many Firm clients: U. S. Gypsum; Smiths Industries; Reliance Electric; Federal Express; C&P Telephone Company; Thomson McKinnon, Inc.; Contel (later part of GTE); Advacare; Buckeye Pipe Line; USPCI; Pepco; Allied Van Lines; Security Federal Savings Bank; Amerace; Mobay (later Miles Inc.); Unisys; Federal Pacific Electric; Merrill Lynch & Co.; Jefferies & Company; and Pilkington plc.

Pilkington, an ML&B client since 1912, has already been dealt with in Chapter 6. Gardner led the defense when Pilkington was sued in Dade County, Florida, by Visual Scene, Inc. (VS) in 1985. Pilkington had invested in VS and supplied blanks to VS for sunglasses. At VS's direction, the blanks were sent to its fabricator in Taiwan to be made into sunglasses. When VS's financial condition precluded its paying for and taking delivery of the glasses, they were stored in a warehouse in Taiwan. The warehouse was humid, and a fungus damaged the lenses by the time VS finally received them. VS said that they were inherently defective; Pilkington counter-claimed on grounds that VS had mismanaged its business, caused its own loss, and jeopardized Pilkington's investment in VS.

The suit generated seventy depositions and 300,000 documents by way of discovery, as well as 12,000 pages of testimony at a four-month trial. VS claimed $16 million in compensatory damages and $65 million in punitive damages. In settlement discussions, VS demanded $36 million, a figure from which it never retreated, even during the trial in 1990. But after four days of deliberation, the jury returned a verdict against VS on all counts and awarded $1 million to Pilkington.

Gardner's facility with juries was matched by Buscemi's skill at the appellate level. That skill derived in part from his four years in the Solicitor General's office, during which he argued ten cases before the Supreme Court and had primary responsibility for twenty-five briefs. After joining ML&B, he took part in all the Firm's Supreme Court cases, as well as appellate cases in other courts. Among his more colorful assignments was *Allegheny County v. Greater Pittsburgh ACLU*, a 1989 Supreme Court case in which he represented Allegheny County and the city of Pittsburgh.[21] They had authorized the display of a Christmas nativity scene by the Holy Name Society, a Roman Catholic organization, on the grand stair-case of the county court house. They had also authorized the display by a Jewish organization of an eighteen-foot menorah set up next to a forty-five-foot Christmas tree outside a municipal office building.

Not surprisingly, the Pittsburgh displays were challenged by civil liberties organizations and local residents, primarily on grounds that they represented "an establishment of religion" contrary to the First Amendment. The district court found both displays permis-sible, the Court of Appeals for the Third Circuit found neither permissible, and the Supreme Court found the menorah permissible but not the nativity scene. During argument before the Supreme Court, there were references to an earlier case in which the Court had allowed Pawtucket to display a nativity scene alongside a Santa Claus house, reindeer pulling Santa's sleigh, candy-striped poles, and a wishing well. Buscemi argued that a decision rendering the Pittsburgh creche impermissible while approving it in Pawtucket would elevate plastic Santas and candy canes to a level of constitu-tional significance. Justice John Paul Stevens, who obviously opposed the Pittsburgh display, remarked that it was easy to make fun of such distinctions but difficult to establish what the correct rule should be. As it turned out, the distinction prevailed: What Pittsburgh needed were plastic Santas and candy canes.

■ ■ ■ ■ ■

In 1962, a book appeared that joined *Uncle Tom's Cabin* and *The Jungle* in dramatically affecting the course of American history. It was Rachel Carson's *Silent Spring*.[22] Aimed at DDT, an insecticide credited with saving millions of lives during World War II, the author argued that it had become a biocide. Translated into twenty-two languages, *Silent Spring* was a best-seller and a wake-up call. In the years immediately following the book's publication, the word ecology entered common parlance, the Cuyahoga River caught fire, Lake Erie was pronounced "dead," and an oil spill near Santa Barbara provoked a national outcry. Passions climaxed on Earth Day, April 22, 1970. According to the media, it was the biggest outpouring of American people onto the streets since the Japanese surrender in 1945.

The states and the federal government rushed to respond. Caught up in that rush was John Quarles, a young Boston lawyer who had opted in 1969 for "two years of government experience," as he put it. Employed by the Interior Department under Secretary Walter Hickel, Quarles worked on President Nixon's first environmental message to Congress early in 1970 and assisted in forming the Environmental Protection Agency (EPA). Present at the creation, Quarles was asked by William Ruckelshaus, the EPA's first administrator, to become the agency's general counsel and lead its enforcement program.

In April 1973, as Watergate intensified, Nixon named Ruckelshaus, a white hat in his administration, to head the FBI.[23] As a result, Quarles was tapped to move into the EPA's number-two position, serving four years as its deputy administrator, with two stints as acting administrator. All told, Quarles spent eight years in the government at the forefront of all emerging environmental initiatives. He launched a nationwide water pollution permit program, built a tough enforcement arm, testified before congressional committees on some seventy-five occasions, and wrote a book: *Cleaning Up America, An Insider's View of the Environmental Protection Agency*.[24] The book, a personal account of the political crosscurrents attending the birth and early years of the EPA, was published by Houghton Mifflin, the publisher of *Silent Spring*. However, Quarles noted ruefully that his piece never achieved the popularity of Carson's pioneering effort. After Jimmy Carter's election in 1976, Quarles returned to private practice, joined ML&B early in 1977, and eventually served on both the Firm's Executive and Allocation committees.[25]

Arriving at ML&B, Quarles found its Philadelphia office already engaged in environmental work for Delaware Valley clients. But his designs were grander: a national environmental practice. Although it took him "time to adjust to the private sector and also for clients to welcome assistance from a former nemesis," he was soon engaged in environmental matters for labor client Anheuser-Busch and litigation client Rollins Environmental Services, Inc. Eventually, whole industries became clients, including the American Petroleum Institute, and later the Chemical Manufacturers Association. Also attracted were groups of companies with problems under specific environmental laws. An example was the representation over a twelve-year period of twenty major corporations with respect to clean air legislation. They included General Motors, IBM, Chevron, ARCO, and Proctor & Gamble.

Another important environmental lawyer was Kenneth Rubin, who arrived in 1974, became a partner in 1981, and originated Olin Corporation as a client while still an associate. For many years, the Firm worked for Olin on litigation in more than a dozen states involving over twenty manufacturing sites. In addition to Quarles and Rubin, ML&B's environmental practice was fleshed out in the 1980s as the Firm attracted a number of lawyers who were already leaders in their subspecialties. Among them was William Lewis, who joined the Firm as a partner in 1984. He had served as executive officer of the California Air Resources Board and subsequently as director of the National Commission on Air Quality. Another was Steven Schatzow, a lateral entrant in 1986, who had spent ten years with the EPA, the last two as director of its Office of Pesticide Programs. Finally, Michael Steinberg returned to the Firm in 1987, becoming a partner in 1988. Earlier, he had been an associate before leaving to serve five years as assistant chief of the Environmental Defense Section of the Justice Department.

Environmental regulation "began to sputter," according to Quarles, after Ronald Reagan took office in 1981. Still, the Comprehensive Environmental Response, Compensation and Liability Act[26] (CERCLA) had been enacted the previous year. CERCLA created the Superfund program and was a bonanza for lawyers, especially since the liability it imposed was strict and retroactive, as well as joint and several (by judicial interpretation), on owners and operators of waste sites, transporters to waste sites, and generators or persons who arranged for the disposal of waste to such sites.

Considering CERCLA's broad reach, it was not surprising that detectives were hired to identify "potentially responsible parties" (PRPs) who could be held liable. PRPs soon became so numerous they revolutionized the forms routinely circulated inside the Firm to avoid representing clients with adverse interests. Called conflicts reports, they normally named the client, the opposing party, and one or two other affected interests. With CERCLA, extra pages had to be attached to designate scores and sometimes hundreds of PRPs at a Superfund site. According to Quarles, CERCLA was "ponderous, costly, and inefficient, but it pushed the Firm into prominence in the field." By 1993, ML&B had been involved in 200 Superfund proceedings in thirty-five states for more than fifty clients, including ICI Americas, Inc.; Olin Corporation; Mobay Corporation (later Miles Inc.); Rollins Environmental Services, Inc.; North American Philips Corporation; Genesco; AT&T; and CIBA-Geigy, Inc.

Under Quarles, ML&B became a leader among law firms in keeping clients informed about EPA regulations focusing on air pollution, water pollution, pesticides, toxic substances, and hazardous waste. The Firm even published popular handbooks in the field. One was the *Environmental Deskbook*, first issued in 1988. It received *Of Counsel's* yearly award for the "best guidebook, source book, or other report," accompanied by the comment: "With the visibility of lawyers like former EPA general counsel and deputy administrator John Quarles, Morgan, Lewis has established a reputation as having one of the top environmental departments anywhere."[27]

The *Environmental Deskbook* enjoyed a circulation of 7,500 copies. Demand was even greater for *The NEW Clean Air Act*, requiring distribution of more than 20,000 copies. It was used not only by industry but even by the EPA in its training courses. Finally, there was the *PRP Organization Handbook*, first published by the Firm in 1989 for The Information Network for Superfund Settlements, a group of over 150 leading companies, law firms, public agencies, educational institutions, and nonprofit organizations. The work was widely recognized as *the* definitive guide in establishing a framework for structuring large groups of defendants in Superfund proceedings, resolving disputes among them and with the government, and managing work at Superfund sites.

By 1993, seventy Firm lawyers, mostly in the government regulation and litigation sections, were busy with ML&B's environmental practice in seven offices. Although J. Tyson Stokes's centennial history never mentioned environmental law, twenty years after its publication, the number of ML&B lawyers working in the environmental field was more than half the number of lawyers in the entire

Firm as Stokes knew it.

■ ■ ■ ■ ■

Starting with World War II, as the United States government became the world's largest purchaser of goods and services, government-contracts law evolved into a highly developed specialty. Four of the Firm's Washington partners practiced in that field: Thomas Williamson, who arrived in 1980 and became a partner in 1984; Marcia Madsen, who arrived in 1981 and became a partner in 1986; and Roy Mitchell and Andrew Ness who joined the Firm laterally as partners in 1987. Mitchell's clients included Mobil Oil Corporation, Arabian American Oil Company (ARAMCO), and Dillingham Corporation. His coverage was global, taking him regularly to Saudi Arabia, Kuwait, Europe, and the Far East. One matter required four trips to Bahrain and involved the building of the Shaikh Isa Airbase in Suman, Bahrain, an outpost base for the Desert Shield staging in 1990 and the Desert Storm liberation of Kuwait in 1991. An unusually exotic international matter, its protagonists included the Bahrain defense forces as the base owner, a Taiwanese contractor, Bahraini subcontractors, and a United States engineering firm.

From involvement in an occasional international matter, the Firm's Washington office took a significant step in 1986 with the lateral addition of three full-time international partners: Markham Ball, Mark Joelson, and Joseph Griffin. They became available with the fragmentation of Wald, Harkrader & Ross, a Washington firm of which Griffin had served as managing partner. The trio brought with them Mark Bravin, an international associate who became an ML&B partner in 1993. As detailed in Chapter 24, they also brought thirty Iranian claims cases being tried in The Hague, as well as work for the British and Australian governments, subsequently adding the Republic of China and British Aerospace PLC to their client list. With the arrival of international section lawyers in 1986, all eight of the Firm's sections were finally represented in Washington.[28]

■ ■ ■ ■ ■

In 1989, a government relations lawyer, the first in the Firm's history, was added to the government regulation section. He was lateral partner Stanton Sender, and his arrival generated a collective filing by the Firm as one of Washington's 8,000 registered lobbyists. The Firm's lawyers had certainly influenced legislation before, but never on a full-time basis. A lobbying specialist was inevitable, Sender opined, because "Washington, D. C., is twenty square miles surrounded by reality," a commodity that frequently eludes bureau-crats and sometimes legislators but never lobbyists. For three decades before joining ML&B, Sender had served on the legal staff of the Interstate Commerce Commission, and later as legislative counsel in Washington for Sears, Roebuck & Co. He brought Sears as a client in the transportation field. He also brought unusual office furnishings: His walls were adorned with presidential pens given to him at White House signing ceremonies of legislation he shepherded while in the government and at Sears.

Since Congress moves slowly, lobbyists normally have the luxury of time as they analyze, strategize, inform, and cajole. But some-times there is a Mission Impossible, as Sender described one assignment that produced a law in twenty-two hours from start to finish, including the President's signature. For many months, the Firm had been representing the National Railway Labor Conference in collective bargaining. Led by Curtin, Rissetto, and Burton, the effort would ultimately produce extraordinary cost savings for the railroads through greatly reduced crew sizes. Obviously, reduced crew sizes were repugnant to the railway unions. So, anticipating an impending collision between railroads and unions, Sender's forces were ready when union pickets gathered to precipitate a nationwide rail strike on the morning of April 17, 1991.

In view of Sender's careful preparations, it was not surprising that the House and Senate were deluged with calls, faxes, and letters from shippers, including manufacturers who were desperate for just-in-time deliveries, and from farmers who threatened to slaugh-ter their chickens for want of feed grain. Media reports underscored the urgency. The campaign crescendoed as the House Energy and Commerce Committee held an early-morning hearing. House floor action followed to end the nascent strike and implement the recom-mendations of a Presidential Emergency Board, which the Firm supported. Later in the day, the Senate debated and passed the House bill without a committee hearing or even a mark-up. The bill was then rushed to the President for signature after midnight. Fourteen months later, on June 24, 1992, there was an encore, which Sender called Round Two of Mission Impossible. By that time, the unions knew the strategy and mobilized to defeat or at least stall the emergency legislation. They were again overwhelmed, but this time the campaign took thirty-six hours.

Back in 1947, Monarch had dissuaded Mason from locating the Firm's new Washington office in the Mayflower Hotel. He was reflecting Harry Truman's well-known prejudice against lobbyists. But starting with the Kennedy years, a more cordial view prevailed.

Lobbyists had achieved respectability, as well as global recognition. On one occasion, trying to describe lobbyists to German lawyers in Berlin, the author said, "We call them lobbyists." The German lawyers replied, "So do we."

■ ■ ■ ■ ■

ML&B's Washington office attests to the fallibility of strategic plans. Although it was conceived to handle tax matters, years would pass before the Firm developed a significant Washington tax practice. Meanwhile, the office would have, lose, and regenerate an expertise in natural gas law. Its labor specialty, unimagined at the outset, would eventually become its most successful area of activity. Not only the practice of the Washington office, but also its fundamental role would turn out different than anticipated: In 1947, the office was intended to provide only a window on Washington, whereas by 1986 all the Firm's eight sections were represented, most of them in depth. And of paramount importance, the practice of each section was freestanding: Washington had long ceased to be a satellite of Philadelphia.

Three aspects of ML&B's Washington experience were especially remarkable: that in 1947 the Firm decided to open a Washington office at all; that in 1968 it resolved to go full service; and that twenty years were needed to implement its full-service resolution. The first two aspects evince the Firm's innovative thinking. The third underscores the perennial difficulty of finding the right people in the right place at the right time. Solid growth for law firms is generally a slow process. Various combinations of practitioners must be tried before a law office operates effectively and becomes an institution. ML&B enjoyed an early start, thanks to Mason and MacIntosh. The result would certainly have given them joy forty-six years later.

By 1993, there were 160 lawyers in ML&B's Washington office, plus 187 nonlawyers. The office was larger than all but twelve law firms headquartered in the nation's capital and was the third-largest law firm headquartered elsewhere.

CHAPTER 21

NORTH TO NEW YORK

The Washington and New York offices compared ■ *The Harrisburg office* ■ *National practice as uncharted waters* ■ *The special challenge of New York* ■ *The role of leveraged leasing* ■ *The New York office opens in 1972* ■ *The labor practice* ■ *Latter-day clipper ships* ■ *The New York office imports and exports its practice* ■ *Wickes Riddell* ■ *Enter Samuel Fortenbaugh* ■ *Reading Company redux* ■ *Favorable and unfavorable leases* ■ *Yuppies and fat years* ■ *Riding the roller coaster* ■ *Superman and a sacrificial lamb* ■ *Full circle to leveraged leasing*

The history of ML&B's Washington office is a study in evolution. Founded in 1947, it began to transform itself in 1968 from a gas and labor boutique into a full-service office. For a law firm then to have more than one full-service office was extraordinary. But Washington had already existed as a boutique for two decades. The foundation was there. Only the transformation was necessary.

Next in the chronology came the Harrisburg office, which opened on January 1, 1961. Since Harrisburg is Pennsylvania's capital and is only 105 miles from Philadelphia, the Harrisburg office was conceived as a special-purpose satellite of the Firm's Philadelphia headquarters. Its practice initially encompassed Pennsylvania corporate and tax questions, legislative matters, and utility regulation. For eight years, Samuel Harry, a state tax specialist, was the Firm's only resident partner in Harrisburg, having previously served in the Philadelphia office. Other lawyers commuted between Philadelphia and Harrisburg. So it was with the labor practice until the arrival in 1972 of lateral entrant Thomas Lane, whose clients included hospitals, municipalities, and school districts. So it was also with the public utility practice until the arrival in 1975 of lateral entrant Russell Hoerner, whose clients comprised prominent electric, gas, and water companies. In 1977, Lane was joined by labor lawyer William Flannery, and Hoerner by government regulation lawyer Michael Gang. Both Flannery and Gang became partners in

1984. In 1993, Charles O'Brien arrived laterally and became Harrisburg's first business and finance partner.

The office in New York city, which opened in 1972, was fundamentally different from both Washington and Harrisburg. Washington started as a boutique and did not adopt a full-service agenda until twenty years later. Harrisburg started as a boutique and remained one. But New York was conceived as a full-service operation from the outset.

Today this sounds commonplace. By the mid-1980s, law firms were opening offices across the nation, sometimes by transplanting homegrown talent or alternatively by acquiring firms already in place. But back in 1972, it was a revolutionary idea that a non-New York firm would have a New York office of any kind, not to mention a full-service one. Commentators on the Firm's hubris might have applied other adjectives, including unrealistic or just plain dumb. But adjectives aside, it was the next logical step in the Firm's daring plan to go national.

ML&B was clearly a trailblazer when it opened in New York. The Firm's Long Range Planning Committee Report of 1971 noted that, except for the Firm's Washington office, practically no large law firm had a significant office outside its headquarters state.[1] The report predicted that:

> [U]nless the identity and geographical location of the Firm's major clients change . . . (either by chance or by conscious effort on the Firm's part), it seems likely that the major source of the Firm's business will continue to be generated in the eastern Pennsylvania area, and that its Washington business will continue to be primarily administrative in character and center upon government agencies located in the Washington area.[2]

This pronouncement certainly did not encourage a venture into New York, or anywhere else for that matter.

Moreover, in those days there were other perceived impediments to multiple offices. One was that a law firm could not style itself by the names of deceased partners who had not actually practiced in the jurisdiction being infiltrated—in this case New York. (Morgan, Lewis, and Bockius had never graced the New York bar.) Another concern involved referral business. At that time, the law was more geographically compartmentalized, and ML&B was *the* Philadelphia firm for referrals from many of its New York counterparts. Would that business evaporate if the New York bar regarded ML&B as a competitor? Ultimately, it turned out that both concerns were misplaced. Examined closely, the name problem really did not exist, and referrals continued undiminished after the opening of the New York office.

A further facet of the Firm's thinking was the New York market itself. That market presented an important advantage and an equally important disadvantage. On the plus side, New York was and is as open as any city in the world. Its fluid social and business structure is freely accessible to anyone. Prospective entrants need not worry about their provincial origins, whether they hail from Philadelphia, Phoenix, or Peoria. But on the minus side, the traditional Wall Street law firms were conceded to have a lock on the cream of the country's corporate law business. That business was concentrated in huge, deeply entrenched firms with towering reputations and aggregates of outstanding skills. There was no void to be filled in New York, even by the best "Philadelphia lawyers."

■ ■ ■ ■ ■

Considering this state of play, how did it happen that the Firm planted its flag in New York? There are at least five principal reasons. First, the Firm was encouraged—perhaps speciously, since the cases were hardly identical—by its success in Washington. Second, there was the influence of W. James MacIntosh. As a bold expansionist, he constantly cited the example of the major accounting firms (then the Big Eight) in urging the proposition that the Firm could and should be "everywhere," as he put it. Third, by 1972 the mantle of Firm leadership had effectively passed to the Quadriviri. In their innocence they believed the Firm could do anything. Anything included a full-service office in New York. More seasoned management might have been warier.

The fourth reason has a peculiarly indigenous ring. Typical of Philadelphia law firms, ML&B had a relatively generous partnership policy, certainly by comparison with the major New York and Chicago firms. This helped preserve the Firm's reputation for compassion in dealing with its people and, as the Firm grew, avoided its characterization as a "factory," a term applied to many large law firms. ML&B's admission policy attracted excellent lawyers. But it also exerted constant pressure for expansion to provide fulfilling opportunities and suitable incomes for an ever-increasing number of partners.

Could the Philadelphia and Washington offices satisfy this need by growing indefinitely? It was hard to predict Washington's possibilities, considering how recently it had embarked upon its full-service agenda. As to Philadelphia, while the Firm had more than its share of important local clients, the city's economy held limited promise for the future. Also, like other large firms, ML&B was already feeling the constraints inevitably imposed by conflicts of interest among its clients. So the Firm's leaders were forced to broaden their vistas, despite their affection for Philadelphia and its traditions.

The fifth and final impetus for establishing a New York office derived from the Firm's achievements in the leveraged-leasing field. (That Archimedean specialty, as practiced by Thomas Lefevre in the Philadelphia office, has already been mentioned in Chapter 19.) Some leveraged-leasing clients of the Philadelphia office had trained bright apprentices who went off to join New York investment-banking firms, including Institutional Leasing, Inc. (the leasing arm of Lazard Freres & Co.) and Dillon Reed & Co. These apprentices persuaded their new employers to use the Firm. Also, they preached the gospel in New York, with the result that additional leveraged-leasing brokers in that city became clients. Lefevre was sure more business would follow if the Firm actually established an office in Manhattan.

After weighing all the arguments, the new Executive Committee, chaired in that critical year by Lefevre, created a subcommittee to oversee the opening of a New York office. The subcommittee comprised Lefevre, John Brittain, Stuart Odell, and Jules Schlezinger. Like Lefevre, who had practiced in New York with Sullivan & Cromwell, Brittain had practiced in New York with Breed, Abbott & Morgan. Brittain was also a leveraged-leasing lawyer and the Firm's principal contact with client Lease Financing Corporation. Odell, who had become a partner in 1970, would acquire a reputation as one of the country's leading leveraged-leasing tax lawyers before leaving the Firm in 1988. The last member of the New York subcommittee was Schlezinger, a partner in the Washington office. Although all four members of the subcommittee played their roles, the venture would not have been undertaken but for Lefevre, who should be regarded as the vital force behind the creation of the Firm's New York office.

From the outset, it was contemplated that many of those involved in the enterprise to the north would commute from Philadelphia. (Regular trains made the run in about ninety minutes; Metroliner service, inaugurated in 1969, did better by about twenty minutes.) Even so, at least one resident New York associate would be required. Several Firm lawyers had dealt with Michael Thoyer, then employed by Cravath, Swaine & Moore, and had been impressed by his work in leasing transactions. He was recruited a month before the office opened and was the Firm's first New York associate, becoming a partner a year later.

So on October 16, 1972, the Firm set up shop in space subleased from the Atlantic Richfield Company on the eighth floor of the Corning Glass Building (717 Fifth Avenue) at the corner of Fifty-sixth Street and Fifth Avenue. The Firm's quarters comprised 3,675 square feet with separate offices for six attorneys. Ignoring the itinerant presences of Lefevre, Brittain, Odell, and others from time to time, the original resident staff consisted of exactly two people. They were Thoyer and Esther Weisgrau, whose job description, according to Thoyer, included "secretary, office librarian, reception-ist, xerox operator and various other administrative capacities, as well as keeper and dispenser of petty cash."[3]

Empty offices are like vacuums, which nature abhors. Even with several transient lawyers on the premises, ML&B still had some available space at 717 Fifth Avenue. To help fill that space, the Firm decided to capitalize on one of its special strengths by attracting a labor lawyer. He was Noel Arnold Levin, who arrived as a partner on October 1, 1973. Arnold, as everyone called him, was a prolific writer on labor law, especially in the pension field. He brought his practice with him, and his addition made possible a little puffing: The office could characterize itself in *Martindale-Hubbell* as engaged in "General Financial and Labor Practice." But at heart Levin was uncomfortable with the regimen of a large firm, and in 1983 he left to spend more time writing, while continuing to operate essentially as a sole practitioner.[4]

In 1985, two years after Levin's departure, the Firm hired Jay Madigan as a lateral labor associate. He brought with him *Newsday* and Ottaway Newspapers. But in 1988, a year after becoming a partner, he was stricken with cancer and died at the age of thirty-seven.

In the 1980s, some of the Firm's Washington labor lawyers joined the ranks of regular commuters to the New York office. One was partner George Stohner who relocated permanently to New York in 1987. He was followed by Bradford Coupe and Anita Coupe in 1989 and 1990, respectively. The Coupes had started their professional lives separately as labor associates in Washington before they became partners, moved to New York, and were married in 1990.[5]

Ultimately, the New York labor practice would include among its clients Ampco-Pittsburgh Corp.; Cablevision Industries Corpora-tion; Schlumberger Ltd.; Sanofi; Olympia & York Developments

Limited; GATX Corp.; International Paper Company; and Tropicana Products, Inc. But that would be years in the future. So back to the early days and the leveraged-leasing practice.

That practice got off to a flying start. In addition to existing leasing clients, the New York office picked up among investment bankers: Equilease; Blyth Eastman Dillon & Co.; A.G. Becker & Co.; and Donaldson Lufkin & Jenrette, Inc. The New York office also functioned as leveraged-leasing counsel for both owners-lessors and lenders, including West Penn Power Company; General Electric Credit Corp.; ARCO; ILI; ConAgra, Inc.; the State of Wisconsin Investment Board; Salomon Brothers Inc.; Shearson Leasing Corporation; Warburg Paribas Becker; Kidder Peabody & Co.; and State Farm Life Insurance Company. Many kinds of heavy equipment were leased: aircraft (including Boeing 747s), storage facilities for petroleum and gas products, railroad rolling stock, and ocean-going and coastal maritime vessels.

The Firm had definitely found a niche. Leveraged-lease financing, still in its embryonic stage, was regarded by investment bankers as a hot product. Most of them had their short lists of approved counsel. The traditional New York law firms were listed; ML&B was not, or at least not yet. But rarely did the traditional firms then have the exact mix of specialized tax and corporate expertise that leveraged leasing required. Accordingly, the approved lists were often trashed, as the investment bankers scorned formality and embraced competence. They also embraced economy, saying that ML&B was significantly less expensive than the New York competition.

Considering the volume of leveraged-leasing business, the New York office needed additional staffing virtually from the start. But in its infancy, it could ill afford to hire inexperienced lawyers straight from law school. They would require training, and there was simply no time for training. Instead, the office needed lawyers with three to five years' experience in general lease financing. Although such people existed, they were hard to lure from old-line firms. Still, some lawyers cannot resist being pioneers. So the Firm succeeded in attracting Bruce Fritch and Howard Mindus in 1973, Stephanie Abramson in 1976, and Raymond Warman in 1977.[6]

Fritch deserves particular mention, since like Lefevre he was one of the earliest specialists in leveraged leasing. He regularly chaired Practicing Law Institute seminars on the subject and in 1977 coedited *Equipment Leasing—Leveraged Leasing*, a book that became the bible in its field. After Fritch's sudden death in 1985, Ian Shrank succeeded him as coeditor when a third edition of the work was published in 1988. It is noteworthy that Shrank came to the Firm directly from law school in 1978 and became a partner in 1984. He was the first associate trained entirely in the New York office to achieve that distinction. A new office may be said to come of age when it makes partners from the ranks of associates who are entirely homegrown.

ML&B's New York office was a front runner in developing variants on leveraged-lease products, including so-called Title XI financings under the Merchant Marine Act of 1936, as expanded and restructured in 1972 pursuant to the Federal Ship Financing Act.[7] When the Maritime Administration agreed to guarantee obligations issued by equity participants in leveraged chartered financings of vessels, an irresistible financial package was created. It combined the federal government's credit with the benefits of a tax-advantaged leveraged lease. In 1973, Thoyer handled an early transaction of this kind. It involved a financing by Offshore Logistics, Inc., of ten supply ships for oil drilling operations in the North Sea, Gulf of Mexico, and waters off Southeast Asia.

The owner-trustee in the transaction was the Hartford National Bank. Since vessels are normally registered at the Coast Guard office nearest the principal place of business of the owner, the closing was held in Hartford, which thereby became the vessels' home port. In the old days, the Coast Guard had maintained an office in Hartford when Yankee clipper ships plied the Connecticut River to Hartford. Although no clipper ship had made the run for almost a century, the Coast Guard kept a nominal office in Hartford, but it was in a post office and no bigger than a closet.

Still, the Hartford National Bank wanted to make a splash, figuratively as well as literally. Accordingly, a Coast Guard officer was sent from New Haven. Also, a large sign bearing the legend "United States Coast Guard" was affixed to the door of the board-room in which the closing was held. Photographs were taken of the bank's chairman together with Offshore's president. Thoyer was also pictured. The event was televised and made headlines the following day in the *Hartford Courant* and *Hartford Times*. Unfortunately, Thoyer's recollections of the closing are mixed. Normally, he kept his car in a garage several blocks from his Riverside Drive apartment. But on the night before the closing, he parked his car on the street to ensure an early getaway to Hartford. In the wee hours, its hood was stolen—remarkable in a city where cars are more apt to disappear in their entirety.

■ ■ ■ ■ ■

From the beginning, the Firm hoped its New York office would not only develop an indigenous practice but would also provide opportunities for synergy among the Firm's other offices. Back in 1972, this was a wholly new idea. No one could foresee just how it would work, if at all. But by the mid-1970s, it was actually happening: New York lawyers were generating work for export to other Firm offices. Conversely, transactions originating in the Firm's other offices were being done in New York—business that probably would have been lost to the Firm without a New York presence.

One example involved client Buckeye Pipe Line Company. Robert Young had initiated the representation, which by the mid-1970s required legal work in New York relating to the placement of institutional debt and revolving credit facilities, as well as the restructuring of pipeline lease financings. Another example was Citibank, which Park Dilks attracted as a client in 1976. In those days, Dilks, Clive Anderson, and George Loveless regularly commuted to New York to do Citibank work. Because of scheduling differences (New Yorkers start their day later than Philadelphians), it was possible for the ML&B team to commute and still arrive at the bank before the bankers reported to work. (Of course, at the other end of the day, it meant very late suppers for the Philadelphians.) While the bankers realized the team was stationed in Philadelphia, they drew comfort from knowing that the Firm had a New York office, although they never visited it.

During the 1970s, there was a pioneer intimacy at ML&B New York. Dinner meetings were held at least once a month at the Harvard Club, Yale Club, Atrium Club, or Williams Club. All partners and associates were invited, and even the most minuscule office problems were painstakingly massaged.

One not-so-minuscule problem pertained to office space. From its original quarters on the eighth floor at 717 Fifth Avenue, the office had spread over parts of three floors. The space was noncontiguous, and no additional space was available in the building. There were fourteen lawyers by the summer of 1977, and the office was bursting at its seams.

In October 1977, the problem was solved when the Firm moved one block north and half a block west to a new building at 9 West Fifty-seventh Street. Viewed from the side, the building had an Eiffel Tower silhouette. Constructed by landlord Sheldon Solow during the mid-1970s recession, its lower twenty-four floors were leased to Avon Products, Inc. As anchor tenant, Avon thought it had negotiated a lease provision by which the building would carry Avon's name. Solow disagreed. The name question was litigated and Solow won. But whatever the building's name, it was easy to identify after Solow placed a huge orange number "9" on the front sidewalk like a work of pop art.[8]

The Firm's accommodations at "9 West" were glorious. The lease covered the entire forty-seventh floor with options to space on the forty-sixth floor. All told, sixty lawyers could be accommodated: forty on the forty-seventh floor and twenty more on the forty-sixth floor. The north side of the reception area offered breathtaking views of Central Park framed by elegant residential buildings along Fifth Avenue on one side and Central Park West on the other. Arriving clients were drawn to the windows of the reception area as if by a magnet. They were loathe to tear themselves away, even after they had been announced and the lawyer whom they were visiting had come to get them. One client said he hoped the "meter was not running," as he delayed getting down to business and stood transfixed by the view. A receptionist commented that she had heard dozens of clients say, "On a clear day, you can see forever." In this case, forever included Connecticut.[9]

With seventeen lawyers at the time of the move and room for sixty, a vacuum again existed, which nature again abhorred. Normally, the Firm attracted lateral entrants much as Noah had filled his ark, a couple here and a couple there. By contrast, on January 1, 1979, ML&B acquired a whole Wall Street firm, the small but well-regarded Wickes, Riddel, Jacobi & McGuire. One of its distinctions was that it had handled the incorporation in the United States of Shell Oil Company (originally Shell Union Oil Company) in 1922 and had served as Shell's general counsel for almost fifty years until Shell moved to Houston in 1971. The firm consisted of twenty full-time lawyers, eight of whom were partners. One of its partners was William O'Connor, whose brother Joseph (Joc) O'Connor was a partner in ML&B's Philadelphia office.

The Wickes acquisition was much debated in the Firm. The Noah's ark approach permitted picking and choosing, whereas selection became impossible with the acquisition of an entire firm as a package. On the other hand, the Wickes culture seemed remarkably similar to ML&B's. Also, Wickes had clients like Industrial Bank of Japan and Eastern States Bankcard Association (both handled by Wickes banking partner John Higgs), as well as Publishers Clearing House, a name known to anyone with a mailing address. The Wickes acquisition would give the New York office immediate competence in banking, litigation, and personal law. It would double the Firm's size

1. Charles Eldridge Morgan, Jr. (1844-1917) was born in Philadelphia. He saw Civil War service at Carlisle during the battle of Gettysburg in 1863 and graduated from the College of the University of Pennsylvania in 1864. After "reading law," he was admitted to the bar in 1868, founded the Firm with Francis Draper Lewis in 1873, and led it until 1908.

2. Francis Draper Lewis (1849-1930) was born in Boston. He graduated from Amherst College in 1869 and from Harvard Law School in 1871. His Harvard diploma was signed by Christopher Columbus Langdell. According to Lewis's diary, he "moved [his] table into Morgan's office" on March 11, 1873—a graphic description of the Firm's beginning.

3. Randal Morgan (1853-1926) was a younger brother of Charles Eldridge Morgan, Jr. He "read law" at Morgan & Lewis, was admitted to the bar in 1877, and was a partner from 1885 to 1895. In 1882, Randal also became inside general counsel to UGI, the Firm's first major client and still a client today. By 1900, UGI was the largest public utility holding company in the United States.

4. Wyndmoor was Randal Morgan's baronial estate in Chestnut Hill, Philadelphia. Late in December every year, the numerous Morgans would gather there to perform Dickens's *A Christmas Carol*. According to Firm lore, Morris Rex Bockius was the only non-Morgan invited to attend. The site of Wyndmoor is now occupied by a residential development with high- and low-rise apartments and a shopping center.

5, 6. Morris Rex Bockius (1859-1939), the great firm builder, was born in Philadelphia, graduated from the College of the University of Pennsylvania and its law school (1883), joined Morgan & Lewis, and became a partner in 1898. He was made a name partner in 1908 and led the Firm from that time until his death. The early photograph (left) dates from about 1880; the later photograph, from about 1937.

7. In 1906, Morris Bockius built his residence at 528 Church Lane in Germantown, just across the street from Charles Eldridge Morgan's residence. During the Bockius halcyon years, his home was the scene of much client and partner entertaining. The building still stands, although the character of Germantown has changed dramatically since Bockius's time.

8. The first office of Morgan & Lewis in 1873 was at 623 Walnut Street opposite Washington Square and just around the corner from State House Row, including Independence Hall. The block comprised once fashionable Georgian residences, many of them later converted into lawyers' offices. In the photograph, which looks northeast from Seventh Street, the Firm was located in the eighth property from the left. The block was demolished in 1908 to make way for the Curtis Publishing Building.

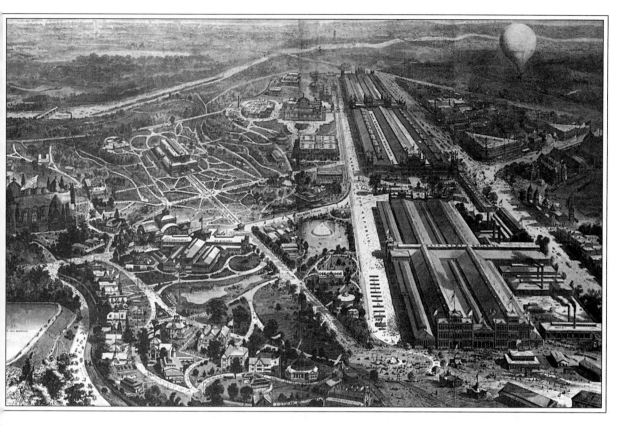

9. The Centennial Exposition of 1876, held in Fairmount Park, was a high point in Philadelphia's history. There, Alexander Graham Bell demonstrated his newly invented telephone to astounded spectators. The illustration is an artist's rendering, since aerial photographs (from balloons) were are in those days. Of the few surviving Exposition buildings, Memorial Hall can still be seen in the distance from the Firm's offices at One Logan Square.

10. The Girard National Bank was an original Firm client starting 1873. In 1926, it merged with the Philadelphia National Bank, which then became a client. The Firm was so identified with the Girard National Bank that, starting in 1889, the *Hubbell* directory listed Morgan & Lewis as "Attorneys to Girard National Bank." The Girard's bank building, shown here left, was constructed in 1795-97 for the First Bank of the United States and is now part of Independence National Historical Park.

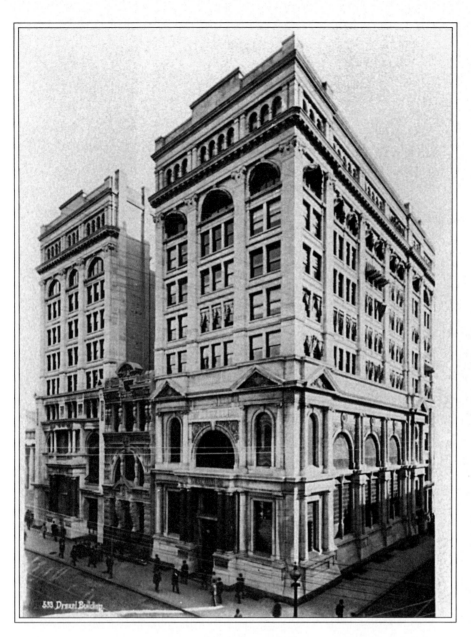

11. Between 1896 and 1904, the Firm occupied
suite 501-09 in the Drexel Building, located at
the southeast corner of Fifth and Chestnut
streets. Eleven stories high with a grand stair-
case, the building was "said to be the handsomest private bank in the world," containing "398
rooms . . . and 22 toilet rooms." It was the
headquarters of Drexel & Co., which later
evolved into Drexel Burnham Lambert.

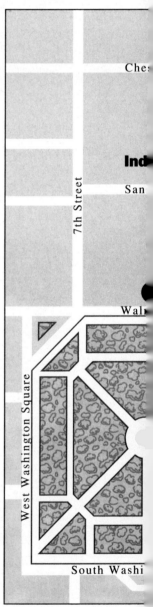

12. Until about 1900, when Philadelphia's present City Hall opened, lawyers clustered around State House Row. It extended along the south side of Chestnut Street between Fifth and Sixth streets and included Independence Hall. State House Row had been the lively seat of the city's government since colonial times, housing the city council, the state and city courts, the sheriff, the recorder of deeds, the register of wills, and the police and fire commissioners. All the Firm's locations from 1873 to 1904 were within two blocks of State House Row.

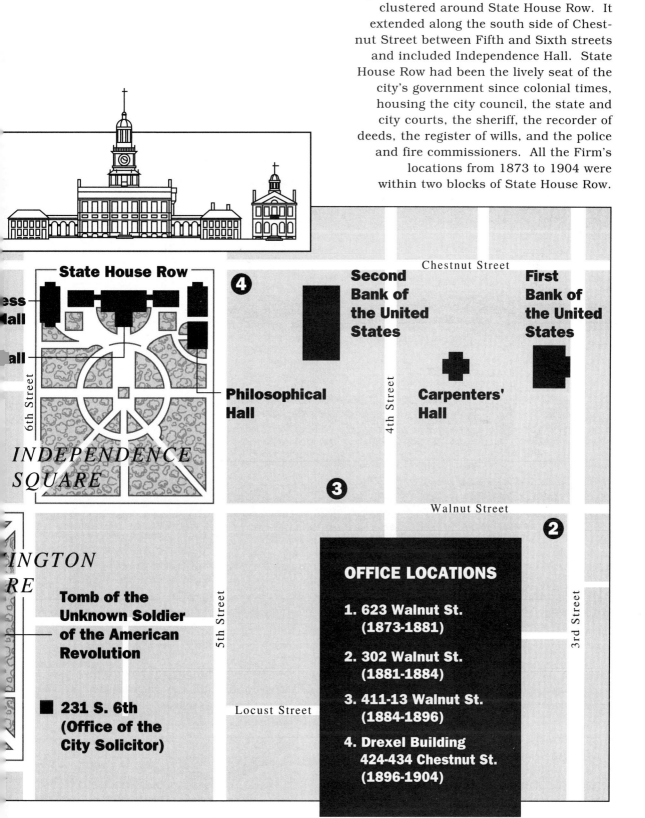

State House Row

Chestnut Street

4

Second Bank of the United States

First Bank of the United States

ess all

all

6th Street

Philosophical Hall

4th Street

Carpenters' Hall

INDEPENDENCE SQUARE

3

Walnut Street

2

3rd Street

INGTON RE

Tomb of the Unknown Soldier of the American Revolution

5th Street

OFFICE LOCATIONS

1. **623 Walnut St.**
   (1873-1881)

2. **302 Walnut St.**
   (1881-1884)

3. **411-13 Walnut St.**
   (1884-1896)

4. **Drexel Building**
   424-434 Chestnut St.
   (1896-1904)

■ **231 S. 6th (Office of the City Solicitor)**

Locust Street

13. In July 1874, sixteen months after the Firm was founded, the cornerstone was laid for Philadelphia's new City Hall at Broad and Market streets to the west of the Old City and roughly equidistant between the Delaware River and the Schuylkill. This Second Empire structure took a quarter of a century to build and cost a then astronomical $25 million. It is still the tallest building with load-bearing walls in North America.

14. After the new City Hall opened, Philadelphia's legal community moved
west. The Firm relocated in 1904 to the Land Title Building at Broad and
Chestnut streets, just a block south of City Hall. Farther south of the
Land Title Building and partly visible at lower left is the Union League,
a sometime Firm client. Its clubhouse was built in the 1860s.

15. The Fidelity Building at 123 South Broad
Street was the Firm's Philadelphia home from
1928 to 1983. In the 1920s, Morris Bockius
chaired a committee set up by the Fidelity
Bank (then the Fidelity-Philadelphia Trust
Company) to supervise the design and
construction of the building. When finished,
the thirty-story structure was the ninth-
largest office building in the world. In the
Italian Renaissance style and with a multi-
story banking floor, it was the city's premier
office structure for four decades.

16. After fifty-five years in the Fidelity Building,
the Firm's Philadelphia office moved in 1983 to
One Logan Square. That office building was
part of a newly constructed complex offering
terraced gardens and a Four Seasons Hotel.
Logan Square, once the site of public executions, had become a circle by 1919 with the
development of Philadelphia's Parkway. In
recent years, other major law firms have followed ML&B to the Logan Square area, previously considered off the beaten track for offices.

In Philadelphia nearly everybody reads The Bulletin

17. ML&B represented Philadelphia's *Bulletin* from 1909 until it ceased publishing in 1982. Once the largest evening newspaper in the Western Hemisphere, its slogan was: "In Philadelphia nearly everybody reads The Bulletin." A series of cartoons drawn by Richard Decker made the point. They featured Philadelphia scenes with all but one person reading the *Bulletin*. This cartoon shows the Philadelphia skyline and a traffic jam on the Schuylkill Expressway to the west.

18. The Baldwin Locomotive Works, once the largest locomotive
manufacturer in the world (and the Firm's largest client), was
represented by ML&B from 1917 until it disappeared in 1972
after several mergers. The Firm was active for Baldwin worldwide in the 1920s, requiring trips by Morris Bockius to Europe
and Latin America. This view is of Baldwin's old plant in Center
City Philadelphia, looking west from Broad Street. In the left
background is the Cathedral of Saints Peter and Paul, just a
block from the Firm's present location at One Logan Square.
Most of the twenty-acre plant was demolished starting in 1928
when Baldwin moved the last of its operations to a 600-acre
facility at Eddystone south of Philadelphia.

19. In 1933, Baldwin Locomotive No. 60000, a 4-10-2 engine weighing 350 tons and measuring 101 feet in length, was moved for permanent exhibition to the Franklin Institute, a long-time ML&B client. To accomplish the move, overhead wires had to be removed and temporary tracks laid over city streets. No. 60000 travels back and forth on a short section of track inside the Institute.

20. Morris Bockius (center) and Samuel Vauclain (right), the CEO of the Baldwin Locomotive Works, visited devastated Eastern Europe in 1920 to negotiate sales by Baldwin of its locomotives to the governments of Poland and Romania. They are shown here with Romania's King Ferdinand I (left). Since Romania had little foreign exchange, the transaction Bockius and Vauclain worked out permitted Romania to pay in either dollars or oil for the fifty locomotives it bought. Vauclain commented that during the trip, which lasted a month, Bockius "worked harder than he had ever done in Philadelphia."

21. The Victor Talking Machine Company was represented by the Firm from 1920 to 1927 in negotiating recording contracts with its artists and in litigation matters. During that period, electrical recording and reproduction replaced the acoustical process. Victor's plant occupied 2.5 million square feet of space in thirty-one buildings on fifty-eight acres of waterfront in Camden, New Jersey. The company was sold to investment bankers in 1927 and resold to RCA in 1929.

22. William Clarke Mason began representing the Reading Railroad in 1903. He brought that client with him when he joined ML&B in 1922. The Reading remained an active client (spawning thousands of FELA cases) until its fourth and final bankruptcy in 1971 and its takeover by Conrail in 1976. Shown here is Reading Terminal, through which 22 million passengers passed each year. The eight-story pink granite headhouse, which opened in 1893, was acquired by the city of Philadelphia in 1993 as the gateway to the city's new half-billion-dollar convention center.

23. Whitemarsh Hall, northwest of Philadelphia, was the residence of Edward Stotesbury, a senior partner in Drexel & Co. and J. P. Morgan & Co. Stotesbury, a close friend and client of Morris Bockius, was said to be worth $200 million in 1929 and "the richest man at Morgan's." Whitemarsh Hall was built between 1916 and 1921 on a 305-acre tract. Called the Versailles of America, it beggared the Gilded Age homes at Newport. Bockius was a frequent visitor at Whitemarsh Hall, which was demolished in 1982.

24. Bockius (left) was in his seventies and Stotesbury (right) in his eighties when this 1930s photograph was taken at El Mirasol, Stotesbury's winter residence at Palm Beach. The Firm handled Stotesbury's estate after he died in 1938. Bockius died a year later.

25, 26. William Clarke Mason (1881-1957) led the Firm from 1939 until his death. He graduated from Penn Law School in 1903, formed his own firm named Mason & Edmunds (known today as Obermayer, Rebmann, Maxwell & Hippel), and was attracted to ML&B by Bockius in 1922. One of Philadelphia's all-time great trial lawyers, he was especially successful with juries. He cultivated eccentricities: polka-dot bow ties, carnations in his buttonhole, a raglan coat in winter, and battered felt hats. Mason served as chancellor of the Philadelphia Bar Association and president of the Pennsylvania Bar Association. In the picture at left, he was about twenty-two; at right, he is shown in 1957, just before his death at seventy-six.

27. Francis B. Bracken (1869-1937) joined the Firm laterally in 1918 and remained until he died. Like William Clarke Mason, Bracken served as chancellor of the Philadelphia Bar Association. Remembered as an extraordinary legal technician, he was also an outstanding trial lawyer, although very different from Mason: Bracken hated juries and tried his cases to the record. Handled gingerly by his partners, he was not given to mirth.

28. Below, Thomas B. K. Ringe (1902-1957) graduated from Penn Law School in 1926 and joined ML&B laterally in 1937. He was a born leader, a dynamic trial lawyer, and a tireless worker. He kept two secretaries busy transcribing his dictation—from four dictating machines, including one in his car. He specialized in big-case litigation for clients like UGI, Scott Paper Company, and the Philadelphia Electric Company.

29. Above, Kenneth Souser (1905-1970), who graduated from Penn Law School in 1930, practiced labor law starting in the mid-1930s, and came to the Firm laterally when his firm (Souser & Kleeb) merged with ML&B in 1959. Following the merger, ML&B boasted seven labor lawyers (there would be more than 100 by 1993) and was the preeminent management labor firm in Philadelphia. Souser's many avocations included Sherlock Holmes and railroads: He maintained a narrow-gauge railroad in an apple orchard on his thirty-six-acre farm in Berwyn, Pennsylvania.

30. Stephen Girard may have been the richest man in America when he died in 1831, leaving the bulk of his $6-million estate (later worth more than $200 million) to the city of Philadelphia to create a "college" for "poor male white orphans." Between 1957 and 1968, the Firm represented the Girard trustees in their effort to carry out the literal terms of the will. The courts finally held that the exclusionary language of the will was unconstitutional, since Girard had provided for "state action" by naming the city as trustee. Starting in 1968, the school was opened to black boys; and starting in 1984, also to girls.

31, 32. Arthur Littleton (1895-1973) graduated from Penn Law School in 1920, joined ML&B, became a partner in 1926, and led the Firm from 1957 through 1966. At left, he is shown in about 1920; at right, in about 1955. Perhaps the most eloquent orator in the Firm's history, Littleton often functioned as a lawyer's lawyer when brought into litigation at the appellate stage. Exemplifying the Firm's culture of cooperation and deference, he is remembered for the epigram: "There is no limit to what can be accomplished if it makes no difference who receives the credit."

33. W. James MacIntosh (1901-1989) taught at the Wharton School while attending Penn Law School, from which he graduated in 1926. He immediately joined ML&B, became a partner in 1932, and led the Firm from 1967 to 1971. Occasionally and affectionately called Mac the Knife by his partners, he was a shrewd businessman who did not shrink from tough decisions. Long before law practices went national (and international), he foretold the day when law firms would be "everywhere." He was the last of the five individual senior partners who, one after the other, had run the Firm for ninety-eight years.

34, 35, 36. Pictured clockwise from upper left are Ernest R. von Starck, John P. Bracken, and Brady O. Bryson. Von Starck, an authority on public utility law, succeeded Littleton as the Firm's leading appellate lawyer. Bracken, a nephew of Francis Bracken, served as the Firm's managing partner from 1958 to 1972. Chairing the Firm's tax section, Bryson functioned in its Philadelphia and Washington offices. Both Bracken and Bryson took part in the Nuremburg trials.

37, 38, 39, 40. According to the *American Lawyer*: "In 1971 MacIntosh turned the Firm over to a Gang of Four—[William] Curtin in Washington and three Philadelphia partners: utilities lawyer Robert Young, corporate and international lawyer Park Dilks, Jr., and tax specialist Thomas Lefevre—who proceeded to implement his vision of expansion." Pictured clockwise from upper left are Lefevre, Young, Curtin, and Dilks. The Gang of Four effectively ran the Firm from 1971 to 1988. During that period, it increased in size from 125 lawyers to more than 600, went national and international, and opened offices in New York, Los Angeles, Miami, London, and Tokyo.

41. In 1947, ML&B opened its Washington office in the Insurance Building at Fifteenth and I streets (above). The office was staffed by two associates, Louis Monarch and John P. Bracken, and a secretary. Monarch was previously an appellate tax lawyer with the Department of Justice.

42. After expansion required several moves, the Firm's Washington office settled into spacious quarters at 1800 M Street in 1975. Starting with 60,000 square feet, ML&B increased its occupancy to 150,000 square feet by 1993. At that time, there were 160 lawyers and 187 other personnel in the Firm's Washington office.

43.The Firm moved its New York office to 9 West Fifty-seventh Street (right) in 1977. Viewed from the side, the building had an Eiffel Tower silhouette. It also featured a marvelous view of Central Park and beyond, leading visiting clients to say: "On a clear day, you can see forever." The Firm's New York operations expanded quickly, and by 1981 the Firm was out of space at "9 West."

44. In 1981, the Firm took floors forty-three through forty-six in a newly constructed building at 101 Park Avenue (left). The space could accommodate 128 lawyers. By 1993, the New York office comprised 115 lawyers.

45. The Firm established its Los Angeles office in 1976 in the Security Bank Building, 800 West Sixth Street (upper left). Opening earlier than planned, the Firm's telephone number was at first unlisted, its furniture was rented, and its library was set up on packing crates.

46. In 1978, ML&B moved its Los Angeles office to the Crocker National Bank Building at 611 West Sixth Street (lower left). Another law firm was vacating the space, which had been designed by a former Philadelphia lawyer and featured dark wood trim and floors. The space looked more like Philadelphia than Philadelphia itself.

47. Rapid expansion by the Firm in Los Angeles required that it move in 1987 to a new building, Chase Plaza, at 801 South Grand Avenue (right). By then, the Firm had 100 lawyers in Los Angeles, forty-three of them having just arrived when Hahn, Cazier & Smaltz joined ML&B.

48. After opening in Miami in 1977, the Firm moved twice, the second time in 1987 to the Southeast Financial Center (later First Union Financial Center) whose sawtooth design made possible many corner offices on the upper floors. On August 24, 1992, the building sustained damage by Hurricane Andrew, the costliest storm in American history, with a price tag of almost $30 billion. The Miami office was closed for a week—the only such closing in the Firm's history.

49. When the London office opened in 1981, the Firm took two floors at 4 Carlton Gardens, just off Pall Mall and next to Marlborough House. Clients and Firm personnel approved the convenience of a location in the West End rather than in the City. During World War II, the building had housed the *Quartier-General* of the Free French led by General Charles de Gaulle.

50. The Firm's Tokyo office opened informally in 1988 and for a year was located in a deluxe apartment complex that provided living, entertaining, and work space. Then, in 1989, the Firm moved to the CS Tower, 1-11-30 Akasaka, Minato-Ku, shown above. Its space there could accommodate two lawyers and four staff.

51. In 1989, responding to the excitement of "EC '92," the Firm opened an office at 220 Rue de la Loi in Brussels, shown above right. The press noted that the Firm's "view of the Berlaymont building [home of the European Commission] across the Schuman traffic circle screams access."

52. Also in 1989, the Firm opened a Frankfurt office in a villa already occupied by future partner Robert Daly. Located at Siesmayerstrasse 44, it was opposite the American consulate.

53. On July 29, 1966, Firm partner William Curtin, representing the airlines, and P. I. Siemiller, president of the International Association of Machinists, lined up at the White House for photographs with President Lyndon B. Johnson, who took credit for settling the worst airline strike in the nation's history. But the celebration was premature, as the strike continued until August 15. Similar photographs appeared in newspapers throughout the world. Partner Brady Bryson, while vacationing abroad, saw one in Milan and "did a double take."

54. In 1968, the Firm negotiated a labor contract that made possible the construction of Walt Disney World. William Curtin led the effort, producing a forty-seven-month agreement with sixteen building trade unions and the Teamsters. This unique agreement was the prototype for a 1974 labor contract, also negotiated by the Firm, that permitted construction of the $7.7-billion Alyeska Pipeline.

55. The Philadelphia Museum of Art is one of the city's outstanding cultural attractions. Among other treasures, it houses 1,279 paintings collected by John G. Johnson, whom the *New York Times* in a 1917 obituary described as arguably "the greatest lawyer in the English-speaking world." After six years of court proceedings, the Firm got a court order in 1989 permitting the museum to retain the Johnson collection until the year 2083. The museum was also permitted to juxtapose the collection with other art works, despite contrary provisions in the Johnson will.

56. The Philadelphia Orchestra, another outstanding cultural attraction, has been called the city's "chief contribution to civilization." Since 1959, the Firm has represented the Philadelphia Orchestra Association in labor matters, including two strikes, both in the 1960s. One of them, in 1966, lasted fifty-seven days, threatened the Orchestra's existence, and seemed to sweep the entire city into the dispute. The photograph shows the Orchestra in 1967, the year after the strike.

57. For many years, the Firm represented John T. Dorrance, Jr., chairman of the Campbell Soup Company, whose forty-nine-acre estate in Gladwyne, just outside Philadelphia, featured block-long greenhouses with prize-winning orchids, English and boxwood gardens, pet roosters and Labrador retrievers, collections of cars and firearms, and an extraordinary assemblage of paintings and other art objects. After Dorrance's death in 1989, the Firm negotiated with Sotheby's the disposition of his art collection, which brought $140 million at auction.

58. The Philadelphia Electric Company (later PECO Energy Company) became a client in 1887. Its two biggest projects involving the Firm were the Conowingo hydro-electric plant on the Susquehanna River, finished in 1927, and the Limerick nuclear plant (above), constructed along the Schuylkill between 1974 and 1990. During that period, several teams of the Firm's lawyers sustained the nuclear project against attacks by environmentalists, consumer groups, and regulatory authorities. Ultimately costing $7 billion, it was the last undertaking of its kind to be completed and actually go into operation in the United States.

59. Strawbridge & Clothier, which became a client in 1937, operates thirty-six department and dis-count stores, and employs 12,700 people. In 1986, it was the target of a hostile takeover attempt. The effort was repulsed, and the company maintained its independence. The Firm's corporate team was led by Donald Scott (left), and its litigation team by Gregory Harvey (right). Interviewed by the media, G. Stockton Strawbridge (center), then the company's CEO, said: "[ML&B is] just one hundred percent perfection from our point of view."

60, 61, 62, 63. After the Gang of Four (1971-1988), ML&B's governance widened, as many partners participated in the Firm's management. Shown clockwise from top left are Samuel B. Fortenbaugh, Alan L. Reed, Michael L. Klowden, and John R. Quarles. Fortenbaugh, a business and finance lawyer who headed the New York office, and Reed, a government regulation lawyer, both served terms as Firm chair. Klowden, who headed the Los Angeles office, was also active in management, along with Quarles, who served on the Allocation Committee and the Governing Board before being elected chair in 1994.

in New York and confer the critical mass of which Young spoke so often. After much deliberation, the deal was done, most of the forty-seventh floor was occupied, and only part of the forty-sixth floor was left for further expansion.

With the Wickes addition, the Firm had ample resources to handle any corporate transaction without drawing upon Philadelphia personnel. The timing was perfect, as the legal services boom of the 1980s was poised to explode. What the New York office needed next was a significant rainmaker to spearhead its growth in the general corporate field.

■ ■ ■ ■ ■

The right lawyer appeared at the right moment. He was Samuel Fortenbaugh III, who joined the Firm on January 1, 1980. A graduate of Williams College and Harvard Law School, he came laterally from Kelley Drye & Warren where he had served on that firm's executive committee. He brought with him a sizable corporate practice, something the New York office was now equipped to handle. In addition, he had leadership qualities and expansionist ideas like the Quadriviri. Specifically, his objective was to develop the New York office so that it could hold its own in comparison with any leading New York firm. Urged on by him, the office reached out and acquired many exceptional lawyers during the 1980s. In the business and finance area, they included Stephen Farrell (1980); Gerald Freedman and Paul Roberts (1984); Mitchell Baron (1987); and Catherine Ludden, William Lynch, and Robert Mendelson (1989). Fortenbaugh's efforts continued into the early 1990s and produced James Lillie (1990); and Robert Robison, Philip Werner, and David Blea (1991). Fortenbaugh also attracted additions to the litigation and tax sections, as well as the government regulation section—discussed later in this chapter.

The Firm's culture fit Fortenbaugh as if he were born to it. In a sense he was, as the son of a distinguished Philadelphia lawyer. (His father had been a name partner in Clark, Ladner, Fortenbaugh & Young.) In his expansion program, Fortenbaugh was aggressive but also sensitive to the overarching need for collegiality and shared objectives. Most of his acquisitions lived up to their billings, qualitatively as well as quantitatively; and a number of them exceeded expectations, as the Firm furnished a springboard for their talents.

Fortenbaugh kept his eye on synergy as well as the Firm's culture. As the Quadriviri preached, there was no point in having multiple offices if each simply went its own way. Two plus two exceeded four only if the offices cross-fertilized. The most felicitous transactions were those in which lawyers from various offices and specialties cooperated to generate a product of national or even international significance. Soon after Fortenbaugh arrived in the New York office, such an ideal transaction came along. It involved the Reading Company, which had been a major client since 1922 when William Clarke Mason brought it with him to the Firm.

In 1971, the Reading had filed for bankruptcy and five years later lost its railroad to Conrail. In this respect it was like Penn Central, although on a much smaller scale. Also, like Penn Central, the Reading retained its nonrailroad properties (including real estate that became the site of Philadelphia's Convention Center in 1993), its condemnation claim against the government (ultimately settled for about $160 million), and a huge net operating loss carryover.

The Reading finally emerged from bankruptcy on January 1, 1981. By then, the Firm's long-time representation had wound down, except for a few old FELA cases, as well as tax questions concerning the loss carryovers. But those tax questions became pivotal when the Reading decided to make an enormous acquisition in 1981. So the Firm was engaged to handle the entire transaction, which was managed out of the New York office. The matter stands as an early case study of law practice on a national scale, as literally every office of the Firm became involved in some way. Moreover, except for a few lawyers in the litigation and personal law sections, every lawyer in the New York office played a role.

In the transaction, Reading acquired the so-called industrial products group of Gould, Inc. The purchase price was $355 million, plus an assumption of debt and other obligations. For almost a year, the Firm worked on the project, which finally closed on September 28, 1981, and was, by the standards of its day, a monumental leveraged buy-out.

The acquired entities were parts of a global conglomerate engaged in manufacturing engine parts, valves, and metal products, with about thirty facilities around the world. In addition to operating assets, Gould's industrial products group owned stock in metallurgical and manufacturing firms in Mexico, India, Brazil, Japan, Australia, Belgium, Canada, France, Singapore, as well as the United States. Some of its holdings had the exotic ring of the old Baldwin Locomotive subfiles mentioned in Chapter 8. For example, there were 212,500 shares of common stock of Bimetal Bearings, Ltd., of 114 Race Course Road, Coimbatore, India; and 390,640 shares of common stock of Nippon Dia Clevite Co. of Marashino City, Chiba Prefecture, Japan. Also, there was factory real estate in Bridgeport, Ohio; Eau Claire, Wisconsin; and Barrie, Ontario; along with some twenty-seven other manufacturing and distribution facilities.

The Reading/Gould transaction was the stuff of which lawyers' dreams are made—at least postclosing dreams. (Preclosing dreams are often nightmares.) Under the overall supervision of Fortenbaugh and Farrell, this extraordinarily complicated acquisition not only showcased the technical skills and energy of the many participants but also constituted a rite of passage for the New York office. Reading/Gould was also a harbinger of several of the largest transactions the New York office handled during the 1980s. They were in the real estate field and involved acquisitions by Prime Motor Inns and Aoki American, Inc.

The Prime Motor Inns transaction took place in 1985-86 when that client purchased the Howard Johnson chain of motor lodges for $235 million. The Firm's team was led by Roberts and included Stohner, Farrell, and William Low.[10] The Prime Motor Inns transaction was followed by a much larger acquisition in 1987-88 when client Aoki purchased the Westin Hotel chain, which then included New York's celebrated Plaza Hotel. That transaction was, to paraphrase the Duke of Wellington's comment on Waterloo, "a near run thing." Aoki and Westin had been negotiating endlessly and inconclusively. After Black Monday, October 19, 1987, when the Dow Jones Industrial Average plunged 508 points, Aoki issued an ultimatum. It offered Westin an additional $50 million, thus raising the purchase price to $1.53 billion. According to Roberts, it also told Westin to "take it or leave it." Westin took it. The Firm's team comprised Roberts, Farrell, Freedman, and Franklin Bloomer in New York; James Hunter and Lee Snyder in Philadelphia; and Sheldon Cohen and Adrian Morchower in Washington.

■ ■ ■ ■ ■

Successful law firms never seem to have just the right amount of space. Where too few lawyers are rattling around in too much space, the vacuum theory applies. (Another statement of the vacuum theory is a variant on Parkinson's law: Personnel expands to fill available space.) But as soon as nature has done its job by banishing the vacuum, there are again too many people and too little space. In theory, it should be possible to stop with just the right number of lawyers in the right amount of space. A law firm would then stabilize and upgrade its practice, rejecting routine matters of minimal intellectual stimulation and low profitability. But it does not work that way. Clients make demands, and lawyers reject stasis. By 1981, the Firm's New York office was out of space again.

Leases for office space start their lives at market rates. Then, as time passes, they may become either favorable or unfavorable to their tenants. In times of space glut, rental rates can be negotiated that become favorable in later times of space shortage. Conversely, in times of space shortage, tenants will agree to rates that often become unfavorable in later times of glut. Thus, office buildings are different from widgets, the price of which sorts itself out daily by reference to supply and demand. It takes years to acquire a site, demolish existing buildings, design a new building, erect it, and fill it with tenants. The idea is to build when there is undercapacity— a landlord's market. But developers move like lemmings: They begin building at the same moment. By the time they have finished, there is overcapacity and another real estate recession. It is this bite-and-chew approach to space consumption that generates favorable and unfavorable leases.

During the Firm's five years at 9 West, its lease progressed from market to favorable. The citywide glut of space in 1977 turned into a space shortage by 1981. If the Firm moved, its space could be rented to a new tenant at almost twice what the Firm was paying. So, when the Firm sought more space at 9 West, the landlord's answer was a resounding no. He wanted the Firm out. The Firm toyed briefly with the idea of adding noncontiguous space in another building on Fifty-seventh Street. But the New York office wanted to remain under one roof. As one New York partner announced, "New York will not bifurcate." Once again, the Firm would have to relocate.

But 1981 was a bad time for tenants in terms of prevailing rentals. In fact, the Firm is still waiting, as of 1993, for its lease at 101 Park Avenue to go favorable. That pinwheel-shaped building was then under construction as the flagship of Peter Kalikow's real estate empire. Situated at Fortieth Street just south of Grand Central Station, it was on prestigious Park Avenue. Like 9 West, it offered spectacular views, although to the east, south, and west, and not over Central Park. Law firms and other professional organizations were flocking to it. ML&B joined them on November 1, 1981.

The Firm took floors forty-three through forty-six at 101 Park. It then leased to subtenants all of the forty-third floor and most of the forty-fourth floor—space that could be recaptured on a staggered basis as the New York office grew during the initial fifteen-year lease term. Altogether, the four floors could accommodate up to 128 lawyers. The ensuing decade would justify the Firm's optimism about the growth of its New York office.

■ ■ ■ ■ ■

With the upheaval of moving behind it, the New York office turned back to business, which dealt increasingly during the 1980s with financial transactions. Investment bankers reigned supreme. Savvy young graduates clutching their MBA degrees emerged from the Harvard Business School and the Wharton School. Their gratification was instant (if short term, as it turned out) in a job market where remunerations were obscene, at least compared with the compensations of nurses and school teachers.

When social phenomena become sufficiently rife, new words are coined to describe them. So it was with Yuppies—a quasi-acronym for young urban professionals. They toiled inexhaustibly, buying and selling pieces of paper. Flaunting their successes, they acquired million-dollar condominiums and mandatory BMWs. Their raison d'etre was to do deals and collect fees. Never mind tomorrow, economic reality, or the generation of any real wealth.

During the seven fat years, 1983 through 1989, the lubricant was borrowed money, as leverage was king and cash passé. Also passé were those few remaining veterans in the brokerage houses who had seen the 1920s become the 1930s. With quavering voices, they told their tales. Years ago they had witnessed "extraordinary popular delusions and the madness of crowds."[11] But who had time for the warnings of wizened sages when so much money cried out to be made? The old-timers were dismissed as Cassandras or indulged as anachronisms.

One sage was MacIntosh. He had lived through it all, as a bond salesman in 1922, as a Wharton School instructor in finance while at law school, and as a lawyer at ML&B starting in 1926. He repeatedly predicted crashes in the financial markets, first in the 1970s and then in the 1980s. But he could never reconcile his ominous predictions with his exuberant temperament. So he disregarded all his warnings when investing for his own account, and did well.

The 1980s saw much misguided talent and misspent energy, with New York as the epicenter. Following in the wake of the investment bankers, some New York law firms, barely known before, became shockingly successful during that decade. Their premium fees, righteously called value billings, gave them money to burn. They burned some of it by overpaying neophyte associates, often better compensated than the judges before whom they appeared. The track was too fast for some medium-sized New York firms. They broke up. But the boutique firms survived with their niches. And generally so did the big firms with their economies of scale.

ML&B had not been in New York long enough to play a major role in the feeding frenzy of the 1980s. But it did represent a number of investment bankers in a variety of transactions. They included Bear, Stearns & Co., Inc.; PaineWebber Incorporated; Oppenheimer & Co., Inc.; Drexel Burnham Lambert Incorporated; Advest, Inc.; Mabon Nugent Securities Corp.; Dean Witter Reynolds Inc.; Robertson, Stephens & Company; and Thomson McKinnon, Inc. (TM). In representing the last, the Firm experienced one of the more spectacular roller-coaster rides of the decade.

TM started life as a cash grain business in 1885. By 1987, it had assets of $4 billion and was the country's ninth-largest stock brokerage house, with 170 offices throughout the United States and Europe, and 2,400 account executives serving 750,000 customers. In addition to its retail securities business, TM had capital markets and investment-banking operations, as well as its own family of mutual funds.

Fortenbaugh first attracted TM as a client in 1982. Thereafter, the Firm became TM's principal outside counsel, and TM became a major client of the Firm. The Firm represented TM in middle-market underwritings: Canadian and Florida telephone companies, savings and loans, chemicals, automobile components, and collateralized mortgage obligations (CMOs). In addition, the Firm handled major financings of TM itself, involving Bankers Trust Company, Connecticut General Life Insurance Company, and the Hartford Insurance Group. There were also acquisitions of regional securities firms, a major restructuring of the TM companies, and a constant flow of regulatory matters. Those were busy days—even frantic days—for any New York law firm with an active investment-banking client like TM.

But it did not last. Toward the end of the 1980s, many old-line investment-banking firms disappeared through mergers and bankruptcies—victims of the times, mismanagement, or just bad luck. TM suffered in all three categories. Between August and October 1987, the Dow Jones Industrial Average dropped almost 1,000 points. In the aftermath, small investors were frightened off, and TM's retail volume declined by more than one-third. Underwritings dried up, as did mergers and acquisitions. Next, TM sustained an arbitrage loss of $20 million and a repurchase agreement (REPO) loss of $25 million. Finally, TM suffered from tragic timing: Before the crash, it had contracted to move from 200,000 square feet at One State Street Plaza to 600,000 square feet at One Financial Square. It was unable to sublease its old space before moving to its twenty floors of new space. So it paid rent on both its old and new space. The former remained empty; and the latter, considering TM's shrunken operations, had the population density, as one TM vice-president put it, of a "bowling alley on an off night." As the decade ended, space was vacant all over the financial district.

With time running out, TM looked for a buyer. Fortenbaugh was encouraged when Prudential-Bache Securities Inc. seemed interested. But ultimately, in 1989, it bought only TM's remaining 158 retail branches for a modest $60 million. Less than nine months later, TM filed for bankruptcy. Recriminations followed. *Forbes* magazine wrote of "management excess . . . a 97-foot yacht and fancy company apartments in Puerto Rico and Manhattan . . . interest-free million-dollar loans and salaries exorbitant even by Wall Street standards."[12]

■ ■ ■ ■ ■

So far, the progress of ML&B's New York office during the 1980s has been traced largely by reference to the Firm's business and finance practice, as well as its activities in the labor field. But the litigation section was also actively building capacity during that period. Entering the 1980s, the office had but one litigation partner, James Harbison (who came with Wickes Riddel), and two associates. Ten years later, there were ten litigation partners and more than twice as many associates. Also, the office had developed a specialty in securities litigation and a subspecialty in cases pertaining to broker-dealer problems.

The first new litigator to arrive was John Linsenmeyer in 1980. Previously, his clients had included one of the IOS funds. His work for that client brought him into contact with Philadelphia partner John Lewis, then handling litigation for Fund of Funds, as recounted in Chapter 36. Lewis admired Linsenmeyer's sardonic wit and encyclopedic mind. Linsenmeyer came to the Firm with a mélange of petroleum, toxic tort, and Canadian securities cases.

Next, in 1986, Charles Manuel arrived with his banking and general commercial litigation.[13] Then, in several high-profile acquisitions, the Firm was joined in 1987 by John Peloso and Robert Romano, shortly followed by Anne Flannery (from the SEC) as of counsel (she became a partner in 1989), and finally by Joseph Cyr (1990). Peloso had previously chaired the management committee of Sage, Gray, Todd & Sims, a medium-sized New York firm. But it was a time when many such firms were breaking up. They were neither boutiques nor did they enjoy the economies of scale that favored the large firms. Sage Gray, founded in 1842, was among the ill-fated, and Peloso had presided over its demise.

By the late 1980s, the New York litigation section was handling matters for clients as varied as alleged polluters and toxic tortfeasors, through Wall Street investment bankers, and all the way to Christopher Reeve, well known to moviegoers for his portrayal of Superman, the Man of Steel. The Reeve matter was another example of multioffice, multisection synergy. It was originated by international section personnel in the London office before moving to New York, where it was handled by the litigation and personal law sections.

The case involved a palimony claim against Reeve by a former companion who was the mother of two of his children. Given considerable play by the tabloids, it also provided a charmed moment for William O'Connor and a vignette for this narrative. Reeve was seated with O'Connor outside a conference room awaiting settlement discussions. He was out of uniform, out of character, and dispirited. Finally, the conference was called. As he and O'Connor rose to enter the conference room, O'Connor whispered to him, "Steel yourself." There was no time for Reeve to change clothes in a telephone booth, but he responded anyway. The resulting settlement was satisfactory all around.

Reeve's affairs were of vital interest to the popular press. Of little interest to that press but with enormous implications for the securities industry was a case for Peloso's client PaineWebber. It was precipitated by the nefarious conduct of a Maimi stockbroker named Dennis Greenman, who was indicted, convicted, and sentenced to ten years in prison.[14] On the civil side, his misdeeds begat litigation that certainly highlighted the Firm's investment-banking specialty and broker-dealer subspecialty.

For almost four years, Greenman ran what he called a "special arbitrage program," initially as a registered representative with Merrill Lynch, then with PaineWebber for nineteen months, and finally with a small discount brokerage firm. The results were dismal. But not to worry: He would cheer his clients by sending them bogus account statements showing total annual returns as high as 70 percent. Of course, he would have to intercept his employers' real account statements. Generally, he did this by directing them to post office boxes under his control. His customers never saw them. Instead, they rejoiced in their apparent good fortune, sent him additional money, and referred further prospects to him.

Meanwhile, Greenman churned his customers' accounts, diverted distribution payments, forged endorsements, and generally treated his customers' money as his own. By 1981, when the FBI closed in, "[o]ver 600 people . . . invested approximately $86 million, of which they lost over $50 million."[15] Considering the financial carnage and Greenman's limited ability to make restitution, deeper pockets had to be sought, along with sacrificial lambs. Merrill Lynch, PaineWebber, and a clearing broker had such pockets and responded accordingly, so that almost 90 percent of the loss was recovered. In the lamb department, two of PaineWebber's employees with direct supervisory authority over Greenman were disciplined by the SEC.

That should have been the end of it. But almost as an afterthought, the SEC cast a wider net. It pursued another PaineWebber employee, Arthur James Huff. He was a compliance officer without direct supervisory authority over Greenman. Terror spread in the investment community. An article in the *Legal Times* noted that a victory for the SEC in the *Huff* case could "have a more profound impact on post-meltdown securities markets than all the corrective measures proposed by Congress, the Federal Reserve System, and industry regulators combined."[16]

The securities industry was shocked as Huff was marched to the block by the SEC and held culpable by an administrative law judge.[17] PaineWebber then retained the Firm, not previously involved in the matter, to represent Huff. Peloso led a team that included Romano and Flannery in New York, and A. A. Sommer and Lloyd Feller in Washington. Peloso argued the appeal to a packed SEC chamber, as interest ran high both at the commission and in financial circles generally.

The commission reversed the decision of the administrative law judge and dismissed the charges.[18] The SEC had cast its net too widely. The *New York Law Journal* noted that the "long-awaited decision . . . [was] being hailed as a victory by the securities industry."[19]

■ ■ ■ ■ ■

As the New York office was fleshed out, it still lacked capacity in the international and government regulation fields. In the international area, the void was filled with the transfer to the New

York office in 1987 of Bloomer from the Firm's London office, where he had spent six years. Bloomer's homeward journey took seven weeks. With two mates, he came by sea as captain of his own twenty-nine-foot sailboat. They sailed from Holyhead, Wales, with stops at the Outer Hebrides, Faeroe Islands, Iceland, Newfoundland, Nova Scotia, and Nantucket. They finally made port at Bloomer's hometown of Riverside, Connecticut.

The next year, in 1988, John Richardson joined the Firm laterally. His main activities were in the highly specialized field of representing Lloyd's of London in United States tax matters.[20] Then, in 1990, partner Alan Neuwirth and of counsel Alvin Kassel came to the Firm with their extensive Japanese practice, to be described in Chapter 24. They brought with them partners William Huss, who joined the Firm's Tokyo office, and Richard Mescon, who joined the New York office's litigation section. Also in 1990, the government regulation section got its turn when Eric Rothenberg, a specialist in environmental law, joined the New York office as a lateral-entry partner.

By 1993, the 115 lawyers of the Firm's New York office represented seven of the Firm's eight practice sections. There were forty-seven lawyers in the business and finance section, thirty-four in the litigation section, seventeen in the labor section, seven in the tax section, four in the government regulation section, three in the personal law section, and three in the international section. Only the trade regulation section was unrepresented; most of its members continued to practice peripatetically from the Firm's Washington office. The development of the New York office had taken almost twenty-one years, but by 1993 that office clearly had depth and versatility.

■ ■ ■ ■ ■

Now back to how it all started with leveraged leasing. Did that original specialty serve its purpose and fade away? On the contrary, leveraged leasing continued to be a mainstay of the New York practice for two decades. Despite numerous changes in the tax law, the rewards of such transactions remained imposing, especially since big-ticket items were involved. Moreover, those changes made the legal aspects of leveraged leasing even more esoteric. And it acquired an international flavor, as transactions were frequently cross-border.

On the corporate side of leveraged leasing, the Firm's star performers remained those from the 1970s, including Thoyer, Warman, and Shrank, joined later by Bloomer and Low. On the tax side,

William Macan, a transplant from the Philadelphia office, acquired a national and international reputation in the field. Many of the Firm's original clients continued in its leveraged-leasing stable. Over the years, they were joined by Qantas Airways Ltd.; Industrial Bank of Japan Trust Company; Pitney-Bowes Credit Corporation; Westinghouse Financial Services, Inc.; Security Pacific Leasing Corporation; NCNB Lease Investments, Inc.; U.S. West Capital Corp.; and Chrysler Capital Corporation.

If Lefevre had fantasized in 1972 how the New York office might evolve, he could have done no better than to imagine what actually took place. Unlike the Firm's experience in Washington, ML&B knew from the start what it wanted in New York. Consequently, it achieved its interim goals relatively quickly. By the 1990s, the New York office was a mature and indispensable component of the Firm's practice.

CHAPTER 22

MANIFEST DESTINY

Overspreading the continent ■ Labor law as the immediate cause ■ William Emanuel and an urgent opening ■ Michael Klowden arrives ■ A woody office and the Crazy Climber ■ Citibank west tries ML&B ■ Peering over the rim ■ The Catch-22 of expansion ■ Satellite offices ■ A major acquisition ■ An even woodier office ■ The resort business ■ The Jefferies story ■ The third market and street sweeps ■ Boesky tells all ■ Drexel pleads guilty ■ A beauty contest ■ Executive Life fails ■ MAAF and Altus Finance ■ A $3.25-billion junk-bond purchase

In 1845, a New York magazine heralded America's "manifest destiny to overspread the continent allotted by Providence for the free development of our yearly multiplying millions."[1] By 1976, with offices in Philadelphia, Washington, Harrisburg, and New York, the Firm was ready to accept the allocation of Providence. This it did on March 1, 1976, by overspreading the continent and opening an office in Los Angeles.

A West Coast office had been on the Firm's screen for several years. The idea of acquiring a prestigious antitrust boutique in San Francisco had already been considered. Certainly that city held its attractions: In the 1970s, law school graduates were eager to settle there. But acquiring a whole firm at such a distance would have posed problems of supervision and cultural integration for which the Firm was not then ready. Although the idea was shelved, the seed of manifest destiny had been planted.

When that seed sprouted in 1976, the venue was different: The fog and cable cars of San Francisco had yielded to the smog and film studios of Los Angeles. Moreover, supervision and cultural integration in Los Angeles would be minimized, because ML&B would not acquire an existing firm but would start from scratch. It would set up with one lawyer who knew the Firm's culture, and it would operate initially in a field of high potential synergy. The lawyer was William Emanuel and the field was labor.

_250_   Morgan, Lewis & Bockius, A Law Firm and Its Times, 1873-1993

Just as the perceived need for tax services had launched Washington in 1947, and leveraged leasing did the same for New York in 1972, so the Firm's burgeoning labor practice is generally considered the immediate cause for the Los Angeles office. Or was the labor practice really a convenient rationalization for what the Firm wanted to do anyway? Consciously or unconsciously, ML&B may have been evolving a strategic plan. But strategic plans are suspect, or at least debatable. It was safer to justify each new office as client driven in some specific area of the Firm's expertise. For Los Angeles it was labor.

From the start, William Curtin was naturally a strong proponent of the Los Angeles initiative. In 1968, he had negotiated a landmark labor agreement that made possible the construction of Walt Disney World, as recounted in Chapter 26. Labor work was ongoing for the Disney interests, with intimations that what was being done by the Firm for Disney east could also be done for Disney west. Different coasts but the same mouse.

As to Emanuel, he had clerked in the Firm's Washington office while studying at Georgetown University Law School, from which he graduated in 1963. The Firm's culture came naturally to him. Manifest destiny did too: He had moved to Los Angeles in 1965, developed a labor law practice there, and by 1975 was ready to leave his firm for something more challenging. He was thrilled at Curtin's suggestion that he become ML&B's first lawyer on the West Coast.

It remained for Curtin to convince the other Quadriviri and for them to convince all others who needed convincing. But a technical problem arose while the proposition was percolating. The problem was reminiscent of the New York experience four years earlier. Although in New York the problem turned out to be imaginary, in California it was very real: A rule designed to keep non-California firms from entering the state was being considered by the California bar. It would have prevented non-California firms from practicing in that state under their firm names unless their name partners passed the California bar examination. This would have been disabling for ML&B. Its name partners could no longer pass the bar, having already crossed it.

Fortunately, the exclusionary proposal was dropped, and ML&B became one of the earliest out-of-state firms to open a California office. Today, with scores of out-of-state firms in California, all this seems quaint. Indeed, the current question is not whether American firms can practice in other states but whether (and what) they can practice in foreign countries.

The opening of the Los Angeles office on March 1, 1976, was accelerated when word leaked out about Emanuel's plans to leave his old firm: He immediately became persona non grata and faced "being thrown out on the street," as he put it. So there was no time to schedule a grand opening with specially chosen wines (he is a wine connoisseur), exquisite hors d'oeuvres, and gorgeous flowers. Instead, in his words:

> For the first several days of our office's existence, we had an unlisted telephone number. Our furniture was obtained from a rental agency, and our library consisted of a set of labor law books piled on top of packing crates.

The Firm's first office was situated in downtown Los Angeles at 800 West Sixth Street. The building was known affectionately as "Little Security," to distinguish it from the taller Security Bank Building located a few blocks away. The first space was only temporary while other space was being fitted up in the building. When the office opened, the staff comprised two people: Emanuel and his secretary.

To support Emanuel in those early days, a number of labor section associates rotated to Los Angeles from Philadelphia and Washington. East also supported west by opening doors. For example, Curtin arranged for Emanuel to make a presentation involving a major labor law case at Disneyland. On arriving at Disney's office in Burbank, Emanuel noted the presence of labor lawyers from other firms and realized that a beauty contest was in progress. One contestant was wearing a Mickey Mouse necktie. Emanuel considered this an unctuous ploy. Maybe the client did too. In any event, substance triumphed: The Firm got the work.

The Los Angeles office operated as a labor law boutique for almost two years. At first, the practice was dominated by hospital clients. One of them, the Anaheim Memorial Hospital, sent the office its first fee check. Combining sentimentality with a fondness for revenue, Emanuel photocopied the check for the Firm's archives. Then, despite its historical significance, it was deposited.

Those were the days of union organizational campaigns against California hospitals. When hospitals in Maywood and San Gabriel were struck, the Firm opined that striking employees could be replaced. They were, but not without some violence. Ultimately, the union lost both strikes, was decertified at one hospital, and never returned to the other. During another hospital strike, goons went to Emanuel's home at night to vandalize it. Fortunately, the police had infiltrated the union. Emanuel was alerted and evacuated his family. When the vandals arrived, the police were waiting in the bushes.

During those first two years, the office added several labor lawyers, including associate (later partner) Michael Wolfram, as well as litigation lawyer Kenneth Wright, who became the Firm's second partner in Los Angeles. Then, on April 1, 1978, Michael Klowden joined the Firm as its first business and finance partner in Los Angeles. He was a natural leader who quickly moved center stage in the development of the Los Angeles office.

Raised in Chicago, Klowden won every possible honor in high school, while working part time selling inexpensive women's shoes, something he continued to do as an undergraduate at the University of Chicago. (He would later become a trustee of that university.) He learned to wait on many customers at once: "One day before Easter in 1967, my senior year in college, I made $75 on straight commission selling 200 pairs of shoes in eight hours." He also discovered that "if you carried a shoe box, walked fast, and seemed to know where you were going, people thought you were busy and successful." These lessons would serve him well. Later, as one of the Firm's most successful partners, he would wait on many customers.

After graduating from Harvard Law School, Klowden settled in Los Angeles to work for a mid-sized firm identified with the entertainment industry. He became that firm's "hiring partner" in his second year as an associate and was made a partner in his sixth year. Two years later, in 1978, he was attracted to ML&B by its commitment to national practice and its collegiality. But at least three other factors influenced him. One was the message contained in a fortune cookie. It said: "You will have an opportunity to make a change to your advantage." Another was the reaction by his former firm to his proposed departure. One senior partner said: "You can't leave; you are the only partner who is on speaking terms with all the other partners." That certainly confirmed his judgment.

The third factor dealt with ML&B's space situation in Los Angeles. By the time Klowden arrived, the office in Little Security comprised seven lawyers and was fully occupied. Normally, the next step would have been to take additional space in the building. But there was a more grandiose proposal on the table. It paralleled Klowden's vision of manifest destiny and clinched his decision to join ML&B. The proposal was that the Firm rent space about to be vacated by a law firm in the Crocker National Bank Building at 611 West Sixth Street, space vastly beyond ML&B's foreseeable needs. Reactions to the proposal varied among the Quadriviri. Thomas Lefevre was agreeable and Robert Young, enthusiastic. William Curtin, who felt a special interest in Los Angeles, was supportive. Not Park Dilks: He thought it was too much too soon. Was it really necessary to rent an entire floor to house seven lawyers and a vision?

But Klowden had a knack for conciliation. On a visit to the Los Angeles office, Dilks was taken by Klowden to see the new space. The floors were finished in very dark wood, with chair rail and moldings everywhere. Klowden knew that Dilks was a wood junkie.[2] Actually, the Crocker space looked more like Philadelphia than Philadelphia itself. As it turned out, the design was by an ex-Philadelphia lawyer who, before going west, had practiced with Saul, Ewing, Remick & Saul. No Philadelphia firm was "woodier" than Saul. Dilks acquiesced in Klowden's vision—for the wrong reason.

The Los Angeles office celebrated Bastille Day by relocating on July 14, 1978, to its new quarters on the twenty-third floor of the Crocker National Bank Building, later renamed the AT&T Building. The building was cruciform, and the space comprised 17,000 square feet with twenty-seven perimeter offices. The floors were impossible to partition for sublease. After the Firm moved in, only one-third of its offices were occupied, with one wing left completely vacant.

Although vacant of human habitation, that wing housed the Crazy Climber. He, she, or it was a large electronic arcade game featuring a giant gorilla that wreaked havoc while climbing office buildings and fighting off airplanes. The Crazy Climber was on loan from a Japanese game manufacturer then being defended by the Firm in a trademark infringement case. An enterprising associate had urged that the Firm acquire a working copy of the machine to study it as part of the defense. The machine ingested coins, but the coin slot had been left open so the money passed right through. Thus, it cost nothing for Firm personnel to play the game. Many did, and not because they were working on the case.

No revenue could be expected from the wing of the office occupied by the Crazy Climber. But revenue was expected from lawyers scattered around the other wings, including from Klowden, especially considering his costly vision. Only thirty-three years old, he had everything: a broad range of legal knowledge, a quick mind, limitless energy, organizing ability, and great personal charm. But in terms of client following he was, as he said, "naked." How to cover his nakedness? Fig leaves would generate no revenue. Only clients would serve.

One prospective client was Citibank, for which the Firm was doing substantial work in Philadelphia and New York. Dilks, who had originated the Citibank representation, knew of the bank's expansion plans into southern California. With Klowden in place, Dilks asked a senior bank officer if the bank would "try ML&B." The answer was encouraging. One of Klowden's favorite stories about multioffice synergy recounts how, during Klowden's first week with the Firm, Dilks and Clive Anderson came to Los Angeles to introduce Klowden to Citibank personnel. Klowden struck up an instant rapport with the bank's personnel and continued to enjoy that rapport over the ensuing fifteen years as bank officers came and went. Through Klowden's efforts, Citibank became one of the Firm's major clients on the West Coast, loaning literally billions of dollars secured by real estate in California, Arizona, Washington, Nevada, Colorado, Hawaii, and western Canada. At one point, Citibank was actually the largest construction lender in southern California—a distinction it would live to regret during the real estate debacle of the early 1990s.

As Klowden's practice grew, so did the office. It is doubtful if any Firm partner ever relished office development as much as he. Unrestrained and left to Klowden's own devices, the Los Angeles office would probably have grown twice as fast. Even restrained, no other ML&B office grew more rapidly, so that by the early 1990s it temporarily outpaced New York, which was four years older.

One of Klowden's lateral acquisitions was John Forry, who joined the Los Angeles office in 1980 as its fourth partner and twentieth lawyer. Like William Clarke Mason, Forry left his own firm, of which he was a name partner, to play on a bigger stage. Forry's practice was international, with a client base comprised largely of wealthy Iranian expatriates who had taken up real estate development in the United States. His specialty was international taxation, on which he wrote and lectured extensively.

In 1980, no law firm based in Los Angeles had a significant overseas presence. Nor did ML&B. But the Firm had an international section, and that section had plans coinciding with Forry's. They included the Pacific Rim. Forry knew that his Iranian practice would wind down, and he envisioned opportunities in Tokyo, Seoul, Hong Kong, and points south and west. Over the years, Forry would give the Los Angeles office its international cast.

In a sense, Klowden's attraction of Forry was lucky. While Forry's practice required that the Firm have many offices, it did not require that the Los Angeles office have the critical mass that Young preached so constantly. But other desirable candidates for the Los

Angeles office insisted on that mass. So Klowden soon faced the same challenge as New York before 1979 when it acquired Wickes, Riddel, Jacobi & McGuire. It was a Catch-22 dilemma: An office cannot attract the lawyers it needs until it gets large enough, and it cannot get large enough until it attracts the lawyers it needs. Moreover, as earlier in New York, there was the branch stigma. Despite Klowden's persuasiveness, it was hard for lateral candidates to believe that the Los Angeles office of a Philadelphia law firm was not a branch.

Nevertheless, by a major acquisition in 1981, Klowden attracted five partners from Adams, Duque & Hazeltine. They were Loyd Derby, Robert Redford, Charles Cale, Jack Liebau, and Charles Stimson. Stimson retired in 1984, Liebau left the Firm in 1990, and Cale's primary interest turned out to be the Olympics—before leaving the Firm in 1990, he served at various times as vice-president/sports of the Los Angeles Olympic Committee and as assistant to the president of the United States Olympic Committee. Still, the Adams Duque lawyers provided mass, and by 1982 the lawyer count in Los Angeles was twenty-eight.

Klowden continued his efforts and attracted on an individual basis Thomas Coleman and John Shultz in 1983, Orville (Jack) Orr and James Wawro in 1984, and Frank Smith in 1985. Randolph (Randy) Visser, who would develop a strong environmental practice in the Los Angeles office, also became a partner in 1985. By the end of 1986, there were sixty lawyers. One hundred was Klowden's objective.

In 1987, he achieved that objective when Hahn, Cazier & Smaltz (HC&S) combined its practice with ML&B. The combination added forty-three lawyers, including a small San Diego office. The San Diego facet raised a nagging question. Should the Firm also aim for mass there, or should San Diego function as a satellite of Los Angeles? If the Firm adopted the satellite approach (Harrisburg had been a special case from the beginning), should Philadelphia have a satellite in Great Valley; should Washington have one in Tyson's Corner; and should New York have one in Stamford? Regional firms have satellites. National and international firms generally stick to the major cities. (Of course, major accounting firms have offices "everywhere," as W. James MacIntosh kept pointing out.) Although San Diego was included in the merger, its role continued to be debated. Six years later, in 1993, having shown little development, it was closed. While other firms seemed to close offices indiscriminately, ML&B had never before done so. But there was a consolation: The Firm could still say it had never closed an office *it* had opened.

Another consolation was that at least the number of the Firm's offices remained at eleven when it set up a Princeton, New Jersey, office late in 1993.[3]

HC&S specialized in corporate and litigation law. Its two principals were Edward Cazier and Donald Smaltz. Cazier, then sixty-two years old, was a seasoned lawyer capable of handling any kind of corporate transaction. He was on the board of E. F. Hutton Group, Inc., before it merged with Shearson Lehman Bros., Inc., in 1988. As with Emanuel and Klowden, the ML&B culture came naturally to Cazier, whose addition enhanced the Firm's prestige in the corporate world. Cazier commented to *California Law Business* that other firms had approached HC&S, but the Firm's "expertise in running a multi-city practice was an important factor in the choice of ML&B." As Cazier put it:

> Two things were important to us: the collegial relationships the partners have with each other, not only in the Los Angeles office but also from one office to another, and the fact that Morgan, Lewis & Bockius was not going to be learning how to run a multi-city practice using us as the test material.[4]

Smaltz was younger than Cazier, forty-nine at the time of the merger. He was a trial lawyer through and through. As he told the press: "In addition to in-depth talent over a wide variety of fields, being with a national firm like this one enables you to have appropriate support and to function exclusively in your chosen endeavor. I like to try cases."[5] But so fierce was Smaltz's commitment to the trial of cases for long-standing clients that he withdrew from the Firm in 1992 after much agonizing rather than be conflicted out of major litigation involving such a client.

Although by 1993 Cazier had retired and Smaltz had withdrawn, most other HC&S lawyers had comfortably settled in as part of ML&B, including corporate lawyer Robert Fraser and litigator Paul Richler. One product of the HC&S acquisition was that ML&B's Los Angeles office was swarming with litigators. HC&S brought twenty, and by 1990 there were sixty altogether. At the time, this made it the largest single sectional group in any of the Firm's offices—appropriate for California where imaginative lawyers and permissive courts are constantly spawning new rights and duties.

With the HC&S acquisition, the Crocker National Bank Building became inadequate. Actually, HC&S could not join ML&B until new space was fitted up at Chase Plaza, 801 South Grand Avenue. After the moving date, May 3, 1987, visiting ML&B lawyers inspecting the new Chase Plaza space declared that it outdid any other ML&B office in terms of dark wood, chair rail, and moldings. These had become the Firm's signature in Los Angeles, as Klowden again demonstrated his political acumen.

At first, the Firm occupied only the twentieth through twenty-second floors at Chase Plaza. (The nineteenth and thirteenth floors were picked up subsequently.) But even so, there was a surplus of space, part of which was filled when David Ellsworth, Richard Davis, Douglas Dodds, and Michael Simondi became lateral-entry partners in December, 1987. The first three joined in Los Angeles; the last, in Newport Beach. In order to make clear that the Firm had not surrendered to the satellite office concept, the Newport Beach office was called a "facility" instead of an office. Lawyers are sticklers for terminology, and this seemed to satisfy everyone.

In its Citibank work, the Firm had handled real estate transactions from the lender's viewpoint. By contrast, Ellsworth represented developers. He was best known as one of the country's leading lawyers handling the development of resorts, especially master-planned golf communities. While his work centered on resort areas in the United States and Mexico (Los Cabos, Puerto Vallarta, Cancun, Ixtapa, Acapulco, and Huatulco), it also took him to Europe, Costa Rica, Tahiti, Malaysia, and Australia. One of Ellsworth's clients was the largest construction company in Latin America, Mexico's Industrial ICA Sociedad de Fomento, S. A. de C. V., also known as GRUPO ICA. In 1990, the Firm handled a $650-million acquisition for GRUPO ICA from United Kingdom interests. In a reprise of New York's Reading/Gould transaction ten years earlier, forty-four lawyers were involved in the GRUPO ICA deal from four of the Firm's domestic offices, plus its London office and its Newport Beach facility.

After the arrival of the Ellsworth group, the growth of the Los Angeles office continued largely from within, as partner ranks were increasingly filled by associates trained at the Firm. But some lateral-entry partners continued to be attracted in specific areas: Jeffrey Grausam in tax (1989), Dean Heller and Barry Freeman in business and finance (1991), and Joseph Herman in labor (1991). In 1973, Herman had founded the Los Angeles branch of another law firm, built it to forty lawyers, and became its "managing partner and key rainmaker."[6] His clients included ITT Sheraton Corporation, Prudential Insurance Company of America, California Table Grape Commission, and Gallo Wine Company. His discussions with the Firm commenced in 1986, and their five-year gestation period probably established some kind of record. Not an impulsive man. A year later, in 1992, two of Herman's former colleagues joined him. They were labor lawyers Raymond Kepner and Gary Moss. (Moss brought with him a sizable Nevada labor practice, which required that the Firm establish a presence there without actually opening an office.) Finally, in 1993, Cynthia Cohen, a bankruptcy litigator, joined the Firm, as did Peter Dolan, a securities litigator, and Andrea Ordin, a former United States attorney and prominent litigator.

■ ■ ■ ■ ■

The excesses of the 1980s, including the fall of the house of Thomson McKinnon, have been mentioned in Chapter 21. They also included the much more celebrated demise of Drexel Burnham Lambert, largely precipitated by the collapse of junk bonds marketed by its Beverly Hills office. Drexel's history has already been traced in Chapter 11: its founding as a Philadelphia enterprise in 1838; its attraction of young J. P. Morgan; Morris Bockius's relationship with Edward Stotesbury; the spinoff of Morgan Stanley in 1935; the split between the New York and Philadelphia houses in 1940; and the many iterations of Drexel before it became Drexel Burnham Lambert in 1976. ML&B's Los Angeles office was involved between 1986 and 1993 in three high-profile matters related to the Drexel phenomenon: the Jefferies affair; the SEC's investigation of Drexel; and matters relating to Executive Life Insurance Company, including its acquisition by client Mutuelle Assurance Artisanale de France, as well as the purchase of its $3.25-billion junk-bond portfolio by client Altus Finance.

The Jefferies story had a modest beginning. In 1980, Jefferies & Co. was a relatively small Los Angeles brokerage house specializing in the block trading of listed securities off the stock exchange, the so-called third market. After acquiring a broker affiliate named Waggenseller & Durst, Jefferies had some legal questions about its rights under the acquisition agreement. Normally, these questions would have gone to Jefferies's regular counsel. But, according to Klowden, Jefferies's regular counsel "was unable to put somebody on the matter for a few days." So Klowden was called in as a second choice. He answered the questions, as well as others, and soon ML&B became Waggenseller's principal outside counsel. (No law firm can afford to be unavailable to any client even for a few days.) Klowden then moved on to Jefferies. That company soon found that ML&B had solutions to securities law questions Jefferies's regular counsel said were unsolvable. (The answers frequently came from Lloyd Feller in the Firm's Washington office.) Consequently, after eighteen months of work for Jefferies, the Firm became its general counsel and represented it in a 1983 public offering.

Jefferies & Co. was renowned for the work habits of its founder, Boyd Jefferies. He was at his desk by 3 a.m. Los Angeles time in order to prepare for the opening of the stock market some hours later on the East Coast. (He did not require the same dedication from his employees: They were permitted to trickle in at 4:30 a.m.) As the takeover craze of the 1980s intensified, it became essential that raiders accumulate large blocks of stock, often in the third market. Jefferies & Co. made a specialty of assembling such blocks, sometimes through "street sweeps." In one example of a street sweep, Jefferies put together stock of Allied Stores for delivery to Robert Campeau in what was probably the largest block trade ever. The transaction was attacked, but the Firm's New York office defended it and prevailed: Jefferies & Co. had carefully followed a procedure for street sweeps laid out by the Firm.

Unfortunately, Boyd Jefferies was not so careful in his own practices. He was an impatient man who sometimes hung up on his lawyers. Ultimately, he was brought down by that most notorious of arbitragers, Ivan Boesky. With prosecutors closing in, Boesky told all, paid the government $100 million, and was sentenced to three years in jail. (He served two years and eleven days.) The "all" that Boesky told included information about Jefferies & Co., and specifically about Boyd Jefferies. According to Boesky, he had "parked" securities with Jefferies. Under the parking arrangement, Boesky's books recorded the securities as sold, but they actually remained Boesky's property. Thus, he circumvented the filing of disclosure documents with the SEC.

The SEC investigated Boyd Jefferies and Jefferies & Co. The potential for conflict was obvious, so the Firm recommended that Boyd Jefferies engage other counsel, while the Firm represented Jefferies & Co. The matter was handled by Klowden and Feller, as well as by John Hartigan, who had come to the Los Angeles office from the SEC in 1984 and became a partner in 1986. A satisfactory settlement with the SEC was negotiated in March 1987. It resulted in the mildest of sanctions against Jefferies & Co., which consented to an injunction not to violate securities laws in the future. The consent order also provided that an independent reviewer would audit Jefferies's operations to confirm that they complied with the law. The Firm was directed by the SEC to conduct the review.

Jefferies himself, represented by other counsel, did not fare quite so well. He pleaded guilty to charges of parking and manipulating securities and was suspended by the SEC from any relationship with a brokerage firm for five years, fined $250,000, and put on probation. Still, he was the only major figure involved in the Wall Street scandals of the 1980s who did not receive a jail sentence. Instead, he became a perennial witness for the SEC as he testified in high-profile prosecutions. Meantime, Jefferies Group, Inc., as it was called by then, continued without its founder and in 1991 bought back his 10-percent interest for $11 million.

That the Firm was directed by the SEC to act as its own client's watchdog was certainly an unusual feature of the Jefferies & Co. settlement. ML&B's appointment attested to the SEC's high regard for the Firm's integrity and competence in the securities field. It was also a warmup for an even more remarkable assignment with respect to Drexel Burnham Lambert.

In December 1988, to avoid racketeering charges, Drexel agreed to plead guilty to six criminal charges and pay fines totaling $650 million. It also consented to the appointment of an independent consultant to review and make recommendations regarding Drexel's internal procedures and controls. After a beauty contest for this coveted engagement, the Firm was named. It had the necessary securities expertise, particularly in the broker/dealer area, and it uniquely offered the depth of lawyers required in three critical locations: Los Angeles, New York, and Washington. A team of sixteen ML&B lawyers was fielded for the project. The team included partners John Hartigan in Los Angeles, Robert Romano in New York, and Lloyd Feller in Washington. All three had previously held important posts with the SEC.

The Firm worked intensively on the matter from the time the decree was signed in September 1989 until February 13, 1990, when Drexel filed for bankruptcy, as described in Chapter 11. Without Michael Milken to make a market for junk bonds, that market had collapsed. Heavily invested in junk bonds, Drexel also collapsed, as did more than 200 savings and loan associations and several insurance companies. When Drexel filed, Hartigan was working on the case in Tokyo. News of the filing reached him by telephone at about 3:30 a.m. Tokyo time. He recalls that top Drexel officials who had just arrived to meet with him "scrambled to find their way home." Almost no one had foreseen the filing. It ended the Firm's engagement as independent consultant.

■ ■ ■ ■ ■

Executive Life Insurance Company (ELIC) was another "victim of the collapse of the junk bond market."[7] On April 11, 1991, fourteen month after the Drexel filing, the California insurance commissioner put ELIC into conservation proceedings. At that time, it was the largest failure of an insurance company in the nation's history. To rid ELIC of its junk bonds and rehabilitate rather than liquidate the company, the commissioner began discussions with several groups of interested investors. One such group, represented by the Firm, comprised a consortium of Altus Finance (a subsidiary of Credit Lyonnais) and a group of French insurance companies led by Mutuelle Assurance Artisanale de France (MAAF). Starting in the spring of 1991 and lasting for two and a half years, the matter received literally round-the-clock attention by ML&B personnel and generated two extraordinary acquisitions. The first was by Altus. In March 1992, it purchased substantially all ELIC's low-grade junk-bond portfolio for $3.25 billion—the largest cash portfolio purchase in the nation's history. The second transaction closed in September 1993 when the MAAF consortium acquired approximately $7 billion in ELIC's assets together with substantially all its restructured liabilities.[8]

The Firm's Altus/MAAF team included lawyers from Los Angeles, New York, Philadelphia, Washington, and Brussels. With Hartigan leading the effort, important roles were played by Robert Miller in Los Angeles; Allen Stewart, David Harbaugh, and Thomas Vallone in Philadelphia; Robert Schlossberg in Washington; and John Richardson, Robert Robison, and Robert Mendelson in New York. Of Hartigan, the *Los Angeles Business Journal* said:

> The Georgetown law graduate is well briefed for his current duties.
> . . . He is a former Securities and Exchange Commission assistant
> director of enforcement and helped clean up the Baldwin-United
> insurance collapse, in the mid-1980s. . . . [He was also] the man
> tapped in 1989 by the SEC to write, implement and monitor a new
> compliance manual for Drexel Burnham Lambert, the now-defunct
> brokerage house. The manual would have specified procedures for
> Drexel to follow to comply with securities laws—"but Drexel went
> bankrupt before I could finish the review," said Hartigan."[9]

ELIC was a creature of the 1980s. From a sleepy, regional enterprise it had become one of the fastest-growing insurers in the nation. That growth was fueled largely by sales of insurance products offering above-market returns. Such returns were supported by junk bonds, which comprised 50 percent of ELIC's assets. That concentration proved fatal when the market collapsed.

Despite chaos in the market and the extreme size of the portfolio, Altus was an interested buyer. It instructed the Firm to negotiate a purchase of the portfolio and generate a plan for ELIC's rehabilitation. In Hartigan's words:

Negotiations reached their peak during the summer of 1991, as teams of negotiators literally camped out on the Los Angeles office's thirteenth floor conference facility for weeks at a time, night and day, pausing only occasionally for meals. Sleep, if any, was often caught while documents were being revised and printed by word processor operators.

On August 7, 1991, the commissioner held a televised press conference to unveil the rehabilitation plan. As part of that plan, he conducted a de facto auction of the junk-bond portfolio. Following three rounds of bidding, a $3.25-billion offer by Altus was accepted by the commissioner in another televised press conference on November 14, 1991. After confirmation by the court, a closing on the junk-bond purchase was held on March 3, 1992, in the Firm's Los Angeles office beginning at 5 a.m. to take advantage of New York banking hours.

Participants at the closing will long tell stories about it. In addition to the enormous size of the transaction, it was plagued by the logistics involved in moving the certificates evidencing the securities from Los Angeles to the client's New York-based custodian. Many of the certificates were bearer bonds. In order for Brinks, the carrier selected for the task, to satisfy its insurance requirements, the movement was broken into six shipments involving separate trucks to transport each shipment to the airport, with the proviso that only two shipments could be in the air simultaneously. These procedures were assiduously followed, and the movements were accomplished without incident. But corporate lawyers know that transactions of this magnitude rarely close without at least one glitch. That glitch came when a banker present at the closing announced that a $1-billion wire transfer had been lost. Of course, it was found and the closing proceeded.

In addition to real problems, one was staged for comic relief. As the closing wound down and everyone believed the securities were safely on their way, a messenger bearing a sealed bag from Security Pacific National Bank (at that time the principal custodian for ELIC) appeared and announced that he was making a special delivery of bearer bonds—$12 million in the bag with another $400 million waiting in a truck outside. He asked if the appropriate person could please sign the waybill. A few seconds of stunned silence were followed by pandemonium until it was revealed that the bag contained no securities and the messenger was simply acting out a prank. The prank had the desired effect: Tensions eased, and the client kept the securities bag as a souvenir.

With the junk-bond portfolio sold, the disposition of ELIC's insurance operations moved to center stage. There were furious attacks on the rehabilitation plan by trustees of $1.85 billion in municipal bonds previously backed by ELIC—the so-called muni-GICs. Not only were they opposed to the rehabilitation plan, they also wanted to rescind the junk-bond sale of a year earlier, the market for such securities having rebounded. Despite their attacks, MAAF's acquisition of ELIC's insurance operations closed on September 3, 1993, as the ill-fated ELIC was transformed into the appropriately named Aurora National Life Assurance Company. This time, again in Hartigan's words, "only a mere (by comparison) $300-million wire transfer was lost en route." At this second closing, there were no impersonations: The parties were too exhausted for any pranks. Instead, there was other excitement even at the last minute when the muni-GICs made a desperate bid for a stay by the California Supreme Court. It was denied.

■ ■ ■ ■ ■

Jefferies, Drexel, and ELIC were landmarks in the nation's financial history during the 1980s and early 1990s. The Firm's involvement showed that it had come of age in Los Angeles. No transaction would henceforth lie beyond the grasp of that office—listed by the September 20, 1993, *Los Angeles Business Journal* as the eleventh-largest law office in the city and substantially larger than any other non-California headquartered firm. The Firm had answered the call of manifest destiny.

CHAPTER 23

SOUTHERN EXPOSURE

Ponce de León and taxes ■ *Disney World* ■ *Florida's multiple markets* ■ *Florida Progress Corporation* ■ *The Bacardi family* ■ *Labor practice in the public sector* ■ *A restructuring* ■ *Snake oil and lead poison* ■ *A Latin American renaissance* ■ *Marble halls* ■ *Hurricane Andrew* ■ *Talking to God* ■ *Persistence and rewards*

Florida became a state in 1845, the same year the press proclaimed manifest destiny. Immigration followed slowly: There was no gold rush to Florida. But by the 1920s, America's "yearly multiplying millions" were definitely making their way south. Many were following in the footsteps of Ponce de León, as they sought the fountain of youth, or at least the prolongation of life. Some also sought low taxes: While California's income taxes were among the highest in the nation, Florida's constitution forbad the imposition of any income taxes. Nor were there any inheritance taxes. Thus, Florida was a good place both to live and die. It was also a good place to visit. Northerners considered it familiar territory, and children of all ages regarded Walt Disney World as a kind of mecca following its opening in 1971. (Chapter 26 recounts the Firm's role in making Disney World possible.)

Familiarity certainly affected the choice of Florida for the Firm's next office. Indeed, two Philadelphia partners during the 1970s had Florida roots: Thomas Lefevre and Herbert Odell. Lefevre, who was raised in Saint Petersburg, thought Florida a good bet for an ML&B office, perhaps confusing nostalgia with economics. Odell also thought it a good bet. He was a tax lawyer who came to the Firm in 1967, became a partner in 1970, and left the Firm in 1989. His objective was to generate a practice in Florida while continuing to serve major Philadelphia tax clients. He succeeded in the latter, but not in the former, and returned to the Philadelphia office in 1982.

Whether the Firm should have a Florida office seemed easier to decide than where it should be located. More than most states,

Florida comprises a number of quite different markets: Orlando had to be considered because of labor work for Disney World; Jacksonville, for banking matters; Tallahassee, for regulatory work; Palm Beach, for estate work; and Miami, for its size and the variety of opportunities it afforded, including its gateway to Latin America. As the analysis proceeded, there were no votes for Jacksonville or Tallahassee. Nor was William Curtin a proponent of Orlando: Disney's interests were being well served from Washington. The personal law section had wealthy clients in the Palm Beach area. But their needs could be met from Miami. So the choice fell to Miami, where the Firm opened an office on the twenty-sixth floor of One Biscayne Tower on September 1, 1977.

Despite space for five lawyers, only Odell was there full time. Assisting him was Beverly Jermyn, his secretary, who was later named Miami's office manager. He was also supported by peripatetic lawyers from the Firm's other eastern offices. In 1978, the Firm attracted two real estate lawyers whose tenures were short. They were followed, in 1979, by George Mayrosh, an experienced real estate lawyer who transferred to Miami from Philadelphia and remained there until he retired in 1988. Terence Connor also joined the Miami office in 1979 as a labor lawyer, becoming a partner in 1984.

A noteworthy acquisition in 1980 was Richard McGonigal. He played a strong leadership role in the Miami office before transferring to the New York office in 1990. Prior to joining ML&B, McGonigal had already spent two years in Florida setting up the Miami office of a Cleveland firm. He was a seasoned corporate lawyer who understood the operations of large firms.

McGonigal's major clients during the 1980s included Florida Westcoast Banks, Inc.; VGC Corp.; Florida Progress Corporation (FPC); the Comas family group (Bacardi); and Burnup & Sims, Inc. Florida Westcoast Banks was a commercial bank holding company headquartered in Venice, Florida. (It would be acquired by SunTrust in 1992.) VGC Corp., located in Fort Lauderdale, acted as the acquisitions vehicle of VRG Groep-N.V., its Dutch parent and a corporation with $3 billion in annual revenues.

ML&B's representation of FPC exemplified interoffice cross-fertilization. Starting in the 1970s, the government regulation section of the Firm's Washington office had been active in utility regulatory matters for Florida Power Corporation, the principal subsidiary of FPC. Consequently, when FPC embarked upon a diversification program during the 1980s, the Firm handled its acquisitions as it branched into data processing, insurance, printing, financial services, and building supplies. In another example of cross-fertilization, Progress Credit Corporation, FPC's financial services subsidiary, would later use the Firm's New York office to accumulate a $1-billion lease portfolio.

The Comas family comprised a line of descendants of the Bacardi empire's founder. Few proper names are as identified with any single product as Bacardi is with rum. After the Castro revolution and the confiscation in 1960 of the vast Bacardi holdings in Cuba, the business redomiciled in Puerto Rico and established its American bottling operations in Jacksonville through Bacardi Corp., a Delaware public company owned 75 percent by Bacardi descendants.

As generations of Bacardi descendants proliferated, some took part in the multibillion-dollar family business, while others were passive shareholders, living as citizens of the world in Spain, Costa Rica, the Bahamas, Puerto Rico, Canada, and the United States. Most of the passive shareholders had other interests, but all enjoyed their Bacardi dividends. Consequently, they were alarmed when Bacardi's management proposed to take the company private through a reverse split that would eliminate many of them as shareholders. (Falling below a threshold value test, their interests would have been cashed out.) Going private would also have terminated Bacardi's registration with the SEC, thus relaxing its disclosure obligations.

To defeat management's move, the Comas family and another line of Bacardi descendants, each with 12-percent positions, arranged to split their forty former holdings into 240 trusts. As a result, the company then had more than 300 shareholders and could not terminate its SEC registration. Management countered by attacking the validity of the trusts. After lengthy SEC proceedings, a family settlement was worked out. It guaranteed a minimum dividend, required increased corporate disclosure, and provided for board representation by the dissenters. Having prevailed, the two lines of the family then collapsed their trusts, and the number of the company's shareholders fell to 236.

The Firm's Miami office orchestrated the effort for the Comas family, generated the trusts, and helped mastermind the negotiations. The matter extended over a seven-year period, during which McGonigal came to admire the cohesiveness and civility of the Bacardis. As he put it, "They are considered by the Latin business press to be the Hispanic version of the Rockefeller family."

■ ■ ■ ■ ■

ML&B's Miami office experienced a greater turnover of lawyers than other nascent offices of the Firm. By 1993, only three lawyers remained in Miami of those who had become partners before the mid-1980s. They were Connor, Richard Pettigrew, and Peter Hurtgen. Pettigrew had been a prominent Democrat in Florida politics before joining the Firm in 1981. He served as a member of the Florida House of Representatives from 1963 to 1972 (as speaker from 1970 to 1972) and as a state senator from 1972 to 1974. Although trained as a litigator, his practice increasingly dealt with environmental matters.

Hurtgen, who joined the Firm as a partner in 1983, brought with him a significant labor practice, including GATX Corporation and the cities of Miami, Miami Beach, and West Palm Beach, as well as Palm Beach County. Hurtgen's public-sector practice enjoyed high visibility and generated occasional media events. One followed the firing of Miami's police chief. The chief's suit against the city triggered depositions in the Firm's conference room with television cameras and special lighting. In another case, Hurtgen presented arguments to a total of twenty judges over a seven-year period before the Florida Supreme Court finally ruled that police officers suspected of illegal drug use could be tested by their employers without the agreement of their union. Characterizing the case as "one of great public importance," the court opined that "[p]ublic safety and protection cannot wait for a bargaining session under these circumstances."[1]

Hurtgen increasingly took over leadership of the office from McGonigal during the late 1980s. In 1989, he was joined by E. Barclay Cale, a Philadelphia litigation partner steeped in the Firm's culture since 1962. Cale was also an experienced administrator, having served as the Firm's managing partner from 1972 to 1978. Together, Hurtgen and Cale undertook a reappraisal of the Miami office. It had grown to a peak of fifty-one lawyers by the late 1980s. But its practice had not kept pace with its personnel. Moreover, its disparate assemblage of partners lacked a common vision, and their areas of expertise did not always mesh with the Firm's national practice groups. A restructuring was inevitable.

When the dust settled in 1991, the office had shrunk to thirty-one lawyers. Then the rebuilding process began. By 1993, the number had risen to thirty-seven. Of these, fifteen were partners. Of the fifteen, four were stalwarts: Connor, Pettigrew, Hurtgen, and Cale. In addition, there were four partners who started in Miami as associates during the 1980s and came up through the ranks: John Fletcher, named a business and finance partner in 1986; Sergio Alvarez-Mena, named a litigation partner in 1989; Mark Zelek, named a labor partner in 1991; and Robert Brochin, who became a litigation partner in 1988, left the Firm in 1991 to serve as deputy general counsel to Governor Lawton Chiles, and returned in 1993. Finally, there was a new wave of lateral entrants: William Radford, named a labor partner in 1988; Peter Pinney, named a business and finance partner in 1990; Bennett Falk and Keith Olin, who became litigation partners in 1991; Carlos Mendez-Peñate, named a business and finance partner in 1992; and Douglas Bischoff, named a business and finance partner in 1993.

Falk and his protégé Olin arrived at the Firm as a team. They brought an outstanding securities litigation practice: Olin served Kidder Peabody, while Falk's clients included Merrill Lynch, Pierce, Fenner & Smith Incorporated; PaineWebber Incorporated; Smith Barney; Harris Upham & Co. Incorporated; Raymond James & Associates, Inc.; Dillon Reed & Co.; Donaldson Lufkin & Jenrette, Inc.; Dean Witter Reynolds Inc.; Bear, Stearns & Co.; Prudential-Bache Securities Inc.; and Shearson Lehman Brothers Inc. Thus, Falk and Olin shared kinds of matters and even clients with John Peloso and Robert Romano in the Firm's New York office. Frequently, those matters involved defending against claims by investors that they had been victimized by securities dealers, hardly the favorites of Miami juries, especially in cases that savored of churning. Large verdicts were the rule.

So it was with special satisfaction that Falk won a case in 1993 for Merrill Lynch involving a $2-million claim for damages asserted by the patriarch of one of Venezuela's leading industrial families. The patriarch's lawyers dubbed Merrill Lynch's representative a "snake-oil salesman," saying he had traded $3.5 million of "lead poison" for the patriarch, thereby generating $655,000 in commissions for Merrill Lynch. "Lead poison" referred to zero-coupon United States treasury bonds (STRIPS), coupled with a sophisticated options trading strategy. If held to maturity, the STRIPS would have been worth almost $25 million. Unfortunately, the bond market tumbled in March 1987, and the patriarch ordered the STRIPS sold. Their disposition was contrary to Merrill Lynch's advice and before the market recovered.

After disposing of the STRIPS, the patriarch claimed they had been unsuitable investments from the beginning, that Merrill Lynch had not advised him about the risks involved, and that Merrill Lynch had not kept him informed as the market soured. Merrill Lynch countered that the investments fit squarely within the patriarch's objectives as set forth in his handwritten instructions, that Merrill Lynch expected a recovery of the STRIPS after the crash and had advised him to hold them, and that Merrill Lynch actually spent 1,000 minutes in telephone conversations with the patriarch and his family during the period when they alleged Merrill Lynch was incommunicado. The ML&B trial team also had to discredit two impressive expert witnesses from Venezuela, one of whom was finally brought to his knees and testified: "I'm very confused and don't really know what happened."

About ten minutes into his closing argument, Falk leaned toward the jury and made eye contact with each juror as he slowly put the question: "Now, ladies and gentlemen, who is attempting to manipulate—here? Who is intending to deceive whom? Think about that. Think about that."

The jurors answered by turning toward the patriarch. Their gesture foreshadowed the outcome: The three-week trial ended with a jury verdict for Merrill Lynch on all the claims.[2]

■ ■ ■ ■ ■

The desire for a gateway to Latin America had played a role in the Firm's decision to open a Miami office in 1977. While the reasoning was correct, it was also premature, especially as Latin America went into an economic tailspin shortly after the office opened. But by the early 1990s, there was cause for optimism: The Latin economies were stabilizing, privatizing, and beginning to enjoy a renaissance. Also, Cuba excited great expectations. With communism discredited and Castro's regime nearing its likely end, there was talk among Cuban expatriates that Miami would one day become the effective capital of Cuba, as investment and entrepreneurship flowed into that country through the Miami community. Expropriation claims would be filed and new businesses created. Lawyers would be in demand, especially Spanish-speaking lawyers in the Miami offices of major American law firms.

Havana-born, Yale-trained Mendez-Peñate figured prominently in this class. After his arrival at the Firm in 1992, he established a subgroup of Spanish-speaking ML&B lawyers who regularly made the rounds to Central and South America. Their clients included such industrial giants as Exxon, Merck & Co., and Phelps Dodge International, as well as banks, brokerage houses, and mutual funds investing in Latin American securities.

■ ■ ■ ■ ■

The fluidity that characterized ML&B's Miami personnel also extended to its office locations. From One Biscayne Tower, which it occupied in 1977, it moved to Miami Center in 1983, only to leave Miami Center for Southeast Financial Center (later First Union Financial Center) in 1987. All three locations were striking, although the wood was always a lighter shade than in Los Angeles: Miami never fancied itself more like Philadelphia than Philadelphia itself. At Southeast Financial Center, where the Firm was spread over three floors, an extraordinary number of lawyers could occupy corner offices due to the building's sawtooth design.

But by far the Firm's most exotic location in Florida was Miami Center. Initially called the Edward Ball Building, it contained 750,000 square feet of office space, was thirty-five stories tall, and seemed to rise from the sea nearby. Covered with specially quarried Italian dark brown travertine marble, it featured bronze reflective-glass picture windows. Adjoining the office building as part of the same development was the Hotel Intercontinental (initially called the Pavillon), also thirty-five stories tall, grandiose, and boasting Belgian tapestries and a Henry Moore sculpture. But funding ran out, and the buildings were never finished as designed. When the situation worsened, the developer filed for Chapter 11 protection in 1984. He raised a flag in front of the hotel bearing the slogan, "Don't tread on me."[3] The bankruptcy judge (who later recused himself) called the developer "a madman."[4] In such an atmosphere, and with building services deteriorating, the Firm had no choice in 1987 but to relocate, which it did to the just-completed Southeast Financial Center, at that time the premier office building in Miami.

Still, the inconveniences of Miami's multiple office relocations were nothing compared with Hurricane Andrew, which struck the area in the early morning hours of August 24, 1992. The costliest storm in American history, it carried a total national price tag of almost $30 billion. The devastation in Dade County was of epic proportions. Seven ML&B personnel suffered severe damage to their homes, and almost everyone in the area with the Firm sustained some losses: windows broken, trees uprooted, roof tiles blown down, and cars damaged. Hurtgen was hard-hit; he and his sons barri-caded the front entrance door of their home for almost two hours against 150-mile-per-hour winds.

Firm personnel were not allowed in the office building for two days after the hurricane passed. The destruction was shocking. Sixteen windows in seven lawyers' offices had to be boarded up where winds and flying debris had crashed through the double glazing. Clerestory glass was also smashed, ceiling tiles were down, and duct work was exposed. Window blinds were mangled. Files and furniture were wet and filled with glass. Carpets were destroyed. The office was closed for a week.

When it did reopen on August 31, car pools were established, flexible working hours instituted, and lunch for all personnel was provided, since no restaurants were yet operating in the area. The Firm organized cleanup crews, developed lists of suitable building contractors, and arranged for legal clinics to assist employees with insurance claims. In addition, the Firm and personnel from other offices raised $28,000 for distribution to those Miami office employees whose homes sustained the worst damage.

But black clouds often have silver linings. Wherever Hurricane Andrew struck, it turned a real estate recession into a miniboom. Suddenly, there was a shortage of operating properties and a demand for developers and contractors. Among the beneficiaries was the estate of Stuart Perlman, which owned substantial Florida property. Philadelphia partner Howard Shecter had attracted the representation, aspects of which were then being handled by Cale in Miami. Before Perlman's death in 1988, he and his brother had made fortunes by developing a national chain of restaurants called Lums, acquiring control of Caesars' Palace in Las Vegas, and building Caesars' Casino and Hotel in Atlantic City. But the brothers subsequently suffered reverses that triggered massive litigation after Stuart Perlman's death. The estate's difficulties required help from Washington partner Sheldon Cohen to fight a multimillion-dollar tax battle with the IRS. They also required help from the Firm's New York bankruptcy team and from William Zeiter in the Philadelphia office, as he dealt with several complicated Pennsylvania partnership issues.

Zeiter's involvement caused a stir in the Palm Beach probate court to which Cale presented a fee petition. The presiding judge seized upon a Zeiter time entry. He had charged for one-half hour at $325 an hour. Who could possibly be worth $325 an hour, demanded the judge? Cale responded that Zeiter had written Pennsylvania's business laws, and that it was often better to get an authoritative answer to an arcane question from Zeiter in thirty minutes than an equivocal answer after a day of legal research by a lawyer with a lower rate. "Like talking directly to God," mused the judge. "Fee petition approved." Divine interoffice synergy.

■ ■ ■ ■

Over the years, many prominent national law firms that succeeded elsewhere failed in Florida. While they opened and closed their offices, ML&B persisted for sixteen years in seeking the right combination of lawyers and matters for its Miami office. Rewards for the Firm's patience have come only recently, and it cannot be denied that ML&B's Miami experience put a damper on the Firm's expansion program. Until Miami, the Firm had enjoyed extraordinary successes wherever it went. So it kept going.

Miami was different, as the Firm settled down to nurse its problems there. Consequently, no new domestic offices were added during the 1980s, except San Diego and Newport Beach, which were by-products of acquisitions by the Los Angeles office. Instead, having pioneered in Washington in 1947, Harrisburg in 1961, New York in 1972, Los Angeles in 1976, and Miami in 1977, ML&B concentrated during the 1980s on adding depth to its existing domestic offices. While it flirted briefly with the possibility of a Chicago office, all four of its new offices during the 1980s would be abroad. The Firm had gone national. Now it was time to go international.

CHAPTER 24

THE WORLD WAS ALL BEFORE THEM[1]

Early contacts with international law ■ *USIF's liquid real estate* ■ *The missing link* ■ *Onto something* ■ *A section proclaimed* ■ *IOS, Cornfeld, and Vesco* ■ *The SEC and a rogue elephant* ■ *The oldest jail in Europe* ■ *An American in Paris* ■ *Telephones and dogs* ■ *A Korean restaurant and a London office* ■ *Iranian claims in The Hague* ■ *The Pacific Rim* ■ *The fortieth* gaiben ■ *Doing the deal ML&B-style* ■ *Screaming access in Brussels* ■ *The satellites come unglued* ■ *The German practice and the Frankfurt office* ■ *Chipping the wall* ■ *Russia goes public* ■ *Adam and Eve*

ML&B's contacts with international law were sporadic before the 1970s—not strange for a Philadelphia firm with a developing office in Washington and a satellite office in Harrisburg. True, the Firm had represented Pilkington in the United States since 1912, as described in Chapter 6. For Pilkington, the Firm handled matters typical of foreign clients: transactions with licensees and vendees, acquisitions, trademarks, and regulatory problems. International lawyers call such work inbound. Although cultural differences must still be bridged, the work is largely performed in the United States and the applicable law is generally domestic law.

Greater expertise is required for outbound work. When a domestic client goes abroad, the lawyer should be familiar with the legal system and mind-set of the host country. An American client or lawyer who thinks and acts American in a foreign country is at a disadvantage. That disadvantage may be negligible in the United Kingdom, but it can be serious in continental Europe, and it is often disabling elsewhere.

The Firm certainly faced the challenge of outbound assignments between 1917 and the Depression years when it represented the Baldwin Locomotive Works. As mentioned in Chapter 8, the file titles were exotic: Chinese Notes, National Railways of Mexico, Polish Bond Issue, Egyptian State Railway, to recall just a few. These matters brought the Firm into contact with foreign lawyers and legal systems. Moreover, Morris Bockius took extended trips abroad with Baldwin's flamboyant CEO to negotiate and document major transactions.

But as the 1920s ended, so did international legal work. Capital formation ceased and trade withered as nations beggared each other with protective tariffs. Then came World War II. It certainly touched off unprecedented international activity. But that activity was under governmental auspices, normally involving public rather than private international law.

It was not until after World War II that international work for lawyers in the private sector moved center stage. American industry set up shop abroad, and American money-center banks opened near Threadneedle Street in London and the Place Vendôme in Paris. Their law firms frequently followed them. But ML&B had no international banking client to follow. Also, the Firm was otherwise engaged, especially with the development of its new Washington office starting in 1947. International law would have to wait, as it did until 1972 when ML&B was suddenly thrust into the affairs of United States Investment Fund (USIF), followed nine months later by Investors Overseas Services (IOS). They were the two largest offshore mutual funds in history.

■ ■ ■ ■ ■

USIF was an open-ended fund in the form of a Bahamian trust. Its shares had been sold to 18,000 shareholders in 100 countries, excluding the United States to avoid American securities regulation. The proceeds had been invested by USIF in more than 100 wholly owned American subsidiaries. The subsidiaries then acquired or developed real estate, primarily apartment buildings, office buildings, and shopping centers. By 1969, only two years after its founding, USIF was the world's largest offshore real estate fund, with $1 billion of assets. Such success was not surprising. In the heady 1960s, the American economy towered above all the rest. Foreigners wanted to invest in that economy, including real estate.

Another reason for USIF's success was an oxymoron: It offered "liquid real estate," or so it said. Since the fund was open-ended, an investor could always cash out at the net asset value of the investor's shares as reported daily in the financial press. But what the fund really offered was a Ponzi scheme on a vast scale. The investor cashing out did not receive money from the liquidation of the fund's real estate. Instead, the investor received money coming in from other investors. Like all Ponzi schemes, it worked smoothly as long as new money came in faster than old money went out.

But starting late in 1969, the flow of money reversed, as Germans stopped investing and began redeeming their shares. (German tax law had been changed to discourage the export of capital into offshore funds like USIF.) When the flow of cash to USIF went negative, it could not liquidate its real estate fast enough to service redemption requests. So, in 1971, it invoked its right to suspend redemptions. It also went incommunicado.

Such was the state of affairs in March 1972, when Park Dilks happened to be in Geneva on another assignment. He was the house guest of a Swiss banker who asked if he had ever heard of USIF. He had not. So the banker gave him a fat file of papers in German with instructions to read them overnight.

As they discussed the papers the next morning, the banker recounted how he had directed the marketing of USIF's stock in Germany. After redemptions were suspended, he had been barraged by questions from his salespeople and their customers. With the fund incommunicado, he could not answer them. Beleaguered, he had engaged a Munich law firm. It said he needed an expert on American real estate and English trust law—called "the missing link" by the Munich firm—to excite interest and support from the prestigious Deutsche Schutzvereinigung für Wertpapierbesitz.

The Schutz, as ML&B lawyers would call it for short, was a German nonprofit shareholders protective association that had helped Germans locate and authenticate their security holdings in the chaos following World War II. If USIF had been a German entity, the Schutz would surely have plunged into USIF's affairs on behalf of its German shareholders. But USIF was a Bahamian trust, and the Schutz did not consort with non-German enterprises, much less Bahamian trusts. Desperately seizing upon Dilks as a possible missing link, the banker and his lawyers arranged presentations to the Schutz in Munich, after which Dilks flew back to Philadelphia and involved Clive Anderson.

Anderson, an Oxford graduate and young English barrister, had come to the United States to teach legal writing at Penn Law School. Bright and tireless, he needed money more than sleep. So he took a second job moonlighting with the Firm. In due course, he severed his relationship with Penn, became an associate with the Firm in 1969, and was made a partner in 1977. (Still bright and tireless, he served as ML&B's managing partner from 1983 to 1987.) Dilks told

Anderson: "I think we are onto something." What they were onto was not only the reorganization of a billion-dollar offshore fund but also the creation of the Firm's international section.

Dilks and Anderson went to Nassau to confront USIF's trustees. One of them, the managing trustee, had ceased operations, leaving the other, the custodian trustee, holding the bag. The bagholder was Trust Corporation of the Bahamas, Ltd. (TCB), presently known as Coutts & Co., a subsidiary of National Westminster Bank PLC. As a trust company, TCB was ill-equipped to run active businesses, much less real estate operations all over the United States. The result was a custodian's nightmare. TCB was looking for a new managing trustee on which to unload the fund's operating burdens. Meantime, it wanted to hear from no one, especially shareholders.

Informed of the situation, the Schutz resolved to take action. But first it would have to proceed in its usual way by raising a *Kriegs-kasse* (war chest). The Swiss banker furnished to the Schutz a list of USIF's German shareholders. The Schutz then solicited contributions from them in proportion to their shares in the fund. ML&B lawyers thought this naive. Surely the Schutz's solicitation letters would end up in trash baskets all over Germany. But the Firm's lawyers did not understand the Germans. The Germans sent money. ML&B was engaged.

Months of negotiations ensued in Nassau, London, New York, Luxembourg, Düsseldorf (the Schutz's headquarters), and Munich. Ultimately, TCB and its advisers recognized that USIF could not be reorganized without shareholder participation, which meant the Schutz. So the Schutz and ML&B became the principal spokesmen for the shareholders. As such, they shaped USIF's restructuring and played an essential role in lengthy reorganization proceedings before the Supreme Court of the Bahamas.

As part of that restructuring, a trust board was formed to act for the shareholders. The Schutz was given the right to name four of the board's twelve members. It named three Germans and Dilks. A year later, Dilks was elected the board's chairman, when its original chairman, a London barrister, was designated a high court judge and later a member of the House of Lords and Privy Councilor. Anderson was appointed the board's clerk, pronounced in the English manner "clark." During the ensuing twenty years, the Firm's work for USIF has continued through two further restructurings of the fund.

Meanwhile, only six weeks after the original Munich meeting, a memo was issued to all the Firm's lawyers from Thomas Lefevre, chairman of the Executive Committee. Dated May 4, 1972, the memo declared it was "now appropriate to create an international section within the Firm." (The memo also directed the establishment of a Paris office, discussed later.) In more recent times, the Firm has appointed committees to debate every conceivable aspect of its operations. But in those early Quadriviri days, fast action was still possible—a holdover from a century of what Lefevre called the deity system.

That same month, May 1972, the Firm installed its first telex machine in Philadelphia, followed by one in Washington. Before that, urgent overseas communications had come and gone by cablegram. For many years, the Firm's stationery bore the cable address Morlebock. But cablegrams were less efficient than telexes, which could be processed within the office and could even be received when the office was closed. In fact, the Firm's very first telex message arrived at 4 a.m. from Munich (10 a.m. Munich time). Five hours later, at the morning meeting, the partners were amazed to hear that the machine had started to type all by itself during the night. But modern technology moves quickly. Less than twenty years later, fax machines replaced telexes. No more amazement. No more morning meetings either.

■ ■ ■ ■ ■

Even more exciting than USIF were ML&B's adventures in connection with IOS and one of its progeny, Fund of Funds (FOF). The brainchild of Bernie Cornfeld, IOS had $2.6 billion under management during the late 1960s and was the largest offshore fund complex in history. Headquartered in Geneva,[2] it comprised 160 companies arranged to maximize obfuscation and minimize effective governmental regulation anywhere. Its half-million investors resided in virtually every country of the world (again the United States was off limits to avoid SEC intervention), including as many as 40,000 in Germany, ten times the number of German shareholders in USIF. With so many Germans involved and USIF largely under its belt, the Schutz did not resist joining the fray when IOS's problems made headlines late in 1972. This time ML&B was engaged by the Schutz as a matter of course.

Was there ever a financial vehicle as exotic as IOS? The feats of its salespeople, the legerdemain of its management, and its impenetrable structure were the stuff of legend. Journalists found it irresistible. One book about it was entitled *Do You Sincerely Want To Be Rich?*[3] The title derived from a recruiting pitch made by

Cornfeld to attract salespeople. Many were attracted and some became rich.

Cornfeld personified IOS. His résumé recalls a favorite Gilbert and Sullivan patter song: born in Istanbul, raised in Brooklyn, a social worker in Philadelphia, an American in Paris selling mutual funds, created some funds of his own, hounded by the French police, sought sanctuary in Switzerland, achieved fame and fortune with a sprinkling of infamy. As success begat sybaritism, Cornfeld turned to chateaus, backgammon, all-night parties, and the company of beautiful people. He had boundless marketing skills but little financial acumen.

IOS experienced a cash crunch in 1971. Or at least it thought it did—it was so big and had so many pockets for its money that its cash problems may have been illusory. But illusory or not, it looked for a savior. A false one appeared in the form of Robert Vesco. Unlike Cornfeld, Vesco eschewed sybaritism. Nor was he interested in marketing. But his appetite for money was as insatiable as his scruples were scant. He toppled Cornfeld and took control of the IOS empire. He then began to loot its funds.

Vesco's game was spoiled in November 1972 when the SEC filed a suit in the Southern District of New York targeting him and forty-one other defendants. The complaint recited that they had stolen $224 million from various IOS funds. The SEC called it "one of the largest securities frauds ever perpetrated."[4]

After the SEC filed its suit, the Schutz's German lawyers discovered that an IOS employee had made off with computer tapes containing the names and addresses of IOS fund shareholders worldwide. The employee was tracked down in Amsterdam and induced to turn over the tapes. A Schutz *Kriegskasse* letter went forward. This time it was written in several languages and was sent to others beside Germans. Back came some $1 million, with more to follow.

During the first half of 1973, members of the Firm's IOS team, led by Dilks and Anderson, were deployed to Geneva, Ferney-Voltaire, Nassau, London, Luxembourg, Amsterdam, Düsseldorf, Munich, Berlin, and Paris. ML&B's instructions from the Schutz were to get control of IOS's books and records, perform a legal audit, secure existing assets, retrieve lost assets, and restructure the IOS funds to protect their shareholders in the future. Working with the Schutz's German lawyers, most of those instructions were carried out, although twenty years later many questions remain unanswered. Still, the effort failed in one crucial respect: There would be no restructuring of IOS as there had been of USIF.

The Schutz and the SEC disagreed on whether the IOS funds should be restructured or liquidated. The Schutz favored restructure, urging also that each fund be dealt with according to the law of its domicile. The SEC, which regarded IOS as a rogue elephant, wanted all the IOS funds liquidated by a single receiver operating under the supervision of a federal judge in New York. The Schutz retorted that the interposition of such a superreceiver would incite jurisdictional contests and play into the hands of Vesco and his cronies by protracting the proceedings. But although adverse to the SEC, the Schutz wanted access to the SEC's investigation. And although adverse to the Schutz, the SEC wanted shareholder support, which the Schutz could deliver. An uneasy relationship.

While proceedings were grinding on in New York, the denouement came in Luxembourg at a summit conference held on June 29, 1973. It was attended by the SEC and regulatory agencies from other countries in which IOS entities were chartered. The Schutz's German lawyers were there, as were Dilks and Anderson. But tiny Luxembourg strong-armed the proceedings. Although it had granted a safe-conduct pass to the senior IOS delegate, it had him arrested on arrival and "confined to the oldest jail still in continuous operation in Europe," according to a gleeful announcement by the Luxembourg banking commissioner.

Like a roaring mouse, Luxembourg then rejected the arguments of the Schutz that the funds should be restructured. It also rejected the arguments of the SEC that the funds should be liquidated in New York. But if the Schutz lost on the restructure question, it prevailed on the question of applicable law: The Luxembourg authorities announced that they would unilaterally liquidate in Luxembourg a large IOS fund domiciled there. The inference was that the other funds should also be liquidated in their respective jurisdictions. The SEC was shocked. The *Wall Street Journal* spoke of liquidations "the likes of which the world has never seen."[5]

As proceedings closed in Luxembourg, a line of demarcation was drawn by the Schutz: It directed that its German lawyers shepherd the liquidation of funds domiciled in the Eastern Hemisphere and that ML&B to do the same for the Western Hemisphere funds. The leading Western Hemisphere fund was FOF, an Ontario corporation. ML&B's assignment to liquidate FOF would give rise to years of litigation and a stunning victory for the Firm in 1980, as chronicled in Chapter 36.

USIF and FOF are still active files at the Firm after two decades. Matters for USIF have continued, particularly in Nassau and London. For FOF, additional assets are recovered from time to time, with a large recovery—from Vesco himself—still a possibility for the future. The Firm's $225-million judgment (including interest) against him remains on record and awaits his return from Cuba, where he is currently a fugitive from justice in the United States.

■ ■ ■ ■ ■

Returning to Lefevre's memo of May 4, 1972, it not only announced the creation of the Firm's international section, it also mandated the Firm's first foreign office. Paris was then the fashionable place for the overseas offices of American law firms. From 1972 until 1981, the Firm's stationery listed its associated office in Paris at 130, rue du Faubourg, Saint-Honoré. Cartesian reasoning required that the Firm actually lease space in Paris in order to have an office there. But Cartesian reasoning did not specify the area. So the area was minimal, leading some partners to characterize ML&B's Paris office as a broom closet.

Whatever its size, it was located in the offices of a law firm then known as Badinter, Bredin, Jouanneau et Prat. (Robert Badinter, the firm's senior partner, was subsequently minister of justice in the Mitterrand government and later a member of the French constitutional court.) For some years, a brass plaque bearing the Firm's name adorned the building's entrance. Taken down and stored by the French firm, it surfaced in 1990 when delivered by that firm to ML&B's recently opened Brussels office.

As the Firm's European practice developed during the 1970s, Dilks and Anderson operated out of the Paris office. But the lawyer there the most was Joseph Hennessy, the third original member of the international section as designated by Lefevre's memo. Since Dilks was the section's chairman and Anderson was its administrator, Hennessy was its only nontitled member, giving rise to his boast (or admission) that two lawyers were needed to supervise him. A Ph.D. in political science from Notre Dame, he had lived in Paris while writing his doctoral dissertation. His French was good. Increasingly, it was Hennessy who handled the Firm's French matters, culminating in a nine-month sojourn at the Badinter firm in 1977.

During his Paris sojourn, Hennessy learned not only French legal drafting but also something about French telecommunications and canines. Using a public telephone to reach a client, he once called the same number seven times while trying to understand a recorded message. He had almost exhausted his supply of *jetons* before realizing that the message, delivered in supersonic French, was telling him to call still another number.

He also had trouble with French dogs. Before the American fitness obsession caught on in Europe, he jogged early each morning in the Champs de Mars, thereby attracting attention and sometimes disapproval. Once he noticed two Doberman pinschers running toward him. He tried to elude them, but they cornered him, jumped up, and effectively pinned him against a wall along the Seine. In leisurely fashion, the dogs' owner arrived carrying their leashes. She called the dogs off but did not apologize. Instead, she glowered at Hennessy. Pulling himself together, Hennessy explained in his most polite French that the dogs had attacked him. Deflecting the point, the dogs' owner announced with unassailable Gallic logic: "Sir, you were running!" Victorious, she then strode off, preceded by her dogs, still unleashed.

But the real lesson Hennessy learned in Paris did not relate to telecommunications, canines, or even drafting legal documents in French. It was simply that the best European location for an American law firm at that time was London, not Paris. While undeniably charming, Paris was not the financial center that London had once been and was again becoming. Considering the Firm's growing European practice and the burdens of commuting, even the most conservative projections argued for an ML&B office in London, instead of a broom closet in Paris. Studies also showed that the Firm should build its London office around an American lawyer who was already there, who expected to stay there, and who had a free-standing practice.

As word got around that ML&B was looking in London, an American lawyer named Franklin Bloomer made himself known. He was working in London for a Saudi investment company that was about to close its London office. Also, he was the nephew of Millard Bloomer, who had been a partner in the New York firm of Wickes, Riddel, Jacobi & McGuire, which merged with ML&B in 1979. In effect, Bloomer wanted to join his late uncle's successor firm, and he wanted to do so in London. He satisfied two of the three criteria: He was an American lawyer in London and he wanted to stay there. But he missed on the third: He had no free-standing practice.

Recognizing his shortcoming, Bloomer countered with a proposition. He would undertake to find the right American lawyer in London; and if he did so, the Firm would make Bloomer a partner in

London to assist the lawyer he found. Bloomer's proposition was accepted, and for months he interviewed every suitable American lawyer in London. On one ground or another, they were all inappropriate except Charles (Chuck) Lubar. Lubar had practiced in London since 1971 and was the senior partner of a prospering firm of four lawyers in Saint James Place. He had previously been approached by several major New York law firms, but he preferred his independence and had rejected their overtures. Also, he feared that a large firm would be repressive and stuffy.

ML&B launched a selling effort at Lubar, but to no avail. Finally, late in 1980, he and Dilks had a long dinner together at a Korean restaurant in New York. It will never be known whether Lubar would have surrendered but for the presence at the dinner of two women. One was Lubar's wife, who said simply, "Do it, Chuck." The other was Dilks's wife, who was wearing jeans. As Lubar tells it, the choice of a Korean restaurant and the presence of a senior partner's wife wearing jeans overcame his concern about stuffiness. He capitulated, and ML&B's London office opened on March 1, 1981. (More about Lubar in Chapter 34.)

Ideal space for the London office was found at 4 Carlton Gardens, just off Pall Mall and next to Marlborough House. Two floors were gutted and rebuilt for a maximum of nine lawyers. Bloomer was there, as agreed. Also, the ubiquitous Hennessy was dispatched and spent twenty-eight months in London. His job, he said, was to stamp ML&B on Lubar's forehead. When Hennessy returned to the United States in 1983, he was given a framed picture displaying the national flags of all personnel in the London office. There were nine different flags.

Lubar, Bloomer, and Hennessy may be regarded as the Firm's pioneers in London. They were soon joined by Michael Pfeifer, who arrived in 1981 as an associate, was made a partner in 1984, and left the Firm in 1993 to become special assistant to the associate chief counsel (international) of the Interval Revenue Service. Then, with Bloomer's return to New York (he went by sea, as described in Chapter 21), Thomas Benz joined the Firm laterally as a partner in 1987. Finally, Robert Rakison became a partner in 1993, leaving a firm of solicitors named for him and of which he was the senior partner. His addition was made possible when the Law Society adopted the Multinational Partnership Rules that permitted solicitors to form partnerships with foreign lawyers while continuing to practice local law. ML&B was among the first firms to create a multinational partnership in London.

■ ■ ■ ■ ■

Turning from London, the international section's next initiative was in Washington, where three partners arrived laterally in 1986: Markham Ball, Mark Joelson, and Joseph Griffin. All three had attended Oxford University, a credential Anderson naturally found endearing. Joelson and Griffin were former chairs of the American Bar Association's Section on International Law and Practice, and Ball had seen prior government service as general counsel of the United States Agency for International Development. They brought with them such prestigious clients as the governments of Australia and Great Britain. They also brought some thirty Iranian claims cases.

The Iranian claims cases had their genesis in the November 4, 1979, seizure of the United States embassy in Tehran by Iranian militants, euphemistically called "students" by their government. The students held fifty-two American hostages for an agonizing 444 days. In retaliation, the United States government froze $8 billion in Iranian assets, meanwhile seeking a release of the hostages and mounting an unsuccessful military rescue attempt. President Jimmy Carter's inability to deal with the hostage ordeal contributed to his defeat by Ronald Reagan in the 1980 election. On the day Reagan took office, there was a settlement. The hostages were released, some assets were unfrozen for return to Iran, and an Iran-United States claims tribunal was constituted in The Hague to adjudicate claims for the rest. There were 3,800 claims totaling $60 billion.

The Firm's Iranian team tried half its thirty cases and settled the others. The team's largest claim was for Phillips Petroleum Company, which was awarded more than $100 million in a decision that established a precedent by calculating damages on the basis of discounted cash flow. While the result in the Phillips case was ultimately gratifying to the client, the proceedings started badly, according to Ball and Griffin. The Iranians arrived early at the hearing room in The Hague's Peace Palace and removed all the chairs from their side of the room. Then they insisted on postponing the hearing because there was no place for them to sit. Other chairs were found. But the Iranians continued to delay the proceedings on various grounds. In an unrelated case, a seventy-year-old neutral arbitrator was beaten by two forty-year-old Iranian arbitrators, resulting in a suspension of all proceedings for more than a year. Such are the niceties of international law practice.

A year after Ball, Joelson, and Griffin joined the Firm in Washington, it was time to address the other side of the world, as
championed by John Forry. Forry had arrived in 1980 as a lateral
partner in Los Angeles. He was an international tax expert, active
on the lecture circuit, and widely published. To him, the future lay
with the Pacific Rim. His travels regularly took him to Tokyo, Hong
Kong, and Singapore. International section members marveled at
his exhausting itineraries. No one covered more ground: He was the
perfect caller. He also kept records on everything. With them he
could demonstrate that Tokyo was the ideal location for the Firm's
first office in the Far East. Moreover, Anderson's financial projections confirmed that such an office could be cost-effective, considering the business it would generate for the Firm's other offices.

Still, such projections were strictly academic until 1986, when the
Department of Commerce finally succeeded in opening the door for
American lawyers to practice in Japan. That year, the Japanese
enacted the Special Measures Law Concerning the Engagement in
Legal Practice by Foreign Lawyers. For the first time since the early
1950s, non-Japanese lawyers would be permitted to establish
offices in Japan. But the rules were strict. Foreign lawyers could
only practice the law of their home jurisdiction. Also, they could not
associate with Japanese lawyers.

The Firm's Tokyo office, which officially opened on July 1, 1988,
had two torchbearers: Forry, who was Tokyo's most vigorous proponent, and Elmer Stone, who actually went to the scene. It was a
stroke of luck that Stone had become an of counsel to the Firm in
1984. Working for thirty years with Japanese clients, he traveled
regularly to Japan, spoke Japanese, empathized with Japanese
culture, and often took Japanese exchange students into his home.
His clients included Fuji Heavy Industries; Subaru of America, Inc.;
Mitsubishi International Corporation; Shin Meiwa Industry Co.; and
Yamada International. Best of all, Stone was eager to carry the
Firm's flag to Tokyo. He arrived there in September 1987, made
application to become a *gaikokuho-jimu-bengoshi* (*gaiben* for short),
satisfied the requirements, and was admitted the following year.
(The official records list him as Japan's fortieth *gaiben*.) For the first
time in the Firm's history, the stationery of one of its offices
displayed characters unintelligible to all but a few ML&B lawyers.

On Stone's arrival in Tokyo, he settled into an apartment at Ark
Towers, 3-40 Roppongi, 1 Chome, Minato-ku. There, starting in
1987, he had his residence and unofficial office; he could not have
an official office until he became a *gaiben*. By Japanese standards,
the apartment was huge—2,000 square feet with a large dining

room, ideal for entertaining, and a balcony with spectacular views of the city below. (The rent was equally spectacular: $18,000 per month furnished.) Of course, Stone and his staff worked there. But since the facility was residential, discretion was advised: As Stone put it, "The landlord admonished that the telephone not be answered with the Firm's name."

Entertainment is an important part of Japanese business life, and the Ark Towers apartment was a magnet. Business lunches were served, followed by early-evening cocktails and sushi. Most meals were prepared by Mrs. Stone. Demonstrating their versatility, she and paralegal Takako Muramatsu also functioned as postprandial cleanup crew. These were pioneering times for the Firm in Tokyo. In a sense, they ended on April 1, 1989, when the Tokyo office relocated to CS Tower, 1-11-30 Akasaka, Minato-ku, the Firm's first real office in Japan. Many stories about those early days will surely be told in years to come by Stone's successors.

One such successor was Frank Gniffke. Recruited by Stone in advance of his return to the United States late in 1991, Gniffke became a partner in 1989 and left the Firm in 1993. In 1990, a year after Gniffke's arrival, the Firm's Japanese practice grew dramatically as international lawyers Alan Neuwirth and William Huss (both partners) and Alvin Kassel (special counsel) joined the Firm.[6] (Both Huss and Kassel became *gaibens*, numbers seventy-eight and eighty respectively.) The *New York Observer* reported that a "team with the biggest Japanese business left Webster & Sheffield to join the Manhattan office of Morgan, Lewis & Bockius—taking an estimated $5 million in annual billings with them."[7]

The Neuwirth group's clients included Hitachi, Sumitomo, Asahi, Daikin, and Ricoh. Neuwirth and Kassel moved into ML&B's New York office, while Huss was immediately assigned to the Tokyo office. Married to a Japanese woman, Huss had previously spent six years living and working in Japan. Kassel was the group's father figure, having originated its Japanese practice in the 1950s. Exceptionally energetic, he was seventy-two when he came to the Firm and thus venerable by Japanese standards. His energy, his many contacts, and his zest for business development made him another extraordinary caller in the Far East.

Like the Firm's London office, its Tokyo office was a success right from the start. Some of its business was outbound from the United States, but mostly its matters went in the other direction. There was also an unusual ingredient, a third-country practice. That practice involved matters for American, Japanese, and European clients in

Korea, Taiwan, and Hong Kong. Those clients often instructed the Firm's Tokyo office to "do the deal American-style." Sometimes their instructions were even more specific, and flattering: "Do the deal ML&B-style."

The Tokyo office presented challenges never experienced by the Firm's domestic lawyers. The *Los Angeles Times* wrote:

> Elmer Stone's life spans half the globe, sustained by the telephone, facsimile machine, overnight mail and the longest of work days.
>
> As an American lawyer in Tokyo, he is on the phone at home well before he heads off to the Morgan, Lewis & Bockius law offices in the city's Roppongi district—at 6 a.m., dialing New York, where it is 4 in the afternoon. Shortly, he is in touch with the law firm's office in Los Angeles. Less than 12 hours later, London is calling.[8]

With no real overlap between the working hours of the Firm's Tokyo office and its domestic offices, some means of communication had to be found other than the telephone. Faxes and computer modems were the answer. Also, in order to service Tokyo's requirements, the Firm created something called Tokyo Office East within the Los Angeles office. Tokyo East was staffed by three partners (John Forry, Michael Karlin, and Kenneth Slade) and three paralegals. They were responsible for routing and answering the bulk of Tokyo's inquiries. They also undertook to edit the work product of other Firm offices into what they called Japanese English. Tokyo East labored while Tokyo West slept, and vice versa.

■ ■ ■ ■ ■

The Brussels and Frankfurt offices opened almost simultaneously in 1989, a year after the Tokyo office. The Single European Act of 1986, which amended the 1957 Treaty of Rome, envisaged a barrier-free market of 340 million people in the twelve European countries then comprising the European Community (EC). Applying the act, so-called Eurocrats holed up in Brussels and turned out directives by the hundreds. The directives contemplated common product standards and, someday, a single corporate law, currency, and tax system. No detail escaped the Eurocrats' attention: Yorkshire pudding had to come from Yorkshire, and a vehicle that was otherwise a moped could go no faster than fifteen miles per hour and still be called a moped. The Eurocrats also threatened long traditions: In some countries, stores remained open on Sundays, while in others they closed. The Germans pushed for a directive requiring all to close. Would it be adopted? And if so, would it be enforced?

Shades of Pennsylvania's Sunday blue law litigation handled by the Firm in the 1960s, as discussed in Chapter 16.

Americans watched with exhilaration and anxiety the phenomenon called EC '92, with its December 31, 1992, target date. The EC might rationalize the European market and facilitate American competition. Alternatively, it might erect a Fortress Europe. This was a tremendously important question for the American economy, with 25 percent of its gross national product devoted to foreign trade and 30 percent of its exports to Western Europe. American interests needed advice, the job of lawyers. Many American law firms were setting up in Brussels. ML&B joined them on November 1, 1989.

The right space was found at 227 Rue de la Loi. A *Business Week* article remarked that the Firm's "view of the Berlaymont building [home of the European Commission] across the Schuman traffic circle screams access."[9] The article also sported a small map of Berlaymont and environs. The map pinpointed the locations of the European Parliament, the Council of Ministers, the European Commission, three well-known restaurants, and Morgan, Lewis & Bockius.

A French-speaking associate from the New York office was dispatched to Brussels, as was Griffin on a part-time basis. A major client, for which John Shenefield was the responsible attorney, appeared handily on the scene. It was Sky Television Ltd., an affiliate of News Corporation Limited, and it was concerned about the level of "European content" the Eurocrats would require for its film and television programs.

A search began for an EC lawyer to head the Firm's Brussels office. Ideally, that lawyer should be an ex-Commission official, preferably high-ranking and proficient in at least three languages. Helmut Kreis filled the bill. Before becoming a partner on January 1, 1992, he had headed a division in the Commission's powerful Directorate General for Competition (DG IV). Fluent in German, French, English, and Dutch, he could also manage in Italian and Russian and was the only Firm partner known to have a Cyrillic typewriter.

■ ■ ■ ■ ■

For almost two decades, the Firm had handled important matters for German clients, but without a German specialist or an office in Germany. In 1989, the long-sought German specialist materialized as a lateral entrant: Peter Solmssen. Admitted in Germany as a Rechtskundiger, he spoke German fluently and was from a respected German family. (His great-grandfather had been the first chairman of Deutsche Bank.) Solmssen had made a discovery: No matter how good their English, German clients preferred having someone parse with them in their native tongue such exotica as the Federal Reserve's approach to calculating bank capitalizations, the IRS's loss carryover regulations, and the SEC's tender offer rules. By doing these things superbly, Solmssen attracted a fine stable of German clients, including Krupp Stahl AG; Klöckner-Humboldt-Deutz AG; Bayerische Vereinsbank AG; Metallgesellschaft AG; and MAN Aktiengesellschaft.

Solmssen came to ML&B from another Philadelphia firm that had maintained a relationship in Frankfurt with Robert Daly. Solmssen brought that relationship with him to ML&B. Daly had practiced in Frankfurt since 1968. His office was in a villa on Siesmayerstrasse, opposite the American consulate where he was known as Mr. American Lawyer. Married to a German, he was such a part of the German scene that his children had to learn English in school. Solmssen and other ML&B personnel operating in Germany used space rented from Daly, and ML&B's Frankfurt office formally dates from the Firm's lease of that space and Solmssen's arrival at the Firm on September 1, 1989. Subsequently, Daly merged his firm with ML&B and became a partner in 1991.

In 1993, Christopher King was made a partner in the Frankfurt office. He had been domiciled in more ML&B offices than any other Firm lawyer, first in Los Angeles (he arrived in 1987 with Hahn, Cazier & Smaltz), then in Philadelphia with long periods in New York, and finally after 1991 in Frankfurt. Also in 1993, Herman Bolton became an of counsel to the Firm. As a licensed German lawyer, he made it possible for the Frankfurt office to practice German law.

■ ■ ■ ■ ■

The Brussels and Frankfurt offices were established at a time of world-shaking events. However seductive in theory, communism had shown itself a monstrous hoax in practice, neither utilitarian nor efficient, just totalitarian. The Soviet Union had achieved blazing triumphs in space and weaponry, but it could not feed its population. As it imploded, its former satellites looked westward, with Germany as the pivot. Just 250 miles northeast of Frankfurt, the Berlin Wall fell on November 9, 1989. A symbolic event for human freedom during Europe's *annus mirabilis*, it touched off round-the-clock celebrations. Pieces of the wall were sold as souvenirs. Chipping their own tokens was the preference of some collectors, including Anderson and Griffin. The Firm archives include a picture of them in the act.

Reunification of the two Germanys had become inevitable. After forty-five years of separation, the German Federal Republic absorbed the misnamed German Democratic Republic on October 3, 1990. A month later, all the powers of Europe—East and West—met in Paris to declare an end to the Cold War. Finally, on December 26, 1991, the crumbling Soviet Union was officially dissolved. Since the late 1940s, the two superpowers had spent trillions of dollars and rubles on a vicious arms race. After a truly Manichean struggle, one power had been ruined, and the other's solvency and quality of life threatened. Now it was over, without a shooting war, and the forces of light had seemingly triumphed. But with communism discredited, the question remained whether free enterprise, if given the chance, could do any better, considering resurgent nationalism and ethnicity, as well as global resource exhaustion, pollution, overpopulation, and hordes of peoples on the move.

As lawyers rediscovered the East, ML&B's Frankfurt office filed dozens of claims for properties in the former German Democratic Republic, some confiscated during the 1930s by the Nazis and others by the communists after World War II. Separately, Hennessy handled acquisitions in Budapest and Bucharest. In the former, he found a functioning infrastructure and good food. In the latter, he witnessed something like the desolation Bockius encountered in 1920. Also, according to Hennessy, "the Romanians, once renowned for their cuisine, have completely forgotten how to cook." Like Napoleon's army, international lawyers travel on their stomachs.

Anderson went repeatedly to Warsaw in connection with the installation of cable television and cellular telephone systems in four major Polish cities. Communication networks are essential for an efficient economy. The Polish telephone system functioned indifferently. The authorities were in a hurry: There was no time to tear out ancient wires and install new ones. Cellular systems were the answer. But did the Poles have the foreign exchange to pay for them? (Again shades of problems that Bockius faced in Eastern Europe in the 1920s.) Not to worry, Anderson was told by a high-ranking figure in the Telecommunications Ministry: The Poles had plenty of dollars, an estimated $9 billion. Over the years, the money had been sent by Americans of Polish descent and horded by the recipients in mattresses. The trick was to get the money out of the mattresses and into circulation, said the official.

Leningrad's city council heard about the Polish transaction. The Russians also wished to jump-start their communications network through a cellular system. Anderson went to Leningrad in June 1990 (it became Saint Petersburg again the next year), where he was impressed by Russia's engineering but depressed by its bureaucracy: The Russians had been isolated from economic reality since World War I, the Poles only since World War II.

While in Leningrad, Anderson was afflicted by jet lag. He looked out his hotel window at 3 a.m. It was daylight, the season of "the white nights." So he jogged. Like Hennessy earlier in Paris, Anderson was a pioneer: There were no other joggers on the streets, just some ragtag troops drilling and women sweeping. But unlike Hennessy, Anderson was not attacked by dogs, or bears. Instead, his visits led to a joint venture named Petersburg Long Distance Inc. It went public on February 18, 1993, and became "the first Russian-related issue to trade on a U.S. stock market since the imposition of Communist rule in the former Soviet Union about 75 years ago."[10]

■ ■ ■ ■ ■

Back in 1972, the Firm's seven practice sections became eight with the creation of the international section. The Firm was "onto something," as Dilks told Anderson. It remained onto something: By 1993, the section comprised thirty-five lawyers, compared with the original three. Local and regional practices had been comfortable. So also, it turned out, was national practice. But now there were no limits. The Firm shared the feelings of Adam and Eve as they ventured from Eden: "The world was all before them."

CHAPTER 25

THE SKIES WERE SILENT

A nonconfrontational style ■ *The grocery chains are struck in 1964* ■ *A go-go union* ■ *The airlines bargain jointly* ■ *Souser serendipity* ■ *An ox in the ditch* ■ *Guns and butter* ■ *Wage guidelines* ■ *Wirtz's bargain basement* ■ *Silent skies in 1966* ■ *L.B.J. and the media* ■ *The sausage phase* ■ *Get me to the church on time* ■ *The settlement* ■ *Curtin's New Frontier image* ■ *Their futures are made*

O f ML&B's eight practice divisions, none has attracted more media attention than its labor section, flowing from the many matters of national significance handled by it since the 1960s. Five such matters will be covered in this and ensuing chapters: the nationwide airlines strike by the machinists union in 1966; the labor negotiations that made possible Walt Disney World and the Alyeska pipeline; the 1981 strike by the air traffic controllers against the United States government; and the unique labor relations that characterize professional baseball. William Curtin led the Firm's efforts in the airline industry strike, the Disney and Alyeska negotiations, and the air traffic controllers strike. Charles O'Connor was widely acclaimed for his handling of the baseball representation.

■ ■ ■ ■ ■

Before Souser & Kleeb merged with ML&B in 1959, labor law was practiced part time by two lawyers in the Firm's Philadelphia office. With that merger, ML&B added five full-time labor lawyers and immediately became the preeminent labor law firm representing management in the Philadelphia area. Then Curtin joined the Washington office in 1960. By the late 1970s, largely due to his efforts, ML&B was widely regarded as having the most prestigious labor law practice in the United States. As the 1990s began, more than 100 of the Firm's lawyers in six of its domestic offices were full-time members of the labor section. Kenneth Souser's heirs were fully realizing on his legacy.

Part of that legacy was a nonconfrontational and nonideological approach to organized labor and collective bargaining. While some management labor lawyers make names for themselves as union busters, that was not Souser's style. Instead, he believed that with time even the most intractable disputes could be coaxed to a solution. So he hung on his office wall a large framed rendering of Thomas Babington Macaulay's words: "Men are never so likely to settle a question rightly as when they discuss it freely."[1]

Not that Souser was a pushover. Few bargainers ever negotiated longer and conceded less, while still enjoying the respect and even the affection of their opponents. (When Souser finally did make a move, he always seemed to be parting with his last dime.) Curtin had a similar nonconfrontational approach to bargaining. Both Souser and Curtin trained their disciples in the importance of respectful relationships with the other side as a way to reach fair settlements and keep the wheels of commerce turning.

Another facet of their labor practices, and therefore of the Firm's practice, was multiparty bargaining. Souser's clients had included the regional bakeries, laundries, and meatpackers. Curtin's three years with the Teamsters had honed his skills in multiemployer bargaining. In fact, it was in multiemployer Teamster bargaining that he first attracted the Firm's attention and was persuaded to move from the union side of the table to the management side. And it was in multiemployer bargaining as an ML&B associate that Curtin first achieved national recognition in 1964 when the grocery chains were struck in the Baltimore and Washington areas by the Retail Clerks Union. That recognition led five major airlines to retain the Firm for negotiations which culminated in a nationwide strike by the machinists union in 1966.

At that time, the International Association of Machinists (IAM) had 894,000 members, was the country's fourth-largest union, and represented the highly skilled maintenance personnel servicing aircraft on the ground. Its then president, P. I. Siemiller, called it "the go-go union for workers who want action."[2] So action was what the airlines expected and got after their labor contracts with the IAM expired at the end of 1965. In August of that year, five of them (Eastern, Northwest, TWA, National, and United) took the unprecedented step of banding together for negotiations. They engaged the Firm, and specifically Curtin.

Initially, the Firm's mandate was a narrow one. Curtin was to bargain with the union and function as spokesman for the carriers. He would have no responsibility for any proceedings before a

Presidential Emergency Board (PEB), if such a board were convened.[3] Any such proceedings would presumably be orchestrated by a veteran Washington hand and not by Curtin, who was only thirty-five years old.

But that presumption failed to reckon with what the labor section calls "Souser serendipity." By early April 1966, it seemed inevitable that President Lyndon Johnson would convene a PEB. In an effort to ascertain the likely appointees, representatives of the five airlines met in the Firm's Washington office and asked Curtin to call Assistant Secretary of Labor James Reynolds. Curtin placed the call on a speaker phone as the airline representatives listened. With Reynolds away from his office, the call was taken by his deputy. As luck would have it, the deputy was a former law school classmate of Curtin's. He obviously held Curtin in high regard and provided the desired information. The clients were impressed with Curtin's easy access to the Department of Labor. They huddled and asked him to handle the PEB presentation. In due course, Curtin would act as their spokesman not only to the PEB, but also to several congressional committees, the media, and President Johnson.

Appointments to the PEB were publicly announced on April 21, 1966. The chair went to Johnson's friend, Senator Wayne Morse (D., Ore.). To him, Johnson said: "Wayne, my ox is in the ditch and I want you to help me get it out."[4] Hearings got underway on May 6. To organize their presentation, the airlines literally appropriated the Firm's modest offices at 1120 Connecticut Avenue. Curtin led the campaign with the aid of a thirty-one-year-old associate, Richard Hotvedt. Although Hotvedt would later become a senior member of the Firm's Washington labor section, he recalls that his duties in those early days included handfeeding a state-of-the-art photocopying machine one sheet at a time.

The PEB's deliberations were colored by prevailing social and economic conditions. In July 1965, Johnson had made his disastrous commitment to escalate America's involvement in the continuing Vietnam war, to which opposition at home was steadily mounting. Simultaneously, his Great Society programs were transforming the domestic scene. With demands for both guns and butter fueling inflation, the administration had promulgated wage guidelines. For 1966, those guidelines aimed to cap wage increases at 3.6 percent.

The PEB delivered its report on June 8, 1966. "At no time did we consider the guideposts," said Senator Morse.[5] Nevertheless, the board recommended an increase that exactly replicated the 1966 guideline percentage. Under the Railway Labor Act, a cooling-off period then followed while the parties tried to resolve their dispute based on the PEB's recommendations. The cooling-off period would last until July 8. If the dispute remained unsettled at that time, the union was free to strike.

The airlines quickly announced their acceptance of the board's report, although the recommended settlement went beyond their offer. As their spokesman, Curtin wrote to the President on June 13, 1966:

> Careful study shows that effectuation of the Board's recommendations would be very costly to the Five Carriers. We recognize, however, that a just and prompt settlement of this dispute is clearly in the national interest.

Curtin signed the letter "Chairman, Five Carriers Negotiating Committee."[6]

The IAM did not accept the board's recommendations, which gave the union little more than half of what it was demanding. Nor did it reject them. To the union they were simply a way station in the bargaining. As negotiations resumed, Johnson became increasingly involved. However historians may treat him, he was definitely a hands-on President. He determined that Secretary of Labor W. Willard Wirtz should personally officiate on behalf of the government at the bargaining, which shifted to the Labor Department and was held in a conference center colloquially called "Wirtz's bargain basement." All the while, the President jawboned his friends at the AFL-CIO, hoping they would induce the IAM to moderate its demands.

But it was to no avail. When the cooling-off period expired on July 8, 1966, the worst airline strike in United States history commenced at 6 a.m. The five carriers were struck by 35,400 ground crew workers at seventy-four locations in thirty-five states. The five normally transported 150,000 people per day, served 231 cities and twenty-three foreign countries, and accounted for 62 percent of the country's airline passenger miles and 70 percent of its airmail movements. Air transportation in the United States was effectively paralyzed. To cop a phrase used later by the Professional Air Traffic Controllers Organization (PATCO): The skies were silent. (PATCO's 1981 strike, during which the skies were *not* silent, is described in Chapter 28.)

As the strike continued, so did the bargaining. For the President's convenience, there was another change of venue, this time to the suite of Vice-President Hubert Humphrey in the Executive Office Building next to the White House. Hovering over the proceedings, Johnson was obviously torn by conflicting objectives. First, he simply had to end the disruption and restore the country's airline service. Second, he was committed to fighting inflation through his guidelines, which meant the 3.6-percent settlement recommended by the PEB. And third, he would do nothing to alienate organized labor, one of his most powerful constituencies.

For three weeks, Curtin and his union counterparts inched closer to a settlement. Finally, there was a climactic twelve-hour session on July 29. When it appeared that a breakthrough was imminent, Johnson wanted to be the first to tell the public. He sent his domestic policy assistant, Joseph Califano, trotting back and forth between the Oval Office and the Executive Office Building next door. Califano wanted to know when there would be a settlement the President could announce on national television. The Huntley-Brinkley NBC Evening News had already concluded. The President's next target was Walter Cronkite's CBS Evening News. Now Reynolds joined Califano in shuttling between the negotiators and the President. Johnson had moved from impatient to frantic. Suddenly, the settlement itself seemed less important to him than the possibility of missing the prime-time television audience altogether. When the settlement finally came, Johnson announced it by interrupting a popular Friday evening series, the *Man from U.N.C.L.E.*

Curtin recalls that the parties were lined up in an unlighted walkway overlooking the Rose Garden after leaving the Oval Office and before entering the White House movie-television studio. Having been briefed, Johnson, who was famous for putting his arms around people, put his arm around Curtin and said, "Tell that industry of yours I saved 'em $134 million!" It was a rule with Johnson that he always took the credit no matter how farfetched. A photo opportunity followed. It featured a three-way handshake by Johnson, Curtin, and Siemiller. Partner Brady Bryson, who was traveling abroad, said he "did a double take" when he saw the photograph on the front page of a newspaper in Milan.[7]

But the rejoicing was premature. Although Siemiller undertook to recommend ratification, many local union leaders urged rejection, and the vote ran three to one against the proposal. The *Wall Street Journal* called it a "defeat . . . for President Johnson, who had committed his power and prestige in personally intervening in [the] negotiations."[8]

With the executive branch rebuffed, the strike moved into what

Curtin and Hotvedt called "the legislative phase" or, as Otto von Bismarck might have put it, "the sausage phase." (To Bismarck is attributed the observation: "If you like laws and sausages, you should never watch either one being made."[9]) What would Congress do in response to the fury of constituents and damage to the economy? Congress would do what it always does in such cases: It would hold hearings. It would even hold a nonhearing.

The nonhearing was convened on August 1 by Representative Adam Clayton Powell (D., N.Y.), the charismatic pastor of the Abyssinian Baptist Church in Harlem. An avowed basker in the limelight, he chaired the House Labor and Education Committee. When Powell was told by the congressional leadership that his committee lacked jurisdiction, the congressman gathered its membership anyway and cheerfully announced: "This is a *non*-hearing; now we would like to hear from Mr. Siemiller and Mr. Curtin." The two witnesses were then placed at the same table in the hearing room, so that various committee members, depending upon their views and desires for publicity back home, could put hard or easy questions to one or the other.

The committee that actually had jurisdiction was the House Interstate and Foreign Commerce Committee, chaired by Harley Staggers (D., W.V.). The question was whether there should be legislation to force the machinists back to work and prevent similar strikes in the future. One witness was Secretary Wirtz. His task was impossible: He had to carry out Johnson's policy of pleasing everyone. Thus, he had to deplore inflation and public hardship, but at the same time he could not advocate legislation to end the strike.

Wirtz also had a logistical problem. It was Saturday, August 6, the day Luci Baines Johnson and Patrick John Nugent were to be married at Washington's National Shrine of the Immaculate Conception. Naturally, Wirtz was invited. So in his opening remarks to the House committee he agreed to answer all questions but pleaded "just get me to the church on time."[10] Later, Wirtz learned that his quote from *My Fair Lady* reached Johnson. Apparently, the President was not amused.

The Johnson nuptials also precipitated a near miss for Curtin and the airlines. August weather in Washington can be stifling, especially for those in formal attire at a wedding ceremony. White House secretary Liz Carpenter had an inspiration. With the carriers strike-bound, why not have them move their idle air-conditioning trucks from Baltimore airport to Washington to chill the church? Somehow word of the plan reached Wirtz. He called Curtin. They quickly agreed the Carpenter initiative could backfire if furnishing the equipment were seen as a favor by the airlines to the President's family. Carpenter had arranged for the Maryland police to escort the trucks down the Washington-Baltimore Parkway. With the equipment already on its way, Wirtz ordered the FBI to head off the caravan just short of the church and send it back to the airport. The church remained unchilled.

Meanwhile, negotiations were proceeding parallel with the legislative (sausage) phase and the Johnson wedding. On August 15, after twenty hours of nearly continuous talks, the parties again reached a settlement. The contract was ratified by the union membership four days later, thus ending the forty-two-day strike. When Assistant Secretary Reynolds was asked if the pact was inflationary, he "declined to characterize it 'in any way whatsoever.' "[11] Curtin calculated the cost at 4.8 percent, essentially the amount the IAM's membership had voted to reject on August 1.

The settlement was finally accepted for a number of reasons. First, Curtin and his clients managed to convince the union that the airlines absolutely would not increase their offer. Also, airline witnesses testified they were not opposed to legislation. Conversely, the AFL-CIO was vitally concerned, as always, about any congressional action to end a strike by legislation. Furthermore, public outrage at the terribly disruptive strike was less directed at the carriers than at the union, whose demands were perceived as excessive. Finally, the parties repackaged the settlement to make it appear more generous. While considerably below the 6 percent the IAM sought, it clearly penetrated the 3.6-percent guidelines. Indeed, the guidelines ceased to have any meaning after the settlement.[12] Also forgotten was the legislative initiative.

In retrospect, considering Curtin's youth and the political and economic complexities of the matter, it is amazing that he held the disparate carriers together for an entire year. It was a bravura performance, but one without an encore. They never again bargained as a group.

During the strike and its aftermath, the Firm and Curtin received the highest praise. Relationships by the Firm with the airline industry were established that have endured to the present time. According to the Washington *Sunday Star,* Curtin "exude[d] an easy self-confidence" and was a "partner in the massive law firm of Morgan, Lewis & Bockius."[13] (The Firm then numbered eighty lawyers.) The July 13, 1966, *Wall Street Journal* was equally laudatory, observing:

Athletically handsome Bill Curtin, articulate and polished, a persuasive, even-tempered advocate, is molded in the New Frontier image, even down to such details as a love for touch football and a daughter named Caroline.

With Johnson's ox out of the ditch and the skies no longer silent, Souser wrote to Secretary Wirtz, expressing his appreciation for the Secretary's contribution to the negotiations. He also correctly appraised the prospects for Curtin and Hotvedt, to whom he said, "Gentlemen, your futures are made."

CHAPTER 26

THE MAGIC KINGDOM

On the side of the angels ■ *The Associated General Contractors of America* ■ *Walt's dream* ■ *Twice the area of Manhattan* ■ *A free hand from Roy* ■ *Sitting down together* ■ *The Purple Tree* ■ *Seventeen unions agree* ■ *The miracle of arbitration* ■ *Local negotiations* ■ *Disney World opens in 1971* ■ *The Mad Hatter out of action* ■ *Epcot* ■ *Amusement not salvation*

Kenneth Souser was right about the futures of his young Washington protégés William Curtin and Richard Hotvedt. The airlines strike was closely watched. For the first time, a major sector of that industry bargained together. It did so impeccably and under enormous pressure, while being subject to intense scrutiny by the public, the media, and all three branches of the United States government. It took a strike and held its ground, even though it could have capitulated and turned to the Civil Aeronautics Board for rate relief in those days before deregulation. In short, the airlines were on the side of the angels at a time when escalating inflation was a serious national concern.

One group paying special attention to the IAM strike was the Associated General Contractors of America (AGC), the umbrella organization for employer associations dealing with building-trades unions all over the United States. In no industry were wages and benefits rising faster than in construction. So it was not surprising that the AGC asked Curtin to deliver a keynote address at its September 1966 convention in Hawaii and thereafter engaged the Firm to advise it in the labor field.

Nor was it surprising that the AGC recommended the Firm and Curtin to contractors and owners. One such owner was Walt Disney Productions, which had a unique undertaking on its drawing board. That undertaking would require Curtin to negotiate with seventeen unions a landmark labor agreement designed to ensure labor peace while building "the biggest nongovernmental project in the world."[1]

In 1964, the Disney interests had quietly begun buying up land twenty miles southwest of Orlando, Florida. By the time Walt Disney World was announced publicly in November 1965, they had acquired 27,400 acres of bog, saw grass, and palmetto. The site comprised forty-three square miles, about twice the area of Manhattan. On it they would construct an entertainment park five times the size of Disneyland in Anaheim, California. Among the project's many superlatives was the creation of a lake requiring "the largest earth-moving job since the Hoover Dam."[2] As it turned out, Walt Disney World would be the posthumous achievement of the legendary Walt Disney, who died on December 15, 1966.

After Walt's death, his brother Roy took control of the Disney entertainment empire. It was Roy, then seventy-three-years old, who asked Curtin to visit Anaheim in April 1968 and see Disneyland from the inside. While there, Curtin learned more about Disney's mind-boggling plans. The first phase of the project, to be called the Magic Kingdom, would cover 2,500 acres with six theme areas: Main Street USA, Adventureland, Frontierland, Liberty Square, Fantasyland, and Tomorrowland. Curtin also learned about Disney's insistence upon perfection. (*Time* later noted: "[T]hey vacuum the streets at night and disinfect the public telephones with Lysol."[3]) Already, that perfection was being endangered, as Disney ran into union problems while simply engaged in preliminary site clearance. ML&B and Curtin were presented with a challenge: Could Walt's dream be realized and so extraordinary a project actually be built?

Looking back, Curtin might well ask how he ever brought it off. Never in anyone's memory had a private owner or contractor negotiated simultaneously with so many building-trades unions (as well as the Teamsters) to generate a single contract that would extend four years until the completion of such an unprecedented construction project. The idea was logical enough, but the building-trades unions were not accustomed to bargaining together. Not only were they in constant conflict with employers, they also nursed ancient grievances against each other based on generations of jurisdictional haggling.

Curtin's strategy was first to have Roy Disney shut down completely all activity on the site. Curtin doubted if the client would agree. But the client did, thereby dealing Curtin the cards he needed. With those cards, Curtin approached the Building and Construction Trades Department of the AFL-CIO, the coordinating entity for the many separate trades, with the proposition that a "single construction project agreement" would have to be negotiated before another spadeful of earth was turned.

For the internationals in Washington to sit down together was itself a signal event. In May 1968, there were two opening meetings at the Madison Hotel. One was strictly ceremonial: The international representatives were shown what Disney's lieutenants called "Walt's last film." In that film, the entertainment genius spoke figuratively from the grave about his concept of Walt Disney World. After that ceremonial meeting, there was a second opening meeting at which negotiations actually got started. Then the sessions adjourned to the old Hamilton Hotel at Fourteenth and K streets, a favorite haunt for union types. Sometimes they met in its cocktail lounge, called "The Purple Tree."

From the first bargaining meeting, it was evident that the parties were sailing in uncharted seas. Generalities were easy and safe, so the Disney representatives waxed eloquent about negotiating the most innovative collective bargaining agreement in history. The old salts representing almost a score of unions listened patiently if skeptically. Finally, the building-trades chairman asked: "Please give us an example of what you are talking about." One Disney representative responded that there would have to be an exceptionally tight grievance and arbitration provision to avoid any work stoppages. The union chairman said he understood: Indeed, he had just the right provision in his desk drawer. When produced at the next meeting, it read:

> In the event there is a dispute on the job which cannot be resolved between the contractor and the union, the matter shall be referred to the International Union where the General President or his employment representative will make the final decision.

Obviously, Disney and the unions were approaching the problem from entirely different backgrounds. The former had in mind a typical industrial union contract, while the latter were thinking in terms of the building trades. An industrial union contract contemplates a fixed employment relationship, whereas building-trades workers are not so much attached to employers as they are referred to jobs by hiring halls. Consequently, workers in the construction industry are treated as interchangeable parts. If a problem arises, one worker is taken off the job and another is supplied. Also, when a building-trades union regards a problem as serious, it will get management's attention by shutting down a job at will. Elaborate no-strike clauses and multipage grievance and arbitration provisions were practically unknown in building-trades contracts at that time.

Nevertheless, Curtin ultimately persuaded the unions to move all the way from nothing to the strongest possible no-strike and arbitration provisions. Since uninterrupted construction was Disney's primary objective, the contract as finally executed provided for no stoppages of any kind, a permanent arbitrator, hearings within twenty-four hours of any dispute, a single-session hearing (to avoid delays), awards within three hours of the close of a hearing, and enforcement of such awards in the courts. It is a miracle that such a provision was obtained.

The provision also overcame a then peculiar problem in the labor law. In 1962, the Supreme Court had held that the Norris-LaGuardia Act prohibited federal courts from enjoining violations of no-strike clauses.[4] On the other hand, a case in the Fifth Circuit (which at that time included Florida) had just declared arbitrators' awards enforceable by the courts, including awards enforcing no-strike clauses.[5] Since an employer could thereby achieve indirectly through an arbitrator's award what it could not achieve directly by a court order, an absolutely efficient arbitration system became indispensable to deal with work stoppages. The language the Firm negotiated in the Disney contract would be much imitated.

The Disney bargaining was unique in form as well as substance. From the beginning, the Disney representatives had displayed very different personalities, agendas, and techniques. They appeared to be working at cross-purposes, and they knew it. So they appointed Curtin to meet alone and speak for them with the assembled union leaders. It was an extraordinary format—a single management representative facing a score of union delegates. It certainly put Curtin on his mettle. It also accounted in large measure for what was accomplished.

That accomplishment, after two and a half months of bargaining, took the form of the Walt Disney World Project Agreement dated August 1, 1968. No private-sector labor contract like it had ever been negotiated. While only one signature was necessary for the employer (a contractor designated by Disney), twenty signatures were necessary for the Building Trades Council, the internationals, the Orlando Building Trades Council, and the Teamsters.[6] The contract was also extraordinary for its duration. It ran for forty-seven months, until June 30, 1972. Walt Disney World planned to open late in 1971. But management was taking no chances. The master agreement had to cover the entire construction period, including any delays.

The master agreement set forth overall terms and conditions. It did not specify individual rates of pay for the various trades. These would be the local rates already in place. But no trade in the Orlando area had negotiated rates that extended all the way to the termination date of the master agreement. Thus, it was necessary to reopen all local contracts and bargain appropriate rates beyond those then in force. This was the Firm's next assignment, which was completed by the fall of 1968. The results could not have pleased the client more: Rates were locked in for the duration of the project, there were no significant work stoppages, and the project was completed with time to spare.

The Magic Kingdom opened to the public on October 1, 1971. "Its heart . . . is in the late 1950s, America's last happy time," noted *Newsweek*, which also described the working conditions of the more than eighty Disney characters, including a famous mouse and almost equally famous duck:

> The worst occupational hazard is Florida's sun, at least in summer. Those with enough room in their suits get cooled by a little battery-powered fan that draws a miniature breeze across a chunk of dry ice. The next worst hazard is obscured vision. The Mad Hatter fell off a curb the other day and has been out of action ever since.[7]

Typical of Disney, opening day left nothing to chance. It was intentionally scheduled for a Friday, the slowest day, to iron out any operational kinks. There were only 10,000 in attendance that day. Less than a month later, the number reached 45,000 on a holiday. All told, there were 10.7 million visitors the first year.

Walt Disney's original dream included Epcot (an acronym for Experimental Prototype Community of Tomorrow), later built south of the Magic Kingdom at a cost of $1.2 billion. Epcot opened in 1982 and was followed, still farther south, by Disney-MGM Studios in 1989. During these additions, the Firm continued to serve the Disney interests, as the 1968 labor agreement with appropriate amendments and reiterations remained the construction bible. So when Walt Disney World celebrated its twentieth anniversary on October 1, 1991, it was fitting that Curtin was among the honored guests. By then, Walt Disney World had become the planet's top tourist destination, a mecca presenting Norman Rockwell's view of America—life as children of all ages think it should be.

During the Middle Ages, western Europeans made pilgrimages to the shrine of Saint James the Apostle at Santiago de Compostela in northwestern Spain. They joined their fellow travelers at assembly points along the way. The perilous journey might last months, and some travelers never returned. Pilgrimages were the package tours of their time.

Today's package tours are less arduous. Getting to Walt Disney World and back rarely takes more than two days. Airports are the assembly points: Cities from Rio de Janeiro to Frankfurt have direct flights to Orlando, which means to Walt Disney World. But whatever the parallels between pilgrimages past and present, today's quest is for amusement not salvation. The mouse has supplanted the grail.

CHAPTER 27

THE LARGEST PRIVATE PROJECT EVER UNDERTAKEN

Progeny of Disney ■ Discovering oil in 1968 ■ Permafrost and mosquitoes ■ Also environmentalists ■ The OPEC embargo ■ The light flashes green ■ The oil companies organize ■ Peculiarities of the building trades ■ Seven pages for fifty signatures ■ Local 959 is king of the hill ■ A self-serving anatomical feat ■ A fight in Pawtucket ■ Camp followers ■ Working magic ■ The unthinkable happens ■ Oil flows in 1977 ■ A landmark achievement

The Walt Disney Project Agreement begat progeny handled by the Firm. In 1986, there was the Yerba Buena development in San Francisco, a joint venture of Marriott and Olympia & York. Another project was the Toyota installation in Kentucky, one of the largest industrial facilities in North America, with nearly 8 million square feet under roof. Still another, in 1990, was the $6.1-billion Boston harbor cleanup. But Disney's most immediate offspring was (and remains) the undisputed king of them all, the 1974 Trans-Alaska pipeline.

Only a few human creations are allegedly visible from the moon. One is the 1,500-mile Great Wall of China. Another is the 800-mile Trans-Alaska Pipeline. Half its length is above ground on supports. If it were entirely buried, like most pipelines, it would collapse as hot oil passing through it melted the surrounding permafrost into jelly. Among its other peculiarities are 550 crossings built to accommodate migrating caribou.

Few people had heard of Prudhoe Bay when oil was struck there in March 1968. The field was estimated to contain some 10 billion barrels, the largest oil deposit ever found in the United States. Major petroleum companies scrambled for leases. In 1970, eight of those companies set up a consortium called the Alyeska Pipeline Service Co. (Alyeska).[1] In old Aleut, Alyeska means "the Great Land." One of the word's variants is Alaska. Twice the size of Texas, Alaska then had a population of 300,000, fewer people than Norfolk, Virginia.

Prudhoe Bay is above the Arctic Circle and frozen nine months of the year. The question: How to get the oil out? The answer: Pipe it south to terminals on ice-free Prince William Sound. On its way, the 48-inch line would cross three mountain ranges, as well as 800 rivers and streams.

Construction posed fantastic challenges. Winter temperatures descend to minus-70 degrees Fahrenheit, thaws generate impassable mud, and wind velocities sometimes reach fifty miles an hour. One of the Apollo astronauts and an American who scaled Mount Everest were consulted about the effects of cold-weather stress and isolation on the ability of workers to perform their tasks. Other difficulties included mosquitoes in summer and environmentalists all year round.

The latter thwarted the project from 1970 to 1973. But their courtroom victories were cut short by the gasoline crisis of 1973. OPEC pricing caused sticker shock at the pump. Motorists who expected gasoline to cost little more than water were indignant. President Richard Nixon responded to their indignation. On November 7, he proposed a program to render the country self-sufficient in the energy field by 1980. It was an easy sell. Congress passed the Trans-Alaska Pipeline Authorization Act,[2] and Nixon signed it on November 16, 1973. The light flashed green.

During the years when environmental litigation stalled construction, some pipeline contractors and their unions in Alaska negotiated contracts that would apply if, as, and when. The contractors were bargaining over the heads of the oil companies, and the companies were alarmed at what they saw. An air of unreality pervaded the negotiations. For example, one contract provided for a "stay-on-the-job bonus" of 6 percent if employees worked eight weeks, with an additional 10 percent if they worked the entire season. What should the oil companies do?

The oil companies responded by creating a special task force to investigate the possibility that they, not the contractors, might negotiate a single-construction-project agreement. Such an agreement would cover the enterprise from beginning to end and involve a score of unions at both the international and local levels. There was only one true analog: the agreement the Firm had created for Walt Disney World in 1968. All roads led to ML&B, and specifically to William Curtin.

On October 7, 1971, a group of senior Alyeska executives met at the Firm's Washington office. Curtin briefed them about the building-trades unions, their multiplicity, traditions, personalities, and conflicts, all with frequent references to the Disney experience. Bradford Coupe found it riveting. As the Washington labor section's newest associate, he was fated to spend years on the Alyeska project.

Building construction is not susceptible to automation. It is labor-intensive and fragmented. Each local in the field rules its fiefdom. Relations between the far-flung locals and their internationals in Washington are often uneasy. In addition, each trade, both locally and through its international, fights constant jurisdictional battles with the other trades, while engaging simultaneously in warfare with management. But American engineering and construction management techniques are unsurpassed, as are the skills of workers in the trades. Buildings get built.[3]

Curtin's strategy from the outset was to sidestep the agreements negotiated by the pipeline contractors with their unions. He also decided to start with the international unions in Washington, instead of with the local unions in Alaska. This approach had worked for Disney in Florida. Would it work for Alyeska in Alaska? Detractors of the idea argued that the internationals could not control the locals and that the oil companies might just as well go to Alaska and prostrate themselves before the local union potentates. Coupe summarized the situation: "Before 1974, Alaska was still a surprisingly primitive state. Power was exercised in all of its forms with only occasional reliance on the rule of law."

But Curtin knew what he was doing. With his Disney background and by intensive bargaining over a five-month period, he put the pieces together, starting in Washington, moving to Alaska, then to the West Coast, and finally back to Washington. He was sensitive to the jurisdictional aspirations of the trades and the personalities of the union leaders. And he had infinite patience in helping to work out the internationals' problems with their locals and the locals' problems with one another.

The result was a construction project agreement dated April 29, 1974. Like the Disney contract, it was easy for management to execute: Only one line was required for the signature of Alyeska's president. But this time, seven pages were required for fifty signatures reflecting the agreements of fourteen separate building-trades unions both internationally and locally. In addition, there was the Building and Construction Trades Department of the AFL-CIO, the umbrella organization for all the trades. Finally, there were the Teamsters, at both the international and local levels, as well as the Hotel and Restaurant Employees and Bartenders International

Union. At the core of the agreement was a no-strike clause and mechanisms to keep work going while disputes of all kinds were adjusted through a grievance and arbitration procedure even more complex and comprehensive than in the Disney contract.

No union group proved more obstreperous than the Teamsters. But as a former Teamster lawyer, Curtin also knew their personalities and politics. He bargained simultaneously with the international in Washington and with Local 959 in Alaska. The local's 23,000 members enjoyed shutting down work at will. They laughed at any employer who proposed a no-strike clause.[4] But even they finally signed. In no case was Coupe's observation about the exercise of power more appropriate. When violence erupted at a construction camp in 1975, Alyeska's president said: "It's a 'king of the hill' contest. The welders consider themselves to be the Marine Corps of the national labor movement. Teamsters Local 959 thinks it runs the state of Alaska."[5]

Local 959 was dominated by Jesse Carr. In a series of articles about him and his local, the *Anchorage Daily News* recounted how his "empire has evolved in just 18 years into a complex maze of political, economic and social power which towers above the rest of Alaska's labor movement—and challenges at times both mighty industry and the state government itself."[6] Another publication put it more simply by asking "whether Carr is the most powerful man in Alaska," and noting his disarming answer: "Power is like being a lady—if you have to tell them you are, you ain't."[7]

Carr had an assistant named Jefferson Barry. On one occasion, Barry caused a break off in negotiations. It was a warm spring day in 1974 at the Hay Adams Hotel in Washington, across from the AFL-CIO headquarters. In the presence of dozens of union executives, Barry flaunted the power and perversity of Local 959. Information had to be furnished, and Curtin undertook to gather it. Everyone was satisfied with Curtin's undertaking except Barry. He questioned whether Curtin could be trusted. There was an uneasy silence. Curtin stood up, slammed shut his notebook, and left the room, but not before inviting Barry to perform a self-serving anatomical feat. When negotiations resumed, the ploy had worked: Barry had been banished by the other union officials and did not appear again during negotiations or later during construction.

Many union leaders thrive on confrontation. Others act tough but are really quite amiable on the inside. Some have delightful senses of humor. One such was Joe Maloney, who represented the ironworkers. Maloney had been a heavyweight boxer. But he also enjoyed quoting Shakespeare and Robert Frost. Curtin once summarized a contract provision by using the word "comity." Maloney reflected aloud in his flat south Boston accent: "Camoddy, I fought a guy by that name in Pawtucket in 1952."

Construction was in high gear within three months of the contract's effective date. The *Wall Street Journal* reported 3,500 workers on the job, forecasted 6,000 two months later, and said that employment would peak at 12,000 to 14,000. Workers were housed in twelve construction camps, most of them spotted in remote locations along the 800-mile front. The *Journal* also noted that housing in Alaska was so scarce that a jury in Fairbanks sat up all night because no hotel rooms were available. Reference was also made to camp followers, a phenomenon characteristic of armies and well-paid workers stationed in distant places: "[O]ne woman . . . disguised her true activity at the oil field by selling subscriptions to a men's magazine. In one week she reportedly made $5,300."[8]

In addition to camp followers, there were lawyers trafficking in other wares, including ML&B's ten-lawyer team. All told, Coupe recorded fifty-five visits and spent the summer of 1975 living in Anchorage. For a while, it was even rumored that the Firm might open an office there.

It is one thing to negotiate a labor contract and another to implement it, particularly under the frontier conditions then prevailing in Alaska. During the three years of construction, there were almost daily legal problems. Some involved stoppages or threats of stoppages. In most cases, they were resolved informally as Curtin worked his magic. (One veteran oil industry bargainer spoke of Curtin's "golden touch" and "deceptively soft gloves" as he "[went] in for the kill.")[9] Other disputes, seventy in all, were arbitrated. But on August 4, 1976, the unthinkable happened: Teamsters Local 959 brought the project to a halt. Planes were chartered by Alyeska to airlift an estimated 4,000 workers from the scene.

Coupe flew to Alaska, invoked the expedited arbitration procedure, prepared the case in one day, and had it heard by an arbitrator for twelve straight hours the next day. The arbitrator found the dispute arbitrable and the stoppage a violation of the no-strike clause. Just days earlier, a federal district court judge had found to the contrary (the Firm had not been involved) and declined relief. Relying on the district court's earlier ruling, Local 959 refused to comply with the arbitrator's award. Coupe went back to the same judge with the argument that the judge should defer to the arbitrator. The judge deferred, the award was enforced, and work resumed.

Thanks to the provision first negotiated in the Disney contract, the Firm enjoyed a stunning victory that was widely noted and subsequently upheld by the Court of Appeals for the Ninth Circuit.[10]

The Alyeska Pipeline was officially completed on June 20, 1977, at a cost of $7.7 billion. It could deliver 2 million barrels of oil per day, representing 25 percent of the country's domestic needs. The *Wall Street Journal* described it as the "largest private [project] . . . ever undertaken."[11] Presumably the Great Wall of China was in the *public* sector.

There is no evidence that the Firm's founding partners were involved in the 1890s Klondike Gold Rush. But obviously the Firm atoned for this deficiency during the 1970s oil rush. Never before had a single labor agreement covered so much private-sector activity on any project by so many unions. It was a landmark achievement for the Firm and its labor section.

CHAPTER 28

THE SKIES
WERE NOT SILENT

Strikes against the public interest ■ PATCO ■ Glowing in the dark ■ The Department of Transportation retains the Firm ■ Wage guidelines again ■ Lunch at Tiberos ■ A handshake ■ Perfidy ■ A Greek tragedy vintage 1981 ■ Planes fly anyway ■ Reagan in the Rose Garden ■ Compassion and amnesty ■ Rebuilding the system ■ The union is decertified ■ The public is supportive ■ A grievous episode

A ffluent societies scorn old duties and coin new rights. Take strikes for example. At common law, stoppages by workers in concert with one another were illegal conspiracies. Then, by virtue of the Clayton Act of 1914, the Anti-Injunction Act of 1932, and the National Labor Relations Act of 1935, strikes achieved an odor of sanctity and almost Bill of Rights respect. But what about strikes that adversely affect the public health and welfare, whether in the public or private sector?

As noted in Chapter 10, President Lincoln seized the railroads in 1864 when they were struck by the nascent Brotherhood of the Footboard (later the Brotherhood of Locomotive Engineers) and had them operated by the army. Then, in 1902, just a year before William Clarke Mason began representing the Reading Company, a miners strike imperiled the nation's anthracite coal supply. President Theodore Roosevelt threatened to send federal troops. The miners returned to work when the operators agreed to a governmental investigation. During that strike, Reading's president earned lasting notoriety by asserting the divine right of management.

Calvin Coolidge was next. In 1919, while governor of Massachusetts, he used the militia to break up a Boston police strike. His words are still quoted: "There is no right to strike against the public any time, anywhere."[1] Still later, in 1943, Franklin Roosevelt had the government seize and operate both the struck mines and railroads. His successor, Harry Truman, repeated the process with the same industries in 1946.

The problem remains. In 1970, when 200,000 postal workers staged a nine-day strike, Richard Nixon sent federal troops to take over the post offices. Then it was Ronald Reagan's turn in 1981, when the air traffic controllers threatened to halt the nation's air transportation. They said "the skies shall be silent."[2] But they were wrong. This time, the skies were not silent, as they had been during the 1966 IAM strike recounted in Chapter 25. Most of the controllers were fired, their jobs taken by others, and their union decertified. It was a sad chapter in union history, and it left the labor movement scarred. In that epic battle, the Firm had as its clients the United States Department of Transportation (DOT) and one of its agencies, the Federal Aviation Administration (FAA).

In 1981, the Professional Air Traffic Controllers Organization (PATCO) represented about 85 percent of the 17,500 federal employees who orchestrated the nation's air traffic. To the uninitiated, their functions were mysterious. As a *Time* correspondent put it:

> There is a swaggering style, a macho flair to O'Hare's ace controllers. In near darkness, they hunch over their radarscopes like teenage boys playing electronic games. Their faces glow in the greenish-yellow light, as each sweep of the radar reveals a constantly changing configuration of planes. They have developed their own special mystique. They chain smoke and drink countless cups of coffee while placating their upset stomachs with chalky Maalox tablets from the big glass candy jars that are standard in every control room.[3]

But mystery aside, the controllers had been disgruntled for years. They said their jobs subjected them to unique tensions and early burnout. They considered themselves grossly underpaid and overworked. They also considered themselves indispensable.

Until 1968, the controllers had been part of the National Association of Government Employees. That year they split off to form their own organization, PATCO. To gain concessions they staged sickouts. But these were no more than thinly veiled strikes, and strikes by federal employees are illegal.[4] The FAA responded by suspending the "sick" controllers and firing their leaders. Furthermore, an injunction was issued in 1970 forbidding the controllers to strike.

In 1980, PATCO replaced its more moderate president with a zealot named Robert Poli. He was bearded, scholarly in appearance, forty-four years old, and a former controller. From the time of Poli's election, PATCO made little effort to conceal its plans. Despite both the law and the injunction, it distributed a strike manual and raised a strike fund that ultimately grew to $3.5 million. The Carter administration reacted by drafting a contingency plan to keep air traffic moving if the controllers went out.

PATCO's labor contract with the FAA expired on March 15, 1981. Thus, the dispute became a legacy from Carter to Reagan, who took office on January 20, 1981. DOT's newly designated secretary was Drew Lewis. Lewis was from the Philadelphia area. Over the years, he had enjoyed many contacts with the Firm: as CEO of client Snelling & Snelling, Inc.; as a trustee of client Reading Company during its bankruptcy; as a consultant to client Builders Investment Group; and later as CEO of sometime client Union Pacific Corp.

In addition to these contacts, Lewis and W. James MacIntosh had worked closely as board members of the Philadelphia Suburban Water Company. They had also been colleagues in Republican politics: Lewis served as chairman of the Republican Finance Committee when MacIntosh was counsel to the Republican State Committee. (Lewis ran unsuccessfully for governor of Pennsylvania in 1974.) After his DOT appointment, Lewis discussed with MacIntosh the forthcoming PATCO confrontation. MacIntosh urged the use of the Firm's Washington office, and particularly William Curtin. Lewis made other inquiries. They confirmed that Curtin was the right choice. Lewis was in touch with Curtin in December 1980, even before the inauguration, and the Firm was engaged.

George Stohner, a fourth-year associate at the Firm, was designated to work with Curtin. From February through April, Stohner attended thirty-seven unproductive bargaining sessions between the FAA and PATCO, as the contract expiration date of March 15 came and went. They were peculiar negotiations. An Executive Order did not permit federal labor unions to bargain about wages and benefits, only about "personnel policies and practices and matters affecting working conditions."[5] Complicating matters, Reagan had inherited from Carter an overheated economy. In 1980, the Consumer Price Index rose by 13.5 percent. Reagan was determined to reduce inflation. In 1981, he established 4.8 percent as the benchmark for increases in the compensations of federal employees. Shades of Lyndon Johnson and the 1966 guidelines, as described in Chapter 25.

None of this made any impression on Poli. He insisted that PATCO's members be treated like airline pilots. Pilots were paid $100,000 a year, more than twice what controllers were getting. Furthermore, he demanded a cut in the work week from forty hours to thirty-two hours without any reduction in pay. He also demanded retirement at 75 percent of pay after twenty years of service, regardless of age. The parties were speaking two different languages.

By May, the FAA had concluded that Poli was obsessed with power and oblivious of reality. Someone had to open his eyes. Curtin, who had not previously met Poli, was asked by Lewis to contact him. Curtin called Poli and they agreed to meet for lunch at Tiberos, Poli's choice and one of Washington's most expensive restaurants. When Poli arrived, he was greeted like a king and seated at his favorite table.

Curtin tried for three hours to disabuse Poli of his fantasies. He repeatedly told Poli that the administration simply would not tolerate an illegal strike.[6] But Poli was unmoved. He brushed aside Curtin's warnings and intimated that he had an ace in the hole: Only three labor organizations had backed Reagan for the presidency, and PATCO was one of them. Moreover, Poli added, he had actually been a passenger in the same car as Reagan on the campaign trail. Curtin was incredulous. He tried again and again, but not even Curtin at his most persuasive could divert Poli from his collision course. Soon after his meeting with Curtin, Poli left Washington for a May 22 PATCO convention in New Orleans. There, according to FAA sources, Poli fanned the flames by threatening to "silence the skies," as well as by arguing that "the only illegal strike is an unsuccessful one."[7]

Back in Washington from the convention, Poli set June 22 as the strike date. Negotiations resumed at the headquarters of the Federal Mediation and Conciliation Service. The final bargaining session lasted thirty-six hours, during which Curtin noticed that Lewis, a remarkably cool bargainer, never even unbuttoned his shirt collar. Such a contrast in styles: An almost hysterical Poli opposite an utterly unflappable Lewis and a gracious Curtin. Still, the marathon session did produce a breakthrough. The administration had come up with a plan to secure special funding from Congress for the controllers. By a handshake, the parties agreed to a new contract at 6:30 a.m. on June 22. Several hours later, the terms had been reduced to an agreement that Poli signed and undertook to support in ratification proceedings by PATCO's membership.

But on July 2, Poli reneged. Despite his earlier handshake, he and eight other members of the PATCO Executive Board actually recommended that the controllers reject the agreement. It was turned down by 95 percent of those who voted.

When negotiations resumed on July 31, Poli's conduct became even more bizarre, according to Curtin. Poli put back on the table his original ninety-nine contract language proposals, together with economic demands costing seventeen times the amount previously bargained. Curtin took him aside and again described vividly the consequences of an illegal strike. Curtin explained that Lewis had spoken with Reagan, who simply would not countenance such conduct. Again Poli was unmoved. He vowed there would be a strike, adding that it would bankrupt three airlines in one week, followed shortly by several hotel chains. Events were unfolding with the inevitability of a Greek tragedy.

On August 3, 1981, the long-threatened strike finally took place as 13,000 of the 17,500 controllers left their work and began picketing. There were two main questions: Would air traffic be paralyzed, and how strongly would the administration react?

The controllers exulted. After more than ten years of frustration, they would finally demonstrate their stranglehold on the nation's air traffic, humble the administration, and get their just deserts. But they miscalculated. Not only did 1,600 controllers refuse to strike, but also 3,000 supervisors and 500 military controllers filled the breach. Although many flights were canceled, 65 percent flew on the first day, 67 percent on the second day, 72 percent on the third day, and 83 percent on the fourth day.

On that first day, Stohner remembers meeting with Lewis and other DOT personnel in Lewis's office. It was L-shaped and imposing as befits a cabinet officer's quarters. It also had an unobstructed view over the Potomac to National Airport. While the group sat on the windowsills watching the planes take off, Lewis admitted he was praying. Yes, the contingency plan was working, but was it as safe as the operations people boasted? There was always the possibility of a tragic mishap.

Meanwhile, at the White House, someone pointed to Calvin Coolidge's portrait in the Cabinet Room and cited the police strike of 1919. History was repeating itself. Lewis briefed Reagan in advance of a press conference scheduled for 11 a.m. in the Rose Garden. The President's staff had prepared a statement for him to deliver. But he put it aside in favor of one he wrote on a yellow pad at Camp David the day before. Exemplifying the Great Communicator at his best, it included an anecdote, made a personal reference, and stressed the controller's statutory oath not to strike:

> At National Airport a traffic controller told a news person he had resigned from the union and reported to work because, "How can I ask my kids to obey the law if I don't?" This is a great

tribute to America.

Let me make one thing plain: I respect the right of workers in the private sector to strike. Indeed as president of my own union I led the first strike ever called by that union [the Screen Actors Guild in 1959]. I guess I'm the first one to ever hold this office who is a lifetime member of an A.F.L.-C.I.O. union. But we cannot compare labor management relations in the private sector with Government. . . .

Let me read the solemn oath taken by each of these employees: "I am not participating in any strike against the Government of the United States or any agency thereof, and I will not so participate."[8]

Reagan was a disengaged President—the details were left to others. He was also a compassionate man, some said a softie. But with the PATCO strike, he was wholly engaged and certainly no softie. It involved matters about which he felt strongly: obedience to the law, the performance of duty, and the sanctity of an oath.

Still, when the question of an amnesty arose, Reagan showed his compassion. The Department of Justice took a hard line, insisting that any amnesty would be incompatible with the statutory provision that striking controllers automatically forfeited their jobs. Lewis, advised differently by the Firm, argued for a seventy-two-hour amnesty. The President also inclined toward an amnesty, on the theory that the controllers might not have been adequately warned by their leaders that their jobs were really at stake. Ultimately, he compromised between Lewis's recommendation and the Department of Justice's position: Controllers who returned within forty-eight hours could have their jobs back. Approximately 1,200 did so, and another 300 were later reinstated based on extenuating circumstances.

Interviewed by the *New York Times*, a PATCO spokesperson declared: "This battle is . . . going to be won on the picket line." While acknowledging that the law required the dismissal of striking federal employees, the spokesperson suggested the President could settle the matter by giving pardons to the controllers, "just like Richard Nixon got."[9]

But the controllers did not receive the Nixon treatment. About 11,500 who ignored the deadline were fired. Three days into the strike, Lewis announced: "To all intents and purposes, the strike is over. Our concern is to rebuild the system."[10] The FAA began accepting applications for replacements. *Time* reported that during a five-hour period in New York City alone, 1,763 people applied.[11]

Not only were the striking controllers fired and banned from reemployment,[12] but PATCO was held in contempt of court and fines were imposed for its violation of the 1970 injunction. Finally, on October 22, 1981, PATCO was decertified by the Federal Labor Relations Authority as a labor organization entitled to represent federal employees.[13]

Despite their zeal, the controllers failed to recognize that they were expendable. They also failed to anticipate the resolve of the President and the hostility of the public. Six weeks before the strike, a *Washington Post* editorial recited their predicament:

> The air controllers are barred by law from striking and are under a federal court order not to strike or to engage in slow-down tactics. For them to deny those twin injunctions, as their president has said they will, would demonstrate a contempt for the orderly processes of government so serious as to justify harsh retaliation.[14]

In fact, the public supported the President by a nearly two-to-one margin.

Of course, there were several dissenting voices. One was the American Civil Liberties Union. It questioned the distinction between private employees who by statute can legally strike, and federal employees who cannot. In its view, the distinction was "unfair and irrational, and a violation of fundamental civil liberty."[15] The AFL-CIO also dissented, though halfheartedly. It acknowledged that the strike was illegal but added that the controllers and "other working people had a basic human right, the right to withdraw their services, not to work under conditions they no longer find tolerable."[16] At least that was the labor movement's *public* position.

But *privately* the AFL-CIO was furious with PATCO and especially with Poli. Before the strike, Lewis and Curtin had called top AFL-CIO officials with a plea that they reason with Poli and somehow control him. But word came back that reasoning with him was futile and that he was uncontrollable. As it turned out, the union officials had grounds for anger. The PATCO strike was a grievous episode that hurt the cause of organized labor for years to come.

CHAPTER 29

PLAY BALL

The PRC engages the Firm ■ *O'Connor's special role* ■ *The Game in the old days* ■ *Television and million-dollar players* ■ *The reserve system and salary arbitration* ■ *Justice Holmes on a bad day* ■ *Demise of the system* ■ *A powerful ratchet* ■ *Pushing the red button* ■ *The collusion era* ■ *A $280-million settlement* ■ *The 1990 negotiation* ■ *Another lockout* ■ *An intelligent statement* ■ *Divine peace*

Collective bargaining between baseball players and their clubs is conducted by the players union and the Major League Baseball Player Relations Committee, Inc. (PRC), a nonprofit corporation owned by the clubs. In 1982, when the PRC first engaged ML&B, baseball was in the throes of a revolution. As that revolution intensified over the following ten years, so did the Firm's involvement. It was a high-profile engagement for the Firm, and especially for Washington labor partner Charles (Chuck) O'Connor. During the 1990 contract negotiations, he served full time as the PRC's exclusive counsel and principal spokesperson.

Older ML&B lawyers remember The Game of their youth. Through the 1940s, it was played by sixteen major league teams representing ten cities mostly in the country's northeast quadrant. Fans arrived at neighborhood parks by trolley, bus, and subway. Games were reported (some said created) over the radio by chatty sportscasters like Red Barber and Mel Allen. (In his early days, Ronald Reagan was an ingratiating sportscaster.) Costs were kept down by the reserve system, and teams were operated like family stores by their owners. One such owner was Connie Mack, who led the Philadelphia Athletics from 1901 until 1950, when he was in his nineties.

The Game began to change in the 1950s. Kansas City attracted the Athletics. And Milwaukee, new home of the old Boston Braves, became the first municipal government to finance the construction of a ballpark. Other cities vied to support their teams: During the 1960s and 1970s, sixteen new stadiums were built at public expense. Major league clubs proliferated. By 1977, there were twenty-six from coast to coast and in Canada. Two more were added in 1993, and still more are a possibility.

Television propelled The Game into a new age. By 1989, media revenue from all sources was running $500 million a year. At that level, it actually exceeded gate receipts, which twenty years before had been seven times media revenue. Considering subsidized stadiums and the bonanza of television, club owners should have enjoyed spectacular profits.

But the owners were not so blessed. Their primary problem was skyrocketing payrolls: The average player earned $52,000 in 1976; $114,000 in 1979; $369,000 in 1985; $580,000 in 1990; and $1.1 million in 1992, with some players' salaries running five times that much. The explosion in baseball salaries had its roots in two developments the Firm would confront. One was the abolition of the reserve system in 1975. The other was arbitration as a means for setting player salaries.

Dating back to 1879, baseball's reserve system had long been fundamental to the relationship between players and their teams. They could not leave the team that originally signed them unless they retired or were traded unilaterally to another team. The system encouraged the clubs to develop their players for the long term and prevented raids by the richest clubs to monopolize the best talent. All teams agreed to respect the system and not compete with one another.

In 1922, the legality of the reserve system was tested and upheld in *Federal Baseball Club of Baltimore, Inc. v. National League of Professional Baseball Clubs.*[1] Speaking for a unanimous Court, Justice Oliver Wendell Holmes declared that baseball was not in interstate commerce and was therefore immune from the antitrust laws. (Court of Appeals Judge Henry Friendly would later remark that "*Federal Baseball* was not one of Mr. Justice Holmes' happiest days."[2]) In 1953, the Court revisited the question in *Toolson v. New York Yankees Inc.*,[3] when George Toolson resisted being sent down to the Binghamton farm team by the Yankees. But the Court declined to overrule *Federal Baseball*, noting that Congress had considered legislation to do so but had not acted.

Next came *Flood v. Kuhn* in 1972.[4] Curt Flood had been a star outfielder for the Cardinals. In 1969, when he was thirty-one and making $90,000 in Saint Louis, he was traded to the Phillies. With the Phillies he would have played the 1970 season for a salary of

$100,000. But he was not consulted about the trade, refused to relocate, and asked the commissioner (then Bowie Kuhn) to make him a free agent so he could bargain with other major league teams. When Flood's request was denied, he instituted an antitrust suit. Somewhat sheepishly, the Court affirmed *Federal Baseball* and *Toolson*, again observing that Congress had not acted and that baseball's exemption from the antitrust laws was "an aberration that has been with us now for half a century . . . [and is] entitled to the benefit of *stare decisis*."[5]

But what George Toolson and Curt Flood failed to achieve in the courts, two other players won in a 1975 arbitration. They were pitchers Andy Messersmith of the Los Angeles Dodgers and Dave McNally of the Montreal Expos. When their contracts expired, they refused to sign new ones for a year. After that, they argued they had become free agents, not subject to the reserve system. Arbitrator Peter Seitz agreed.[6] Dubbed "baseball's Abe Lincoln,"[7] he effectively laid to rest a system that had been "indispensable"[8] to baseball for ninety-seven years. Free agency was introduced in 1976. Salaries soared as players proclaimed "freedom from slavery" and owners predicted "chaos and ruin."[9]

In a related development, baseball's union contract (called the Basic Agreement) had been amended in 1973 to provide for arbitration in cases where a player and his club could not agree on his renewal salary. The amendment prescribed final-offer arbitration, which required the arbitrator to adopt either the salary figure submitted by the player or the one submitted by the club. By itself, salary arbitration might not have been remarkable. But when free agency became the rule in 1976, the effects were stunning. Free agents, defined as players with six years' experience in the major leagues, set an economic pattern in the open market. Arbitrators would then apply that pattern in fixing the salaries of players who were not yet free agents. Working together, free agency and salary arbitration created "a powerful ratchet."[10]

Due to that ratchet, the clubs piled up $277 million in operating losses from 1980 to 1984, despite stadium subsidies and burgeoning media royalties. Peter Ueberroth, who had run the profitable 1984 Summer Olympics in Los Angeles, became baseball commissioner in 1985. He insisted that the clubs open their books to one another. It was found that twenty-one of the twenty-six were losing money. He chided them:

> Let's say I sat each of you down in front of a red button and a black button. . . . Push the red button and you'd win the World Series but

lose $10 million. Push the black button and you would make $4 million and finish somewhere in the middle. . . . The problem is most of you would push the red one.[11]

The commissioner's lectures on profitability encouraged peer pressure, which in turn discouraged bidding. Without bidding, free agent salaries actually retreated in 1985-87. The union grieved, alleging that the owners were depressing salaries by collusion, which the Basic Agreement expressly prohibited. There were three separate grievances, one each for 1985, 1986, and 1987. The first was filed in February 1986. Six months later, the PRC asked the Firm to join in the defense.

ML&B came to the proceedings with a strong background in baseball salary arbitrations. Starting in 1983, O'Connor, together with Washington labor partners Robert Dufek and Francis Casey, had compiled an impressive won-lost record in handling important salary cases for the Pittsburgh Pirates and Atlanta Braves. They also advised concerning other cases for the Chicago Cubs, Montreal Expos, Cleveland Indians, and Milwaukee Brewers. All these engagements had their genesis in the Firm's Anheuser-Busch labor work, which went back to 1970. Handling such work over the years, O'Connor had developed a close relationship with the Busch family, owners of the Saint Louis Cardinals. Like them, O'Connor was an avid fan.

In the three collusion cases, 32,193 pages of transcript were filled by the testimony of 120 witnesses over 186 days of hearings. Clearly, the owners had not agreed to collude de jure. But collusion could arguably be inferred de facto from evidence the union pieced together. In 1987, the owners lost on the liability issue in the first case. The arbitrator noted "the sudden and abrupt termination of all efforts to secure the services of free agents from other clubs. They surely had a value at some price and yet *no* offers were advanced."[12]

If liability in the collusion cases was complicated, damages were even more so. Washington partner Michael Kelly was drafted from the Firm's antitrust section to mastermind complex financial models. Multiyear contracts had to be analyzed covering hundreds of players over at least a six-year period. What would the players have been paid if the clubs had acted without restraint? Late in 1990, before a final award was handed down in the last of the three cases, the parties negotiated a comprehensive settlement. The players would receive $280 million, to be borne $10.8 million by each of the twenty-six clubs.

Baseball's financial picture had improved during the "collusion era."[13] In 1988, revenues reached $1 billion and operating profits $121 million. Also in 1988, four-year media contracts were negotiated under which the clubs would receive approximately $500 million per year from all sources.

But the clubs' prosperity was short-lived. Even as hearings were being held in the collusion cases, fierce competition resumed for players, and salaries soared to new highs: The owners were again pushing Ueberroth's red button. Also, CBS and ESPN said they were losing hundreds of millions of dollars on their television contracts, raising fears about renewal terms in 1993. Ten teams would lose money in 1990, whereas all had been profitable in 1989.

Such was the climate in November 1989 when the Firm was further engaged by the PRC to prepare for the 1990 round of collective bargaining. Unprecedented difficulties would attend those negotiations. Distrust by the players was rife after the collusion cases. Moreover, the clubs had a basic business problem: In the wonderland of free agency and salary arbitration, they could not predict their costs, unlike other unionized employers. To normalize such costs, the owners offered a "partnership" to share revenue with the players. According to the *New York Times*, O'Connor was "unmistakably the architect of the owners' radical proposal for revenue-sharing."[14]

Under the clubs' proposal, the players would receive 48 percent of pooled income from ticket sales and broadcast rights. That percentage would be distributed on the basis of performance to players with less than six years of service. Free agency would continue for players with six or more years of service, but subject to a collective salary cap. Salary arbitration would be abolished along with multiyear player contracts. A precedent arguably existed for the clubs' proposal: The National Basketball Association had a similar arrangement with its players by which they received 53 percent of revenue.

Although some baseball players would have earned more under the owners' proposal, the players union rejected it. They considered it complicated, they feared the unknown, and they mistrusted the clubs and their accounting methods. In addition, they were "in the catbird seat," a favorite expression of sportscaster Red Barber. Nevertheless, according to O'Connor, "the groundwork was laid out [for revenue participation], and the concept embodied in the proposal remains as one of the important goals of Major League Baseball."

Having rebuffed management, the players union countered with a demand to reduce from three to two the number of years of service required to make a player eligible for salary arbitration, as had been the case before the 1985 negotiations. Obviously, the parties were far apart: The clubs wanted to abolish salary arbitration altogether, while the union wanted to increase the number of players eligible. The result was a lockout: Spring training did not commence as scheduled on February 15, 1990, nor was the first game played on April 2.

During the 1970s and 1980s, work stoppages plagued baseball, interrupting The Game in 1971, 1973, 1976, 1980, 1981, and 1985. According to a *New York Times* tally: "For the last 18 years, the score reads: Strikes 4, Lockouts 2."[15] And that was before the 1990 lockout. It lasted thirty-two days, until a settlement was hammered out at 5:45 a.m. on March 19, after a weekend of hard bargaining. The press gave O'Connor credit for finding the key: The clubs would agree to make 17 percent of the two-year players eligible for salary arbitration, instead of 100 percent as the union had demanded. A panel was also constituted to consider reforms for the future.

Experienced labor negotiators know there is more to contract bargaining than wages, hours, and working conditions. When the tumult and shouting die, how do the parties view each other and the settlement? Everyone regarded baseball's 1990 negotiation as a breakthrough for the cause of amity. Five looseleaf scrapbooks in the Firm's archives attest to the esteem in which O'Connor was held by all concerned, including the Fourth Estate. The *National Sports Daily* called him "management's first diplomatic negotiator."[16] Regarding O'Connor's background, the *New York Times* wrote:

> O'Connor was born in Boston 49 years ago and grew up cheering for the Red Sox. He graduated from Holy Cross in 1963 and from Boston College Law School in 1966, and he had no doubt what he wanted to do, even when he was working as a bricklayer: he wanted to be a labor lawyer. . . . He got his start in the general counsel's office of the National Labor Relations Board in Washington. Then, 21 years ago, he joined . . . Morgan, Lewis & Bockius."[17]

One reason O'Connor enjoyed such an admiring press was that he reported events accurately and never used the media as a bargaining tool. Thus, he attracted the same media encomia as his mentor William Curtin twenty-four years earlier during the airlines' strike. Also, O'Connor was philosophical. After the all-night bargaining session on March 19, he was quoted by the *National Sports Daily*:

They [the players] have just taken part in one of the most important parts of our society, the right of self-negotiation, the union movement and the collective bargaining process. I hope that's viewed as a major accomplishment.[18]

Marvin Miller, who led the players union from 1965 to 1983, wrote a book in which he quoted O'Connor's statement and commented: "A statement that intelligent has never before been uttered by baseball officialdom. I wish I had said it."[19]

Baseball is a high-profile activity: No business excites more passion relative to the number of people employed. (There were 700 major league players in 1993.) Baseball is also an economic anomaly: Because neither the players nor the owners have any market competitors, they both enjoy effective monopolies. But each has its Achilles' heel. Athletes have short careers: In terms of lifetime records, days lost due to work stoppages can never be recaptured. And "the owners . . . [who can't] agree on what to have for breakfast"[20] are so disparate that the revenues of some are less than the payrolls of others. Then there are the fans. They love The Game and are frustrated by battles between millionaire players and millionaire owners over a billion-dollar pie. Also, they know that money does not necessarily buy championships: Since 1979 the teams receiving the highest salaries have made it to the World Series less often than the more modestly paid contenders. How different is The Game of the 1990s from the days of Tinker to Evers to Chance.[21]

Jacques Barzun wrote: "Whoever wants to know the heart and mind of America had better learn baseball."[22] Of course, he meant the rules of the game, not its economics. Like divine peace, baseball's economics pass all understanding.

CHAPTER 30

THE JOLLY TESTATOR

The Firm in the arts ■ Grist for the barrister's mill ■ The greatest lawyer in the English-speaking world draws his own will ■ Johnson as a collector ■ Van Eyck to Eakins ■ The mansion on South Broad Street ■ Botticelli and the bathtub ■ Prohibitions against removal and commingling ■ The judge's ire ■ Six years in the Orphans' Court ■ An international art mafia ■ The court approves the new layout ■ Good until 2083

Chapters 25 through 29 dealt with the Firm's labor practice, down-to-earth stuff. Ascending now to more ethereal realms, Chapters 30 through 34 will consider the Firm in the arts. Three stories will be about paintings: court proceedings for the Philadelphia Museum of Art dealing with the John G. Johnson collection; a landmark auction of the John T. Dorrance collection by Sotheby's; and high-profile litigation for Philadelphia's Union League concerning the authenticity of a putative Bierstadt. The remaining two artistic stories will be musical: the Firm's long-time relationship with the Philadelphia Orchestra; and a transaction in which the Firm's London office acted for Michael Jackson in his acquisition of rights to music by the legendary Beatles.

■ ■ ■ ■ ■

There is a tale, perhaps apocryphal, that barristers at London's Inns of Court raise a toast each year to jolly testators who make their own wills. What grist for the barrister's mill these do-it-yourself scriveners provide. They are mostly nonlawyers, so maybe they deserve their fate. Which is not to say that all lawyer-drawn wills are impeccable. Remember the lawyer-drawn will in Dickens's *Bleak House?* Based on an actual chancery case, it gave rise to *Jarndyce v. Jarndyce*, litigation lasting for decades. The grist provided by Jarndyce's will ultimately consumed the estate. Still, lawyers generally do a better job than nonlawyers.

But what about a will drawn by a testator who is a lawyer? If grist is thereby provided, more pity is felt than scorn. Such was the case with John G. Johnson, whose many relationships with the Firm are recounted in Chapter 3. He may have been "the greatest lawyer in the English speaking world,"[1] but the will he drew furnished employment for three generations of lawyers, including ML&B during the 1980s.

Wealthier people in other walks of life have occasionally amassed more valuable art collections than Johnson. One of them, Peter A. B. Widener, was a Johnson client, a UGI and PE founder, and a traction magnate. But even Widener, whose collection went to Washington's National Gallery in 1942, did not collect on Johnson's scale or with his scholarship.

In the days when the courts closed for the summer and lawyers took real vacations, Johnson would spend his holidays in Europe seeking out and buying paintings. Widener tells the story of a visit they made to an art dealer in Paris. The dealer unveiled painting after painting. Before the dealer could speak, Johnson identified each painting, indicated when it was painted, explained how it reflected the artist's style, and recited who its owners had been over the years. Obviously, Johnson researched art as he researched law. And he retained what he researched. His studies enabled him to anticipate what would become valuable and buy it before its cost became prohibitive.

Johnson began collecting in the 1880s. By the time he died in 1917, he had what has been described as "probably the largest art collection ever assembled by one American and certainly the most comprehensive."[2] Initially, he collected artists of his own time. He then shifted to Italian primitives, and still later to early Flemish, German, and Spanish works, before they appreciated in value. He constantly upgraded his collection, which eventually spanned almost seven centuries and ranged from paintings by van Eyck, van der Weyden, Botticelli, Titian, and El Greco, to works by Turner, Manet, Whistler, and Eakins.

What Johnson assembled was a veritable encyclopedia of Western painting. His approach was eclectic and historical. He rarely acquired the best picture by any artist, but nowhere else in a private American collection could be found such a panorama of representative works by major painters of so many periods.

Johnson lived in a mansion at 506 South Broad Street, near the center of Philadelphia, where his staggering collection of 1,279 paintings ultimately filled every wall from floor to ceiling and overflowed into servants quarters, closets, and even onto the backs of chairs. There is a story that Johnson was discussing the Italian renaissance with a visitor. To make his point he dispatched a servant upstairs to bring down a Botticelli that Johnson said was leaning against a bathtub.[3]

Five years before he died, Johnson prepared a will leaving his collection to the city of Philadelphia, subject to certain conditions. If the city failed to accept the conditions, the collection would go to New York's Metropolitan Museum of Art. One condition was that the city "erect a suitable gallery to house the collection." Another condition was that the city pay the required inheritance taxes. (At Johnson's death, his collection was valued for inheritance tax purposes at $4.2 million. When it was appraised in 1988, estimates of its value ranged up to $1 billion.)

The will also provided that "the collection must always be kept together as a whole and must not be commingled in any way with any other collection of paintings or works of art." The Firm would subsequently be involved in litigation construing this restriction.

After Johnson signed his will, he bought a still larger home just down the block at 510 South Broad Street, a massive yellow-brick French chateau. He then made a codicil relieving the city of erecting a suitable gallery and instead provided that the city should equip his house as a gallery and exhibit the collection there. Finally, the codicil stated: "The art objects should not be removed for permanent exhibition, to any other place, unless some extraordinary situation shall arise, making it exceedingly injudicious [sic]." This provision would also be litigated, but not until after the collection was actually removed.

Why did Johnson make the codicil providing for the maintenance of his home as a museum? Perhaps he thought the city would never build the long-contemplated Philadelphia Museum of Art, which in fact was built and opened in 1928 just nine years after his death. Even so, it is hard to understand why he wanted the collection displayed in his home. Not only were the premises inadequate for the purpose, they were also a fire hazard in a neighborhood that Johnson surely knew was deteriorating.

After Johnson died in 1917, the city accepted the bequest, thus defeating the Metropolitan Museum's claim. Then in 1921, the city and Johnson's trustee petitioned the Philadelphia Orphans' Court to sell the house on grounds that the collection could not fully or safely be exhibited there. But the will was clear, and in 1921 the Orphans' Court dismissed the petition. In 1923, the fire marshal approved only two of the house's four floors for public occupancy. Half the collection had to be stored.

By the time of the Depression, the expenses of maintaining Johnson's residence as a museum could not be met. The city refused to meet them, and the trust created by his will was not adequate. It had been invested, as he stipulated, in fixed-income securities. As a result, the trust had not benefited from the boom of the 1920s and was now suffering from the defaults of the 1930s. So in 1933, the collection was simply packed up and removed without judicial authorization to the city's newly constructed art museum on the Parkway. Gradually, the museum built many galleries to display parts of the collection, and ultimately about 350 paintings were exhibited, less than one-quarter of the total number.

It was not until 1954 that the collection's relocation was officially brought to the attention of the Orphans' Court, which in 1958 filed an opinion excoriating the trustee.[4] The opinion noted that the relocation had taken place "without the knowledge or approval of the orphans' court . . . [and] in open defiance of" the court's earlier order.[5] "The complications in this case . . . result entirely from the improper conduct of those to whom the testator entrusted his precious possessions. The persons responsible for the illegal re-moval of the collection must be censured."[6] Nevertheless, the court said it was faced with a fait accompli, and it gave permission "albeit reluctantly"[7] for the museum to continue its display of the collection on a temporary basis.

Only the city and the trustee were involved in these proceedings. The museum had not participated and was therefore spared the judge's ire. But the museum had two problems. First, it wanted to extend its dominion over the collection for a long period, if not permanently. Second, it wanted to display the collection in a historical context with other works of art in the museum. Its second objective violated the will's clear direction that the collection must always be shown as a unit: Commingling was not permitted.

ML&B partner William Wood had been president of the museum from 1976 to 1980, and partner John Lombard had represented the museum since the 1970s.[8] The Firm's assignment was to obtain a court order securing the Johnson collection for the museum over a long period and also permitting display of the collection in juxtaposition with the museum's other paintings. Obviously, such an order would conflict with the will on two counts. Moreover, the order would have to be secured from the same judge who had taken the trustee to task in 1958.

Nevertheless, the Firm discharged its assignment. By a decree dated April 30, 1987, the court authorized the formulation of a juxtaposition plan, which the court said will be "in the best interests of the Johnson Collection and will provide a better understanding by the viewing public of its significance as one of the most important collections of European paintings in the United States." Finally, by a decree dated February 23, 1989, the court not only approved the implementation of the juxtaposition plan but also extended until 2083 the period during which the museum would have dominion over the Johnson collection.

Here is Lombard's summary of how the juxtaposition and extension questions were approached:

> First we had the advantage that Judge Klein himself initiated the proceedings. The judge was interested in the collection. He had heard that the museum's new air-conditioning system had caused water damage in one of the period rooms. He felt the collection might be at risk. We got into exhibition techniques, climate control, and conservation.
>
> The judge seemed interested and satisfied. So we decided to press our luck. We made the point that the museum contained two parallel collections of paintings, Johnson's and all the rest. Separating them was disadvantageous, despite what Johnson's will said. The judge gave the museum three years to conduct a study about alternative means of exhibiting the collection.
>
> The museum got a grant from the National Endowment for the Humanities to do a study and consulted with a number of world-renowned figures in the art history field, including Michel Laclotte, presently director of the Louvre. At that time, he was working on the new Musee d'Orsay in Paris, an enormous belle epoch railroad station on the Left Bank being converted into a museum. It would display the Louvre's collection of paintings from 1850 to about 1905 which had been in the Jeu de Paume. The judge appeared fascinated by Laclotte and at one point asked him if there were some sort of association to which museum directors from all over the world belonged. Laclotte answered: "Ah yes, we all belong to a kind of 'International Art Mafia,' I should say." Even Judge Klein joined in the merriment.
>
> It was the expert consensus that the Johnson collection should be divided into five elements and juxtaposed with the museum's other materials from the same periods. There would be fourteenth- and fifteenth-century Italian paintings, fourteenth- and fifteenth-cen-

tury North European paintings, seventeenth-century Dutch paintings, nineteenth-century paintings by European artists, and finally works from all of these areas which would be shown as a study collection.

Plans were submitted to the court for approval. While permitting juxtaposition, the judge insisted that the Johnson items receive special treatment, be suitably marked and be shown in specifically designated areas. This worked out just fine. When it was all over, the judge was so pleased with the product that he invited us to submit a decree further extending the museum's stewardship of the collection until 2083.

The hearings took six years, from 1983 until 1989, and the reinstallation of the collection at the museum will not be completed until 1994.

It was a big job but a very satisfying one.[9]

So once again, a jolly testator provided grist for the litigation mill. But unlike the outcome in *Jarndyce v. Jarndyce*, the Johnson estate was not consumed by fees and costs. Instead, the collection is there for all to see—at least until 2083, when the Firm's lawyers will presumably petition the court to extend the arrangement into the twenty-second century.

CHAPTER 31

A COLLECTOR WITH NO MONEY OF HIS OWN

A good eye ■ *Condensed soup* ■ *Taxes and lawyers* ■ *Doubling the fee* ■ *The family patriarch* ■ *Dorrance's lifestyle* ■ *Sotheby's and Christie's battle it out* ■ *The Firm's hard bargain* ■ *A night to remember* ■ *Matisse and Picasso* ■ *Van Gogh and Monet* ■ *A sea change in the market* ■ *Hitting it just right in 1989*

Lawyer John G. Johnson bought art as an expert and collected as an encyclopedist. Client John T. Dorrance, Jr. (everyone called him Jack) eschewed expertise and collected only what he liked. But he had a good eye. After his death on April 9, 1989, his collection accounted for $140 million of his $225-million estate.

Also after his death, some $2 billion passed to his three children from a trust created by his father, Dr. John T. Dorrance, Sr. With degrees from the Massachusetts Institute of Technology and Goettingen University, Dr. Dorrance was a chemist by profession. He is credited with inventing condensed soup, and at his death in 1930 he was the sole owner of the Campbell Soup Company.[1]

With only a life estate in his father's trust, Jack Dorrance enjoyed saying, "I really have no money of my own, just the income from a trust." But before he died, that income amounted to roughly $40 million a year and nicely supported his avocation. Collecting what he liked, Dorrance would replace paintings that no longer pleased him with paintings that did. Capital gains taxes were often attracted. They annoyed him. What business was it of the government that he now liked new painting A better than old painting B?

The annoyance that Dorrance felt toward tax complexities also extended to lawyers. From the time he became a client of the Firm in 1960, he received especially solicitous attention, first from W. James MacIntosh, then from Peter Somers, and finally from Frank Mirabello. Although Dorrance was dubious about lawyers, he appreciated a job well done. Early in his relationship with the Firm, he received a $25,000 bill from MacIntosh. Dorrance struck out $25,000, wrote $50,000, and sent a check for the larger amount. The check was deposited, but the annotated bill was kept for many years by MacIntosh in his desk drawer as a souvenir. It is not every day that a client doubles a lawyer's bill.

For forty years, twenty-two of them as chairman, Dorrance was associated with the Campbell Soup Company, running the company with a kindly hand. He also promoted Campbell products by serving them along with gourmet foods at his formal dinner parties. Spanning two generations, he functioned as patriarch and focal point of the Dorrance family, which comprised his children, sisters, nephews and nieces, and their respective spouses and descendants. Following his death, the press speculated whether the family would fragment and even sell the company.

Dorrance presided over his empire from a forty-nine-acre estate in Gladwyne, just outside Philadelphia. Twenty-eight employees maintained his great home, block-long greenhouses with their prize-winning orchids, English and boxwood gardens, pet roosters and Labrador retrievers, collection of cars and firearms, hundreds of jade and porcelain objects, French and English antique furniture, wine cellar, and above all his spectacular collection of paintings.

Since Dorrance served as chair of the Philadelphia Museum of Art from 1986 until his death, it was surmised that he would leave his collection or at least part of it to the museum. Although modest compared with the number of paintings John G. Johnson had amassed, Dorrance's collection consisted of highly prized impressionistic art. Most of his paintings were individually more valuable than all but a dozen or so in the Johnson collection.

But Dorrance had no intention of bequeathing his collection to the museum. Instead, he followed his father's example and left the bulk of his wealth to his grandchildren. To pay the resulting death taxes, the collection had to be sold. A team of Firm partners was assembled to mastermind the sale: William Wood was knowledgeable about the art market and a collector in his own right; Lawrence Berger was experienced in documenting sales of art objects; and Frank Mirabello was a nationally recognized authority on the taxation of estates.[2]

The Firm's team did not have to ring doorbells. The art world came to it. That world included the two arch rival auction houses, Sotheby's and Christie's. In November 1988, Christie's had disposed of the William and Edith Mayer Goetz collection. That auction had brought $85 million and was the largest sale of it kind up to that time. The Dorrance collection was even more valuable. Competition to dispose of it was fierce. Christie's wanted another triumph. Sotheby's was determined to trump Christie's.

Sotheby's offered to provide expert appraisals, transportation, shipping and insurance, and a world tour to exhibit the objects, all without cost. It also offered to waive the 10-percent seller's premium and look solely to the 10-percent buyer's premium for its compensation. Christie's made a similar proposal, but ultimately lost out when Sotheby's met the Firm's demand that the auction house guarantee $100 million in net proceeds to the estate.

Thus, the risk of the giant sale was effectively shifted to Sotheby's. It would suffer a severe loss if it had overestimated the value of the collection or if the art market collapsed, as actually happened some months later. On the other hand, if the market continued strong, the estate would enjoy the upside. Finally, the Firm's team even insisted that Sotheby's prepay the guaranteed amount, so it could be invested and generate income for the estate prior to the auction.

The arrangement was unusual and controversial. Although auction houses sometimes guaranteed floors under the prices of individual works, none had previously guaranteed the sale of so extensive a collection. Dealers speculated whether this portended the end of auction houses as disinterested market makers. As Sotheby's gloated, Christie's sulked, arguing that its role was "as an auction house . . . and not as a bank."[3]

With so much at stake, Sotheby's lost no opportunity to promote the sale. It exhibited important parts of the collection in Los Angeles, Paris, Zurich, Tokyo, Philadelphia, and New York. The private showing in Philadelphia was at the Museum of Art on September 28, 1989. It was an exciting social event, attended by many Firm lawyers, clients, and local art cognoscenti. Finally, the collection moved to New York for the grand finale, which entailed four days of auctions covering 919 lots.

The auction's main event commenced at 7 p.m. on October 18, 1989, when forty-four lots were offered, comprising forty-three of the best paintings and one sculpture. More than a thousand people attended by invitation, some in formal attire. Bids were received in person or transmitted over sixty dedicated telephone lines. The first night alone, bids totaled a record $116,182,000. Of the forty-four items, sixteen were sold to Japanese bidders, five to Europeans, and the balance to Americans. The Firm's team watched the proceedings from a private upstairs room.

On that first night, there was a colossal sale of paintings by Matisse, Picasso, Van Gogh, Monet, Renoir, Manet, Degas, Cézanne, and Gauguin, among others. Matisse's *Woman With a Red Umbrella Seated in Profile* brought $12.4 million. (The previous record for a Matisse was $5.7 million, and Sotheby's presale estimate was $5 million to $7 million.) Picasso's *At the Moulin Rouge,* an early painting (1901) of a world-weary woman in a Paris cabaret, went for $8.5 million. As the auctioneer's gavel fell, Paloma Picasso, the artist's daughter, craned her neck to see who had bid it in. Another Picasso, *Pitcher Bowl and Lemon,* brought $4.8 million. A Van Gogh, *Man at Sea,* went for $7.1 million, and Renoir's *Young Woman With a Red Corsage,* for $5.8 million.

Many of the Firm's partners who attended the presale exhibit at the Philadelphia Museum of Art had chosen Monet's *Riverbank at Argenteuil* as the painting they wanted most to take home. It had originally been bought from Monet's agent in Paris a century earlier by Peter A. B. Widener, perhaps during one of his trips there with John G. Johnson. It went for $6.6 million, but unfortunately not to anyone from ML&B. Another Monet, *Haystacks in the Morning Snow,* brought $8.5 million.

It was a night to remember, not only because of the crowd, the excitement of the art, and the fabulous prices, but also because the sale took place as values, especially in impressionistic and contemporary art, were at or near their zenith. A year later, it would all be very different. One reason for the difference was the retreat of the Japanese as vigorous (some said reckless) bidders, when the Nikkei stock index dropped almost 40 percent during 1990.

Sotheby's felt this sea change in November 1990 at an auction of paintings owned by the late Henry Ford II. It had guaranteed roughly $58 million to Ford's estate but took in only about $49 million. Of the thirty-six paintings offered, thirteen failed to sell at their guaranteed prices, thus becoming the property of Sotheby's. The sea change also affected Sotheby's stock. Selling for $35 a share at the time of the Dorrance auction, it dropped to $10 a year later. As *Time* magazine put it: "The Great Auction Wave in contemporary art, which rose amid the financial euphoria of 1982 and crested in late 1989, is now over."[4]

Collectibles are subject to wide swings in value. Hitting it just right, the Dorrance sale established a high watermark that lasted for years. Jack Dorrance would have been gratified—he had done pretty well for someone with no money of his own.

CHAPTER 32

THE BOMBARDMENT
OF THE UNION LEAGUE

Sharp-eyed dealers and a stodgy club ■ *Key versus Bierstadt* ■ *First-year law school* ■ *The South declares war* ■ *Ironclads and monitors* ■ *A subsequent bombardment* ■ *Comparing styles* ■ *A deal is a deal* ■ *The experts lie low* ■ *Innocence and attribution* ■ *No help from the courts* ■ *The murky art world* ■ *New Vermeers* ■ *A rationale of repose*

I n 1987, an art expert wrote: "Two sharp-eyed dealers thought they had gotten a good deal from a stodgy old men's club and they made a mistake."[1]

The "two sharp-eyed dealers" were Steven Juvelis and Firestone & Parson, Inc. The "stodgy old men's club" was the Union League of Philadelphia. The "good deal" was that in 1981 the dealers had paid the league only $500,000 for a celebrated painting by Albert Bierstadt. The "mistake" was that the painting, called *The Bombardment of Fort Sumter,* was apparently not by Bierstadt but by John Ross Key.

The two painters should be distinguished at the outset. Bierstadt, who lived from 1830 to 1902, is a renowned American artist best known for his hugh canvases of grandiose Western scenery. Key, who lived from 1837 to 1902, is best known for having a grandfather whose poem "The Defense of Fort McHenry" became "The Star Spangled Banner," adopted as the national anthem in 1931. The twenty-six-by-sixty-eight-inch *Bombardment of Fort Sumter* hung prominently in the Union League between 1937 and 1981. It had always been considered a Bierstadt and had been loaned as such to major exhibitions of American art. It bore what purported to be Bierstadt's signature, which had once been examined and verified by a painting conservator at the Metropolitan Museum of Art.

As a Bierstadt, the painting was probably worth $1 million. As a Key, it might have brought $50,000. Or at least so the sharp-eyed dealers said on October 6, 1986, when they sued the Union League in the United States District Court for the Eastern District of Pennsylvania. The dealers wanted their money back. They claimed there had been a mutual mistake of material fact entitling them to rescind. Shades of first-year law school.

Was the painting a Bierstadt or a Key? To understand the problem, turn back to 1860. In the presidential election that year, Abraham Lincoln was not even on the ballot in ten states (out of thirty-three) and received only 40 percent of the popular vote in a four-way race. He was committed to maintaining the Union. The South obviously did not share his commitment. Nor did everyone in the North, at least at the cost of war. Many Northerners thought the South had a right to secede. Some said good riddance. Lincoln's problem was to unite the North against secession by the South. The South effectively played into Lincoln's hands by bombarding Fort Sumter, a federal installation in Charleston harbor, on April 12-13, 1861. Some 40,000 shells rained down for thirty-four hours before the fort surrendered, badly damaged but with no loss of life. The South had effectively declared war on the North.

The bombardment of Fort Sumter was a landmark event. Such events often generate important art by important artists. So it was with the Bierstadt. Or so it was until the publication of an article in the *Magazine Antiques* for February 1986 by Alfred C. Harrison, Jr., an art historian and dealer in San Francisco. Harrison contended that the *Bombardment* was not painted by Bierstadt in 1861 but by Key in 1863.

Harrison asserted that the painting could not date from April 1861, since it showed the presence in Charleston harbor of Confederate ironclads and Union monitors. Such vessels were not used until the epic battle of the *Merrimac* and the *Monitor* at Hampton Roads in March 1862. But they were used during a subsequent bombardment of Fort Sumter in the fall of 1863, when the positions were reversed: The Confederates held the fort, and the Union was doing the bombarding. Moreover, by 1863, the fort was in ruins, as shown in the painting, not largely intact as it would have been in 1861. Thus, Harrison argued, the painting depicted the later bombardment and not the landmark event that triggered the Civil War two years earlier.

Moving from the date to the artist, Harrison noted that Bierstadt was away in the West when the 1863 bombardment occurred, whereas Key was a lieutenant in the Confederate engineers and was stationed near Charleston at the time. Also Bierstadt's works were romantic, idealistic, dramatic, and colorful. Key's were cold, crude, flat, and even primitive. The *Bombardment* was in the latter style. It certainly looked bad for Bierstadt.

It also looked bad for the Union League. What should it do? It had scores of paintings on its walls, and it had only skimpy records regarding their provenance. Its officers were not art historians and had given no warranties. They had simply taken advantage of fast-rising art prices to generate some needed funds for the club. They had sold a well-regarded painting, whoever the artist. Still, as pillars of the community, they were in an awkward position. They agonized but ultimately declined recision. "A deal is a deal," said the club's president.

ML&B was instructed to defend the suit. A team was assembled, led by Lawrence Berger and Kell Damsgaard. Berger had a subspecialty in sales transactions under the Uniform Commercial Code. Damsgaard was a litigator.

Everyone assumed the case would involve a battle of the experts. Some would testify the painting was a Bierstadt, while others would testify it was by Key. But the Harrison article scared off the Bierstadt partisans. Where were all those art authorities who had exhibited the painting for so many years as a Bierstadt?

Authenticity aside, there was a threshold question. Was the suit timely? The applicable statute of limitations was probably four years, and the sharp-eyed dealers had waited longer than that before starting their action. Of course, they said they had no choice, being unaware that they had a recision claim until publication of the Harrison article. Consequently, they contended they had four years from the time they "knew or should have known."

The Firm's lawyers filed a motion for summary judgment, arguing that the statute of limitations had begun to run when the painting was sold, not when the buyers learned of the Harrison article. If the court sustained the motion, lengthy depositions regarding authenticity, credibility, and good faith could be avoided.

Chief Judge John P. Fullam granted the Firm's motion, holding that the plaintiffs' claim was time-barred. Then, in a widely quoted opinion going beyond the question of timeliness, he wrote:

> [M]y ruling that plaintiffs' claims are time-barred should not be interpreted as suggesting that plaintiffs' claims would otherwise have been valid: in the arcane world of high-priced art, market value is affected by market perceptions; the market value of a painting is determined by prevailing views of the marketplace concerning its attribution. Post-sale fluctuations in generally accepted attributions do not necessarily establish that there was a mutual mistake of fact at the time of the sale.[2]

The art world is often murky. What was once considered a Rembrandt might not be considered one today, and vice versa. Art historians spend their lives attributing and reattributing. Auction houses like Christie's and Sotheby's protect themselves by disclaimers: Attributions are matters of scholarly opinion, which can change. Even John G. Johnson, that most assiduous of private collectors, was occasionally taken in. It is a game of classy detective work and high stakes.

Sometimes the stakes are literally life or death. Between 1937 and 1943, some "new" Vermeers came to light in Holland. Since only thirty-three paintings by Vermeer were known to exist, the discoveries stunned the art world. But scientific tests showed the newly found paintings dated from the seventeenth century. They were so convincing that one was bought by the Rijksmuseum. Another was bought in 1942 by Hermann Goering. They were offered for sale by Hans van Meegeren, who after World War II was charged with treason by the Dutch government for selling a national treasure to the Nazis. The crime carried the death penalty. His defense was that the new Vermeers were not national treasures at all. The reason: He had faked them. (Better embarrassment than death.) He prevailed and was sentenced to one year in prison for fraud. There was egg on many expert faces.

Judge Fullam's rationale of repose would not have helped in the van Meegeren case, since it does not apply where the seller is guilty of fraud. But in the absence of fraud, it did apply to the *Bombardment*. Consequently, the "stodgy old men's club" kept its money and the "sharp-eyed dealers" kept their Bierstadt/Key.

CHAPTER 33

THOSE FABULOUS PHILADELPHIANS[1]

Economics and the performing arts ■ *Philadelphia's chief contribution to civilization* ■ *The musicians mobilize* ■ *The 1961 strike* ■ *Politicians need love* ■ *A mediator misses the concert* ■ *The grand design* ■ *Year-round paychecks* ■ *A backbreaking workload* ■ *The strike of 1966* ■ *A Roman carnival* ■ *The board goes on record* ■ *Losing their public* ■ *Translating beauty into money*

The Philadelphia Orchestra—or the Orchestra, as it is invariably called in Philadelphia—was founded in 1900. It was unremarkable until 1912, when a conductor named Leopold Stokowski was hired.[2] He was thirty years old, an Adonis, and a binder of spells. In the field of classical music, Stokowski was the greatest showman since the legendary Franz Liszt, at whose concerts the audience swooned. By the 1920s, the Orchestra was regarded as among the world's finest, some said *the* finest. For seventy years, under the leadership of Stokowski, Eugene Ormandy, Riccardo Muti, and Wolfgang Sawallisch, Philadelphia's "chief contribution to civilization [has been] her incomparable orchestra."[3]

But whatever their quality, American symphony orchestras do not earn their keep, a condition typical also of opera companies, ballets, and theater groups. Their European counterparts are heavily subsidized, while in the United States, deficits in the performing arts are generally defrayed by tax-deductible contributions. Years ago, the Orchestra's deficit was made up by just a handful of people who wrote checks at year-end. The Depression and high taxes put an end to that era of noblesse oblige. As the amounts written on the checks decreased, the number of people writing the checks had to increase. Today, deficits and constant fund raising (euphemistically called "development") are central to the Orchestra's existence.

The Orchestra's members have long been represented in collective bargaining by the American Federation of Musicians. However, the members themselves took no part in the bargaining process until

1959. That year, their union permitted them for the first time to send a committee to observe the negotiations. It also permitted them to engage a lawyer, although at their own expense. When the Orchestra musicians engaged a lawyer, the Orchestra management had no choice but to do likewise. So Kenneth Souser was engaged. He had just come to ML&B and was recognized as the dean of those Philadelphia lawyers who specialized in collective bargaining.

Going into the 1959 season, the base pay of the Orchestra musicians was $157.50 per week, and the concert year lasted only twenty-nine weeks. Souser bargained a 1959-61 contract without a strike. The basic wage increased significantly; the length of the season did not. Although the musicians made only modest progress, they held Souser in high regard. A group of them came to him after the negotiations and asked if he would switch sides and represent them the next time around. Souser could not and did not switch sides, but he was touched.

Negotiations for a new contract in 1961 were very different. This time the musicians got authority from their union not merely to observe but also to speak up. They did more than that: In short order, they took over the negotiations. (Eventually, their union ceased to play any role other than sign the contracts they negotiated.) The musicians wanted more money and a much longer employment year than their twenty-nine-week season.

There was a twenty-day strike in 1961, and the scene shifted to the Philadelphia office of the Federal Mediation and Conciliation Service. After acceptable terms had been hammered out in lengthy and complex negotiations, Mayor Richardson Dilworth arrived by prearrangement at the bargaining table. He took off his coat, rolled up his sleeves, and was photographed with the parties. The media credited him with settling the strike. Souser was not offended. "Politicians need love too," he told the mediators, who were invited to sit in the manager's box for the season's delayed opening concert that night. One mediator who was not a music lover respectfully declined to attend, commenting to Souser: "I miss 'em when I can."

Souser had been joined in the 1961 negotiations by Park Dilks, whose education included musical training. It was Souser's view that a whole new approach to symphonic labor relations would have to be found, and it was Dilks's assignment to find it. Souser was right about the need for a new approach: Symphonic musicians were becoming militant all over the country, as they followed Philadelphia's example, side-stepped their union, and bargained directly with their managements.

The new approach was the Orchestra's 1963-66 labor contract. It increased the weeks of employment in each year, so that by the last year the musicians received fifty-two paychecks for forty-six weeks of work, with six weeks of paid vacation. Up to that time, no American orchestra had been guaranteed year-round pay. The guarantee became possible because the Orchestra undertook to increase its touring and contracted to spend part of each summer at a new festival in Saratoga Springs, New York. As a result of the guarantee, the musicians finally got what they wanted. Now, as several of them said, "We won't have to play every wedding and bar mitzvah to make ends meet."

But those who get what they want do not always want what they get, as became apparent in 1966 when the next contract was negotiated. Now, instead of wanting more performance time, they wanted less. They said their workload had become "back-breaking," threatening the legendary artistry of the Philadelphia Orchestra. In response, management offered to reduce the number of work weeks. After all, the fewer weeks the musician played, the lower the deficit. But this assumed they would not be paid when they did not play. And there was the rub. Fifty-two paychecks were welcome. Performing for them was not. What Souser had called the "grand design" of 1963 had been no solution.

A strike by the musicians between September 19 and November 15, 1966, had all the aspects of a Roman carnival. They set up a strike headquarters. And they picketed, distributed leaflets, and issued extravagant press releases. Seizing upon such statements, the media reported that the musicians' lives were unbearable, "[a] typical 'easy' home week . . . consist[ed] of 74 hours . . . of activity,"[4] the musicians were on the road constantly, they rarely saw their families, and they were not reimbursed for their travel expenses. Letters to the editors were published almost daily, decrying the inhumanity of the Orchestra's board. Some were written by people who had never attended a concert.

The public was swept up in the dispute. A Save the Orchestra Committee emerged with the suggestion that the board be replaced by a new one that would meet the musicians' demands. Governor William Scranton sent word that his good offices were available for dispute resolution. Excitement reached a peak when the musicians organized a concert at Philadelphia's Convention Hall on October 14 for the benefit of their strike fund. It was conducted by the eighty-four-year-old Stokowski, who had resigned in a huff as music director thirty years before. He enjoyed tweaking the board. The event was attended by 9,000 people and raised more than $15,000.

As the strike lengthened, public sympathy was generally with the musicians. They were fine artists, overworked and underpaid. By contrast, the board was judged insensitive and arrogant. Comprising some of the people who defrayed the deficit, it remained aloof. Its theory was that answering the musicians' charges would simply exacerbate the dispute and impair fund raising when the strike ended.

But increasingly it appeared that the strike might not end, that the concert season might have to be canceled, and that the Orchestra might even cease operations. Maestro Ormandy was asked privately whether he could form a new Philadelphia Orchestra if the old one was disbanded. He said it was possible, provided he could retain the Orchestra's dozen solo players. He called them his "diamond necklace."

The bargaining continued into November without any sign of a breakthrough. Finally, as a last resort, the board did what it had steadfastly resisted doing. It went public by taking full-page ads in the *Bulletin* and the *Philadelphia Inquirer*. The ads explained exactly how much the musicians were paid and how long they worked. Detailed examples were given of their work days and work weeks. Their actual eighteen-hour week of performances and rehearsals bore no similarity to the hyperbolic seventy-four-hour week they and their union had publicized.

Public support for the musicians eroded swiftly after revelations about their real working conditions. Mayor James Tate seized the opportunity by appointing a Board of Public Accountability.[5] He also arranged for bargaining to continue at his conference center on the sixteenth floor of Philadelphia's Municipal Services Building, saying: "Don't come out until you have a contract."

But another fifteen days passed before the parties reached agreement. It came after a thirteen-hour bargaining session that lasted until 1:30 a.m. on November 15. While the mayor's committee met with the musicians' committee, Dilks and the Orchestra's managers drafted contract language, Souser played solitaire, and the board's chairman napped on the mayor's conference table. In repackaged form, the final settlement was not essentially different from terms offered earlier. Nevertheless, the musicians voted two to one to accept it. Explaining their change of heart, they said simply: "We lost our public." A scapegoat had to be found, so they fired their lawyer.

■ ■ ■ ■ ■

For many years, Souser represented the Philco Corporation in its labor relations. He would remark that 10,000 employees could go on strike at Philco and cause less furor than 100 members of the Philadelphia Orchestra. There are at least four reasons for this. First, cultural institutions are public treasures, so the entire community has a stake in their operation, or thinks it has. Second, disputes regarding public treasures are often complicated by excessive and inflammatory media coverage. Third, the usual marketplace guidelines are absent in the case of cultural enterprises operating at a loss. And fourth, there is simply no way to translate beauty into money.

After Souser's death in 1970, Dilks took over the bargaining, aided by Mark Dichter who, in turn, succeeded Dilks in 1993. Since 1966, nine contracts have been negotiated at three-year intervals, and the Orchestra has undergone a substantial turnover in its membership. But the old timers still tell tales of the "great strike of '66." Maybe such tales have had a restraining influence: There has been no strike since the great strike. By 1993, the base pay had increased to $1,290 per week (almost all the musicians receive more than the base), with ten weeks of paid vacation. The musicians still declare their frustrations, and the operating deficits rise every year. But the music is as glorious as ever.

CHAPTER 34

A LONG AND
WINDING TRANSACTION

A menu of entertainers ■ *Irresistible targets for taxing authorities* ■ *Charles Lubar's stock in trade* ■ *The Beatles' catalog* ■ *Michael Jackson bids it in* ■ *The pinball machine* ■ *Passing through the Bahamas* ■ *A visit in full regalia* ■ *A rock Mozart* ■ *Relics from an earlier age* ■ *A gold Rolls-Royce* ■ *Reflecting the results achieved*

Michael Jackson and the Beatles are as incomparable in their genre as the Philadelphia Orchestra is in its. For this last story about the Firm in the arts, the scene shifts from Philadelphia to ML&B's London office and from classical music to rock. The story also spotlights the rarefied international tax practice of partner Charles (Chuck) Lubar.

There are law firms, generally boutiques, that specialize in entertainment law. ML&B is not one of them. Still, the Firm has represented many entertainers in recent years, including Yehudi Menuhin, Ivo Pogorelich, Thomas Hampson, Catherine Malfitano, Paata Burchuladze, Douglas Fairbanks, Jr., Jane Seymour, Albert Finney, John Hurt, Christopher Reeve, Eric Segal, David Merrick, and Michael Jackson. Assorted Muppets are also clients: On Lubar's office wall hang photographs of Kermit the Frog and Miss Piggy. These photos, which include warm personal messages, purport to be autographed.

The Firm's attraction for entertainers is its expertise in planning the affairs of high-net-worth clients, especially in the tax area. Entertainers often have impressive balance sheets and even more astounding income statements. The compensations of industry titans pale in comparison with the incomes of top entertainers. Moreover, entertainers derive their income from all over the world. Consequently, they are irresistible targets for a multitude of taxing authorities. They and their managers urgently require international tax advice. Lubar is one of a handful of lawyers who specialize in giving such advice.

So it was natural that Michael Jackson's lawyers would turn to Lubar when their client wished to acquire the music publishing catalog of Associated Communications Corporation plc. That catalog contained 57,000 songs from the 1930s through the 1970s. But the crown jewels were 251 pieces written between 1964 and 1970 by John Lennon and Paul McCartney, and performed by them with two other Liverpudlians, George Harrison and Ringo Starr.

Everyone but a Rip Van Winkle knows that Lennon, McCartney, Harrison, and Starr comprised the Beatles, who dominated rock music in the 1960s. Although they stopped performing together publicly in 1966 (they were only in their mid-twenties), they made recordings until 1969 before going their separate ways. Their tours between 1963 and 1966 drew crowds like World Cup soccer. At Adelaide, Australia, 300,000 people were present just to see them arrive. It was a phenomenon called Beatlemania.

The Beatles produced many great hits, including "I Want to Hold Your Hand," "Let It Be," "A Hard Day's Night," "Something," "Penny Lane," "Yellow Submarine," "Yesterday," and "Hey Jude." Another was "The Long and Winding Road," which the *Los Angeles Times* said summed up the "10 months of intense, complicated and confusing on-again, off-again negotiations" that finally culminated in the purchase of the Beatles' catalog by Michael Jackson for $47.5 million.[1]

Others besides Jackson had been interested in buying the Beatles' songs, including CBS, Coca-Cola, and EMI. It was also reported that Paul McCartney and Lennon's widow, Yoko Ono, had offered $40 million for the songs. When they were outbid by Jackson, McCartney blamed Ono's "penny-pinching ways for a delay that allowed Michael Jackson to buy . . . the Beatles classics."[2]

In making what the press called "the most expensive publishing purchase ever by an individual,"[3] Jackson did not have to pinch pennies. His *Thriller* collection had sold almost 40 million copies worldwide and was the best-selling record album of all time. *Time* magazine reported in 1985 that "his posters were plastered on Burger King drive-thrus, his trademark lone white glove was a hip street item, and not only youngsters but their parents, too, were scurrying to snap up tickets to his Victory concert tour."[4] When he acquired the Beatles' catalog, Jackson was on a sentimental journey. In a *Rolling Stone* magazine interview, a source close to him said "the Beatles . . . [were] special to him as a fan, not just as a businessman."[5]

As buyer and seller negotiated, tax considerations became crucial. Could Lubar transform eight affiliated United Kingdom corporations that owned the rights into a United States sole proprietorship, namely Jackson? And could Lubar transform the fully depreciated copyrights of the United Kingdom corporations into a $47.5-million tax basis for Jackson? (This would provide Jackson with sizable depreciation deductions to offset his other personal income from record royalties and performing.) And finally, could Lubar do all this without attracting any United Kingdom or United States taxes to either the buyer or the seller? A tall order.

Models were constructed. They were like pinball machines. If the ball did not strike one bumper, it struck another. And with each contact, a light went on. It signaled that a tax was payable somewhere. Finally, Lubar devised the perfect model. No lights.

If the United Kingdom taxing authorities would so rule, the corporations could become nonresident United Kingdom corporations in the Bahamas. Under United Kingdom law as it then stood, they would be subject only to Bahamian taxes, of which there were mercifully none. After a suitable time, the corporations could liquidate and distribute their assets to Jackson. Under United States law, Jackson could avoid tax on the distribution and step up his basis to the purchase price. Meantime, withholding taxes could be skirted on royalties payable to the Bahamian corporations, if such payments were legitimately deferred until after the transaction closed. Miraculously, it worked just that way.

A cynic might say Lubar took advantage of then existing loopholes in the United Kingdom and United States tax structures. But that is one function of the tax lawyer. By the same token, one function of the taxing authorities is to close loopholes as fast as private practitioners reveal them. The loopholes have since been closed: The structure would not achieve the same tax result today.

The acquisition attracted much publicity in both the entertainment and tax worlds. For the latter, Lubar wrote an article published in the *International Financial Law Review* (January 1987) and the *Tax Planning International Review* (October 1987). Honoring Jackson's best-selling album, Lubar's exposition was entitled "Tax Thriller."

Entertainment clients are often invisible to their lawyers. They are engrossed in their art. Some find business transactions incomprehensible, and have lost fortunes due to inattention. But Jackson was attentive. On September 3, 1985, at 5:30 p.m., accompanied only by his driver, Jackson arrived at the Firm's London office. He was staying at the Montcalm Hotel, where scores of his fans maintained a constant vigil hoping to catch a glimpse of him. He gave them the slip by using the hotel's back door.

Jackson joined the negotiations in the Firm's main conference room on the first floor (second floor to Americans) at 4 Carlton Gardens. The seller's counsel was surprised and delighted to see him. (A question had been raised whether Jackson was really the buyer.) Jackson ingratiated himself immediately. He spoke softly: "Man, that's a lotta paper. You sure are working hard for me." He then settled in and discussed substantive issues with the seller's counsel. Lubar, who has seen many entertainers, says Jackson is one with his eye on the bottom line.

In due course, the seller's counsel left the meeting, and Jackson was alone with his own team. He sounded no different from clients everywhere when he said, "Please close the deal quickly." Lubar studied him. His face had an androgynous quality. His eyes were haunted and doelike. He was tiny. (The press set his weight at 115 pounds.) But such talent. A rock Mozart.

Jackson was a showman even when not performing. He arrived at the London office dressed in his stage regalia and signed autographs all around. It was a memorable event, especially for young people on the Firm's staff. Some were so overwhelmed by his visit they seemed preoccupied for days.

Jackson made his first record ("I Want You Back") for Motown in 1969 as part of the Jackson 5 when he was eleven years old. That was the year the Beatles made their last album (*Abbey Road*). The Beatles were already legends when Jackson was scarcely out of short pants. To him their songs were sacred relics of bygone times. His quest ended, Jackson signaled his exhilaration and gratitude by giving a gold Rolls-Royce to his entertainment lawyer.

Jackson understood the tax miracle Lubar had wrought for him, and with a little encouragement Jackson might also have given Lubar a gold Rolls-Royce. But Lubar furnished no encouragement. Gold Rolls-Royces are ostentatious and inappropriate for lawyers in old conservative firms, especially those with roots in Philadelphia.

Even more important, Lubar knew very well the financial and tax implications of such a "gift." The Inland Revenue and/or Internal Revenue Service would presumably treat the car as income to Lubar and/or the Firm. In such case, if Lubar kept the car, the Firm would reduce Lubar's partnership distribution to the extent of the car's value. Alternatively, the Firm might try to allocate the car among its then 200 partners, entitling each one to drive it for so many days and minutes during the year, depending upon the distributive share of such partner.

None of this seemed feasible to Lubar. So he rejected any idea of compensation in kind. Instead, he applied the legal profession's traditional billing criteria, including the notion that a bill should reflect the results achieved. They were extraordinary, so it did.

CHAPTER 35

THE GREAT TRAIN WRECK

Lawyers as gladiators ■ *No fingerprints* ■ *The Standard Railroad of the World* ■ *Trailblazing enterprises* ■ *The slow decline* ■ *A disastrous merger* ■ *Section 77 of the Bankruptcy Act* ■ *Buckeye Pipe Line Company* ■ *Amtrak and Conrail* ■ *No railroads in the Northeast* ■ *A market glut* ■ *Assets in liquidation* ■ *Four years of valuation* ■ *A weighty affidavit* ■ *A worthless certificate* ■ *Vacationing in Patagonia* ■ *The Firm's debt to railroads*

Having dealt with the Firm in labor (Chapters 25-29) and the arts (Chapters 30-34), five miscellaneous matters remain to be considered (Chapters 35-39). All five occurred within the last two decades and involved huge stakes. In three of them, the client's survival depended on the outcome. Two stemmed from the Firm's public utility practice going back more than a century. The others involved international securities law, a hostile takeover attempt, and antitrust law. Either immediately or eventually they all reached the courts, demonstrating that lawyers are still basically gladiators.

■ ■ ■ ■ ■

Some times are more felicitous than others for the government to perform a politically delicate but unavoidable act. The interregnum between administrations is one such time, especially if there has been a change of party. So it was with the settlement of the so-called Penn Central Valuation Case. The settlement terms were informally announced on election eve, November 3, 1980, when the announcement was swamped by other news. The settlement agreement was dated November 16, 1980, a Sunday twelve days after Jimmy Carter became a lame duck. And the closing, at which the government paid the Penn Central Transportation Company $2.1 billion, was on January 15, 1981, five days before Ronald Reagan was inaugurated. No fingerprints.

It was clear that effective April 1, 1976, the government had appropriated most of the Penn Central's railroad properties, along with five smaller railroads in the Northeast.[1] But it was not at all clear what the government owed for them. Having taken them, the government was operating them through the Consolidated Rail Corporation (Conrail) and was losing shocking sums in the process, $421 million in the first year alone. As to Penn Central, the government had repeatedly asserted that its value in liquidation was no more than $587 million. Obviously, a settlement of $2.1 billion was a long way from $587 million. Three law firms were instrumental in achieving that settlement. ML&B was one of them.

The Pennsylvania Railroad was chartered in 1846 to build a railroad between Harrisburg and Pittsburgh. In the ensuing decade, it linked the Atlantic seaboard and the Ohio-Mississippi valley. With the railroad in place, New Orleans finally ceased to be the route of choice for goods moving between Philadelphia and Pittsburgh. After the Civil War, railroads dominated the American scene, and the Pennsy with its Tuscan-red rolling stock dominated the railroads. It was nicknamed "the Standard Railroad of the World."[2]

The Pennsy's power was enormous: It was even rumored to control the legislature and Supreme Court of Pennsylvania. Just after the turn of the century, it reached its apogee when it tunneled under the Hudson River and linked up with another of its holdings, the Long Island Railroad. At their junction in Manhattan, the railroad constructed Penn Station. Inspired by the Baths of Caracalla, it was a colossal landmark from its opening in 1911 until its demolition in 1963-64.

During World War I, the railroads were operated by the government. After the war, they began their long, slow decline. But the Pennsy maintained its commanding position as America's largest transportation enterprise. In *No Way to Run a Railroad*, Stephen Salsbury could still describe the Pennsy at midcentury:

> With assets of almost $3 billion, its more than 10,100 miles of tracks stretched westward from New York City to Chicago and St. Louis. . . . Only three of *Fortune's* 500 largest industrial corporations, General Motors, Standard Oil of New Jersey, and United States Steel, had more assets than the Pennsylvania. And among the utilities, only the giant American Telephone and Telegraph surpassed the Pennsy.[3]

In today's world of fabulous multinational corporations, it is hard to imagine railroads as trailblazing ventures. But a century ago, when other businesses were local and sedentary, railroads functioned as unique operations on an unparalleled geographical scale.

Their dispersion required revolutionary management and accounting techniques. They were less like conventional enterprises and more like whole governments or the medieval church.

Because of their natural monopoly, railroads attracted regulation by the Interstate Commerce Commission (ICC). Created in 1887, it was the prototypical federal agency. Railroads also attracted the labor movement, and by 1920 the rail unions were stronger than organized labor in any industry except possibly coal mining. The unions froze work rules and sanctified featherbedding. The ICC ossified operations and regulated rates. The railroads lost their ability to innovate, as well as their capacity to raise capital.

Even worse for the railroads was the construction of the country's great highway networks, especially after World War II. Trucks used publicly furnished roads to go where privately laid tracks did not reach. Finally, railroads such as the Pennsy and New York Central were obliged to provide unprofitable passenger service, including that worst loser of all, twice-a-day peak-period commuter service.

Facing the trucking threat and stymied by government regulation and crippling union rules, the railroads took refuge in mergers. Among the eastern systems, the Chesapeake & Ohio absorbed the Baltimore & Ohio. To the north, the Pennsy and the New York Central contracted in 1962 to merge the nation's first- and second-largest railroad corporations, with a total of $7 billion in assets, 19,600 miles of track, and 106,000 employees.

What followed was a nightmare. Six years were consumed in litigation and ICC proceedings. The merger was opposed by nine railroads, which exacted concessions. The unions also resisted, acceding only after they won expensive job-protection guarantees.

Although the merger was finally consummated in 1968, there had been virtually no functional planning during the years of litigation. Consequently, nothing worked. The computer systems of the two railroads were incompatible. So were their operating structures: The Pennsy was decentralized by regions, while the New York Central was run entirely out of New York City. Other afflictions included internecine management battles, chaos in labor relations, and a cash crunch: The day of the merger the two railroads had only $13.1 million between them in their banks. To top it off, the 1969-70 winter weather was the worst in a century.

By early 1970, Penn Central was so desperate it tried for a government bailout. When none was forthcoming, its directors fired

---

top management, including CEO Stuart Saunders, one of W. James MacIntosh's poker-playing buddies. Then on June 21, 1970, it filed in Philadelphia for reorganization pursuant to Section 77 of the Bankruptcy Act. The Penn Central's bankruptcy was by far the largest up to that time.[4]

The filing was by the Penn Central Transportation Company, which owned and operated the railroad. It had a subsidiary, Pennsylvania Company (Pennco), which did not file and remained remarkably unaffected by its parent's reorganization. Pennco held nonrailroad assets, including amusement parks, office buildings, coal fields, the Waldorf Astoria and Biltmore hotels, and the Arvida Corporation with its Boca Raton Hotel complex. Pennco also owned the Buckeye Pipe Line Company. Buckeye was a profitable enterprise, with earnings that helped reduce the railroad's losses. Its pipelines extended from Long Island through New Jersey, Pennsylvania, Ohio, Indiana, and Illinois, with other segments in Florida and the state of Washington.

The Firm's involvement with Penn Central came through Buckeye, which was building a new pipeline from Linden, New Jersey, to Allentown, Pennsylvania. In 1972, Buckeye approached Robert Young for advice. His performance so impressed Buckeye that it soon retained ML&B generally, embarked upon a program of acquisitions, and became a valued client of the Firm.

Meanwhile, the railroad went from bad to worse as it lurched along in reorganization. Losses mounted, financing dried up, strikes disrupted operations, and creditors insisted that any further delays in the reorganization proceedings would violate their constitutional rights. While Penn Central's liquidation was inconceivable, it also seemed inescapable.

But the real issue was even broader. It pertained to the whole future of railroads in the Northeast and lay beyond the competence of any bankruptcy court. Legislation was required. In 1971, Congress created the National Railroad Passenger Corporation (Amtrak) to relieve the railroads of their long-haul passenger service burdens. Then, in 1973, the Regional Rail Reorganization Act was passed. It charged the United States Railway Association (USRA) with designing a new rail system in the Northeast and designating the lines to be included. The act also sired Conrail to operate the new system and established a special court to value the properties taken for the system.

Pursuant to its mandate, USRA developed a Final System Plan, which was certified by the special court on March 12, 1976. The plan covered designated portions of the six railroads. These designated portions were then conveyed to Conrail effective April 1, 1976.

As Conrail took over, Penn Central went out of the railroad business but continued in reorganization. It retained its Pennco subsidiary, its billion-dollar tax loss carryover, and its claim against the government. Ultimately, it emerged from reorganization in 1978, changed its name from Penn Central Transportation Company to Penn Central Corporation, became a conglomerate, and moved its headquarters to Cincinnati.

But what about Penn Central's claim against the government? USRA said it was worth no more than $587 million, thus reflecting USRA's concept that railroads in the Northeast had no going-concern value and would have to be liquidated. That meant there would be no rail lines whatsoever east of the Mississippi and north of the Ohio rivers. That also meant there would be a market glut of rolling stock and track. Tunnels and bridges would require huge conversion or shut-down costs. Countless rights-of-way would revert to prior owners. In short, many of the Penn Central's presumed assets would have no value or would turn into liabilities.

Through its Buckeye relationship, ML&B entered the Penn Central Valuation Case in October 1976. The Washington law firm of Covington & Burling had already been engaged by Penn Central and was developing what it called "an alternate rail use theory" on the railroad's behalf. The idea was to prove that at least some of the trackage in the Northeast was essential and could be profitable, especially if acquired by railroads in the West. Such a going-concern approach would support a much higher valuation of Penn Central's railroad assets than the government was then conceding.

But someone had to wrestle with USRA's downside arguments. So the Firm's assignment was to ignore the going-concern approach and value the assets themselves: those not used pursuant to the alternate rail theory or, if that theory failed, then all assets thrown on the market by virtue of the liquidation. In the latter case, the Firm would confront the glut concept on which USRA relied to minimize values. Dozens of the Firm's lawyers worked intermittently for almost four years, from early 1977 into 1980, organizing and supervising the valuation of Penn Central's assets.

Finally, the parties were ready for settlement discussions beginning in the summer of 1980. Robert Young and William Zeiter were among those representing Penn Central. As the parties talked, a settlement seemed feasible if it offset the roughly $2 billion in indebtedness that Penn Central carried with it out of reorganization two years earlier.

But under the statute, the settlement could not exceed the "net liquidation value" of the properties taken. So affidavits were filed with the special court valuing the railroad's voluminous properties as if in liquidation. Zeiter's affidavit was among them. It was dated November 26, 1980, and dealt with "facilities, equipment and other assets." It included an exhibit that listed the assignments of the Firm's lawyers who had worked on the project. Just the assignments and the names of the lawyers covered eleven pages.

The Zeiter affidavit analyzed tracks, ballast, ties, locomotives and other rolling stock, communication systems, down to small tools and Penn Central's in-house law library. Along the way there were oddments. For example, cabooses were conceded to have only scrap value, and bridges and tunnels were assumed to have neither a positive nor a negative value. The affidavit was crucial to the proceedings. In reviewing the methodology and the years of work performed by the Firm's lawyers, it provided the required comfort to the government and the special court and supported the $2.1-billion settlement.

Still, there might have been no settlement at all if Zeiter had not researched in advance a point everyone else apparently took for granted. That point involved the mechanics of payment. The statute provided that USRA would issue a certificate of value to Penn Central. The certificate would then be exchanged for Treasury obligations which Penn Central could immediately convert to cash. At least, so everyone thought. But Zeiter was unable to find any provision in the act specifically authorizing the exchange of the certificate of value for Treasury obligations. His detective work revealed that the language permitting the exchange had been stapled onto the printer's copy of the committee report, but the required change had never been made in the act itself. Thus, the certificate of value would have been worthless. The problem was resolved when ten words were added at the end of a thousand-word section of the Staggers Rail Act that the President signed on October 1, 1980. Only a few people knew the import of those inscrutable ten words.[5]

Zeiter, whose proclivity to analyze every conceivable (and some-times inconceivable) issue made him an exceptional resource, had one further concern: However unlikely, Congress might hold hearings during the presidential interregnum. He was fully prepared to defend his thesis. Still, if hearings were held, would the settlement become a political football? Zeiter thought hearings might be discouraged if he distanced himself from the nation's capital. He pondered an appropriate locus for a well-earned three-week vacation. He chose Patagonia and descended toward the bottom of the world. There were no hearings, and the $2.1-billion closing was held as scheduled on January 15, 1981.

The Penn Central Valuation Case did not end the Firm's contact with railroads. Since 1977, ML&B has provided labor representation for Conrail, which became a profitable business and was privatized in 1987. Two years later, an ML&B team led by partner Dennis Morikawa won a landmark case in the Supreme Court upholding Conrail's right to test its employees for drugs.[6] Separately, during the 1980s, the Firm received Silver Liner Club awards from Amtrak as the second-largest user of passenger services along the Northeast Corridor between Washington and New York. Finally, in 1990, the Firm began its representation of the National Railway Labor Conference.

For seventy years, railroads have been good to the Firm: the Reading and the Central Railroad of New Jersey; Penn Central; Conrail; and recently the whole industry in labor relations. As award-winning train users, the Firm's lawyers acknowledge every day their debt to this historically dominant force in American economic life. They have reason to be grateful. If all railroads in the Northeast had been dismantled, as USRA proposed, ML&B might today be the second-largest user of buses in the Northeast corridor. Not an alluring alternative.

CHAPTER 36

THE GIANT BIRD[1]

IOS again ■ *Vesco takes the money* ■ *Ontario appoints a liquidator* ■ *Aiders and abettors* ■ *LPI and FUBAR* ■ *Fiduciary paralysis* ■ *David and Goliath at the trial* ■ *Closing arguments and a hurdy-gurdy* ■ *A little firm beats a big one* ■ *Recoveries for FOF's shareholders*

T he groundwork has been laid in Chapter 24: the creation of Investors Overseas Services (IOS) by Bernie Cornfeld; its development into the largest offshore fund complex in history, with $2.6 billion under management; its plundering by Robert Vesco; its collapse in 1972; the SEC's campaign to have IOS liquidated in New York; the Firm's involvement in the Luxembourg summit conference; the decision to liquidate the IOS funds in their respective countries of domicile; and the direction of the Deutsche Schutzvereinigung für Wertpapierbesitz (the Schutz) that ML&B pursue liquidations of IOS funds domiciled in the Western Hemisphere.

The main IOS fund in the Western Hemisphere was Fund of Funds (FOF), an Ontario corporation. Pursuant to the Schutz's mandate, the Firm instigated the appointment of a liquidator for FOF by the Supreme Court of Ontario. He was John Orr, formerly senior partner in Canada of the Touche Ross accounting firm (more recently Deloitte & Touche). Orr then engaged the Firm to pursue the looters of FOF.

Vesco and his confederates had sacked various IOS entities in different ways. As to FOF, Vesco recognized that many of its shareholders lived in countries with exchange controls. These shareholders had acted illegally when they converted their currencies into dollars and invested outside their native lands. Considering their vulnerability, Vesco contrived a scheme for reorganizing FOF. FOF shareholders would either have to redeem their shares or lose their interests. If they redeemed, they could face criminal proceedings at home. So Vesco assumed many would not redeem.

On that assumption, he simply appropriated their interests, which he calculated at $60 million. Having taken the $60 million, he ran it through a chain of bank accounts until only he knew where it was. Its location is still unknown today.

Vesco presumably thought no one would complain as he fleeced IOS. When there was a worldwide outcry, he fled first to the Bahamas, then to Costa Rica, and later to Cuba. The Firm got a default judgment against him in 1979. With interest, the still-unsatisfied judgment amounted to $225 million by 1993. Satisfaction awaits repatriation.

But Vesco and his confederates could not have raped the IOS funds without assistance. The Firm's investigation turned up putative aiders and abettors. They included FOF's counsel, Willkie Farr & Gallagher (WFG), and FOF's custodian, the Bank of New York (BONY). By December 1973, it was obvious to the liquidator that FOF would have to pursue them. Firm litigators John Lewis and Jay (Jerry) Calvert moved center stage.

WFG, a highly regarded New York law firm, had been counsel to FOF for years. With Vesco now running FOF, WFG found itself taking orders from him. Its files were explicit concerning its services to Vesco as he plotted his depredations. For example, LPI stood for Looting & Plundering, Inc., a hypothetical corporation to which Vesco referred as he discussed with WFG's lawyers how he would sack FOF. Another file referred to FUBAR, an acronym that in sanitized form stood for Fouled Up Beyond All Recognition. In still another reference, WFG's lawyers displayed their erudition by using the Greek word *krasis*. It means watering the wine, and it described the way Vesco would dilute the shareholders' interests.

Of course, the WFG lawyers were concerned about involvement by the SEC: Their time entries spoke of the extraterritorial effect of SEC antifraud laws. Nevertheless, they undertook their tasks with good humor. One WFG lawyer, while sunbathing on a beach in the Bahamas, was approached by a Vesco henchman with a scheme to bleed an IOS entity named Venture Fund. When the scheme was described and the WFG lawyer was asked to do some fast drafting, he commented amiably: "This sure is venturesome."[2]

Over the years. WFG had received sizable fees from the IOS entities. Naturally, the handful of WFG lawyers who managed the IOS account did not wish to lose this valuable business. So they accommodated Vesco when they should have known better. Few other WFG partners probably had any idea what the handful was up to, but the partnership was liable just the same. There are lessons here for lawyers: Do not follow your clients over the line, and know your partners.

A similar paper trail implicated BONY. The bank was suspicious of Vesco, and bank personnel reflected their suspicions in file memos about how the bank should improve its procedural safeguards to avoid releasing funds to him. Some of the memos recited mistakes the bank had made in the past and listed steps to be taken in the future. When the steps were not taken, still other memos were written reemphasizing what absolutely had to be done. The bank suffered from bureaucratic paralysis and was still flagellating itself when Vesco made off with the $60 million.

Years ago, doctors resisted testifying against one another, and lawyers overlooked the indiscretions and incapacities of other lawyers. But WFG's role in the FOF frauds could not be ignored by the liquidator, who was directed by the Ontario Supreme Court to take action. After much soul-searching by the Firm's senior partners, a suit was instituted against WFG and BONY on May 8, 1974. There followed six years of acrimonious motions and pretrial discovery, including almost 100 depositions. Ultimately, WFG paid a substantial sum to the liquidator and was released. By agreement, the terms of the settlement were never made public.

That left BONY, represented by Sullivan & Cromwell, which offered $500,000 to settle its share of a claim for $60 million plus interest. Lewis considered the $500,000 offer absurd. The liquidator and the Ontario Supreme Court agreed and directed that the case be tried. The trial commenced on June 13 (a Friday), 1980, and lasted five weeks.

The approaches of the two law firms—ML&B and Sullivan & Cromwell—were in striking contrast. Indeed, Lewis highlighted the contrast whenever possible. Sullivan & Cromwell occupied two counsel tables at which as many as seven lawyers appeared busily engaged, with paralegals scurrying in the background. Lewis and Calvert occupied the other counsel table, with one paralegal discreetly delivering documents from time to time.[3] Other ML&B personnel in the courtroom were instructed by Lewis to distance themselves from the Firm's trial team. The jury could easily distinguish David from Goliath.

The panel consisted of six women, some of whom came from Brooklyn and the Bronx. They must have regarded as bizarre the closing argument of the senior Sullivan & Cromwell attorney. He asked them to look out their back windows over their lawns and disregard any trash they saw in the distance. By trash he was presumably referring to Lewis's arguments. In short, he wanted them to ignore the trees and concentrate on the forest. The trouble was, their vistas offered no lawns or trees, much less forests. Another lesson for lawyers.

During his closing argument, the Sullivan & Cromwell lawyer labored under an additional disability. It was a hot day, the air conditioning was not functioning, and the courtroom windows were open. From below in Foley Square came the music of a hurdy-gurdy. The argument of the Sullivan & Cromwell lawyer was lengthy and analytical. The jury had difficulty hearing it, not to mention concentrating.

Lewis's argument followed. It was shorter, clearer, and intelligible to ordinary mortals. Just before Lewis began, the hurdy-gurdy stopped. A few minutes earlier, an ML&B associate had gone below to negotiate a buy-out of the music. But he found the organ grinder packing up to leave. No buy-out was necessary.[4]

The Sullivan & Cromwell lawyers must have observed their senior colleague straining to compete with the hurdy-gurdy. With so many lawyers at their counsel tables, surely it occurred to at least one to go below and end the music. But none of them stirred. Perhaps it was beneath their dignity to bargain with an organ grinder. Still another lesson.

The jury brought in a $60-million verdict for FOF, of which $25.2 million was assessed against BONY and $34.8 million against WFG. Of course, WFG had settled earlier. Judgment was entered against BONY for $35.6 million, which included interest. BONY had never increased its offer beyond the original $500,000. After the jury was discharged and was leaving the courtroom, one juror approached Calvert and said, "Isn't it wonderful that a little law firm like yours can beat that big firm of Sullivan & Cromwell!" At the time, ML&B was roughly twice the size of Sullivan & Cromwell. Modesty has its rewards.

Rewards include fees. Having undertaken the massive FOF litigation on a contingent basis, the Firm was appropriately compensated for its labors. Over the years, and from all sources, more than $100 million was recovered for the FOF shareholders.

CHAPTER 37

TWO VAST AND
TRUNKLESS LEGS[1]

Client for a century ■ *PE's hydroelectric plant at Conowingo* ■ *Rate-making proceedings at the Mayflower Hotel* ■ *Limerick's fifty-story towers* ■ *Supplying 2 million people* ■ *A $7-billion price tag* ■ *Public opposition* ■ *The PUC and the courts* ■ *An additional team of lawyers* ■ *A bet-the-company inquiry* ■ *The solution is a cap* ■ *Exhaustion and vindication* ■ *The fire that lights the sun*

Philadelphia Electric Company (PE) was created in 1881 by some of the same Philadelphia entrepreneurs (including client William G. Warden) who founded UGI a year later.[2] After Randal Morgan went to work for UGI in 1882, the Firm made a specialty of utility law. Considering that specialty and the principals active in both UGI and PE, it is not surprising that PE became a client in 1887.

During the 1920s, a major Firm project for PE involved the construction of the Conowingo hydroelectric power plant on the Susquehanna River in Maryland. The project had to be financed, contracts had to be let, and a dam almost one mile across had to be built. The dam created a lake fourteen miles long. PE had to acquire the land covered by the lake, as well as land for transmission lines. The Firm set up its own title plant near the construction site, in order to search titles and render opinions on the thousands of properties being acquired. When Conowingo was finished, it was second only to the Niagara Falls plant in size and output. That was in 1927, just a year before UGI acquired PE, thus bringing two major Firm clients together.

The Conowingo project cost $52.2 million, an immense sum in those days. During the 1930s, Conowingo's costs were reviewed for rate-making purposes by the Federal Power Commission. William Clarke Mason led the Firm's team. As described in Chapter 20, it set up shop in the Mayflower Hotel, just a block from subsequent locations of the Firm's Washington office. According to J. Tyson Stokes, an entire floor of the hotel was occupied by the files and personnel required for the case. The proceedings were not finally over until 1947.

By the 1960s, PE's interests had moved from water power to nuclear power. Today, two buildings fifty stories tall stand in lush fields along the Schuylkill, just south of Pottstown, Pennsylvania. The buildings are hyperbolic in shape and so large that the base of each could accommodate Philadelphia's Veterans Stadium, where the Eagles (a Firm client) and the Phillies perform. They are the cooling towers of PE's two nuclear generating plants, called Limerick I and Limerick II. The plants can produce approximately 2.1 million kilowatts of power and satisfy the energy needs of 2 million people.

Limerick was constructed over a sixteen-year period between 1974 and 1990. During PE's century-long history, nothing embroiled it in so much controversy, and few undertakings of the Firm consumed the time of so many of its lawyers over so long a period. During the 1960s, it was possible to build a nuclear power plant without significant public opposition. During the 1970s, it became much more difficult. After the accident at Three Mile Island in 1979 (Chernobyl followed in 1986), it became virtually impossible.

The Limerick project was conceived in 1968 and was to have been completed by 1975 at a cost of $760 million. But the site was near heavily populated areas, so the Nuclear Regulatory Commission (NRC) did not issue the construction permit until 1974.[3] When the permit was finally issued, PE extended the prospective completion dates for the two plants to 1981 and 1982. But due to problems of technology, financing, and regulation, Limerick I was not actually completed until 1985 and Limerick II not until 1990. And the total cost was not $760 million but $7 billion.

By the 1980s, it seemed that everyone opposed the continued construction of Limerick: the city of Philadelphia; an organization called the Philadelphia Area Energy Users Group; numerous environmental groups; consumer groups; the Office of Consumer Advocate (OCA); the trial staff of the Pennsylvania Public Utility Commission (PUC); the Pennsylvania legislature; and the governor's office. The media were also active. The *Philadelphia Inquirer* declared war on Limerick from its inception, and for two decades it regularly condemned the project and PE's management. Even fishermen were disaffected: In March 1983, protestors paddling about in canoes delayed construction of the Point Pleasant Pumping Station on the Delaware River because half its output was earmarked for Limerick's cooling towers. Against such opposition, PE's senior management and the Firm stood virtually alone.

The issue was squarely joined in August 1980 when the OCA petitioned the PUC for an order requiring PE to show cause why the continued construction of Limerick was in the public interest. Lengthy hearings ensued before the PUC. Robert Young headed the Firm's team, as the project was assailed on all sides. Nevertheless, the PUC decided in August 1982 that PE's plan to build Limerick I, then well underway, was sound.

But as to Limerick II, the PUC held that the project should either be delayed or canceled. The Firm argued that the PUC had no authority to make such an order and appealed to the Commonwealth Court, which reversed.[4] But there was a further appeal to the Pennsylvania Supreme Court, which in May 1983 reversed the Commonwealth Court.[5] PE then advised the PUC that it would suspend Limerick II until it completed Limerick I, after which it would immediately recommence Limerick II, in order not to lose the project's momentum and the services of specialized contractors on the job. The PUC rejected this proposal in December 1983 and ordered that nothing be done on Limerick II, at least until Limerick I commenced operation about two years later.

As if this were not bad enough, the political pot boiled over in August 1984 when the PUC ordered a comprehensive investigation of the impact that Limerick II would have on PE's overall financial health and what should be done about the expenditures (approximately $500 million) already incurred for it.

At this point, Young's team was already overwhelmed by preparations for a monumental rate case involving Limerick I, which commenced service in 1985. So a whole new team was organized. Lawyers were seconded from the litigation and the business and finance sections to join government regulation lawyers in this bet-the-company inquiry. Jay (Jerry) Calvert effectively led the additional team, as hearing preparations went forward around-the-clock. The PUC wanted everything: PE's anticipated capacity; the area's needs in the early twenty-first century; an analysis of all PE's existing plants and their potential lives; consideration of alternate sources of power and their projected costs; and the possibility of converting Limerick II into a coal-fired plant. Even utilities in neighboring states had to be studied and questions regarding their potential capacities examined.

As these no-holds-barred proceedings commenced in 1984 and continued into 1985, Young suggested a vehicle for compromise: With Limerick I now operational and with a half-billion dollars already invested in Limerick II, the PUC might be induced to approve the completion of Limerick II if the company would offer to cap its construction costs for rate-making purposes. Obviously, this would be risky for PE. But PE's management agreed and offered to cap the cost of Limerick II at $2.7 billion. As is normal with caps, conditions were attached. As is normal with regulatory authorities, the conditions were ignored when the caps were accepted. So the company was on its own. But it turned out that the gamble was a good one. When Limerick II was put into service in January 1990, its cost was within the cap.

PE got what it wanted. During the 1980s, it completed two nuclear power plants at a time when other utilities were surrendering or were continuing the battle with disastrous consequences.[6] But PE did suffer some casualties along the way, including its CEO and president. Having fought the battle for nuclear energy, they took early retirement in 1988 after the NRC shut down Peachbottom, a smaller PE nuclear plant where control-room operators had been found sleeping on the job.

By 1990, it seemed that PE's determination to complete Limerick was farsighted. The pendulum had swung, and the press was forecasting brownouts and blackouts along the East Coast.[7] Now the complaint was that utilities had not built enough capacity. Then came a further energy crisis: Iraq annexed Kuwait on August 2, 1990, and oil prices temporarily exceeded $40 per barrel. How did PE fare? The *Wall Street Journal* reported that PE would hardly be affected by the invasion of Kuwait since it "depends on oil to generate less than 5% of its electricity. Instead, the company depends on nuclear power plants for about three-fourths of its energy needs."[8]

Still, the ultimate answer remains elusive. While some countries, France for example, generate as much as 70 percent of their electricity by nuclear fission, no new nuclear plants have been commissioned since 1978 in the United States, where the number of commercial reactors stands at 112. Admittedly, such reactors produce deadly nuclear waste and have an operational life of forty years at best before they must be phased out. So nuclear fission is a short-term solution. Longer-term solutions include power from the sun and wind, as well as from within the earth and the seas. The best solution may ultimately be nuclear fusion—the thermonuclear fire that lights the sun. Someday, it may provide energy that is cheap, clean, and virtually inexhaustible. Meantime, Limerick stands among the last of its ilk in the United States.

CHAPTER 38

HANDS OFF
THE FAMILY STORE

The legislative initiative ■ Monopoly with real money ■ Retailers on the hit list ■ White knights and greenmail ■ A predator's agenda ■ Shark repellents ■ A tender offer ■ The market reacts ■ The family is not for sale ■ In the courtroom ■ Reclassifying the stock ■ In the courtroom again ■ A study in contrasts ■ The shareholders speak ■ 100-percent perfection

As noted in Chapter 7, the Firm's work during the 1980s for client Scott Paper Company included an initiative in the Pennsylvania legislature to fashion defenses against corporate predators. In 1986, some of those defenses proved critical in averting a hostile takeover of client Strawbridge & Clothier (S&C).

During that acquisitive decade, it was not enough that a corporation made a good product, sold a good service, and was well-managed and profitable. It was safe from predators only if it was loaded with debt or its stock price was prohibitively high. Otherwise, it could be put in play, as the expression went, and targeted by anyone with sufficient capacity to borrow. Junk bonds were often the vehicle, many of them marketed by Michael Milken and the Beverly Hills office of Drexel Burnham Lambert.

It was a period when literally thousands of takeovers, mergers, and buy-outs were completed at a cost of at least a trillion dollars. All the while, threats of hostile takeovers diverted businesses from improving their products and increasing their sales. Domestic enterprises fell behind their foreign competitors, as the nation's best brainpower was squandered playing Monopoly with real money.

Some predators came equipped with their own capital. Others bootstrapped their way. Novice predators who did a few deals gained entry to the club. The more they played, the more they could borrow. And the more they could borrow, the less they had at risk. In fact, their downsides were often negligible. Either they acquired their targets and stripped them to pay their debts, or their targets paid them greenmail to go away. Such profits were the best of all. The players never had to dirty their hands with operations.

Retailers led the hit list. Household names like Brooks Brothers, B. Altman, Bonwit Teller, Ames, Zayre, R. H. Macy, Jordan Marsh, Marshall Field's, Neiman Marcus, Bergdorf Goodman, and Abraham & Straus were all affected. In many cases, ownership changed hands. In almost all cases, massive debt was incurred. Debt-service burdens caused some stores to be closed, some to be sold, and some to file for bankruptcy.

By the early 1980s, only eight of the nation's top fifty department stores were independent. The others had been acquired by national chains. In twenty-sixth place nationally and second place as an independent was Woodward & Lothrop in Washington, D.C. In thirty-third place nationally and fifth place as an independent was S&C.

Woodward & Lothrop is significant because toward the end of 1983 it was the object of a hostile tender, had recourse to a white knight, and did its own leveraged buy-out. The raider was Ronald Baron. He neither took over the company nor received greenmail. Instead, having put the company in play, he and his clients benefited from a run-up in the stock price as they unloaded their holdings at a profit of at least $15 million.

Even before the Woodward & Lothrop transaction, S&C was on Baron's screen. Interviewed by *Barron's* in May 1983, Baron said he was acquiring S&C stock, that "[t]he book is understated by half, and there is $3 in equity for $1 in debt." The article was headlined: "Stock Picker for the Pros When Ron Baron Talks, Big Investors Listen."[1]

From 1983 through 1986, Baron increased his and his clients' holdings in S&C. He also announced his agenda for the company. That agenda included merging S&C with a national chain, borrowing huge sums to expand S&C's Clover division, and borrowing to redeem some of S&C's stock.

S&C's management had different ideas. It counseled with the Firm during the spring of 1984 and adopted state-of-the-art shark repellents. In accordance with Donald Scott's advice, these included blank-check preferred stock, the elimination of cumulative voting, an increase in the percentage of shares required to call a special meeting from 20 percent to 50 percent, and an increase in the vote required for shareholder action without board approval from a majority to two-thirds.

Baron complained in the press that S&C would not give him a seat on its board, despite his and his clients' holdings. Nor, he said, would the company discuss with him its operations or plans. The easy victory he enjoyed at Woodward & Lothrop was not to be repeated at S&C.

With the parties at an impasse, the stage was set for a dramatic gesture. It took the form of a tender offer announced by Baron on April 21, 1986. He offered to acquire 4.16 million S&C shares, representing approximately two-thirds of the company's stock, at $60 per share for a total outlay of $249.6 million.

The stock market had anticipated the move. A year before, in 1985, the stock had sold for as little as $29.50 per share. But by March 1986, it was up to $48.50. The day before the offer, it advanced to $56.50, and the day after the offer it reached $62.63. And this was just the beginning, according to the *Philadelphia Daily News*, as analysts speculated that S&C's stock was worth $100 a share and that the company would find a white knight to outbid Baron.[2]

S&C retained Kidder Peabody & Co. and Drexel Burnham Lambert as its investment bankers to join ML&B in repelling the attack. The Kidder team was led by Martin Siegel. Despite Siegel's subsequent notoriety, Scott credits him with performing effectively for S&C.[3]

At the time of the offer, about 44 percent of the company's 6.2 million shares were held by family members. The investment bankers and the Firm urged the creation of a "13D group," by which family members, officers, and other major shareholders holding a total of 48 percent ultimately agreed not to sell their shares for at least six months. Obviously, such solidarity spelled trouble for Baron.[4]

S&C's board met on April 30, 1986. Advised by the Firm and the investment bankers, the board rejected Baron's $60-per-share offer. S&C's press release called the offer "highly speculative," "inadequate," "coercive," and a "transparent scare technique." According to Scott, a key element in the board's rejection was the Shareholder Protection Act of 1983. It had amended the Pennsylvania Business Corporation Law to permit a board of directors, when faced with a takeover offer, to "consider the effects of any action upon employees, suppliers and customers of the corporation [and] communities in which offices or other establishments of the corporation are located."[5] The role of the Firm in drafting and shepherding the act through the legislature has already been noted in Chapter 7.

Simultaneously with its rejection of Baron's offer, the company mounted a publicity campaign. A full-page ad in area newspapers on May 2, 1986, declared:

> The family is not for sale. More than 12,000 employees. Over 3,000 shareholders. Third, fourth and fifth generation Strawbridge and Clothier descendants. We are the family.

Another ad put it even more succinctly: "The family is not for sale. No sale. No way. Not today. Not tomorrow."

There was a spontaneous outpouring of goodwill toward the company from the general public, with television interviews as well as favorable letters to newspaper editors. One company employee was quoted as saying: "This guy won't pull this off. The Strawbridge family will . . . take care of us . . . again."[6]

To gain access to S&C's shareholders list, Baron filed suit on April 29, 1986, in the United States District Court for the Eastern District of Pennsylvania. Firm partner Gregory Harvey defended, arguing that the company had mailed Baron's offer to its shareholders and had no further obligation to him under federal law. On cross-examination, Harvey repeatedly asked Baron whether he had the funds to implement his offer. But the judge ruled the financing issue premature and directed that S&C produce its shareholders list. Still, Harvey had made his point.

With Harvey in the courtroom, Scott and the corporate team unveiled a plan to reclassify S&C's stock. Under the plan, the number of authorized shares would be doubled and divided into two classes: Class A with one vote per share, and Class B with ten votes per share. The one-vote stock would be entitled to dividends at least 10 percent higher than the ten-vote stock. The ten-vote stock would be transferable only to "any lineal descendant of a great-grandparent of the shareholder and such lineal descendant's spouse," as well as the shareholder's spouse and certain trusts and estates. Shareholders had a right to choose either the one-vote or ten-vote stock. Once chosen, the ten-vote stock could be converted into one-vote stock but not vice versa. Of course, the family was expected to choose the ten-vote stock.

Baron sued again on May 14, 1986, just a few days after distribution of the proxy statements that proposed the reclassification. In seeking to enjoin a shareholders meeting set for June 11, he alleged that "the reclassification plan would permanently lock up control for management of the company and insulate the controlling group from any challenge."[7] By way of insult, he included allegations under the Racketeer Influenced and Corrupt Organizations Act (RICO).[8] The annual meeting was postponed until July 23, 1986, to allow time for court proceedings.

Those proceedings included four days of trial and highlighted a classic study in contrasts, which Harvey exploited in masterly fashion. Baron, a quick, bright, bearded man in his forties, had no interest in the local scene or social questions. For him it was simply a matter of money.

On the other hand, Francis and Peter Strawbridge showed themselves as caring employers and concerned citizens. Peter Strawbridge testified in detail regarding the tragic effects the proposed takeover could have on S&C's employees, customers, and the communities in which the company operated. His testimony was emotional and compelling. It may also have helped S&C that the courthouse was less than two blocks from its main store in Center City Philadelphia, where judges and court employees shopped and sometimes ate their lunches.

On July 21, the court rejected Baron's contentions, holding that the reclassification served legitimate corporate purposes and was not motivated by fraud, bad faith, or self-interest. The stock closed down at $49.25.

There was cause for celebration, as Harvey told the *Philadelphia Daily News:* "I speak from 25 years' experience, with a lot of it having been in cases of this sort. This is as sweeping a victory on all legal and factual issues as there can be."[9]

The annual meeting went forward on July 23. There was a festive air as 700 shareholders filled S&C's main auditorium and 1,000 people turned out to watch the event on closed-circuit television in the Center City store. The reclassification was approved by a vote of five to one. Holders of 45 percent of the stock chose the Class B shares. Overwhelmingly, they were family members. In view of the restrictions applicable to the Class B shares, Baron chose the Class A shares. The final count showed that only 1.23 million shares had been tendered of the 4.16 million he had solicited and of the 6.2 million outstanding.

Although Baron filed an appeal, the contest was effectively over. He had been beaten by the family's cohesiveness, the community's support, and the Firm's legal strategy. In January 1987, he capitulated by agreeing not to purchase more S&C stock or incite further efforts to take over the company for three and a half years. He also wrote a letter to the company's directors apologizing for the RICO allegations in the complaint.

Considering the outcome, the following is appropriate from an *American Lawyer* article in September 1990 about the Firm:

> "They're [ML&B] just one hundred percent perfection from our point of view," says G. Stockton Strawbridge, whose family still controls the department store.[10]

CHAPTER 39

NO SLURRY

The most exciting thing in South Dakota's history ■ *A judgment for $844.2 million* ■ *The OPEC embargo of 1973* ■ *ETSI has the answer* ■ *Five railroads join forces* ■ *Water become crucial* ■ *The project is cancelled* ■ *Sherman Act violations are alleged* ■ *Winter in the old Sioux empire* ■ *Bowling on Tuesday nights* ■ *A governor testifies* ■ *Good guys and bad guys* ■ *The Supreme Court spoils the game* ■ *In the Eighth Circuit* ■ *Savoring ecstasy*

In another bet-the-company case, Morgan, Lewis & Bockius defended Kansas City Southern Industries, Inc., and its principal subsidiary, Kansas City Southern Railway Company (jointly hereafter called KCS).[1] KCS was sued in 1983 by the state of South Dakota in the United States District Court for that state. On April 12, 1988, after a ten-week jury trial, there was a treble damage award against KCS for $600 million plus costs, interest, and attorneys' fees under Section 1 of the Sherman Act.[2] "The jury verdict is the most exciting thing to happen in the state's history," said George Mickelson, then governor of South Dakota.[3]

When the judgment was entered, it totaled $844.2 million. The population of South Dakota was then roughly 700,000. As a result, each man, woman, and child in the state could claim to be richer by some $1,200. That included the jurors. Of course, collecting would have been something else. The judgment greatly exceeded KCS's net worth.

John Shenefield and Peter Halle brought the KCS case with them when they arrived in the Firm's Washington office as lateral partners in 1986. At that time, Shenefield was already one of the country's leading antitrust practitioners. He had served as assistant attorney general in charge of the Justice Department's Antitrust Division (1977-79) and then as associate attorney general of the United States (1979-81). At ML&B, he organized two teams of lawyers who spent four years working on the KCS litigation. In addition to

Shenefield and Halle, the teams eventually included partners Donald Klawiter, Joseph Fay, Jay (Jerry) Calvert, and Thomas Murrell.

The KCS case was a by-product of the 1973 OPEC oil embargo, a phenomenon also immediately responsible for the Trans-Alaska pipeline, detailed in Chapter 27. The embargo left no doubt that domestic oil production was inadequate to serve the country's needs and that imported oil would henceforth be both expensive and unreliable. Other energy sources would have to be found. One was nuclear power, as in the case of PE's Limerick complex discussed in Chapter 37. Another was coal. There were huge coal deposits in the Powder River Basin in Wyoming. The object was to transport that coal to the electric utilities in the south-central United States. Normally, the railroads would have done the job. Indeed, they derived 25 percent of their revenue from moving coal. But was there a cheaper and better way? Energy Transportation Systems, Inc. (ETSI) thought it had the answer.

Formed in 1974, ETSI was based in Houston, Texas, and included joint-venture partners Bechtel Corporation, Lehman Bros., Texas Eastern Corp., ARCO, and Kansas-Nebraska Gas Co. ETSI proposed to build a 1,400-mile pipeline through the heartland of the nation from Wyoming to the Gulf of Mexico. The pipes would have a diameter of twenty-eight to thirty-six inches, and through them would be pumped a slurry consisting of water and coal in roughly equal parts. The project would cost an estimated $689 million. It would also require rights-of-way, environmental clearances, and enormous supplies of water.

The railroads saw an obvious threat to their interests and resolved to thwart the project. Five of them joined forces with KCS: Burlington Northern Railway Co.; Union Pacific Railroad Co.; Missouri Railway Co.; Chicago Northwestern Transportation Co.; and Santa Fe Railway Co. They divided their labors. For example, Burlington Northern would fight ETSI's efforts to obtain powers of eminent domain, Santa Fe would oppose ETSI's applications for track crossings, and KCS would raise environmental issues.

One major environmental issue pertained to the project's water supply. In 1981, South Dakota had contracted with ETSI to furnish water from that state's Oahe Reservoir for fifty years. South Dakota expected up to $1.4 billion in revenue from the contract. But KCS challenged South Dakota's legal competence to furnish the water. It formed a coalition, including three states (Iowa, Nebraska, and Missouri) and the Sierra Club, to litigate the issue. They ultimately prevailed when the United States Supreme Court held in 1988 that

South Dakota had not obtained the requisite authority from the federal government to sell the water.[4]

By 1984, four years before the Supreme Court finally ruled against South Dakota on the water question, the estimated cost of the pipeline had increased to $3 billion, ETSI had canceled its contract with South Dakota, and the entire project had collapsed. ETSI sued the railroads, claiming they had violated the Sherman Act by combining to sabotage the project. Four of the railroads eventually settled. (KCS's contribution was $82 million.) Only Santa Fe went to trial. In 1989, a jury in Beaumont, Texas, assessed damages against Santa Fe. When trebled, the award amounted to $1.035 billion. That judgment, as compromised for approximately $350 million, brought ETSI's total recovery to about $635 million.

Running parallel with ETSI's suit against the railroads was South Dakota's separate suit against KCS. As a potential supplier of water, what rights did South Dakota have under the antitrust laws? And what rights did KCS have to organize opposition challenging South Dakota's authority to sell the water? In January 1988, after five years of discovery, the scene shifted to Sioux Falls, South Dakota, as the trial began.

The Firm's team settled into more than a floor at the Holiday Inn in downtown Sioux Falls, about six blocks from the federal court-house. Fay reported on conditions:

> Gradually, we acclimated to winter in the old Sioux Empire, where early morning temperatures of twenty-below-zero were common, and wind-chill factors of fifty-below not unheard of. Most of our time—I would estimate typically, all but six to twelve hours per week—was spent either in court or in the Holiday Inn, where we all had both rooms and offices. Most meals were eaten in the hotel, and pizza was delivered frequently. It was a highly confined existence.

Fortunately, the Firm's lawyers were treated as welcome guests and not as city-slickers from back East. Court personnel provided home-baked cookies for the attorneys and witnesses. Jury members then began bringing food, also prepared at home, to share with the attorneys and other court personnel. There were other intimate touches. For example, everybody knew the posttrial-day evidentiary conferences on Tuesdays would be brief: It was the judge's bowling night.

But despite the amenities, the home team definitely had the advantage. As their first witness they called former South Dakota Governor William J. Janklow. A popular lawyer, he was plain spoken and radiated a rough charisma. While in office, he had been a leading proponent of South Dakota's contract with ETSI. He knew all the local lawyers in the case on a first-name basis. Although not qualified as an expert, he was allowed by the judge to pontificate on a wide variety of subjects. But they all boiled down to letting the jury know, in Fay's words, "who were the good guys and who were the bad guys. The good guys were from South Dakota. The bad guys were from that intermeddling railroad 'downstream.'" Janklow emphasized how beneficial the water contract would have been for South Dakota and how meritless were KCS's attacks on South Dakota's right to sell the water. Again in Fay's words: "By the time Governor Janklow finished, the jury must have felt it was their civic duty, as South Dakotans, to find for the plaintiff."

Then a problem arose for South Dakota. On February 22, 1988, while the trial was in progress, the United States Supreme Court held that the state had no right to sell the water in the first place. But the judge refused to dismiss the suit, ignoring the argument that if South Dakota had no water to sell, KCS's conduct, even if improper, could hardly cause the state any loss. He also rejected KCS's contention, under *Noerr-Pennington*, that KCS had a constitutional right, regardless of the Sherman Act, to combine with others to seek executive and legislative redress.[5]

In his closing argument to the jury, Shenefield did a superb job organizing and summarizing the many facets of a complex case. By comparison, South Dakota's closing argument, particularly its rebuttal, was largely an emotional appeal to the jury, urging that KCS be made to "pay the piper." The presentation resembled a prosecutor's summation in a criminal trial.

After a week of deliberation, the jury delivered its verdict. The result was not unexpected, although a $200-million award when trebled with interest is daunting all the same. KCS appealed to the Court of Appeals for the Eighth Circuit. In the manner of Francis Bracken, Shenefield had made an excellent record. As always, the errors of the trial judge that so hurt the losing party with the jury could now be invoked for its benefit on appeal. Attentive and well-prepared, the court allowed each side an hour for argument. In due course, it unanimously reversed the $844.2-million judgment against KCS and dismissed the suit.[6] Its decision was filed on June 28, 1989, after the stock market closed. The next day KCS's stock soared 25 percent.

The Eight Circuit held that South Dakota had no standing, since its "interest does not constitute the interest of a competitor in the coal transportation market."[7] Moreover, as to KCS's activities in organizing opposition to the pipeline, the court found "no proximate causation between the alleged market restraint and the harm sustained by [South Dakota]."[8] Finally, the court said that even if KCS's activities did contribute to the cancellation of the contract between ETSI and South Dakota, such "activities . . . were protected by the *Noerr-Pennington* doctrine."[9] A clean sweep.

The appeals court's analysis was dispositive, and the United States Supreme Court denied certiorari on January 8, 1990.[10] In classic fashion, the Firm had snatched victory from the jaws of defeat. Such are the shifting tides of battle, albeit rarely on so grandiose a scale. How often do lawyers savor the ecstasy of nullifying a $844.2-million judgment?

Just as there was no joy in Mudville after mighty Casey struck out, so there was no longer excitement in South Dakota. On the contrary, there was KCS's bill for court costs amounting to $175,531.68, which was graciously paid. Over time, life returned to normal, as KCS went back to operating its railroad, South Dakota sat on its water, and the trial judge continued to bowl on Tuesday nights.

CHAPTER 40

METAMORPHOSES

Recapitulation ■ Succeeding the Gang of Four ■ Democracy and decentralization ■ An embarrassment of riches ■ Public interest law ■ Even an obscenity case ■ Bockius might not be pleased ■ Lawyers advertise ■ Bids and beauty contests ■ A Director of Client Relations ■ Technology explodes ■ Drowning in IBM cards ■ Mops and buckets ■ Lawyers and the information revolution

Much has been covered since Chapter 19: the Firm's national offices outside Philadelphia, its international practice and foreign offices, its high-profile labor cases, its engagements in the arts, and its successes in some landmark legal controversies. Turning back to that chapter, it is now time to speak further about the Firm's governance, identify some rising young leaders in the Philadelphia office, mention the Firm's pro bono activities, note the advent of marketing by lawyers, and reflect on the impact of evolving technology at the Firm.

As Chapter 19 ended, so did the age of the Quadriviri. They had run the Firm since 1971, took it national and international, and quintupled its size. ML&B had enjoyed Saturnian times. But Thomas Lefevre left the Firm in 1979 to head UGI, and Robert Young and Park Dilks withdrew from management in 1988. Only William Curtin, the youngest of the Gang of Four, remained.

When W. James MacIntosh stepped down in 1971, the partners thought another single senior partner would surely succeed him. By the same token, they thought another Gang of Four, or some other modest number, would surely succeed the Quadriviri in the late 1980s. Considering the Firm's size, no one expected a reversion to one-lawyer rule. Also, considering the Firm's accomplishments during the Quadriviri period, it was certainly hoped that another such group would emerge. But instead, between 1988 and 1993, a much broader form of governance evolved. The Executive Committee, which had grown from eight to twelve partners between 1971 and 1990, became a Governing Board in 1990, numbering about seventeen. It included the chairs of the five major office management committees, the chairs of five practice sections, and members-at-large. The old four-partner Management Committee was rechristened an Executive Committee and given jurisdiction over conflicts and sensitive personnel questions.

The new Governing Board was more democratic than the Quadriviri, just as they had been more democratic than a single senior partner. There were even complaints about too much democracy: Where everybody is responsible, nobody is responsible. But on balance, the changes were healthy. Many lawyers became more involved in the Firm's operations. Committees largely honorary during the Quadriviri years actually met and took action. Still, the spread of democracy and decentralization admittedly slowed consensus building and diluted the authority of the Firm's chairman, by this time called the chair. Curtin held that office in 1988-89 for the last time. He was followed in 1990-91 by Samuel Fortenbaugh, discussed in Chapter 21.

Alan Lyndal Reed then served as chair in 1992-93. His father had been a career foreign service officer stationed at various times in Havana, Madrid, Brussels, Rome, and Buenos Aires. Reed's two siblings were born abroad, and he would have been born in Havana had his parents not insisted on "one native-born American child." So his mother went to Washington for his delivery in 1933. He has childhood recollections of 1937 to 1940 in Rome, where he heard Mussolini address throngs in the Piazza Venezia and recalls the fanfare over a visit by Hitler. Reed attended boarding school in Washington and subsequently The Hill School, from which he graduated in 1951. A fine athlete, he was active in football, wrestling, and tennis in prep school, as well as at Williams College, from which he graduated in 1955. He and Fortenbaugh were college classmates.

After college, Reed spent three years as a naval officer, including fifteen months as a communications intelligence officer in the Taiwan Defense Command at Taipei and a year as an air intelligence officer at Moffett Field near San Francisco. At his latter post, his job was to "brief bomber pilots about their designated targets in Communist China or Siberia if the 'big bell' ever rang." Fortunately, it never did.

While in the navy, Reed "fell in love with San Francisco" and intended to return there after his three years at Harvard Law School, which he recalls as "not enjoyable." However, during the summer following his second year of law school, he house-sat at his brother's home in Paoli, a suburb of Philadelphia. He also worked that summer at ML&B, which he chose after "research made clear that ML&B was the Philadelphia firm with the best reputation outside Philadelphia, so when I later interviewed firms in San Francisco or elsewhere they would be more impressed."[1]

That summer in Philadelphia was a revelation to Reed about law practice and living in Philadelphia. Consequently, when Ernest von Starck gave him twenty-four hours to accept an offer then outstanding from the Firm, he opted for Philadelphia on grounds that "San Francisco was a great place for singles, but Philadelphia was a far better place for raising a family." His starting salary at the Firm in 1961 was $6,600.

Initially, Reed was assigned to the litigation section, handling discovery matters for the Reading Company in FELA cases. He also worked in the trade regulation area, monitoring a long criminal antitrust trial involving the bread industry. (Client Stroehmann Bakeries, Inc., had already pleaded nolo contendere and was awaiting sentencing, so it was important to know what the other defendants were saying about Stroehmann.) Reed also acquired some expertise in bankruptcy matters before being approached by von Starck and Young to join the public utility section. (It was renamed the government regulation section in 1972.) When Reed said the move was agreeable but he also wanted to do corporate work, von Starck replied: "I don't understand your interest in corporate work—it's just cutting and pasting."

Reed's early experience in the government regulation section included assignments for long-time clients Philadelphia Suburban Water Company and American Water Works Company. He also handled motor-carrier applications generated by Pop Shertz's arrival at the Firm in 1961, as recounted in Chapter 15. From being "Young's bag carrier," Reed graduated to trying water rate cases and eventually took charge of all the Firm's rate-making practice, succeeding Young as chair of the government regulation section and as the Firm's partner responsible for its century-old relationship with Philadelphia Electric Company. Over the years, major clients developed by Reed included Safeguard Scientifics, Inc., Severn Trent (U.S.), Inc., and O'Brien Environmental Energy, Inc.

As chair, Reed remarked that the main challenge was to implement decisions, however difficult, arrived at by the Firm's leadership. In doing so, he was aided by Jay (Jerry) Calvert. Calvert succeeded Clive Anderson as managing partner in 1988 and served under chairs Curtin, Fortenbaugh, and Reed during the ensuing five years. Calvert had attended Amherst College, where he played lacrosse, and then chose the University of Virginia Law School for its "relaxed atmosphere." Although headed for "rural practice," he wanted first to sample urban life with a large firm. Becoming an ML&B associate in 1970, he soon took a one-year leave to work with Community Legal Services where he "spent some time suing Firm clients." Calvert returned to the Firm as a litigator, assisting John Lewis in Curtis Publishing Company matters and von Starck in antitrust cases, including the representation of Twentieth Century Fox Corporation. He subsequently figured prominently in major litigation for Penn Central Corporation, Fund of Funds, Philadelphia Electric, and Exxon Company, U.S.A. He also inherited responsibility from Young for Independence Blue Cross. As managing partner, he was, as he put it, "the Firm's first lawyer asked officially to spend full time managing." Considering his tirelessness, full time meant 3,000 hours a year.

■ ■ ■ ■ ■

That no obvious successors emerged to the Gang of Four may derive from an embarrassment of riches. During the Quadriviri years, the Firm's practice had broadened. Consequently, by the late 1980s, many younger partners enjoyed extensive client followings, compared with just a few previous rainmakers who towered over the rest. Some of those younger partners outside Philadelphia have already been recognized: Stephanie Abramson, Alan Neuwirth, John Peloso, and George Stohner in New York; Caswell Hobbs, Charles O'Connor, John Quarles, Harry Rissetto, and John Shenefield in Washington; Michael Klowden and John Hartigan in Los Angeles; Bennett Falk and Peter Hurtgen in Miami; and Charles Lubar in London.

In addition, at least thirteen younger partners in Philadelphia deserve special mention: one in the tax section, one in the government regulation section, eight in the business and finance section, and three in the labor section. The tax lawyer was Robert Comfort; and the government regulation lawyer, Kenneth Myers. Especially prominent younger members of the business and finance section in Philadelphia included Howard Shecter, David King, James Jennings, Howard Meyers, William Doran, Lawrence Berger, Michael Bloom, and Edward Cloues. Among Philadelphia's labor section lawyers, three will be noted here: Mark Dichter, Francis Milone, and Timothy O'Reilly.

Comfort always wanted to be a tax lawyer. After serving as a

United States Supreme Court clerk, he joined the Firm in 1978 and eleven years later became manager of the tax section, fielding questions in his specialty from all over the Firm. No matter how arcane the inquiry, Comfort's responses were always prompt, clear, and compelling.

By comparison, Myers ended up in a field not even imagined when he was in law school. Trained at the Massachusetts Institute of Technology as an electrical engineer, he became a lawyer, joined the Firm in 1968, and was assigned to the public utility section. Myers's career changed when MacIntosh read a newspaper report about Earth Day 1970 and decided that clients might eventually need help with environmental matters. MacIntosh wrote a memo to von Starck, who bucked it to Young, who bucked it to Myers, then an associate. Since Myers could not buck the memo further, he became the Firm's first environmental lawyer. He continued to function within the public utility section which, as he put it, "tussled in those days with the widest range of governmental licensing and regulatory programs." Profiting from his engineering background, Myers handled environmental cases over the years for Philco Ford, Cities Service, Oscar Mayer, and more recently for Cookson America, Inc., and SmithKline Beecham.

Among the younger Philadelphia business and finance partners, Shecter was an outstanding performer. He managed the section starting in 1990, was the Firm's managing partner from 1979 to 1982, and chaired the Executive Committee in 1985. An expert in mergers and acquisitions, his clients included the Brand Companies; Charming Shoppes, Inc; American Integrity Corporation; Union Pacific Corp.; and Norsk Hydro A.S.

King was one of Shecter's protégés. He also apprenticed under MacIntosh in venture capital situations. They set his destiny: He later came to head the Firm's venture capital practice, handling matters for both emerging businesses and investors. His clients included Legg Mason Corp.; Cephalon, Inc.; Intermagnetics General; and CSS Industries, Inc.; as well as long-time Firm client Enterra Corporation after it was spun off by Philadelphia Suburban Corporation.

Jennings was also active in the business and finance section's management. He inherited responsibility for such established Firm clients as Janney Montgomery Scott; E. F. Houghton & Co. (subsequently Houghton International, Inc.); LFC Financial Corp.; and Provident Mutual Life Insurance Company. In addition, he took charge of the Firm's relationship with Rhône-Poulenc Rorer, a $3.2-

billion combination of the French chemical conglomerate and the Rorer Group, a suburban Philadelphia-based pharmaceutical company famous for Maalox.

Meyers, who also had a hand in managing the business and finance section, was a Young protégé. With Young, Meyers handled transactions for Buckeye Pipe Line Company and Exide Corporation, assuming responsibility for those clients after Young's retirement. Meyers masterminded the 1986 spin-off of Buckeye from Penn Central Corporation. The transaction involved $540 million in debt and equity, together with a public offering of master limited partnership interests. Buckeye's assets included 40,000 rights-of-way. They had to be identified and transferred with myriad regulatory approvals to newly formed operating partnerships.[2]

Two partners, Doran and Berger, were associated with the municipal and banking subsections, respectively, of the business and finance section. Doran's main client was SEI Corporation. By 1993, it managed $40 billion of assets and functioned as the main provider of data processing services for banks and trust departments throughout the United States. Doran's introduction to SEI was roundabout. In 1968, SEI's founder, a young Wharton MBA candidate, told his father he needed a lawyer in Philadelphia. The father contacted Thomas S. Gates, Jr., a former secretary of the navy and then chairman of Morgan Guaranty Trust Company. Gates knew of ML&B through *his* late father, who had been a Drexel partner, chairman of the University of Pennsylvania, and a client of William Clarke Mason, as noted in Chapter 2. Gates recommended Arthur Littleton, who in turn assigned young associate Doran to create SEI.

While Doran handled one of the Firm's newest clients from the start, Berger did the opposite when he inherited responsibility from Dilks for one of the Firm's oldest clients, CoreStates Bank, N. A., formerly Philadelphia National Bank. In addition, he represented Chase Home Mortgage Corporation in designing and documenting new mortgage products. He also succeeded to the Firm's long-time relationship with the Franklin Institute and represented the institute when it received its final distribution in 1993 from the estate of Benjamin Franklin, who died more than two centuries earlier.

Bloom arrived laterally at the Philadelphia office in 1988, just in time to capitalize on what he forgivably called "the bloom" in his bankruptcy and reorganization specialty. "Starting in 1989, it was like being an emergency room surgeon in triage. They just kept bringing in the bodies." His diverse practice included representing Apollo Investment Fund in an exchange of debt for equity, leading to the takeover of Interco Incorporated (with brand names including Florsheim, Converse, Lane, and Broyhill); debtors like Mortgage & Realty Trust and Motor Freight Express in Chapter 11 cases; major creditors of Lomas Financial Corporation, Continental Airlines, and Circle K; and official creditors and equity committees in bankruptcy proceedings involving Carter Hawley Hale, Wall to Wall Sound & Video, and Record World. Bloom also served for many years as chairman of the legal ethics and professional responsibility committee of the Pennsylvania Bar Association. When continuing legal education became mandatory in Pennsylvania, he found himself giving formal courses for credit on legal ethics. ML&B lawyers were among his students.

While many partners spent significant time on the operations of the 170-lawyer business and finance section, Edward Cloues regarded as a distraction anything but day-to-day law practice. His main client was K-Tron International, the world's largest manufacturer of precision feeders and blenders. But his practice was diversified: Once, while representing a joint venturer in a gold mining enterprise, he attended a meeting in a small Utah town (population 200) to negotiate with Mormons. His client had warned that Mormons were generally suspicious of lawyers and particularly of Philadelphia lawyers. So Cloues wore his oldest clothes, including jeans with a hole in one knee. His client later reported how relieved the Mormons were that "the Philadelphia lawyer didn't show up."

Turning to Philadelphia's labor section, surely Mark Dichter was its highest-profile partner. Already mentioned in connection with the *Bulletin* and the Philadelphia Orchestra, Dichter's clients included General Motors, General Electric, International Paper, Boise Cascade, ARCO, Aon Corporation, and GTE. As one of the country's leading employment discrimination lawyers, Dichter became immersed in the fallout from corporate downsizing starting in the 1980s. Even employees in high-ranking positions became vulnerable, and Dichter regularly defended major employers against claims brought by discharged professionals, executives, and investment bankers.

One of Dichter's many jury trials was presented on *Court TV* in 1992—the first time an ML&B lawyer was so featured. His client was General Motors (GM), and the case involved an age discrimination claim asserted by a fifty-five-year-old zone manager whose employment GM had terminated. The trial lasted a week and a half, and portions of it were shown on television over a four-day period. Dichter especially recalls the voir dire during which several prospective jurors were excused who complained about the quality of their

GM cars. One said he could not be fair and objective "if GM treated its employees the way it treats its cars." Despite this inauspicious start, the jury returned a verdict for GM.

Two other prominent labor lawyers in the Philadelphia office were Francis Milone and Timothy O'Reilly. Milone was a nationally recognized employment discrimination litigator whose clients included Cigna Corporation and Unisys Corporation. O'Reilly numbered among his representations Stroehmann Bakeries, Inc. (originally a Souser client); Delaware County; and the Philadelphia Eagles Football Club, Inc.

■ ■ ■ ■ ■

Lawyers have always done pro bono work. Going back to the turn of the century, it is Firm lore that CEM never turned down a worthy cause, despite the disapproval of Morris Bockius. CEM's causes involved the downtrodden—needy persons who simply walked in off the street or got his name and looked him up. He also served on Philadelphia's Board of Education and Board of City Trusts.

In addition to good works by individual practitioners, every major law firm then had its cultural and charitable clients, particularly hospitals, that were rarely charged for legal services. But after World War II, many such organizations underwent radical changes. Some grew beyond recognition, came to dwarf traditional clients, and grappled with the same problems as large commercial enterprises. Law firms began sending them bills.

As some nonprofit institutions ceased to be pro bono clients, the spotlight shifted to public-interest causes. Many were triggered by increasing civil rights awareness, starting in the 1960s. Lawyers and the courts had once been regarded as luxuries, not necessities. But the post-World War II era saw heightened expectations. As new rights were defined and old ones vitalized, lawyers and the courts had to be made accessible to the general public, including those who could not pay. How should major law firms address these issues? While senior partners dithered, younger lawyers acted. With a passion for equality and justice, arriving law school graduates forced their firms to reach out for causes. ML&B did so sporadically starting in the late 1960s. In 1971, a milestone was passed when Richard Brown convinced MacIntosh that ML&B should become a frontrunner among major law firms in the area of public-interest law.

Also in 1971, Joseph Torregrossa arrived as an associate. With the Firm's encouragement, he spent much of his time on civil rights matters, organized the Firm's pro bono efforts, and by the 1990s coordinated almost $4 million of time spent annually on such causes. Immediately after his arrival at the Firm, he and his wife (who dedicated her legal career solely to serving the poor), with the support of the Firm's litigation section, began work on *Goosby v. Osser.*[3] Reaching the Supreme Court in 1973, it decided that Pennsylvania could not withhold voting rights from persons awaiting trial in prison because they were unable to raise bail or were charged with nonbailable offenses.[4]

What Brown urged, MacIntosh approved, and Torregrossa exemplified, spread rapidly to the Firm's other offices in the 1970s. Unlike law firms that informally permitted pro bono work, ML&B formally prescribed it. Structures were put in place, time records kept, credit given, and the same enthusiasm accorded it as ML&B's regular practice. Other firms caught up in the 1980s when Republican administrations reduced the funding and purview of public legal-service programs, thus obliging the private sector to fill the void. By the late 1980s, even the legal press was tracking the pro bono activities of major law firms.

In recent years, the Firm has served the public interest in scores of causes involving indigents; the homeless; the elderly; battered women; unwed mothers; women in military service; abused children; handicapped and exceptional children; children in custody disputes; day care centers; food banks; housing discrimination; slum rehabilitation; illegal hospital confinement; public asylum petitions; death-row appeals; nature conservancies; and First Amendment cases. Running the gamut, some matters achieved high visibility: a political asylum case for a Chinese who played a leadership role in that country's pro-democracy political movement; a Court of Claims case for reinstatement of an air force officer discharged because he expressed reservations about America's nuclear policy; a case holding that confinement on bread and water violated Article 55 of the Uniform Code of Military Justice; a landmark settlement in massive housing discrimination matters for the Fair Housing Council of Greater Washington; and even an obscenity case.

Not surprisingly, the obscenity case drew the widest media attention. Decided by the United States District Court for the Central District of California, the case held that the National Endowment for the Arts (NEA), having awarded a grant to client Bella Lewitzky Dance Foundation, had no power to withhold the grant when the Foundation declined to certify that the funds would not be used "to promote . . . materials which in the judgment of the [NEA] . . . may be considered obscene." The court struck down the certification provision as vague in violation of the Fifth Amendment, adding that it had a chilling effect in violation of the First Amendment.[5] The Justice Department filed no appeal, and subsequently the NEA dropped the pledge requirement—a complete victory for the Firm.

By 1993, more than half the Firm's lawyers were participating in its public interest programs. CEM would presumably be pleased (Bockius might not), while marveling at the variety of the causes espoused.

■ ■ ■ ■ ■

In recent years, it has been necessary for lawyers not only to champion the downtrodden but also their own interests. Formerly, lawyers could not advertise, and it was considered wicked for a dignified law firm to extol its virtues to anyone not already a client. At cocktail parties, lawyers in major firms might identify themselves as lawyers, but they rarely mentioned their firms unless asked. And, of course, they did not sell their own or their firm's expertise. Ambulance chasing was unsavory, no matter how subtle.

Then came the Supreme Court's holding in *Bates v. State Bar of Arizona* allowing lawyers to advertise. Decided in 1977, the vote was five to four. Among the dissenters, Justice Powell wrote: "[T]oday's decision will effect profound changes in the practice of law, viewed for centuries as a learned profession."[6] He was right.

Following *Bates*, domestic relations and negligence practitioners lost no time. They glorified themselves on radio and television, in the Yellow Pages, and by transit ads. At first, the major firms did nothing. Competition among them remained discreet, never overt, with each continuing to enjoy a stable coterie of loyal clients. But as the 1980s wore on, clients increasingly shopped and divided their legal work among firms, often on the basis of bids and beauty contests. The time had finally come, more than two centuries after Adam Smith, for the legal profession to enter the marketplace.

Arthur Littleton had been the Firm's senior partner from 1957 through 1966. That saintly man would have agreed with Justice Powell's dictum and been repelled by any hint of commercialism in the profession. But by 1976, a year before *Bates*, the Quadriviri sensed what was in the wind when they formed a Firm Practice Committee. As noted in Chapter 19, it was a means by which the Gang of Four—on or off the Executive Committee—ran the Firm.

Still, its justification was the need, recognized for the first time, to study the Firm's clientele and determine how to expand it. This included taking positive steps to supersede other firms through "cross-selling," an expression that committee member von Starck, reflecting traditional thinking, found "embarrassing."

A decade later, there would be no embarrassment. Major firms, including ML&B, embarked upon programs to alert the business community to their particular areas of expertise. Vehicles included client seminars, newsletters, white papers, client receptions, and firm brochures. Words like "marketing" and "practice development" that troubled von Starck and would have appalled Littleton became standard vernacular.

By 1986, the burdens of client development were too heavy for the Firm's busy partners to bear in their spare time. Luckily, Stacy West was fascinated by the challenge. An associate in the Philadelphia office's government regulation section, she presented a proposal: She would cease to practice law and devote herself full time to Firm promotion. The Executive Committee knew it was crossing a Rubicon when it accepted her offer and engaged her as the Firm's first Director of Client Relations. Her job was difficult: She had to raise the visibility of the Firm to the outside world, as well as convince many reluctant ML&B lawyers to promote their skills.

When West left the Firm in 1992 to raise a family, there was general agreement that she had done a difficult job well. In her final year, ML&B held fourteen seminars in six cities attended by 1,500 clients and "friends" of the Firm; it published five specialized news periodicals with mailing lists of up to 11,000; it issued 180 pieces of literature for use in presentations describing the Firm's practice; and it published ninety white papers, speeches, and articles concerning important legal developments. In addition, during her incumbency, over 3,500 references to the Firm appeared in domestic and foreign media.

Still, other firms did more. With its conservative traditions, ML&B was hardly a leader in the marketing revolution.

■ ■ ■ ■ ■

The Firm adjusted more easily to the information revolution, as technology literally exploded in the 1980s. When the Firm was founded back in 1873, information was exchanged in person or by written words using steel-tipped pens. There were no telephones or typewriters. By the 1890s, both were prevalent. Letter presses and then carbon paper made possible the copying of written communications. After World War II, wet photocopying machines came and went, followed by xerography. The paper industry prospered, since lawyers always want more copies of everything than they need.

Also after World War II, early data processing machines, some using punch cards, invaded accounting departments and helped lawyers keep time records. According to William Zeiter, ML&B was "drowning in IBM cards by the 1970s, sending out for processing by a service bureau approximately twenty cartons—200,000 cards— each and every month." In 1978, the Firm replaced punch cards with scanners that read time sheets. It also acquired its first mainframe computer and brought its information system in-house. Now, for the first time, the back office could generate any data desired. Information flowed until it clogged lawyers' desks and briefcases. As in Disney's adaptation of the *Sorcerer's Apprentice,* mops and buckets kept multiplying.

The revolution extended to the front office as well. Beginning in the 1950s, manual typewriters were replaced by electric ones, some with easy correcting devices. Then, in 1977, the Firm also created a centralized word processing system. But this was nothing compared with word processing by personal computers at secretarial workstations. The first were installed by the Firm in 1986. They also multiplied like mops and buckets, and soon every secretary had one. Originally, the function of personal computers was simply to increase secretarial output, like typewriters. But unlike typewriters, they also made their way into lawyers' offices.

Actually, personal computers reached some lawyers' offices before they reached secretarial stations. In 1980, Robert Bildersee joined the Firm laterally. An expert in employee benefit law, he brought with him his computer and an extraordinary database compiled over many years. Other lawyers, especially in bank lending and real estate, saw the possibilities, acquired their own computers, and built databases in their fields. When they asked the Firm for reimbursement, the answer was no. If one was reimbursed, others would request computers, and eventually every lawyer would want one. What could be more ludicrous than every lawyer with a computer!

This was the state of affairs until 1986 when, again according to Zeiter, "the dam broke because young associates began using their modest savings to buy computers, which then cost $5,000, instead of household furniture." From refusing to reimburse anyone, the Firm agreed to furnish a computer to every lawyer who requested one. Almost all did, and by 1993 there were 1,700 personal computers throughout the Firm.[7]

Now, for the first time in the history of the legal profession, attorneys at their workstations could retrieve vast libraries of information without leaving their desks or even rising from their chairs. Using their computers, they could do research, write briefs, compose opinions, draft documents, and transmit them electronically within or outside the Firm. Moreover, when they left their desks, they could carry their gear with them. Computers, printers, and telephones were now portable: Lawyers began arriving at courts and bargaining tables linked to huge data bases. They were formidable combatants.

What long-term effects will this technological revolution have on the legal profession? For one thing, it has been suggested that the practice of law will become paperless. But the paperless office is an idea whose time has already passed. As more hard copy can be produced, more is produced. Human beings prefer the tangible. Also, like pack rats, they collect things.

Another suggestion is that lawyers and law firms may fade away. (Clients will presumably survive but be called something else.) These possibilities have an alluring simplicity, especially for those who dislike lawyers. But neither is apt to occur.

Instead of rendering lawyers extinct, technology will probably multiply their number. Human beings are obsessed with their behavior and its regulation. Mature societies, while espousing freedom, require ever more regulation. And more regulation generates an even greater demand for lawyers.

Nor will law firms fade away. Lawyers need to solve problems by analyzing them with other lawyers. Two, three, or more minds will remain better than one. Specialties as yet unimagined will be hatched, requiring constantly larger networks of lawyers to service client needs. Moreover, firms will grow geographically as practices become increasingly global. Back offices will also thrive and generate still more data, while also supporting the growing technology used by front offices.[8]

Beside burgeoning, future law firms will also be more stratified. With information readily at their fingertips, nonlawyers will perform many functions formerly reserved for lawyers. Less experienced lawyers will generate information packages for use by more experienced lawyers. And the most seasoned lawyers of all will continue to spot the critical issues, ask the telling questions in the courtroom, and organize the discussion at the bargaining table. Wisdom will remain beyond the grasp of machinery.

So exploding technology will not wipe out lawyers and the legal profession. Instead, the contrary is likely to be true, leading to the inquiry: How did lawyers ever function before computers, and even before telephones and typewriters? But even to pose that question exalts form over substance: Messers Morgan and Lewis seem to have functioned very well.

CHAPTER 41

LEARNING ABOUT NUMBERS

Troelsch lectures the partners ■ A gentlemen's profession ■ Charging like a carpenter ■ A gracious ritual ■ Billing nights ■ Trifling with lawyers ■ Cash flow ■ Expenses in 1917 ■ The revolution in associate salaries ■ No free lunch ■ Hours, rates, and profits ■ A banner year in 1920 ■ $100 million of revenue in 1986 ■ $200 million in 1990 ■ Numbers for the public ■ Reexamining commitments ■ Demise of the allocation list ■ A fair division ■ Wiser and sadder

Reference has already been made in Chapter 5 to Kitty Mulligan/Munshower, who knew everything about the files. She came to the Firm in 1923 and retired in 1970. Her counterpart in the Firm's accounting department was Louis Troelsch, who actually *was* the accounting department. Unlike Mulligan/Munshower (seldom called by her first name), who was patient and slow-moving, Troelsch (always called Louie) was impatient and moved at a half trot. He was, as one longtime secretary put it, "always two minutes from a fit."[1] He arrived in 1926 and retired in 1967. Every lawyer saw him at least once a month because he delivered the pay and draw checks. He was treated with respect mingled with fear. After all, he had been hired by Morris Bockius, knew more inside information about the Firm than anyone, had seniority over almost everyone, and was indispensable.

When Troelsch joined the Firm, all accounting entries were made by hand in cash books, ledgers, and journals. He made them. There were sixteen lawyers, and revenue totaled $414,000. When he retired, there were eighty-six lawyers, and revenue totaled $5.1 million. The era of the computer had begun, but Troelsch was still the heart of the back office.

On his retirement, Troelsch was invited to join the partners at their annual Union League dinner. No nonpartner in memory had been so honored. It was intended that he be mentioned during the proceedings and rise gratefully to receive his clock or other token of the Firm's esteem. But it did not happen quite that way. He *was* mentioned, he *did* rise, and he *did* receive his token. But then he remained on his feet, berating the partners for being so inattentive to accounting functions over the years. The first few minutes of Troelsch's diatribe were greeted with good humor. It was vintage Troelsch. But as he continued, the partners cast embarrassed glances at one another. Arthur Littleton, then the senior partner, rose on the theory that Troelsch was finished or should be finished. But he was not finished, so Littleton sat down. By the time Troelsch ceased venting his frustrations, the partners were appropriately chastised.

Troelsch had a point. While lawyers enjoy receiving their pay or draw checks, they do not enjoy keeping track of their time and expenses. Nor do they enjoy billing and collecting. Their resistance to billing and collecting may have a historical basis. The law was once a gentleman's profession, and gentlemen did not sully their hands with money. In ancient Rome, lawyers were forbidden to charge for their services. They did very well by subterfuge, as Cicero demonstrated.

The same was true of early English lawyers. With the demise of ordeal by fire or water, someone might defend a friend against the king's writ. Obviously the friend, being a friend, did not charge. In later centuries, that friend became a barrister, and the fiction continued that his services were untainted by coin of the realm. Indeed, barristers would not even discuss money. That was done by their clerks. So it remains today.

What should be the basis for a lawyer's charges? Abraham Lincoln regarded time as a lawyer's stock in trade. Presumably that means charging by the hour. Littleton demurred, saying that if he had wished to charge by the hour, he would have been a carpenter. He was not demeaning carpenters. He was merely suggesting that lawyers add value beyond completion of the job in accordance with the plans and specifications.

The Firm kept no time records through the mid-1940s, as noted in Chapter 10. Primitive records began to be maintained in the late 1940s, although many partners spurned timekeeping as unprofessional and offensive. Starting in the 1950s, time records became compulsory. They were submitted in longhand and posted the same way. "The lawyers kicked and screamed," according to Howard Kellogg. On the last day of the year, one partner recalled "composing and submitting five months of time sheets." Obviously, the time he reported bore little resemblance to the actual time. But neither did the bills in those days.

Before billings were based on time records, they were based on trust and relationships, which seem to have been more robust in times past. For example, in the early 1950s when William Clarke Mason managed the Firm's engagement by the Philadelphia National Bank, the Firm charged for most of its services to the bank in a lump sum each year. It is doubtful if time records determined that sum. Nor was there much explanation, since the bills merely referred to "services rendered." The ritual was gracious. Mason made his annual trip to see Frederic A. Potts, then CEO of the bank. Mason would hand Potts an envelope, saying, "Mr. Potts, I am delivering to you our Firm's statement for services rendered beyond the retainer last year." Potts would respond, "Thank you, Mr. Mason, I will see that it is paid."

Billing was a low-priority item even during the spit-and-polish Bockius years. The Firm's archives refer to "billing nights." On two evenings each year, the lawyers (who normally were in the office anyway) and their secretaries (who normally were not) turned their attention to billing. Then toward year-end, Troelsch would tell Bockius how the revenue stood, which clients were overdue for billing, and which clients were indebted to the Firm. If necessary, a few more bills could be sent and a few telephone calls made.

A relaxed attitude toward bills was possible in those days for two reasons. First, client relationships were such that lawyers' bills would generally be paid whenever they were rendered, timely or otherwise. Clients held their lawyers in some awe. Lawyers were not to be trifled with, much less stiffed. But today, lawyers are as apt to be stiffed as other creditors. They fight back by suing clients. Unimpressed, clients assert counterclaims for malpractice, almost as frivolous as they are automatic. Indeed, malpractice claims of all kinds are so prevalent these days that the professional career of the average lawyer will be marked by about three of them, and this number will surely increase if the present trend continues. Better to be feared than loved, exhorted Machiavelli. Long ago, lawyers gave up being loved, but at least they were feared. Now, they may be neither.

The second reason for relaxed billings and collections in former times was dramatically lower expense ratios. Lawyers need revenue to pay their expenses. If their expenses are modest, they are working largely for themselves, and they can bill and collect as they see fit. But if their expenses are substantial, they need more revenue and they need it faster. It is a question of cash flow.

There is a rule of thumb these days that about 65 percent of a large law firm's revenue goes to pay its expenses, with the rest available to the partners as net income. But the ratios were very different years ago. The first year for which the Firm's financial records still exist is 1913. Expenses were lumped, and the expense ratio was 15 percent. For 1917, a breakout of expenses has survived; it shows that the ratio was 13 percent. Revenue was $244,385 that year, and expenses were $31,873. Of these, the bulk was for salaries and wages, amounting to $16,680. There were six partners and five associates. In those days, according to W. James MacIntosh, each partner and senior associate had a secretary. (The newer associates scrambled.) So the Firm probably had about nine secretaries, plus a bookkeeper, and perhaps a receptionist. Apparently, five associates, nine secretaries, a bookkeeper, and a receptionist shared $16,680 of compensation, worth $189,000 in 1993. Quite a feat. Incidentally, the six partners divided net income of $212,511, for an average per-partner profit of $35,418, worth $401,000 in 1993.

While all expenses have increased over the years, associate salaries have climbed meteorically. Formerly, young lawyers sought clerkships. They were apprentices learning their trade and were grateful to their mentors for the opportunity. Any payments they received were due to their mentors' generosity. It was also recognized that their output might be of little value to their mentors' clients. W. James MacIntosh said the starting salary in 1926 was $1,200, worth $9,800 in 1993. Robert Young remembered that in 1948 it was $3,300, worth $19,900 in 1993. A century earlier, there were negative starting salaries. Clerks paid their preceptors for the privilege of "reading law."

Associates' salaries exploded in 1968. Conventional wisdom holds that the Wall Street firms needed ever more associates but simply could not find them, as the best and brightest rejected business law practice and embraced causes and public-interest work. It was a time when traditional icons were being smashed—the critical year of anti-Vietnam war protests, the civil rights movement, the generation gap, and antiestablishment activism. But the establishment was as savvy as it was suspect. It bet that many young lawyers, despite their idealism, would succumb to the lure of really big money. So that year, starting salaries for New York associates were raised 58 percent from $9,500 to $15,000, worth $62,500 in 1993. Firms outside New York made comparable adjustments. The trend went nationwide for two decades, as law firms seemed insatiable for lawyers during the 1970s and 1980s.

Philosophers seek eternal verities. They find few they can agree upon. Laymen are more successful. They have correctly identified the inevitability of death and taxes, the swinging of the pendulum, and the illusion of the free lunch. If there is no free lunch, something has to give to support higher associate salaries. In fact, three things give. Associates support themselves by working more hours. Clients support them by paying higher rates for their time. And partners support them by sharing with them a larger percentage of the revenue. These three phenomena have profoundly affected the practice of law in recent years.

First, more hours. When the author came laterally to ML&B in 1961, he was told by another associate: "There is absolutely no pressure for hours—they are only interested in quality." More than thirty years later, the Firm is still interested in quality. But in 1961, the number of billable hours logged by associates averaged only 1,350. Beginning in the 1970s, as associates' salaries increased, firms could not be satisfied with such low time inputs. Financial types began doing computations. If an associate's overhead and direct and indirect payroll costs were totaled, how many hours of that associate's time would be required before any profit was realized by the firm? While these are elementary calculations, apparently no one bothered making them at the Firm until the late 1960s.

Second, higher rates. In 1961, the hourly rate for a new ML&B associate was $8, worth $39 in 1993. But by 1993, the hourly rates for starting associates at the Firm reached $80 to $100, depending upon the location of the office—different markets carried different rates. One effect of such high rates for starting associates was that clients demanded leaner staffing, or no junior associates at all. Another effect was to shorten the permissible learning curve of junior lawyers. To justify their rates, they had to specialize earlier. They also had to abbreviate that mystic process by which, over long periods, they absorbed the experience, perspective, and judgmental sensitivity of senior lawyers. Still another by-product of higher associates' rates was the proliferation of paralegal assistants. They are at their best in repetitive processes that do not require compre- hensive legal training.

Are today's associates worth their rates? In a free market, that is really not the question. The real question is whether clients will pay their rates. In the early 1960s, the author's hourly rate as a senior associate was raised from $24 to $28. He protested to Thomas Lefevre, "I am not worth $28, and clients won't pay it." Lefevre responded: "You're not worth it, but they *will* pay it." Thirty years later, many senior partners were charging more than ten times that rate. Clients continued to pay, and grumble.

Third, profit sharing. In addition to the contributions made to their higher salaries by associates in terms of more billable hours and by clients in terms of higher rates, there is the contribution made by the partners in terms of reduced net income. To pay associates the going rate and keep up with other expenses, the net incomes of some firms have declined sharply, leading them to fragment and sometimes disband altogether.

■ ■ ■ ■ ■

What has been the impact of these financial trends in the final analysis? Some historical highlights will tell the tale. As noted, the earliest year for which the Firm still retains even the most fragmentary financial records is 1913. Revenue was $130,000, the expense ratio was 15 percent, there were six partners, and the average per-partner profit was $18,000, worth $264,000 in 1993. The Firm had a banner year in 1920, when the average per-partner profit was $61,000, worth $442,000 in 1993. (Incidentally, the highest marginal tax bracket for someone making $61,000 in 1920 was 38 percent.) The Firm's last good year before the Depression was 1929, when the average per-partner profit was $42,000, worth $356,000 in 1993. Then came 1935, the worst year of the Depression for the Firm, when the average per-partner profit was $25,000, worth $265,000 in 1993.

The Firm's revenue did not pass the $1-million mark until 1945. It was an outstanding year, generating an average per-partner profit of $53,000, worth $430,000 in 1993. (Joy was no doubt tempered by then prevailing income tax rates: At $50,000, a taxpayer was already in the 70-percent bracket.) After modest growth during the 1950s and 1960s, the Firm expanded dramatically in the 1970s and 1980s, with revenue exceeding $100 million in 1986 and $200 million in 1990.

Curiously, the Firm's average per-partner profits were unaffected by its exploding top line. Expense ratios were the reason. They climbed from 15 percent in 1913, to 26 percent in 1945, to 41 percent in 1960, and to more than 60 percent today. Everything costs more: space, technology, and especially people. In inflation-adjusted dollars, direct and indirect payroll costs have increased tenfold for associates and fourfold for nonlawyers. (Indirect payroll costs were negligible in the early years.) Not only do people cost more, but there are also more of them, despite labor-saving technology. Presently, the Firm has 945 employees whose time is not billed. This compares with 734 timekeepers, comprising 254 partners, 353 associates, 29 of counsel and 98 paralegal assistants. Obviously, there has been a redistribution of the wealth. It has been driven by supply and demand, higher skills, and increased egalitarianism. And its effect has been that partners at ML&B and comparable large law firms have generally run in place during most of the century, despite ever-expanding operations and the illusion of progress conferred by inflation. But even in place, it has been a good run.

■ ■ ■ ■ ■

What has just been written about the economics of law practice today is less remarkable than the fact that it has been written at all. It certainly would not have been written twenty years ago. In those days, every law firm's numbers were its own business. No one knew how other firms were doing, and no one tried to find out. Then came the information revolution, including the emergence of something called the legal press. It pandered to the morbid curiosity of lawyers about one another. Firm A was said to be doing well and Firm B was in trouble. Several years later, Firm B was said to be doing well and Firm A was in trouble. Lawyers vowed not to read such trash. But they could not resist. Nothing fascinated them more than the fortunes and misfortunes, real and imagined, of other law firms.

In 1985, the *American Lawyer* published its first survey of law-firm finances. ML&B provided no numbers, but putative numbers for the Firm appeared in the survey anyway. Several years later, dozens of the Firm's partners were called by the *American Lawyer* staff in an effort to find someone who would divulge the actual numbers. No one was found, but again putative numbers were published. Still, the *American Lawyer* was onto something. The numbers game was riveting. It was like the exception to the hearsay rule in which truth or falsity does not matter. Saying it suffices.

Over the years, ML&B's lawyers have become inured to hearing numbers every month about the Firm and to reading correct or incorrect numbers in the media about law firms generally. Quaint concepts of privacy and modesty have yielded to life in a fishbowl. Perhaps the Troelsch days were better. Only he and the senior partner worried about the numbers, leaving the other partners to practice law. During John Bracken's term as managing partner (1958-1972), he would announce that any partner could inspect the Firm's financial statements by coming to his office. No one came.

It is not that lawyers have only recently become interested in their finances. They were always interested. But before the information revolution, there was no basis for comparisons. Now the veils have been cast off and every law firm's finances, real or alleged, are public knowledge. As a result, short-term advantages have supplanted long-term objectives. The same malaise that afflicts American businesses—earnings per share as published quarterly—now afflicts American law firms. Lawyers who were committed to their firms are reexamining their commitments. Sometimes these reexaminations are based on questions of collegiality and client service. More often they are based on numbers.

■ ■ ■ ■ ■

One of ML&B's great blessings has been an allocation system in which its partners repose complete confidence. The seasoned partners elected to three-year terms on the Allocation Committee spend a month each year studying the financial data, visiting the Firm's major offices, and hearing from almost everyone about everyone. ML&B has no point system, and all evaluations are retrospective in the context of each partner's past history and likely future contribution.

How satisfied are the partners with their allocations? Through 1976, each partner received a list of every partner's allocation in descending order, as made before 1971 by the senior partner and later by the Allocation Committee. Partner X first looked at his number and swelled with pride. (It is permissible to say X looked at *his* number: Until 1980 all the partners were men.) X was doing just fine. Then X studied the list and noted the allocations of Y and Z, partners X barely knew. They were also doing fine. X was seized by doubt: Was it possible that Y and Z were overpaid or that X was underpaid? Considering the Firm's size, X was in no position to answer the question. The list had become an anachronism.

Then, in 1976, a relatively new lateral partner absentmindedly took home his copy of the list. (As embellished, the story is untrue: He did not tape it to his refrigerator door.) Somehow his wife saw it and, based on having met several other partners at a Firm social function, decided that compared with them her husband was undercompensated. She urged him to complain to his seniors. He did so sheepishly, invoking the ancient doctrine of spousal pressure. He got no more money, but he sealed the fate of the old list.

In 1977, the Firm scrapped the old list in favor of a streamlined procedure. Henceforth, X would be told how X had fared, how the Firm had fared, and the number of partners whose allocations fell within each $25,000 bracket. Individual names and numbers could be ascertained only by visiting an allocator or the chairman of the

Executive Committee and examining the official list. To hamper comparisons, the official list was arranged alphabetically instead of by amounts in descending order, and note-taking was proscribed. Only a handful of partners ever visited. Instead, there was general relief at the demise of the old list. X continued to be properly compensated and no longer felt threatened by Y and Z. The perception that allocations are fair remains one of the Firm's glories.

In recent years, lawyers have learned much about the economics of law practice, while watching a profession turn into a business. They are probably wiser, and certainly sadder.

CHAPTER 42

LEARNING ABOUT PEOPLE

Revolutionary changes ■ *Lawyers proliferate* ■ *Specializations narrow* ■ *Relationships erode* ■ *Bride for a year* ■ *The Firm's first partnership agreement in 1978* ■ *The brotherhood from cradle to grave* ■ *Jewish lawyers* ■ *African-American lawyers* ■ *Women lawyers* ■ *Problems with the quality of life* ■ *Information overload* ■ *Alienation and burnout* ■ *Management by nonlawyers* ■ *Going public* ■ *Lawyers as survivors* ■ *Horizontal structures* ■ *For their eccentricities as for their achievements* ■ *A golden age* ■ *Curiosity and nostalgia*

During its 120 years, ML&B has witnessed revolutionary changes in the way the law is practiced and in the kinds of people who practice it. Charles Eldridge Morgan, Jr., and Francis Draper Lewis would not recognize their profession or firm today.

Into the 1950s, it was still possible for a Philadelphia lawyer to know every other Philadelphia lawyer by name if not personally. The law was actually so insular that until 1968 Pennsylvania lawyers were admitted to practice in only a single county. Now, ML&B partners and associates are everywhere, all over the country and frequently abroad. Their paths converge in airports and train stations just as often as they see one another in their offices.

As lawyers have proliferated, specialties have narrowed, requiring more practitioners for a full-service firm. Small firms have become medium-sized, medium-sized firms have become large, and large firms have become megafirms. Size and specialization have begotten depersonalization both outside and inside law firms. There is presently no counterpart at ML&B to the outside relationships enjoyed by Morris Bockius with William McLean of the *Bulletin*, Thomas McCabe of Scott Paper Company, Samuel Vauclain of Baldwin Locomotive Works, Edward Stotesbury of Drexel & Co., and Joseph Wayne of Philadelphia National Bank. A lawyer who had such relationships was literally the CEO's alter ego. Today, few such lawyers exist. Moreover, CEOs themselves have become hired managers who come and go, instead of entrepreneurs who devote their lives to the businesses that personify them.

Inside ML&B, there have been parallel changes. Recall Chapter 18 and the infamous report of September 28, 1962, by which the Young Turks involved themselves in the Firm's long-range planning and incurred the wrath of their elders, at least until the glorious revolution of 1971. The report stated:

> The Committee doubts the future wisdom of indefinite and unlimited Firm expansion . . . there would be a loss to the members of the intimacy and collegiality which are now a valued part of professional life.

By 1962, even as the committee recorded its views, much intimacy had already been lost. Orvel Sebring was a first-year associate when he married in 1933. In a touching story, his wife recounted how she was, as she put it, "bride for a year," since all the partners regularly had the Sebrings to dinner and kept them well stocked with theater and concert tickets. Few people bother anymore. The brotherhood (not yet a sisterhood) that was once a law firm rarely survives as such today.[1]

One mark of that brotherhood was trust. Consequently, during the first sixty-eight years of the Firm's existence, it flourished without a partnership agreement. And even when, in 1941, the partners adopted a two-page "Memorandum of Agreement," it comprised a single paragraph simply reiterating the historic prerogative of the senior partner to determine what amount, if any, the partnership would pay for the interest of a deceased partner. (The partners did not need the reiteration, which was really aimed at the taxing authorities.) It was not until 1978 that William Zeiter prepared and the partners executed a document resembling a comprehensive partnership agreement. By then, brotherhoods were becoming businesses. Trust was no longer enough.

There were other marks of the law-firm brotherhood in the old days, at least in Philadelphia. One was the likelihood that lawyers accepted as associates would one day become partners. Another was that as partners they would be compensated as much by reference to their seniority as their achievements. In effect, they were tenured as partners and remained with their firms as long as they wanted. Their colleagues would support them even after they had ceased to be productive lawyers. For the anointed, a law firm was a partner's family, and the legal profession extended virtually from cradle to grave.

Little of this remains in major law firms today. Now, associates are more likely *not* to become partners than the other way around. And if they become partners, they discover that seniority counts for little and merit for much. Also, the day will come when they must retire, ready or not, to make way for the next generation. Moreover, they may find themselves involuntarily terminated long before retirement if they are deemed insufficiently productive.

■ ■ ■ ■ ■

The former brotherhood, while comfortable for the anointed, had a baser side: To be Jewish, African-American, or a woman was virtually disqualifying. Fortunately, that shameful situation has changed dramatically in recent times, as inroads have been made against discrimination. It is unlikely that the Firm's newer lawyers have any idea how the profession has been transformed since World War II. Today, that transformation is taken for granted. It would be well to review it.

When that war ended, there were gentile and Jewish law firms in Philadelphia, and almost no African-Americans or women in the major ones. The situation of the Jewish lawyer was preposterous. Unlike African-Americans and women, there was no shortage of Jewish lawyers. From millennia of construing Talmudic law, Jews obviously had a proclivity for the legal profession.

But at least in Philadelphia, Jewish lawyers generally exercised that proclivity with other Jewish lawyers. Just after World War II, a Jewish lawyer arrived as an associate at the firm (not ML&B) where the author clerked. That firm's senior partner suggested the young man avoid offending gentile clients by not being too visible. An appalling story today. But not then. Indeed, that senior partner was proud to be a libertarian: He had actually reached out to hire his firm's first Jewish lawyer.

The first Jewish lawyer at ML&B arrived through the back door. He was Henry Gross. Born in Lithuania in 1877 and hired by the Firm as a stenographer in 1904, he attended Temple Law School at night, became an associate, retired in 1955, and died in 1960. Through the early 1930s when taxation was a kind of subculture practiced by accountants, Gross functioned part time as the Firm's first tax lawyer. In the days when associates had their own stationery and kept all their own fees (a custom lasting into the early 1960s), it is Firm lore that Gross's income exceeded that of some

ML&B partners. In exaggerated form, the story even claims he made more than Bockius. The first part of the story is credible, even if the exaggeration is not. But whatever his income, Gross never became a partner. The first Jewish lawyer to become a partner, William Goldstein, arrived in 1961 and made partner in record time six years later. Today, whether a lawyer is Gentile or Jewish has no more relevance than hair color.

The situation has been very different for African-American lawyers. In his landmark study of black Philadelphians, W. E. B. DuBois pointed out that at the turn of the century, there were only "10 practicing Negro lawyers in the city."[2] None was employed by a major firm, a condition that prevailed until after World War II. Moreover, according to Judge A. Leon Higginbotham, "in September 1949, there was not one black on the faculty of any Ivy League law school, and there was not even a single black federal judge."[3]

In the 1970s, affirmative action became the rule. Law schools busily recruited African-American students, and law firms busily recruited African-American lawyers. But it was unrealistic to suppose that centuries of deprivation would instantly be swept away and that legions of qualified graduates would spring forth eager to engage in big-firm practice. ML&B employed its first African-American associate in 1970, and others followed. Some left to form their own firms, become investment bankers, or go into government. The competition for them was and is keen. Gerald Brawner became the Firm's first African-American partner when he arrived laterally in 1985. He was followed by Edward S. G. Dennis in 1990. Dennis brought with him a nationwide reputation as assistant attorney general in charge of the criminal division of the United States Department of Justice.[4] They were followed in 1991 by Grace Speights, who had come to the Firm in 1984 as an associate and rose through the ranks to become ML&B's first African-American woman partner.[5]

It has been easier for major law firms to hire white women than African-Americans of either sex. Starting in the 1970s, white women gravitated to the law schools in droves. As that decade began, women comprised 10 percent of the law school population. By the mid-1980s their number had climbed to 40 percent. The Firm employed its first woman associate, Gail Beckman, in 1963. In a letter dated February 8, 1991, Ms. Beckman applauded the courage of those Firm partners who urged that she be hired, especially considering J. Tyson Stokes's views "about why ML&B would never have a woman partner."[6] Ms. Beckman also wondered if the Firm's courage was "moot," since she intended to stay only a short time before leaving to teach law. Still, the presence of women in the Firm grew steadily through the 1960s and 1970s. In 1980, Stephanie Abramson became the Firm's first woman partner. (Her progress was swift: In 1989, she was elected to the Firm's Executive Committee.) By 1993, twenty-three women had followed her into the partnership.

The Firm has grappled to accommodate women in the profession as they face challenges for which there are no precedents. Some accommodations have been strictly ministerial. One pertained to the ML&B Office Memorandum Form, which had to be reprinted: It had previously included the words "To: Mr." and "From: Mr." Easily remedied. Other problems have required more creative solutions. For example, the Firm was among the profession's leaders in 1982 when it formally adopted a three-month paid maternity leave. Seemingly unremarkable today, the leave policy was viewed by the Firm's affected women as a breakthrough, according to Jami McKeon. McKeon, who became a partner in 1989, credits to this policy the Firm's high retention rate among women electing to have families. Although similar leaves were granted by some other firms, their approaches were generally ad hoc. Consequently, they placed the affected women in the position of supplicants. At ML&B there was no need to supplicate.

A more difficult issue pertains to employment on a less than full-time basis for those working mothers who desire to strike a different balance between their home and professional responsibilities. Of course, Bockius would have rejected the idea that anyone could be a lawyer who did not regularly work five and a half days and three nights a week, plus such other nights and weekends as required. Still, recent years have seen more flexible and innovative approaches to work schedules, as the role of women in the profession and the Firm continues to evolve.[7]

But much lies ahead. Undeniably, the practice of law by the major firms exacts a time commitment that a considerable number of lawyers, men as well as women, find incompatible with the quality of their lives outside the profession. For this reason, many women have abandoned such firms to take positions with more civilized demands, while those who remain must constantly deal with their competing obligations. Another reason they leave is more subtle: their concern that advancement in the profession, at least in the major firms, is still not actually open to them. While the statistics arguably belie their concern about a glass ceiling, their perception of it is no less deeply felt.[8]

■ ■ ■ ■ ■

In earlier ages, the human quest was simply for food and shelter. Now, in more affluent societies, food and shelter have become matters of right, and the quest is for a life of better quality. But this poses a special problem for lawyers, as clients insist that more be done in less time and as firms set ever higher hourly targets. Equally stressful is the information revolution: Knowledge has so exploded that if today's lawyers just keep up on their reading, they will have little time left for their practices. But they must support themselves by practicing, so it is their free time that really suffers. Hard working by tradition, they can always find more to do and do better. Still, they had more freedom in the old days. For example, the courts used to close in the summer, allowing John G. Johnson, that busiest of lawyers, to take lengthy European vacations and thereby stock Philadelphia's future art museum.

Thirty years ago, ML&B partners were expected to take off a month in summer and two weeks in winter. (Associates got a month off in summer.) Lawyers who did not take their vacations were asked by the managing partner if they were properly looking after themselves. In recent years, no one has asked, as extended vacations have ceased to be practicable, much less mandatory. The average ML&B partner now takes off between three and four weeks, sometimes in bits and pieces.

Moreover, today's vacations are inferior in quality as well as duration. A lawyer is never really away. En route, there are laptop computers, as well as telephones in cars, trains, and airplanes. At destinations, there are telephones, fax machines, and computers. And their use is not restricted to emergencies. The lawyer is reached regardless.

Vacations were admittedly interrupted even in the old days. But since reaching a lawyer on vacation was then more difficult, only cosmic questions were posed. While summering in Europe, John G. Johnson once received a three-page cable from his office. The cable described a proposed megamerger and asked if it were possible. Johnson cabled back: "Merger possible, jail certain."[9] Reputedly his fee for the advice was $5,000, which is $1,250 per word, not counting punctuation. After all, his vacation had been interrupted.

Traditional time frames have been collapsed by the technology explosion, as described in Chapter 40. In the old days, documents from clients generally arrived by mail. A day might be required for delivery. Then the lawyer would take several days to read the documents, ponder the problems and respond, sometimes by telephone but quite often by mail. Now, documents arrive by fax or E-mail, and clients are on the telephone twenty minutes later asking for their lawyers' views. Another innovation is voicemail. It has ruined the classic stall: "I didn't get your message."

Plugged into such communication devices and victims of information overload, lawyers are always in touch, whether at or away from their offices. And being always in touch, they suffer pressures unknown to their predecessors. Because time and the law then moved more slowly, those predecessors practiced to a ripe old age. But today's lawyers are caught up by Henry Adams's law of acceleration. They cannot run fast enough. Nor can they ever be sure they have mastered all aspects of a problem before it must be resolved. These concerns, at least in cutting-edge law firms, have caused lawyers to wonder how long they can endure such a frantic pace. In recent years, the result has been some disenchantment with the profession, alienation, and burnout.

■ ■ ■ ■ ■

So law firms have grown exponentially, specialties have narrowed, relationships have depersonalized, discrimination has faded, and pressures have intensified. As firms have become institutions, questions have increasingly been raised about their governance. One popular idea is that they should be run by professional managers who are not lawyers.

For more than two decades, ML&B has had a nonlawyer as executive director or its equivalent. (In earlier iterations, the title was less exalted.) Harry Applestein held the position from 1971 to 1973, Frank Parkin from 1973 to 1986, and Francis Fee from 1986 to the present. Before coming to the Firm, Fee was the assistant comptroller general of the United States responsible for the functioning of the General Accounting Office. After twenty-three years spent wrestling with the federal bureaucracy, he arrived well equipped to confront the complexities and personalities of a large law firm.

The theory is that having a nonlawyer run a law firm will leave the lawyers free to do what they like to do most and almost always do best, namely practice law. But lawyers resist taking orders from nonlawyers, to the extent they take orders from anyone. So, at the moment, lawyers continue to govern their firms, although they are increasingly assisted by nonlawyer operating personnel.

Another popular idea is that all law firms will inevitably incorporate, thus arguably improving their tax positions, facilitating management, and limiting vicarious liability. (Partnerships are, after all, nineteenth-century structures rarely recommended by lawyers to their clients, absent tax considerations.) The corporate form would also permit the retention of earnings and the payment of dividends, features that could commend firms to outside investors. If and when such investment is permitted by liberalized regulations, megafirms might well go public. Or they might be acquired by major corporations, as has been the case recently with investment banking firms. Putting aside questions of conflicts (which presently limit the natural growth of law firms), a captive law firm would benefit from the financial strength of its parent and could expand "everywhere," as W. James MacIntosh liked to say. Also, its former partners would reap a one-time gain as they sold their heritage.

■ ■ ■ ■ ■

If major law firms become public companies, will they survive as such or go the way of dinosaurs? To shed light on this Darwinian inquiry, compare the leading business corporations of seventy-five years ago with the leading law firms of the same era. Why can so few of the former be recalled, whereas the latter still exist and many dominate their field?

The answer may derive from the inherently horizontal structure of a law firm. By contrast, most business corporations are managed vertically and produce a standardized product. In time, they lose their sensitivity to the marketplace. Examples include the Baldwin Locomotive Works and the *Bulletin,* as well as more recently General Motors, IBM, and Sears. But while law firms also try to standardize their products and manage themselves hierarchically, their *practices* are necessarily conducted day after day by individual lawyers handling discrete matters in direct personal contact with their clients. Consciously or not, those lawyers are ceaselessly adjusting to market forces and reinventing their wares, while ignoring memos from on-high pleading for standardization. Thus, the same maverick idiom that renders law firms so difficult to govern may also account for their adaptability and longevity at the practice level regardless of size.

If law firms are natural survivors, then ML&B's future prospects should be especially bright. The Firm enjoys a long tradition of collegiality, exceptionally sound financial underpinnings, and a diversified practice. It has been a pacesetter in anticipating the challenges of specialization, multimarket practice, and changing governance. It has certainly demonstrated its capacity to adapt. Of course, the Firm of the future will be as incomprehensible to its present generation of lawyers as the Firm of today would be to its founding partners. But change is the price that natural selection exacts for survival.

Just as law firms are preternaturally adaptable, so they also encourage singularity. All efforts to render them homogenous are doomed to failure. As collections of individualists, they cannot help sporting a Morris Bockius, a William Clarke Mason, a Kenneth Souser, and a W. James MacIntosh, not to mention more recent company. These ghosts of ML&B past have spiced this narrative and validated Stokes's thesis that people are as memorable for their eccentricities as for their achievements. So be of good cheer: In law firms of the future—no matter how big, and even if publicly owned—their counterparts will thrive as before.

■ ■ ■ ■ ■

ML&B's six-score years have spanned a golden age: from the aftermath of the Civil War in which CEM served, through Philadelphia's blossoming as the Workshop of the World, to the nation's hegemony following World War II. No institution could have chosen better its period and place in history.

Moreover, during the past two decades, American law firms have gone national, with ML&B in their forefront. And they have gone international, spreading their style of law practice throughout the world. Today, more than ever, rights are asserted, disputes are resolved, and transactions are arranged the American way.

But every wave crests and ebbs. As exhilaration inevitably turns to afterglow, lawyers may look back on Saturnian time and, at ML&B, ponder their roots. Present and future generations of the Firm's family may marvel at how a modest enterprise set up 120 years ago—when Lewis "moved [his] table into Morgan's office"— grew to command international acclaim and engage the talents of some 1650 people in 11 cities at home and abroad. Those present and future generations may also be curious, perhaps nostalgic, about the personalities and events that shaped the Firm's character and set its destiny. May this book gratify their curiosity and quicken their nostalgia.

NOTES

CHAPTER 1 In the Beginning (pages 1-12)

1. The 1870s were vintage years for law firms. In addition to ML&B, the following firms, among others, trace or stretch their lineage back to that decade: Hughes Hubbard & Reed; Rogers & Wells; Shearman & Sterling; Pillsbury Madison & Sutro; Dechert Price & Rhoads; Paul, Weiss, Rifkind, Wharton & Garrison; Proskauer Rose Goetz & Mendelsohn; Stroock & Stroock & Lavan; Reed Smith Shaw & McClay; and Sullivan & Cromwell.

2. CEM's home at 547 Church Lane in the Germantown section of Philadelphia was torn down in 1926, nine years after his death. Lewis lived farther north in Chestnut Hill, also a suburb within Philadelphia. His home at 516 West Moreland Avenue was torn down in 1958, twenty-eight years after his death.

3. Frank H. Taylor, *Philadelphia in the Civil War 1861-1865* (published by the City of Philadelphia, 1913), p. 248.

4. A. J. Pleasonton, *The Home Guard of the City of Philadelphia: Third Annual Report.* (Philadelphia: King & Baird, 1864), extract from the Report of Thomas B. Dwight, p. 89.

5. Pleasonton, *The Home Guard of the City of Philadelphia*, p. 90.

6. Pleasonton, *The Home Guard of the City of Philadelphia*, p. 92.

7. During the Civil War, Stuart operated systematically behind Union lines. Civil War aficionados still debate whether the outcome of Gettysburg might have been different if Stuart and Lee had kept in contact so Lee could have benefited from intelligence gathered by Stuart concerning the whereabouts and strength of the federal forces, as well as if Stuart's cavalry had reached Gettysburg earlier.

8. *The Philadelphia Tradition of Work* (Philadelphia: Philadelphia Area Cultural Consortium, 1979), p. 4.

9. Russell F. Weigley, editor, *Philadelphia: A 300-Year History* (New York: W. W. Norton & Company, Inc., 1982), pp. 481-82.

10. J. Tyson Stokes, *Morgan, Lewis and Bockius, Memoir of a Law Firm, One Hundred Years, 1873-1973* (Philadelphia, 1973), p. 2.

11. Stokes, *Morgan, Lewis and Bockius* p. 6.

12. In *Curtis Estate*, 452 Pa. 527 (1973), the Firm prevailed in asserting ownership of the Curtis Arboretum by the Cyrus Curtis estate. The arboretum was later sold by the estate to Cheltenham Township in Montgomery County, Pennsylvania.

13. *Philadelphia and Popular Philadelphians*, (Philadelphia: The North American, 1891), pp. 76-77.

14. *Independence, a Guide to Independence National Historic Park*, (Washington, D.C.: Government Printing Office, 1982), p. 50.

15. *Fortune*, June 1936, p. 176.

16. Lincoln Steffens, *The Shame of the Cities* (New York: Hill and Wang, 1957), p. 136. Steffens's article, "Philadelphia: Corrupt and Contented," first appeared in the July 1903 issue of *McClure's Magazine*.

17. Stokes, *Morgan, Lewis and Bockius*, p. 13, would seem to be incorrect in giving the date of the move as between 1906 and 1912. Philadelphia city directories show the Firm at the Drexel Building address in 1903 and at the Land Title Building in 1904.

18. The economics of practicing law in the late 1800s in Philadelphia are considered in Barnie F. Winkelman, *John G. Johnson, Lawyer and Art Collector* (Philadelphia: University of Pennsylvania Press, 1942), p. 112.

19. Mark Frazier Lloyd, *A History of Caring for the Sick Since 1863*, published by Germantown Hospital and Medical Center, Philadelphia, Pa., 1981, p. 15.

20. Lloyd, *History of Caring for the Sick*, p. 15.

21. Philadelphia *Public Ledger*, March 5, 1917.

CHAPTER 2 A Client for All Seasons (pages 13-23)

1. Some of the Firm's earliest cases in the Pennsylvania Supreme Court concerned utilities, including *Guest v. The Lower Merion Water Co.*, 142 Pa. 610 (1891), *Commonwealth v. Northern Electric Light & Power Co.*, 145 Pa. 105 (1891), *Commonwealth v. Brush Electric Light Co.*, 145 Pa. 147 (1891), and *Fay Gas-Fixture Co. v. Welsbach Light Co.*, 189 Pa. 20 (1899).

2. Regarding assumption of risk cases in the days before workers compensation insurance, the Firm knew whereof it spoke. It prevailed in *Smith v. Drake*, 125 Pa. 501 (1899), on behalf of an excavation contractor who was sued by an employee

whose foot had been crushed by a cart pulled by a "fractious" horse. The court noted that "it was [the employee's] business . . . to know about the horses, to know whether they were safe and fit to work with. . . . If there was any negligence, it was his own negligence in not sending that horse back to the stable." At 502-03.

3. Atlantic Refining Company ceased to be controlled by the Standard Oil trust following *Standard Oil Company of New Jersey v. United States*, 221 U.S. 1 (1910), in which John G. Johnson represented the Rockefeller interests and lost. After the Standard Oil companies were split up in 1911, Atlantic Refining was an occasional client of the Philadelphia office until it moved out of Philadelphia in 1968, following its merger in 1966 with the Richfield Company to form Atlantic Richfield Company (ARCO). Subsequently headquartered in Los Angeles, ARCO in recent years has occasionally used the Firm's Los Angeles office in litigation matters.

4. *Philadelphia and Popular Philadelphians*, p. 130.

5. Weigley, *Philadelphia: A 300-Year History*, p. 623.

6. Charles A. Howland, *Philadelphia's Gas Problem*, Bureau of Municipal Research of Philadelphia, 1926, p. 23.

7. Howland, *Philadelphia's Gas Problem*, pp. 13-14.

8. Weigley, *Philadelphia: A 300-Year History*, p. 540.

9. Weigley, *Philadelphia: A 300-Year History*, p. 541.

10. Philadelphia *Evening Bulletin*, December 15, 1937.

11. Howland, *Philadelphia's Gas Problem*, pp. 50-51.

12. Weigley, *Philadelphia: A 300-Year History*, p. 623.

13. *Philadelphia Gas Works Company v. Philadelphia*, 331 Pa. 321, 356 (1938).

14. Philadelphia *Evening Bulletin*, April 15, 1938.

15. Philadelphia *Evening Bulletin*, December 4, 1962.

CHAPTER 3 The Great Precipitator (pages 24-31)

1. Other major Philadelphia firms in 1920 were Henry, Pepper, Bodine & Stokes (later Pepper, Hamilton & Scheetz) with twelve lawyers; Prichard, Saul, Bayard & Evans with eleven lawyers; Duane, Morris & Heckscher with ten; Dickson, Beitler & McCouch (later Drinker Biddle & Reath) with nine; Roberts, Montgomery & McKeehan (later Montgomery, McCracken, Walker & Rhoads) with nine; Stern & Wolf (later Wolf, Block, Schorr & Solis-Cohen) with seven; Barnes & Brinton (later Dechert Price & Rhoads) with five; and Ballard, Spahr & Andrews (later Ballard, Spahr, Andrews & Ingersoll) with four.

2. *New York Times*, April 15, 1917.

3. Johnson was born three years before CEM and died the same year, in 1917. In 1863, they served together as members of Battery A. Later, they were office neighbors, first on Walnut Street and then in the Land Title Building. Johnson was a sole practitioner and not a partner in any firm. But the Firm's archives disclose that the Firm and he handled many matters together. He was such an authority on every phase of the law that in transactions of great moment it was considered prudent for his name to appear with the Firm's name on joint opinions. Occasionally, he was enlisted to join the Firm as co-counsel in an important appeal. After his death, his practice was divided. The Firm picked up one of its crown jewels, the Baldwin Locomotive Works, described in Chapter 8. Johnson's extraordinary art collection generated interminable court proceedings, some of them handled by the Firm, as recounted in Chapter 30.

4. Stokes, *Morgan, Lewis and Bockius*, p. 15. Stokes gives Bockius's birth date as October 12, 1860. Other authorities, including obituaries, use October 3, 1859.

5. Stokes, *Morgan, Lewis and Bockius*, p. 16.

6. *Germantown Guide*, May 28, 1892.

7. Philadelphia *Record*, April 14, 1939.

8. The Clayton Act of 1914 struck at interlocking directorships, but it was not really enforced until the 1940s. See Kramer, *Interlocking Directorships and The Clayton Act after 35 Years*, 59 Yale L.J. 1266 (1950).

9. After Johnson's death, some of his former employees formed a firm called Prichard, Saul, Bayard & Evans. The firm was effectively led by Maurice Bower Saul, who retained Johnson's valuable Pennsylvania Company, John Wanamaker, and John B. Stetson (hat company) business. In 1923, the firm split into Saul, Ewing, Remick & Saul and Evans, Bayard & Frick. The former firm remains today. In 1954, the latter firm merged into what is now Pepper, Hamilton & Scheetz.

10. J. Tyson Stokes, *No Axe to Grind*

(Wayne, Pa., Haverford House, 1982), p. 31. Nine years after his centennial history of the Firm, Stokes published a book of reminiscences. *Axe* ranges widely and offers a more intimate view of Bockius than the Firm history.

11. Stokes, *No Axe to Grind*, p. 30.

12. Stokes, *Morgan, Lewis and Bockius*, p. 19.

13. Francis Bacon, *Essays, Civil and Moral, VIII. Of Marriage and Single Life.*

CHAPTER 4 Banks and Trust Companies (pages 32-41)

1. The National Banking Act was not passed until 1863. A year later and pursuant to the act, the Philadelphia Bank became the Philadelphia National Bank and the Girard Bank became the Girard National Bank.

2. The need for a central bank became manifest again during the War of 1812, and the Second Bank of the United States was formed in 1816. Its constitutionality survived an attack by strict constructionists in *McCulloch v. Maryland*, 4 Wheaton 315 (1819). It had a twenty-year charter, good until 1836. Andrew Jackson, who hated all banks, declared war on the Second Bank and in 1832 vetoed efforts to renew and extend its charter. No more central banking for the United States until the creation of the Federal Reserve System in 1913.

3. Nicholas Wainwright, *The Philadelphia National Bank, 1803-1953* (Philadelphia: Wm. F. Fell Co., 1953), p. 20.

4. In 1930, the publishers of *Martindale's American Law Directory* purchased the publishing rights of *Hubbell*, and in 1931 the first *Martindale-Hubbell* appeared.

5. *Harvey v. Girard National Bank*, 119 Pa. 212 (1888).

6. Wainwright, *Philadelphia National Bank*, p. 197.

7. As told to the author by G. Morris Dorrance, Jr., on November 12, 1992.

8. Memorandum entitled *A History of Fidelcor, Inc. and Fidelity Bank*, sent to the author by John McKelvie of Fidelity Bank in June 1989.

9. Robert Davidson Coxe, *Legal Philadelphia, Comments and Memories* (Philadelphia: Campbell, 1908), pp. 44-46.

10. Logan Square was laid out in 1683 as Northwest Square, one of Philadelphia's five original squares. In 1825, its name was changed to honor William Penn's secretary, James Logan, who was also chief justice of Pennsylvania from 1731 to 1739. The square was once used as a burying ground and a grazing spot for cattle. It was also the site of public executions, the last one in 1823. By 1919, as a result of the Parkway development, Logan Square became a circle, but it is still called a square. Today, a focal point of the square is the Swann Memorial Fountain, also known as the Fountain of the Three Rivers, with sculptures by Alexander Stirling Calder honoring the Delaware, the Schuylkill, and the Wissahickon. In 1988-90, the fountain was rehabilitated. The Firm contributed financially, and partner William Zeiter headed the effort.

11. *United States v. The Philadelphia National Bank*, 201 F. Supp. 348 (E.D. Pa. 1962).

12. *United States v. The Philadelphia National Bank*, 374 U.S. 321 (1963).

CHAPTER 5 In Philadelphia Nearly Everybody Read the *Bulletin* (pages 42-48)

1. The *Bulletin* so described itself in its last edition of January 29, 1982. Its nearest competitor was William Randolph Hearst's *Herald Examiner*, an evening newspaper in Los Angeles. The *Herald Examiner's* circulation fell from 729,000 in 1967 to 238,000 in 1989, when it finally closed.

2. *Fortune*, June 1936, p. 179.

3. Joseph Marie de Maistre, *Lettres et Opuscules Inédits du Comte J. de Maistre*, 5th Edition, Book I, (1869), p. 264. "Toute nation a le gouvernement qu'elle mérite."

4. *Time*, April 14, 1947.

5. *Taylor and Selby Appeals*, 412 Pa. 32 (1963).

6. Robert E. L. Taylor, *Robert McLean's Bulletin and a Look at Our Free Press in 1987* (Bryn Mawr, Pa.: Dorrance & Company, 1988), p. 24.

CHAPTER 6 Washing Up (pages 49-54)

1. *Moody's Industrial Manual* (New York: Moody's Investors Service, Inc. 1990), Vol. 2, p. 3315.

2. T. C. Barker, *The Glassmakers, Pilkington: The Rise of an International Company, 1826-1976*, (London: Weidenfeld and Nicolson, 1977), p. xxviii.

3. *Fortune*, July 1968, p. 91.

4. *Fortune*, p. 90.

5. *Pilkington Float Glass*, HBS Case

Services, Harvard Business School, 1971, p. 12.

6. Sir Alastair Pilkington letter dated July 6, 1973, to Arthur Littleton.

CHAPTER 7 McCabe's Marketing Miracle (pages 55-63)

1. Thomas McCabe letter dated August 2, 1973, to W. James MacIntosh.

2. *ScotTissue Broadcast*, June/July 1979. Mason served on the Scott Paper Company's board from 1941 to 1957. He was preceded by Firm partner Clement Wood, who served from 1931 to 1940.

3. *Wall Street Journal*, December 20, 1989.

4. *Philadelphia Inquirer*, January 15, 1990.

5. *Business Philadelphia*, December 1990.

6. *Wall Street Journal*, April 3, 1990.

7. *New York Times*, April 6, 1990.

8. *Wall Street Journal*, April 3, 1990.

9. *Wall Street Journal*, February 1, 1990.

10. *Philadelphia Business Journal*, April 9, 1990.

11. *New York Times*, April 4, 1990.

12. *Philadelphia Business Journal*, June 4, 1990.

CHAPTER 8 An Affair with Steam (pages 64-72)

1. Philip Scranton and Walter Licht, *Work Sights: Industrial Philadelphia, 1890-1950* (Philadelphia: Temple University Press, 1986), p. 181.

2. Weigley, *Philadelphia: A 300-Year History*, p. 479.

3. *Luellen v. Baldwin Locomotive Works*, 11 F.2d 390 (3rd Cir. 1926); 20 F.2d 449 (3rd Cir. 1927).

4. *National Labor Relations Board v. Baldwin Locomotive Works*, 128 F.2d 39 (3rd Cir. 1942).

5. Robin Bruce Lockhart, *Reilly: Ace of Spies* (New York: Penguin Books Ltd., 1984).

6. Lockhart, *Reilly*, p. 7.

7. *Sidney G. Reilly v. Baldwin Locomotive Works, Eddystone Ammunition Corporation and Samuel M. Vauclain*, Supreme Court, New York County, 4768-1920.

8. Lockhart, *Reilly*, p. 153.

9. After World War II, Danzig became Gdánsk. The great shipyard gave birth to the Solidarity movement that helped spark the liberation of Eastern Europe from Communist domination during the 1980s and ultimately the dismemberment of the Soviet Union.

10. Samuel M. Vauclain, *Confidential Memoranda, Descriptive of Conditions in Poland, Rumania and France, Spring of 1920*, p. 42.

11. Petition of Morgan, Lewis & Bockius, Attorneys for Debtor, for Allowance for Professional Services, dated January 6, 1938, *In the Matter of The Baldwin Locomotive Works, Debtor;* in the District Court of the United States for the Eastern District of Pennsylvania, No. 18519.

12. *Steere v. Baldwin Locomotive Works*, 98 F.2d 889 (3rd Cir. 1938).

13. Smoke and cinders had always been a problem with steam locomotives, although less so after the introduction of air conditioning for passenger cars in 1931.

14. In the early 1970s, when oil prices exceeded $30 per barrel for the first time, there was talk of a return to steam locomotives powered by inexpensive coal. Nothing came of it.

CHAPTER 9 Immortal Sounds (pages 73-76)

1. In its heyday, between 1896 and 1954, Willow Grove Park was the Philadelphia area's outstanding entertainment attraction. Comprising 110 acres of then lush countryside north of the city, it was created by traction magnate Peter A. B. Widener (also a founder of UGI and the Philadelphia Electric Company) to generate revenue for his trolley lines. There was no admission charge, just the cost of a round-trip trolley fare. The park sometimes drew a hundred thousand people on a single day. It featured a Ferris wheel, three roller coasters, a scenic railway, a lake for boating, and concerts led by Victor Herbert, Walter Damrosch, and John Philip Sousa. Today, a shopping mall stands on the site. In a nostalgic gesture, the developer erected a statue of Sousa.

2. The Philco Corporation was another Firm client in the sound industry. In the 1960s, it also disappeared. (See Chapter 15.)

CHAPTER 10 Black Diamonds (pages 77-84)

1. Act of April 22, 1908, Ch. 149, 35 Stat. 65; 45 U.S.C. §§ 51-59.

2. *Pennell v. Philadelphia & Reading Railway Company*, 231 U.S. 675 (1914). *Farrugia v. Philadelphia & Reading Railway Company*, 233 U.S. 352 (1914). *McGovern, Administratrix v. Philadelphia & Reading Railway Company*, 235 U.S. 389 (1914). *Reese v. Philadelphia Reading Railway Company*, 239 U.S. 463 (1915).

3. The *Legal Intelligencer* is Philadelphia's official daily publication for legal notices. Founded in 1843, it is the oldest periodical of its kind in the United States and is owned by Legal Communications, Ltd., an ML&B client.

4. Masterson left the Firm in 1967 to become a judge of the United States District Court for the Eastern District of Pennsylvania. He returned in 1973.

5. The site of CNJ's Manhattan terminal later became part of Battery Park City, a 92-acre landfill project that includes the 6-million-square-foot World Financial Center (WFC) developed by Olympia & York (O&Y). The Firm, with William Curtin and Bradford Coupe leading the effort, represented O&Y in 1982-89 regarding the labor aspects of the $1.5-billion WFC project. Although the old CNJ site is now landlocked, a successor ferry plies the Hudson River today from the WFC Plaza to Hoboken.

6. *In re Philadelphia & Reading Coal & Iron Company*, 105 F.2d 354 (3rd Cir. 1939); *In re Philadelphia & Reading Coal & Iron Company*, 105 F.2d 357 (3rd Cir. 1939); and *In re Philadelphia & Reading Coal & Iron Company*, 141 F.2d 954 (3rd Cir. 1944).

7. *In re Philadelphia & Reading Coal & Iron Co.*, 61 F. Supp. 120, 126 (E.D. Pa. 1945).

8. James L. Holton, *The Reading Railroad: History of a Coal Age Empire, Volume II: The Nineteenth Century* (Laurys Station, Pa.: Garrigues House, 1992), p. 113.

9. Holton, *The Reading Railroad, Vol. II*, p. 30.

10. Holton, *The Reading Railroad, Vol. II*, p. 34.

11. *Continental Insurance Company v. Reading Co.*, 259 U.S. 156 (1922).

12. *Noerr Motor Freight, Inc. v. Eastern Railroad Presidents Conference*, 155 F. Supp. 768 (E.D. Pa. 1957), 166 F. Supp. 163 (E.D. Pa. 1958), 273 F.2d 218 (3rd Cir. 1959), 365 U.S. 127 (1961).

13. *In the Matter of Reading Company*, 524 F.2d 324 (3rd Cir. 1975).

14. *Philadelphia Inquirer*, July 4, 1993.

CHAPTER 11 Drexel and Stotesbury (pages 85-92)

1. "Hoist with" seems preferable to "hoist by." Shakespeare has Hamlet say (III, iv): "For 'tis sport to have the engineer hoist with his own petard." See *Brewer's Dictionary of Phrase and Fable*, 14th ed. (New York: Harper & Row, 1989), p. 843.

2. Morgan Grenfell was acquired in November 1989 by a sometime ML&B client Deutsche Bank for $1.41 billion in what the financial press described as the world's most expensive acquisition of an investment bank.

3. James T. Maher, *The Twilight of Splendor, Chronicles of the Age of American Palaces* (Boston: Little, Brown and Company, 1975), p. 27.

4. Drexel & Co. remained in the Drexel Building until 1927 when it moved to a newly constructed Florentine palace that stands today at Fifteenth and Walnut streets.

5. Philadelphia *Evening Bulletin*, May 17, 1938.

6. Stokes, *Morgan, Lewis and Bockius*, p. 82.

7. The author still recalls those magic moments during the 1930s when the car would stop on Willow Grove Avenue during Sunday afternoon drives so the family could catch a glimpse of Whitemarsh Hall in the distance.

8. Nathaniel Burt, *The Perennial Philadelphians: The Anatomy of an American Aristocracy* (Boston: Little, Brown and Company, 1963), p. 163.

9. Maher, *Twilight of Splendor*, p. 78.

10. Interviewed by a Stotesbury biographer in 1985, a footman (there had once been a small army of footmen and gardeners) recalled Bockius and his many visits to Whitemarsh Hall.

11. George and Mary Roberts, *Triumph on Fairmount: Fiske Kimball and the Philadelphia Museum of Art* (Philadelphia: J. B. Lippincott, 1959), p. 231.

12. Roberts, *Triumph on Fairmount*, p. 231, quoting from *Grandeurs and Miseries of Whitemarsh Hall*, a typescript dating from 1945 by Fiske Kimball.

13. Maher, *Twilight of Splendor*, p. 87.

14. The Metropolitan Museum of Art sent for safekeeping "ninety vanloads of art, including French furniture, medieval ivories, renaissance bronzes, gothic tapestries, and five hundred

paintings." Maher, *Twilight of Splendor*, p. 20

15. Maher, *Twilight of Splendor*, p. 86.

CHAPTER 12 The Man in the Battered Hat (pages 93-101)

1. George D. Gibson letter dated June 12, 1973, to Orvel Sebring. Gibson, then a senior partner of Hunton, Williams, Gay & Gibson, wrote to thank Sebring for a copy of Stokes's centennial history of the Firm.

2. Thomas McE. Johnston letter dated August 3, 1973, to John Bracken. Johnston, then a senior partner in Mershon, Sawyer, Johnston, Dunwoody & Cole, wrote to thank John Bracken for a copy of Stokes's centennial history of the Firm.

3. Fictional barrister Horace Rumpole is the creation of real barrister John Mortimer.

4. The journal of the Philadelphia Bar Association was then called *The Shingle*. It is now called the *Philadelphia Lawyer*.

5. *The Shingle*, May 1952.

6. Stokes, *Morgan, Lewis and Bockius*, p. 32.

7. J. Tyson Stokes, "William Clarke Mason, 1881-1957," *American Bar Association Journal*, January 1958.

8. *The Shingle*, May 1952.

9. Robert McLean letter dated May 30, 1973, to J. Tyson Stokes.

10. Obermayer clerked for Mason & Edmonds during the summers of 1906 and 1907. After graduating from the University of Pennsylvania Law School in 1908, he went to work for that firm (today Obermayer, Rebmann, Maxwell & Hippel), with which he maintained a connection until 1984, when he died at the age of ninety-eight.

CHAPTER 13 The Depression Years (pages 102-115)

1. A reference to baseball is not out of bounds. In 1982, the Firm began its labor representation of the Player Relations Committee of Major League Baseball, as discussed in Chapter 29.

2. *The Survey*, May 15, 1931, p. 217.

3. Wainwright, *Philadelphia National Bank*, p. 207.

4. Stokes, *Morgan, Lewis and Bockius*, p. 26.

5. Theodore G. Joslin, *Hoover Off the Record* (Garden City: Doubleday, Doran &

Company, Inc., 1934), p. 366.

6. Hoover won in Philadelphia that year. While the city remained Republican in local elections until 1951, it voted for Democratic presidential candidates starting in 1936, when the Democratic Convention was held in Philadelphia. But that year the Union League, a sometime Firm client (Chapter 32), sported a large electric sign favoring Republican candidates Landon and Knox.

7. The bank closing is the first event of national importance within the author's recall. Newsboys on the streets in the early morning darkness shouted: "Extra, extra, banks closed." The family awoke. A paper was bought and the situation explained. But the word moratorium is not in the vocabulary of a five-year old.

8. The FDIC and FSLIC guarantees were raised in stages until they reached $100,000 in 1980. Thereafter, thrifts virtually printed money through deposit insurance. The result, starting in 1990, was a federal bailout of thrifts that may cost an estimated $1 trillion (including interest) over a thirty-year period.

9. *United States v. Butler*, 297 U.S. 1 (1936)

10. *NLRB v. Jones & Laughlin Steel Corp.*, 301 U.S. 1 (1937).

11. *Steward Machine Company v. Davis*, 301 U.S. 548 (1937).

12. Peter A. B. Widener worked his magic with the transportation systems of other cities besides Philadelphia. When he died in 1915, he left an estate valued at up to $100 million. He had also amassed one of the finest private art collections in the world, which his son, Joseph Widener, gave to the National Gallery in Washington in 1942. (See Chapter 30.)

13. John G. Johnson drew the leases, which were regarded as unassailable.

14. *Report of C. C. McChord to The Public Service Commission of the Commonwealth of Pennsylvania in re Philadelphia Transit Situation*, 1927, p. 14.

15. This is one of Sebring's favorite Francis Bracken stories. It is also recounted in Stokes, *Morgan, Lewis and Bockius*, p. 55.

16. *Application of Philadelphia Rapid Transit Company*, 19 PUC 340, 344 (1938).

17. Sebring was referring to the elaborate Second Empire-style federal courthouse and post office building on Ninth Street between Market and Chestnut streets. Built between 1873 and 1884 on land previously occupied by the University of

Pennsylvania, it was demolished in the late 1930s not long after the trial. Its courtrooms were not air conditioned. It was replaced by a structure that opened in 1939 and was air conditioned. In 1975, the federal courts moved to their present site at Sixth and Market streets overlooking Independence Mall.

18. *Humble Oil & Refining Co. v. Smith*, 412 Pa. 78 (1963).

19. The author remembers working many years ago on a marigold project for Burpee. It involved the legal aspects of feeding marigolds to hens so they would lay eggs with more colorful yokes.

20. *Philadelphia Inquirer*, June 25, 1980.

21. *Enterra Corporation v. SGS Associates*, 600 F. Supp. 678 (E.D. Pa. 1985).

22. Edwin Wolf, 2nd, *Philadelphia, Portrait of an American City* (Harrisburg: Stackpole Books, 1975), p. 299.

CHAPTER 14 World War II
(pages 116-129)

1. A plaque on the wall at 4 Carlton Gardens quotes de Gaulle at length. "*La France a perdu une bataille! Mais la France n'a pas perdu la guerre! . . . Elle retrouvera sa liberté et sa grandeur. Tel est mon but, mon seul but! . . . Notre patrie est en péril de mort. Luttons tous pour la sauver! Vive la France.*" Every July 14 (Bastille Day), French patriots gather outside the building, de Gaulle's words are read, and the *La Marseillaise* is sung. Every year those who gather are older and fewer.

2. War Department Price Adjustment Board Citation to W. James MacIntosh, August 1944.

3. Long after returning to civilian life and law practice, Snyder also made his mark as the author of *City of Independence, Views of Philadelphia Before 1800* (New York: Praeger, 1975). He also served on the boards of the Pennsylvania Academy of the Fine Arts and the Historical Society of Pennsylvania.

4. Peter Strawbridge, S&C's president, once told the author: "There are three quintessential Philadelphia business institutions: S&C, PNB, and ML&B. I'm happy to head the first, be on the board of the second, and be advised by the third."

5. Nicholas B. Wainwright, *History of the Philadelphia Electric Company 1881-1961* (Philadelphia, 1961), p. 212.

6. Wainwright, *History of Philadelphia Electric*, pp. 227-28.

7. Rexford G. Tugwell, *The Democratic*

Roosevelt, A Biography of Franklin D. Roosevelt (New York: Doubleday & Co., 1957), p. 168.

8. Edward Robb Ellis, *A Nation in Torment, The Great American Depression, 1929-1939* (New York: Coward-McCann, 1970), p. 49.

9. Ellis, *Nation in Torment*, p. 49.

10. Ellis, *Nation in Torment*, p. 60.

11. Wainwright, *History of Philadelphia Electric*, p. 222.

12. Ellis, *Nation in Torment*, p. 54.

13. Wainwright, *History of Philadelphia Electric*, p. 228.

14. *Electric Bond & Share Company v. SEC*, 303 U.S. 419 (1938).

15. James Allen, *Democracy and Finance, The Addresses and Public Statements of William O. Douglas as Member and Chairman of the Securities and Exchange Commission* (New Haven: Yale University Press, 1940), pp. 130-31.

16. *The Shingle*, May 1952.

17. *New York Times*, May 26, 1940.

18. There may be a fourth reason for UGI's preeminence in PUHCA litigation. Between 1942 and 1947, the SEC was located in Philadelphia in the former Penn Athletic Club building on the east side of Rittenhouse Square. With UGI's headquarters at Broad and Arch streets, the antagonist were only eight blocks apart and conveniently situated for battle.

19. *Securities and Exchange Commission v. Morgan, Lewis & Bockius*, 209 F.2d 44, 45-47 (3rd Cir. 1953).

CHAPTER 15 The Age of Specialization
(pages 130-141)

1. Weigley, *Philadelphia: A 300-Year History*, p. 653.

2. Weigley, *Philadelphia: A 300-Year History*, p. 652.

3. On June 6, 1990, Dilworth's former assistant district attorneys, including the author, held a reunion. Of the thirty-two original appointees, nineteen survived. Of the survivors, two were federal court judges and seven were state court judges. Although old salts on their feet, several choked up and had to leave off as they spoke about their adulation of Dilworth and the excitement of that shining hour.

4. George Wilson, *Yesterday's Philadelphia* (Miami: E. A. Seemann Publishing Co., Inc., 1975), p. 147.

5. The burdens Ringe imposed on secretaries were legendary. When Alma Meyer, who retired in 1979, reported to the Firm in 1950 for her first day as one of Ringe's secretaries, she overheard the telephone operator say, "She won't last three weeks with Ringe!" Letter dated January 29, 1993, from Alma Meyer to the author.

6. Philadelphia *Evening Bulletin*, January 22, 1957.

7. Souser pronounced his name SOW-ser, remarking: "You can't make a silk purse out of a Souser."

8. Codicil dated October 15, 1961, to Last Will and Testament of Kenneth Souser dated January 11, 1950.

9. The little railroad's vicissitudes are recounted in *Railfan & Railroad*, October 1992.

10. Archilochus, *Satires*, Frag. 83. (c. 700 B.C.).

CHAPTER 16 Changing Times in Philadelphia (pages 142-155)

1. Act of August 10, 1959, P.L. 212, No. 18 P.S. §4699.10.

2. *Two Guys From Harrison-Allentown, Inc. v. Paul A. McGinley*, 179 F. Supp. 944 (E.D. Pa. 1959).

3. *Two Guys From Harrison-Allentown, Inc. v. Paul A. McGinley*, 366 U.S. 582 (1961).

4. *Two Guys From Harrison-Allentown, Inc. v. Paul A. McGinley*, p. 595.

5. *Bargain City U. S. A., Inc. v. Dilworth*, 407 Pa. 129 (1962).

6. *Kroger Co. v. O'Hara Township*, 481 Pa. 101 (1978).

7. *Kroger Co. v. O'Hara Township*, p. 116.

8. *Fidelity-Philadelphia Trust Company, Trustee v. Philadelphia Transportation Company*, 404 Pa. 541 (1962).

9. *Philadelphia Inquirer*, March 14, 1962.

10. Act of August 14, 1963, P.L. 984, No. 66 P.S. § 2001 et seq.

11. Pursuant to the Regional Rail Reorganization Act of 1973, six bankrupt railroads (including the Penn Central and Reading) in the Northeast and Midwest were taken over by Conrail effective April 1, 1976. (See Chapter 35.) The Philadelphia-area commuter lines were part of the package. Conrail operated them for SEPTA until they were divested on January 1, 1983, as required by the Northeast Rail Service Act of 1981. When SEPTA assumed direct operation of the lines, there was a 108-day work stoppage. With rare support from the public and the politicians, SEPTA prevailed against the unions. Outdated work rules were scrapped, salaries were cut, and 40 percent of the union jobs were eliminated as a railroad operation metamorphosed into a local transit system.

12. *Philadelphia Inquirer*, October 13, 1965.

13. *Southeastern Pennsylvania Transportation Authority v. Philadelphia Transportation Company*, 419 Pa. 471 (1965).

14. *Southeastern Pennsylvania Transportation Authority v. Philadelphia Transportation Company*, 426 Pa. 377 (1967).

15. *Philadelphia Inquirer*, October 1, 1968.

16. *Wall Street Journal*, September 27, 1990.

17. Stephen Girard Will, Article XXI.

18. Stephen Girard Will, Article XXI.

19. *Vidal v. Girard's Executors*, 43 U.S. (2 How.) 127 (1844).

20. *Brown v. Board of Education of Topeka*, 347 U.S. 483 (1954).

21. *Girard Estate*, 4 Pa. D&C 2d 671 (1955).

22. *In re Estate of Stephen Girard, Deceased*, 386 Pa. 548 (1956).

23. *In re Estate of Stephen Girard, Deceased*, p. 557.

24. *Pennsylvania v. Board of Directors of City Trusts of the City of Philadelphia*, 353 U.S. 230, 231 (1957).

25. *Girard Estate*, 7 Fiduc. Rep. (Pa.) 555 (1957).

26. *In re Girard College Trusteeship*, 391 Pa. 434 (1958).

27. *Pennsylvania v. Board of Directors of City Trusts of the City of Philadelphia*, 357 U.S. 570 (1958).

28. *New York Herald Tribune*, December 19, 1965.

29. *Philadelphia Inquirer*, May 13, 1965.

30. See generally Arthur C. Willis, *Cecil's City, A History of Blacks in Philadelphia 1638-1979* (New York: Carlton Press, 1990).

31. *Philadelphia Inquirer*, August 4, 1965.

32. *New York Herald Tribune*, December 19, 1965.

33. *New York Herald Tribune*, December 19, 1965.

34. *Commonwealth of Pennsylvania v. Brown*, 260 F. Supp. 323 (E.D. Pa. 1966) and 260 F. Supp. 358 (E.D. Pa. 1966).

35. *Philadelphia Inquirer*, November 12, 1966, and December 21, 1966.

36. *Commonwealth of Pennsylvania v. Brown*, 270 F. Supp. 482 (E.D. Pa. 1967).

37. *Commonwealth of Pennsylvania v. Brown*, 392 F.2d 120, 123 (3rd Cir. 1968).

38. *Brown v. Pennsylvania*, 391 U.S. 921 (1968).

39. *New York Herald Tribune*, December 19, 1965.

40. The details are set forth in two biographies of Girard: John B. McMaster, *The Life and Times of Stephen Girard, Vol. II* (Philadelphia: J.B. Lippincott, 1918), p. 449; and Harry Emerson Wildes, *Lonely Midas, The Story of Stephen Girard* (New York: Farrar & Rinehart, 1943), p. 99.

CHAPTER 17 A Saintly Man and Mac the Knife (pages 156-169)

1. The author had been at the Firm less than a year. He was trying to impress a prospective client. So he arranged a luncheon to which he invited the prospective client and MacIntosh. Wanting to appear important, the author asked MacIntosh's permission to call him by his first name during the luncheon. Looking puzzled, MacIntosh asked: "Doesn't everybody call me Jim?"

2. *Apocrypha*, Ecclesiasticus 44:1.

3. Stokes, *Morgan, Lewis and Bockius*, p. 39.

4. Arthur Littleton letter dated January 15, 1959, to the partners.

5. Stokes, *Morgan, Lewis and Bockius*, p. vii.

6. J. Tyson Stokes letter dated July 13, 1966, to W. James MacIntosh.

7. Philadelphia *Evening Bulletin*, December 20, 1973.

8. *Philadelphia Electric Company v. City of Philadelphia*, 301 Pa. 291 (1930). Philadelphia Electric won below, but the Supreme Court reversed.

9. Jerry A. Sacchetti, ed., *Reflections on Water, A Centennial History of Philadelphia Suburban Water Company 1886-1986* (Bryn Mawr, Pa., 1986), pp. 58-59.

10. Gilbert Cross, *A Dynasty of Water, The Story of American Water Works* (Voorhees, N.J., 1991), pp. 1-2.

11. Cross, *A Dynasty of Water*, p. xii.

12. John Galsworthy, *The Forsyte Saga* (New York: Charles Scribner's Sons, 1933), p. 843. Consols are interest-bearing bonds with no fixed maturity issued by the British government.

CHAPTER 18 The Old Order Yields (pages 170-183)

1. The leading *Gold Clause* case is *Norman v. Baltimore & Ohio Railroad*, 294 U.S. 240 (1935), in which the Supreme Court upheld a joint resolution of Congress, passed June 5, 1933, which *inter alia* abrogated the right of an obligee to receive gold in discharge of a private contractual obligation.

2. In 1993, Bracken privately published a book commemorating the adventures of the USS *Marblehead*, including its engagement against Japanese warships on February 4, 1942, the damage it sustained, and its amazing 17,011-mile journey from Java to New York with no rudder control over much of the distance, steering only by engine speed changes.

3. Eugene Davidson, *The Trial of the Germans* (New York: Macmillan, 1966), p. 421. In response to a questionnaire submitted to him by Doenitz's counsel, Nimitz confirmed that an American submarine was not expected to rescue survivors if such rescue would constitute an undue or additional hazard to the submarine.

4. Telford Taylor, *The Anatomy of the Nuremburg Trials* (New York: Alfred A. Knopf, 1992), p. 403. The British passenger ship *Laconia* was torpedoed by the Germans in the South Atlantic on September 12, 1942. The *Laconia* carried 2,732 passengers and crew. As the ship was sinking, the Germans learned that 1,800 Italian prisoners of war were among the passengers. Primarily for that reason, the Germans dispatched three U-boats and mounted an extraordinary rescue effort that miraculously saved almost half of those on board, including 500 Italians. Instead of sending rescue ships, American planes bombed the U-boats, disabling one of them.

5. Davidson, *Trial of the Germans*, p. 418. The Soviets were right. Doenitz later told his interrogators that his continued resistance following Hitler's death had saved 3.5-million German soldiers from Soviet captivity.

6. Davidson, *Trial of the Germans*, p. 424.

7. Apparently, Bryson's responsibilities did not converge with those of Henry

Gross, a sometime-tax lawyer and perennial associate. (More about Gross in Chapter 42.)

8. Taylor, *The Anatomy of the Nuremberg Trials*, pp. 264-65.

9. *New York Times*, January 12, 1946.

10. During the 1870s, Schacht's parents lived in the United States and greatly admired Horace Greeley.

11. Hillary Gaskin, *Eyewitnesses at Nuremberg* (London: Arms & Armour Press, 1990), p. 169.

12. *New York Times*, October 2, 1946.

13. *UGI v. Commissioner*, 240 F.2d 312 (3rd Cir. 1956). UGI acquired a subsidiary that had issued preferred stock. Dividends on the preferred stock were guaranteed by a third party. UGI assumed the third-party guarantee and contributed $1.4 million to the subsidiary so that it could pay the required dividends. Was the contribution an ordinary business expense deductible against gross income or (after the subsidiary failed) a capital loss deductible only against capital gains? The majority held the payments deductible as a business expense. The dissent spoke of "an enormous windfall to the petitioner [and] a new course . . . charted for tax avoidance." At p. 323.

14. George J. Miller conversations with the author as summarized in a letter, dated May 8, 1991, from the author to Miller.

CHAPTER 19 The Quadriviri (pages 184-202)

1. John Bracken chaired the Executive Committee in 1973, Ernest von Starck in 1974, Miles Kirkpatrick in 1980, Donald Scott in 1983, and Howard Shecter in 1985.

2. The *American Lawyer*, September 1990.

3. Shultz was later at various times an educator, business leader, and public servant, as dean of the University of Chicago Business School, CEO of Bechtel Corp., secretary of labor, secretary of treasury, and secretary of state.

4. Peet, who was a partner from 1964 to 1966, left the Firm and later became vice-president and general counsel of client RLC Corp.

5. During the Quadriviri period, whether or not they were on the Allocation Committee, Young and Dilks went through all the allocation statistics and generated their own allocation lists. While there was certainly no warrant for this, the legiti-

mate allocators, out of deference or perhaps curiosity, would inevitably ask Young and Dilks for their lists. Amazingly, the conclusions of the Allocation Committee and the two shadow allocators were essentially the same.

6. *New York Times*, September 21, 1982.

7. Geoffrey Chaucer, *Canterbury Tales*, Prologue, l. 308.

CHAPTER 20 In the Nation's Capital (pages 203-229)

1. Chapter 14.

2. Stokes, *Morgan, Lewis and Bockius*, p. 85.

3. Reor. Plan No. 1 of 1952, 17 Fed. Reg. 2243, 66 Stat. 823.

4. Mason had already been in touch with the Mayflower. According to his file memo of December 31, 1946, "I stated that we desired a sitting room and two bedrooms adjoining it, to be converted to office space."

5. *Phillips Petroleum Co. v. State of Wisconsin*, 347 U.S. 672 (1954).

6. In addition to Monarch, Holtzinger, and Curtin, there was William Ross, an ML&B associate from 1959 to 1965 and subsequently a name partner in Wald, Harkrader & Ross.

7. At the time of the demonstrations, partner John Quarles was general counsel of the Environmental Protection Agency. He recalls how he and other high-ranking government officials were ordered to report for work at 5 a.m., so demonstrators could not make good their threat to shut down the government. Even at that early hour, he passed a car set on fire and burning by the dawn's early light at the base of the Key Bridge.

8. They were Paul Keck, Karol Lyn Newman, John Stough, James Vasile, and Thomas Schmutz, as well as George Edgar, who joined them a few weeks later.

9. UDC had split off from AGD in 1969 and eventually exceeded it in size.

10. *Mobil Oil Exploration & Producing Southeast, Inc. v. United Distribution Companies*, 498 U.S. 211 (1991).

11. 45 U.S.C. § 797(g).

12. *Hinds v. Consolidated Rail Corporation*, 518 F. Supp. 1350 (R.R.R.A., Special Court 1981), *cert. denied*, 454 U.S. 1145 (1982); *United Transportation Union v. Consolidated Rail Corporation*, 535 F. Supp. 697 (R.R.R.A., Special Court 1982), *cert. denied*, 457 U.S. 1133 (1982).

13. *Building and Construction Trades Council v. Associated Builders and Contractors of Massachusetts,* 113 S.Ct. 1190 (1993). Uehlein and Curtin appeared as counsel of record for the Massachusetts Water Resources Authority and Kaiser Engineers, Inc., to ward off an attack by nonunion contractors against an agreement Uehlein had negotiated on behalf of Kaiser with the Building and Construction Trades Council. The authority, the unions, and Kaiser determined that the case should be argued in the Supreme Court by former Solicitor General Charles Fried.

14. Schmeltzer and Aptaker subsequently formed their own firm called Schmeltzer, Aptaker & Shepard.

15. Escudero left the Firm in 1993 to become vice-president and general counsel of a corporation then being formed to acquire PRMSA's assets.

16. The Cohen group comprised Henry Zapruder, Norman Schwartz, Adrian Morchower, Roger Pies, Julie Gilbert, Bradley Waterman, and Ellen Harrison. (By 1993, only Morchower, Gilbert, and Harrison remained.) Tax lawyer Carol Calhoun predated the Cohen group; arriving in 1980, she became a partner in 1988. Employee benefit specialist Gary Quintiere arrived laterally as a partner in 1985, six months after the Cohen merger.

17. *Estate of Samuel I. Newhouse v. Commissioner of Internal Revenue,* 94 USTC 193 (1990).

18. From 1977 to 1979, Shenefield was assistant attorney general in charge of the antitrust division. From 1979 to 1981, he was associate attorney general.

19. The *New Yorker,* February 15, 1993.

20. H. R. Haldeman with Joseph DiMona, *The Ends of Power* (New York: Times Books, 1978), pp. 135-37.

21. *Allegheny County v. Greater Pittsburgh ACLU,* 492 U.S. 573 (1989).

22. Rachel Carson, *Silent Spring* (Boston: Houghton Mifflin, 1962).

23. Ruckelshaus's hat was so white that later, as assistant attorney general, he refused Nixon's order to fire special Watergate prosecutor Archibald Cox. For his refusal, he himself was fired on October 20, 1973, as part of the so-called Saturday Night Massacre.

24. John Quarles, *Cleaning Up America, An Insider's View of the Environmental Protection Agency* (Boston: Houghton Mifflin Company, 1976). The book's dust jacket includes the comment of Edmund S. Muskie, then a United States senator

and previously, in 1968, a candidate for the vice-presidency: "I cannot recall when a sitting political appointee so candidly described the political machinations which have attempted to compromise important public policy decisions."

25. In 1994, Quarles was elected chair of the Firm's Governing Board.

26. 42 U.S.C. § 9601-9675.

27. *Of Counsel,* Volume 9, Number 3, February 5, 1990.

28. The personal law section was represented by Ellen Harrison, who had arrived in 1985 with Sheldon Cohen's group.

CHAPTER 21 North to New York (pages 230-249)

1. An exception was Baker & McKenzie, a Chicago firm that then had offices in New York and San Francisco, as well as abroad.

2. ML&B Long Range Planning Committee Report of 1971, pp. 27-28.

3. In her role as "keeper and dispenser of petty cash," Ms. Weisgrau, a woman of unquestionable integrity, was involved in a mystery still unsolved twenty years later. In 1973, she wrote the following memo:

> About three weeks ago I realized that about $30 was missing from petty cash. I thought that perhaps I had made an error and that therefore I should personally absorb the loss. Approximately Wednesday of last week I was analyzing the cash and expenses and discovered an additional $30 missing. Then on Friday, April 27, I placed $89.32 in an envelope, sealed it and placed it under the top tray in the petty cash box. To verify the fact that $89.32 was actually in the box, I noted that figure on a slip of paper and placed it in a small notebook in which I kept a record of expenses. The petty cash box is always locked and the drawer in which the box is kept is opened only while I am at my desk. On Monday, April 30, I found that a substitution of envelopes had been made and the new envelope showed the figure "$59.32" written thereon, which amount evidently covered the theft of an additional $30.

4. Levin died in 1986.

5. By 1993, the Firm had two partner-couples; the other, Joseph and Elizabeth Fay in the Philadelphia office. For some years during the 1970s, the Firm had proscribed connubial relationships between its lawyers; one would have to

leave. The rule succumbed to Cupid's arrows and the overriding need for the best and brightest, even if married to each other. Such relationships would have been inconceivable to Morris Bockius. As already noted, he deplored marriage for lawyers: Nothing should distract them from the swift completion of their appointed tasks. And as for women lawyers, there were almost none in his day, not to mention women married to other lawyers in the Firm.

6. Fritch died in 1985; Mindus in 1991.

7. 46 U.S.C. §§ 1271-1280.

8. At one point, the Firm considered litigation against Solow. A search of court records turned up numerous cases involving him. He was certainly no stranger to controversy. Even his mother sued him. *Solow v. Solow*, 171 N.Y. S.2d 539 (1958).

9. ML&B was not the only law firm to enjoy the view. After the Firm outgrew the space in 1981 and left the building, the space was occupied by Gibson Dunn & Crutcher, and subsequently by Paul, Hastings, Janofsky & Walker.

10. Low left the Firm in 1993 to become vice-president and general counsel of client Publishers Clearing House. Later in 1993, Roberts left to practice in Colorado.

11. Charles MacKay, *Extraordinary Popular Delusions and the Madness of Crowds* (Boston: L.C. Page, 1932). First published in London in 1841, it is a seminal text on crashes and mania in the financial markets.

12. *Forbes*, August 20, 1990.

13. Manuel left the Firm in 1992 when recurring conflicts between his and other ML&B clients limited his practice development efforts.

14. *United States v. Dennis E. Greenman*, 81-137-Cr. T. GC (U.S.D.C., M.D. Fla.) (1982).

15. *In re Dennis Greenman Securities Litigation*, 829 F.2d 1539, 1541 (11th Cir. 1987).

16. *Legal Times*, July 25, 1988; reprinted in *Manhattan Lawyer*, September 20-26, 1988.

17. *In the Matter of Arthur James Huff*, SEC Administrative Proceeding File No. 3-6700 (1987).

18. *In the Matter of Arthur James Huff*, SEC Opinion No. 34-29017 (1991). The case was decided by four commissioners. Two said that even if, *arguendo*, Huff had supervisory authority, his conduct was not deficient. The other opinion did not reach the question of Huff's conduct, saying that he simply did not have supervisory authority.

19. *New York Law Journal*, April 14, 1991.

20. In 1993, Richardson took early retirement from the Firm to raise Scottish Highlander cattle on his New Hampshire farm.

CHAPTER 22 Manifest Destiny (pages 250-264)

1. John Louis O'Sullivan, *United States Magazine and Democratic Review*, July-August 1845, p. 5.

2. In 1983, Dilks would indulge his penchant for dark wood, chair rail, and moldings in fitting up the Firm's new offices at One Logan Square.

3. Robert White, an experienced New Jersey trial lawyer, became a partner when the Firm opened a Princeton office on September 13, 1993.

4. *California Law Business*, November 7, 1988.

5. *California Law Business*, November 7, 1988.

6. *American Lawyer*, November 1991.

7. *Wall Street Journal*, March 23, 1993.

8. The acquisition was by Aurora Life Assurance Company, a new company owned two-thirds by MAAF and one-third by Los Angeles-based SunAmerica, Inc.

9. *Los Angeles Business Journal*, November 18, 1991.

CHAPTER 23 Southern Exposure (pages 265-273)

1. *Fraternal Order of Police v. City of Miami*, 609 So.2d 31, 32, 35 (1992).

2. *Blue Gray Corporation, First Sunset Corporation and Duilio Pizzolante v. Merrill Lynch, Pierce, Fenner & Smith, Inc.*, 89-1886-Civ-Moreno (S.D. Fla.) (1993).

3. *Miami Herald*, January 4, 1985.

4. *Miami Herald*, August 29, 1987.

CHAPTER 24 The World Was All Before Them (pages 274-291)

1 Milton, *Paradise Lost*, bk. xii, 1. 647.

2. Although IOS was permitted by the Swiss authorities to have a nominal headquarters in Geneva, the bulk of its operations had to be conducted across the French border at Ferney-Voltaire. Voltaire

had lived there during periods when his nonconformity rendered him persona non grata in Paris.

3. Charles Raw, Bruce Page and Godfrey Hodgson, *Do You Sincerely Want To Be Rich?* (New York: Viking Press, 1971).

4. *New York Times*, November 30, 1972.

5. *Wall Street Journal*, July 2, 1973.

6. The group also included Richard Mescon, a litigator who joined the New York office.

7. *New York Observer*, June 17, 1991.

8. *Los Angeles Times*, December 11, 1988.

9. *Business Week*, November 19, 1990.

10. *Wall Street Journal*, February 19, 1993.

CHAPTER 25 The Skies Were Silent (pages 292-299)

1. Thomas Babington Macaulay, *Southey's Colloquies on Society*, January 1830.

2. *Time*, July 15, 1966.

3. In 1936, the airlines were brought under the Railway Labor Act of 1926 with its distinctive procedures for dispute resolution, including the appointment of an emergency board to find facts and make nonbinding recommendations. In time, the act's intricacies as applied to both railroads and airlines became a subspecialty of the Firm's labor practice.

4. The President was so quoted by syndicated columnist Drew Pearson in the *Washington Post* on June 26, 1966.

5. *Wall Street Journal*, June 9, 1966.

6. Curtin wrote his letter on the Firm's Philadelphia letterhead, which incorporated the Washington and Harrisburg addresses and listed all the Firm's partners and associates. The names of six (of the seven) Washington lawyers were asterisked to acknowledge that they were not admitted in Pennsylvania.

7. The newspaper was the *Rome Daily American*, July 31-August 1, 1966.

8. *Wall Street Journal*, August 1, 1966.

9. *Respectfully Quoted* (Washington: Library of Congress, 1989), p. 190.

10. In Lerner & Loewe's musical, *My Fair Lady*, dustman Alfred P. Doolittle finally agrees to marry the woman with whom he has been living. On his final night of freedom, he sings about "gettin'

married in the morning" and admonishes his buddies to "get me to the church on time."

11. *Wall Street Journal*, August 16, 1966.

12. The Consumer Price Index increased 1.6 percent in 1965 and 3.0 percent in 1966. It rose 5.9 percent in 1970 and 13.5 percent in 1980, its highest one-year climb since 1920.

13. Washington *Sunday Star*, July 17, 1966.

CHAPTER 26 The Magic Kingdom (pages 300-305)

1. *New York Times*, December 29, 1970.

2. *Philadelphia Inquirer*, October 27, 1991.

3. *Time*, May 27, 1991.

4. *Sinclair Refining Co. v. Atkinson*, 370 U.S. 195 (1962); later overruled by *Boys Markets, Inc. v. Retail Clerks Union, Local 770*, 398 U.S. 235 (1970).

5. *New Orleans Steamship Association v. General Longshore Workers*, 389 F.2d 369 (5th Cir. 1968).

6. The unions were:

- Bricklayers, Masons & Plasterers International Union
- Brotherhood of Painters, Decorators and Paperhangers of America
- Granite Cutters' International Association of America
- International Association of Bridge, Structural & Ornamental Iron Workers
- International Association of Heat and Frost Insulators and Asbestos Workers
- International Association of Marble, Slate and Stone Polishers, Rubbers and Sawyers, Tile Helpers and Finishers, Marble Setters Helpers, Marble Mosaic and Terrazzo Workers Helpers
- International Brotherhood of Boilermakers, Iron Ship Builders, Blacksmiths, Forgers and Helpers
- International Brotherhood of Electrical Workers
- International Brotherhood of Teamsters, Chauffeurs, Warehousemen and Helpers of America
- International Union of Operating Engineers
- Laborers' International Union of North America
- Operative Plasterers and Cement Masons International Association
- Sheet Metal Workers' International Association
- United Association of Journey-

men and Apprentices of the
Plumbing and Pipe Fitting
Industry of the United States and
Canada
• United Brotherhood of Carpenters and Joiners of America
• United Slate, Tile and Composition Roofers, Damp and Water proof Workers Association
• Wood, Wire and Metal Lathers International Union

7. *Newsweek*, October 18, 1971.

CHAPTER 27 The Largest Private Project Ever Undertaken (pages 306-311)

1. The consortium consisted of Phillips Petroleum Co., Standard Oil Co. (New Jersey), ARCO, Standard Oil Co. (Ohio), Mobil Oil Corp., Amerada Hess Corp., Union Oil Co. of California, and Home Oil Co.

2. 43 U.S.C. § 1651 et seq.

3. Kenneth Souser used to tell of a dialogue, probably apocryphal, between Walter Reuther, the legendary president of the United Auto Workers, and George Meany, the equally legendary former plumber and long-time president of the AFL-CIO. Reuther supposedly remarked to Meany that if cars were manufactured by the building-trades unions, they would have to cost at least $100,000 each. And that was at a time when they cost less than $5,000.

4. *Anchorage Daily News*, December 15, 1975.

5. James P. Roscow, *800 Miles To Valdez, The Building of the Alaska Pipeline* (Englewood Cliffs, N.J.: Prentice-Hall, Inc., 1977), p. 153.

6. *Anchorage Daily News*, December 4, 1975.

7. *Fairbanks Daily News-Miner*, October 25, 1975.

8. *Wall Street Journal*, July 25, 1974.

9. Vincent R. D'Allesandro, chief negotiator for ARCO and liaison to the Alyeska Owner Committee, letter dated September 19, 1992, to William Curtin.

10. *Alyeska Pipeline Service Co. v. Teamsters Local 959*, 557 F.2d 1263 (9th Cir. 1977).

11. *Wall Street Journal*, August 31, 1970.

CHAPTER 28 The Skies Were Not Silent (pages 312-318)

1. Calvin Coolidge, governor of Massachusetts, telegram to Samuel Gompers, September 14, 1919, regarding the Boston police strike. *Respectfully Quoted* (Washington: Library of Congress, 1989), p. 334.

2. *Washington Post*, August 4, 1981.

3. *Time*, August 17, 1981.

4. 18 U.S.C. § 1918 imposes fines and imprisonment for any violation of 5 U.S.C. § 7311(3), which prohibits federal employees from participating in a strike against the government.

5. Exec. Order No. 11,491, reprinted in 5 U.S.C. § 7102 *et seq.*

6. Not only was the PATCO dispute important in its own right, but it would also affect negotiations with 600,000 Postal Service employees, whose contract expired on July 20, 1981. If PATCO got away with an illegal strike, the postal employees might try to do the same.

7. Edward V. Curran, Theodore N. Maher, and John F. Leyden, *Air Traffic Controllers Out of Control (The inside story of a strike that failed);* unpublished typescript, pp. 112 and 196.

8. *New York Times*, August 4, 1981.

9. *New York Times*, August 6, 1981.

10. *Time*, August 17, 1981.

11. *Time*, August 17, 1981.

12. The ban was not lifted until August 12, 1993.

13. In 1986, a new organization, the National Air Traffic Controllers Association, was recognized by the FAA. By 1991, approximately 70 percent of the controllers had joined.

14. *Washington Post*, June 20, 1981.

15. *New York Times*, August 4, 1981.

16. *New York Times*, August 4, 1981.

CHAPTER 29 Play Ball (pages 319-325)

1. *Federal Baseball Club of Baltimore, Inc. v. National League of Professional Baseball Clubs*, 259 U.S. 200 (1922).

2. *Salerno v. American League*, 429 F.2d 1003, 1005 (2nd Cir. 1970), *cert. denied, sub nom. Salerno v. Kuhn*, 400 U.S. 1001 (1971).

3. *Toolson v. New York Yankees, Inc.*, 346 U.S. 356 (1953).

4. *Flood v. Kuhn et al*, 407 U.S. 258 (1972).

5. *Flood v. Kuhn*, p. 282.

6. *In re The Twelve Clubs Comprising National League of Professional Baseball Clubs*, 66 LA 101 (1975).

7. *New York Times*, March 4, 1990.

8. *In re The Twelve Clubs*, at p. 112.

9. *New York Times*, September 27, 1987.

10. Neil J. Sullivan, *The Diamond Revolution* (New York: Saint Martin's Press, 1992), p. 196.

11. *Wall Street Journal*, May 20, 1991.

12. *New York Times*, September 22, 1987. By agreement of the parties, the arbitrator's opinion remains unpublished.

13. *Wall Street Journal*, May 20, 1991.

14. *New York Times*, February 9, 1990.

15. *New York Times*, November 27, 1989.

16. *National Sports Daily*, February 1991.

17. *New York Times*, February 9, 1990.

18. *National Sports Daily*, March 20, 1990.

19. Marvin Miller, *A Whole Different Ball Game: The Sport and Business of Baseball* (New York: Carol, 1991), p. 362.

20. Peter Ueberroth as quoted in the *Wall Street Journal*, May 20, 1991.

21. The Chicago Cubs double-play combination of shortstop Joe Tinker, second-baseman Johnny Evers, and first-baseman Frank Chance was immortalized (to baseball fans) by Franklin P. Adams's eight lines of doggerel entitled *Baseball's Sad Lexicon*, published by the *New York Daily Mail*, July 1910.

22. Jacques Barzun, *God's Country and Mine* (Boston: Little, Brown and Company, 1954), p. 159.

CHAPTER 30 The Jolly Testator (pages 326-331)

1. *New York Times*, April 14, 1917.

2. *Newsweek*, November 10, 1941.

3. Burt, *The Perennial Philadelphians*, p. 349.

4. *Johnson Trust*, 15 Pa. D&C2d 407 (1958).

5. *Johnson Trust*, p. 425.

6. *Johnson Trust*, pp. 427-28.

7. *Johnson Trust*, p. 431.

8. Wood was the son of former Firm partner Clement Wood, referred to in Chapters 3, 7, 12, and 13. Lombard came to the Firm laterally in 1984, having previously been a partner in Obermayer, Maxwell, Rebmann & Hippel, the firm founded by William Clark Mason as Mason & Edmonds in 1904.

9. To make the project possible, the Philadelphia Museum of Art raised more than $60 million, of which about $10 million was to be spent by 1994 to rework eighty-three galleries, create ten new ones, and restore more than 225 paintings.

CHAPTER 31 A Collector with No Money of His Own (pages 332-335)

1. In 1954, there was a public offering of 13 percent of Campbell's stock, leaving 87 percent for the family, who by 1990 still retained 59 percent.

2. Mirabello became a partner in 1985. He had joined the Firm laterally as an associate in 1981, having come cross-country from Irell & Manella in Los Angeles.

3. *Wall Street Journal*, October 19, 1989.

4. *Time*, December 3, 1990.

CHAPTER 32 The Bombardment of the Union League (pages 336-339)

1. Russell Burke, vice-president of Kennedy Galleries (New York), as quoted by Lita Solis-Cohen in *Maine Antique Digest*, June 1987.

2. *Firestone & Parson, Inc. v. The Union League of Philadelphia*, 672 F. Supp. 819, 822-23 (E.D., Pa. 1987); affirmed *per curiam*, 833 F.2d 304 (3rd Cir. 1987).

CHAPTER 33 Those Fabulous Philadelphians (pages 340-344)

1. Herbert Kupferberg, *Those Fabulous Philadelphians, The Life and Times of a Great Orchestra* (New York: C. Scribners Sons, 1969).

2. In 1939, Stokowski and the Philadelphia Orchestra made the landmark film *Fantasia* for Disney Productions. Since 1968, various Disney interests have been represented by the Firm, as noted in Chapters 22 and 26.

3. Kupferberg, *Those Fabulous Philadelphians*, p. 64, citing critic Lawrence Gilman writing for the *New York Herald Tribune*.

4. *Philadelphia Inquirer*, October 13, 1966.

5. The chairman of the Board of Public Accountability was Dr. George W. Taylor,

a national authority on labor relations and the first Gaylord Harnwell Distinguished Professor at the University of Pennsylvania. Taylor had been chairman of the War Labor Board during World War II and chairman of the National Wage Stabilization Board during the Korean War.

CHAPTER 34 A Long and Winding Transaction (pages (345-349)

1. *Los Angeles Times*, September 22, 1985.

2. *Washington Times*, April 14, 1990.

3. *Los Angeles Times*, September 22, 1985.

4. *Time*, August 26, 1985.

5. *Rolling Stone*, September 26, 1985.

CHAPTER 35 The Great Train Wreck (pages 350-356)

1. They were Central Railroad Company of New Jersey, Erie Lackawanna Railway Company, Lehigh & Hudson River Railway Company, Lehigh Valley Railroad Company, and the Reading Railroad.

2. Stephen Salsbury, *No Way to Run a Railroad* (New York: McGraw-Hill, Inc., 1982), p. xiii.

3. Salsbury, *No Way to Run a Railroad*, p. 29.

4. A year after the filing, the Penn Central trustees retained the Firm (the matter was led by William Curtin) in connection with proceedings designed to achieve reduced crew sizes. The matter led to Executive Order 11664 and the naming of Presidential Emergency Board No. 180. While the proceedings were in progress, the Firm's efforts were superseded by congressional action, including passage of the Regional Rail Reorganization Act and the establishment of Conrail. Thereafter, the Firm represented Conrail in major labor matters and finally the rail industry as a whole to achieve such savings. (See Chapter 20.)

5. They were: "or under subsection (a) of section 306 of this Act." P.L. 96-448, Sec. 703(f)(3); 45 U.S.C. § 720.

6. *Consolidated Rail Corporation v. Railway Labor Executives' Association*, 491 U.S. 299 (1989).

CHAPTER 36 The Giant Bird (pages 357-360)

1. In 1971, a German lawyer remarked that his USIF work with ML&B was causing him to be "brushed by the wings of the giant bird." The bird was IOS, thousands of whose shareholders would be gathered up a year later by the Deutsche Schutzvereinigung für Wertpapierbesitz and represented by the Firm, as described in Chapter 24.

2. Arthur Herzog, *Vesco* (New York: Doubleday, 1987), p. 149.

3. The paralegal was Susan Drumheller, who spent many years in this and other cases organizing what Lewis called his "war rooms." By far, Lewis's largest war rooms would later be for United States Gypsum Company (USG), which came to the Firm in 1966 and by the late 1980s was among its most active clients. For USG, Lewis organized what he called his A Team. It comprised up to forty lawyers who defended asbestos property-damage claims against USG in thirty-five states.

4. The associate was William Carr, who later became an assistant United States attorney in Philadelphia. Hyperbole has it that Carr actually arranged in the first place for the hurdy-gurdy during the Sullivan & Cromwell closing argument. Such was not the case.

CHAPTER 37 Two Vast and Trunkless Legs (pages 361-364)

1. Percy Bysshe Shelley, "Ozymandias" (1818). Shelley is thought to have been inspired by the ruins of the Temple of Rameses II at ancient Thebes. He could have been writing about the cooling towers of Limerick I and II.

2. Philadelphia Electric Company changed its name to PECO Energy Company effective January 1, 1994.

3. The *Philadelphia Inquirer*, in an editorial on June 9, 1980, wrote there was "little doubt that if Philadelphia Electric engineers went to the Nuclear Regulatory Commission for the first time today with their plans for Limerick, located 26 miles from center city Philadelphia, they would be rejected."

4. *Philadelphia Electric Company v. Pennsylvania Public Utility Commission*, 71 Pa. Commonwealth Ct. 424 (1983).

5. *Pennsylvania Public Utility Commission v. Philadelphia Electric Company*, 501 Pa. 153 (1983).

6. Antinuclear groups effectively blocked the opening of LILCO's $5.5-billion Shoreham nuclear power plant in Suffolk County on Long Island. The plant was completed but never put into service. In 1989, by agreement with the state of New York, it was decommissioned as a nuclear plant and sold to a public authority for $1 and a commitment by the state to allow a ten-year rate increase in favor of LILCO. Actual destruction of the plant's nuclear

facilities commenced in 1992. Separately, in another case, more than 3,000 protestors were arrested over the seventeen-year period required to construct the $6.5-billion Seabrook plant in New Hampshire. Before the plant was completed and began to deliver power in 1990, Public Service Company of New Hampshire filed for bankruptcy in 1988, the first bankruptcy of an investor-owned electric utility since the Depression.

7. *Wall Street Journal*, February 28, 1990.

8. *Wall Street Journal*, August 7, 1990.

CHAPTER 38 Hands Off the Family Store (pages 365-370)

1. *Barron's*, May 30, 1983.

2. *Philadelphia Daily News*, April 22, 1986.

3. In 1990, Siegel paid about $10 million in fines and was sentenced to two months in prison and 3,000 hours of community service following his guilty plea on charges of tax evasion and conspiracy to violate securities laws. He acknowledged receiving suitcases containing $800,000 in cash from convicted arbitrager Ivan Boesky in return for inside information.

4. A 13D group derives its name from a provision in the Securities Exchange Act of 1934 that any group holding more than 5 percent of the stock of a registered company must file a Schedule 13D disclosing that fact and such group's intentions.

5. Act of December 23, 1983, P.L. 92, No. 395, Sec. 408B.

6. *Philadelphia Daily News*, April 29, 1986.

7. *Ronald Baron v. Strawbridge & Clothier*, 646 F. Supp. 690, 692 (E.D. Pa. 1986).

8. 18 U.S.C. § 1961 et seq.

9. *Philadelphia Daily News*, July 22, 1986.

10. *American Lawyer*, September 1990, p. 64.

CHAPTER 39 No Slurry (pages 371-375)

1. KCS's rail system comprised 2,500 miles of trackage through Missouri, Kansas, Arkansas, Oklahoma, Louisiana, and Texas.

2. 15 U.S.C. § 1.

3. United Press International, April 9, 1988.

4. *Missouri v. Andrews*, 586 F. Supp. 1268 (D. Neb. 1984), *aff'd.*, 787 F.2d 270 (8th

Cir. 1986), *aff'd. sub nom. ETSI Pipeline Project v. Missouri*, 484 U.S. 495 (1988).

5. See *Eastern Railroad Presidents Conference v. Noerr Motor Freight*, 365 U.S. 127 (1961), and *United Mine Workers of America v. Pennington*, 381 U.S. 657 (1965). In the *Noerr* case, the Firm had earlier represented some of the victorious railroads, which included Chesapeake & Ohio Railway Company; Delaware, Lackawanna & Western Railroad Company; Erie Reading Company; Lehigh & Hudson River Railway Company; New York, Chicago & Saint Louis Railway Company; and Reading Company. (See Chapter 10.)

6. *State of South Dakota v. Kansas City Southern Industries*, 880 F.2d 40 (8th Cir. 1989).

7. *State of South Dakota v. Kansas City Southern Industries*, p. 48.

8. *State of South Dakota v. Kansas City Southern Industries*, p. 49.

9. *State of South Dakota v. Kansas City Southern Industries*, pp. 52-53.

10. *State of South Dakota v. Kansas City Southern Industries*, 493 U.S. 1023 (1990).

CHAPTER 40 Metamorphoses (pages 376-389)

1. Gregory Harvey tells a similar story about John Lewis who started with the Firm in 1961. Interviewing in Philadelphia, Lewis reportedly asked each of the major firms: "Which is the best Philadelphia firm?" Each responded that *it* was. Lewis then asked: "Which is the second-best Philadelphia firm?" Uniformly, they responded, "Morgan, Lewis & Bockius." Lewis knew exactly what choice to make. Harvey, a sometime law school roommate of Lewis's, benefited from Lewis's research by coming to the Firm a year later.

2. Meyers succeeded Calvert as the Firm's managing partner in 1994.

3. *Goosby v. Osser*, 409 U.S. 512 (1973).

4. Torregrossa and his wife, Ann, agreed that she would argue the case in the Supreme Court, with Joseph sitting at the counsel table. Ann was eight months pregnant. Noting her condition, the Court was unusually gracious, and Justice William Brennan in particular answered some questions put to her by the other Justices. When the Torregrossas's son was born a month later, he was named Brennan after the Justice, thus setting in motion a relationship that endured even after Brennan retired from the Court in 1990.

5. The matter was handled by Anthony

Russo in the Firm's Los Angeles office, assisted by Peter Buscemi in the Firm's Washington office. Stephen English, another Los Angeles partner, was a recipient in 1993 of the President's Pro Bono Service Award that recognizes outstanding service by lawyers to California's poor and disadvantaged. A Firm team led by English had obtained a substantial verdict for low-income tenants against their landlord in a matter referred by the Inner City Law Center in Los Angeles.

6. *Bates v. State Bar of Arizona*, 433 U.S. 350, 389 (1977).

7. ML&B's caution conformed with a policy implemented by the Firm's then Executive Director Frank Parkin that "ML&B will never be the first." Parkin had come to ML&B from a major New York law firm that invested millions of dollars in computer equipment only to find several years later, in the fast-changing world of technology, that more powerful and compact equipment could be purchased for a fraction of the cost. Parkin's policy served the Firm well when he considered and rejected terminals at secretarial stations hardwired to a central mainframe. Stand-alone personal computers turned out to be a better solution. They did not entail a huge start-up cost, were more flexible, and could easily be upgraded as innovations came on line.

8. By 1993, ML&B's information needs were served by sixty-two employees. Of these, twenty-seven were assigned to the back office and thirty-five to the front office. The effort was led by Director of Information Systems Donald Sternfeld.

CHAPTER 41 Learning About Numbers (pages 390-398)

1. Alma Meyer, letter dated January 13, 1993, to the author. Ms. Meyer was a secretary at the Firm from 1950 to 1979, working at various times inter alia for Thomas Ringe and John Bracken.

CHAPTER 42 Learning About People (pages 399-407)

1. In 1975, the Firm issued its first *Directory of Lawyers*, setting forth their names, significant dates, law schools, and pictures. The directory has been reissued each year since and is generally called "the picture book." By issuing it, the Firm conceded that all its lawyers no longer knew one another. And there were only 210 of them in 1975.

2. W. E. B. DuBois, *The Philadelphia Negro: A Social Study* (New York: Schocken Books, 1967), p. 114.

3. A. Leon Higginbotham, Jr., *A Tribute to Thurgood Marshall*, 105 Harvard Law Review 59 (1991).

4. In December 1992, Dennis was named by the attorney general of Pennsylvania as special counsel to oversee an investigation of the Pennsylvania Supreme Court. In June 1993, he was appointed by the United States Department of Justice to conduct an independent review of its handling of the fifty-one-day siege of the Branch Davidian compound in Waco, Texas, which ended in eighty-six deaths from fire and gunshots.

5. Speights was president of the Women's Lawyers Division of the National Bar Association. She also served on the Blue Ribbon Panel of the District of Columbia to recommend appointments for United States District Court judges, United States attorneys, and United States marshals.

6. Gail Beckman letter dated February 8, 1991, to the author.

7. See American Bar Association Commission on Women in the Profession, *Lawyers and Balanced Lives: A guide to drafting and implementing workplace policies for lawyers*, 1990.

8. The problem was discussed in the *National Law Journal*, January 27, 1992.

9. Roberts, *Triumph on Fairmount*, p. 132.

APPENDIX

Chronological list of members of Morgan, Lewis & Bockius to May 10, 1994

	Year of Admission	Year of Retirement/Withdrawal
Charles E. Morgan, Jr.	1873	1917
Francis D. Lewis	1873	1930
Randal Morgan	1885	1895
Morris R. Bockius	1898	1939
William Findlay Brown	1898	1902
R. Stuart Smith	1908	1922
Charles E. Morgan III	1910	1944
Clement B. Wood	1910	1940
Francis B. Bracken	1918	1937
William Clarke Mason	1922	1957
W. Heyward Myers, Jr.	1922	1958
Bevan A. Pennypacker	1922	1954
A. Allen Woodruff	1922	1949
Arthur Littleton	1926	1967
John Murdoch Clarke	1929	1933
John Russell, Jr.	1929	1974
Henry R. Heebner	1932	1967
W. James MacIntosh[1]	1932	1979
Frederick H. Knight	1933	1964
Thomas B. K. Ringe	1938	1957
J. Tyson Stokes[2]	1939	1974
Howard H. Rapp	1941	1974
Anthony H. Whitaker	1941	1968
William E. Lingelbach, Jr.	1941	1975
H. Orvel Sebring, Jr.	1941	1976
Jesse R. Fillman	1945	1957
Leonard A. Spalding	1947	1954
Ernest R. von Starck	1948	1978
Randal Morgan III	1949	1955
Arthur F. McCarthy	1951	1969
Alfred J. McDowell	1951	1973
Martin P. Snyder	1951	1979
John N. Schaeffer, Jr.	1951	1979
Howard W. Taylor, Jr.	1951	1980
Oscar M. Hansen	1953	1976
John R. McConnell	1953	1982
Brady O. Bryson	1955	1980
John P. Bracken	1955	1977
Norman R. Dutton	1955	1959
Miles W. Kirkpatrick[3]	1955	1985
J. Wesley Oler	1955	1974
Richard P. Brown, Jr.	1956	1988
Norman T. Hayes, Jr.	1956	1977

Howard Kellogg	1956	1978
J. David Mann, Jr.	1956	1983
Thomas V. Lefevre	1956	1979
Benjamin M. Quigg, Jr.	1956	1983
Robert H. Young	1956	1991
Henry C. Beerits	1957	1972
Kenneth Souser	1959	1970
Ronald Souser	1959	1976
Robert H. Kleeb	1959	1979
Robert C. McAdoo	1960	1980
David W. O'Brien	1960	1989
Allen M. Woodruff	1960	1961
H. Peter Somers	1961	1988
Thomas A. Masterson[4]	1961	
Arthur R. Littleton	1961	1985
John S. Brittain	1961	1988
Samuel W. Morris	1961	1968
Robert H. Shertz	1961	1962
James M. Ballengee	1962	1962
Samuel C. Harry	1963	1981
E. Jackson Bonney	1964	1989
Park B. Dilks, Jr.	1964	
Ralph Earle II[5]	1964	1973
John E. Holtzinger, Jr.	1964	1983
George F. Mayrosh	1964	1988
John C. Peet, Jr.	1964	1966
Donald A. Scott	1964	
William J. Taylor	1964	1982
William P. Wood	1964	1991
William J. Curtin	1965	
George M. Aman III	1967	1993
Lee H. Snyder	1967	
V. Baker Smith	1967	1975
David A. Sutherland	1967	1972
Peter D. Walther	1967	1975
William E. Zeiter	1967	1994
William M. Goldstein[6]	1967	1982
James A. Matthews, Jr.	1967	1990
Ansel S. Luxford	1968	1971
Neil D. Naiden	1968	1983
John W. Pehle	1968	1975
Julius Schlezinger	1968	1978
Richard C. Hotvedt	1969	
Alan L. Reed	1969	
E. Barclay Cale, Jr.	1969	
Gregory M. Harvey	1969	
Frederick H. Knight III	1969	1991
Edwin Kronfeld	1969	1979

John H. Lewis, Jr.	1969	
Frederick Moring	1969	1978
Angus M. Russell	1969	1987
Fred Speaker	1969	1970
Walter M. Strine, Jr.	1969	1986
Robert H. Zimmerman	1969	1985
Mario F. Escudero	1970	1993
Denis V. Brenan	1970	
James W. Jennings	1970	
Herbert Odell	1970	1989
Stuart I. Odell	1970	1988
Loren K. Olson	1970	1981
Harry Reagan	1970	
Edward Schmeltzer	1970	1976
Peter C. Ward	1970	1972
Stanley Weiss	1970	1977
Edward Aptaker	1971	1976
Henry S. Klaiman	1971	1981
Warren M. Laddon	1971	1986
Kenneth R. Myers	1971	
W. Wesley Nagle	1971	
Charles P. O'Connor	1971	
Robert A. Peavy	1971	
Thomas H. Lane	1972	1985
Joseph A. O'Connor, Jr.	1972	
Noel Arnold Levin	1973	1983
George L. Edgar	1973	1983
Miles J. Gibbons, Jr.	1973	1981
Kenneth F. Hickey	1973	1992
Frank P. Saponaro, Jr.	1973	1989
Howard L. Shecter	1973	
Michael E. Thoyer	1973	
E. Carl Uehlein, Jr.	1973	
Fred F. Fielding	1974	1981
W. Russel Hoerner	1975	1985
Dennis N. Barnes	1975	
Bruce E. Fritch	1975	1985
Robert S. Hodavance	1975	
Paul H. Keck	1975	1983
Thomas M. Kittredge	1975	
Harry A. Rissetto	1975	
William J. Emanuel	1976	
John F. Bales III	1976	
Bradford W. Coupe	1976	
Raymond T. Cullen	1976	
George W. Davies	1976	1990
Mark S. Dichter	1976	
William M. Doran	1976	

Caswell O. Hobbs	1976	
George G. Loveless	1976	
William A. Macan IV	1976	
John Quarles	1977	
E. Clive Anderson	1977	
James A. Hunter, Jr.	1977	
Arthur L. Klein	1977	1993
George E. Lieberman	1977	1988
Allen W. Stewart	1977	1994
Joseph A. Torregrossa	1977	
Orris S. Hiestand	1978	1985
Kenneth B. Wright	1978	
Michael L. Klowden	1978	
Vincent Butler	1978	1981
Burton A. Hartman	1978	1982
Richard S. Koffey	1978	1987
Jay H. Calvert, Jr.	1978	
Joseph H. Hennessy	1978	
Robert J. Kane	1978	1985
Robert A. Mallow	1978	1983
Howard V. Mindus	1978	1991
Timothy P. O'Reilly	1978	
Paul G. Russell	1978	1984
Marc J. Sonnenfeld	1978	
Thomas C. Watson	1978	1979
Thomas F. Cunningham	1979	1988
James W. Harbison, Jr.	1979	
George M. Hasen	1979	1988
John H. Higgs	1979	
J. Howard Marshall, Jr.	1979	1988
William B. O'Connor	1979	
D. Brooke Taylor	1979	1989
William J. Rennert	1979	1980
Donald C. Alexander	1979	1985
A. A. Sommer, Jr.	1979	
Lawrence H. Berger	1979	
Edward B. Cloues II	1979	
John E. Krampf	1979	
Charles W. Smith	1979	1983
Robert J. Smith	1979	
Robert Thornton Smith	1979	1982
Michael L. Wolfram	1979	
James S. Wright, Jr.	1979	1984
Samuel B. Fortenbaugh III	1980	
John I. Forry	1980	
John M. Linsenmeyer	1980	
Robert A. Bildersee	1980	
Richard M. McGonigal	1980	

Stephanie W. Abramson	1980	
Walter R. Hall II	1980	1989
James J. Kelley II	1980	
Frederick J. M. LaValley	1980	
Howard L. Meyers	1980	
Karol Lyn Newman	1980	1983
John T. Stough, Jr.	1980	1983
Elihu Fier	1980	1983
H. Franklin Bloomer, Jr.	1981	
Charles G. Lubar	1981	
Richard A. Pettigrew	1981	
Charles G. Cale	1981	1990
Loyd P. Derby	1981	
F. Jack Liebau	1981	1987
Robert D. Redford	1981	
Charles E. Stimson, Jr.	1981	1984
Kell M. Damsgaard	1981	
Lloyd H. Feller	1981	
Allen J. Gross	1981	1989
Michael S. Kelly	1981	
David R. King	1981	
Paul J. Levine	1981	1987
Stephen P. Mahinka	1981	
Francis M. Milone	1981	
Dennis J. Morikawa	1981	
Thomas W. Murrell III	1981	
Kenneth A. Rubin	1981	
Richard J. Sabat	1981	
Peter S. Sartorius	1981	
James B. Vasile	1981	1983
Frank L. Skillern, Jr.	1981	1983
Morris C. Brown	1982	1991
Richard J. Bischoff	1982	1989
Harry W. Burton	1982	
Robert D. Comfort	1982	
Stephen P. Farrell	1982	
Robert B. Miller	1982	1993
George A. Stohner	1982	
Raymond E. Warman	1982	
Thomas K. Wotring	1982	
Renato Beghe	1983	1989
Peter J. Hurtgen	1983	
Robert A. Dufek	1983	
Thomas P. Gadsden	1983	
Thomas B. Kenworthy	1983	
Susan S. Sauntry	1983	
Thomas A. Schmutz	1983	1983
Thomas H. Coleman	1983	

Lowell L. Garrett	1983	1991
John D. Shultz	1983	
Orville O. Orr, Jr.	1984	
William L. Gardner	1984	
Paul E. Roberts	1984	1993
Gerald M. Freedman	1984	
Robert D. Heyde	1984	1989
William H. Lewis, Jr.	1984	
John E. Scheifly	1984	1990
Terence G. Connor	1984	
H. Steven Durrett	1984	
Lawrence B. Fine	1984	
William J. Flannery	1984	
Michael W. Gang	1984	
Harold W. Low	1984	1993
Michael G. Pfeifer	1984	1993
Ian S. Shrank	1984	
Thomas F. Williamson	1984	
George G. Yearsich	1984	
B. John Williams, Jr.[7]	1984	
John J. Lombard, Jr.	1984	
James Wawro	1984	
Sheldon S. Cohen	1985	
Norman L. Schwartz	1985	1988
Henry G. Zapruder	1985	1989
Adrian L. Morchower	1985	
Roger A. Pies	1985	1989
Julie N. Gilbert	1985	
Bradley S. Waterman	1985	1987
Gerald T. Brawner	1985	
Thomas V. Vakerics	1985	1988
Frank H. Smith, Jr.	1985	
Stephen R. English	1985	
Robert M. Lawrence	1985	
David B. MacGregor	1985	
Richard F. McMenamin	1985	
Francis J. Mirabello	1985	
Eric A. Sisco	1985	1994
Steven D. Spencer	1985	
Kathleen E. Topelius	1985	1993
Randolph C. Visser	1985	
I. Lee Falk	1985	
Gary G. Quintiere	1985	
Markham Ball	1986	
Mark R. Joelson	1986	
Joseph P. Griffin	1986	
Charles B. Manuel, Jr.	1986	1992
John H. Shenefield	1986	

Peter E. Halle	1986	
Steven Schatzow	1986	
Theodore W. Mason	1986	
James R. Silkenat	1986	1989
Mary E. Baluss	1986	
John E. Bussian III	1986	1992
John S. Fletcher	1986	
Margery Sinder Friedman	1986	1989
Ellen K. Harrison	1986	
John F. Hartigan	1986	
Pamela Daley Kendrick	1986	1989
N. Jeffrey Klauder	1986	
Gregory S. Lewis	1986	1994
Marcia G. Madsen	1986	
David W. Pollak	1986	
Howard T. Weir III	1986	
Roberta Lee Halladay	1987	
Edward C. Cazier, Jr.	1987	1991
Donald C. Smaltz	1987	1992
Allen L. Neelley	1987	1992
Dirk T. Metzger	1987	1989
Robert B. Fraser	1987	
Mark S. Rapaport	1987	
William R. Kuntz, Jr.	1987	1988
Paul A. Richler	1987	
Vernon C. Gauntt	1987	1987
John B. Nauman	1987	1993
Leighton M. Anderson	1987	1992
Stephen J. M. Morris	1987	1991
John G. Davies	1987	1993
C. G. Gordon Martin	1987	
Robert L. Hess	1987	1992
Lois A. Anderson	1987	1987
Michael D. Weiner	1987	1992
John F. X. Peloso	1987	
Robert M. Romano	1987	
Thomas J. Benz	1987	
David C. Goodwin	1987	1992
Ralph N. Albright, Jr.	1987	
Peter Buscemi	1987	
Stephen A. Edwards	1987	
Linda L. Griggs	1987	
Keith J. Kosco	1987	
James D. Madigan III	1987	1988
Frank M. Thomas, Jr.	1987	
Joel C. Weiss	1987	1989
Mitchell N. Baron	1987	
Martin E. Weisberg	1987	1991

Roy S. Mitchell	1987	
Andrew D. Ness	1987	
David G. Ellsworth	1987	
Richard F. Davis	1987	1992
Michael P. Simondi	1987	
Douglas A. Dodds	1987	
Allen L. Raiken	1988	
Michael A. Bloom	1988	
William R. Radford	1988	
Robert M. Brochin[8]	1988	
Carol V. Calhoun	1988	
Francis L. Casey III	1988	
Michael F. Clayton	1988	
Robert L. Collings	1988	
Elizabeth Hoop Fay	1988	
Kathryn A. Kapusta	1988	
Michael J. A. Karlin	1988	
Donald C. Klawiter	1988	
Stephen M. Lowry	1988	
Thomas H. Mabie	1988	
Michael J. Ossip	1988	
James D. Pagliaro	1988	
Thomas E. Reinert, Jr.	1988	
Anthony Russo	1988	
Michael W. Steinberg	1988	
Thomas J. Sharbaugh	1988	
Robert J. Lichtenstein	1988	
John C. Richardson	1988	1993
Frank R. Goldstein	1989	
Jeffrey L. Grausam	1989	
Frank L. Gniffke	1989	1993
Richard W. Grant	1989	
Peter Y. Solmssen	1989	
Stanton P. Sender	1989	
Sergio Alvarez-Mena III	1989	
Michael L. Banks	1989	
Joseph B. G. Fay	1989	
Anne C. Flannery	1989	
Kathryn L. Gleason	1989	
David L. Harbaugh	1989	
Donald L. Havermann	1989	
Christopher T. Jensen	1989	
Jami Wintz McKeon	1989	
Andrew J. Schaffran	1989	
Barbara S. Schilberg	1989	
Anita W. Coupe	1989	
Kenneth H. Slade	1989	1993
Catherine A. Ludden	1989	

Robert C. Mendelson	1989	
William J. Lynch	1989	
Peter R. Pinney	1990	
Eric B. Rothenberg	1990	
James W. Lillie, Jr.	1990	
Joseph H. Golant	1990	1992
Kathryn B. McGrath	1990	
Edward S. G. Dennis, Jr.	1990	
Jeffrey N. Brown	1990	
Joseph P. Cyr	1990	
William D. Ellis	1990	
Kathleen C. Johnson	1990	
Eric Kraeutler	1990	
Lowell F. Martin	1990	
Robert S. Schlossberg	1990	
Alan J. Neuwirth	1990	
Richard A. Mescon	1990	
William R. Huss	1990	
Robert L. Abramowitz	1990	
Brian J. Dougherty	1990	
J. Dean Heller	1991	
Robert V. Daly, Jr.	1991	
Philip H. Werner	1991	
Robert G. Robison	1991	
David P. Blea	1991	
Bennett Falk	1991	
Keith Olin	1991	
Barry V. Freeman	1991	
Robert D. Manfred, Jr.	1991	
Edward J. Matey, Jr.	1991	
Greer L. Phillips	1991	
William P. Quinn, Jr.	1991	
Grace E. Speights	1991	
Scott A. Stempel	1991	
Richard L. Umbrecht	1991	
Lisa Klein Wager	1991	
Steven R. Wall	1991	
Mark E. Zelek	1991	
Joseph E. Herman	1991	
Helmut W. R. Kreis	1992	
Raymond R. Kepner	1992	
Carlos E. Méndez-Peñate	1992	
Gary C. Moss	1992	
Anthony Ciasulli	1992	
J. Gordon Cooney, Jr.	1992	
Gregory S. Feis	1992	
Stanley F. Lechner	1992	
Timothy Maxwell	1992	

Sara Anne McClintock	1992	1993
Robert M. Moore	1992	
D. Michael Underhill	1992	
Thomas J. Vallone	1992	
Cynthia M. Cohen `	1993	
Douglas K. Bischoff	1993	
Charles L. O'Brien	1993	
Peter Brown Dolan	1993	
Robert A. White	1993	
Andrea Sheridan Ordin	1993	
Mark N. Bravin	1993	
Christopher C. King	1993	
David G. Nichols, Jr.	1993	
Michael A. Putetti	1993	
Joseph E. Santucci, Jr.	1993	
Stuart M. Sarnoff	1993	
Roseann C. Stevenson	1993	
Glen R. Stuart	1993	
Mark R. Yanowitz	1993	
Robert Rakison	1993	
Howard M. Liebman	1994	
Judith E. Harris	1994	
Richard E. Lutringer	1994	

[1]General Counsel, War Contracts Price Adjustment Board 1943-44.
[2]Vice President, Baldwin Locomotive Works 1940-46.
[3]Chairman, Federal Trade Commission 1970-73.
[4]United States Judge, Eastern District of Pennsylvania 1967-73.
[5]Deputy Assistant Secretary of Defense and Defense Adviser, United States Mission to NATO in Brussels 1968-72.
[6]Deputy Assistant Secretary of Treasury for Tax Policy, Department of Treasury 1975-77.
[7]Judge, United States Tax Court 1986-90.
[8]Deputy General Counsel/Inspector General for Florida Governor Lawton Chiles 1991-93.

SENIOR PARTNERS/CHAIRS

1873-08	Charles E. Morgan, Jr.		1985	Howard L. Shecter
1908-39	Morris R. Bockius		1986	Robert H. Young
1939-57	William Clarke Mason		1987	Robert H. Young
1957-66	Arthur Littleton		1988-89	William J. Curtin
1967-71	W. James MacIntosh			Robert H. Young (1/88-7/88)
1971-72	Thomas V. Lefevre		1990-91	Samuel B. Fortenbaugh III
1973	John P. Bracken		1992-93	Alan L. Reed
1974	Ernest R. von Starck		1994-	John R. Quarles
1975	Park B. Dilks, Jr.			
1976	Robert H. Young			
1977	William J. Curtin		**MANAGING PARTNERS**	
1978	Thomas V. Lefevre		1946-57	J. Tyson Stokes
1979	Robert H. Young		1958-72	John P. Bracken
1980	Miles W. Kirkpatrick		1972-78	E. Barclay Cale, Jr.
1981	Park B. Dilks, Jr.		1979-82	Howard L. Shecter
1982	William J. Curtin		1983-87	E. Clive Anderson
1983	Donald A. Scott		1988-93	Jay H. Calvert, Jr.
1984	Robert H. Young		1994-	Howard L. Meyers

INDEX

A. G. Becker & Co., 235
A&P, 136, 197
Abraham & Straus, 366
Abramson, Stephanie, 235, 379, 403
Academy of Music (Philadelphia), 10, 99, 120, 158
Acme Markets, 158, 187, 197
Act of August 10, 1959, P.L. 212, No. 18, 415
Act of August 14, 1963, P.L. 984, No. 66, 415
Act of December 23, 1983, P.L. 92, No. 395, 424
Act of April 27, 1990, P.L. 129, No. 36, 61
Adams, Duque & Hazeltine, 256
Adams, Franklin P., 422
Adams, Henry, 405
Advacare, 222
Advertising by lawyers, 385-86
Advest, Inc., 244
AFL-CIO, 196, 295, 298, 301, 308-09, 317-18, 421
African-American lawyers, 401-02
Agricultural Adjustment Act, 108
Air traffic controllers (PATCO) strike (1981), 197, 292, 295, 312-18, 421
Al-Tajir, Mahdi, 38
Alan Wood Steel Company, 187, 193
Albright, Ralph, 222
Alexander, Donald, 216
Alexander, Raymond Pace, 150, 152
Allegheny County v. Greater Pittsburgh ACLU, 223-24, 418
Allen, James, 414
Allen, Mel, 319
Allied Stores, 260
Allied Van Lines, 222
Allocation Committee, 159, 182-85, 188, 191, 194, 199, 201, 211, 225, 397, 417
Altus Finance, 259, 262-63
Alvarez-Mena, Sergio, 269
Alyeska Owner Committee, 421
Alyeska Pipeline Service Co. (Trans-Alaska Pipeline), 197, 213, 292, 306-311, 372
Alyeska Pipeline Service Co. v. Teamsters Local 959, 421
Amerace, 222
Amerada Hess Corp., 421
American Airlines, 212
American Bar Association, 27, 95, 98, 158-59, 162, 167, 174, 190, 284, 425
American Civil Liberties Union, 318
American College of Trial Lawyers, 158
American Container Company, 158
American Federation of Musicians, 340
American Institute of Certified Public Accountants' Oversight Board, 217
American Integrity Corporation, 380
American Lawyer, 160, 180, 185, 194, 201-02, 370, 396, 417
American Petroleum Institute, 225

American Red Cross, 213
American Security Bank, 214
American Stores, 187
American Surety Company, 158
American Telephone & Telegraph, *see* AT&T.
American Water Works Company, 133, 166-67, 190, 378
American Window Glass Company, 50-51
Ames (department store), 366
Amherst College, 6, 379
Ampco-Pittsburgh Corp., 234
Amtorg, 117
Amtrak, 353
Anaheim Memorial Hospital, 252
Anderson, Clive, 237, 255, 276-77, 279-81, 285, 289-91, 378
Andover, 189
Anheuser-Busch, 225, 322
Annenberg, Walter, 47, 168, 221
Anti-Injunction Act of 1932, 312
Antitrust law practice, 219
Aoki American, Inc., 218, 241
Aon Corporation, 382
APA calculation, 194
Apollo Investment Fund, 381
Applestein, Harry, 405
Application of Philadelphia-Rapid Transit Company, 413
Aptaker, Edward, 215, 418
Arabian American Oil Company, 227
Archilochus, 140, 415
ARCO, 225, 235, 372, 382, 409, 421
Ark Towers (Tokyo), 285-86
Armour & Co., 72
Armstrong World Industries, 61-62
Arts, ML&B in the, 326-49
Arvida Corporation, 353
Asahi, 286
Ashland Oil, 61
Associated Communications Corporation plc, 346
Associated Gas Distributors (AGD), 191, 207, 209-10, 417
Associated General Contractors of America (AGC), 300
AT&T, 220, 226, 351; Building, 254
Atlanta Braves, 322
Atlanta Gas Light Company, 209
Atlantic Refining Company, 16, 43, 409
Atlantic Richfield Company, 234, 409
Atochem North America, Inc., 61, 92
Atomic Energy Commission, 214
Aurelius, Marcus, 159
Aurora National Life Assurance Company, 264, 419
Avon Products, Inc., 237-38

B. Altman, 366
Bacardi Corp., 266-67
Bacon, Francis, 30, 410
Badinter, Bredin, Jouanneau et Prat, 281

379, 412, 417-18, 420-21, 423
Curtis Arboretum, 408
Curtis, Cyrus H. K., estate of, 5, 408
Curtis Publishing Company, 5, 379
Cyr, Joseph, 246

D'Allesandro, Vincent R., 421
Dabney, Morgan & Co., 86
Daikin, 286
Daly, Robert, 289
Damrosch, Walter, 411
Damsgaard, Kell, 78, 338
Dante, Alighieri, 161
Danzig (Gdánsk), 68, 411
Darrow, Clarence, 82
Dartmouth College case, 149
Dauphin Deposit Trust Company, 158
Davidson, Eugene, 416
Davis, Richard, 258
Dean, John, 221
Dean Witter Reynolds Inc., 244, 269
"Death Sentence" (PUHCA), 124-27
Dechert Price & Rhoads, 130, 408-09
Deep Throat, 222
"Defense of Fort McHenry, The," 336
Degas, Edgar, 335
de Gaulle, Charles, 116, 414
"Deity system," 182, 278
Delaware County (Pennsylvania), 383
Delaware, Lackawanna & Western Rail-
    road Company, 424
Deloitte & Touche, 357
Dennis, Edward S. G., 402, 425
Depersonalization, 399-400
Depression, 11, 19, 32, 40, 58, 69, 76,
    80, 90-92, 102-16, 121, 133, 135, 145,
    148, 185, 195, 329, 340, 395, 424
Derby, Loyd, 256
Desert Storm, 227, 364
Deutsche Bank, 41, 289, 412
Deutsche Schutzvereinigung für Wert-
    papierbesitz (the Schutz), 276-80, 357,
    423
Dichter, Mark, 48, 344, 379, 382-83
Dickens, Charles, 326
Dickey, Charles D., Jr., 23, 59,
Dickey, Charles D., Sr., 23, 59, 89
Dickinson, Oliver, 70
Dickson, Beitler & McCouch, 409
Dictating machines, 134, 165
Diemand, John A., 150
Diesel locomotives, 71
Dilks, Park Bankert, Jr., 184-85, 192-95,
    199-201, 237, 254-55, 276-81, 283,
    291, 341, 343-44, 376, 381, 417, 419
Dillingham Corporation, 227
Dillon Reed & Co., 233, 269
Dilworth, Paxson, Kalish & Kauffman,
    130
Dilworth, Richardson, 21, 40, 83, 130-31,
    135, 146, 192, 341, 414
DiMona, Joseph, 418
Director of Client Relations, 386
Director of Information Systems, 425

Directory of Lawyers, 425
Discrimination law practice, 213, 383
Disney Productions, 422
Disney, Roy E., 114, 301
Disney, Walt, 301
Disneyland, 252, 301
Dodds, Douglas, 258
Doenitz, Karl, 172-73, 416
Dolan, Peter, 259
Dolan, Thomas, 16, 18-19
Donaldson Lufkin & Jenrette, Inc., 235,
    269
Donovan, William, 173
Doran, William, 379, 381
Dorrance, G. Morris, Jr., 36, 410
Dorrance, John T., Jr., 168, 332-35
Dorrance, John T., Jr., Collection, 326,
    332-35
Dorrance, John T., Sr., 332
Douglas, William O., 125-26
Doyle, Arthur Conan, 139
Dred Scott decision, 153
Drexel & Co., 8, 22-23, 31, 57, 59, 80,
    85-89, 106, 123, 259, 381, 399, 412
Drexel, Harjes & Co., 87
Drexel, Anthony J., 87
Drexel Building (Philadelphia), 7-8, 42,
    88, 131, 408, 412
Drexel Burnham, 86
Drexel Burnham Lambert Incorporated,
    85-86, 244, 259, 261-62, 264, 365, 367
Drexel Firestone & Co., 86
Drexel, Francis Martin, 86-87
Drexel Harriman Ripley, 86
Drexel, Morgan & Co., 87-88
Drinker Biddle & Reath, 6, 409
Drumheller, Susan, 423
Duane, Morris & Heckscher, 8, 409
DuBois, W. E. B., 402, 425
Dufek, Robert, 212-13, 322
Duke University, 189
Duke Ziebert's, 208
Dukenfield, William Claude, 120
Dunning, Harrison, 59
Durham, Israel, 18-19
Dutton, Norman, 133, 136
Duveen, Joseph, 91

E. Brooke Matlack, Inc. 140
E. F. Hutton Group, 257
Eagles Football Club, Inc., 362, 383
Eakins, Thomas, 327
Earle George, H., 166
Earth Day, 224, 380
East Texas Motor Freight, 211
Eastern Airlines, 197
Eastern Conference of Teamsters, 196
Eastern Conference of Water Companies,
    193
*Eastern Railroad Presidents Conference v.
    Noerr Motor Freight,* 424
Eastern Railroad Presidents Conference,
    83
Eastern States Bankcard Association,

238
Edgar, George, 417
Edison Electric Institute, 124
Edison, Thomas, 74, 123, 134
Edmonds & Obermayer, 95
Edmonds, Franklin Spencer, 95
Eighteenth and M streets (Washington, D.C.), 208
800 West Sixth Street (Los Angeles), 252
El Greco, Domenico Teotocopulo, 327
El Mirasol (Palm Beach), 89
Electric Bond & Share Company, 103, 123, 126
Electric Bond & Share Company v. SEC, 126, 414
Electro-Motive Corporation, 70
Electrolux AB, 137
Elkins, William L., 16, 109
Eller, Karl, 47
Ellis, Edward Robb, 414
Ellsworth, David, 258
Emanuel, William, 250-53, 257
EMI, 346
Empire Machine Company, 50-51
Employment law practice, 45
Energy law practice, 209-10
Energy Transportation Systems, Inc., 372-73
English, Stephen, 425
Enterra Corporation, 114, 380
Enterra Corporation v. SGS Associates, 414
Entertainment law practice, 345-49
Environmental Deskbook, 226
Environmental law practice, 213, 224-27, 248, 256, 380
Environmental Protection Agency, 224, 417
Epcot, 304
Equal Employment Opportunity Commission, 211
Equilease, 235
Equipment Leasing—Leveraged Leasing, 235
Erie Lackawanna Railway Company, 423
Erie Reading Company, 424
Escudero, Mario, 215, 418
ESPN, 323
Esso Standard Oil Company, 112-13
Estate law practice, 132-33
Estate of Samuel Newhouse v. Commissioner of Internal Revenue, 418
ETSI Pipeline Project v. Missouri, 424
European Community (EC), 287-88
Evans, Bayard & Frick, 95, 130, 409
Evans, Ralph, 95
Evers, Johnny, 325, 422
Excess Profits Tax Act, 174
Executive Committee, 28, 52, 179-80, 182-85, 188, 191, 194, 198-99, 201, 211-12, 214, 225, 233, 278, 376-77, 380, 385-86, 398, 403, 417
Executive Life Insurance Company (ELIC), 259, 261-64

Executive Order 11664, 423
Exide Corporation, 191, 381
Expense ratios, 392-93
Exxon Corp., 112-113, 187, 270, 379
Exxon Company, U. S. A., 379
Eyck, Hubert van, 327

Fair Housing Council of Greater Washington, 384
Fairbanks, Douglas, Jr., 345
Falk, Bennett, 269-70, 379
Fall, Albert B., 95
Fantasia, 422
Farrell, Stephen, 239, 241
Farrugia v. Philadelphia & Reading Railway Company, 412
Fay, Elizabeth, 418
Fay Gas-Fixture Co. v. Welsbach Light Co., 408
Fay, Joseph, 372-74, 418
Federal Aviation Administration (FAA), 313-15, 317, 421
Federal Baseball Club of Baltimore, Inc. v. National League of Professional Baseball Clubs, 320-21, 421
Federal Deposit Insurance Corporation (FDIC), 40, 107, 217, 413
Federal Employers' Liability Act (FELA), 15, 78, 84, 132, 240, 378
Federal Energy Regulatory Commission, 210
Federal Express, 222
Federal Home Loan Bank, 217
Federal Labor Relations Authority, 318
Federal Maritime Commission, 215
Federal Mediation and Conciliation Service, 137, 315, 341
Federal Pacific Electric, 222
Federal Power Commission (FPC), 125, 203-07, 209, 361
Federal Reserve Board, 217
Federal Reserve System, 58, 107, 247, 289, 410
Federal Savings and Loan Insurance Corporation (FSLIC), 107, 413
Federal Ship Financing Act, 236
Federal Trade Commission, 52-54, 57, 219
Fee, Francis, 405
FELA, *see* Federal Employers' Liability Act.
Feller, Lloyd, 217, 247, 259-61
Ferdinand I, King, 69
Fidelity & Deposit Company of Maryland, 111, 158
Fidelity Bank, 31, 35, 36, 38, 40, 145, 158, 167, 410
Fidelity Building (Philadelphia), 21, 29, 37-39, 42, 80, 94, 99, 101, 118, 170
Fidelity Building Corporation, 37-38, 158
Fidelity Insurance Trust & Safe Deposit Company, 36
Fidelity Trust Company, 26, 31, 36, 88
Fidelity-Philadelphia Trust Company, 26,

Lloyd's of London, 248
Local 959 (Teamsters), 309-10, 421
Lockhart, Robin Bruce, 411
Logan, James, 410
Logan Square (Philadelphia), 39, 410
Lomas Financial Corporation, 382
Lombard, John, 329-31, 422
London office, 116, 246, 248, 282-84,
    286, 326, 348, 379
London Stock Exchange, 216
Long Island Lighting Company, 207
Long Range Planning Subcommittee, 180-
    81, 184, 194, 231, 400, 418
Looting & Plundering, Inc., 358
Lord, Joseph, 153
Los Angeles Dodgers, 321
Los Angeles office, 199, 250-64, 273, 287,
    289, 379, 409, 425
Los Angeles Olympic Committee, 256
Loveless, George, 237
Low, William, 241, 248, 419
Lubar, Charles (Chuck), 283, 345-49, 379
Ludden, Catherine, 239
Luellen v. Baldwin Locomotive Works, 411
Lums (restaurant chain), 272
Luxembourg, 280, 357
Luxford, Ansel, 214
Lynch, William, 239
Lyons, Albert, 148

MAAF, *see* Mutuelle Assurance Artisanale
    de France.
Maalox, 313, 381
Mabon Nugent Securities Corp., 244
Macan, William, 249
MacArthur, Douglas, 160, 177
Macaulay, Thomas Babington, 293, 420
MacGregor, David, 22
Machiavelli, Niccolò, 392
Machinists Union strike (1966), 292-99,
    300, 313
MacIntosh, William James, 20-21, 27, 40,
    55, 57, 71, 100, 103-04, 107, 117-18,
    121, 131, 133-35, 139, 143, 156-57,
    159, 163-71, 173, 178-84, 188, 190,
    193-94, 198, 203-06, 210, 213, 229,
    232, 243, 256, 314, 332-33, 353, 376,
    380, 383-84, 393, 406-07, 411, 414,
    416
Mack, Connie, 102, 319
MacKay, Charles, 419
Macy, R. H., 366
Madigan, Jay, 234
Madsen, Marcia, 227
Magazine Antiques, 337
Magic Kingdom, 301-05
Maher, James T., 412-13
Maher, Theodore N., 421
Mahinka, Stephen, 214
Maine Antique Digest, 422
Maistre, Joseph de, 44, 410
Major League Baseball Player Relations
    Committee, Inc. (PRC), 319, 322-25
Malfitano, Catherine, 345

Maloney, Joe, 309-10
MAN Aktiengesellschaft, 289
Management Committee, 377
Management Review Committee, 179-80,
    182-83, 194
Manet, Edouard, 327, 335
Manifest Destiny, 250-51, 253, 264-65
Mann, J. David, 206-09
Manuel, Charles, 245, 419
Marine Midland Bank, 40-41
Maritime law practice, 215
Marketing, by lawyers, 385-86
Marriott, 306
Marshall Field's, 366
Martin-Marietta Corp., 213
Martindale's American Law Directory, 410
Martindale-Hubbell, 234, 410
Maryland National Financial Corp., 214
Mason & Edmonds, 95-96, 413, 422
Mason, Mary Townsend, 98-99
Mason, William Clarke, 15, 20, 23, 27,
    29-30, 35, 55, 58, 63, 66, 69, 75-78,
    82, 91-92, 93-101, 112-13, 121, 124-
    29, 132-35, 137, 156-57, 159, 165, 167,
    170-71, 173-74, 176, 180, 203-06, 208,
    217, 219, 228-29, 240, 255, 312, 361,
    381, 392, 407, 411, 417, 422
Massachusetts Institute of Technology,
    332, 380
Massachusetts Water Resources Author-
    ity, 213, 418
Masterson, Thomas, 78, 412
Maternity leave, 403
Matisse, Henri, 335
Matthews, James, 136
Mayflower Hotel (Washington, D.C.), 203,
    205, 208, 228, 361, 417
Mayrosh, George, 266
McCabe, Thomas Bayard, 55, 57-59, 103,
    399, 411
McCartney, Paul, 346
McCaw Cellular Communications, Inc.,
    220
McClellan, John, 196
McClelland, George, 157
McConnell, John, 45, 78, 118, 132-33
McCracken, Robert T., 95-96, 99, 101,
    112, 127
McCulloch v. Maryland, 149, 410
McDevitt, Vincent P., 95
McDowell, Alfred, 134, 187
McGonigal, Richard, 266-68
*McGovern, Administratrix v. Philadelphia &
    Reading Railway Company*, 412
McGrath, Kathryn, 217
MCI Communications Corporation, 213
McKelvie, John, 410
McKeon, Jami, 403
McLean, Robert, 44, 101, 410, 413
McLean, William, 43-44, 399
McMaster, John B., 416
McNally, Dave, 321
Meany, George, 421
Meegeren, Hans van, 339

Controllers Organization.
Paul, Hastings, Janofsky & Walker, 419
Paul, Weiss, Rifkind, Wharton & Garrison, 186, 408
Paul Young's (restaurant), 208
PE, *see* Philadelphia Electric Company.
Peachbottom Nuclear Plant, 364
Pearson, Drew, 420
Peavy, Robert, 215-16
PECO Energy Company, 423
Pedro II, Dom, 7
Peet, John (Jay), 196-97, 417
Pehle, John, 214
Pehle, Luxford, Schlezinger & Naiden, 214
Peloso, John, 245-47, 269, 379
Penn Center (Philadelphia), 131
Penn Central Corporation, 354, 379, 381
Penn Central Transportation Company, 32, 83-84, 168, 191, 219, 240, 350-56, 415, 423
Penn Central Valuation Case, 350-56
Penn Fuel Gas, 133
Penn Mutual Life Insurance Company, 10, 113
Penn, William, 9, 410
Pennell v. Philadelphia & Reading Railway Company, 412
Pennsylvania Academy of the Fine Arts, 99, 414
Pennsylvania Bar Association, 27, 98, 158, 162, 382
Pennsylvania Building (Washington, D.C.), 208
Pennsylvania Business Corporation Law, 367
Pennsylvania Chamber of Commerce, 60
Pennsylvania Company (Pennco), 353
Pennsylvania Company, 36, 40, 104, 409
Pennsylvania Department of Revenue, 113
Pennsylvania Dock & Warehouse Company, 111-12
Pennsylvania Motor Truck Association, 140
Pennsylvania Newspaper Publishing Association, 135
Pennsylvania Power & Light Company, 63
Pennsylvania Public Accommodations Act, 153
Pennsylvania Public Utility Commission (PUC), 111, 145-46, 362-63
Pennsylvania Public Utility Commission v. Philadelphia Electric Company, 423
Pennsylvania Railroad, 32, 70, 79, 84, 111-12, 131, 147, 168, 351-52
Pennsylvania Republican State Committee, 156, 314
Pennsylvania Retailers Association, 143
Pennsylvania Salt Manufacturing Company, 92
Pennsylvania State Employees Retirement Fund, 62
Pennsylvania Station (New York), 351

Pennsylvania Turnpike, 79-80
Pennsylvania v. Board of Directors of City Trusts of the City of Philadelphia, 415
Pennwalt Corp., 61-62, 92
Pension law practice, 213
Peoples Natural Gas, 191
Pepco, 222
Pepper, Claude, 186
Pepper, George Wharton, 8, 95
Pepper, Hamilton & Scheetz, 8, 95, 409
Perlman, Stuart, estate of, 272
Personal law practice, 194, 238, 266
Petersburg Long Distance Inc., 291
Pettigrew, Richard, 268
Pfeifer, Michael, 283
Phelps Dodge International, 270
Phi Beta Kappa, 157, 192
Philadelphia & Reading Coal & Iron Company, 80-82, 109, 112, 158
Philadelphia and Reading Corporation, 158
Philadelphia Area Energy Users Group, 362
Philadelphia Athletics, 102, 319
Philadelphia Bank, 33-34
Philadelphia Bar Association, 27, 96, 98, 133, 158, 162, 413
Philadelphia Chamber of Commerce, 193
Philadelphia Charter Commission, 135
Philadelphia Clearing House, 107
Philadelphia Convention Center, 84, 240
Philadelphia Daily News, 47, 367, 369
Philadelphia Electric Company (PE; PECO Energy Company), 15, 26, 31, 35, 63, 94-95, 105, 109, 122-24, 128, 133, 135, 141, 166, 178, 191, 203-04, 207, 210, 327, 361-64, 378-79, 411, 414, 416, 423
Philadelphia Electric Company v. City of Philadelphia, 416
Philadelphia Electric Company v. Pennsylvania Public Utility Commission, 423
Philadelphia Gas Works (PGW), 15, 18-22, 105, 131, 158, 204-07, 210
Philadelphia Gas Works Company v. Philadelphia, 409
Philadelphia, Germantown & Norristown Railroad, 64
Philadelphia-Girard National Bank, 31, 35
Philadelphia Inquirer, 26, 44, 47, 168, 221, 362, 423
Philadelphia Lawyer, 413
"Philadelphia Lawyer," 8, 162, 232
Philadelphia Museum of Art, 9, 65, 90-91, 326, 328-31, 333-35, 422
Philadelphia National Bank (PNB), 26, 31-32, 33-36, 40-41, 97, 101, 103-04, 107, 141, 158, 174, 187, 194, 381, 392, 399, 410
Philadelphia Orchestra, 10, 74-75, 158, 326, 340-45, 382, 422
Philadelphia Phillies, 320
Philadelphia *Public Ledger,* 26, 408

Philadelphia Rapid Transit Company
(PRT), 109-11, 135, 145-46, 166
Philadelphia Suburban Water Company,
109, 112, 114, 166-67, 187, 314, 378,
380
Philadelphia Traction Company, 109
Philadelphia Transportation Company
(PTC), 109, 111, 142, 145-49, 158, 178
Philadelphia Trust Company, 36
Philco Corporation, 136-37, 344, 380,
411
Philips Gloeilampenfabrieken N.V., 137
Phillips Petroleum Co. v. State of Wisconsin, 417
Phillips Petroleum Company, 284, 421
Picasso, Pablo, 335
Picasso, Paloma, 335
Pickens, T. Boone, 61
Pierpont Morgan Library, 87
Pies, Roger, 418
Pilkington plc, 31, 49-54, 222-23, 274
Pilkington, Sir Alastair, 49, 52, 54, 411
Pilkington, Sir Harry, 52
Pillsbury Madison & Sutro, 408
Pinchot, Gifford, 106, 122
Pinkerton Detective Agency, 66, 82
Pinney, Peter, 269
Piper & Marbury, 217
Pitney-Bowes Credit Corporation, 249
Pittsburgh Pirates, 322
Players Relations Committee of Major
League Baseball, 413
Plaza Hotel (New York), 241
Pleasanton, A. J., 408
PNB, *see* Philadelphia National Bank.
PNB Financial Corporation, 40
Pogorelich, Ivo, 345
Point Pleasant Pumping Station, 362
Poland, 68, 89; telephone system, 290
Poli, Robert, 313-16, 318
Porter, William A., 6
Potomac Electric Power Company, 212
Potts, Frederic A., 392
Pound, Roscoe, 189
Powder River Basin (Wyoming), 372
Powell, Adam Clayton, 297
Powell, Lewis F., 385
PPG Industries, 52, 211
Practice development, 385-86
Practicing Law Institute, 235
Presbyterian Hospital of Philadelphia,
158
Presidential Emergency Board, 228, 294-
96, 423
Prichard, Saul, Bayard & Evans, 409
Prime Motor Inns, 241
Princeton office, 257, 419
Princeton University, 177, 189
Pro Bono Service Award, 425
Pro bono work, 383-85
Proctor & Gamble, 225
Professional Air Traffic Controllers
Organization (PATCO), 295, 313-18
Professional Personnel Committee, 188,

191
Profits, per partner, 395-96
Progress Credit Corporation, 267
Proskauer Rose Goetz & Mendelsohn, 408
Provident Life and Trust Company of
Philadelphia, 26, 31, 36
Provident Mutual Life Insurance Company, 26, 31, 380
Provident National Bank, 40
Provident Trust Company, 26, 31, 158
PRP Organization Handbook, 226
Prudential Insurance Company of
America, 258
Prudential-Bache Securities, Inc., 245,
269
Prudhoe Bay (Alaska), 306-07
PTC, *see* Philadelphia Transportation
Company.
Public interest law practice, 383-85, 425
Public Service Company of New Hampshire, 424
Public Service Corporation of New Jersey,
128
Public Service Electric & Gas Company,
207
Public Service of New Mexico, 209
Public Utility Holding Company Act of
1935 (PUHCA), 15-16, 107-08, 121,
124-28, 217, 414
Publishers Clearing House, 238, 419
Puerto Rico, Commonwealth of, 215
Puerto Rico Maritime Shipping Authority
(PRMSA), 215, 418
Purple Tree, 302

Qantas Airways Ltd., 249
Quadriviri, 184-202, 207, 232, 239, 251,
253, 278, 376-77, 379, 385, 417
Quarles, John, 224-26, 379, 417-18
Quigg, Benjamin, 30-31, 93, 133-34, 143,
161, 190, 219
Quinn, Arthur Hobson, 157
Quintiere, Gary, 418

Racketeer Influenced and Corrupt Organizations Act (RICO), 369-70
Radford, William, 269
Radio Corporation of America, 75-76
Raiken, Allen, 217
Railway Labor Act of 1926, 212, 294, 420
Rainmakers, 24
Rakison, Robert, 283
Randal Morgan Physics Laboratory, 14
Rank Organization, 221
Rapp, Howard, 105, 133
Raw, Charles, 420
Raymond James & Associates Inc., 269
Reading Eagle Company, 158
Reading/Gould Transaction, 84, 240-41
Reading law, 6, 14, 393
Reading Railroad, 4, 15, 31-32, 71, 77-
84, 88, 92, 95, 132, 138, 147, 240, 312,
314, 356, 378, 415, 423-24
Reading Terminal (Philadelphia), 79-80,

Securities Exchange Act of 1934, 107, 424
Security Federal Savings Bank, 222
Security Pacific Leasing Corporation, 249
Security Pacific National Bank, 41, 263
Segal, Eric, 345
SEI Corp., 63, 381
Seitz, Peter, 321
Seligman, J. W., 76
Sender, Stanton, 227-28
Senior Council, 183
SEPTA, *see* Southeastern Pennsylvania Transportation Authority.
Severn Trent (U. S.), Inc., 378
Seymour, Jane, 345
Shamrock Holdings, Inc., 114
Shareholder Protection Act of 1983, 60, 367
Shearman & Sterling, 408
Shearson Leasing Corporation, 235
Shearson Lehman Brothers Inc., 257, 269
Shecter, Howard, 215, 272, 379-80, 417
Sheet Metal Workers' International Association, 420
Shell Oil Company, 219, 238
Shelley, Percy Bysshe, 423
Shenefield, John, 219-21, 288, 371-72, 374, 379, 418
Sherman Act, 40, 83, 373-74
Shertz, Barnes & Shertz, 139-40
Shertz, Harold (Pop), 140, 378
Shin Meiwa Industry Co., 285
Shingle, The, 96, 101, 161, 413-14
Shoreham nuclear power plant, 423
Shrank, Ian, 235-36, 248
Shultz, George P., 189, 417
Shultz, John, 256
Shumaker, Edward E., 76
Sidney G. Reilly v. Baldwin Locomotive Works, Eddystone Ammunition Corporation and Samuel M. Vauclain, 411
Siegel, Martin, 367, 424
Siemiller, P. I., 293, 296-97
Sierra Club, 372
Silent Spring (Carson), 224, 418
Silver Liner Club awards, 356
Simmonds Precision Products, Inc., 214
Simondi, Michael, 258
Sinclair Refining Co. v. Atkinson, 420
Single European Act of 1986, 287
Sioux Falls (South Dakota), 373
Sirica, John, 212
Skillern, Frank, 217
Sky Television Ltd., 288
Slade, Kenneth, 287
Slocum, Richard, 45-46, 136
Smaltz, Donald, 257
Smith, Adam, 4, 141, 385
Smith, Baker, 140
Smith Barney, 269
Smith, Frank, 256
Smith, Nelson Lee, 206
Smith, R. Stuart, 27, 96
Smith, Robert, 212-13

Smith v. Drake, 408-09
SmithKline Beecham, 380
Smiths Industries, 222
Smithsonian Institution, 76
Snellenburg, N. (department store), 120
Snelling & Snelling, Inc., 314
Snyder, Lee, 241
Snyder, Martin, 118-19, 133, 414
Société General Elf Aquitaine, 61
Socony Mobil Oil Co., 136
Solidarity movement, 411
Solis-Cohen, Lita, 422
Solmssen, Peter, 288-89
Solow, Sheldon, 237-38, 419
Somers, Peter, 332
Somerville, Ernest, 163
Sommer, A. A., 216-18, 247
Sonnenfeld, Marc, 78
Sotheby's, 326, 333-35, 339
Sousa, John Philip, 411
Souser & Kleeb, 15, 46, 133, 136, 139, 292
Souser, Kenneth, 45-46, 112, 136-39, 170, 193, 197-98, 200, 210, 212-13, 292-93, 299-300, 341-44, 383, 407, 415, 421
Souser, Ronald, 136, 138
South Carolina Electric and Gas Company, 209
South Dakota, 371-75
Southdown, Inc., 220
Southeast Financial Center (Miami), 271
Southeastern Pennsylvania Transportation Authority (SEPTA), 109, 146-47, 415
Southeastern Pennsylvania Transportation Authority v. Philadelphia Transportation Company, 415
Southern Pennsylvania Traction Company, 158
Southern Surety Company, 158
Southland Corp., 61
Southwestern Bell, 220
Soviet Union, dissolution of, 290
Special Committee on Labor Rackets, 196
Specialization, 130-141, 399
Specter, Arlen, 45
Speights, Grace, 222, 402, 425
Speyer & Co., 76
Staggers, Harley, 297
Staggers Rail Act of 1980, 212, 355
Standard Oil Company of New Jersey, 16, 43, 112-13, 187, 351, 409, 421
Standard Oil Company of New Jersey v. United States, 409
Standard Oil Company of Ohio, 421
Standard Power & Light Corporation, 123
Star (newspaper), 221
Starr, Ringo, 346
State Farm Life Insurance Company, 235
State House Row, 8-9
State of South Dakota v. Kansas City Southern Industries, 424
State of Wisconsin Investment Board, 235
Steere v. Baldwin Locomotive Works, 411